MAVERICK GUIDE TO
MOROCCO

mav•er•ick (mav'er-ik), *n* 1. an unbranded steer. Hence [colloq.] 2. a person not labeled as belonging to any one faction, group, etc., who acts independently. 3. one who moves in a different direction than the rest of the herd—often a nonconformist. 4. a person using individual judgment, even when it runs against majority opinion.

The Maverick Guide Series
The Maverick Guide to Australia
The Maverick Guide to Hawaii
The Maverick Guide to New Zealand
The Maverick Guide to Thailand
The Maverick Guide to Bali and Java
The Maverick Guide to Berlin
The Maverick Guide to Malaysia and Singapore
The Maverick Guide to Vietnam, Laos, and Cambodia
The Maverick Guide to Prague
The Maverick Guide to Hong Kong, Macau, and South China
The Maverick Guide to Barcelona
The Maverick Guide to Scotland
The Maverick Guide to Oman
The Maverick Guide to Morocco

MAVERICK GUIDE TO
MOROCCO

Susan Searight

PELICAN PUBLISHING COMPANY
Gretna 1999

ISBN: 1-56554-348-3

The word "Pelican" and the depiction of a pelican are trademarks
of Pelican Publishing Company, Inc., and are registered
in the U.S. Patent and Trademark Office.

Information in this guidebook is based on authoritative data available
at the time of printing. Prices and hours of operation of businesses listed
are subject to change without notice. Readers are asked to take this into
account when consulting this guide.

Maps and photos by Susan Searight and
Moroccon National Tourist Office

Printed in the United States of America

Published by Pelican Publishing Company, Inc.
1000 Burmaster Street, Gretna, Louisiana 70053

Contents

LIST OF MAPS

ACKNOWLEDGMENTS

This book would have been very difficult to produce had I not been helped by many friends, who willingly shared their information and impressions. I am particularly grateful to the following:

Stella Fizazi, Ilse and Charlie Mochan, members of the British, American, and French communities in Casablanca, William Gill, Alexander Moll, Kitty Morse, Juliette Searight-Evans, Alain and Eliane Bozon, Chebihani Ma el-Ainin, Stephanie Sweet, Danielle and Jacques Mamane, Nellie Chaoui, Marie-Christine Henrion-Martinet, Gaëlle Riou, Jacques Guilbert, Aicha Idrissi, the Fédération Nationale de l'Industrie Hotelière in Casablanca, the Moroccan National Tourist Board and, above all, to Guy Martinet for his help with the history of Morocco and all his patience while I spent long hours at the computer.

MAVERICK GUIDE TO
MOROCCO

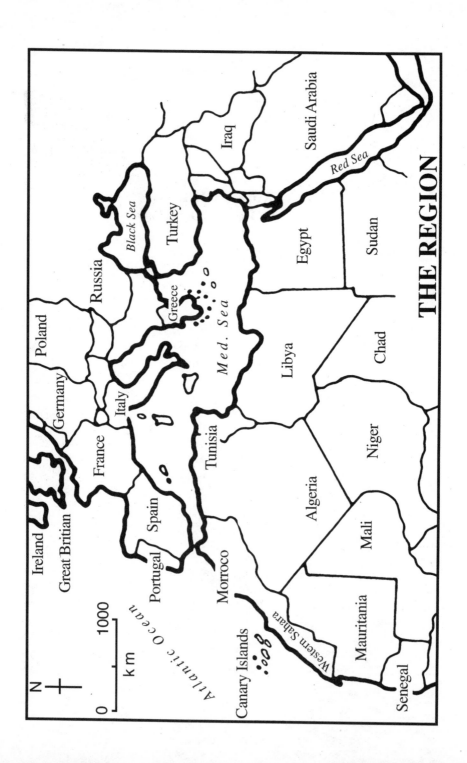

THE REGION

1

Why Go to Morocco?

Morocco is a land of contrasts, of colors, of fascinating scenes of daily life, and of strong traditions still upheld. It is an old country: inhabited for at least one million years and an independent kingdom since the eighth century. Many of the standing monuments are over 500 years old. But its population is young—the streets and the countryside are crowded with children. It is a country of contrasts: sea, snow, and sandy deserts can all be reached in a maximum of two days' travel time. A day's drive takes you from the blue Mediterranean Coast to the snow-covered Atlas Mountains, which have a dozen summits over 4,000 meters, and more than 400 exceeding 3,000 meters. Another day will bring you through cedar forests to the date-palm oases, sand dunes, and stony plateaus of the desert. The features of Morocco's landscapes can all be found in the United States, but here, in this ancient land, they are concentrated in a relatively small, easily accessible space.

The contrasts do not stop with the landscape. The age-old imperial cites of the north give way to mud-brick fortified settlements south of the High Atlas chain. Modern 20-story buildings in the economic capital of

Casablanca are centuries away from the black woven tents of the nomads on the high plateaus. High-powered Mercedes speed down the highways alongside mule-driven carts, mini-skirted young girls rub shoulders with veiled older women, white skins mingle with brown and black, and *jellabas* of all colors in the towns are replaced by somber black draped clothes in the south.

Morocco owes its charm not only to the beauty of the landscapes, but also to its people and their way of life. Traditions are still strong, despite computers and portable telephones. The winding alleys of the old imperial towns have scarcely changed over the centuries and still exercise a fascination over visitors. Handicrafts flourish. Craftsmen still beat away on metal trays, turn wood with simple foot-driven drills, plunge skins into dying vats, thump down lines of weaving, or make carefully-chosen tractor tires into traditionally-shaped water-carriers.

Artists and writers have long been attracted to Morocco by the light, the colors, and the harmony of the traditional architecture. Others come because the country offers a gentle introduction to Islam, welcomes visitors, is sufficiently exotic to be strange without being frightening, and offers a microcosm of civilizations and cultures. In Morocco, indigenous Berber, Andalusian Spain, the Arab Middle East, and "black" Africa have all mingled to produce a unique country. Geographically, Morocco is America's nearest African and Arab neighbor.

You can go to Morocco for all or some of these reasons. You can go, too, because you like to combine sports and culture—beautiful sights for the eyes and healthy exercise for the body. Morocco is a marvelous country for trekking (with mules to carry the baggage!), for going off into the desert on the back of a camel, for improving your golf score on excellent courses designed by international experts, for surfing, or for indulging in a session of water-therapy. You can do all this before or after marveling at the centuries-old Islamic architecture or delicate decoration of the fortified adobe dwellings in southern oases. Many international companies hold seminars or meetings in Morocco. For instance, in the spring of 1998, General Motors brought together 16,000 delegates from all over Europe for a convention in Marrakech. The same town served as host to the international GATT meeting in 1994.

There are excellent hotels throughout the country, and no travel restrictions (except in the south of what used to be known as the Spanish Sahara). Although French is the main language after Arabic and Berber, English is spoken in the big hotels and in the tourist resorts. The main roads are good, and flights are available to the main towns The climate is agreeable, and there are no "horrible" diseases. You don't need to worry about security—Morocco is a well-organized and carefully controlled country.

The Highlights of Morocco include:

- The Imperial Cities of Rabat, Meknès, Fès, and Marrakech, which feature old palaces, mosques, winding covered alleys, crowded markets, and craftsmen at work in tiny booths (as well as superb Moroccan cuisine in Fès and Marrakech).
- Casablanca. Although Rabat is the administrative capital, Casablanca is the business center, with a cosmopolitan and active population, the new Hassan II mosque (a showpiece of Islamic decorative arts), and gourmet restaurants!
- The Atlantic Coast, with its old Portuguese and Spanish fortifications, beautiful beaches, and surfing and sea fishing.
- The High Atlas and Middle Atlas Mountains are great for outdoor activities: trekking, climbing, birdwatching, and kayaking, all in a setting combining natural beauty and contact with a proud and hospitable population that has kept its traditional music, dance, dress, and architecture.
- The fortified, ochre-colored, adobe kasbas nestling in intensive-cultivation oases along the Dades and Draa valleys, and some spectacular gorges.
- The far south—vivid patches of green palm trees along the river valleys in an otherwise barren landscape, sand dunes, stark cliff formations, mud-brick villages, and excursions on camel-back.
- Prehistoric sites where Neolithic man engraved rock surfaces with representations of the animals he hunted or herded, the weapons he used, even the clothes he wore. Roman ruins at Volubilis, Lixus, and Cotta are still capable of evoking their glorious past.

A Personal Note

Although I have lived for 25 years in Morocco—in Casablanca, to be exact—I have not stayed in *all* the hotels (there are 532 classified and a host of unclassified) nor have I eaten in *all* the restaurants (there are too many to count). My work as a researcher in prehistory has generally taken me to places where there are neither hotels nor restaurants. But I have tried out many and I confess I have relied on trustworthy friends to give me information on others. However, in Morocco, as in many countries, hotel stars come and go like fireworks and what may be ★★★★★ today could drop

to **** a year later (the star rating allocated by the state to each hotel is re-
vised every year). Moroccan hotels and restaurants, too, are particularly
vulnerable to staff changes, and the whole affair can crumble almost
overnight. So you *may* find a hotel or restaurant classed as "good" in this
guide to be not to your liking, or one that has not been recommended to
be really top-class. If so, please let me know, so that I can check for future
editions. All your comments, whether positive or negative, will be carefully
considered. This is the moment to say that, like all Maverick Guides, this
one has not been tainted by favors or "string-pulling." No attempts were
made, by any establishment, to sway me one way or another, and I've paid
my way all along the line, from a small cup of black coffee to a ***** hotel.

Getting the Most out of This Book

This guide follows the same pattern as other Maverick Guides. The for-
mat was designed for the Maverick Guide to Hawaii, which came out in
1977, and is now in its 20th edition. Its aim is to present a general view of
the country and its people, without neglecting the practical details that a
visitor should know about.

The first chapter gets you to Morocco, suggests how you can get around
once you are there, and gives information on practical affairs such as what
clothes to wear, money matters, government fiddle-faddle, useful addresses, and tips for tourists. This is followed by chapters discussing the
land and life of Morocco, and the events that have made up its history.

Then the book is divided into nine area chapters: Tangier and the
North; Rabat-Salé and the Surrounding Area; Meknès and the Middle
Atlas Mountains; Fès, the Spiritual Capital; Oujda and the East; Casablanca
and the Atlantic Coast; Agadir, the Anti-Atlas Mountains, and the
Southwest; Marrakech and the High Atlas Mountains; and Ouarzazate, the
Kasbahs, and the Sahara.

Each of the area chapters contains twelve numbered sections. Once you
have mastered this layout in one chapter, it should be easy for you to find
your way around the others. The categories are as follows:

1. The General Picture	7. Guided Tours
2. Getting There	8. Culture
3. Local Transportation	9. Sports
4. The Hotel Scene	10. Shopping
5. Dining and Restaurants	11. Entertainment and Nightlife
6. Sightseeing	12. The Address List

This book is designed to be used in two ways. First, run through it to get
a general feel of the country and the things it offers. Decide what appeals

to you—the classic, unforgettable tour of the Imperial Cities, a hike through the Berber-inhabited High Atlas Mountains with a mule to take the backpack burden off your shoulders, a circuit of the best golf courses, or simple relaxation on the beach.

Below you will find a list of special interests and the chapters in which to find details on each.

- **The Imperial Cities and outstanding Islamic monuments:** see Chapters 6, 7, 8, and 12. For a modern example of Islamic architecture, see Chapter 10 for information on the new Hassan II mosque.
- **Museums:** for **archaeology,** see Chapters 5 and 6. For **ancient craftwork,** see Chapters 5, 6, 7, 8, 11, and 12. For **pottery,** see Chapters 6 and 10. For **ancient weapons,** see Chapter 8.
- **Art Galleries:** most are found in Casablanca, but commercial galleries and cultural centers in Tangier, Rabat, Fès, and Marrakech also regularly exhibit the works of contemporary artists. Essaouira is also an important center for contemporary artists. There is no art gallery of permanent exhibits.
- **Prehistoric and later remains:** for **Phoenician and Roman** sites, see Chapters 5, 6, and 7. For **prehistoric sites,** see Chapters 6,10, and 13, and for **prehistoric rock art,** see Chapters 11, 12, and 13. For old **Portuguese and Spanish fortifications,** see Chapters 5, 6, 10, and 11. For other interesting **relics of the past,** see Chapter 11 for 16th- and 17th-century sugar-working installations and fortified storage granaries, and Chapter 13 for old kasbahs. This list is not exclusive, but aims to pinpoint the most interesting sites.
- **Trekking, Rafting, Skiing, and Climbing:** see Chapters 7, 11, 12, and 13.
- **Birdwatching:** see Chapters 5, 6, 7, 9, 11, 12, and 13.
- **Desert excursions:** see Chapter 13.
- **Windsurfing:** see Chapters 6, 10, and 11.
- **Tennis and Golf:** the big hotels nearly all have hard tennis courts, and many have a professional coach who'll give you a game or a lesson. There are 19 golf courses in Morocco: in Tangier, Cabo Negro, Rabat, Meknès, Fès, Casablanca, Mohammedia, Ben Slimane, Settat, El-Jadida, Agadir, Marrakech, and Ouarzazate. Some are 18 holes, others only 9, but all are located in magnificent surroundings.
- **Shooting and Fishing:** see Chapters 5, 7, 10, 11, and 12.

Then talk things over with your travel agent. Airfares and package tours are their business, but they cannot be expected to know every nook and cranny of Morocco, which was visited by only a little over 87,000 United States visitors in 1997, and only 25,000 Canadians. All agents have to work though a contact established in Morocco but, even so, it is a good idea to express your own ideas on the places you'd like to visit and the hotels that you'd like to stay in.

Here are a few addresses and suggestions to help you before you actually set off on your trip:

General information on Morocco can be obtained from the following:

- Moroccan Embassy: 1601 21st Street, **Washington,** DC 20009 (Tel: 202-462-7979); 38 Range Road, **Ottawa** KIN 814, Ontario (Tel: 416-236-7391/.7392)

- Moroccan Consulate: 767 Third Avenue, 30th floor, **New York,** NY 10017 (Tel: 212-421-1580); 437 Fifth Avenue, **New York,** NY 10016 (Tel: 212-758-2625) 1010 Rue Sherbrooke West, Suite 1510, **Montreal** H3A 2R7 (Tel: 514-288-8750, 514-288-6951)

- Moroccan National Tourist Office: 20E, 46th Street, Suite 1201, **New York,** NY 10017 (Tel: 212-557-2520) Web sites: http://www.kingdomofmorocco.com/html/home.html
  http://www.kingdomofmorocco.com/html/practical information.html
  2 Carlton Street, Suite 1803, **Toronto,** Ontario M5B 1K2 (Tel: 416-598-2208)

- Royal Air Maroc (RAM) Airline Company: 55 East 59th Street, Suite 17B, **New York,** NY 10022 (Tel: 212-750-5115, Fax: 212-754-4215). Reservations: Tel: 212-750-6071, Fax: 212-980-7924. Also 666 Fifth Avenue, 53rd Street, **New York,** NY 10103 (Tel: 212-974-3850, Fax: 212-974-0612)

  1001 de Maisonneuve Ouest, Suite 440, **Montreal,** QC H3A3C8 (Tel: 514-285-1619). Branch at same address, Suite 430 (Tel: 514-285-1689, 514-285-1937). Reservations: Tel: 514-285-1435, Fax: 514-285-1338 Royal Air Maroc web site: http://www.royalairmaroc.co.ma

- General information on Morocco web site: http://maghreb.net/countries/morocco/index.html

Specific Advice

- For **young people:** those wanting to use the Moroccan Youth Hostels will find it easier if they are members of the International Youth Hostel Federation (I.Y.H.F.) The American branch office is: P.O. Box 37613, **Washington,** DC, 20013-7613.
- For **older people:** some firms and airlines offer reductions to seniors 60 and over. This is worth looking into.

- For **people with children:** Moroccans are great with children—they adore them. So that's no problem. Care should be taken with all foodstuffs, only bottled water should be given, and be particularly careful about sunstroke and dehydration. Disposable diapers are on sale in the bigger towns (Babydou is a good brand).
- For **people with a serious, chronic medical condition:** talk things over with your doctor. Hospitals and clinics are available throughout the country, but may not be equipped to deal with your particular problem. There are plenty of drugstores, but they won't have your brand of medication, so check into the European equivalent (for instance, Doliprane is the same as Tylenol).
- For **physically disabled people:** Morocco is not geared for wheelchairs and the like (ramps to pavements, escalators or elevators in railway stations, shops, or restaurants, etc.), but disabled people need have no worries in Morocco. Moroccans are particularly sensitive to people with physical handicaps, and there will always be someone ready to give a helping hand. Hotels particularly suited to wheelchair travelers are indicated in this guide. For advice, get in touch with the Society for the Advancement of Travel for the Handicapped, 347 Fifth Avenue, No. 610, **New York,** NY 10016 (Tel: 212-447-7284).
- For **single women:** this is a tricky point. Some people I have spoken to say there is absolutely no problem for women traveling alone; others say that it is totally out of the question. My feeling is that it all depends on you. Some men will always try and link up with a single woman, but a calm and firm attitude (avoid shouting or screaming if someone speaks to you), combined with care in the places you go (no wandering around the streets late at night or diving into "seedy" bars), will enable the single woman traveler to visit Morocco with no problem. If necessary, appeal to a policeman or older man nearby.
- For people particularly interested in **arts and crafts:** a web site has been created that takes the visitor through workshops in the dozen or so towns with the best reputation for handicrafts (which are indeed an attractive feature of Morocco). Reference: http://www.maghrebnet.ma/artisanat/indexnf.html.
- For the **individual traveler:** while many hotels concentrate on package tours (where prices are greatly reduced), there are plenty of accommodation possibilities for the totally independent traveler. For those wanting a minimum of reservations or a personalized itinerary based on particular interests, contact a specialized agency (a few are listed below). Consider a fly/drive deal, which is cheaper to arrange

in the United States before arriving. Car rental in Morocco can be organized from the United States via the web (companies like Budget or Hertz, for instance, charge, respectively, US$389.35 and US$387.92 weekly for the second smallest car).

Some firms specializing in tours to Morocco:

- Olive Branch Tours, 35 Rue el Oraibi Jilali, **Casablanca,** Morocco (Tel: 22 03 54/22 39 19, Fax: 26 09 76/20 36 79, e-mail: olivetour; open.net.ma). A long-established operator, representing the Smithsonian, art museums across the United States, and many up-scale tour operators in the United States.
- Abercrombie & Kent International, Inc., 1520 Kensington Road, **Oak Brook,** Illinois, 60523-2141 (Tel: 630-954-2944, Fax: 630-954-3324, www.abercrombiekent.com).
- G.W.T. Inc., 190 Moore Street, **Hackensack,** NJ 07601 (Tel: 800-868-7498, e-mail: travelgwt@aol.com, www.travelgwt.com) has been running packaged tours to Morocco and the Middle East for over 20 years. It can also put together customized Jewish interest tours.
- Royal Tours, Inc. (Tel: 800-643-8744) does a cheap one week package (roundtrip air and hotel are included).
- Isram World (Tel: 800-223-7460) offers the standard Imperial Cities, the Kasbah route, or the south, a deluxe chauffeur-driven private-car tour, stays in deluxe hotels, a fly/drive cheaper program for independent travelers, and a "Jewish Heritage Tour," focusing on places with Jewish interest.

Theme travel:

- A British agency, with a long experience of Moroccan travel, based in London but dealing with a great deal of American customers, can plan personalized itineraries for birdwatching, painting and photography, gardens, trekking, horseback riding, camel treks, golf, archaeology, and mountain biking. Contact CLM Morocco Ltd., 69 Knightsbridge, **London** SW1X 7RA, (Tel: 0171 235 0123/2100, Fax: 0171 235 3581).
- In Morocco, a French-run agency proposes adventure travel expeditions: the far south in 4WD vehicles, animal photography accompanied by a professional, rafting on the High Atlas rivers, mountain biking in the desert, horseback riding, private airplane flights (five- or six-seater Cesna) over the mountains and the desert, and visits to

animal reserves in the southwest. Contact Globe Trotters, 65 Rue Lamgranta, **Casablanca,** Morocco 20100 (Tel: 25 13 65, Fax: 25 15 22, web site: www/g.trotters@plvplus.net.ma).

- Another Moroccan agency, with a long experience in theme travel, sport, adventure, and incentive travel (seminars, motivation trips) is Team Travel Services, Résidence Eugénie, 209 Boulevard d'Anfa, Casablanca (Tel: 94 12 22/25, Fax: 94 12 50). (English-speaking).

Once in the country, I hope you will find my recommendations on hotels, restaurants, and shopping helpful to avoid disappointment, but don't be afraid to branch out—after all, you may discover a pearl of a hotel or restaurant that I've overlooked! One word here: Moroccan hotels are given stars according to their category—from * to *****, indicating luxury. But one star should be knocked off to correspond to western standards. The sections on history, culture, and sightseeing will enable you to get the most out of your visit.

A number of maps are included in this volume to give you a general idea of the geography and location of the main towns. Itineraries are proposed, but nothing replaces a good detailed map, on sale in large bookshops and the bigger hotels. Simplified street plans are given to help you get around. Here again, don't hesitate to ask your way. Many people in the tourist towns speak a little English (but don't expect a Berber woman in the mountains to direct you in English to the nearest water source!).

Distances are given in kilometers, since it is best to become accustomed to this locally-used measure. Prices are shown in the local currency, the Moroccan *dirham*. Unlike other countries, there are no "tourist" prices. Locals and overseas visitors pay the same price (in theory, but, of course, everyone tries to get more out of the tourist! Play the game a little, but don't get fleeced . . .). Morocco is a safe, friendly country, and the authorities do all they can to make the visitor's stay enjoyable.

2

Happy Landings

How to Get There

The majority of visitors to Morocco arrive by **plane** at Mohammed V Airport, in Casablanca. From the United States, the easiest way to come is by the state airline, **Royal Air Maroc (RAM),** which runs a flight direct from JFK Airport in New York to Casablanca four times a week. RAM also has a weekly flight from Montreal to Casablanca. It might be useful to know that the airline code for RAM is AT. Departure time for both flights is approximately 8:30 P.M. and arrival is scheduled for about 7:00 A.M. Actual flight time is six and one-half hours, since Morocco is five hours ahead of Eastern Standard Time. The distance between New York and Casablanca "as the crow flies" is 5,800 kilometers (km) and between Montreal and Casablanca it is 5,675 km. With the opening of the skies now imminent, it is possible that the RAM monopoly will be broken and other companies will be able to step in and offer competitive prices.

Another possibility is to come via Europe. This can be done by crossing the Atlantic on one of the many airlines flying to any of the numerous cities in Europe with connecting flights to Morocco, or by simply making a short or long extension to a holiday or business trip to Europe. The first option entails changing planes and having to wait in a transit lounge for the connecting flight; the second obviously provides more room for choice and avoids tedious delays in airports.

Royal Air Maroc has flights to Morocco from all main European cities and from the Canary Islands. In addition, the private Casablanca-based company, **Regional Air Lines,** flies from Malaga, Grenada, and Lisbon to Casablanca; **British Airways/GB Airways** flies from London and Gibraltar; **Air France** from Paris, Bordeaux, Lyons, Marseilles, and Nice; **Lufthansa** from Dusseldorf and Frankfurt; **Sabena** from Brussels; **KLM** from Amsterdam; **Scandinavian Airlines** from Stockholm; **Swissair** from Zurich; **Iberia** from Madrid and Malaga; **Air Portugal (T.A.P)** from Lisbon; and **Alitalia** from Milan and Rome. Some European flights call in at interme- diate airports in Morocco before arriving in Casablanca. Flying time from London is about three and one-half hours, but flights are shorter from air- ports near the Mediterranean coast. Very tempting bargain-price holidays in Morocco are offered in France by agencies such as Dégriftour, Réductour, and Nouvelles Frontières. Once in Europe, it is worth looking around for these bargains, if you are not too pushed for time and can choose your season (these reduced rates generally don't apply during peak holiday periods).

It is also possible to track down cheap flight offers across the Atlantic to London and Paris. Once in Europe, you can go for the scheduled flights or for the bargain offers.

It is perfectly possible to get to Morocco from Europe by that old-fash- ioned form of transport—the **train** (**Gare d'Austerlitz,** Paris). The new ex- press trains (TGV) now operating in France and Spain make the continental departure point, the Spanish port of Algeciras, easily accessi- ble. From there, the standard car ferry will take you to Tangier, where you can pick up a train to Rabat, Casablanca, Fès, or Oujda. Or you can rent a car in Tangier and drive wherever you want.

If you start your trip to Morocco in Europe, you can travel by **car ferry** from France, Spain, or Gibraltar. The Moroccan car-ferry, **Marrakech,** runs twice a week between Sète (near Montpellier, France) and Tangier (Compagnie Marocaine de Navigation, Comanav). The journey takes about 36 hours and is relatively expensive. Two classes of cabin accommo- dations are available, **tourist** and **comfort.** Meals are included in the ticket. In the high season, the round trip in a two-berth outside cabin with a water closet, **comfort** class, currently costs 4,700 DH per person; the **tourist** class has four-berth cabins from 3,120 DH round trip; a car costs from 4,000 DH round trip. From July through to September (the high season), the boat is crowded with Moroccans who work in France coming home for the holidays (early July) or returning to work (end of August/early September). This is not a particularly advantageous system, unless, of course, you have a car and like sea-crossings, billed as "mini-cruises." The same company is opening a similar service from Sète to Nador in the summer. If you **do** come by **car,** you need Green Card Insurance (for Europe), the Vehicle Registration Document, and an International Driver's License. Once on Moroccan soil you have to buy Moroccan Frontier Insurance, which covers you for a maximum stay of three months. European car rental firms may not be keen on you taking their car out of the country, so it is better to rent in Morocco.

The quickest and cheapest boat route is the two-hour crossing from Algeciras (south Spain) to the Spanish enclave of Ceuta, by **Trasmediterranea Company.** A disadvantage is the absence of public transport once in Ceuta, and the often long delays in getting through the frontier (especially in the holiday period mentioned above). A new service from Algeciras to Ceuta started in 1998, by the **Buquebus España SA,** which crosses the 29 km in 35 minutes. Algeciras to Tangier is another route and more hassle-free. Both are served by Morocco (Comanav Company) and Spain (Trasmediterranea, Limadet Ferry). From the Tangier port, it is possible to travel by train to other destinations in Morocco.

Hydrofoils will also take you across the Strait of Gibraltar from Algeciras to Tangier or Ceuta (no cars). Departures depend on the weather—the sea is not always calm—and the trip is not a particularly agreeable one. But it is quick (30 minutes to Ceuta, one hour to Tangier) (Transtour Company, Algeciras). Hydrofoils also operate twice a week between Gibraltar and Tangier (one and one-half hours, Seagle Ltd., Gibraltar). A very hesitant hydrofoil service sometimes runs between Tarifa, on the Spanish side, and Tangier—but, unless you enjoy difficulties, it is best not to count on this crossing.

You can, of course, come to Morocco in your **private boat.** Tangier is the obvious port of call, or Al-Hoceima further east. The Moroccan Atlantic Coast is very poor in good harbors, until you get to Mohammedia (just north of Casablanca), Casablanca itself, or down to Agadir. But you will undoubtedly be treated with great suspicion by the Moroccan Customs officials, who are always on the lookout for drug smuggling. Make sure you have no little, plastic bags filled with suspicious-looking white washing or talcum powder carefully stowed away under the bunks on the boat. Consider yourself warned!

Addresses and Telephone Numbers: Boat tickets can be bought at the following offices or at most travel agencies:

Comanav agent: Compagnie Charles Le Borgne, 3 Quai de la République, BP 99, 34202, Sète Cedex, France (Tel: 33-4-67-46-61-70, Fax: 33-4-67-74-33-04)

Seagle Ltd, 9B St. George's Lane, Gibraltar (Tel: 76763, 71415)

Transtour, Algeciras, Spain (Tel: 956-66-52-00)

Finally, for the hardy or those who are on a tight budget, there is always the **bus.** The journey from London to Tangier takes two days, departing from Victoria Coach Station (reservations from Eurolines, 52, Grosvenor Gardens, London SW1 0AU, Tel: 0170-730-8235, or at the Coach Station). There are departures three times a week. I've done it, and it's not too bad for those used to all-night bus travel, though short legs are an advantage. From Paris, the same company, Eurolines, has buses leaving from the Porte de la Villette (Tel: 01-40-38-93-93) four times a week (slightly shorter journey) to Tangier, right down to Tiznit, and passing through Rabat, Casablanca, Marrakech, and Agadir. Much of the male population in the Tiznit area was recruited many years ago to work in France, which accounts for the popularity of this service during the summer holiday months. The Moroccan bus companies **CTM, SATAS,** and **Supratours** are also authorized to run services from Brussels, Paris, and other European destinations. About 500,000 people travel between Morocco and Europe this way each year. Don't get lured into taking a seat on a cheaper bus—a number of international transport companies are illegal and their buses are uninsured.

Transportation within Morocco

Air. Royal Air Maroc (RAM) has an extensive network of internal flights. The hub of the system is Casablanca. So there are regular flights from Casablanca to Tangier, Tetouan, and Al-Hoceima in the north; to Oujda in the east; to Rabat and Fès in the center; to Er-Rachidia in the southeast; to Marrakech and Ouarzazate in the south; and to Agadir, Laayoune, and Dakhla in the far south. There used to be a flight to Tan-Tan, but this has been stopped. Regional Air Lines, a new company using 19-seater Beechcroft planes follows much the same routes as RAM: Tangier, Oujda, Fès, Marrakech, and Agadir. Hopefully, it will branch out and cover a few new destinations.

Timetables tend to change, as do prices. For some destinations, RAM offers reductions for people under 26 or 60 and over, and for couples traveling together. These airfare discounts depend on a variety of factors, so it is best to check first. Tickets can be bought from RAM or Regional Air Lines city branches (addresses are given in the area sections of this guide), or from almost any travel agency. Confirmation of return flights is essential.

Train. The Moroccan state railway service has greatly improved. A policy of modernization undertaken by the state railway company, the **Office Nationale des Chemins de Fer (ONCF)**, has led to faster and more comfortable trains, though the network is still limited to the north-south axis from Tangier to Marrakech and the west-east axis from Casablanca to Oujda. Recently, the Casablanca-Marrakech service has been extended by a connecting ONCF bus, included in the rail ticket, between Marrakech and Agadir, going on south to Laayoune and Dakhla. The same system has been set up to connect Tetouan to the Tangier-Casablanca train service and Beni Mellal to the Marrakech-Casablanca service. A fast and frequent service between Casablanca and Rabat was introduced a few years ago to serve the numerous commuters between these two cites.

Trains also link Mohammed V airport to the station of Casa Port, Rabat, Salé, and Kénitra roughly every hour, sometimes every two hours. Tickets for these stations, as well as to Meknès, Fès, Tangier, Oujda, and Marrakech, can be bought at the airport (in the lower airport level, just before the train platforms).

A last word on train services within Morocco: check on departure times before turning up at the station (and make sure you're at the right station in towns where there are two). And, alas, bear in mind that the trains usually run late . . .

Bus. Almost anywhere in Morocco can be reached by a **long-distance bus.** However, the only company I can recommend is the CTM, formerly a state enterprise, which has been recently privatized. CTM buses have timetables, leave when they are supposed to, and arrive more or less on time. Once you have bought your ticket, you are sure of a seat. Your baggage is securely stowed away. It's best to book in advance at peak periods, such as Friday and Sunday evenings, or the days before or after a public holiday. Night travel is safer than by the train, because there is little movement of passengers once you have started, and the driver and his assistant are vigilant. The CTM has recently started a service, with air-conditioning and video, from Casablanca to Dakhla via Agadir (covering the 1,684 km in 18 hours—you have to like that sort of thing!).

Other long-haul bus companies, though cheaper, are less reliable, more crowded, the seating accommodations are chancy, and unscheduled stops are frequent. Buses tend not to leave until they have got a full load of passengers—and possibly a few more—just to cover eventualities. But these buses are more fun (if you want to see local life in close quarters), and

more full of "local color" than the CTM. You may travel beside a buxom
peasant woman clutching a chicken or two, there are bound to be dozens
of babies, older children, unidentifiable bundles, and bursting packages
blocking the aisle, as well as the occasional object that falls from a decrepit
baggage rack.

Traveling by bus is an ideal way to come into contact—both physically
and intellectually—with local people who are not particularly obsessed by
the tourist as a source of income. It is unlikely that anyone on board will
speak English, but sign language can work wonders. A fruit or piece of
chocolate shared is worth a whole speech. This way of traveling is just fine
if you don't mind roughing it a bit.

Within the big towns, such as Tangier, Rabat, Casablanca, Fès, and so
on, it is possible to get from place to place by **urban buses.** Some are state-
run, others are private. The latter are slightly more expensive and are supposed to guarantee you a seat. In fact, in either public or private you are
likely to be able to sit down, unless you get on at a terminus. The fares are
between 2 and 4 DH for the trip. These are not recommended unless you
empty your pockets, stow away your money and valuables very carefully,
and enjoy what is, indeed, a very human experience. Thousands of men
and women use these buses up to four times a day to get to and from their
jobs. They are therefore almost always crowded. You are unlikely to see another foreigner on board, but this adds to the charm.

Taxi. Long-distance travel can also be done by **Big Taxi** *(grand taxi),* usually a Mercedes. They have specific pick-up places, and are limited to out-
of-town runs. They take six passengers and only leave when they are
full—unless you are willing to pay for the unsold places. You can also negotiate a particular destination with the driver, and even hire him and his
car for a morning or whole day. This can be quite a good alternative to
renting a car if there are several of you. Otherwise, at the pick-up place,
ask around until you find a driver going where you want to go, find out the
price, and—preferably—choose a vehicle that only needs you in it to set
off. Otherwise you may have to wait around a bit.

Within the big towns, the **Small Taxis** *(petits taxis)* (usually small
Renaults, Fiats, or Peugeots) are a comfortable and rapid alternative to the
bus. They are, of course, more expensive, but well worth it. The vehicle
should have a meter; if not, negotiate beforehand (unless you like to run
the risk of a scene upon arrival if you refuse to pay the exorbitant sum demanded). Luggage on the roof rack is extra, as is night use, and only three
passengers can be carried. These taxis are clearly distinguishable by their
sign, *Petit Taxi,* and their color, which is different in each town.

Rental Cars. For independent travel nothing beats a rented car. What is lost in close contact with your neighbor is more than compensated for by the freedom of choice. You can drive where you like in Morocco, except in the south of what used to be the Spanish Sahara, where there are some travel restrictions. As a tourist you can drive on a national driving license, but it is better to have an International Driver's license (issued by the American Automobile Association). Travel, too, with your national license. Carry your passport and car papers close at hand, as the Gendarmerie frequently stop cars to check on all the documents.

Hosts of car rental firms ply their trade in Morocco. There is not much competition between the big firms, but shopping around can produce better prices. A lot depends on the time of year—peak holiday periods are obviously less open to interesting bargains—and the length of time you want to book. At the Mohammed V Airport in Casablanca, Eurocar, Avis, Hertz, Budget, InterRent, Eurodollar, and Afric Cars are among the leading names. The first does a lot of business with the U.S. government, and may be open to negotiation. Always check carefully what you are getting for your money. A 20 percent VAT (Value Added Tax) has to be added to the figure quoted.

The most usual models offered by the car rental firms start with the Renault 4 or Fiat Uno (1,962 DH/three days from Eurodollar and Avis), moving progressively up to the Renault 19 (3,769 DH/three days from Eurodollar), the VW Minibus (with air-conditioning, 6,072 DH/three days from Avis), and the Mercedes 190E (with air-conditioning, 7,710 DH/three days from Eurodollar). If you are planning to use rough roads, I recommend the Renault 4 if you can get one (I have one myself), but if you want to go really rough or into sand, then you need a 4WD vehicle. These are usually Land Rovers or Mitsubishis. As an indication, average prices are 1,500-2,000 DH/day for a long chassis (six seats with an agency driver), 1,200-1,500 DH/day for short chassis (four seats without a driver). These vehicles are not offered from Mohammed V Airport, but can be ordered from there or obtained in towns such as Marrakech or Agadir. If intending to drive around Morocco—and this is really the best way to see the details—buy a good road map (make sure it has the Western Sahara marked as part of Morocco).

Addresses of car rental firms are given in the appropriate chapters of this guide.

A few words on driving in Morocco. Driving in Morocco is often thought to be a terrifying experience at first, especially in a big city like Casablanca. But after a while, the expatriate (expat) or the temporary visitor gets used to its eccentricities and enters into the swing of things ("swing" is actually quite a good word to describe Casablanca driving). It must be said that the **majority** of Moroccan car drivers do obey the Highway Code (based on the French one)—it's the others that give you a fright. Signposts follow the international code.

Traffic drives on the right, and priority has to be given to all vehicles coming from the right, unless their road has a stop sign (a six-sided sign, with white Arabic letters on a red background). But by the time you've searched for *their* stop, it's probably too late—so you'd best get used to giving way to traffic, including motorcycles, bicycles, and donkey-drawn carts, coming at you from the right, even if their road is a miserable affair compared to yours. When your road has a stop sign, come to a full stop. Traffic light patterns are: red—green—green blinking (very short)—orange (short)—red. You are allowed to pass on the blinking green light, but crossing on the orange and, of course, the red, is likely to get you into trouble. No motorist stops at a pedestrian crossing (called "target areas" by some humorists), or lets a car into the stream from a side road. If you do either of these things, you may well be bumped into by the car behind you. Ambulances, funeral processions, police cars, and Royalty always have priority.

There is a speed limit of 40 km/hour in the towns, which is rigorously enforced in the smaller centers, and rather less so in the big cities. On main out-of-town roads the limit is 100 km/hour, 120 km on the highway (this is not obvious from the speed at which cars will overtake you). A fine is also collected on the spot for a motorist encroaching on the unbroken white line. It is mandatory to fasten your front seatbelts, except in the towns, and crash helmets must (in theory) be worn by motorcycle and moped drivers (most riders just hang the helmet over the handlebars).

The main roads are good, thanks largely to the IMF, which has financed many of the improvements in Morocco's road network. The expressway between Rabat and Casablanca has been open for many years now (15 DH charge for the full journey). A new section continuing north to Tangier is almost completed, as is the stretch from Rabat to Fès via Meknès, and the Casablanca to Settat section has been inaugurated. There are some service stations and cafés along the expressway. A yellow "Help and Safety" van circulates (sometimes also a red one). Roadside telephones are absent, although the number to call—(Tel: 07-74 33 44)—is indicated by the side of the road from time to time.

Rough, unpaved roads range from good to very bad. Weather conditions can make even a good unpaved road impossible in a few hours, and a river suddenly in flood can hold up traffic even on a major road. Always ask at the Gendarmerie for information on road conditions if the weather is unstable. Snow barriers are quickly in position if the High Atlas passes are blocked; damaged bridges are likewise quickly and clearly indicated. Directions are well marked, generally in French and Arabic. However, in the residential areas of towns, the names of many streets are impossible to see or quite simply missing. This can be frustrating, but people will generally help you if you ask.

There are filling stations in all the big towns, with gasoline getting fractionally more expensive as you move away from Casablanca—until you get to the far south, where it is tax-free. The familiar Mobil is well represented. Current prices are as follows: Diesel is 4.64 DH/litre, Regular (becoming rarer) is 7.26 DH/litre, Super is 7.50 DH/liter (has a lower octane rating than its counterpart in the United States), and Unleaded is 7.32 DH/liter (not available everywhere). There are long stretches of road without service stations, so fill your tank whenever you can.

A special word of warning. Watch out for pedestrians walking in the street, or crossing over without looking, motorcycles and scooters weaving in and out of the traffic or coming at you on the wrong side of the road, unlit motorcycles, bicycles, animal-drawn carts at dusk or after dark, and vehicles of all kinds running the lights. Take particular care during the month of Ramadan, when fasting truck drivers tend to sleep at the wheel. As a pedestrian, you should look right and left, even on one-way streets. Don't be afraid to honk your horn. It is advisable to avoid driving in the country after dark, unless you have to. Even the expressway has seen some unpleasant episodes at night. Be vigilant at all times—the roads are often for the boldest and biggest. And keep calm. One of the signs posted along roadsides says the equivalent of "More haste, less speed."

Accidents are frequent in Morocco. Before you take to the road, ask your car rental agency what you should do in the event of getting involved in one of these affairs, which can turn out to be quite unpleasant if a crowd gathers. If personal injury is involved, the police **must** be summoned; otherwise it is simpler to have a "friendly" arrangement between the two parties. This involves the careful filling-in and signing of a form (which should be provided with your car—the *Constat à l'amiable d'Accident Automobile*) by both the drivers involved, giving details of the accident, the positions of the cars involved, and full data on the drivers' insurance companies. The rental agency should be informed at once, and will advise you on what to do next. Normally, the form goes to the insurance company for settlement.

Other transportation within Morocco. Bicycles are a popular means of transport, particularly in Marrakech. They can be rented for the morning, afternoon, or the whole day. Your hotel can give you details on where to rent and how much it will cost. Mountain bikes can also be rented from specialized agencies. There is nothing to beat a **mule** for carrying your gear if you go trekking in the mountains. Current prices for the animal and its driver are 75 DH/day. Rental tariffs and addresses are given in the High Atlas section. Count one mule for two people's "normal" baggage. In the desert, the **camel** is the most suitable beast of burden. With a driver, it costs around 300 DH a day.

Hitchhiking. Plenty of people hitch a ride in Morocco, especially in country districts where transport is rare. Truck drivers who pick up hitch-hikers expect to be paid. I cannot recommend it as a way of getting around, although I have on occasion picked up Moroccan women (yes, Moroccan women hitchhike!) and old men if there are several of us in the vehicle and no normal public transport. **Under no circumstances should you try hitchhiking in the Rif area in north Morocco (see relevant chapter), or pick up anyone trying to get a lift—however pathetic they may seem.** They only need to be caught with a gram of *kif* (marijuana) on them and you are arrested for "transporting drugs," a criminal offense.

Travel Facts

Climate. Morocco is a warm, sunny country. But temperature differences can be big and sudden—between the day and the night, between the midday sun outside and the interior of a house. The hottest months are June, July, and August. Temperatures in Tangier and Casablanca are around 27°C (81°F) in summer and 15°C (59°F) in winter. In Marrakech they can reach 38°C (101°F) in July and August, dropping to a comfortable 18°C (64°F) in winter. Agadir is more temperate: 26°C (78°F) in June and September, a few degrees higher in July and August, and dropping to 21°C (69°F) in December and January.

It does rain in Morocco, but never enough for the farmers. Country people used to be able to count on rain falling towards the end of October/beginning of November, and again in February/March. In recent years the climate has become more erratic, with drought and water shortages a permanent feature. If all goes according to schedule, November through February will see rain, with snow on higher altitudes. Good months for traveling anywhere are March and April, and May and June if you don't go too far south. Another good season is the fall, i.e. September through to October. Spring travel has the advantage of a green landscape, full of flowers and trees in blossom. In the fall, the countryside is dry and parched after the long summer months without rain, but temperatures have normally dropped. In July, August, and September it's hot, too hot to enjoy travel in the far south, which is best done in the winter, from November through February. But if you plan to lie on the beach, then the summer months will suit you fine, and this is, in fact, the busiest tourist season. Trekking in the High Atlas can be done all the year round, but the ideal months are from April through October, keeping to the high valleys in the heat of summer. A rough seasonal guide for activities is given below:

- March, April, May, June, September, and October: good for sight-seeing
- June, July, and August: the time for beach-goers
- April, May, June, July, August, September, and October: ideal for mountain trekking
- November, December, January, and February: good for desert travel

The month of Ramadan, when Moslems fast from dawn to dusk, is considered by some to be a bad month for visitors. The whole normal schedule of activities is certainly upset, with people getting up later, not stopping for lunch, going home from work early in the afternoon—and making merry all night. It's not a very profitable month in which to do business, nor will you be invited in for tea by people you meet on the roads. Otherwise, it's calm and quiet for traveling.

Packing. The advice given to travelers all over the world is to "travel light," and this holds for Morocco. Easy-to-wash, light, comfortable, and casual clothes in natural fabrics will do you most of the time, with a smarter outfit if you are planning to dine out or to go to an evening show (some restaurants require men to wear a tie). Comfortable shoes are essential. A warm sweater is often needed in the evenings, even in summer. A foldaway plastic raincoat is handy for sudden showers and head protection against the sun should certainly be included. Men can go sightseeing in shorts, Bermuda style, not too short, but women are best dressed in a light skirt or loose trousers when walking through the town or visiting museums and monuments. Beachwear is, of course, relaxed. If you are on a business trip, you'll need to dress more formally. Moroccans are very sensitive to appearances, and a T-shirt and blue jeans are less likely to pull off a business deal than a well-cut suit. Whatever type of holiday you are on, you'll be able to use a bathing suit. Micro-bikinis are probably all right on the beach, as are bare shoulders and midriffs, but expect a lot of attention from Moroccan men on the lookout for foreign beauties. If you plan to trek or do some other sport, you should bring the appropriate clothing, as boots and so on are expensive here. Among the non-clothing items that could come in handy are a small flashlight, a penknife for peeling fruit, and your favorite remedy for a queasy stomach—few people avoid a short bout of *tourista*, a diarrhea attack that can spoil your holiday if not treated. Such stomach upsets usually come from a change in eating habits and don't necessarily imply bad food. Take with you a supply of any regular medication. Insect repellent and toilet paper are always useful, but can be easily bought in Morocco.

Public Holidays

There are ten national secular holidays and three religious ones. On these occasions, all state buildings, the post office, banks, factories, and schools are closed. Small grocery shops and bakeries remain open in the mornings, but other food shops may well close for the whole day. Most restaurants and cafés continue to function, as do hotels, trains, buses, and taxis. Watch out for what is called a "bridge"—an additional day taken after a holiday and linking it to a weekend to make a really good break.

Secular holidays:

- January 1   New Year's Day (celebrated in Western fashion)
- January 11   Celebration of the Independence Manifesto
- March 3   Throne Day (lots of patriotic speeches, music, and processions
- May 1   Labor Day (trade unions parade and shout slogans)
- May 23   National Day
- July 9   Celebration of Youth
- August 14   Anniversary of the allegiance of the Saharan province of Wad-Ed-Dahab
- August 20   Celebration of the Revolution of the King and the People
- November 6   Anniversary of the Green March
- November 18 Independence Day

Islamic holidays:

- *Aid es Sghir,* the Little Feast (more correctly *Aid al Fitr*): marks end of Ramadan
- *Aid al Kbir,* the Big Feast (more correctly *Aid al Adha*): 68 days after *Aid al Fitr*
- *Mouloud:* 12th day of Islamic month of Rabia 1.

Morocco follows the Islamic lunar calendar, which means that the year is 11 days shorter than ours. Since this calendar depends on a sighting of the new moon, it is impossible to forecast exactly which day will be a holiday.

Mail and Telephone Services

The postal service is reasonably good, with letters and parcels reaching a local destination within a few days. Overseas mail can be slow: up to ten days or a fortnight to North America (airmail), and five to seven days to Europe (automatically airmail). Surface mail can take weeks or months. The current rate for an ordinary airmail letter to the United States is 11 DH. Important overseas mail, whether letters or parcels, should be registered (presented open to the post office employee and sealed after inspection). The weight limit is 20 kilograms (kgs). DHL World Wide Express will send documents or packages overseas rapidly, and a Poste Rapide service operates from the central post offices (for both overseas and inland mail). A 500 gram (g) parcel to the U.S. by the Poste Rapide costs 300 DH and should arrive within a few days. There is also United Parcel Service in Casablanca (210 Boulevard Zerklouni, Tel: 02-48 36 36, Fax: 02-48 35 56). They also operate in Rabat, Meknès, Fès, Tangier, and Adadir. An office will open soon in Marrakech.

North American companies have been at work recently, improving the Moroccan telecommunications network. While it is not perfect, there has certainly been a big change for the better. A rather complicated system allows cheaper calls at certain periods (within Morocco at lunchtime, between 8:30 P.M. and 7:00 A.M., and during weekends, for instance, and overseas between 10:00 P.M. and 7:00 A.M. and on weekends). There are nine telephone regions, each starting with a 0—07, for instance, is the code for Rabat and its region (the other codes will be found in the appropriate chapters). The 0 is not needed when telephoning within the region. Charges are based on distance and time. They range, at the moment, from 40 centimes to 4 DH per minute during normal hours (calls from hotels cost considerably more). The telephone directories (in French) give full telephoning instructions and useful numbers.

Most countries in the world can be reached direct from Morocco (dial 00, followed at once by the country code and number required). It is generally cheaper to call Morocco from abroad (the international code for Morocco is 212), rather than the other way around. At the moment, a one-minute call to the U.S. or Canada costs 20 DH at the ordinary rate. Recently AT&T set up a service to the U.S. The access code is 00-211-00-11: give your AT&T card and PIN number, then go ahead. The call will be charged as if it originated in the U.S. In fact, there are very little savings, the advantage being that you are billed in the U.S., which can be useful when on holiday. Public telephones used to be very poor—always broken or out of use—but the recent introduction of private *téléboutiques* has revolutionized the scene. These little booths are not only equipped with a number of telephones, but also have fax and photocopying machines and sell stamps (stamps are also sold by many newspaper and tobacco kiosks, which saves time lining up at the post office). They will also act as a fax-receiving station for you and sell phone cards *(télécartes)* for use in card phones (68.50 DH for 50 units, 156 DH for 120 units). Watch out: cards bought from a téléboutique can't be used in all téléboutiques, but only in ones belonging to the same company; cards bought at the post office can only be used at the post office. Fax machines are widely used, e-mail is coming in, and the Internet is used by many. Some 6,000 Moroccans surf the Web, and cybercafés have sprung up in all the big towns. Most of the big hotels are well-equipped in this line. Receiving mail in the big towns, other than at your hotel, works quite well at the "Poste Restante, La Poste Principale" of the town of your choice. They won't keep your letters very long, however, and you need a passport to claim them.

Photocopying must be the second national sport after football, as photocopying machines are everywhere—no self-respecting newsagent would be without one. Phoning or faxing from a hotel is expensive, as hotels charge a very high minimum fee.

Metrics and Electrics

Morocco uses the metric system. You will need to master a few conversions in order to be able to calculate temperatures and distances.

Temperature. Water freezes at 0° and boils at 100° in the Celsius (C) system. If the temperature is 10°C it's cold (50° Farenheit), 20° (68° F) is a pleasant temperature for moving around, at 30° (86°F) it's hot for physical activity, and at 38° (100°F) it's very hot. If you want to do the conversions yourself, Farenheit is converted to Celsius by subtracting 32 and multiplying by $5/9$; to change Celsius to Farenheit, multiply by $9/5$ and add 32.

Distance. Feet and miles are replaced in Morocco by a millimeter (mm), a centimeter (cm; 10 millimeters), a meter (m; 100 centimeters), and a kilometer (km; 1,000 meters). Distances on the roadsides are in kilometers, or fractions of kilometers. A sufficiently close conversion for distances is to count 8 km for 5 miles. So the 240 km shown for the distance between Casablanca and Marrakech, for instance, is the equivalent of 150 miles. On the small scale, 5 centimeters equal 2 inches, 30 cm equal 1 foot, and a meter and a yard are practically the same length.

Electricity. 110 volts and 220 volts coexist in Morocco, within the same town and even within the same house. Older houses (such as my own) are often wired for 110 volts, and new buildings are wired for 220 volts. Always check that you plug in your shaver, hairdryer, or other appliance to the appropriate voltage. You'll usually need a converter before using your

American appliances. Despite the general reliability of the electrical system, it is best to travel with a flashlight.

All the towns have electricity, but not all villages. Ambitious plans are under way to equip even remote areas with electricity. Some village people have joined together to buy a diesel-run motor to produce electricity, while others are slowly and timidly turning to solar panels (especially homes where a member of the family works in Europe and has brought back a satellite dish).

Money and Prices

The Moroccan currency is the *dirham* and its smaller unit, the *centime*. One hundred centimes (cts) make up a dirham (shown here as DH). Bills come in denominations of 10 DH (pink), 20 DH (sort of orange), 50 DH (green), 100 DH (pale brown), and 200 DH (blue). Coins worth 10 DH, 5 DH, 1 DH, and 50 cts are silver-colored, and those worth 20 cts, 10 cts, and 5 cts are brass-colored (the last-named are almost non-existent). The 10 DH coin is easy to confuse with the 5 DH model. Some shopkeepers still count in French francs. Just remove the last two figures to get the right sum in dirhams; for instance, a quoted 10,000 francs means 100 DH. Others use an old-fashioned *rial*. If you are quoted what sounds like an extraordinarily high figure, chances are that it's in rials. There are 20 rials to the dirham. I have my own conversion system, which you may or may not like: I cut the rial sum in half, then put in a decimal point (50 rial—25 rial—2.5 DH). (You won't need this very often!)

Access Mastercard, American Express, and Diners Club credit cards are widely accepted, not only in hotels, but also in up-market restaurants and shops. It is preferable to change travelers' checks at a bank. Plans are afoot for the dirham to be made into a convertible currency, but for the moment exchange controls operate, although the market is pretty free and there is practically no black market. There is no financial advantage in changing money in the street with individuals who may approach you with an apparently tempting offer. Most banks have a counter (marked "Change") where you can change money. Rates vary little. At the moment, a quick system puts the US$ at 10 DH (in fact, ± 9.50 DH). Your passport is needed for transactions. ATM machines exist in Casablanca and Rabat, and some American bankcards can be used to withdraw local currency from an account in the United States. Banking hours vary slightly from branch to branch (see later under "Business Hours").

Prices. A whole book could be written about Moroccan prices and bargaining. To get an idea of prices, see what the following cost: a small black coffee is 3 DH (30 cents); an in-town taxi is 10 DH (US$1); a double room in a *** hotel is 350 DH (US$35); a room in the cheapest hotel is 50 DH (US$5); a middle-range lunch is 200 DH (US$20); and a cheap set (or "fixed") meal in Marrakech is 80 DH (US$8).

There is no such thing as an official "tourist" price and a "local" price, as is in some countries. But, in fact, tourists always get asked more, except where there are fixed prices (in hotels and restaurants, for example). Prices are always quoted in dirhams, although you can settle the bill by credit card or dollars in places used to dealing with tourists, as was stated above. Hotels and restaurants have a fixed price range and do not appreciate attempts to bargain, although the former sometimes have special deals, and you could try negotiating a lower price for a long stay. Drinks at the bar cost at least double what they would in America. Wine served at meals is three to four times more expensive than the bottle you can buy around the corner. When looking at the prices proposed in a restaurant, see if the service charge and taxes are included. The latter could add 17 percent to your bill and cause a nasty surprise.

Hotel prices given in this guide are for a double room (singles are slightly cheaper and triples a bit more expensive). Check whether the price you are quoted includes all taxes. Hotel prices are regulated by the state. The Ministry of Tourism allocates stars to hotels, which can then charge within the limits of their rating. Top of the line are the ***** hotels, going down to the * (and unclassified). At least one star should be knocked off to approach Western standards. Moroccan hotels are good when they are new. Unfortunately, maintenance is often neglected, even in the top hotels. Down the scale, bedroom lighting is often poor, light bulbs are missing, washbasin plugs are absent, the hot water is not always hot, and the plumbing hesitant and noisy. In the cheap hotels, and in many popular restaurants, the toilet facilities are unappealing, with squat water closets. If you haven't come across them yet, note that a squat water closet (toilet) consists of a ceramic, metal, or plastic square with a hole in the middle and two slightly raised foot-shaped areas where you stand. There is generally a bucket and tap available for you to throw water down the hole, while trying not to douse your shoes at the same time. North African standards should not be compared to or confused with what is known back home.

Food shops, including markets, have fixed prices, but you might get a dirham or two knocked off your bill by suggesting to the stall holder that you could buy a kilo of oranges cheaper at his neighbor's. Bargaining is part of the Moroccan commercial scene. It's a miserable affair for the seller if his first price is accepted right away. Lengthy bargaining is part of the pleasure a salesman gets out of selling—if his first price is accepted, he can reckon to have lost a good chance of making more. And all that play-acting strengthens the links established between buyer and seller. The bargaining act comes into play when buying souvenirs, clothing, jewelry, pottery, fossils, and a whole host of other things that make Morocco such a tempting place in which to spend money. However, craftwork centers run by the State *(Ensemble Artisanal, Complexe Artisanal)* have fixed prices, and if you don't enjoy the poker game of bargaining, then you are better off doing your shopping here. The choice is good and the prices reasonable.

Now, let's start the bargaining. You rather fancy a piece of silver jewelry. (But is it really silver? I'll give you some pointers in just a bit!). Have some idea of what it should cost, or at least the top price you are prepared to pay. You ask the price of one or two other items, with interest but without enthusiasm. Then you arrive at the one that you really fancy.

"And that piece?" you ask indifferently.

"500 DH."

You throw up your hands in horror.

"How much then?"

"Well, perhaps 200 DH."

"200 DH? No, no, but you can have it for 450."

You then move away, feigning interest in something quite different, launch into another subject altogether, get out your purse showing ostensibly that you only have 200 DH, make for the door—the choice of strategies is almost limitless. The seller drops his price, you raise yours by 20-30 DH, he drops a bit more, you concede yours another 10 DH . . . and so on. If your last offer is accepted (around 250-260 DH for instance), you must take the goods—it's not considered fair play to cut the affair short at this stage.

A lot depends on how much you want the object. I was flabbergasted once, when coming down by car from a trip in the High Atlas, to find my companion the possessor, for 100 DH, after 30 minutes of discussion, of a rug for which the owner of the roadside stall had originally asked 1,000 DH. But that was an exception—and my friend sincerely didn't want the rug.

A satisfactory price, with neither side losing face, usually ends up at half the starting figure. If you are buying directly from a craftsman, and not from a commercial intermediary, insulting offers should, of course, not be made. You'll have to judge the situation yourself—but in all cases, keep smiling, laugh, agree that the goods are superb, and suggest that you'll come back another time (even if this is unlikely). Enjoy being an actor working out your own script.

Now, is that heavy piece of jewelry really silver? That necklace, is it really amber? The wife of an American Consul General in Casablanca (herself a jewelry-maker) has some advice: practically all the foibles, bracelets, and necklaces you are tempted to buy are not made of silver. Some 80 percent of the jewelry today is made of "German silver," or nickel silver, a metal alloy of copper, zinc, and nickel invented 80 years ago by a German scientist. Don't believe the merchant's trick of rubbing the metal shiny with a piece of cloth, scraping it against a rough surface, or even biting it, then triumphantly showing you the bright spot—"Look, it's all silver!" There is, in fact, no way you can tell the difference for sure unless you have a trained eye. What can you do to avoid being swindled? The answer is to buy from a trustworthy jeweler and have a silver-test done. This means that the jeweler will rub a corner of the jewelry against a touch stone which leaves a trace of metal, then apply a drop of testing acid. If the piece is silver, the metal trace will turn bright red. A pale red means low silver content, and if the trace disappears completely, then it's nickel silver. Testing acid is highly poisonous (even its vapor), so don't dream of taking a bottle of it on your next visit to the souk. And don't be surprised if those honey-colored beads turn out to be plastic (the smell is different when polished). Don't let this put you off buying a pretty piece—but pay accordingly.

Tipping. Most hotels and restaurants add a service charge to the bill (10 percent). If the waiter has been particularly pleasant, or you have been a particularly demanding customer, a few coins left for him will always be appreciated. But don't go in for heavy tipping. Porters in the big hotels are usually already paid for this service, but if the doorman runs errands for you, like getting a packet of cigarettes or a newspaper, then he, too, will appreciate a couple of dirhams or so. There is a fixed rate for baggage at the airport (3 DH per piece), and there is no need to give more. Parking attendants (excluding hotel parking when you are a guest) expect 2-3 DH a session, golf caddies get 100 DH per round (mandatory), and ball boys at tennis clubs receive 10-20 DH/hour, depending on the club. Museum staff and filling station attendants do *not* need tipping (although I give 1 DH if I want air put in the tires).

If a local inhabitant springs out from behind a palm tree you were admiring and asks you into his house for a cup of tea (mint tea), he is, alas, not completely disinterested in a "reward" of some sort. Moroccan hospitality is proverbial, but the advent of tourists has changed things. If you accept the invitation, leave a small present as you go—it could be a 5 or 10 DH piece (depending on how much tea you've had), a small gadget, or some pencils or sweets for the children. You have to play it by ear, as some people definitely prefer the money, while I've met others who have spurned the money with indignation but were pleased to have a couple of cans of sardines.

Although not exactly tipping, there are a number of other ways in which one is urged to part from one's money. I personally am against paying to take a photograph of someone (which is perhaps why I have no photographs of people), although this is, unfortunately, nearly always asked for nowadays (1-2 DH is quite enough—but always ask permission before photographing people close up). Children will constantly solicit you for anything—they particularly like squinting into your car and asking for anything that catches their eye (make sure their eye doesn't catch too much). The normal requests are for dirham, "bonbons," *fanida* (sweets), or "stylo" (a ball-point pen). It is best not to encourage them. A distribution of sweets to 2 or 3 children will quickly turn into a rioting crowd of 20-30 youngsters, all determined to get a share of the goodies. This can be a disagreeable experience. Men will occasionally plead for a cigarette, and if you camp or picnic in the country, and people know you are there, you are likely to have a stream of visitors complaining of stomach pains, eye trouble, and/or headaches, or rolling up a trouser leg to show you a hideous cut or burn. It is helpful to travel with aspirin tablets (to be given out sparingly), and cotton-balls and an antiseptic to clean the wound (if you feel up to it). You can't do much more except advise a visit to the local health center (which may be many miles away).

You will see beggars in Morocco, despite firm efforts by the state to keep them off the streets. What you do when an old woman, small child, or blind man stretches out a hand, imploring alms in the name of God, is very much a personal matter. Not all Moroccans give to chance beggars, though they may have their preferred recipients. If you do decide to put something into the outstretched hand, it need only be one of the brass-colored 10- or 20- centime pieces. Some people feel it more useful to help a collectivity—the school for blind children, a private training center for girls of very modest condition, or a center for the physically handicapped. In the Mohammed V Airport in Casablanca, there is a large glass collection box where you can put all your small change just before leaving and thus help the day-care centers and crèches for needy children run by the Moroccan League for the Protection of Children (*Ligue Marocaine Pour la Protection de l'Enfance*).

Government Fiddle-Faddle

Passports and Visas. Passports are required and must be valid for at least six months. Visas are not needed for visits of under three months (90 days). On arrival, all incoming travelers are required to fill in a form with personal details, including purpose of visit (stay simple and put "tourism") and local address (a hotel will do—you're not penalized for changing your mind and never turning up in the designated hotel). For a stay exceeding 90 days, Americans, like other foreigners, are obliged to have a resident's permit. United States citizens also require a re-entry visa if they intend to return to Morocco for extended periods. The permit *(carte de séjour)* and visa can be requested, before the expiration of the 90-day period, from the immigration section *(Contrôle des Etrangers)* of the central police station. Depending on your situation, it might be just as easy to take a day trip to Ceuta or Melilla, or across the Strait to Gibraltar or Algeciras, and start a new 90-day stay period. This shortcut cannot be practiced indefinitely. Further information concerning entry requirements to Morocco can be obtained from the Moroccan Embassy in Washington, D.C.

In hotels all over Morocco, you have scarcely time to take a breath when you are asked to fill in a police form, with your name, date and place of birth, passport number, and so on. This can be irritating if you have had a long and tiring journey, so the up-market hotels sometimes offer guests a fruit juice to calm them down while the forms are sorted out. It is an essential formality—so just bear with it.

The Moroccan government considers children born to Moroccan fathers as Moroccan citizens. This may be a delicate matter in the case of the child of divorced parents if the father is Moroccan or a resident of Morocco, and the mother is American. Even if the child has an American passport, immigration officers may require proof that the father has approved the child's departure from Morocco. American women married to Moroccans do not need their husband's permission to leave Morocco.

The American Consulate General in Casablanca points out that, regardless of which passport is used to enter Morocco, persons with dual nationality or born of Moroccan fathers are treated as Moroccan citizens while on Moroccan soil, and that U.S. consular protection to such persons can be difficult to assure.

Travel Restrictions. The visitor can go almost anywhere in Morocco. However, with the frontier with Algeria to the east being closed, it is likely that anyone driving too close to this area will arouse suspicion. The same remark holds true for the undefined frontier with Algeria in south Morocco, which is under army surveillance. Travel south from Dakhla towards Mauritania is possible, but subject to restrictions. Vehicles have to travel in convoy and must not deviate from the prepared route. The convoy leaves at 12:00 P.M. on Tuesdays and Fridays. This is not worth doing unless you absolutely must get to Mauritania by car (a visa is needed), and/or enjoy the challenge.

Customs. Customs officials will examine your luggage on arrival.

Bringing in personal effects, including jewelry and a camera with up to 10 rolls of film, will cause no difficulty. Customs officers are courteous and not too inquisitive with tourists, but you should avoid having provocative material easily visible. Books with an obvious Jewish content, video films, and pornographic magazines may attract attention and cause delays if your luggage is opened. You are allowed to bring in 200 cigarettes and a liter of spirits. Drugs, of course, are *totally* forbidden. Don't try and bring in anything that looks like cocaine or *kif.* Don't bring in parcels for other people, or take responsibility for anyone else's luggage.

The amount of money you bring into the country is not restricted, but sums over 25,000 DH have to be declared on arrival. Sporting guns (regarded with suspicion) and electronic equipment such as sophisticated cameras, video equipment, and computers can be imported duty-free for a period not exceeding 90 days. Customs will note the details of these things in your passport and check that you still have them when you leave the country. If any of them have been lost or stolen, you'll have to show a police declaration to this effect. Otherwise, it will be assumed that you have sold them, and you will be subject to a heavy fine. This goes, too, for a car: if you came into the country with one you must leave with one or explain convincingly what has happened to it.

Taking dirhams out of the country is forbidden, except for very small sums if you plead an imminent return (in fact, Moroccan money can be changed in Ceuta, Gibraltar, and in southern Spanish ports). At Mohammed V Airport, on departure, you can change back into dollars half of what you changed during your stay—on condition that you show the currency exchange receipts you received when buying dirhams, so remember to keep them.

Traveler's Guide

Safety. Violent crime is not a serious problem in Morocco. When it does occur, it is usually an affair between Moroccans and the tourist is unlikely to be affected. I myself have never felt in danger in Morocco, even during the Gulf War when feelings ran high in favor of Iraq. Having said this, certain elementary rules should be followed. Take the normal security precautions you would take in any large city, such as New York. Carry a minimum amount of cash, and discard your flashy jewelry and diamond-studded watch. Don't load yourself down with parcels, bags, clothing, etc. Valuables you don't need can be left with the hotel reception or out of sight in your room (shut the windows before going out). If driving around in a car, lock your belongings in the trunk. Stow your passport away carefully in an inner pocket or pouch slung around your neck inside your shirt. Petty theft is common, even in hotels. People will try confidence tricks on unwary travelers, ("would you please help me write a letter in English" is a favorite one) mostly to lure them into a souvenir-selling shop (quite harmless), or sometimes to exchange false money (more serious). It is inadvisable to wander about peripheral areas or medinas (literally "town," but used to indicate the original, very Moroccan part of a town, full of little alleys, shops, and houses) after dark, and, in any case, it is best, whatever the time of day, to choose a well-frequented road rather than an isolated shortcut. This advice, of course, is doubly applicable to single women. Don't hesitate to eat in public places, but avoid a drink or food that looks as though it's been prepared only for you. Most Moroccan dishes have to be cooked a long time, so the microbes die (which is why restaurant food—cooked too fast—sometimes tends not to be very good). Don't be paranoid, enjoy meeting people, but be vigilant.

Business Hours. The normal business week is Monday through Friday. Government offices, post offices, and main banks are closed on Saturdays and Sundays, though some bank branches are open on Saturday mornings. Shops are also open on Saturdays (some even on Sundays). Local city markets are always open all week, including Sunday mornings. The working day in government offices is from 8:00 A.M.-12:00 P.M. and 2:30 P.M.-6:00 or 6:30 P.M., except on Friday, when the lunch break starts at 11:30 A.M. and goes on until 2:30 or 3:00 P.M., to allow time for prayers in the mosque. Banking hours are normally from 8:30 A.M.-11:30 A.M. and from 2:30 P.M.-4:30 P.M., but many branch offices have a different timetable. The post office is open from 8:30 A.M.-12:30 P.M. and from 2:30 P.M.-6:30 P.M. The lunch break is 1½ hours longer on Friday. During Ramadan, almost everybody works without a lunch break from 9:00 A.M.-2:30 P.M. or 3:00 P.M.

Tourist Information. Morocco is a country that is trying to improve its tourism sector. Publicity and general information is widely available. However, this tends to consist mainly of glossy brochures of a rather general nature, and details on hotels or attractions available in the town in which you are staying are disappointingly sparse. The local tourist offices *(Office de Tourisme)* rarely have more than a few of these attractive handouts, and not always in the language you want.

On the other hand, books on most aspects of Morocco have been written by sociologists, anthropologists, and professionals in many fields. If you want to delve further into Moroccan subjects, here are just a few subjective suggestions. Some of these books are best read before the journey, others can be brought along for consultation or bedtime reading. Some of these books may be hard to find, so if you don't have any luck at your local bookstore, try the library.

Morocco, General:
- *Morocco,* by Shirley Kay, Quartett Books Limited, UK, 1981. An easy to read, well-illustrated overall view of Morocco and the Moroccans.
- *Morocco from the Air,* by Yann and Anne Arthus-Bertrand, Vendome Press, 1994. Superb aerial photographs.
- *Culture Shock! Morocco. A Guide to Customs and Etiquette,* by Orin Hargraves, Graphic Arts Center Publishing Company, Portland, Oregon, 1995. An ex-Peace Corps volunteer offers a useful guide to the aspects of Moroccan life that puzzle visitors.

Anthology:
- *Morocco, The Traveller's Companion,* by Margaret and Robin Bidwell, I. B. Tauris & Co., London, New York, 1993. Excerpts from the writings of well-known travelers to Morocco, from the 16th century onwards. A most useful insight into Morocco from works now very difficult to get (recommended for bedtime reading).

Architecture, Decoration, and Design:
- *A Practical Guide to Islamic Monuments in Morocco,* by Richard Parker, one-time U.S. Ambassador to Morocco, The Baraka Press, Charlottesville, Virginia, 1981. Published under the sponsorship of the Aga Khan Program for Islamic Architecture at Harvard University and the Massachusetts Institute of Technology, this excellent book is just what it says it is, and you should have it near you if you are interested in Islamic architecture.
- *Al-Andalus, the Art of Islamic Spain,* ed. Jerrilynn D. Dodds, Metropolitan Museum of Art, New York, 1992. A beautiful book with a chapter on the architectural heritage of Islamic Spain in North Africa.
- *The Hassan II Mosque,* published by Daniel Briand, 1993. Two versions, one is trilingual. The cheaper version is in English, with the same photos and text.
- *Morocco. Designs from Casablanca to Marrakech,* by Lisl and Landt Dennis, Clarkson Potter Publishers, New York, 1995. A beautiful and well-documented book on houses, architecture, pottery, and so on.
- *Moroccan Interiors,* by Lisa Lovatt-Smith, ed. Angelika Muthesius. Taschen (U.S.A.), 1997. Interesting reading with interiors of celebrities' houses from Essaouira, Marrakech, Fès, Rabat, and Tangier.
- *The Kutubiyya Mosque Minbar,* ed. Jonathan M. Bloom. Metropolitan Museum of Art, New York, 1998.

Arts and Crafts:
- *Berber Tribal Carpets and Weavings from Morocco,* by H. Reinisch and W. Stanzer, Reinisch, Graz, 1991. An excellent and well-documented bilingual (French and English) text with good photos, covering far more of Berber life than its title suggests.

- *Arts & Crafts of Morocco,* by James F. Jereb, Thames and Hudson, UK, 1995. A beautiful book by an American living in Santa Fé who has spent many years studying Moroccan architecture and decoration.

Berbers:

- *The Berbers of Morocco,* by Alan Keohane, Hamish Hamilton, UK, 1991 (Library of Congress Catalog Card Number 90-85831). Has excellent photographs, but a very short text.
- *Imazighen, the Vanishing Tradition of Berber Women,* by Margaret Courtney-Clark, Clarkson Potter, 1996.
- *The Berbers (The People of Africa),* by Michael Brett and Elizabeth Fentress, ed. Parker Shipton, Blackwell, 1997. A complete study, highly recom-mended by David Hart, the leading American anthropologist on the northern Moroccan Berbers.

Cooking:

- *Come With Me to the Kasbah, a Cook's Tour of Morocco,* by Kitty Morse, Editions Serar, Casablanca, 1989. Has plenty of good recipes, and much more than that, by a Californian cooking expert and writer, born and brought up in Morocco (a few copies are available through the author: www.kittymorse.com).
- *North Africa: The Vegetarian Table,* by Kitty Morse, Chronicle Books, San Francisco, 1996 (www.chronbooks.com).

History and Politics:

- *Lords of the Atlas,* by Gavin Maxwell, UK, 1966. Most of the book comes from a well-known earlier writer, Walter Harris, with some original comments.
- *The Commander of the Faithful,* by John Waterbury, Columbia University Press, 1970. A fascinating study of the politico-family networks in Morocco by one of America's leading authorities on Morocco.
- *A Year in Marrakech,* by Peter Mayne, Eland Books, London, and Hippocrene Books Inc., New York, 1982. A humorous account of life in Marrakech in the 1950s.

Women:

- *A Street in Marrakech,* by Elizabeth Warnock Fernea, Waveland Press, 1988. An amusing description of a year in Marrakech by the author, her husband, and three children.
- *Beyond the Veil, Male-Female Dynamics in a Modern Muslim Society,* by Fatima Mernissi, Indiana University Press, 1987. An outspoken book by one of Morocco's leading sociologists and feminists, holder of an American Ph.D.
- *Patience & Power, Women's Lives in a Moroccan Village,* by Susan Schaefer Davis, Schenkman Publishing Company, Cambridge,

Massachusetts, 1982. A good insight into daily life by an American anthropologist.

- *The Use and Function of Tattooing on Moroccan Women,* by Susan Searight, Human Relations Area Files, Inc., New Haven, Connecticut, 1984. A 3-volume study on tattooing, undertaken as a doctoral thesis in social anthropology.

News Media. Television is the most popular medium, with almost every town building, and many a village house, sporting a television aerial. In the fall of 1998, the Moroccan Department of Statistics indicated that 72 percent of households had television. Satellite dishes are also a familiar—and ugly—sight in town and country. In fact, the television satellite audience is in full expansion, attracting many European and Saudian operators. I rather think that television has supplanted the radio in people's lives, but small transistors are still favored by the young, be they students or shepherds. Moroccan television has two channels, broadcasting in Arabic and French. One, 2M, used to be private, required payment, and offered some competition to the official service (TVM). But pirating of decoders and frauds of various kinds brought it to untimely end. Now, both channels are run by the state. Unless you know Arabic or French, they are not very interesting, except perhaps to watch a little bit of local news, which is mostly the activities of the Royal Family and the arrival of important foreign dignitaries.

Satellite television is available in most up-market hotels. Dozens of foreign stations can be captured, broadcasting in Arabic, French, English, Italian, German, Spanish, and Portuguese, to name just a few. The bigger dishes catch CNN, NBC, TNT Classic Movies, BBC, and Eurosport in English.

Before satellite television came in with a bang, video films used to be very popular and video clubs sprang up all over the big cities. But this phase seems to have passed and all the video clubs in my area have disappeared. The videotape system in use in Morocco is SECAM.

Local radio broadcasting is in Arabic and French. Spanish programs can be picked up in northern Morocco, and in Tangier it is sometimes possible to get English-language broadcasts from Gibraltar. The Voice of America (V.O.A.) can be heard on shortwave radios at various times of the day. The Press Section of the American Cultural Center *(Dar America)* in Casablanca will supply information on program times. The BBC also broadcasts in English from about 8:00 A.M. until the evening, on different frequencies according to the time of day.

Local newspapers are all in French or Arabic. Most are linked to a political party. *Le Matin du Sahara et du Maghreb* and *Maroc Soir* are both right wing, *L'Opinion* and *Al Alam* are both Istiqal, *Libération* and *Al Ittihad*

Al-Ichtiraki are Socialist, *Al Bayane* and *Bayane Al-Youm* are ex-Communist, and *Almaghrib* is center. A new Arab-language daily came on sale at the end of October 1998, *Ahdat Maghribya*, that is independent left-wing. Imported French newspapers and reviews are available at newsstands catering to a French-speaking public. Many local weeklies are written in French. They cover many shades of opinion and are well worth reading. A useful little booklet, usually free, called *La Quinzaine du Maroc*, gives lots of information on cinemas, restaurants, and other attractions, and you don't have to be a French-language wizard to make use of it.

Time and *Newsweek* are on sale at all big hotels and in many newsstands in the big cities. The *Washington Post* and Chicago's *Herald Tribune* are less easy to come by, but, again, are stocked by the bookshops attached to the big hotels and in certain newsagents in the tourist towns. *The Economist* and the *International Guardian* can also be found in the main centers.

Travel Tips in Morocco

Before you go

- Weigh the advantages of flying direct compared to a stopover in Europe, or even a few days holiday there.
- If your current insurance policy doesn't cover you, it is highly advisable to take out travel insurance, covering you for medical expenses, luggage loss, or theft, and cancellations or important delays in your travel schedule. The amount of the coverage depends on the insurance you take out, so make sure you are satisfied with the terms offered. Some policies arrange to pay doctors and hospitals directly rather than having the burden of paying fall to you, with subsequent claims to make to the insurance company. If the second system is the one used, remember to keep all receipts and details of the expenses incurred. It is a good idea to check if the policy covers ambulances or an emergency flight home. This all makes gloomy reading, and it is unlikely that you will have to make use of any of it, but it is better to start on your travels knowing that if anything does happen, you've done your best to minimize the trouble.
- Travel light—you can always buy local if you are in a pinch. Have comfortable walking shoes. There is a weight limit on checked luggage, and carry-on bags must be small enough to fit under the seat or in an overhead bin.
- Decide what you want to do and choose your season accordingly. If it is a visit to the marvelous monuments, palaces, and mosques that

you are after, try to avoid mid-summer unless you are a glutton for heat. A camel trip in the far south is also definitely not to be undertaken in August.

- Photocopy your passport and other essential documents and keep these copies separate from the originals.
- Check that your passport is valid, that you have with you your American or international driver's license (if you are going to rent a car), credit cards, some U.S. currency, and your ticket before setting off for the airport, and don't be late for the plane. Overbooking can happen and latecomers are the ones who are going to suffer.

While you are away

- If you've planned onward international flights, or even internal flights, confirm them as soon as possible. A computer network operates for most bookings, so there shouldn't be any trouble.
- The U.S. Consulate General in Casablanca (the only one outside of Rabat) recommends that you drop in to the consular section and say you want to register, even if you are only staying a couple of weeks in Morocco. This is helpful if your documents go astray. Remember to advise them of your departure.
- If you've not already done so, photocopy your passport. Photocopying machines are everywhere and it is cheap (so cheap that students spend a lot of time copying books . . .)
- Report lost credit cards at once. The loss of a passport should also be declared at once to the local police (*Déclaration de perte or Déclaration de Vol*) and to the nearest U.S. embassy or consulate.
- Always carry your passport, travel documents, credit cards, and money with you (securely stowed away), as well as essential medical items in case your baggage goes astray (unlikely). You are asked for your "papers" (*papiers*), i.e. passport (and driving documents if you are at the wheel of a car) on many occasions: by the receptionist on arrival in a hotel, by a policeman if he thinks you have committed a driving offense, or by a gendarme if he is doing a road check.
- Be careful of strong sun in summer, even if it is hazy. Drink bottled water or bottled soft drinks (check that they really are unopened). Some people advise peeling all fruit and eating only cooked vegetables. Personally, I think this is going a bit far, but if you have a delicate stomach, it's probably advisable. All fruit and vegetables should be washed before eating.
- Use the restrooms of big hotels and restaurants rather than public toilets (usually of the squat type). Bring your own toilet paper.

- Leave your valuables in the hotel safe deposit while you are sightseeing.
- Dress discreetly when walking around town.
- Get familiar with the local currency, and don't over-tip.
- Don't try and visit a functioning mosque—they are out of bounds to non-Moslems, with the exception of the Hassan II Mosque in Casablanca (disaffected mosques are open to visitors).
- Prudent travelers make use of an official guide or no guide at all. In the tourist towns, such as Marrakech and Fès, plenty of people will come forward with tempting offers. Turn them down firmly and get a guide from your hotel or the tourist office.
- Keep cool, smile, keep your temper, ignore harassers, compromise, and adapt.
- Enjoy yourself! Morocco has lots to recommend it, and talk to people if you feel like it, but shake them off firmly when you've had enough.

Visit the Region

I would say that there was more than enough to do and see in Morocco for most travelers to have little time left to visit other countries in the region, but the following are within a few hours' flying time. Tickets are obtainable from most travel agents or from the carrier's offices. If planning a trip to Mauritania or Senegal, check vaccination requirements first (yellow fever is currently advised for Senegal, tetanus is always useful anywhere, and typhoid and cholera are not generally necessary).

Gibraltar. A short flight from Casablanca or Tangier by British Airways/GB Airways will take you to this historical outpost. A day-trip is also possible, but gives you little time to visit the different sites. Departures are three times a week.

Tunisia is the most accessible North African country, and by far the best geared for tourists. Royal Air Maroc and Tunis Air assure seven flights a week from Casablanca to Tunis and back (1,660 km). The fare is not expensive: 2,000 DH round trip.

Algeria. RAM does a flight to Alger once a week (1,050 km). It is not possible to go by rail or road, since the frontier is, at present, closed.

Libya. Since the lifting of the embargo, it is now possible to fly to Tripoli by RAM.

Mauritania. The difficulties of getting there by car from Morocco were explained in the section "Travel Restrictions" and I cannot at all advise this way of traveling to Mauritania. There are two flights a week from Laayoune to Nouakchott by RAM (1,890 km).

Senegal. Dakar can be reached by RAM twice a week from Casablanca (2,300 km).

Canary Islands. A visit to the Canary Islands can make an attractive excursion from Agadir or Casablanca. RAM has three flights a week from Casablanca to Las Palmas, Gran Canaria, via Agadir (960 km from Casablanca).

Mainland Spain. RAM has a flight every day to Madrid. A mere 460 km separates Casablanca from Malaga, and RAM and Regional Air Lines both fly there. There are daily boat crossings, but the sea journey takes 2½ hours with Trasmediterraea or Limadet Ferry (daily departures).

Portugal. Flying time to Lisbon is about 1 hour. RAM has a flight three times a week and Regional Air Lines flies once a week.

3

The Land and Life of Morocco

A young English friend of mine, who had never been out of England before, arrived in Casablanca. He saw roads, pavements, buses, traffic lights, pedestrian crossings, and modern buildings, and exclaimed, "Why, it's just like London!" A day or two later he changed his mind and realized that, despite appearances, he was in a totally different world.

At first sight, indeed, many aspects of Morocco appear familiar to the Western visitor. But quickly the traveler comes to see that Morocco is not just a pale copy of something else but a country in its own right, with a long and rich cultural heritage. Centuries of adoption and adaptation have produced, by a secret alchemy, a nation that both shares characteristics with others and is yet unique. A country that is truly quite different.

Geography

Situated in the very northwest corner of the African continent, Morocco forms a link between Africa and Europe. Contact between north and south has existed since early prehistoric times. From the east came the Moslem expansion that pushed westwards across North Africa in the seventh century

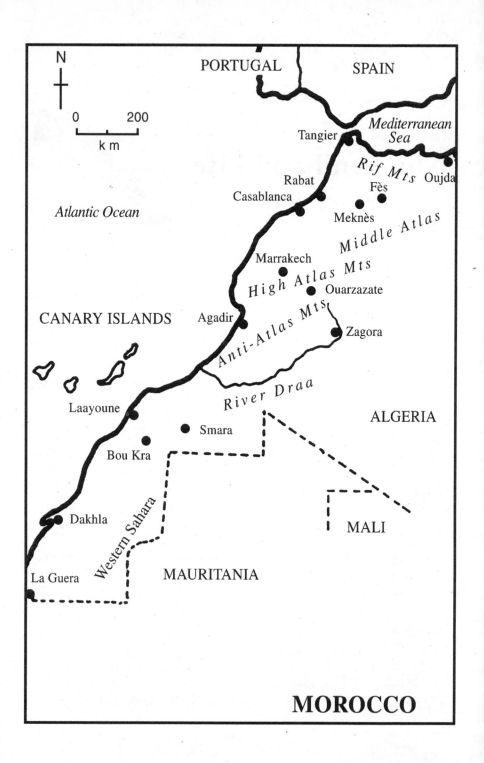

A.D., from Arabia to the Atlantic, finding in Morocco its western terminus. Morocco's northern neighbor is Spain; to the east lies Algeria and to the south Mauritania.

Geologically speaking, Morocco's structure is the result of a series of plate tectonic movements. Put simply, the Anti-Atlas Mountains and part of the Western Sahara were formed over 2 billion years ago. During the Primary era the land was covered by water and the collision of three plates resulted in the creation of the central plateau. The Tertiary era followed, with the formation of the Rif Mountains, the Middle Atlas, and the High Atlas. These geological upheavals have produced extensive fossil and mineral deposits.

The total land surface of the kingdom is 710,850 km² (including the area once known as the Spanish Sahara, still awaiting the results of a referendum). It is difficult to put a map conveniently within the limits of page in a book, since the country is both long—the distance in a diagonal line from the very north (Tangier) to the very south (La Guera) is 2,100 km, and at one point broad (the widest distance from east to west is 820 km— Figuig on the Algerian frontier to Essaouira on the Atlantic coast). All Morocco lies north of the Tropic of Cancer, except for a small area far south, below Dakhla. The Moroccan coastline stretches some 3,500 km along the Mediterranean and down the Atlantic Ocean.

Mountains are an important feature of the landscape. In the north, the Rif chain forms a crescent some 200 km long from east to west, overlooking the Mediterranean and facing the Sierra Nevada Mountains in Spain. Summits over 2,000 m are rare, although the highest peak, the Tiddiriyn, reaches 2,458 m. Despite its relatively low altitude, the Rif receives the most rainfall of all the Moroccan ranges. The Loukkos and Moulouya rivers have their origin here.

Moving south, the eastern end of the 250-km long Middle Atlas range is separated from the Rif by a narrow passage—the Taza Corridor—used by most of the invaders coming from the east. The Middle Atlas branches north from the High Atlas towards its eastern extremity. It is made up of two massifs of differing height and composition—a western limestone plateau of moderate height cut by deep valleys, and an eastern block of folded formation, with the highest peak reaching 3,326 m.

The most important mountain chain in Morocco is that of the High Atlas, known to the Greeks and Phoenicians of antiquity as the "mountain of mountains," the domain of the legendary giant Atlas, who bore the world on his shoulders. The High Atlas range stretches over 700 km from the southwest to the northeast. It divides the country in two: to the north is the Atlantic and Mediterranean Morocco, to the south, Saharan

Morocco. Ten summits reach 4,000 m with the highest peak, the Toubkal, at 4,167 m. More than 400 summits exceed 3,000 m. Today, three passes allow modern motorized traffic to move with ease north and south, while many other routes are accessible only to mules or travelers on foot. The highest of these passes, the Tizi n'Tichka, stands at 2,260 m and a cold wind ensures that, even in summer, the visitor who stops to admire the view is glad to have a sweater. The more westerly Tizi n'Test pass, just over 2,000 m, is another place where a sweater comes in handy.

Forming a link between the High Atlas and the Anti-Atlas, the Sirwa massif is the remains of an old, very large and high volcano, reaching a height of 3,305 m. The Anti-Atlas itself is a range more than 400 km long, stretching from the Atlantic in the west to the Tafilalet in the east. One of its most spectacular sections is the Jbel Sarhro (*jbel* means mountain), rising to a height of 2,712 m. At the western end of the Anti-Atlas, a complex network of generally dry rivers has created an extremely ravined landscape. The last upheaval of the Anti-Atlas, in the south, known as the Jbel Bani, marks the beginning of the pre-Saharan desert.

Unlike its neighbors, Morocco is fortunate to have several important rivers. Most flow into the Atlantic Ocean: the Loukkos, the Sebou, the Bou Regreg, the Oum er-Rbia, the Tensift, the Souss, and the Draa. The Draa starts with a northwest-southeast course, but it suddenly changes after Zagora and heads west to the Atlantic, generally disappearing under the sand for the penultimate stages of its journey. In east Morocco, the rivers Ziz and Rheris run from north to south before they, too, get lost in the desert. The most important north-flowing river, the Moulouya, reaches the Mediterranean close to the Algerian frontier. These rivers are fed by rain and snow falling in the mountains or the high central plateau. Many of them have had their waters harnessed to form dams, supplying water for irrigation, consumer use, and electricity. At the moment, 12 main dams and more than 20 smaller ones are in operation, but others are envisaged as part of an ambitious plan to increase the irrigated zones. Numerous natural lakes form an attractive feature of the Middle Atlas region.

South of the Anti-Atlas Mountains stretch the vast plateaus, the *hamada*. These can be stony or covered with sand dunes. Imperceptibly, these Moroccan, sub-Saharan *hamada* blend into the big Saharan desert.

Climate

As mentioned earlier, Morocco is a warm, sunny country. But you can be scorching at midday and freezing at 8:00 P.M. Temperatures everywhere are at their lowest in December and January, rising slowly to reach peaks in July and August. Rabat and Casablanca, being on the coast, enjoy the benefits of a sea breeze and the thermometer rarely gets beyond 27°C in summer. But when you get inland, to Fès or Marrakech, for instance, peak temperatures can hover around 38°C, with the hot Saharan wind, the *chergui*, blowing dust around and making energetic life difficult. In the far south it is not unusual to be faced with a temperature of nearly 45°C in August. From November through February, most people are glad to heat their houses. Coastal areas can count on temperatures around 15°C in winter, the Atlas Mountains get below freezing point, with snow and ice, and even in the south Sahara temperatures can be low in the winter evenings. Central heating is a feature of modern town buildings—as is air-conditioning for the summer. If you're worried about being cold, check that your hotel is heated if you are planning a winter visit. Solar power has been used in some public buildings and in an increasing number of private houses to supply light and water-heating—and energy to run a television satellite dish where electricity is not otherwise available.

Winds can make life unpleasant, especially in the far south. But they often bring rain if coming from the north or west, and are welcomed for this reason. The northwest tip of Morocco, close to the Strait of Gibraltar, is considered to be one of the windiest places in the country. It is here that the largest wind-powered installation in Africa and the Arab world is under construction, near Tetouan. It should be operational by the end of 1999 and will produce two percent of the country's annual electricity consumption (226 million kilowatts per hour). Individual metal windmills (now replaced by oil-fueled engines) have been used by farmers for many years to pump water.

Rainfall used to be predictable, but El Niño's predecessors have upset the established pattern. For instance, the rainfall recorded in Ifrane (Middle Atlas) was 483 mm in 1994-95, rising to 1,603 mm in 1995-96. Admittedly, 1995-1996 was an exceptional year and saw the dams filled to 83 percent of their capacity. Early in 1998, better figures showed that six of the dams were 100 percent full, with 19 others just behind.

The natural vegetation, so dependent on the climate, is as varied as the country. It ranges from species common around the Mediterranean basin, through mountain-loving trees and shrubs, down to drought-resistant plants in the south. Morocco can proudly claim to have the most extensive forests of North Africa. They cover 7 percent of the country—but this is a low figure compared to the international norm of 15-25 percent. In the north, the holm oak, cedar, and pine are the characteristic trees of the Rif Mountains, with a Mediterranean-type scrub found at lower altitudes. The Middle Atlas still possesses fine cedar forests, though every year they get thinner and thinner, as do those in the Rif. Other Middle Atlas trees are various species of conifers, oaks, junipers, and ash. The High Atlas has stands of cedars at its eastern end, but holm oaks, Aleppo pines, and thuyas are more widespread, with juniper at the higher altitudes. Pink and white flowered oleanders grow along the stream banks. South of the Atlas, trees become rarer, represented mostly by the white-spined accacia. Alfa grass provides some food for grazing flocks. On the Atlantic Coast, moving down from Tangier to Rabat, the cork oak is a familiar tree, while further south, towards Agadir, the acacia, various species of euphorbia, and the Tertiary relic tree, the argan, dominate. The very familiar eucalyptus, growing alongside the main roads or forming small woods, is an import from Australia, introduced by the French. The date palm is another import, but much earlier.

Thanks to this varied biotope, Morocco has some 30,000 plant and animal species. Unfortunately, almost a quarter of the 7,422 plant species have become rare and are threatened with extinction.

If the flora is conditioned by the climate, the fauna is in turn influenced by the vegetational cover and the food resources. Among the more visible wild animals are the Barbary apes in the Rif Mountains and, particularly, in the Middle Atlas. Their natural predator, the leopard, having been practically exterminated, these primates are relatively tame and sometimes come quite close to visitors. The wild boar seems to have had no trouble in maintaining itself and lives all over Morocco. Controlled hunting is allowed—an average of 1,600 animals were killed each year between 1960 and 1971. The jackal was, until very recently, one of the most numerous large wild animals in the country. However, the very adaptable red fox, also with a wide distribution, is now considered to be the most frequent Moroccan carnivore, the jackal having been systematically poisoned, shot, or trapped to protect the flocks of sheep and goats. Foxes can very occasionally be seen in the mountains. Few of the other animal species are easy to spot. Even hares and rabbits are rare, so great is the human pressure on their habitats and the desire to make them into a good stew. The Dorcas gazelle, which could be seen grazing in all the plains of Morocco in the 16th century, now only exists—precariously—in eastern Morocco and in the sub-Saharan regions of the south. The Edmi gazelle, a mountain species, is reported to be still present in the western part of the High Atlas and in the Anti-Atlas. The Barbary sheep used to live in all the mountainous regions, but today its distribution is very limited, due to extensive hunting. A few specimens still exist in the eastern end of the Middle Atlas, where a national park has been created to protect them. A small colony of monk seals exists off Dakhla, in the Western Sahara. Those living in the

Mediterranean near Al-Hoceima have been apparently exterminated. The mongoose, ratel, and porcupine, as well as the hedgehog, are very discreet animals and the casual visitor is unlikely to see them. Toads, frogs, and lizards can be found wherever the habitat is suitable. In the hotter regions, scorpions and snakes can be found, but it is unlikely that they will creep into your sleeping-bag or fall into your lap from a tree (care, however, should be taken when picking up stones or rummaging among rocks).

Over 300 species of birds have been recorded in Morocco. The diversity of habitats and the country's position on migratory routes are responsible for this richness. Only a few species will be mentioned (see the area chapters for specific birdwatching habitats). Common town-birds are sparrows, pigeons, and doves, while coastal areas are the home of various species of seabirds. Birds of prey are noticeable in the country, both in the plains and the mountains, and a whole host of smaller birds such as larks, pipits, swallows, and blackbirds can be seen in town and country. Partridges are hunted. Among the more spectacular birds are the kingfisher, bee-eater, roller, hoopoe, and flamingo. These few lines on Morocco's birds cannot end without a mention of the migrating storks, whose huge nests occupied by complacent parent birds can be seen perched on almost any high point, from treetops to roofs, abandoned chimneys, and even telegraph poles (they are about the only bird respected by the population, and therefore live in complete safety).

The Government

Morocco is a monarchy, and has been for well over a thousand years. The present king, Mohammed Ben Al Hassan, came to the throne at the end of July 1999, upon the sudden death of his father, King Hassan II. The constitution allows for a parliament, although ultimate power rests with the king. Several constitutional amendments in the last forty years have led to changes in the composition of the parliament, most notably the creation of a bicameral system in the fall of 1996. Previously partially elected, partially nominated, all deputies to the lower house were directly elected—by all members of the population eligible to vote—for the first time in the fall of 1997. One-third of the deputies to the newly-created upper house were nominated directly or elected by trade unions, professional bodies, and other non-public organizations.

Many shades of opinion were covered in the 15 political parties that presented candidates in the 1997 elections. In addition to the Socialist Party and Istiqlal, the *Parti du Progrès et du Socialisme* (ex-Communist) and the *Organisation de l'Action Démocratique et Populaire* constituted the bulk of the opposition. On the other side, the most influential parties were the

Mouvement Populaire (Berber), the *Union Constitutionelle,* the *Rassemblement National des Indépendents,* the *Mouvement National Populaire,* and the *Parti National Démocratique.*

These elections led, for the first time in many years, to the victory of the united opposition parties (the *Koutla,* including the socialist USFP party and the nationalist Istiqlal). However, they did not win a sufficient number of seats to enable them to govern without the cooperation of the center party, the RNI *(Rassemblement National des Indépendants).* The announcement of the new left-center government, under the freshly nominated Prime Minister, Mr. Abderrahmane Youssoufi (Socialist Party), was delayed until March 1998 while intense negotiations went on between the various components of the new majority. Nine ministries were allocated to the Socialist party, six to Istiqlal, and five to the RNI. Other opposition parties were rewarded with a ministry or two. Four ministers from the previous right-wing/technocrat government remained in office, including the all-powerful Minister of the Interior and the Minister of Foreign Affairs. The king retained control over national security. The program of the new government was approved by almost all the deputies when it was presented at the end of April 1998. Without going into details, it laid out the general lines of governmental policy, including a settlement of the Western Sahara problem, a reform of the educational system, continuation of the privatizations, reinforcement of the freedom of speech, and specific programs in favor of young people and women (including the elimination of illiteracy). The "hottest" of these questions were undoubtedly education, employment, and the Western Sahara. The upper house continued to be essentially right-wing, representing the parties that have controlled Moroccan politics for the past 30 years.

Morocco has a Minister of Justice and one for Human Rights. The first meeting of organizations concerned with human rights in the Mediterranean area was held in Marrakech in April 1998. The UN High Commissioner for Human Rights, Mary Robinson, was present and several important decisions concerning human rights were made. Law courts, appeal courts, judges, lawyers (prosecution and defense), and all the apparatus of modern justice exist. The system does not work perfectly, but the current Minister of Justice has pledged reform and improvement. There are three trade unions: the oldest is the *Union Marocaine du Travail* (UMT), affiliated to the international trade union body, the C.I.S.L., shortly after its creation in the 1950s. The other two are the *Union Générale des Travailleurs Marocains* (UGTM, close to the nationalist Istiqlal party), and the *Confédération Démocratique du Travail* (Socialist).

Islamic fundamentalists (*barbus,* "bearded," as they are often called) are active in certain spheres of Moroccan life, especially in the universities. No

Islamic party is officially recognized at the political level but the small, quite legal *Mouvement Populaire Démocratique et Constitutionnel* has been allowed to let members of the illegal Islamic party, *Unification et Reforme,* join its party. Several jailed Islamic activists were released in the fall of 1998. The leader of one of the most important illegal groups, *Al Adl Wal Ihsan* (Justice and Charity), has been under house arrest since 1989, but the lifting of this constraint is imminent. Understandably, his party was not allowed to take part in the 1997 elections.

Administratively, Morocco is divided into 65 provinces or prefectures (the latter for the towns) headed by governors. The tendency in recent years has been to increase the number of provinces and prefectures, thus bringing the administration closer to the population (Casablanca, for instance, is made up of seven prefectures). Provinces and prefectures are divided into smaller units ("circles"), which in turn are divided into communes (urban and rural), each with its own administration and elected local council. At the grass roots level, an appointed state agent called the *moqadam* is responsible for keeping an eye on what goes on in his little area, listening to complaints before they reach the police and, in the country, often acting as postman. Of the urban population, 11.9 percent works in the general administration of the country.

In books, and indeed in reality, Morocco is divided into tribes, particularly in rural districts. You will often see references to tribes when buying a rug, or reading a book on textiles. Officially, tribes no longer exist and legislation in 1958 aimed to end the tribal system and replace the tribes by communes. This meant the end of the role played by tribal nobles, their substitution by the central authorities, and the end of the tribe as a part of the administrative system. In point of fact, despite the 1958 measure, rural social structure remains essentially linked to the tribe and nearly everyone knows to which tribe, or part of a tribe, he belongs. The exceptions are second-generation townspeople who have often, but not inevitably, lost their sense of tribal identity.

The Economy

Put briefly, Morocco has a mixed economy based to a large extent on agriculture, fishing, phosphate and other mining, light industry, and tourism. Nearly 350,000 Moroccans emigrated to Europe between 1986 and the beginning of 1995, and their remittances are an important element in the country's economy. In recent years this income has been reduced as many such workers are turning more towards the purchase of property in the host country.

Morocco has been a faithful pupil of the International Monetary Fund (not without some internal difficulties from time to time); privatization schemes have been energetically pursued (including hotels) as the state slims down on many of the activities it took up after independence in 1956, and the national currency is on its way to being fully convertible.

However, Morocco is still a steady borrower, and servicing the debt is a heavy burden on the country's finances. Luckily, Saudi Arabia agreed to forgive a loan of several billion U.S. dollars, and in 1998 France also agreed to forget about a number of loans. The World Bank gives more aid to Morocco than to any other North African and Middle Eastern country. In the spring of 1998, Japan granted a loan of 986 million DH for electrification projects and the construction of the south Casablanca by-pass, bringing loans from Japan's Fund for overseas economic cooperation to some 7.5 billion DH. The European Investment Bank also signed an agreement in Rabat in the spring of 1998 for a loan of approximately 1.3 billion DH, to help local banks finance the competitive reconstruction of Moroccan businesses—and also to improve the electricity supply network. The USAID agency and Morocco cooperate in projects in many parts of the country.

Morocco is a member of the General Agreement on Tariffs and Trade (GATT). High hopes exist of entry to the European Union (Morocco has been presenting its case since 1987), a free trade zone agreement was signed by the two parties in 1996, and a fishing agreement allows European Union boats to fish in Moroccan waters at certain periods. However, Morocco's attempt to join the European Union has brought hostility from a number of Mediterranean countries, which fear competition from Morocco's fruit and vegetables. Morocco tries to maintain friendly relations with Israel, and steps to improve contacts between the two countries were set in motion in 1993. But 1997/1998 events have darkened the outlook.

The union between Morocco, Algeria, Tunisia, and Libya that should help commercial exchanges between these North African countries has never really gotten off the ground. Libya is the country in this group that has the most trading contacts with Morocco (both imports and exports). The Organization of African Unity (OAU), which Morocco left in 1984 because of differences over the question of the ex-Spanish Sahara, has always been an organization more politically than economically oriented, and Moroccan trade with countries south of the Sahara is negligible. The Ivory Coast is the only sub-Saharan country to import significantly from Morocco (25th place out of 31 countries), but Nigeria is quite an important supplier (10th place) (1997 figures).

Inflation stands at around three percent. Unemployment is said to have decreased from 23 percent of the active population to 20 percent, but these figures have to be taken cautiously. The dividing-line between "employed" and "under-employed" is also hard to draw. While the national average for unemployment is given as 18 percent, figures vary considerably from one region to another. The highest figures for male unemployment are in the eastern part of the country, and stood at 19.3 percent in 1997. As the population increases steadily, there is a risk that unemployment will also increase unless efforts are made to boost production. The number of young holders of university doctorates, often trained abroad, who fail to find work is disquieting, and has led to sit-ins and demonstrations. The Prime Minister recognized in May 1998 that unemployment among university degree holders was 33 percent.

It is also generally admitted that Moroccan industry is not ready to face the world competition that is looming. The country lacks skilled human resources, despite a rising population. Unemployment figures could increase dramatically unless a healthier growth rate is maintained. Entry to the European Union may take some time in coming. The gap between the rich and the poor is certainly widening, though, again, figures differ. Using the World Bank criteria, the government has estimated the poor to number approximately four million, but past opposition parties have always contested this figure. The monthly minimum wage (the SMIG) has recently been raised to 1,500 DH/month, but this sum can usually only cover the needs of a single man, if he has rent to pay. Agricultural wages are lower. Many concerns do not even pay this minimum legal wage, although a number of economic experts consider that raising wages would result in an increase in consumption and a consequent healthy increase in local production. There are no unemployment benefits, and only a few workers are affiliated with the Social Security scheme covering illness and accident costs, and a tiny minority contribute to a small pension fund. The vast majority of the population, especially in rural areas, relies on the family for old age and illness support. This basic poverty, while not leaving people on the breadline, combined with ever-increasing numbers of young people in the job market, presents a potentially difficult situation unless the government manages to improve the situation. Very sadly, hundreds of young men die trying to cross the Strait of Gibraltar into Spain in small, un-seaworthy, overcrowded boats, after paying large sums of money to the "transporter."

In more detail, about 40 percent of the country's population is directly engaged in agriculture, forestry, or fishing. Land owners range from small holders with under 10 hectares, to those with many thousands of hectares. Working methods obviously vary according to the situation of the owner:

the "small" man ploughs his plot with mule or donkey, while the "big" man has up-to-date machinery for ploughing and harvesting, some of it imported from the United States. Agricultural cooperatives exist to help the smaller enterprises. The agricultural bank, *Crédit Agricole,* lends money to farmers for equipment, fertilizer, and seeds. At present, agricultural enterprises don't pay tax on their income (however big the income may be!).

Livestock, in the form of sheep and goats, mules, donkeys, and camels (in fact, they are dromedaries, but are always referred to as camels), has always been important in Morocco. Sheep and goats are local breeds, adapted to the terrain and the climate. The cattle stock, too, is mainly made up of local races, supplying milk and meat. It has recently been improved, but milk still has to be imported at certain times of the year. There are about 2½ million cattle, 15½ million sheep, and 5 million goats. It has been estimated that 4½ million sheep were slaughtered at the big Moslem "Feast of the Sacrifice" in 1998. There are well over a million donkeys and mules, used as transport and for farm work. The horse is Morocco's pride and the country boasts superb animals. The late King Hassan II had a number of stud farms where Arab thoroughbreds, Barbs, and Arabo-Barbs were available free for reproduction purposes, in order to maintain the quality of the race, and this is sure to continue under his son. All "small" landholders own a few chickens and industrial poultry concerns flourish.

The main winter crops are wheat, barley, and oats. The latest published figures showed that in the 1996/1997 season 4½ million hectares of these cereals were harvested, as were 372,000 hectares of the spring crops—corn, sorghum, and rice. Leguminous plants covered around 372,000 hectares, while sunflowers and peanuts accounted for another 135,000 hectares. Industrial cultivation of sugar beet (63,000 hectares) and, to a much smaller extent, sugarcane, cotton, and tea, is practiced in certain parts of the country. In spite of all this, Morocco still has to import wheat (2.2 tons in 1996, according to the latest available figures), corn (543,000 tons), tea (28,000 tons), and sugar (513,000 tons). An uncertain climate and drought (such as the one in 1994/1995) make agriculture a rather hazardous affair despite increasing irrigation schemes.

Citrus fruits, on the other hand, are a big Moroccan production (1.2 million tons in 1996/1997). They come in seventh place in the list of exports (*Le Maroc en Chiffres,* published by the Banque Marocaine du Commerce Extériéur) and can be seen in the shops in many European countries, as well as being in constant supply on the home market. Fresh tomatoes are also high among the exports (11th place), a bit above other fresh vegetables (17th). Olives are widely cultivated, and olive oil is exported (16th place).

Recent years have seen a remarkable extension of the cultivation of the Barbary fig, especially in arid regions (north of Marrakech, for instance). It is a useful plant since it can grow on poor soils and protects them from erosion, as well as providing animal fodder.

Fishing agreements exist between Morocco and Japan, as well as with certain European countries. This is a contentious subject, and the Moroccan press frequently carries articles denouncing illegal fishing in territorial waters, the capture of under-sized fish, or fishing during the closed season. Most of the catch goes into by-products, followed by consumer sales (home and export), canning, and freezing. Value-wise, shellfish and mollusks won third place in Moroccan exports, only a little behind phosphoric acid and phosphates. Canned fish came just after citrus fruits (all latest 1997 figures, *Le Maroc en Chiffres*, published by the Banque Marocaine du Commerce Exteriéur).

Morocco is thought to have well over half of the world's phosphate reserves. Annual production rises steadily (20,740,000 tons extracted in 1996 and 29,066,000 in 1997) (*Le Maroc en Chiffres*, published by the Banque Marocaine du Commerce Exteriéur). Phosphoric acid tops the export chart in value, followed closely by fertilizers and untreated phosphate. In 1997, Morocco regained its place as the world's biggest phosphate exporter, with 30.9 percent of the international market. The phosphate industry is run by the *Office Chérifien des Phosphates* (OCP), a semi-public concern. A partnership between an Indian group and the OCP, initiated in 1997, is leading to the construction of a phosphoric acid production line at Jorf Lasfar, which, by 1999, will increase the site's production by 25 percent. One of the brilliant moves by General Hubert Lyautey, in 1920, when he was Résident Général during the French Protectorate, was to nationalize the newly-discovered phosphate reserves to avoid a potential source of wealth to the Moroccan state falling into private hands.

Minerals mined include (in decreasing order of importance) barytes, salt, zinc, lead, fluorite, copper, manganese, iron ore, and silver. Lead, copper, and silver are exported. Coal mining, for local consumption, used to be important in eastern Morocco, but the mines have been going through a bad period and production has almost stopped. Oil prospecting continues intermittently, and it was hoped that a deposit of oil shale being explored near the Atlantic Coast, in the southwest of the country, would prove promising. Oil is imported and is treated in two refineries.

Textiles rank high among the manufacturing industries. A number of foreign firms buy finished or half-finished garments that come out of numerous workshops and small factories in different parts of the country. Ready-made clothing placed third for exports, from a value point of view

(1997). Hosiery, shoes, and rugs are also exported. Rug exports used to be very important a number of years ago, but concern about the use of children in many rug factories, combined with changing tastes and increased competition have pushed rug exports down to 23rd place—a big drop from the 5th place they had in 1979, for instance. Other light industries include fruit and vegetable canning (as well as fish), and jam and fruit-juice bottling. Small factories produce (and export) cloth and cotton thread. A whole host of articles (too long to list) are manufactured locally, sometimes under foreign license, such as automobile parts, household accessories (44 percent of households own a refrigerator), light fittings, and clothing. Trucks, cars, and television sets are assembled in Casablanca, but the majority of new cars licensed each year show a clear domination of French vehicles (Peugeot and Renault). An estimated 1,600,000 cars are on the roads—there were only 306,000 in the 1970s. However, the Moroccan Department of Statistics revealed in the fall of 1998 that only 12 percent of Moroccan families owned a car. Bus sales increased by over 26 percent in 1997, and truck sales showed the same healthy increase, as many businesses renewed their vehicle fleets. Many manufactured items are on sale in two forms: the imported article and the locally-produced (which is cheaper). A total of 26.5 percent of the urban population is engaged in industry (including water, electricity, and other energy sources).

The lion's share of trade, both exports and imports, goes to France. Spain is the No. 2 partner in both ways, but from this point buyers and suppliers differ. The third most important country for Morocco's exports is India, followed by Italy. Trade with the U.S. is quite healthy, with the United States figuring in at 7th place for Moroccan exports and 4th for imports. Moroccan men are enthusiastic smokers, and American cigarettes must figure among the country's imports, since Marlboro and Winston are favorite brands for Moroccans. In 1997, Moroccan smokers consumed 12.68 billion cigarettes.

Morocco always hopes that tourism will be a big moneymaker, in view of the many advantages enjoyed by the country. Unfortunately, this industry has never lived up to the high hopes that have been placed on it. Tourist entries have undoubtedly increased: 1.83 million foreign tourists are recorded as having visited the country in 1997, compared to 1.63 million in 1996. But this is disappointing when one considers that Spain doubles its population in the holiday season, thanks to tourism, and that nearby Tunisia, a smaller country, is above Morocco in the league table (meaning they receive more tourists per year).

Understandably, the vast majority (1.5 million) are Europeans. The number of American tourists rose in 1997 compared to the previous year (87,570 against 77,356), but the Canadian figures remained the same

(25,000 in 1997). With 532 classified hotels, a good communications network by air or road, and a variety of activities offered to visitors, numbers
are certain to rise. Looking at things from another angle, it is surely a
pleasure for a tourist to find himself in a country not absolutely swamped
by non-locals!

The People

Population. According to official figures, Morocco had 27.3 million inhabitants in 1997 (13.72 million are women and 13.58 million are men). It
is estimated to reach 35 million by 2014. Morocco is characterized by a
"young" population. The "under-20s" account for 46 percent of the population. However, the percentage of young people is beginning to drop. For
example, the "under-15s," 44.4 percent of the population in 1960, only
represented 34 percent in 1998. Life expectancy for men is 66.8 years and
for women it is 70 years. The population is increasingly urban: in 1960,
only 29 percent lived in the town. In 1997 this figure had risen to 53 percent, and the trend will certainly continue. In urban areas, out of 4 million
people with jobs, 63.6 percent were salaried workers, while 19.5 percent
were independent.

Population density per km^2 obviously varies. In the economic capital of
Casablanca, and its satellite communities, the density per km^2 is 1,974, in
Rabat-Salé-Temara it is almost as high: 1,236.9. Casablanca's population is
given as 2.8 million, but other estimates put it at over 3 million. This concentration of humanity can easily be felt as one goes through these agglomerations, where the notion of green spaces is limited to a few
privileged zones. The lowest figures are for the eastern, largely rural region
of the country, bordering on Algeria, where the five provinces or prefectures concerned have a total density of a mere 20.0 per km^2.

Berbers and Arabs. The population is made up of people of different
and mixed origins, and skin colors vary from white to black. The country
was originally peopled by Berbers (*imazighen*, "the free men"). It is hard to
give an exact date to this "originally," but let's say that the Berbers were
there in prehistoric times. Small Berber kingdoms existed in Northwest
Africa in the 4th century B.C. and were recorded in Morocco in the 1st century B.C. The Roman occupation, which took place mainly in the first two
centuries A.D., left traces in the form of architecture and customs. Berbers
in the north became "Romanized," but few Moroccans today would claim
to have Roman blood in their veins. The Vandal armies that swept through
North Africa in the 5th century are unlikely to have added much to the
ethnic composition of the country either. The big change came when Arab
invaders arrived for the first time in the 7th century A.D., followed by later

waves from the 12th century onwards. A sub-Saharan, African input is also discernible in southern Morocco, where dark skinned people are the main inhabitants of the oases. They may call themselves Arabs or Berbers, and are often referred to as *Haratin*. Their origin is not very clear. They may have come up from the Sahara with the first Berber conquerors in the middle of the 11th century, they may be the descendants of black slaves, or they may simply be the dark-skinned inhabitants of the southern fringes of the country since time immemorial. I have met, in south Morocco, people who do not define themselves as either Berber or Arab, but *Saharaoui*, (of the Sahara). In passing, no Tuaregs live in Morocco, despite the fashion for the so-called "Tuareg" shops that have sprung up in the south.

Basically, the bulk of the population is made up of a mixture of Berbers and Arabs. Many who call themselves Arabs are, in fact, Berbers who have only recently become "Arabized." Speculation as to the proportional representation of the two major groups is rather fruitless, and many people prefer to use the terms "Arabic-speaking" and "Berber-speaking." It is not uncommon for Arabs and Berbers to intermarry. French policy under the Protectorate emphasized the differences between the two main groups; official policy today is to claim that such differences are minimal and in the process of disappearing. In fact, while all affirm that they are Moroccans, ethnic consciousness remains very much alive, and both groups are very aware of their cultural and linguistic backgrounds and differences. In the past, these differences were accentuated by dress, speech, and behavior. But nowadays outward distinctions tend to become blurred, particularly among the men. In rural areas and among women in particular, however, differences in dress, decoration, and behavior are still striking.

Roughly speaking, the Rif Mountain area in the north is inhabited by Berbers. The Middle and High Atlas Mountains are also largely peopled by Berbers. South of the Atlas, Berbers *(Chleu)* inhabit the Anti-Atlas, the Haratin live in the oases, and the Saharaoui along the desert fringes. In the south, too, are the "blue men," so-called because the indigo dye of their robes colors their skin—not exactly blue, but a rather dark color.

Jews. At the beginning of the Christian era, small groups of Jews, fleeing persecution or simply looking for a better life, arrived in Morocco. Further Jewish populations, forced to leave Spain by the Reconquista and the fall of Grenada in 1492, crossed the Mediterranean and found refuge in towns such as Fès, Tetouan, and Salé. They were noted for their skill as craftsmen, and lived and practiced their faith unmolested much of the time, protected by the sultan. In the 19th and early-20th centuries their commercial talents and contacts with Moslem Morocco made them very useful to the various foreign countries dealing with Morocco. The word *yahoudi* (Jew) is often used as an insult, although Jewish schools, synagogues, and cemeteries still function in a few towns, such as Casablanca. Most of the Jews have left Morocco by now, to take up life in Israel, America, or Canada, but many return each year to their native land, to participate in a religious pilgrimage to a Jewish saint, for instance. The Foundation for the Judeo-Moroccan cultural heritage also has a program for the restoration of abandoned Jewish historical sites in Morocco, which it runs with the support of the Jewish community of Agadir.

Others. An increasing number of Europeans, mainly French and Spanish, started living in Morocco from the beginning of the 20th century. With independence, and the subsequent taking over by the state of foreign-owned farms and property, the number of resident foreigners drastically dropped. At the moment, non-Moroccans (all nationalities taken together) number about 25,000.

Religion

Morocco is an Islamic country and the overwhelming majority of Moroccans are Moslems. It is extremely difficult to be of Moroccan nationality without being a Moslem or a Jew. Some Moroccans have dual-nationality, but this in no way changes their religious status. Non-Moslem women may marry Moroccans without being obliged to become Moslems, but they are then outside Moslem legislation concerning inheritance, for instance, and the children of such marriages must be brought up in the Moslem faith. But if a non-Moslem man wishes to marry a Moroccan woman, he must convert to Islam.

Islam was the religion professed by the prophet Mohammed in the 7th century at Mecca, in Saudi Arabia. Islam means the submission *(islam)* to one single god, Allah, whose message was revealed to his prophet Mohammed in the Koran. By conquest and conversion, Islam spread rapidly throughout the Middle East and North Africa. Its first followers reached Morocco, as invaders, at the end of the 7th century.

Indigenous Christianized populations had lived in Morocco, both in the Romanized towns and in the country far from any Roman influence, from the 2nd century A.D. Indeed, the Christianization of Roman North Africa was widespread and many Berbers became Christian. Saint Augustin, born in Algeria, the son of a modest pagan landowner of Roman origin and a Christianized mother of Berber origin, was baptized a Christian when he was 33 years old and was bishop of Bône in Algeria in 395. There were four Christian bishops in Morocco at the beginning of the 8th century. Some of these Christian communities resisted Islamization, but by the Middle Ages all had merged into the prevailing religion.

After the arrival of Islam, many members of the Jewish groups that arrived

in Morocco in the 15th century and earlier kept their Jewish religion and
were protected by the local authorities on payment of a special tax, while
others converted to Islam.

With the exception of a few small groups, all Moroccan Moslems are
Sunni and follow the Maliki rite. The Maliki School is less rigid in its in-
terpretation of the Koran than other Sunni groups. Morocco does not
apply the *shari'a* (Koranic law) followed in Saudi Arabia and elsewhere.
Hard-line Islam, as in some Arab states, is toned down in Morocco. The
sale and public consumption of alcohol is permitted, but not to young
Moroccans, and the calendar shows a compromise: the Western world's
New Year's Day being as much a holiday as the Islamic New Year's Day.

The Koran, the holy book of Islam, must be studied by children in
Koranic schools *(msid)* before they are allowed to enter the state primary
school. Considered to be God's direct word, through Mohammed, it allows
for no changes or interpretations, such as has been the case with the Bible.
It contains 114 *sourates* (chapters) and lays down the basic rules concerning moral standards and legislation. The Koran is supplemented by a collection of the sayings of the prophet Mohammed, the *Hadith,* which are his
recommendations and remarks on the conduct of everyday life. The Koran
contains many references to Biblical figures such as Adam, Abraham,
Moses, and Jesus, and certain passages are strongly influenced by the
Bible. Ibrahim (Abraham), Moussa (Moses), and Aissa (Jesus) are familiar
Moroccan first names. Moslems recognize that Jews and Christians share
their faith in one God, that they are the "People of the Book," but for
Moslems, Mohammed is the last of God's prophets and Islam inevitably the
last stage in God's design for humanity. For Moslems, therefore, it is only
right and proper that the whole world should follow Islam. You may well
meet a few Moroccans who will try to persuade you of this.

A Moslem has five religious obligations:
- The profession of faith *(shahada)*—"I affirm that there is only one
  God and that Mohammed is his prophet,"
- Prayer *(salat)* five times a day after ritual washing, facing Mecca,
- Alms-giving *(zakat),*
- Fasting during the month of Ramadan *(sawm),*
- And, if he has the means, the pilgrimage to Mecca *(hajj).*

In 1998, 27,000 Moroccans accomplished the pilgrimage to Mecca on
the occasion of the Feast of the Sacrifice. None of these obligations will be
particularly perceptible to the visitor, except for fasting during the month
of Ramadan, if this happens to be the period when he or she is in Morocco.

During this month, the ninth in the Islamic year, the beginning and end of which are identified by the sighting of the new moon, all eating, drinking, smoking, and sexual intercourse is forbidden between dawn and dusk. The whole day's normal timetable is upset. People "break the fast" in the evening, around 6:00 P.M. in the winter (later in summer) when the siren announces that the sun has set. This is a light but nourishing meal, followed a few hours later by a more solid affair, equal to lunch. Then, while it is still dark, the "courageous" (and hungry) leave their beds (temporarily) and have another meal (dinner), which will be the last they are allowed until the following evening. Work starts later, there is no lunch break, and most places close around 3:00 P.M. or 4:00 P.M.

Outside of Ramadan, it is the call to prayer, five times in twenty-four hours, that reminds the visitor that he is in a Moslem country. The *muezzin's* dawn call, from the top of the mosque's minaret (the tower that is an ornamental part of all mosques), is an infallible early morning "wake up" if you happen to be staying nearby— *"Allahu akbar, Allahu akbar."* meaning, "Allah is great, Allah is great." Unfortunately, most mosques are equipped with loudspeakers and make a rather mournful wailing sound as they get under way. But this call to prayer, and the recitation of the Koran on Fridays, can be quite beautiful. Friday's midday prayers are the most important, when the *imam* of the mosque gives his sermon *(khotba)* (prepared nowadays by the Ministry for Religious Affairs, the *Habbous*). Non-Moslems are not allowed into functioning mosques, which is a pity since their decoration is often superb. The exception is the new Hassan II Mosque in Casablanca, and a visit here should not be missed.

Four important events in Islam are celebrated every year. Their date is regulated by the lunar calendar, 11 days shorter than the Gregorian one, which means they fall on a different day each year. Their exact dates depend on the sighting of a new moon, and give rise to a lot of uncertainty and speculation. This is particularly so for the feast that marks the end of the month-long fast of Ramadan, *Aid al Fitr*, also known as *Aid es Sghir* (the "Little Feast"). In fact, it is not only the day of the feast that is uncertain, but also the fixing of the first day of the fast, which has to last until the next new moon is seen. Other Moslem countries such as Saudi Arabia or nearby Algeria are closely watched to see when they begin their fast, since Morocco usually follows a day or two later. The most important feast day, however, is *Aid al Adha* (the "Feast of the Sacrifice"), called more familiarly *Aid el Kbir* (the "Big Feast"), commemorating Abraham's submission to God when asked to sacrifice his son (Ismail for the Moslems, Isaac for the Jews and Christians). This is an occasion for great rejoicing; families buy and slaughter a ram or sheep, and the men visit the mosque. The feast of *Mulud*, the Prophet's birthday, is celebrated more calmly, as is the *ler Moharrem*, the beginning of the Islamic year. These two events are, of course, also mobile.

Two religious or semi-religious classes exist within Islam. One is made up of the alleged lineal descendents of the prophet Mohammed, and claim to derive their power directly from him. The other class consists of the saints. The former are called *chorfa* (singular *cherif*). Women are also counted among the *chorfa* (feminine *cherifa*). *Chorfa* can be found in both Arab and Berber tribes. When they occur in the latter, they are held by most Moroccans to be descendants of Arab immigrants who married into Berber families, or become Berberized in some other way. The oldest family of *chorfa* in Morocco is that descended from Mulay Idriss, the first to establish Islam in the country. There are a lot of *chorfa* in Morocco, but you may hear someone addressed as *cherif* or *cherifa* simply as a matter of courtesy.

As noticeable as the mosque's minaret that rises up among a cluster of houses are the small, domed constructions that stand almost inevitably in isolation in an open space. Whitewashed in northern and central Morocco, they are often ochre-colored in the south. The dome *(kubba)*, too, changes according to region, from polygonal to a simple cone as one moves south. These buildings house the tomb of a saint, a holy man, a *siyyad*, or, very occasionally, that of a holy woman. The saint, through his tomb, is venerated by the population, especially women, who come to seek his blessing *(baraka)* and healing powers for a multitude of ailments: sterility, disease, and mental disorders. The tombs of the very famous *siyyads* are the rallying points for annual pilgrimages and festivities, or *moussems*. They are usually surrounded by simple cemeteries, small upright stones marking the heads and feet of the deceased (two stones for a man, a third one in the middle for women). The cult of the saints exists in a highly developed form in Morocco, alongside orthodox practice. It was undoubtedly a characteristic of Berber life before the arrival of Islam and the Arabs, and was taken over by Islam much in the same way as other religions took over earlier beliefs. Certain trees and springs are also considered to be sacred and have *baraka*, and they too will be visited, mainly by women.

Less noticeable, but nevertheless important in the religious life of the country, are the religious fraternities. Most fraternities have centers for study and prayer throughout Morocco, and often beyond its frontiers. They are formed around a sanctuary, and the building containing the saint's tomb, the dwellings of the fraternity members, and guest houses for visitors constitute a *zaouia*. The *zaouia* gets its income from gifts from pilgrims, but may also own land.

If you have a good ear for languages, you will notice, as you move around Morocco, that a number of phrases with a religious connotation are used regularly by people of all walks of life. The most usual of these is *"B-ism-illah"* ("in the name of God"), pronounced before starting a meal or setting out on a journey; *"inch'allah"* (a favorite phrase meaning "God willing," said whenever some project or work is envisaged); and *"al-hamdu li-llah"* or *"hamdullah"* ("thanks be to God"), which is used when something has turned out well.

Language

The official language is Arabic. A modern version of classical Arabic *(Fuzha)* is taught in all schools. It is the language used in the newspapers, television, and on radio, and for official speeches. It is never used in ordinary conversation, Moroccans, in their daily life, preferring to use a colloquial Arabic *(Darija)*, distinguished from "official" Arabic by pronunciation, syntax, and, to a great extent, vocabulary differences. Moroccan Arabic includes long-established loan words from the Berber dialects and modern borrowings from French and Spanish. If you happen to be a fluent speaker of the Arabic spoken in Saudi Arabia, for instance, you will have difficulty understanding Moroccan Arabic, though many will be able to follow what *you* are saying.

The Arabic language was introduced into Morocco in at least two stages: the first at the end of the 7th century with the first Moslem conquest, the second in the 12th century with the arrival of new Arabic-speaking tribes. At first used and spoken only in the towns, it later spread to include most of lowland Morocco. Those people calling themselves Saharaoui speak *Hassaniya,* a form of Arabic somewhat akin to classical Arabic.

The Berbers have their own language, pre-dating Arabic. The inhabitants of the High Atlas and the Chleuh of the south and southwest speak *Tachelheit,* the populations of the central Moroccan Middle Atlas and some central Rif people speak *Tamazirt,* while other Rifian people speak a linked dialect called *Zenatiya.* There are similarities between these dialects, but a speaker of one will not necessarily be immediately understood by someone using another dialect. Although Berber was the language of many early Moroccan dynasties, it was never used for courtly or literary expression, or made the subject of grammatical studies. It exists today in the spoken form only, although attempts are being made to revive the alphabet. It is probable that some 40 percent of the population speak Berber, but most adult males, and certainly their children, also speak some Arabic. Rural Berber women generally only speak Berber. The spread of schools, even in remote areas, is increasing the Arabization of the population.

What are you going to speak when you arrive in Morocco? As was mentioned earlier, Moroccans on the tourist circuit will know sufficient English

to communicate with the visitor. However, outside this circuit, you will
need either some fairly elementary French, or some Arabic. French is
widely spoken and is the second language in Morocco. Moroccans appreciate French for the opening it provides to further education and modern,
Western ideas. Spanish is spoken in many parts of north Morocco, even by
those too young to have experienced the Spanish occupation. North
Morocco captures Spanish television more easily than programs from
Rabat, and this helps keep the Spanish language alive.

So, where do you go from here? I recommend a simple English/
French phrase book if you are planning to travel as an individual in out-
of-the-way places, especially if you are using a car, since these useful objects may decide to break down in awkward places. Even non-French
speaking mechanics, whether they are Arabs or Berbers, will use French
terms to describe the inside of your car.

Having said that, trying to speak the local Arabic will bring great pleasure to the people you meet and will smooth out many little problems.
Some sounds are difficult for Westerners to pronounce, but it's worth having a try ("kh" is pronounced like a sort of "haa" or Spanish *jota*, while "aa"
is a very guttural "a"). Arabic has two genders, masculine and feminine.
Feminine words end in "a." Incidentally, Peace Corps volunteers who come
to work in Morocco often learn both Arabic and Berber and thus feel at
home with the local population.

Names, I think, are no problem. Common first names for men are
Mohammed (after the Prophet Mohammed), Driss, Kamal, or names beginning with Abd (servant), followed by a word indicating one of Allah's
attributes. So we can have Abd-el-Malik, meaning "Servant of the King,"
Abd-el-Hakim, "Servant of the Just," Abd-er-Rahman, "Servant of the
Clement," and so on. Fatima, Fatna, Fettouma, and Zohra are frequent
names for women, after members of the Prophet's family. Itto is a characteristic Berber name given to women. This first name used to be followed
by "ben" or "bent" ("son" or "daughter" of so-and-so), followed by another
"ben" or "bent" and the name of the father's father. But all this has been
abolished and Moroccans now have a given name and a surname, looking
like this: Mohammed Khattibi, Abdelwahed Zitouni, and Fatima Lahlou.
When addressing a man, you can call him Mr. Khattibi, or by a professional
title (such as Dr. Khattibi), if speaking English, or you can launch out into
a more pleasing *Si* (Arabic for Mr.) Khattibi or *Lalla* (Arabic for Madam)
Lahlou. If you know the person fairly well, you can use his first name.

I don't personally think it is necessary to learn the Arabic numbers, as
fingers will usually do, or you can write down your figure on a piece of
paper. However, I'll list them here.

Numbers

one—*wahad*
two—*zouj* or *tnain*
three—*tlata*
four—*aarba*
five—*khamsa*
six—*stta*
seven—*sebaa*
eight—*tmenia*
nine—*tsa* or *tsaoud*
ten—*aashra*
eleven—*haddach*
fifteen—*khamstach*
twenty—*ashrine*
hundred—*mia*
thousand—*alf*

Days of the Week

These can be useful since the country markets are called after the day of the week on which they are held:

Sunday—*nhar el-had*
(first day)
Monday—*nhar et-thnine*
(second day)
Tuesday—*nhar et-tlata*
(third day)
Wednesday—*nhar el-aarba*
(fourth day)
Thursday—*nhar el-khamis*
(fifth day)
Friday—*nhar el-jemaa*
(mosque day)
Saturday—*nhar es-sebt*
(seventh day)

Greetings

Good morning—*sbah l-khir*
(morning-the-good)
Good afternoon—*msa l-khir*
(afternoon-the-good)
Good night (a farewell)—
laila saida
Peace be with you—*s-salama aa-likum* (a general greeting when entering a room), reply—*wa aalikum s-salam* (and on you peace)
How are you? How are things?—*la-bas?* (no harm?), *la-bas aalik?* (no harm on you?) (can be used interrogatively, or as an affirmative to the same question. A most useful and highly used phrase, good for all occasions and often thrown into the middle of a conversation, just for assurance that the other person really is all right)
What news?—*ash khbar-k?*
Your health OK?—*saaha la-bas* (health, no harm?), reply—*la-bas, hamdullah* (no harm, thanks be to God)
All OK?—*bi-khir?* (with good?), reply—*bi-khir* or *hamdullah*
Goodbye—*b-slama*

General

bad—*khaib*
beautiful—*zwine*
behind—*wara*
cold—*bird*
excuse me—*samhalih-iya*
expensive—*ghali*
far—*beid*
good—*mezian*
how?—*kifash?*
how much?—*shhal?*
inexpensive—*ma-shi-ghali*
(a) little—*shouia*
look—*shouf*

(a) lot—*bezzaf* (very expensive—
    ghali bezzaf)
money—*flouss*
near—*krib*
new—*jdid*
no—*la* (*oho* in Berber)
now—*daba*
OK—*wakha*
old—*kdime*
please—*afak*
thank you—*baraka-laufik* or
    shrukran (more classy)
there is—*kein*
there isn't—*ma-kein-sh*
what?—*shnou?* or *ash?*
when?—*imta?* or *foqash?*
where?—*fin?*
who?—*shkoun?*
why?—*alesh?*
yes—*naam* (classy) or *iyeh*
    (more commonplace)

Food
beef—*begri*
beer—*bira*
bottle—*karaa*
bread—*khobz*
chicken—*djaj*
coffee—*kahwa*
couscous—*seksou*
cup—*kass*
fish—*hout*
glass—*kass*
meat—*lham*
meat balls—*kefta*
milk—*hlib*

mint—*nana*
orange—*limon* (*chin* in the
    east)
salad—*salata*
sausages—*mergez*
sugar—*sukkar*
    (with sugar—*b-sukkar*)
tea—*atay*
water—*ma*
wine—*shr'ab*

Traveling
airplane—*tiyyara*
airport—*matar*
avenue—*sharia*
bus—*tobus*
car—*siyyara*
house—*dar* (*taddart* in Berber)
left—*l-isar*
market—*souk*
mosque—*jemaa*
mountain—*jbel*
    (*adrar* in Berber)
mountain pass—*tizi*
right—*l-limen*
river—*oued* (*assif* in Berber)
route—*trik*
station—*mahatta*
straight on—*nishen*
street—*zankat*
tarmac road—*l-goudron*
town—*medina*
train—*tren*
village—*douar*
watchman (for car,
    for instance)—*assas*

Culture and Lifestyle

Moroccans are strongly attached to their traditions, be they family life
or hospitality, or aspects of their culture such as architecture, decoration,
craftwork, religious festivals, music, and dance. In Morocco you can find

people who are many things all at the same time: Western, Oriental, and African; Arabic-speaking, Berber-speaking, and French-speaking; capable of quoting verses from the Koran or from a French poet; addicted to mint tea but not scorning a whisky or a good wine. You can find others who are pure Berbers, only speak *Tachelheit*, and have never seen a bottle of alcohol. But they all hold strongly to their traditions, whether they are Casablanca bankers or High Atlas shepherds.

Family Life. If I had to single out one, unifying, trait, it would be a strong sense of family life. No packing the old parents off into a home (they don't exist, anyway) or imagining your widowed mother living on her own. The idea of someone living alone is not a pleasant one. An English teacher friend of mine once asked her class of students to describe the situation they would dislike the most—they all replied in chorus, "Being on my own!" The family support system is very strong and takes the place of a non-existent state welfare plan. Linked to this importance of family life is a great love of children. Boys and men are as ready to play with small children and to laugh at their antics as are their wives or sisters. Up to the 1960s and 1970s, a Moroccan woman could be expected to have seven children. This figure has dropped to three. Urban women, understandably, have the smallest number of children, two to three, against four for the rural woman. Women are marrying older now, and this also has an effect on family size. In 1960, the average age for a girl to get married was just over 17; in 1998 it was around 26. Contraception is allowed by the state, the pill and "mechanical" methods of avoiding pregnancy are available, and family planning is becoming widespread among town families. However, the old ideas about male virility, proved by the number of his offspring, are still tenacious. And all couples want a boy in the family!

Women's Issues. Despite this strong sense of family solidarity, the place of women in Moroccan society is not as secure as in the Western world. A Moslem is allowed to have four wives, on the condition that he has the means to treat them all in the same fashion. In rural areas I have noticed that the first wife is sometimes glad to have a second, strong, young wife there to do all the hard work, especially if she remains the mother of the eldest boy. Nowadays, however, most Moroccan men prefer to divorce rather than have the expense of two or more wives (it appears that, today, 1.4 percent of Moroccan men are polygamous). Divorce is easy for a man, who can repudiate his wife by simple unilateral action, but difficult for a woman. Arranged marriages, once the norm, are disappearing. Great strides forward in the emancipation of women have taken place within the last three or four decades, but their legal and economic status remains delicate. Like Moslem women anywhere in the world, the basic Islamic provisions about marriage, divorce, inheritance, and property are applicable to

Moroccan women. A divorced or separated woman may have custody of the male children until they are seven or eight, the female children a couple of years longer, but then they may be legally claimed by the husband. Generally, however, women are granted custody of their children in divorces, but they cannot take them out of the country without the father's approval or radically change their place of residence without the father's permission. A man must make reasonable provisions for his wife after his death, but a daughter inherits from her father only half as much as a son (but without his responsibilities). A woman has full control over her own money or property and may, in theory, dispose of it without asking permission from male relatives. Increasingly, young men like to marry a girl who has a job and this new situation inevitably changes the power struggle within a couple. In urban couples, male-female relationships are becoming much more relaxed, even if the male is still dominant. It is interesting to note that 16 percent of Moroccan families are run by women (particularly in urban areas), generally widowed or divorced (69 percent). A Moroccan couple cannot spend the night together in a hotel without showing their marriage certificate. Sexual relations before marriage is definitely *hshuma* (shameful) for a woman, and the birth of any resulting baby an enormous problem for the unmarried mother. It has been estimated that 40 percent of babies born of single mothers are abandoned. Two non-governmental associations exist in Casablanca to help such women, often very young girls, to keep their babies. But the issue is a very delicate one.

Hospitality. Part and parcel of this family solidarity attitude—which extends, of course, far beyond the nuclear couple—is a sense of hospitality. Once proverbial, now strained by tourism, Moroccan hospitality is such that a visitor will always be offered something to eat and drink, however busy the host and however empty his pocketbook. If you are asked into someone's house, it is correct (but not essential for foreigners) to take off your shoes once inside. If you are invited to a meal it may be that you won't see any women, except servants (if there are any). Never mind—their turn will come later when they and the household children finish off all that is left in the dish. The meal will probably be preceded and followed by glasses of mint tea.

If you have accepted an invitation, you must eat or drink what has been prepared. Even if you are allergic to camel meat, it is really not correct to make a face and refuse it. If you have gotten through various salads, two kinds of meat stew, a flaky pastry pigeon pie, and really feel you can't manage the couscous that follows, you can refuse, pleading complete fullness, after praising the quality of the meal. A few mouthfuls, however, "just to enjoy this marvelous dish," will certainly please your host. The right hand is used for eating out of a large communal dish, after a washing-bowl and towel has been passed around. Bits of meat and gravy are scooped up with a piece of bread. Couscous is also often eaten in the hand, rolled up into small balls and tossed skillfully into the mouth, but the visitor is not obliged to follow—you can politely ask for a spoon. This is better than spraying semolina all over the floor.

Chat. Moroccans often give the impression that they are on the same wavelength as the visitor, but this is sometimes deceptive. As they greatly enjoy talking, conversations can last for hours, sometimes coming back to the beginning and repeating what has already been said. The greetings themselves are lengthy and repetitive. This is where you can run through the last five greetings listed earlier (excluding "good-bye," which would hardly be appropriate). Don't hesitate to use the same one several times. But do be careful over the subjects of conversation. Some subjects are taboo—the king, religion, and the question of the ex-Spanish Sahara. You should not inquire too pressingly about your host's wife (showing a suspicious interest), nor admire too profusely any small child that is presented to you (as it is likely to bring down the evil eye on the unfortunate baby). I should keep away from mentions of Israel and the Palestinians, unless you are against the former and support the latter. Moroccans are proud of their country, and while they freely criticize many aspects of daily life, they do not appreciate *your* condemnation of these things (just like any of us, after all). Nor would I try and justify the Spanish occupation of the two towns of Ceuta (Sebta to the Moroccans) and Melilla, unless you are speaking to a good, open-minded friend or enjoy a heated argument. Moroccans, too, are keen to please, and an outright "no" or "I don't know" are not customary phrases. The visitor should avoid a firm refusal to do something—it is best to hedge, say vaguely "another day" or "I'll see," "if possible," or "God willing" *(inch'allah)*. Sitting around talking is an entertainment in itself for many people, and relatives will regularly pay each other lengthy visits just to exchange news, while filling up with sweet, sticky pastries. However, talk stops during meals, when it is not considered rude to remain silent (thereby showing appreciation of the food).

Education and Health. In theory, primary school should be attended by all children from the age of 7 to 14. The state schools are free, but books, pens, and so on cost money that many parents can ill afford. In the 1997/1998 school year, just over 3 million children followed the first cycle of this primary grade schooling, and a further 900,000 continued into the second cycle. The total of just over 4 million included those in private establishments, the number of which increases every day in the towns. It has been estimated, however, that only 50 percent of Moroccan children of primary grade age actually attend school. These figures vary from region to region. The figure is higher in the towns (69 percent attendance) than in the country, where only 36 percent of school age children go to school. In the country, too, very few pupils are girls (20 percent), the parents preferring to keep them at home to do useful jobs around the house and in the fields. Morocco and the U.S. recently signed an agreement in Washington giving US$1.8 million via USAID to improve the educational chances of rural girls. The latest figures, from 1997, indicate that slightly more than 400,000 first-graders went on to high school, the 14 universities admitted 230,000 students aiming for a degree, and a total of 27 state and higher education institutes trained 9,000 future engineers, public administrators, pilots, forestry officers, and so on. Lower-level technical training was given to some 127,000 students. Moroccans are understandably keen for their children to succeed in an increasingly competitive world, and those who can put a lot of money into schooling. The rich often send their children abroad to complete their higher education. The first private university was founded in Ifrane in 1993, following the initiative of the late King Hassan II. It has an American-style campus and provides an Arabic-American curriculum, with a number of American teachers. It has attracted the children of wealthy Moroccans and Arabs from other countries.

The health service used to be free, but in recent years would-be patients have had to pay for a night's lodging and for any specialized examinations required, such as X-ray or scanner. Slightly over 4,000 doctors and 25,000 paramedical personnel work for the national health system. A larger number of doctors (5,730) are in private practice. There are approximately 3,000 private pharmacists. The distribution of doctors, both public and private, reflects the attraction of the big towns to the detriment of rural areas: 669 state doctors and nearly 2,000 private ones work in Casablanca; 850 state and 747 private doctors work in Rabat-Salé; the remote southern province of Tan-Tan has the lowest number of any kind of doctor—9 in public service and 3 in private practice. Despite the competence of the doctors, many of whom have trained in medical schools abroad, and the sophistication of the equipment available in the large towns, the situation of a poor, sick person is not a comfortable one. Indeed, a 1998 study showed that 4 out of 10 Moroccans don't call on the official health service when they become ill. Great disparities exist here, too, between the town and the country: 69 percent of urban Moroccans go for medical help, while the figure drops to 49 percent in the country. In rural districts, many resort to traditional healing methods in the absence of modern medical care. In 1998, it was estimated that 7 to 8 women died each day in Morocco following childbirth (32 deaths for 10,000 live births). In 1995, 63 percent of births took place in the mother's home, with no professional help. Having a baby at home does not, of course, automatically create problems, but the absence of professional medical help close at hand is obviously a handicap in the event of complications.

Physical Contact. As we all know, hand and body gestures vary in meaning from country to country. Most Americans find that Moroccans stand too close to them. Physical contact is also more generalized; men hold hands, or walk hand in hand. As a matter of course, hands are always shaken when one meets people and are often laid on the arm later to emphasize a point; and men, as well as women, kiss each other on the cheek. As a sign of great respect, one person may kiss the other's shoulder (pupil to ex-teacher situation, for instance). If you want to attract someone's attention—a waiter, for instance—use a palm down, four-bent-finger movement, and not the one with the palm upright, which means "more, more" (usually money).

The body is covered in Morocco, even in high temperatures. Bare-chested men are not seen in the streets, although young men wear shorts. Women visitors should also avoid walking around displaying large expanses of flesh—this should be kept to the beach, where less strict clothing rules apply. In this context, it is a surprise to visitors to see women breast-feeding their babies in public, but this is a perfectly acceptable activity (at least for a Moroccan woman—I'm not too sure about the reaction if a Western woman did the same thing!). In the *hammam* (public baths), men and women keep on their underpants. I have known of street-boys refused entry to a *hammam* in Casablanca because they had no underclothes. Many people visit the *hammam* once a week, even if they have running hot water at home (women often spend long hours in the *hammam* where suitable marriage partners for their children can be an important subject of conversation). Personal cleanliness is important for Moroccans, although this is not evident from the state of the streets or countryside, where plastic bags and litter of all kinds are everywhere. The principle seems to be to clean up in front of one's own house by pushing all those bits of greasy paper in front of the neighbor's.

Green Issues. Environmental issues are slowly coming to the forefront. An association, Afak ("please"), has been formed, and launches clean-up campaigns, providing street trash cans (alas, often never emptied) and car stickers announcing that "the street is not a garbage can." With no conscious feeling for green issues, recuperation and recycling has long been carried out. Old newspapers, glass and plastic, bottles, plastic sandals, grass, rotting vegetables, and almost anything else you'd like to name are all bought or picked up for free by men passing down the road with a little cart or a big sack. Only the ubiquitous black plastic bags seem to be unre-coverable, flying around like grotesque birds or caught flapping in thorny country bushes. I know of two camels that died recently in the far south—the autopsy showed that the cause of death was a stomach full of plastic bags, innocently gobbled up.

A "green belt" has existed south of Rabat for many years now. More than 10,500 hectares of fruit and ornamental trees were planted around Fès in 1991, as part of its "green belt" planned to cover 20,000 hectares. Reforestation plans operate in many parts of the country, but the increas-ing demand by rural populations for firewood for cooking and heating makes the race a rather unequal one. In mid-1998 it was estimated that Morocco loses about 31,000 hectares of woodland each year. Some of this loss is due to forest fires, but man himself is responsible for most of the degradation: over-grazing, extensive use of wood for cooking and heating, and little replacement of destroyed or disappearing forests. The U.S. co-operates with Morocco on a number of green issues.

Drugs and Prostitution. Drugs are a big issue in Morocco and scarcely a day goes by without the Moroccan newspapers announcing a huge bust somewhere. Drug smuggling is the main reason why a number of foreign-ers—both men and women—are in Moroccan jails. It is paradoxically not illegal to cultivate hash, but it is illegal to commercialize it. Both hash and marijuana *(kif)* are smoked by the local people, the latter in a long-stemmed, small-bowled pipe called a *sebsi*.

Several tons of cocaine in small plastic bags were washed up on the beaches around Casablanca in 1997 and eagerly seized by the locals. The result was heavy fines and prison sentences, so, unless you are looking for trouble, it is better to avoid any form of drug taking. U.S. consular au-thorities remind their citizens that they are subject to the laws of the coun-try and risk severe jail sentences and fines for possession, use, or trafficking in drugs.

Prostitution is part of Moroccan life, although not officially approved of, of course. An unmarried man can frequent prostitutes without incur-ring disapproval, and all nightclubs have their quota of "working girls." Homosexuality has become less tolerated by the authorities, and is pun-ishable by imprisonment. Nevertheless, in some towns, young Moroccans still try to catch a tourist. Pedophilia is definitely out.

Arts and Crafts. Alongside the modern sector of the economy, an arts and crafts tradition flourishes, making Morocco the most outstanding North African country in this field. Moroccan leather-ware *(maroquinerie)* has been known throughout Europe for many centuries. Nowadays, the only export items are rugs, the other handmade articles being for home consumption or for the tourist trade. Handmade woven rugs, brass and copperware, pottery and ceramics, woodwork, basketwork, and jewelry are familiar sights in all the markets and form an essential part of Moroccan culture. They are a joy to look at. Few households are without a rug from Rabat, Fès, the High Atlas, Tazenakht, or Ouaouizarht—all with their distinctive designs and techniques. In the Middle Atlas, the flat-woven *hanbel* (used as a blanket or thrown around the shoulders) is a common sight. In the country, donkey bags, mule cloths, and bags of all kinds are woven in the home. Brass and copper are hammered into trays; candlesticks, lamps, mirror frames, hand-washing basins, and pitchers are carefully worked by craftsmen in the medinas. Again, most Moroccan men will own at least one pair of handmade slippers, *belgha*, in white or yellow leather for special occasions; leather, felt, or silk slippers, very colorful and decorated, are favorites with women. The leather hammocks found in most households are, unfortunately, being replaced by plastic ones. Pottery is both very functional, such as the thick glazed *tajine* dish, and more decorative. The blue soup bowls from Fès, the plates, bowls, and coffee sets from the Oulja workshops in Salé, and the decorated *tajine* dishes from Safi combine aesthetics with utility. Polychrome glazed tiles, *zellij*, of traditional design, are a feature of religious buildings, but are also widely used in private houses.

Dress. Most young men wear western-style clothing. The T-shirt is very popular—and very cheap—but blue jeans are not worn all that often, probably on account of their price. The garment the visitor sees most often is the *jellaba*, a loose hooded outfit of wool or some lighter material, worn by both men and women. The former favor browns, blacks, or blues, while the latter go for the brightest colors available. Underneath this, men will be wearing a shirt (no tie) and trousers; women may be in smart town clothes, jogging trousers, or a more traditional long dress over long baggy underpants, designed to be seen. For festive occasions, women will be dressed in silk, long-sleeved kaftans, belted in with sumptuous gold belts. Pointed slippers *(belgha)* are worn by both men and women. Men's headgear varies from the around wool cap, to the turban or the fez (a truncated-cone shaped red hat with a tassel, worn by the doormen of snazzy hotels). Boys and young men prefer the sporty cap, worn back to front in modern fashion. Older town women will still cover the lower part of their face with a silk or cotton veil, not to be confused with the all-around-the-face affair of the Islamic sisters. Only very young girls should go out without their hair being covered in some sort of scarf, but this, too, is not strictly observed. Berber women of the Middle Atlas have splendid woolen capes *(hendira)*, and those around Tangier are noted for their wide pompomed straw hats and for the red and white striped cloth *(fouta)* tied over their white dresses. It is well known that these *fouta* come in useful for hiding contraband articles smuggled in from the Spanish enclaves. South of the Atlas, under a burning sun, women are often surprisingly swathed in layers of black material, decorated with a few lines of colored embroidery. The very traditional *haik*, seven meters of white cotton or wool, which a woman wraps up and down and around, is now seldom seen.

Jewelry and Personal Decoration. Whole books have been written on Moroccan jewelry, especially Berber, and it is difficult here to do justice to this extremely rich aspect of Moroccan culture. Urban jewelry, generally gold or gold-plated, enhanced by pearls or precious stones, recalls that of medieval Andalusia when it is not clearly a modern creation. Berber jewelry, on the other hand, is of silver (or pseudo-silver) and looks more austere, although its shapes are extremely varied and rich in symbolism. It is much sought after by overseas buyers, and one can not always be sure of having acquired a true antique. Many old bits of jewelry, perhaps a bit broken, were sold back to silversmiths who reworked them into more modern forms.

Among the pieces most frequently seen are fibulas, pendants (sometimes in the shape of the hand to repel the evil eye), earrings, diadems, necklaces, rings, and bracelets. Techniques include the incorporation of coral, precious stones, and the use of enamel inlays.

Personal decoration includes henna painting and tattooing, as well as modern lipstick among town women. Henna painting of hands, wrists, ankles, and feet is much practiced. It can be applied at private and public festivities—religious holidays, marriages, births—or simply because one feels like it. The sheep about to be slaughtered at the Feast of the Sacrifice often has its head daubed with henna. Henna is a beneficial plant, approved of by the Prophet Mohammed. It is also used to color or tint the hair. Tattooing, on the other hand, is not well thought of anymore, and is tending to die out. A study of over 1,000 tattooed women, both Arab and Berber, showed that tattooing was definitely not a sign of belonging to a certain tribe, nor a sign of moving into puberty, despite much that has been written to this effect. The bulk of the women interviewed were tattooed "to be like the others" or to "be beautiful." A small minority were tattooed for superstitious reasons. These were generally married but childless women who were trying to exorcise the evil eye that was preventing them from conceiving.

Architecture and Housing. Broadly speaking, the houses and buildings that a traveler is most likely to see can be divided into three groups: European, Hispano-Mauresque, and Berber. Within these groups there are, of course, many sub-groups, often varying from region to region.

Town dwellers live in apartment blocks, houses, or villas. Shantytowns still exist outside the main cities, although efforts are being made to absorb them. In the country, settlements can be made up of scattered houses (as in the Rif) or be grouped (as in the High Atlas or the south, for example). Berber houses of the second type, closely integrated into their landscape, are made of stone or adobe and, in many cases, look like small forts. This fortified appearance is given by the presence of an imposing, turreted building, the kasbah. Other impressive buildings are the *agadir, tighremt,* or fortified storage depot. In the very south, eight or so families are lodged inside an enclosure, the whole thing being called a *ksar* (plural *ksour),* a word which crops up as a place name. Nomadic tribes still live in goat or camel-hair tents *(khaima),* which are often used by hotels and restaurants in the south to give a touch of local color to their establishment. A different type of tent, not lived in but put up on official occasions, is the "government tent," white with a repetition of small black motifs.

Sport, Music, and Dance. Moroccans are fervent footballers (the American equivalent of soccer)—perhaps "fanatical" would be more appropriate than fervent. Fields where young people can play being almost nonexistent, almost any open space in town or country will see 100 percent absorbed players chasing after the round ball and dreaming of being the heroes of the national team—the "Lions of the Atlas." Morocco reached the second round of the World Cup in 1986, and qualified for the 1998 World Cup. Many Moroccans play for French, Spanish, Swiss, or Italian teams and the progression of these teams is followed with passion in Morocco. Other sports pale in comparison with football. To be sure, the N° 1 Moroccan tennis player is 36th in the ATP ranking and beat the world's N° 1 player, American Pete Sampras, a couple of years ago, but tennis is still a game for the elite, as it is too expensive for the majority. Golf, too, is only practiced by the well-heeled. However, Moroccans excel in middle-distance running, where Hicham El Guerrouj is a 1,500 m world champion, Salah Hissou holder of the 10,000 m world record, and Zohra Ouaziz is dominant over 5,000 m. Said Aouita brought athleticism into the limelight back in the 1980s, by winning a gold medal in the 1984 Los Angeles Olympics, while his colleague, Nawal Moutawakil, became the first Arab woman to win a gold medal for the 400 m hurdles.

Music plays an important part in Moroccan life. It can be of the traditional Andalusian type, with musicians in white *jellabas* and red fez solemnly strumming lutes and violins accompanied by a singer; Berber, with drums and other percussion instruments *(bendir, derbouka),* also accompanied by one or several singers; Arabic, with the famous Egyptian Oum Keltoum still at the top of the list, but followed by well-known

Moroccan and Lebanese singers; local pop, such as *rai* (using electric gui-
tars, accordions, and brass instruments); *Gnaoua,* practiced by a religious
fraternity, which combines mysticism, trance, and music; and, of course,
western imports, mostly American.

Andalusian music is an age-old music, combining Spanish, Arab, and
African rhythms that have been handed down by ear over the generations.
It can be heard on the radio or television, and is particularly developed in
Tetouan, Fès, and Rabat. Popular Berber music is usually associated with
community dances, the *ahidous* and the *ahouach.* The latter is the most
popular dance in *Chleu* country. It generally starts with an improvised song
and then suddenly the circle of musicians springs into life and the whole
thing gets faster and faster. Thirty to 150 women dancers, shoulder to
shoulder, form a huge circle that moves slowly around in small steps,
singing songs that can be naïve, religious, or pastoral. The male musicians
squat in the center of the circle, beating on their *bendir,* the rhythm finally
reaching a crescendo while the chorus remains silent.

The Middle Atlas is home to the *ahidous.* It gives an impression of peace
and calm. Men and women dancers line up alternately, singing songs re-
minding one of the Psalms by their questions and replies. The *guedra* is another well-known Moroccan dance, practiced in the far south. In this
dance, a kneeling woman sways and twists in the middle of a circle of musicians, to music, and with fairly erotic gestures.

Singers such as Oum Keltoum or Sappho need no introduction. Their
songs are known the world over and, while they are popular with
Moroccans, do not constitute part of the Moroccan musical heritage. *Rai,*
too, is more Algerian than typically Moroccan, although it flourishes in
eastern Morocco. It is much appreciated by the young. *Gnaoua* music has
its roots in West Africa and is practiced by black-skinned musicians. It has
come to the forefront recently, and the Gnaoui take part in many musical
manifestations, as well as twirling around in the streets, snapping their cas-
tanets, and strumming on their *guembri* (a sort of simple lute), on Fridays.
Randy Weston was the first to introduce Gnaoua music to the western
world and Paul Bowles recorded their music in the 1940s. The Nass el
Ghiwane group, created in the 1970s, rapidly became cult figures. They
profoundly shook the Moroccan musical landscape, with their mixture of
traditional instruments, African, Arab, and Algerian Berber roots, their po-
etry, and the force of their songs. Western, particularly American, music
reaches Morocco via radio and tapes. Not much protection exists in the
way of copyright and tapes are endlessly copied and sold quite openly.
Shops and stalls selling tapes of all kinds can be found in towns and markets all over the country.

Food and Drink

Moroccan cooking is among the finest in the world. Even if you are not particularly hooked on eating, you should not miss out on a meal in a really good Moroccan restaurant (just once, at least). The following are some of the specialties—not in any order of excellence.

Brochettes are kebobs (small pieces of meat on a skewer), often sprinkled with cumin. They are a popular dish and are cooked in all the roadside restaurants as you wait. Those who know about meat will choose their bit from the hunk on the stall, say a ½ kilo, which will then be cooked for you. It is about the safest thing to eat in uncertain places. Fish kebobs are also served.

Bastela is a really top-class dish which you must try. Sheets of flaky pastry encase shredded pigeon (or chicken), ground almonds, chopped-up eggs, cinnamon, and saffron. It is delicious.

Couscous is a national dish, nearly always served on Fridays (the prayer day). It can vary from the complicated to the very simple, traditionally with some meat (beef, lamb, or chicken) hidden beneath the cone of steamed wheat semolina. Other ingredients can include carrots, turnips, onions, raisins, and other vegetables, the whole lot accompanied by a delicious sauce.

Djaj is chicken. It can come in a great variety of stews *(tajine)* or roasted with almonds.

Harira is the traditional soup served as part of the first meal after breaking the fast during Ramadan. It is thick and spicy and can contain all sorts of ingredients such as onions, tomatoes, chickpeas, lentils, favas, and meat. It is very nourishing—and very filling.

Kefta are meatballs, swimming in gravy, sometimes accompanied by eggs. As the meat has been minced and may have been around for a while, they are probably not advisable from wayside cafés.

Mechoui is whole roasted lamb, split open, which one tackles with ones fingers, usually getting slightly burned in the process. It is served on very special occasions, such as a marriage.

Mergez are spicy beef or lamb sausages, and are very hot.

Tajine is a sort of meat stew, but a rather sophisticated one, depending on the ingredients, which can include green beans, favas, peas, prunes, squash, artichokes—my cookbook gives 46 varieties of *tajine!* It is cooked very slowly over a small charcoal brazier, in a dish, also called a *tajine,* in which it is served.

Excellent fish is available and served in towns near the coast, anywhere down the Atlantic from Tangier to Agadir and further south.

These meals are generally accompanied by water, Coca-Cola, or some other fizzy drink. Mint tea will always be served, along with sticky honey or almond pastries. Coca-Cola is everywhere, but Diet Coke is much rarer (sold as "Coca Light").

Good wines are produced in Morocco and can be bought in many supermarkets and grocery shops in the bigger towns. Wine is not served in the smaller restaurants, but is available in all the big hotels and restaurants. The former also have a large range of imported alcohol, from whisky to vodka. A word of warning: restaurants and hotels up-price wine served to guests by approximately 150 percent. Semilant, Coquillages, and Valpierre are popular white wines of average price, Cabernet du President, Guerrouane, Toulal, Ksar, and Ait Souala are good red ones, while Guerrouane and Ksar also come as rosés. An excellent, more expensive red wine is Beau Vallon. Beer, both local and imported (including Budweiser), is widely available, in cans or bottles. Locally-bottled brands are Flag and La Cigogne.

Festivals

These can be divided into two categories: the traditional celebration in honor of a saint and the more recent creation of festivals to promote a region or an activity. Starting with the second group first, the Sacred Music Festival *(Festival de Fès des Musiques sacrées du Monde)* is held in Fès in May, the Rose Festival *(Fête des Roses)* at Kelaa des Mgouna (southern Morocco) late in May, the National Folklore Festival in Marrakech (stopped for a while, but started up again in the summer of 1999), the Cherry Festival *(Fête des Cerises)* in Sefrou (near Fès) in June, the International Arts Festival in Asilal (Atlantic Coast) in August, and the Horse Festival *(Fête du Cheval)* in Tissa (Fès) and the Date Festival *(Fête des Dattes)* in Erfoud, both in October. These types of events are well worth seeing and, as they are not religious, new festivals seem to be added every year. One was born in June 1998 called The First International Festival of Gnaoui Culture (see above for a quick idea of Gnaoua music). Another very new one is the Festival of Camel Racing in Laayoune at the end of February.

It would be impossible to mention all the religious festivals or *moussems* that are held from the spring through the fall. The biggest and most popular are perhaps the *Moussem of Sidi Bou Sellam* (near Kénitra) in May, the *Moussem of Mulay Abdallah* (near El-Jadida) and the *Moussem of Mulay Idriss* (near Meknès), both in June, the *Moussem of Setti Fatma* (near Marrakech) in July, and the *Fête des Fiancés* (Marriage Festival) in Imilchil in late September—this one is a real attraction for tourists, with organized excursions. But there are plenty of others throughout the country and it is well worth stopping to have a look.

Health and Safety

Medical care is available in the towns, although few hospitals outside Rabat and Casablanca have sophisticated facilities of a high standard and specialized care or treatment may not be available. If you need a blood transfusion, hospital staff will often ask you to provide it yourself from friends or neighbors (if they are available!). Non-emergency matters can be dealt with quite adequately, although medical staff will probably not speak English. It is advisable to carry a first-aid kit if trekking in the mountains or in the far south. In the event of a serious accident in the mountains or on the road, the nearest local authorities should be notified, as well as the American Embassy in Rabat or the Consulate in Casablanca. Immediate ambulance service for car accidents is not guaranteed. It is wise to be sure what your insurance covers. The American Consulate will advise on doctors, if requested.

The beaches around Casablanca are particularly dangerous, with a strong undertow. The more frequented beaches are controlled, but not all the local lifesavers have the necessary boats to fish you out of trouble. Avoid sunstroke, even if the sun doesn't seem that hot. Sexually transmitted diseases and AIDS are also present in Morocco.

Be careful—but not hypochondriac—over what you eat and drink. Bottled water is the best, though the water in all the towns is perfectly safe. Don't forget that ice is only as good as the water from which it is made. *Tourista*—tourist stomach upsets—is commonly experienced by visitors. If you have special medical needs, it is best to bring your pills and things with you. Chemists are well stocked, but the brand names are French and you may not be able to find exactly what you need.

Morocco is a safe country in which to travel. Take the usual precautions you would in any big town—keep your money well tucked away, avoid visible, expensive jewelry and flashy watches, and try to time your road journeys to avoid night travel. In the far southwest, in what used to be called the Spanish Sahara, off-road travel is not advisable. Fierce fighting in the past has left minefields and other dangers that have not yet been removed. Further tips about safety in general were given in chapter 2.

Business Opportunities

Every Moroccan newspaper carries articles on the need to find foreign investors. They are said to have risen recently, but they are still thought to be insufficient to infuse new life into the Moroccan economy. An assessment, requested by the Moroccan government and prepared by two international agencies, Moodys and Standard and Poor's, gave Morocco a "B" rating among the countries where it was good to invest. The assessment was based notably on the country's reimbursement capacity. The summer of 1998 saw an important boost to foreign investments with the signing of an agreement with the South Korean Daewoo involving the creation of two specialized production units in Casablanca for an investment of 400 million dollars. Great satisfaction was expressed when Delphi Paccard, a subsidiary of General Motors, recently decided to open a factory in Tangier. The textile industry is a sector that sees a number of foreign investors. The British firm, Courtaulds Textiles, opened a small factory in Rabat in the spring of 1998. Various organizations and banks are ready to help potential investors:

- Foreign Investment Department, Ministère des Finances et des Investissements Extérieurs, 11 Rue Sebou, Rabat-Agdal, Morocco. (Tel: 212-7-68 02 08, Fax: 212-7-68 02 07, Internet address: http// 3W.MFIE.GOV.MA, e-mail: DIEAMSIE@GOV.MA)
- International Department, Wafabank, 163, 163 Avenue Hassan II, Casablanca, Morocco (Tel: 212-2-20 02 00/22 41 05, Fax: 212-2-47 03 08)
- Price Waterhouse publishes the useful, free *Business Guide,* which gives basic information on such things as legal aspects, labor legislation, taxation, investment incentives, the stock exchange, and privatization. They have a range of services available, going well beyond financial auditing. For information contact their branch in Rabat: Résidence Es Saada, 1 Boulevard Mohammed V, 11100 Rabat (Tel: 212-7-72 74 97/72 01 95, Fax: 212-7-73 88 70, Telex 32047 M [PRICEWAT]);
- In Casablanca contact: 4 Rue Colbert, 21100 Casablanca (Tel: 212-2-31 49 68/31 04 05, Fax: 212-2-31 30 91, Telex 21947 M [PRICEWAT] and 22922 M [PRICEWAT])
- The British Chamber of Commerce, 65 Avenue Hassan Seghir, Casablanca (Tel: 212-2-44 88 60/61/65, Fax: 212-2-44 88 68, e-mail britcham@techno.net.ma) (The president is Alexander Moll, OBE.)
- Finally, the U.S. Consulate in Casablanca (8 Boulevard Moulay Youssef, Casablanca) suggests potential investors get in touch with them first. Contact the Commercial Attaché in Casablanca (Tel: 212-2-26 45 50, Fax: 212-2-22 02 59). The Consulate has produced a list of useful contacts including the following:
- U.S. Embassy, 2 Avenue de Marrakech, Rabat (contact the Economic Counselor or the Agricultural Attaché) (Tel: 212-7-76 85 62, Fax: 212-7-76 54 93)

- American Chamber of Commerce, Business Center, Casablanca Hyatt Regency, Place des Nations Unies, Casablanca (contact the Executive Director, Mr. Simon O'Rourke, Tel: 212-2-29 30 28, Fax: 212-2-48 15 97, e-mail: amcham@mtds.com)
- U.S.-Morocco Council on Trade & Investment, BMCE Building, 140 Avenue Hassan II, Casablanca (contact the Director of Programs & Development, Ms. Julianne M. Furman, Tel: 212-2-26 27 30, Fax: 212-2-47 14 17)
- U.S. Deptartment of Commerce, Office of the Near East, 14th & Constitution Avenue NW, Washington, DC 20230 (contact the Morocco Desk Officer, Tel: 202-483-1860, Fax: 202-482-0878)

Investment in Morocco is, unfortunately, still hampered by administrative fiddle-faddle (said to have decreased with the new government), and sound advice is recommended at an early stage.

The Casablanca Stock Exchange was created in 1929, but it is only with recent privatizations that it has become an active organization. Relevant information can be obtained from any of the above addresses.

Visiting businessmen can get a full range of secretarial, interpreting, translating, intensive language courses, and office support services from SEKA Services, 84 Rue Meissonier, Palmier, Casablanca (Director, Gwendolyn Dellar) (Tel: 212-2-99 11 22, Fax: 212-2-99 11 24, e-mail: sekacasanet@net.ma). The British Chamber of Commerce (address above) can also supply the same range of services (without the language courses).

4

Who Are the Moroccans?

Prehistory

Man is known to have been present in Morocco for nearly one million years. Lower Palaeolithic (Acheulian) hand axes, picks, cleavers, choppers, and chopping tools have been found during on-going excavations in Casablanca quarries. Palaeomagnetic data suggests an age of more than 780,000 years. The earliest human remains, those of *Homo erectus,* are younger and are dated to approximately 400,000 B.C. The Acheulian tradition continued for many millennia. Then two almost-complete skulls were found while quarrying near Safi. One was carried off to the United States by the well-known American anthropologist, Carlton Coon. Recent studies of the other skull have suggested that the owner was a primitive *Homo sapiens,* dating to around 120,000 years ago. This discovery is thought to prove the existence of an independent evolution of *Homo erectus* into *Homo sapiens* in Africa.

This rather primitive ancestor of modern man evolved, as did his tools. Then, around 20,000 years ago, he disappeared, to be replaced in east

Morocco by a new human type, a real *Homo sapiens sapiens,* almost like us, a sort of cousin of the European Cro-Magnon. Excavations have revealed that this newcomer made small, microlithic flint tools, buried his dead, and cared for the living. For example, a severely handicapped woman lived to an old age, showing that these people, known as Iberomaurusians, were no primitive savages. Could they be called Proto-Berbers? Certainly their successors, the Capsians, known mostly in Algeria and Tunisia, have been considered by some researchers to be the earliest Berbers. The Iberomaurusians spread over most of north Morocco and down the Atlantic Coast, continuing their hunting way of life until the first ideas of agriculture and animal domestication reached northwest Morocco, proba-bly from Spain, just across the Strait of Gibraltar. It is thought to be un-likely that these innovations were accompanied by massive "invasions" of new people. It is much more likely that existing populations simply adopted the new techniques. Excavations from Tangier to Casablanca have enabled a Neolithic sequence to be built up, starting around 7,500 B.C. (or, if you prefer "calibrated," "truer" dates based on tree-rings, rather than the "pure" radiocarbon ones, then around 9,000 B.C.). Sheep, goats, and cattle were kept, simple farming started a bit later, and pottery of many shapes and sizes was common (much of it closely linked to Iberian models). Several important burial caves have been excavated between Rabat and Casablanca. A sand dune site produced the remains of over 100 individu-als: one-third were children under two, one-third were over two and ado-lescents, and one-third were adults. Grave goods were numerous: pottery, stone vases, polished axes, bone tools, bowls and bracelets in elephant ivory, and decorative objects of ostrich eggshell. The site is dated by radio-carbon to 3,000 B.C. (about 1,000 years earlier by calibrated dates).

South of the High Atlas, rock engravings of domestic cattle showed that a pastoral life was once possible in regions now dry and deserted. This was the time, from about 4,500-2,500 B.C., when the climate was wetter than today, and a grass steppe could provide food for cattle as well as wild ani-mals such as antelopes, gazelles, elephants, and rhinoceros.

Echoes of the European Copper and Bronze Ages began to reach Morocco in the middle of the third millennium B.C., in the shape of a strik-ing pottery goblet known as a "Bell Beaker." Very few copper or bronze ob-jects have been found, but small graves similar to those in Spain showed clearly that new influences were at work. Some rock engravings of daggers and halberds in the High Atlas are thought to be copies of real, Bronze Age, mid-second millennium weapons found in Iberian excavations.

Phoenicians, Mauretanian Berbers, and Romans

Increasingly, Morocco became incorporated into the commercial system of the Mediterranean basin. From the eighth century B.C., the Phoenicians had installed themselves in trading points along the Mediterranean and Atlantic coasts. With their arrival, Morocco's prehistory could be said to have ended, in the sense that they introduced an alphabet and writing. But the inhabitants of the inland regions continued their ancestral way of life, based on crop-raising and animal herding. The introduction by the Phoenicians of iron weapons, along with other more fanciful items designed to attract the local people, probably altered their way of life very little. A number of Phoenician and Carthaginian sites have been excavated in northwest Morocco, mostly of a funerary nature.

The date of the earliest Berber—"Mauretanian"—kingdoms in northwest Africa is unknown. The first was recorded by a Roman historian in the fourth century B.C., but in Morocco the first Berber king to be mentioned by name was Bocchus, who reigned from 118-81 B.C. However, small, probably autonomous, geographically-limited groups under a chief must have existed in one form or another throughout the later prehistoric period, becoming more formalized with the arrival of the Phoenicians and Carthaginians.

In 146 B.C., Rome, having defeated Carthage and having occupied Tunisia, became the new power to be reckoned with in the western Mediterranean. Two Berber kingdoms were dominant at that time in northwest Africa: Mauretania and Numidia (roughly Morocco and Algeria plus Tunisia). Numidian chiefs whose names have gone down in history are Massinissa and his grandson, Jugurtha. Unfortunately for him, Jugurtha's own grandson, the Numidian king Juba I, was on the wrong side in fights against the Romans. He opposed the Roman advance through his country, was defeated, and his young son was taken prisoner and brought up at the Roman court by the Emperor Augustus. But the story has a happy ending, for in 25 B.C., Augustus placed the young prince at the head of a sort of Roman protectorate in Mauretania, where he ruled as Juba II until 23 A.D.

Juba II was a cultivated man, reading Greek and Latin, a patron of the arts, and the author of many books (all were unfortunately lost). His capital was Caesarea (now Cherchell) in Algeria, and his secondary residence or secondary capital was in Morocco, at Volubilis, near Meknès. The country flourished under his rule. A bronze head of a handsome, pouting young man, thought to represent Juba II, was excavated at Volubilis, and is now on view at the Archaeological Museum in Rabat. Juba II married Cleopatra Silene, daughter of the Egyptian Cleopatra and Mark Antony. Their son, Ptolemy, who replaced his father, came to a bad end in 40 A.D., assassinated in Rome by the Roman emperor Caligula. Trouble and disorder arose both in Rome and in the North African provinces, and in 42 A.D. the Romans took direct control over the whole area, which they divided into two: Mauretania Caesariensis (east Morocco and Algeria) and Mauretania Tingitana (the rest of Morocco north of the Middle and High Atlas Mountains).

Under Roman rule, Morocco became particularly prosperous, with an important agriculture that provided Rome with cereals and olive oil. Archaeological discoveries prove that, in the fourth century A.D., the Christian church was no longer persecuted as it had been before the conversion of the Roman Emperor Constantine in 313 A.D. Rome remained present until 285 A.D. in Volubilis and 429 A.D. in the north. However, four or five centuries of Roman domination left few traces, apart from a number of agricultural terms, for Rome never became rooted in Morocco and didn't really change what already existed. By early in the fifth century A.D. the Roman Empire was in pieces, outlying areas such as Morocco were being harassed by local tribes, and the Romans had to pull out completely. The year 429 A.D. saw the rapid raid by the Vandals led by Genseric across northwest Africa, aiming for Carthage, but this had little lasting effect on Moroccan customs or way of life (the Vandals are *not* responsible for the white skins and red hair seen sometimes in north Morocco!). In an attempt to win back North Africa, the Byzantine rulers managed to establish themselves in Tangier and Ceuta, which they occupied until the arrival of the Arabs in the seventh century. The Berber kingdoms and tribes doubtless reverted to their squabbles and battles. Of all the Roman towns, only Volubilis has yielded traces of an occupation by local people, some of them Christianized Berbers, after the departure of the Roman army and the rich landowners. But little is known about Morocco from the fourth to the seventh century, and they have understandably been called the "Dark Ages."

The Arrival of the Arabs and Islam: 681 A.D.

The seventh century saw the emergence of a new power and a new religion: the Arabs from Arabia, intent on spreading their religion, Islam, as far as they could. In 681, an Umayed chief from Damascus, Oqba ibn Nafi, who had founded the city of Kairouan in Tunisia, launched a lightning raid into Morocco. The epic scene, where the Arab leader is seen spurring his horse into the Atlantic Ocean, is well known to Moroccan schoolchildren.

Oqba is said to have claimed that only the sea prevented him from spreading Islam even further. But Oqba and his troops managed to antagonize the Berber populations to such an extent that what began as skirmishes ended in full-scale battles, in one of which, on his return through Algeria, Oqba was defeated and killed by the Berber chief Koseila. Berbers and Byzantine forces combined to put an end to this first Arab incursion into northwest Africa. In 698 the Arabs invaders had another try and this time succeed in chasing out the Byzantines and quelling resistance by the famous Berber princess, Kahina. Tactful, conciliating policies by a new Umayad general, Musa ibn Nosayr, put Morocco in the hands of the Arabs by 710. In 711, Musa continued his conquests by crossing the Strait of Gibraltar with his lieutenant Tariq ibn Ziad (Gibraltar is a corruption of the word *Jbel Tariq*, meaning "Tariq's Mountain"). Pushing northwards through Spain, the invaders reached Poitiers in France in 732 before being forced to retreat. But back in Morocco a fierce revolt, known as the Kharijite Rebellion, arose in 740, triggered by the Arab rulers' tax system. The rebellion was finally quelled, but the situation had dramatically changed: by 740, North Africa had split off from the Oriental Caliphs, all the Arab rulers had gone, and Morocco was never again to come under the direct control of the eastern Arab rulers. At the end of the seventh century North Africa was made up of independent states, hostile to the Caliphs of Baghdad. Islam, however, remained firmly adopted by the Berber populations.

The First Moroccan Moslem Dynasty, the Idrissids: 788-1055 A.D.

Disputes over the Prophet Mohammed's succession in the east led to revolts against the ruling Abbasid caliphs, represented by Harun er-Rashid, of Arabian Nights fame, Caliph of Baghdad. In 786, Idriss ibn Abdullah, a descendant of Ali, the Prophet Mohammed's son-in-law, in revolt against Harun er-Rashid, was obliged to save his life by fleeing from Arabia. He found refuge in Morocco, in the town of Walili (ex-Volubilis of Roman times), and quickly won the allegiance of the local Berbers by his learning and piety. In 788 he was proclaimed *imam* (religious leader), established himself as the head of the first Moroccan dynasty, the Idrissids, and founded, in 789, the first settlement at Fès. However, this was not at all to the liking of Harun er-Rashid, who had him poisoned in 792. Luckily for the new dynasty, Idriss's Berber wife gave birth to a son two months after his death, and the boy was raised to become Idriss II. He brought new areas of Morocco under his authority, organized his state, and enlarged and embellished the town of Fès. Helped by the arrival of skilled refugees

from Cordoba and Kairouan, Fès became the country's cultural and economic center. Upon the death of Idriss II in 828, his kingdom was divided
among his 10 sons. Fès continued to prosper thanks largely to the caravans
laden with gold that arrived there from Guinea. These riches attracted the
attention of the rival Caliphs of Tunisia (Fatimid) and Spain (Umayad).
The former captured Fès in 921, but, undaunted, the Idrissid ruler managed to have himself proclaimed Caliph of Cordoba. All this agitation
ended with the partition of Spain into small kingdoms and the fall of the
Idrissid dynasty in 1055 in the face of the Almoravid tribes of the desert.

Desert Warriors, the Almoravids: 1055-1144 A.D.

A Sanhaja tribe of the western Sahara, the Berber Lemtouna, known as
al mulathamin (the veiled people) became known in the middle of the 5th
century as nomads, getting their wealth from their herds, the caravans
transporting gold, hunting, and fighting. The desire to enlarge their territory combined in the 10th century with a religious fervor. A Lemtuna
leader, on his return from a pilgrimage to Mecca, contacted a Moroccan
holy man, Abdallah ibn Yasin, with the idea of teaching his tribal warriors
more about Islam. Not having much success, Abdallah retreated with several chiefs and founded a *ribat*, a military convent, with a very strict, pure
regime. However, this paid off, as new recruits to the *ribat* poured in and
the *al morabitoum* (men of the ribat) set off with an army of 30,000 men to
spread their new purified Islam, by force if necessary.

In 1053-54 the Almoravids *(al morabitoum)* under their army commander, Abu Bakr, won control of the trans-Saharan commerce by seizing
the caravan town of Sijilmassa in south Morocco. In 1069 they conquered
Fès after a six-year siege, and around 1070 they established their camp
near Marrakech and set about building what was to become their capital,
the town of Marrakech. The town gave its name to their kingdom:
Morocco. Abu Bakr, confronted by troubles in the south, had to leave
Marrakech in the hands of his cousin, Yusef ben Tachfin.

Continuing his campaign of military and religious conquest, Yusef ben
Tachfin reached Algiers in 1082, and invaded Spain shortly thereafter, getting as far as the River Ebro. The Almoravids thus became the masters of a
vast empire including Moslem Spain, western Algeria and Morocco. Yusef
ben Tachfin was succeeded in 1106 by his son, Ali ben Yusef, who reigned
for 37 years. Ali, the son of a Spanish, Christian slave, was born in the town
of Ceuta. Steeped in Andalousian culture, he was not the tough desert
warrior that his father had been. He was nevertheless one of Morocco's
greatest rulers, even if he was unable to cope with the difficulties that were
springing up. In Spain, the Christians were attempting to win back their

country, and in south Morocco a new Berber group, the Almohads, was becoming more and more active. But the Almoravids left a permanent mark on the country by stamping out heresies, installing a unified rule, and introducing Spanish Muslim culture and civilization.

Moslem Unitarians, the Almohads: 1130-1269 A.D.

Considering, as so many do from time to time, that the country was slipping away from the necessary high religious standards, Ibn Tumert, calling himself the *mahdi* (messenger of God), installed himself in 1125 in Tinmal, in the High Atlas foothills south of Marrakech. Here he continued his preaching of purity, rigor, higher moral standards, and the unity of God that had already got him into trouble in Fès and Marrakech. Continuing Ibn Tumert's revolt against the Almoravids, considered decadent, which had started in 1121, his followers, the Almohads (unitarians), managed, not without difficulty, to capture Marrakech in 1147, after a first failure in 1130. Ibn Tumert, who died around 1129, was succeeded by a disciple, Abd el-Mumen, who called himself Caliph, along the lines of the Caliphs of Baghdad or Cordoba, and extended his empire as far as Tunis. Abd el-Mumen died in Rabat in 1163. He was succeeded by his son, Abu Yacub, who, by 1172, had completed the conquest of Moslem Spain. The peak of the Almohad dynasty was reached under Abu Yacub's son, Abu Yusef Yacub (generally known as Yacub el-Mansour, "the Victorious"), who defeated the Portuguese and Spanish armies at the battle of Alarcos in 1195. At the end of the 12th century, the Almohads transferred their capital to Rabat. During their reign the combination of Andalusia and Morocco produced a civilization of great distinction. But after the death of Yacub el-Mansour in 1199, the vast empire started collapsing and Ibn Tumert's doctrine was rejected. On the military front, the army of Yacub el-Mansour's son, Mohammed, lost the battle of Las Navas de Tolosa in Andalusia against the Christian forces united in their reconquest of Spain.

The Merinids, a Third Berber Dynasty: 1269-1465 A.D.

The Beni Marin, Zenata Berbers from eastern Morocco, were already, by 1248, profiting from the weakness of Almohad rule and had seized Fès, Rabat, and Salé. In 1269, the Merinid leader Abu Yusef Yacub occupied Marrakech, and by 1274 they had conquered, by devious means (battles, alliances, and arrangements), the whole of Morocco and had supplanted the Almohad dynasty. Having established themselves firmly in Morocco, the Merinids then tried to build up the crumbling empire by sending expeditions to Spain, Algeria, and Tunisia. The best-known Merinid sultan was Abul Hassan, who reigned from 1331 to 1351. Called the "Black Sultan" (his mother was from "black" Africa), he was defeated in Spain, at the battle of Rio Salado in 1340, although he managed to keep a hold on Gibraltar. After capturing Tlemcen and Tunis in 1347, revolts and the plague soon forced Abul Hassan and the Merinid army to pull out. These failures started the decline of the Merinids, who could not manage to ward off the Portuguese and Spanish, who were invading the Moroccan coasts. A period of revolt and troubles set in, contrasting with the stability the country had known under the Almohads. The last 40 years or so of Merinid rule were in fact dominated by their cousins, the Wattasids, who manipulated the last Merinid princes. Some historians refer to the Wattasids as the fourth Berber dynasty, and they remained at the head of Morocco from around 1420 until 1554. But they, too, were unable to cope with the religious confrontations or prevent the increasing number of Portuguese and Spanish incursions. Indeed, the Portuguese had established themselves in the Atlantic ports by 1508 and were seriously compromising the trans-Saharan trade. Stronger stuff than the Wattasid rulers was needed to redress the situation, and this came in the shape of the Arab tribe of the Beni Saad, encouraged by pious and holy men preaching a holy war against the invaders.

The Saadians, Descendants of the Prophet Mohammed: 1525-1659 A.D.

The ancestors of the Arab Beni Saad tribe, who claimed they were descended from the Prophet, had settled in the valley of the River Draa, in the far south. Stimulated by the holy preachers, they resisted the Portuguese advances in 1509, and in 1525 captured Marrakech. This date is used to mark the official entry of the new Saadian dynasty. Under their leader, Mohammed ech-Cheikh, the Saadians set about chasing the Portuguese from Agadir (1541) and freeing all the other enclaves, with the exception of Mazagan (now El-Jadida). Defeating the Wattasids, they took Fès in 1554, in spite of support for their enemies from the Turks, installed in Algeria. In 1578, the greatest leader of the Saadian dynasty, Ahmed el-Mansur, popularly known as Mansur ad-Dahabi (the Golden Victorious), defeated the Portuguese and Spanish at the Battle of the Three Kings in north Morocco (in which three kings lost their lives). This decisive victory removed the Portuguese danger and the Saadians were able to take back control of the gold route by becoming masters of Timbuktu.

However, history repeated itself. Upon the death of this powerful and intelligent ruler in 1603, who knew how to juggle international politics and keep Spanish, English, and Turks at bay (and at loggerheads with each other), violent fighting took place between his sons and the country fell into a very bad period characterized by anarchy and rival factions. The Moslem Andalusians, expelled from Spain between 1609 and 1611 by the Christian Reconquest, took the opportunity to establish an independent republic in Salé from 1620 to 1639. They lived off pirate raids in the Mediterranean and Atlantic and made a terrifying reputation for themselves. Few merchant sailors of the time had not heard of the "Sallee Rovers."

The Present Dynasty, the Alaouites: from 1666 A.D.

The Alaouites, also descendants of the Prophet, had settled near Sijilmassa in the Tafilalet at the beginning of the 13th century, where they reigned as independent rulers. Profiting from the instability following Ahmed el-Mansur's death, they started to extend their rule from 1633, at first under Mulay Cherif, then under his sons Mulay M'hammed and Mulay Rashid. Local enemies were defeated and an agreement made with the Turks, rulers of Algeria. By 1670, Mulay Rashid had made himself master of Morocco and established himself in Fès. He was succeeded in 1672 by his half-brother, Mulay Ismail, to whom he left an authentic state and the recognized title of Commander of the Believers.

Mulay Ismail is certainly the best known of these 17th century Alaouites. He reigned with energy and intelligence until 1727, wielding absolute power and consolidating the work of his predecessors. To achieve his aim, he created a permanent army, made up of black slaves. By the end of his reign he had about 150,000 of them, rigorously trained both in civil and military matters, to whom he gave specially chosen young black women as wives. In order to ensure a continual supply of new recruits, their male children were all brought up to be soldiers and were enrolled in the army once they had reached the age of 15.

A builder and a soldier, Mulay Ismail constructed a network of 76 forts throughout the country in order to keep his unruly countrymen under control and to ward off constant Spanish and Portuguese encroachments. He won back Larache from the Spanish and Tangier from the English, eliminated hostile local leaders, extended his rule as far as Senegal, and built a series of fortifications throughout the country. But Mulay Ismail was also aware of the need for diplomatic exchanges. In 1698, he sent a mission to France to draw up a political treaty and to negotiate the purchase of French prisoners, and in 1699 the French king Louis XIV received the Moroccan envoy, Ben Aicha (an ex-pirate). He was on writing terms with the English queen Elizabeth I, exchanging ambassadors with both France and England, and kept a keen eye on commercial and economic affairs. The peak of his power was reached in 1700, but upon his death the black guard ran amok, plundering and looting all they could lay their hands on. Seven successive sultans tried without success to rule the country, struggling in the throes of a civil war until, eventually, Sidi Mohammed ben Abdallah, a grandson of Mulay Ismail, took control in 1757 as Mohammed III. His reign was a period of peace and stability: the Portuguese were driven out of El-Jadida and the country opened up to overseas trade. Mohammed III is remembered for having signed a Treaty of Peace and Friendship with George Washington and the newly independent United States in 1787. It was not a purely disinterested treaty, since it aimed at organizing commercial links between the two countries at a time when the Moroccan pirates were roving the high seas, seizing the goods transported by foreign ships, including American ones. The treaty is still in force and makes the U.S. one of Morocco's oldest allies. (When Henry Kissinger visited Morocco in 1973, this treaty was reproduced in the Moroccan newspapers.)

Mohammed III was succeeded in 1790 by his son, Mulay Yazid, who only reigned a couple of years, to be followed by another son, Mulay Sliman. None of these sultans managed to get the same grip on the country as Mulay Ismail, and slowly things such as internal and external political troubles, drought, plague, the end of the pirates, and the decline in maritime trade led to a recession which Mulay Sliman's successors were unable to reverse. Mulay Sliman's isolationist policy (closing of ports to foreigners and banning of Moroccans traveling to Europe) did nothing to help the situation either.

European Penetration in the 19th Century

The Moroccan sultan Mulay Abd er-Rahman (Mulay Sliman's nephew) (1822-59) tried to turn the tide, and started well by signing agreements with Portugal, England, and France. But, rather unwisely as it turned out, he supported the Algerian leader Abd el-Kader in his revolt against the French, who had occupied Algeria in 1830, thereby provoking a French military intervention. The Moroccan troops were defeated at the Battle of Isly in 1844, their first defeat for 200 years, and Mulay Abd er-Rahman could no longer resist the pressure put on him by the business world and the European powers. He was succeeded by his son, Mohammed IV (1859-73), and then by his grandson, Hassan I. Mulay Hassan did try, indeed with some success, to consolidate his power and modernize Morocco, while still remaining independent. One of his actions, for instance, was the reconstitution, at the end of the 19th century, of a modern navy, commanded by a small group of German sailors. But the country fell more and more into debt with overseas banks, and Great Britain, France, and Spain were able to impose treaties favorable to their aims of commercial and territorial expansion.

Upon the death of Hassan I in 1894, his 14-year old son Mulay Abd el-Aziz was proclaimed sultan. In fact, this nomination was quite irregular, having been made by the powerful and ambitious minister Ba Ahmed without the approval of the religious leaders. Intrigues and crises inevitably followed, the people were becoming more and more hostile to foreign penetration, and the young sultan's policies were disastrous. After Ba Ahmed's death, Abd el-Aziz, well intentioned but manipulated by his courtiers, and a prey to rival factions and hard-sell salesmen ready to fascinate him with the latest gadgets, could no longer compete. The state's coffers were rapidly emptied of the little they had, the Saharan provinces revolted under the charismatic chief Cheikh Ma el-Ainin, and the people were increasingly hostile. Abd el-Aziz was seen as the "friend of the Europeans" and his elder brother, Mulay Abd el-Hafid, as the representative of resistance to the ever-increasing European penetration. The tribes were in revolt and the European powers decided that it was time to step in firmly. The British let the French act in Morocco in exchange for British rule in Egypt, the Spanish—with a long history of occupation of Morocco—wanted their share, and the German kaiser William II even landed in Tangier to help the sultan sort out his difficulties. The Conference of Algeciras saw 13 countries—including the United States—come together in January 1906 to end all this confusion, harmful to both Western and Moroccan interests. But it needed the energetic intervention of the American President, Theodore Roosevelt, to ensure the international character of the decisions and to avoid a stalemate caused by the Kaiser's declarations. The treaty allowed for the independence of the sultan, recognized the principle of equal economic chances and free trade for all countries, but let Spain and France be responsible for restoring order. The Bank of Morocco was created with foreign capital (largely French, British, and German) to undertake the modernization of the country. In reality, the Act of Algeciras placed a sort of international protectorate over Morocco and marked the end of the effective independence of the Moroccan sovereigns. Following the decisions taken in Algeciras, in 1907, the French started modernizing the port of Casablanca, involving the construction of a small railroad. Claiming (wrongly) that the line went through a Moslem cemetery, local people killed a number of French and Portuguese workers. A precipitous landing by a small party of French troops led to fighting, which in turn led to the bombardment of the town by the French navy, and the no less prompt sack of Casablanca by local tribes before order was restored. These events undoubtedly precipitated the establishment of a French protectorate five years later. Mulay Hafid declared his brother Abd el-Aziz unfit to rule and had himself proclaimed sultan the same year. His reign was a short one. In 1909 the Spanish started the military occupation of their northern zone. Two years later, Mulay Hafid was forced to call on the French army to free Fès, besieged by furious tribesmen, and in March 1912 had to accept a Protectorate treaty, known as the Treaty of Fès. The sultan effectively retained only his title, with real power passing into the hands of the French. Spain extended her control in the north and very south of the country. Tangier was declared an International Free Zone in 1923. In 1912, Mulay Hafid abdicated and left the throne to his younger brother, Mulay Yusef. The French General Lyautey was appointed Résident Général and a new page opened in Morocco's history.

The French and Spanish Protectorates: 1912-1956

General Lyautey was a confirmed royalist and always showed great respect for the Moroccan sultan. His aim was not merely to pacify the country, but to modernize it in the best interests of the Moroccan people. He built the ports of Casablanca and Kénitra and new, European-style towns in Rabat, Meknès, Fès, and Marrakech. Under his wise and enlightened administration, roads and railways were constructed, the newly discovered phosphate mines nationalized for the benefit of the Moroccan state, modern farming methods introduced, and a countrywide medical service set up.

Opposition to European penetration occurred mainly among the mountain Berber populations. Particularly serious was the uprising under Abdelkrim in the Spanish protectorate in the Rif Mountains in 1921, finally crushed in 1926 by combined Franco-Spanish forces, but not before the latter had suffered heavy military defeats at the hands of the tribesmen. A number of foreign powers had their fingers in this war, sending underhand supplies to the rebels, and fighting was fierce and cruel on both sides. After the departure of General Lyautey in 1925, French rule became more direct and the sultan's power was curtailed. In 1927, Mulay Yusef was succeeded by his son, Mohammed V, father of the late King Hassan II, and grandfather to the present king. Progressively, the French pacified the country and brought it under the sultan's rule. But the young, urban upper- and middle-class intellectuals were growing increasingly restless under this continued foreign occupation and planned actively to win back the country's independence. A law known as the *Dahir Berbèr*, allowing the Berbers to keep their tribal laws, tried to divide the Arabs and Berbers, but backfired completely, only serving to strengthen the nationalist cause. During World War II independence claims were shelved, and Mohammed V asked his people to take up arms for the Allies in the cause of freedom.

After the Allied victory in 1945, France's General de Gaulle decorated Mohammed V with the Order of Companion of the Liberation in recognition of the services rendered by the Moroccan troops. In fact, Mohammed V was the first foreign sovereign to be welcomed in France after the liberation. After the war, an exceptional drought hit Morocco after two years of bad harvests and, at the beginning of 1945, the country's 7 million inhabitants experienced the worst famine and epidemics of the 20th century. At the request of the French authorities, American ships heading for France were re-routed to Casablanca where their cargo of wheat was discharged on the quays for distribution to the population. Canada, Great Britain, Argentine, Portugal, and even France (hard-hit by forced exports to Germany) contributed until early 1946 to nourish the starving population. The 1945 famine killed more Moroccan civilians than the war had killed Moroccan soldiers.

On the Road to Independence: from 1942

The American landings in Morocco in 1942, and President Franklin Roosevelt's promise to Mohammed V during their conversations in Casablanca in 1943 that America would help Morocco regain its independence, added fuel to the nationalists' cause. An official independence political party, *Istiqlal,* was formed and publicly demanded full independence in a declaration in 1944. In 1945, the party sent a request to the San Francisco conference requesting Morocco's admission to the United Nations. In 1947, the sultan gave a public speech in Tangier in favor of independence and the incorporation of Morocco into the Arab League. The same year, the liberal-minded Résident Général, Eric Labonne, was replaced by the tough General Juin. Negotiations with the French government under General de Gaulle had already started, but changes in France led to the talks being abandoned. Assassinations, bombs, and riots in Casablanca in December 1952 forced the French to take a firmer line. With the support of the Pasha of Marrakech, Thami el-Glaoui, an immensely powerful figure who ruled over most of the High Atlas and parts of south Morocco, the French Résident Général organized a "popular" uprising against the sultan, who was promptly deported to Madagascar in August 1953 and replaced by a weak and inoffensive relative, Ben Arafa.

Poor Ben Arafa had a hard time. He was never accepted by the population and was the object of an assassination attempt, which failed. Meanwhile, the exiled Mohammed V became a hero in the eyes of his people (some of the more imaginative of whom swore that they had seen his face in the moon). Murders of French farmers, massacres of French civilians, and reprisals by the French security forces marked the following two years. But troubles in Indochina and Algeria forced the French government to tone down its hard-line policy. Mohammed V was allowed back to his country on the November 16, 1955, and Moroccan independence was recognized by France on the April 7, 1956, and five months later by Spain. Immense scenes of joy greeted the sultan on his first public appearance.

An Independent Nation: from 1956

The sultan Mohammed V had little time in which to engage in reforms and enjoy the newly won independence of his country. His sudden death in 1961 during a banal operation plunged the people into paroxysms of grief. He was succeeded by his son, the Crown Prince, who became Hassan II. A new constitution, largely the work of Mohammed V, was ratified in 1962, declaring that Morocco was a social, democratic, and constitutional monarchy. The first elections to Parliament took place in 1963. Disputes with Algeria over the southern frontiers broke out into fierce fighting the same year. At home, there was considerable political and economic unrest, the socialist leader Ben Barka was assassinated in France, and, in 1965, the king was obliged to declare a state of emergency and rule without parliament. A new constitution drawn up in 1970 reintroduced parliamentary rule, but gave the king considerable control over its decisions. Several unsuccessful attempts were made on the king's life, the most spectacular of which was mounted by army generals in 1971 and resulted in a bloodbath during birthday festivities at the royal place in Skhirat, outside Rabat. A second attempt followed in 1972, when the king's Boeing was attacked by dissident Moroccan Air Force pilots as he returned from a visit to Spain.

The Green March, which saw 350,000 unarmed Moroccans from all over the country walk though the desert in November 1975 to win back the territory known as the Spanish Sahara, had an enormous unifying effect. People and political parties rallied to the national cause, the "recuperation" of their Saharan provinces, although the International Court of Justice at The Hague had given a rather obscure judgement when the affair had been brought before them. Despite help from the Spanish administration, which had obligingly withdrawn (General Franco was on his deathbed and prince Juan Carlos had not yet been proclaimed king), Morocco had to face fierce armed opposition from a local organization, the Polisario, which wanted both Spanish and Moroccans to pull out. A Saharaoui Democratic Arab Republic (R.A.S.D.) was created by this Saharan opposition, with its headquarters in the Tindouf camp just across the frontier in Algeria. The Polisario, supported by Algeria and Libya, waged a fierce war for independence against Morocco for more than ten years. Many lives were lost on both sides. Finally, fighting became more sporadic, and Morocco got the upper hand militarily and started pouring money and people into the area. In 1991, the United Nations called for a cease-fire and decreed that a referendum should be held the following year to determine the country's future. But an enormous problem has been deciding who has the right to vote in this referendum. It has consequently been put off year after year as both sides haggle over the lists of authorized voters. Pushed hard by the United States, irritated by the expense of maintaining a UN Mission in the area, both parties came to an agreement in Houston in 1997. The Secretary General of the United Nations indicated that his patience was running out and appointed James Baker, former U.S. Secretary of State, as special UN envoy to settle the affair. The latest ruling by the UN Secretary-General is that the referendum will be held in July 2000. The Saharan issue is a very important one in Morocco, both for the king's prestige and for the unifying spirit it arouses in all shades of political opinion in the country.

In the Gulf Crisis with Iraq in 1990, the late King Hassan II was active in pushing for a negotiated settlement, personally urging Saddam Hussein to withdraw from Kuwait. When this became impossible, he opted for the anti-Iraq coalition, sending a Moroccan medical force to Saudi Arabia. It has to be said, however, that his people were profoundly pro-Arab and pro-Iraq. In his relations with Israel, the king, although supporting energetically the liberation of Jerusalem, had for long been a discreet host to many Israeli politicians, including Shimon Peres and Yitzak Rabin, and worked actively for a durable peace in the Middle East and full rights for the Palestinian people.

Relations with neighboring Algeria are sometimes good, sometimes bad. At present, the situation in Algeria and mutual accusations led to the closing of the frontier between the two countries in 1995. The French National Day celebrations in Paris on July 14, 1999 saw an unexpected sight. The Moroccan Royal Guard headed the traditional military parade down the Champs Elysées, constituting the first presence of non-European troops in this event. King Hassan himself was present, next to French President Jacques Chirac. The king's sudden death, nine days after his return from Paris, saw the Crown Prince Sidi Mohammed accede to the throne as Mohammed Ben Al Hassan. Hundreds of thousands of grieving Moroccans of all ages—men, women, and children—lined the route of the funeral procession. The presence of more than 70 foreign heads of state or their representatives during the ceremony, including American President Bill Clinton and his wife Hillary, attested to the international esteem in which King Hassan II was held. Despite difficulties, Morocco under King Hassan II managed to steer a middle course. His son will doubtless pursue his father's efforts for peace in the Middle East and increasing democracy in Morocco. All in all, it can be said that today's independent Morocco is a stable country, successfully keeping links with the East and the Moslem world, sub-Saharan Africa, and the West.

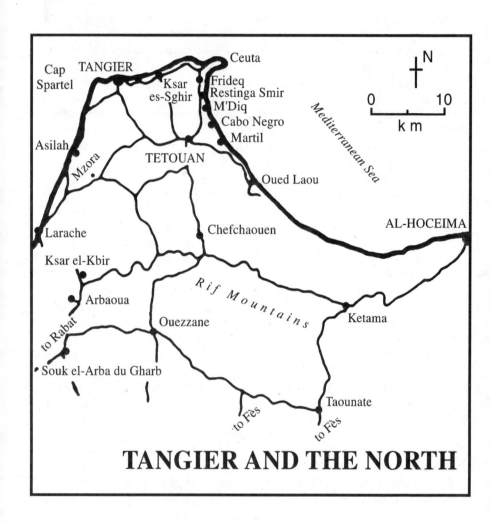

Cap Spartel

TANGIER

Ceuta

Ksar es-Sghir

Frideq
Restinga Smir
M'Diq
Cabo Negro
Martil

Asilah

Mzora

TETOUAN

Oued Laou

Mediterranean Sea

Larache

Chefchaouen

AL-HOCEIMA

Ksar el-Kbir

Arbaoua

Rif Mountains

Ketama

to Rabat

Ouezzane

Souk el-Arba du Gharb

Taounate

to Fès

to Fès

N

0   10

k m

TANGIER AND THE NORTH

5

Tangier and the North

1. The General Picture

Tangier is not the capital of Morocco, nor is it the most evident place in which transatlantic visitors are likely to arrive. However, if one is coming from Europe, it is the gateway to Morocco, lying as it does in the northwest tip of the country, with only a few kilometers of water separating it from Spain. It makes a convenient starting place for this guide, which goes from north to south. Many interesting places are within a day's drive, which also makes it a good base. Sightseeing further afield needs an overnight stop, but Tangier remains the town with the biggest choice of hotels and restaurants.

The Distant Past. Greek mythology would have Tangier founded by Anteus, son of Neptune, god of the sea, and Gaia, goddess of the earth. Anteus was an extremely cruel giant, who named the town after his wife Tingis (Tanjah in Arab, Tangier in English). It was also the site of one of the Labors of Hercules, who was sent to get a golden apple from the Garden of the Hesperides, guarded by the daughters of Atlas (who held the world on his shoulders). Hercules killed Anteus and all ended happily.

More prosaically, Tangier was inhabited from prehistoric times and traces of contact with the Iberian peninsula during the Neolithic and Bronze Age periods are numerous, but not particularly visible, since the modern town has destroyed much of this early past. The Greeks were around early in the first millennium B.C., and the Phoenicians established a trading post about the same time, followed by the Carthaginians. From about 140 B.C. the town was the capital of the Berber kingdom of Mauretania before becoming the capital of the Roman province of Mauretania Tingitania in 40 A.D. The town was one of the last to remain occupied by the Romans after their retreat from Volubilis at the end of the third century A.D. The Vandals paid a brief visit to Tangier at the beginning of the fifth century and the Byzantine rulers established themselves there until they were defeated by Arab invaders in the eighth century A.D.

The newcomers were attracted to Tangier by its strategic position, only a few kilometers from Spain. The Berber general Tarik started his conquest of Spain in 709 and 710 from Tangier. It became the departure point for successive waves of Almoravid invasions of Spain in the 11th century. The Moroccan voyager Ibn Batuta, who traveled far and wide in the 14th century, was a native of Tangier. The town was particularly flourishing in the 15th century, doing business with Marseilles, Genoa, and Venice, as well as with the rest of Morocco. But European interest in the 15th and 16th centuries resulted in its capture by the Portuguese in 1471, and its peaceful occupation by the Spanish in 1580 when Spain and Portugal united. When these two countries separated, Tangier came once again under Portuguese rule. However, in 1661, when the Portuguese princess Catherine of Braganza married the English king Charles II, Tangier formed part of her dowry and thus became an English possession. The English had high hopes that Tangier would become a starting-point for the penetration of British trade in North Africa. But they did not have an easy life in Tangier and spent most of their time building fortifications to ward off attacks by Mulay Ismail's troops or to defend themselves from the Spanish. The English Samuel Pepys, posted to Tangier in 1683, made several uncomplimentary entries in his diary concerning the town and its inhabitants. Neglected by their home country, the English troops were forced to move out in 1684. But European interest in Tangier never waned—it was such an evident entry into Africa. When Mohammed III opened up the country to international trade at the end of the 18th century, foreign governments were quick to respond. By 1830, Tangier had become an "authentic" diplomatic capital, counting 10 consulates, including that of the United States. Around 1832, the artist Eugène Delacroix managed to get himself incorporated in a French military mission to Fès and painted some of his best-known works in Tangier. In the summer of 1998, one of his most famous paintings, the *Choc de Cavaliers Arabes,* painted on his return from Morocco, was put up for sale in Paris and was fiercely bided for by the representative of an American museum and a New York art dealer, going to the latter for a record sum of 45.5 million French francs. In the middle of the 19th century, Mark Twain visited the town in the course of a European tour. He was less impressed by Morocco than Delacroix, and fixed his impressions in *The Innocents Abroad,* including the remark that "the general size of a store in Tangier is about that of an ordinary shower-bath in a civilized land." Amusing accounts of this period, and that which followed, were given by Walter Harris, resident in Tangier and correspondent for the *London Times* from 1887 until his death in 1933. Among his many stories was a description of the bridge parties with the ex-sultan Mulay Abd el-Hafid and a young American dentist, who counted the hours playing bridge in his dentistry fees! Harris also had some admiration for the qualities of Mulay Abd el-Hafid's verses and quoted one of his poems where the people of Tangier came before the Judgement Seat of God. The Supreme Judge told them they were wicked people and asked them how they had lived. They replied "We have sinned! We have sinned! But our Government was international and we were ruled by the representatives of Europe." The Supreme Judge said, "Surely you have been punished enough. Enter into Paradise!" Mulay Abd el-Hafid obviously didn't think much of international government.

Tangier, an International Paradise. Internal confusion and financial chaos in Morocco at the end of the 19th century led to active international intervention. The German kaiser William II landed with great ceremony in Tangier in 1905 and encouraged the Moroccan sultan, Mulay Abd el-Hafid, not to give way to Spanish and French ambitions. The resulting international conference, held in Algeciras in 1906, guaranteed Moroccan independence and equal commercial opportunities for all countries. When France and Spain officially established their protectorates over the country in 1912, Tangier became a bone of contention and the problem was only solved in 1923 when it was declared an International Free Zone. It was administered by diplomats from a dozen countries, including the United States, under the overall supervision of the sultan's representative, and enjoyed complete political, military, and economic neutrality.

In many ways it could be said that this was the heyday of Tangier. Free trade and no taxes encouraged foreign investors and the town became rich. From the start of the international period, Tangier was also a hive of intrigue, smuggling, and spying. In World War II, the British playwright Noel Coward, who lived a while in Tangier, was thought to be merely a

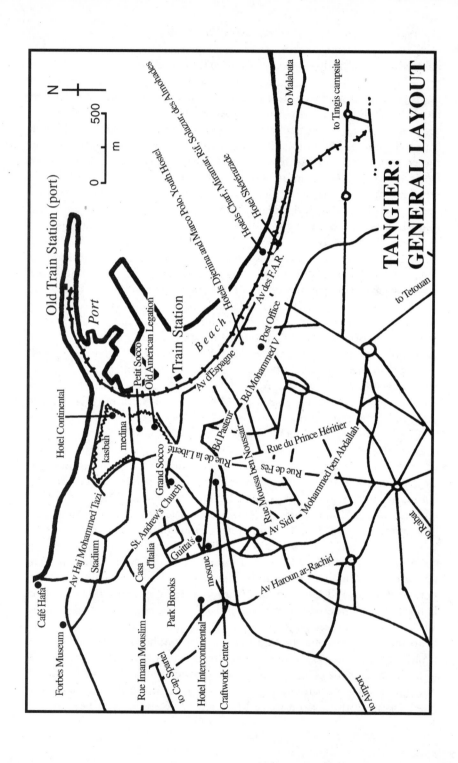

TANGIER: GENERAL LAYOUT

N

500

m

0

Old Train Station (port)

Port

Beach

Train Station

to Malabata

to Tingis campsite

to Tetouan

to Rabat

to Airport

to Cap Spartel

Hotels Djenina and Marco Polo, Youth Hostel

Hotels Chaar, Miramar, Rif, Solazur, les Almohades

Hotel Shéhérazade

Av des F.A.R.

Post Office

Av d'Espagne

Bd Mohammed V

Rue du Prince Héritier

Rue de Fès

Mohammed ben Abdallah

Av Sidi

Av Haroun ar-Rachid

Hotel Continental

kasbah

medina

Petit Socco

Old American Legation

Bd Pasteur

Rue de la Liberté

Bd de Noussair

Rue Moussa ben Noussair

Grand Socco

St. Andrew's Church

Casa d'Italia

Guitta's

mosque

Park Brooks

Rue Imam Mouslim

Hotel Intercontinental

Craftwork Center

Av Haj Mohammed Tazi

Stadium

Café Hafa

Forbes Museum

society gossip—in fact he was spreading misinformation and spying for the Allies. In the 1940s and early 1950s, artists, writers, and celebrities (or on their way to becoming so), crowded into Tangier, attracted by the climate, the mentality, and the almost total freedom to do what they liked. Already the French painter Matisse, who spent three months in Tangier in 1912, had declared—on the strength of his Tangier experience—that "Paradise exists on earth." The writers Tennessee Williams, Paul Bowles, William Burroughs, and Jack Kerouac, as well as a host of beatniks, all found inspiration or freedom in the rambling streets of the Little Socco. Bowles's novel *The Sheltering Sky*, published in 1949, was hailed as a landmark in American literature. His later autobiography, *Without Stopping*, tells how he came to settle in Tangier. The musician Aaron Copland spent a few weeks in the town. Film stars Marlene Dietrich, Elisabeth Taylor, and Errol Flynn flew in from time to time, the Woolworth heiress Barbara Hutton had a house in the kasbah, and Cecil Beaton, Talullah Bankhead, and, later, the Rolling Stones, all made appearances in Tangier, definitely the in-place at that time. Other less desirable characters also found Tangier provided a comfortable hideaway. When Lucky Luciano was the big crime boss, the port of Tangier was an essential part of the cigarettes and drug circuit. A 1998 film by Peter Goedel, *Tanger, Légende d'une Ville*, recalls this "golden age" when mad millionaires, artists, writers, and eccentrics of all nationalities threw fabulous parties and did extraordinary things. This was not the first film shot in Tangier—the city has been the location of many films, including a number of Moroccan productions, as well as the Spanish *The Dream of Tangier*, the American James Bond film, *A License to Kill*, and, more recently, *The Legionnaire* starring Jean-Claude Van Damme.

Today's Tangier is a more prosaic place, with little to recall the wild life of the first half of the century. But the colors and luminosity that fascinated so many artists still remain. During the Second World War, Tangier was left in the hands of the Spanish. In 1947, the Moroccan sultan Mohammed V made his public call for independence in Tangier, an independence that came in 1956. The town returned fully to the Moroccan crown, many foreign investors left, and industrial and commercial activities slowed down. But new industries started up, mainly textile, and tourism began to have an impact. Motorbike and car rallies in northwest Africa all start here, including the annual Harley Davidson motorbike rally. In 1991, a free-trade zone was reintroduced. Publicity for this free zone underlines the advantages of two ports (the present one and the planned Atlantic one), the proximity of the airport, the Tangier-Casablanca expressway and railway service, the Morocco-Spain interconnecting electricity installations, and the presence of the Moroccan end of the Maghreb-Europe gas pipeline.

The port of Tangier is very active: some 900,000 people disembark there each year, for the most part Moroccans working in Europe returning for their holidays. Some 70 percent of these overseas Moroccans go through Tangier between mid-June and mid-September. A tunnel under the Strait of Gibraltar, linking Europe to Africa, is seriously being considered. From an environmental point of view this is not a very agreeable prospect, but economically the advantages are enormous and would take a big load off the port.

The town is spread out around its wide bay and port, with rising ground in the northwest. The "new," European-style town surrounds the medina (old town), which squats behind the port, with the kasbah rising up in the northwest corner. Unfortunately, the railway line has to be crossed to get from the town to the beach, but this is no longer a danger now that the train doesn't come this far. The more classy houses are high up, in the district called "The Mountain," while the hub of the original Tangier is obviously in the medina and kasbah. The local people, now much mixed with newcomers, are the Berber Jbala of the Rif. The town's population has expanded and, with its immediate surroundings, is thought to be around 650,000. But the expatriate colony, perhaps once numbering about 60,000, barely tops 1,000 today (around 200 British, with perhaps 100 Americans). However, there is still the Anglican church, St. Andrew's, and a Spanish Catholic church, complete with a bishop. In fact, north Morocco, as far as Nador to the east and Ksar el-Kbir in the south, forms a diocese. There is also an American school, which takes boarders.

Tangier has a small fishing fleet, but is basically an important port for passenger ships. To the visitor, however, it looks as though the major activity is making money out of the tourist. This is not a particularly pleasant situation, and many people are turned off by the town right away. But if you stick it out, you'll find Tangier an interesting place, with its own atmosphere and culture, quite unique in the Moroccan scene. And there's more nightlife going on than in most other big Moroccan towns, mainly due to the Spanish-style late opening hours of the shops. A word of warning: hustlers are particularly active and aggressive in Tangier, especially around the port and the hotels. The Tangier port is a sleazy place, full of dubious guides and "sharks" of all kinds. You'll need a lot of patience, too, to deal with the officials. Don't linger, especially if you are a woman. Day-trippers from Spain or Gibraltar are quickly disgusted, not only with Tangier, but also with Morocco, and this is a pity, as the town is not representative of the whole country. If you do want to visit the port, try to look as though you know exactly where you want to go, and make it in the morning before the boats arrive, because everyone is waiting to catch the day-trippers. Remain calm and ignore provocation. And avoid being alone in the medina or the beach at night. People say that they have felt insecure in Tangier late at night, and visitors should not forget that unemployment in the area here is very high. More positively, many expats really enjoy life here.

This section cannot end without a word or two about the tragic end that awaits many hundreds of young Moroccans and other Africans each year as they attempt to get into Spain across the Strait of Gibraltar in over-crowded and unseaworthy vessels. Hardly a day goes by in the spring without stories of boats capsizing and young men drowning or disappearing into the sea forever, duped by unscrupulous boat owners (both Moroccan and Spanish), squeezing the maximum amount of money (several thousand DH) for "passage" to what is seen as a rosy future in Europe.

2. Getting There

Transatlantic flights do not land in Tangier, but the town is linked to major European cites by **international airlines.** British Airways, for instance, has a Saturday flight from Gatwick Airport (UK) to Tangier. Royal Air Maroc flights from London stop at Tangier three times a week, and the same company does a direct flight twice a week from Paris. Regional Air Lines, based in Casablanca, runs regular services to Tangier. Ibn Batuta Airport is situated 15 kms from the town. A taxi is needed, since there is no bus or train service (80-100 DH). The energetic can walk a bit over a kilometer to the main highway and pick up a bus (on the other side of the road) going to the center of Tangier. **Car ferries** from France (Marseilles), Spain (Algeciras), and Gibraltar go to and from Tangier daily or weekly. Hydrofoils also run from Algeciras and Gibraltar. A new service from Algeciras to Ceuta started in 1998 (Buquebus España SA), doing the 29 km crossing in 35 minutes. Fast **trains** from France and Spain will get you to Algeciras, and from there you can get the boat across the Strait of Gibraltar. **Continental bus companies** also run services from Europe down to Tangier and further (see chapter 2 for details).

Trains inside Morocco only come to Tangier from one direction— south. The old train stations in the port and just outside it were closed at the beginning of 1999. The new, temporary, Mghogha station is out of town, by the Tangier/Tetouan road, and not as convenient as the old ones, especially as taxis tend to demand a huge price to get you into the center. Coming from Casablanca to Tangier, the best bet is the 6:45 A.M. departure from Casa-Port, reaching Tangier at 12:35 P.M. This is considered to be the "boat train," making a connection with the boats crossing to Spain. The other two day trains from Casablanca mean changing, and both arrive

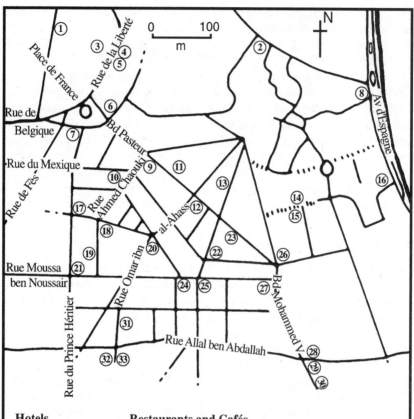

Hotels

1. Ziryab-Le Dawliz
5. El Minzah
8. Valencia
12. de Paris
14. El Muniria
15. Ibn Batuta
16. Biarritz
21. Atlas
24. Ritz
26. Rembrandt
27. Tanjah-Flandria
32. Chellah

Restaurants and Cafés

2. Sandwich Cervantes
4. Saveur de Poisson
6. Café de Paris
7. Café de France
9. Wimpy
   La Marsa
10. Raihani
    Hammadi
13. Romero
17. La Pagode
18. San Remo
19. Las Conchas
20. Pizzaria Piazzi
    Capri
22. Rubis Grill

25. Pâtisserie Rahmouni
30. Pâtisserie Oslo
31. Le Bon Goût
33. El Dorado

Useful Addresses

3. Galeria Delacroix
   (Art Gallery)
11. Tourist Office
23. Librairie les Colonnes
28. Post Office
29. Great Britain
    Consulate

TANGIER TOWN CENTER

rather late in Tangier—at 9:13 P.M. and 11:40 P.M. This is alright if you have a hotel booked or know where you are going, but not so good if you have to look around for a night's lodging. If you are coming from Fès or further east you'll have to change at Meknès, where there is often a long wait. Tangier can be reached from Marrakech during the day, changing trains in Casablanca, or there is the very convenient direct night train with couchettes. The station for the long-distance **CTM bus** is opposite the Tangier railway station (*gare*). CTM buses arrive six times a day from Casablanca (the seven-hour journey is 110 DH) via Rabat, four times a day from Fès, and twice from Meknès, often calling in at smaller intermediate towns (including Asilah, Larache, Chefchaouen, and Ouezzane). Buses from Tetouan are much more frequent. Cream-colored, long-distance **big taxis** (*grands taxis*) are also a possibility, but turn out to be rather expensive. They drop passengers near the main bus station (*gare routière*), which is the terminus of the non-CTM buses, some way from the center of town. By **road,** Tangier can be reached via all the major towns. A new **expressway** is under construction, linking Tangier with Casablanca and Rabat. By the fall of 1998 it was completed as far as Larache (255 km from Casablanca), leaving 88 km to be covered by the old P2.

3. Local Transportation

If you have come by **car,** you'll have difficulty parking, as in all big towns. In Tangier there are local **buses,** but the easiest is to take a **small taxi** (*petit taxi*, pale blue with a yellow stripe) or walk. Negotiate the price of the taxi before starting, or make sure that the meter works. From the Place de France out to the Forbes Museum will cost around 5 DH. The hills on which Tangier is located makes biking rather unappealing, but the town is not so big as to exclude walking.

4. The Hotel Scene

There are 37 classified hotels in the Tangier area and any number of un-classified ones, ranging from the ★★★★★ luxury to the very cheap (50 DH). Low-season hotel charges fixed for this region are as follows (they vary ac-cording to the presence or absence of showers and water closets in the room): ★★★★ 403-503 DH or 516-613 DH, breakfast 61 DH for both; ★★★ 201-319 DH or 227-363 DH, breakfast 45 DH for both; ★★ 110-191 DH or 119-239 DH, breakfast 29 DH for both; ★ 100-147 DH or 105-169 DH, breakfast 22 DH for both. Add 30-100 DH in the high season. Tangier is steeped in memories of famous (and less famous) Americans who've stayed in the town. But if you are a hunter of literary souvenirs, you'll be disappointed if you try to book in at any of the medina hotels made famous by writers such as Tennessee Williams. Best stay with your imagination.

The **regional telephone code** is 09 (0 omitted for in-region calls).

EXPENSIVE HOTELS

These are hotels classed as ***** or ****. Top of my list for character is the ***** **Hotel El Minzah** (100 rooms, from 1,000-1,250 DH, 85 Rue de la Liberté, Tel: 93 58 85, Fax: 93 45 46). It is well situated, near the Big Socco, fully-equipped, and has air-conditioned rooms, some of which are rather small (the best ones overlook the sea). The hotel has a delightful interior courtyard with a fountain, a pleasant garden, swimming pool, several restaurants, bars, car park, conference room, fitness center (with sauna and Jacuzzi), tennis courts, and mini-golf. Among the El Minzah's famous clients have been King Juan Carlos of Spain, Winston Churchill, and Rita Hayworth. During World War II, Americans were prominent customers.

After that there are a number of **** hotels. One is the **** **Hotel Rif** (130 rooms, 152 Avenue des F.A.R., Tel: 94 17 31, Fax: 94 17 94). It is situated on the seafront and has a nice garden, a pool, and a tennis court.

The vast **** **Hotel Solazur** (360 rooms, Avenue des F.A.R., Tel: 94 01 64, Fax: 94 52 86) is also well placed overlooking the sea, but caters to package tours. It has restaurants, bars, and a swimming pool.

The **** **Hotel Tanjah-Flandria** (150 rooms, 6 Boulevard Mohammed V, Tel: 93 32 79, Fax: 93 43 47), although rather drab, is centrally located, with a good view from the small top-floor swimming pool.

The **** **Hotel Intercontinental** (125 rooms, Park Brooks, Tel: 93 53 63, Fax: 93 79 45) has improved and can be recommended for those who like peace and calm. It lies in an agreeable park setting, with a spring, and lots of running water and vegetation, about 15 minutes from the center of town. It has a restaurant and swimming pool.

Back in the center, the **** **Hotel des Almohades** (138, Avenue des F.A.R., Tel: 94 00 26, Fax: 94 63 71), which was recently renovated, overlooks the sea and has restaurants, tennis courts, a conference room, and a sauna. It is run by the French Accor group and accommodates package tours, so it's rather institutional and lacks character.

Part of a group with other establishments in Casablanca and Rabat, the **** **Hotel Ziryab/Le Dawliz** (22 rooms and 6 suites, 42 Rue de Hollande, Tel: 33 18 12/13/14/15, Fax: 33 18 23) is an attractively designed and decorated hotel set in a complex of shops, cinemas, and restaurants. It has a restaurant specializing in Moroccan and international dishes and another serving Asian food. It has a nice little swimming pool, a piano bar, and a coffee shop—and splendid views from the terrace.

The **** **Hotel Shérérazade** (Avenue des F.A.R., Tel: 94 05 02, Fax: 94 08 01) is agreeable, as you can go down directly to the beach.

A much-praised hotel, 20 minutes from the center of town, on the Atlantic Coast near Cap Spartel, south of Tangier, is **Le Mirage** (classified as a first-class club, Grottes d'Hercule, Tel: 33 33 32). The view is marvelous, steps lead down to the beach, and the bungalows are new and grouped around the swimming pool. The recently-retired owner, Ali, is married to an English woman. The hotel and restaurant close for six weeks during Ramadan.

Another hotel just outside Tangier on the road to Rabat is the **** **Ahlen Village** (Km 5, Route de Rabat, Tel: 35 00 01/02, Fax: 35 00 03/05), which is a holiday club type place, unfortunately more and more hemmed in by ugly new buildings. It has a restaurant, bar, tennis courts, and a night-club, and proposes a variety of activities.

MEDIUM-PRICE HOTELS

The *** **Hotel Rembrandt** (80 rooms, corner Boulevard Mohammed V/ Boulevard Pasteur, Tel: 93 78 70, Fax: 93 04 43) has memories of Tangier's "good old days." Not particularly attractive from the outside, it has recently been renovated and is not a bad value.

I'm afraid the *** **Hotel Chellah** (94 Rue Allal ben Abdallah, Tel: 94 20 03/ 94 33 88, Fax: 94 55 36) has gone down in recent years, but the *** **Hotel Atlas** (50 Rue Moussa ben Noussair, Tel: 93 64 35/36/67, Fax: 93 30 95) is friendly, calm, and well run, with large bedrooms and bathrooms. It hasn't much character, but those who stay there return regularly.

Well out of town, along by Cap Spartel (about 17 km from the center), the *** **Hotel Robinson Plage** (116 rooms, Cap Spartel), just next to Le Mirage hotel, is ideal for those who like to be right on the beach. The little bungalows, looking across the sea, are attractively furnished, and the establishment has a swimming pool, bar, and a restaurant.

The ** **Hotel Djenina** (30 rooms, 8 Rue al-Antaki, Tel: 94 22 44) has recently been renovated. It's well kept and has a restaurant and bar.

The ** **Hotel Charf** (19 rooms, 25 Rue el-Farabi, Tel: 93 44 93/94 29 38) is another place that is clean and pleasant, with marvelous views. Down that way, the ** **Hotel Valencia** (72 Avenue des F.A.R., Tel: 93 07 70) tends to be full, but it's a nice place and useful for the bus station.

The ** **Hotel de Paris** (42 Boulevard Pasteur, Tel: 93 18 77/93 81 26), right on the main commercial street, is a good choice in this category, with clean and comfortable bedrooms with showers.

The ** **Hotel Astoria** (29 rooms, 10 Rue Ahmed Chaouki, Tel: 93 72 01), just off the Boulevard Pasteur, is conveniently placed, but is noisy from the traffic. It has a restaurant. The ** **Hotel Ritz** (1 Rue Sorolla, Tel: 93 80 75, Fax: 94 10 02) will do, but can no longer be recommended as warmly as before.

I used to go to the **Hotel Lutetia** (3 Rue Prince Mulay Abdallah, Tel: 93 18 66) quite often, but it is now definitely *not* the place to stay—there is noisy activity all night.

In the medina, the best is undoubtedly the ** **Hotel Continental** (68 rooms, 36 Rue Dar el-Baroud, Tel: 93 10 24/93 11 43), and I would say it is one of the best in the ** range anywhere in town. On the edge of the medina, accessible by road (but get a taxi at night if you are a single woman), this white-painted hotel is superbly placed overlooking the port, with a delightful large terrace from which to admire the view. It's one of Tangier's old hotels, and full of memories. It's a popular place and Si Abdesslem makes visitors very welcome.

Another good hotel in the medina is the ** **Hotel Mamora** (30 rooms, 19 Avenue Mokhtar Ahardan, Tel: 93 41 05), which is clean and quiet (though you are likely to be woken up by the *muezzin* in the mosque calling the faithful to prayer), with good sea views.

BUDGET ACCOMMODATIONS

The * **Hotel Biarritz** (29 rooms, 102 Avenue des F.A.R., Tel: 93 24 73) is a good place to head for. Its rooms are comfortable and quite spacious. The * **Andalucia** (25 rooms, 14 Rue ibn Hazem, Tel: 94 13 34) has a good reputation and is quiet, despite being above a garage. I can't recommend the * **Hotel Miramar,** on the same road (168 Avenue des F.A.R., Tel: 93 89 48). The same goes for the * **Hotel Marco Polo** (2 Rue al-Antaki, Tel: 94 11 24), because it is nearly always full.

Further down the scale are the two unclassified hotels, **Hotel Ibn Batuta** (Tel: 93 71 70) and **Hotel el-Muniria** (Tel: 93 53 97), both in Rue Magellan, not far from the seafront. Both are clean, with good views. The latter is British-run and a place enjoyed by the younger set interested in Tangier's history. Prices are around 100 DH. At the bottom end of the market, there are many pretty, rustic Spanish-style *pensiones* in the medina. The **Youth Hostel** *(Auberge Jeunesse)* (8 Rue el-Antaki, off the Avenue d'Espagne, Tel: 94 61 27) was clean and well kept at the time of writing. A bed in the dormitory costs about 25 DH, and hot showers are extra. It is open from 8:00 A.M.-10:00 A.M., from 12:00 P.M.-3:00 P.M., and from 6:00 P.M.-10:30 P.M.

The campsite **Camping Miramonte** is about 3 km out of town to the west (indicated in the Place de France). It could be good (it is near a beach, and has a restaurant and a small pool), but is, in fact, badly maintained and pretty dirty, generally. The **Camping Tingis,** going the other way, out towards Malabata, looks okay from the outside, but is, in fact, worse. The **Camping Robinson** at Cap Spartel is the best of a bad lot, but can't be recommended. The **Camping Ashakar,** too, is another unprepossessing place.

5. Dining and Restaurants

Tangier offers a good choice of places to eat and drink, ranging from the simple fried fish joints to more sophisticated restaurants. As usual, wine—when available—is expensive (two to three times what you'd pay in a shop).

HOTEL RESTAURANTS

The **Hotel El Minzah** produces a Moroccan meal in its El Korsan restaurant (the prices are high, in line with the hotel's standing—expect to pay about 150 DH for the main dish). There is sometimes a floorshow. One can, in fact, eat better in its wine bar (the main dish is around 100 DH), but this is usually rather crowded.

Friends have found the food disappointing in the **Hotel le Mirage,** out of town by Cap Spartel (it is closed for 40 days during Ramadan, and the main dish begins around 60 DH).

Out of town, too, on the Rabat road, it's worth having a meal in a big Moroccan tent and watching a *fantasia* (a display of warlike horsemanship) at the **Ahlen Hotel.** Of course, it's done for tourists, but if you think you may not have the chance to see a more "natural" one, it's worth going to.

If you're staying at the **Hotel Robinson Plage,** it might be convenient to eat in their restaurant, which serves a pretty standard meal (the main dish is 60 DH). Apart from these, all the big hotels have restaurants, but they tend to follow the usual tourist pattern and present little interest to the visitor who wants to take in a bit of the town's atmosphere.

OTHER RESTAURANTS

Starting with the more expensive, there is the **Restaurant San Remo** (15 Rue Ahmed Chaouki), which serves French and Italian cooking, and is often very full (it's closed on Mondays).

London's Pub (15 Rue Mansour ed-Dahabi, Tel: 94 20 94) had definitely closed down by the fall of 1998.

The **Restaurant Las Conchas** (30 Rue Ahmed Chaouki, Tel: 93 16 43) has a good reputation (with pasta from 30 DH, and the main dish from 60 DH).

Guitta's (on the corner of Avenue Sidi Mohammed ben Abdallah/Rue de Belgique, Tel: 93 73 33), run by the polyglot Mercedes, is hidden away in a garden behind quite a high wall, its name at present masked by planks from the adjacent building site. The restaurant has an interesting history, and has been frequented by the Anglo-American community since it opened many years ago. The Duke of York lunched there, and so did King Juan Carlos of Spain when he was Crown Prince. British Ambassadors occasionally drop in and the British community still has Sunday lunch there (they were recently joined by the French and the Spanish). When the late sultan Mohammed V visited Tangier, his food was cooked by Guitta. The garden is beautiful and the food excellent (a three-course Sunday lunch is 150 DH).

The restaurant **Le Marquis** (18 Rue el-Bouhtouri, Tel: 94 11 32, open from 12:00 P.M.-8:00 P.M., and closed on Sundays), specializes in fish dishes, but is said to have gone down lately.

An excellent little restaurant, recently opened, about 50 m up from the Hotel Chellah, is **Le Bon Goût,** run by Nacer and Carine Kadiri (63 Rue Omar ibn al-Ahass, Tel: 33 03 30). Carine is Belgian and the dishes she proposes are delicious and a real pleasure (it's about 350 DH for a meal for two, with a ½ bottle of wine).

If you want to eat Moroccan food, you could try the **Restaurant Raihani** (10 Rue Ahmed Chaouki, Tel: 93 48 66), just down from the Hotel Astoria. It is not up to Hotel El Minzah standards, but is a heap cheaper (the set menu is 90 DH, with the main course around 60 DH). The decor is a bit touristy.

The restaurant **Hammadi** (2 Rue d'Italie, Tel: 93 45 14) also does a reasonable Moroccan meal at a fairly low price (around 40 DH for the main dish), but it, too, is a bit touristy, with a musician and a floorshow from time to time.

The **Restaurant-Bar Rubis Grill** (3 Rue ibn Rochd) was disappointing. To be sure, it was hung with animal heads, African sculptures, and strings of onions, but the service was slow and the food quite ordinary (the pasta—which was cold—was 50 DH, and the main dish starts at 80 DH). It has live guitar music some nights, and an animated bar.

You don't have to be Italian to go to the **Casa d'Italia** (Avenue Hassan II) and enjoy a good Italian meal. The **Restaurant Romero** (12 Avenue Prince Mulay Abdallah, Tel: 93 22 77) is said to be one of the best fish restaurants in town. It does an excellent Spanish *paella,* and sometimes lobster, but order in advance (the main course is around 70 DH).

A more simple fish restaurant recommended by friends in Tangier and Casablanca is the **Saveur de Poisson** (Tel: 33 63 26), at the foot of the steps in the Rue de la Liberté, just downhill from the Hotel El Minzah (indicated by a sign), where the main dish costs from 50 DH.

If you're hankering after oriental food, the best place is **La Pagode** (the corner of Rue el-Boussiri/Rue du Prince Héritier, Tel: 93 80 86), which specializes in Vietnamese cooking (the main dish from 65 DH, with 20 percent tax included, credit cards are accepted, and it is open from 12:00 P.M.-2:00 P.M. and 7:30 P.M.-11:00 P.M., but closed on Mondays).

Down the scale, friends eat in the **Restaurant Agadir** (21 Rue du Prince Héritier, near Rue du Méxique), where the *tajines* are good and you can get a simple three-course meal for 53 DH.

The **Restaurant el-Dorado** (21 Rue Allal ben Abdallah) is another small restaurant recommended for a fairly cheap meal (with a main dish from 50 DH). In the medina, the **Café du Détroit,** overlooking the kasbah gardens, is a favorite tea-and-pastries halt for tourists, and serves a reasonable *tajine* both morning and evening (for 50 DH). It has a superb view of the port. Out of town, the **Golf Club** serves a good meal, and in summer it's nice to sit and eat outside.

OTHER PLACES TO EAT AND DRINK

If you are more interested in snacks, fast food, or pastries, or just want to drink a cup of coffee or tea, you could try **Wimpy** (which has now replaced Big Mac at the corner of Boulevard Pasteur and Rue Ahmed Chaouki). They have pizzas and hamburgers from 20 DH.

The **Restaurant La Marsa** (92 Avenue d'Espagne) serves pizzas and salads, as well as the set menu, or you can enjoy coffee, milk shakes, and ice cream on the terrace. The **Pizzaria Piazzi Capri** (2 Rue de la Croix) also serves pizzas. The comfortable **Café de Paris** (1 Place de France) was a well-known rendezvous in the 1920s; a lower salon overlooks the bay. The **Café de France,** just opposite, also has comfortable armchairs and is a good place for a breakfast coffee.

The **Café Central** in the Little Socco used to be frequented by the "Beat Generation" in Tangier's heyday. Good sandwiches can be bought at **Sandwich Cervantes** (Rue Salah ed-Din el-Ayoubi). For cakes and pastries, head for **La Española** (Rue de la Liberté) or **Salon Roxy** (30 Rue Allal ben Abdallah). Just down the road, (at 27 Rue Allal ben Abdallah) **La Heladerca Colonna** specializes in ice cream. The **Salon de Thé Vienne** (corner Rue du Mexique and Rue el-Moutanesi) and the **Pâtisserie Oslo** (Boulevard Pasteur, next to the British Consulate) have good reputations for pastries. The latter also does pizzas. The **Pâtisserie Rahmouni** (35 Rue du Prince Mulay Abdallah) specializes in Moroccan pastries.

If you are near the Forbes Museum, don't miss a visit to the **Café Hafa** (in the Marshan area). This is another relic of the 1920s, with tables scattered in the middle of luxuriant vegetation and a superb view over the Bay of Tangier. It only serves mint tea and pastries.

6. Sightseeing

Some of the most interesting, and unique, things to see in Tangier are linked to the period when Tangier was an international town.

IN TANGIER

You should try and see the **Big** and **Little Socco** *(Grand Socco, Petit Socco),* the **Old American Legation,** the **kasbah** and **Dar el-Makhzen, St. Andrew's Church** and **churchyard,** and the **Palais Mendoub,** housing the Forbes collection of miniature soldiers. To take in the atmosphere of Tangier's international past, there are the cafés mentioned above and a drink in the Hotel El Minzah is worth the price to admire this old palace, built by French architects for the Scottish Marquess of Bute before being converted into a hotel in 1933.

The **Grand Socco** (Place du 9 Avril 1947, a few minutes from the northwest end of the Boulevard Pasteur) links the new town with the medina. It really only comes to life on Thursdays and Sundays, when countrywomen from the surrounding area come in to sell their goods, still wearing their traditional, wide-brimmed pom-pomed straw hats and red and white striped shawls *(fouta).* Before plunging into the medina, the **Old American Legation** can be visited by taking the Rue Salah ed-Din el-Ayoubi, then the Rue du Portugal. Climb the steps on the left opposite the taxi stand (a small sign says "Old Legation") and look for Zankat America, a narrow street which will lead you to the Legation. The building, used by the newly appointed diplomatic representative of George Washington in the 1770s, now functions as a museum and has a first-class English-language research library on Morocco and North Africa. Even if you are not a museum fan, the Old American Legation is well worth the visit for its memories. It was offered to the newly-born United States by the Moroccan sultan in 1821, and was America's first overseas property. It is the only building classified as an U.S. National Historical Landmark not located on American soil (see the "Culture" section). From the Big Socco, take the Rue Semmarine into the medina, then right into the Rue es-Siaghin. The old Jewish quarter *(mellah)* was near here. Pass the 19th-century Church of the Immaculate Conception (which is closed) to reach the **Petit Socco,** a hive of activity at all times. One of the cafés here, the Tingis, was a popular meeting place in the international days. The European administrative center of Tangier used to be here, though this is hard to believe now. There were fancy hotels, banks, the French and Spanish postal services (the latter is now a small hotel), and the Spanish Legation. From the Petit Socco, through a maze of steep little roads, the Rue des Almohades (once named the Road of the Christians) takes you to the Bab el-Assa entrance to the **kasbah,** at the end of the Rue ben Raissouli. The gate to this old stronghold opens onto a courtyard, once containing the stables. Straight on, the Bab er-Raha allows a splendid view across the Strait to Spain on a clear day. To the left is the **Dar el-Makhzen,** once the sultan's palace, now a museum. The palace was built by that tireless builder, Mulay Ismail, in the 17th century. It was enlarged by succeeding sultans, and Mulay Abd el-Hafid even lived here in 1912 with his wives and concubines before departing to France. The gardens, designed in Andalusian style, are a pleasant place in which to wander. A number of houses in the kasbah are owned by wealthy foreigners, but they don't spend much time here. The nearby Sidi Hosni Palace was occupied at one time by Barbara Hutton, the Woolworth heiress, and Paul Bowles has a small house here. The medina is surprisingly clean, thanks to an association that has recently been formed, the *Fondation Tanger-Al Madina,* to improve the living conditions of the inhabitants, by providing trash-cans and a garbage disposal service.

Just outside the medina, south of the Grand Socco, stands **St. Andrew's Church** (on Rue d'Angleterre). The land was given to the British Crown at the end of the 19th century by the sultan Mulay Hassan, and the present church was consecrated in 1905. This historic monument has undergone extensive repairs recently and is always in need of financial support. Many British people who have played an important part in Tangier life are buried in its graveyard: Walter Harris, who was the *London Times* correspondent; Emily Keene, wife of the Cherif of Ouezzane; and "Caid" Maclean, a Scottish military adviser to the sultans Mulay Abd el-Aziz and Mulay Abd el-Hafid. The Dogs' Cemetery, unique to Tangier, is not here but in the upper town, "The Mountain." Pet cats are also buried here, with their names engraved on the tombstones. It seems that this interesting little side of old Tangier life is about to be built over. In a different part of the town, the **Palais Mendoub** (Rue Shakespeare) lies about a 30-minute walk from the Grand Socco, going northwest towards the Stade Marshan. Before becoming the home of the millionaire Malcolm Forbes, which was then turned into the **Forbes Museum** (see "Culture" section), it was the palace of the Moroccan sultan's representative (the *mendoub)* in the International Free Zone from 1923 to 1956. The private apartments cannot be visited, but the interior decoration gives an idea of what this palace must have looked like in its prime. The gardens here, too, are beautifully kept up and a joy to walk around.

AROUND TANGIER

Ten km east of Tangier, **Cap Malabata,** dominated by a lighthouse, offers a fine view over the town and bay of Tangier. The N° 15 bus from
Tangier (Grand Socco) comes here, as well as going on to Ksar es-Sghir.
On the way out, you pass the French holiday village, **Club Méditerranée**
(first-class category, Tel: 94 06 88). This has taken over the villa lived in for
a short time by Walter Harris before constant raiding by the local tribes
drove him back into Tangier. Here, too, is the framework of a huge concrete building, designed to be the Malabata Casino and ***** hotel (the
future Sheraton, so they say). Nine km from Tangier, a short road to the
left leads to the lighthouse; the strange building on the right looking like
a medieval castle is, in fact, a 20th-century creation. The beaches here
are better than those in Tangier. Important roadworks are going on to
widen and improve the road to Ksar es-Sghir and increase its tourist
potential.

Going the other way, 14 km west from Tangier brings you, through a
pleasantly wooded zone, to Cap Spartel, the most northwesterly point of
Africa (there is no public transport, but a big taxi will take you if you don't
have a car). In the past, thick forests surrounded Tangier and the British
Consul in Tangier, Drummond Hay, recorded that a lion was killed near
Tangier as late as 1846. A lighthouse was built on Cap Spartel by the
European powers in the 1870s to stop the endless shipwrecks off this dangerous coast. Just south of Cap Spartel stretches Robinson Plage (the
Hotels Le Mirage and Robinson are here), with the nearby **Grottes
d'Hercule** (there used to be a small entrance fee). These sea-formed caves
were occupied by Neolithic populations some 5,000 years ago and extensive excavations recovered stone tools, ceramics, and animal bones. The
American School of Prehistoric Research worked on the sites between
1936 and 1947, with Carlton Coon as one of its later directors. More recently, the limestone was quarried to make grinding stones (no fabulous
Barbara Hutton parties in the caves now). The hero Hercules is said to
have rested here after his twelve exploits. The well-preserved ruins of the
Roman site of **Cotta** can be seen about 500 yards from the Grottes. It, too,
has been well excavated and dated to the second and third centuries A.D.
Cotta is one of the best conserved of the many establishments set up by the
Romans for salting fish and preparing a sort of fish-paste, *garum,* which was
much appreciated throughout the Empire. Cotta contains the essentials of
such an establishment: salting basins, water cistern, hot water baths, storage rooms, and a watchtower set in a corner of the main wall, from which
a lookout could locate the schools of fish as they approached the shore.
When the salting and fish-paste operations were over, amphoras were filled

with the mixtures, hermetically sealed, and deposited in the storerooms to await dispatching. A Saudi prince has a residence and private beach nearby.

EAST OF TANGIER

Continuing from Cap Malabata, the S704 road goes to **Ksar es-Sghir** (37 km from Tangier), running along the coast, with tempting creeks and beaches once you leave the center. Ksar es-Sghir has had an active past. It was one of the embarkation points for the Almoravid and Almohad armies invading Spain in the 11th and 12th centuries, then the Portuguese captured it in 1458, after a short siege. It remained an important Portuguese stronghold for almost 100 years. Seven seasons of excavations were carried out, beginning in 1972, by the American Archaeological Mission to Morocco, with the financial support of the Smithsonian Institution. Some of the old Moslem and Portuguese structures remain and are well worth visiting, if you like historical ruins (they contain ramparts, gateways, towers, vestiges of mosque, baths, and tiled floors). Ksar es-Sghir is now a small fishing village, with good beaches, and is very popular and a bit crowded in summer. Market day is Saturday. Two simple restaurants, **Restaurant Laachiri** and **Restaurant Dakhla,** both serve reasonable fishmeals.

With a car you can continue along the hilly and picturesque coastal route to the Spanish enclave of **Ceuta** (Sebta to the Moroccans), built on a rocky peninsula just opposite Gibraltar (from Tangier to Ceuta it is 63 km). After passing behind the wooded hill forming Punta Cires, a long climb allows beautiful views back along the coast, the Strait, and across to Andalusia, before approaching Jbel Moussa (842 m). At the foot of this mountain lies the bay of **Belyounesh,** from which the Arabs and Berbers probably set off on their conquest of Spain in the 8th century. A naval battle almost certainly took place here in 1342 between a Merinid fleet, helped by the King of Grenada, and boats sent by the Spanish Alfonso XI. You can see a ruined tower and house foundations revealed by recent excavations. Just off the coast is the **Island of Pereghil,** with its cave where Homer's Ulysses is said to have been bewitched by Calypso for many years. The road then drops down (and offers good views) towards the frontier village of **Fnideq** (which has a polluted beach) and Ceuta. Nearly 800 **gold and silver coins** dated to the Almohad period (12th and 13th centuries) were found in Fnideq in 1953, during house construction. Some of them had been minted in Ceuta. Spanish nuns have a community in Fnideq (Adoratrices Esclavas del Ssmo Sacramento, Mision Catolica, Tel: 97 60 13).

As Ceuta is Spanish, you'll need a passport and be prepared for a harassing time getting through Moroccan and Spanish police and Customs, to say nothing of the gangs of so-called "helpers" trying to get money out of you for unnecessary services rendered. Be prepared for long delays. This is not really advisable, unless you wish to leave Morocco by this route. The town is 5 km from the frontier post (a bus runs every half-hour). Ceuta's history is much like other towns along this Mediterranean/Atlantic Coast. Rome had a trading post here, the Byzantine emperors held it awhile, until the beginning of the 10th century, and it was then ruled by the Umayad dynasty of Spain. It was used by the Almoravids in their many invasion-crossings to Spain. The Spanish captured it in 1309. Then it was taken by the Portuguese in 1415. In 1580, Portugal and Spain were united and when, in 1640, they split up again, Spain kept Ceuta. (And still keeps it, despite permanent, but diplomatic, attempts by Morocco to get it back.) The Spanish army, duty-free goods, and a great deal of smuggling characterize Ceuta. Some 75,000 people are crowded into its 20 km², so the weekend exodus of Spaniards across the border to the Moroccan beaches is understandable.

Ceuta can be reached by a frequent **car ferry** service from Algeciras (Spain) run by Trasmediterranea. The company Buquebus España SA started a new service in the fall of 1998, with eight 35-minute crossings a day to and from Algeciras.

The **hotel scene** includes the two top-category hotels, **Hotel Melia Confort** (2 Calle Alcalde Sanchez Prados, Tel: 51 12 00, Fax: 51 15 01) and the **Hotel La Muralla** (★★★★, 15 Plaza de Africa, Tel: 51 49 40, Fax: 51 49 47).

Medium-priced hotels that can be mentioned are the **Hotel Residencia Africa** (9 Avenida Muelle Canoñero Dato, Tel: 50 94 67, Fax: 50 75 27) and the **Gran Hotel Ulises** (5 Calle Camoens, Tel: 51 45 40, Fax: 51 45 46). The campsite, **Camping Marguerita** (Tel: 50 38 40) is up the hill and hard to find, as well as being at least 4 km from the town.

Dining and restaurants in Ceuta are nothing out of this world. There are a number of places serving fish meals, pizzas, and *tapas*. The **Maritime Park** *(Parque Marítimo del Mediterráneo)*—a new complex by the sea—has restaurants, cafés, ice-creameries, a swimming pool, and a host of other attractions. It is, perhaps, a good place in which to while away an afternoon, but hardly worth a special visit to Ceuta.

Sightseeing will be quickly over with a visit to the **Fortaleza de Hacho,** on the top of Monte Hacho, from where there is a fine view across to Gibraltar. The fort was originally built by the Byzantines, but successive occupants of Ceuta have added to it. There are a few Spanish-style churches, including the one containing the body of the Portuguese king killed in the Battle of the Three Kings in 1578, Iglesia de San Francisco.

For those interest in culture, there is a small but interesting **archaeological**

collection housed in the municipal museum (*Museo Municipal,* corner of
Paseo del Revellín and Calle Ingenieros, open from 10:00 A.M.-2:00 P.M.
and 5:00 P.M.-8:30 P.M.) containing many ancient amphora and other objects found in the waters around Ceuta.

Entertainment and **nightlife** can best be satisfied in the casino in the
Maritime Park or the disco **Rives** (off Calle Real and down the steps, beside the cake shop, Argentina).

The **Ceuta Address List** is short—the banks are mostly along the main
street, Paseo de Revellín. Information about crossings to Spain can be obtained from offices in the port. The post office is in the Plaza de España
and the Tourist Information office is in Muelle Canoñero Dieto (but it is
usually shut). Tax-free petrol can be bought from around the port.

SOUTH OF TANGIER

Instead of taking the coastal road to Ceuta from Tangier via Ksar es-Sghir,
a good day excursion from Tangier is to the town of **Tetouan** by the P38,
southeast, then east (about 50 km). Return either by the same route or by
Ceuta and the northern coast (but it's hardly worth the trouble of getting
in and out of Ceuta). You can also get to Tetouan by **plane** from
Casablanca once a week. There is no **train** service but it is possible to link
up twice a day with the Casablanca-Tangier line by Supratour bus at Souk
Tnine de Sidi Yamani (arrivals are at Rue Achra Mai, off the Place Moulay
el-Mehdi, near the Cinema Avenida). Tetouan can be reached by CTM **bus**
from Tangier (departures are roughly every half-hour) and from
Casablanca by two services a day. Big communal **taxis** are frequent since
this is a busy route.

A few kilometers south of the present town, Tetouan's predecessor, the
Berber settlement of Tamuda, certainly existed in the third century B.C. In
the first century A.D., it was destroyed by the Romans, who established a
military camp on the site. In 1307, the Merinid sultan decided to build a
new, fortified city opposite the ruins of Tamuda, to control the eastern end
of the Rif Mountains. As well as being a military stronghold, Tetouan rapidly became a base for pirates and privateers scouring the Mediterranean
for easy prey, to such an extent that, in 1399, Henry III of Castilla decided
to put an end to their activities by destroying the town and deporting most
of the population. Almost a century passed before Tetouan came to life
again. In 1492, the Christian rulers captured Grenada from the Moslems,
marking the end of Moslem Spain. Fleeing Jews and Moslems installed
themselves in Tetouan and greatly contributed to a revival of the town's
prosperity. However, piracy started up again, with the same result: the
Spanish king Philip II blockaded the town and its commercial activity

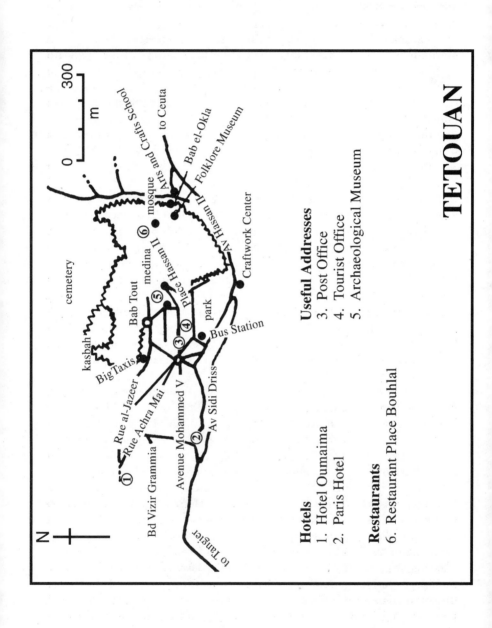

TETOUAN

Hotels
1. Hotel Oumaima
2. Paris Hotel

Restaurants
6. Restaurant Place Bouhlal

Useful Addresses
3. Post Office
4. Tourist Office
5. Archaeological Museum

N

300
m
0

cemetery

kasbah

Bab Tout

medina

Place Hassan II

mosque

Arts and Crafts School

to Ceuta

Bab el-Okla

Folklore Museum

Av Hassan II

Craftwork Center

park

Bus Station

Big Taxis

Rue al-Jazeer

Rue Achra Mai

Avenue Mohammed V

Bd Vizir Grammia

Av Sidi Driss

to Tangier

declined. Things looked up again when Mulay Ismail started encouraging commercial relations with the west. Foreign consuls established themselves in the town and one or two religious orders arrived. Relations with Spain suddenly deteriorated in 1859, and Spanish troops occupied the town for three years. When the Spanish Protectorate over northern Morocco was declared in 1912, it was only natural that Spain should choose Tetouan as its capital, Tangier having been declared an International Free Zone. The modern town outside Mulay Ismail's ramparts was built by the Spanish, and it remained Spanish until Moroccan independence in 1956.

Unlike Tangier, Tetouan has no international feel to it. It is basically a mixture of Arab and Spanish influences, of Mauresque and Andalusian architecture and decoration. The urban population of the province of Tetouan amounts to 390,000, the majority of whom live in the city itself. Despite having been the Spaniard's capital under the Protectorate, it does not have the same attraction for visitors as Tangier, which is why I recommend a short visit, unless you want to lounge around on the beach at one of the resorts along the coast going north towards Ceuta (it is 40 km from Tetouan to Ceuta).

The Tetouan region has its own scale of hotel charges, different from that of Tangier. Low season tariffs are as follows (they vary according to the presence or absence of showers and water closets in the room): **** 318-396 DH or 407-484 DH, breakfast 50 DH for both; *** 158-252 DH or 179-287 DH, breakfast 37 DH for both; ** 87-152 DH or 94-188 DH, breakfast 24-30 DH for both; * 79-117 DH or 83-133 DH, breakfast 18 DH for both. Add 30-80 DH for high season charges.

The most expensive accommodation is at the **** **Hotel Safir** (96 rooms, Avenue Kennedy, 3 km from the town on the way to Ceuta, Tel: 97 01 44, Fax: 97 06 92). It has a restaurant, swimming pool, tennis courts, and a nightclub, and is one of a chain of hotels concentrating on package tours. There is also the **** **Hotel Chems** (74 rooms, but it is also about 3 km from the town, on the way to Ceuta, Tel: 90 09 01, Fax: 99 09 07).

If you really do want, or need, to spend a night in Tetouan itself, the best hotel is probably the ** **Paris Hotel** (40 rooms, 11 Rue Chakib Arssalane, Tel: 96 67 50). The ** **Hotel Oumaima** (36 rooms, Rue Achra Mai, Tel: 96 34 73) is in much the same category. There are plenty of cheap places, most of a rather dubious nature, at much lower prices.

For a meal, the top of the range is the **Restaurant Place Bouhlal** (N° 48, next to the big mosque, Jamaa el-Kbir, in the medina, about 300 m from the main road out to Martil and Ceuta). It serves good Moroccan food (set menu is 80 DH), but attracts tourist groups. The **Restaurant Zerhoun**

(7 Rue Mohammed ben Larbi Torres, parallel to the main street, Avenue Mohammed V, the principal town street, which is for pedestrians only) serves Spanish and Moroccan food, but the service is slow. On the same road, at N°2, the **Restaurant Saigon** (which is Moroccan, not Vietnamese!) does *harira* (soup), couscous, and kebobs at reasonable prices (about 30 DH for the main dish). A bit difficult to find, hidden away in a little square, is the **Restaurant Popular** (around the corner from the Saigon), which serves good, cheap Moroccan food. If you are looking for cakes, it's difficult to choose between the **Café Pâtisserie Smir** (17 Avenue Mohammed V), which is open all day and female-friendly, and the **Copacabana** (one street down, on Rue Mohammed ben Larbi Torres). The **Pâtisserie Rahmouni** (10 Youssef ben Tachfine) is a branch of the Rahmouni pastries shop in Tangier and has the same good reputation for Moroccan cakes. The best ice-cream place at the moment is the **Heladería Atlas** (Rue Achra Mai, same as the Hotel Oumaima).

Sightseeing and Culture. I personally head for the **Archaeological Museum** (just off the Place al-Jala at the end of the Avenue Mohammed V). It's small, but has objects from the Phoenician/Roman site of Lixus, as well as a few mosaics, and some Roman coins and pottery from Tamuda. The small front garden has interesting tombs with Phoenician inscriptions and other mortuary stones (open 9:00 A.M.-12:00 P.M. and 2:30 P.M.-6:30 P.M.— with a longer lunch break on Fridays—closed Saturdays and Sundays, 10 DH entry fee). Other sightseeing could include the **medina,** with an entrance by Bab er-Rouah, next to the old Spanish consulate. It's full of Spanish-style houses and has some specialized markets: Souk el-Hout (fish), Souk el-Houdz, a market selling the famous red and white striped cloth used by the Rifian women, and Souk el-Kbir (fruit and vegetables). But watch out for pickpockets, pseudo-guides, and other nuisances. It is not really the place for shopping, unless Tetouan is the only town you're going to visit, but it's full of interest all the same. The Tetouan medina is one of the six sites recognized by UNESCO as part of the world's cultural heritage. It is included in an improvement scheme sponsored by the Spanish Andalusian government as part of the program underlining the links between Andalusia and Tetouan. The old Roman settlement of **Tamuda** is on the other side of Rio Martil, about 5 km away. It should be an interesting place for the archaeologically-minded, but, unfortunately, all that one can see is an overgrown piece of wasteland with a few stumps of columns. Apart from the Archaeological Museum, there is the **Folklore Museum** *(Musée d'art Folklorique),* housed in a tower in the town wall, near the Bab el-Okla, close to the main road to Ceuta (open 9:00 A.M.-12:00 P.M. and 2:30 P.M.-6:00 P.M., closed Saturdays and Sundays). It contains very fine examples of traditional clothing (predominately Jewish), jewelry, carpets, and other specimens of past life in north Morocco. The **Craftwork Center** (*Centre Artisanal*, Avenue Hassan II, quite close to the Folklore Museum) is really not worth the visit if you've been to the Tangier one. But the **Arts and Crafts School** (*Ecole d'Arts et de Métiers*, just opposite Bab el-Okla), is a fascinating place in which to see young Moroccans learning leatherwork, woodwork, weaving, *zellij* ceramic tile making, and other traditional crafts, under the tuition of master craftsmen (open 8:30 A.M.-12:00 P.M. and 2:30 P.M.-5:30 P.M., closed Saturdays and Sundays).

North from Tetouan, the road leading to Ceuta (about 40 km) runs along the coast. This used to be a place of blue Mediterranean water, sandy beaches, and scrub land, with hosts of unorganized campers in the summer. In recent years, the potential of this attractive sector has been recognized and a mass of holiday hotels and villages have sprung up. The first port of call is **Martil** (10 km away). I find this quite a scruffy place, with a lot of houses built by Moroccans working in Europe who only come during the holidays. But it has a beach, a number of cafés, and a seaside resort atmosphere if you like to mingle with the locals (there are few tourists). If you decide to stay here, the best **hotel** is the ★★ **Estrella del Mar** (32 rooms, half-board only in summer, Avenue Moulay Hassan, Tel: 97 92 76). The campsite is not recommended, for the usual reasons. Spanish nuns have a community here—the *Franciscanas Misioneras de Maria*, 21 Rue Khalid Walid (Tel: 97 90 74). Moving north, you come to the **Cabo Negro** complex—hotels, holiday homes, restaurants, nightclubs, and discos. Hotels here are the ★★★ **Petit Merou** (Tel/Fax: 97 80 65) and the ★★★ **Yasmine Negro** (Tel: 97 73 24). The former has a very good **restaurant.** The Moroccan government put a lot of money into creating this seaside resort in the 1960s.

The French Club Med, with its rather special type of holidays, has a village here (a first-class club), **Club Med Yasmina** (Tel: 97 82 65, Fax: 96 81 99). Then comes **M'Diq** (which has a polluted beach) and **Restinga Smir,** followed by **Marina Smir,** followed by **Ceuta.** M'Diq has a reputation for being an important smuggling center—but then, most of this part of Morocco indulges in this pastime.

The best hotel here is the whitewashed, attractively laid out ★★★★ **Hotel Kabila** (96 rooms, Km 20, Route de Sebta, Tel: 97 50 13, Fax: 66 62 03). I found the ★★★ **Hotel Golden Beach** (88 rooms, Tel: 97 50 77) much less imaginative in its conception, but it's functional enough. More modest is the ★ **Hotel Playa** (20 rooms, Boulevard Lalla Nozha, Tel: 97 51 66). There are heaps of restaurants around, but they suffer from a lack of trade, since many of the visitors—often Spanish—prefer to come with their own cheap

wine and alcohol and eat, drink, and be merry at a lower cost in their
rented apartments or bungalows.

Restinga Smir is a rather exclusive seaside resort, with the ***** **Hyatt
Regency Hotel** and two first-class club establishments: the **Club
Méditerranée** and **Restinga Smir VVT.** It used to be a quiet little fishing village, but has also become an important tourist center, with bungalows,
apartments, two hotels, shops, and nightclubs. Bathing is safe and watched
over by trained personnel, and water-skiing, sailing, and sea fishing are also
possible here. Southeast from Tetouan, a secondary road (S608), which
branches east off the south-going P28 just after it turns west for Tangier,
follows a very picturesque route along the coast. It's worth taking it as far
as **Oued Laou** (20 km), and even a further 10 km, where there is a very
good view over the Mediterranean. There are buses there from Tetouan
several times a day, and, of course, the big collective taxis. Oued Laou was
once a quiet little fishing port and, although it has become more "touristy"
over the years, it still doesn't lack charm. Its mosque is noted for its octagonal minaret. There is an interesting market on Saturday, 4 km out of town
on the Chefchaouen road. There are two rather primitive hotels, but the
Café-Restaurant Rosa will produce a reasonable meal.

The Tetouan address list:

Airlines—Royal Air Maroc, 5 Avenue Mohammed V (Tel: 96 12 60).

Banks—Place Moulay el-Mehdi (town center).

Buses—Supratours for train connections (Rue du 10 Mai). Local buses
to Cabo Negro, Avenue al-Massira (near the Spanish Consulate),
and Martil from Rue Moulay Abbas. Main bus station, Rue Sidi
Mandri/Rue Moulay Abbas.

Church—Spanish-language mass at Nostra Sra de la Victorias, 4, Place
Moulay el-Mehdi (Tel: 96 32 27).

Consulates—Spain is the only country with consular representation in
Tetouan: Avenue al-Massira (Tel: 97 39 41, Fax: 97 39 46), closed
over the weekend.

Drugstore, Night *(Pharmacie de Garde)*—Rue al-Ouhada (Tel: 96 67 77).
They should also be able to help you with a doctor (if you can get
them to understand you!).

Fire—(Tel: 15)

Police—19 Avenue Sidi Driss (Tel: 19).

Post Office—Place Moulay el-Mehdi.

Public Telephone—next door to the post office (Rue al-Ouhada) and
téléboutiques.

Taxis—Big taxis to Martil and Ceuta, Rue Mourakah Anual; to Tangier
and Chefchaouen, from taxi stand in Rue al-Jazeer.

Tourist information—ONMT, 30 Avenue Mohammed V (Tel: 96 44 07).
Generally not able to provide much information.

SOUTHWEST OF TANGIER

An agreeable excursion from Tangier is to continue down the coast by
the main road to the charming little coastal town of **Asilah** (45 km from
Tangier). It can be reached by **bus** or **train** (the train station is 2 km out of
town). About 13 km northeast of Asilah, current Franco-Moroccan excavations have identified the remains of the town of **Zilis,** once thought to
have been those of the Roman post of Ad Mercuri. The stratigraphy has
shown that the town lasted from the second century B.C. to the beginning
of the fifth century A.D. The Idrissids constructed part of Asilah, which
later came under the rule of the Caliphs of Cordoba. In 1471, a Portuguese
fleet captured it from the Merinids and began important fortifications
(ramparts and monumental gates), now the oldest visible part of the town.
In 1578, the Portuguese king, Sebastian I, landed in Asilah at the head of
an army of 30,000 men, against the advice of all his counselors, determined to conquer all Morocco. However, his crushing defeat the same year
at the Battle of the Three Kings, near Larache and Ksar el-Kbir, just east of
Asilah, and his death on the battlefield—along with two Moroccan sultans—put an end to Portuguese control over the town. The Portuguese
were soon replaced by the Spanish, who were only evicted by Mulay Ismail
in 1691. Asilah is intimately linked to the bandit, Raisouli, who spread
destruction and panic around Tangier and Tetouan at the end of the 19th
century, amassing riches from the tribes he plundered. He was also adept
at kidnapping. One of his first victims was Walter Harris (of the London
Times), whom he captured in 1903, but his most sensational kidnapping
was that of Ion Perdicaris, a wealthy Greek-American businessman, and his
stepson, in 1904. The bandit swooped down on Perdicaris's estate near
Tangier and carried off the two Americans, then demanded a ransom of
US$70,000, the release of his own men held in the Tangier prison, and the
position of Pasha of Tangier. When President Theodore Roosevelt heard
of all this, he had a message sent to the U.S. Consul in Tangier that became
famous: "I want Perdicaris alive or Raisouli dead." To prove that he was serious, Roosevelt sent seven U.S. Navy warships to Tangier, even threatening
to land the Marines to attack Raisouli in his stronghold unless something
was done. Finally, the sultan Abd el-Aziz managed to arrange things, and

Perdicaris and his stepson returned home to Tangier. Asilah became Raisouli's stronghold from 1906 until his final arrest and imprisonment by Abdelkrim, another Rif rebel. Raisouli died in 1925. Today, Asilah attracts visitors of all nationalities, including many Moroccan artists, who enjoy the charm of the town, its extensive beaches (unfortunately, some were found to have a high level of pollution in the summer of 1998), and its July/August cultural festival (concerts, plays, exhibitions, discussions, and dances). (It is not always easy to get the program.)

The **hotel scene** is limited (based on the Tangier scale of charges). The most **expensive** is the *** **Hotel Zelis,** in the town (Tel: 91 70 69, Fax: 91 70 98), which has a restaurant, a coffee shop, and a swimming pool, followed by the roadside *** **Hotel el-Khaima** (110 rooms, Tel: 91 72 28, Fax: 91 75 66). This is an attractive-looking establishment, with a restaurant, bar, disco, and a pool. The manager can arrange horseback riding and windsurfing. It's near the station, so it is useful for visitors coming by train.

For **medium-price accommodations** you have the ** **Hotel Las Palmas** (7 Rue Imam Assili, Tel: 91 76 94), the ** **Hotel Mansour** (49 Avenue Mohammed V, Tel: 91 73 90, Fax: 91 75 33), and the ** **Hotel Oued el-Makhazine** (Avenue Melilla, Tel: 91 70 90, Fax: 91 75 00). All have rooms with showers and water closets. The last two have restaurants, and the last one has a small swimming pool open to non-clients.

Budget accommodations come in the shape of * hotels such as the * **Hotel Asilah** (79 Avenue Hassan II, Tel: 91 72 86) and the * **Hotel Sahara** (9 Rue Tarfaya, Tel: 91 71 85). There are a number of reasonable **camp-sites** along the beach as you come into the town, but they become very crowded at Easter and in July and August (often with European tourists). As always, in Moroccan campsites, the sanitary arrangements generally leave much to be desired. A few are open throughout the year. Prices are around 10 DH per person/per tent. It is also possible to rent a **holiday apartment.** Try the agency at 14 Rue Imam al-Assili (Tel: 91 74 97, Fax: 91 74 97), but book well in advance. Prices are from 150 DH a day and up, depending on size.

The recommended **restaurants** are **Casa Pepe** (8 Place Zellaka, Tel: 91 73 95) or **Restaurant Sevilla** (18 Rue Iman al-Assili)—but the former is getting a bit too popular. The specialty in both places is fish, with main courses around 50 DH. If you are tempted by the street stalls selling fish, choose grills or *tajine* rather than the fried (the cooking oil is sometimes a bit doubtful).

Sightseeing will be limited to visiting the old part, within the 15th-century **Portuguese ramparts** and the **medina.** Follow the sign *Centre Ville*, go through the Bab el-Bahr, and follow the path towards the pier, leaving the

Raisouli Palace on your left (there is no furniture but it is an interesting building). There are good views of the ramparts, the old cemetery, and the shrine of Sidi Marzouk, a local saint. The walk through the medina, white-washed, clean, and decorated with modern murals, is very pleasant. You should be able to see a very worn Portuguese royal coat of arms atop one of the gates.

The best **entertainment** and **nightlife** is probably just to watch the crowd from a café table. For a quiet, relaxing drink, the **Hotel Oued el- Makhazine** is a good place, and if you want something "hotter," the **Hotel el-Khaima** has a disco.

The Spanish-speaking Catholic **church** is the Parroquia de San Bartolomé, Mision Católica, 24 Rue Horria (telephone the nuns at 41 71 00 for information).

If you have a car, like seeing prehistoric remains, and don't mind walking, the **Cromlech of Mzora** is only some 16 km away. This impressive monument is unique in Morocco. Continue on the road to Larache, turn left after 16 km for the Tetouan road, then take, almost at once, a road up the hill on the left to the village of Souk Tnine de Sidi Yamani (market on Monday). From here it is best to follow the track on foot a few kilometers (there'll be lots of people to guide you). The monument is composed of a stone circle made up of 167 standing stones, averaging 1.5 m in height, surrounding a tumulus 55 m in diameter by 5 m in height. A retaining wall of carefully-trimmed sandstone slabs is clearly visible at the base of the tumulus. The monument is considered to be the tomb of a local Mauretanian prince under Punic influence, though the standing stones are probably older. At the moment it is almost submerged by a mass of corrugated tin-roofed houses, which are steadily encroaching on the site. You can get back to Tangier (about 60 km) by continuing down the main road towards Tetouan until you come to the left turn for Tangier.

The final reasonable day excursion south of Tangier without changing your base is a continuation from Asilah to **Larache** (about 48 km from Tangier), that is best reached by **car**, or **bus** from Tangier or Asilah, and the site of Lixus. The latter is situated on a hill (altitude 80 m), 4 km before Larache, on the right bank of the River Loukkos, just before the road to Plage Ras r'Mal. Access is by foot, though a track does lead up to the top. The site has an official, uniformed guardian. Lixus is considered to be one of the oldest Phoenician trading posts in the western world. Archaeological research has indeed shown that the Phoenician occupation goes back to the beginning of the eighth century B.C., though no visible structures date from this period. In the fifth century B.C., the Carthaginian Admiral Hanno established a colony. The fish-salting workshops (beside the current road) are among the oldest and most important of the Western Mediterranean. Starting at the end of the first century B.C., their activity continued after the founding of a Roman colony at the beginning of the first century A.D., and went on until the end of the sixth century A.D. On the right, as you climb up, is the **Roman amphitheater/theater,** dating to the first century A.D., its semi-circular stone tiers still marvelously well-preserved (numbers were carved behind some of them to show reserved seats!). In the thermal establishment beside the theater, the mosaic depicting a fierce head of Neptune is, unfortunately, rather damaged. The other mosaics have been taken to various museums.

Considerable archaeological excavation has taken place on the site, first by the Spanish, then by the French and, more recently, by combined Morocco-Spanish teams, but it is a very complex one and the visitor has a hard time distinguishing one ruin from another. However, almost at the top can be seen, on the right, the ruins of small houses built by the local Mauretanian populations, dating to the second century B.C. They had their own way of building, but they were very influenced by Phoenician styles and customs, although the idea of a massive influx of "invaders" is quite definitely excluded. As you continue towards the top of the hill, the semi-circular walling on the right was thought to have been a seventh century Phoenician temple, but trial digging has recently reduced the date to the end of the first century B.C. The building nearby is a tower that was part of the defensive enclosure built in the fourth century A.D., when the Romans were under pressure. The whole top of the hill is considered to be a religious focal point: the columns of several temples are clear enough, as are a number of walls. What was thought to have been a Christian basilica (on the right) has now been shown to be a mosque, and to never have had any Christian function—so today's archaeologists are constantly changing the picture one has of the past! From here the view is magnificent all around—the sea, the town of Larache, and the meanders of the River Loukkos.

Larache itself is a pleasant enough town, a bit bigger than Asilah, but without very much to see. It is a fishing port, with a strong Spanish feeling, painted white and pale blue. Like Asilah, it is hassle-free and less visited by tourists. The first Arab invaders made their camp there in the 7th century A.D. When the Portuguese established themselves in Tangier and Asilah in 1471, they chased out the inhabitants and the town was empty until the Wattasid sultan, Mohammed ech-Cheikh, decided to build a fortress there at the end of the 15th century. The city became rich and important and attracted the unwelcome attention of the Portuguese, the Spanish, and the French. Their attacks were repulsed, however, and in 1491 the kasbah became a pirate stronghold, then passed into Spanish hands in 1610, to be taken back by Mulay Ismail in 1689, before becoming a Spanish possession again in 1911 until Moroccan independence. It is little wonder that the Spanish influence is omnipresent.

The **hotel scene** has the medium-priced ✱✱✱ **Hotel Riad Larache** in the top category (24 rooms, Avenue Mohammed ben Abdallah, Tel: 91 26 26, Fax: 91 26 29) (the direction is well indicated in the center of town). Once a big house belonging to the French Conte de Paris, then a rather crumbling hotel, it has been renovated and is now part of the Kasbah Tours Hotel (KTH) chain. It has a restaurant, bar, garden, tennis courts, and a swimming pool. The ✱✱ **Hotel España** (50 rooms, Place de la Libération, Tel: 91 31 95, Fax: 91 56 38) is a bit shabby and noisy since it faces the main square, but is clean and agreeable.

The best **budget accommodations** are supplied by the **Pension Malaga** (60 DH, 4 Rue de Salé, Tel: 91 18 68) and the **Pension Amal** (80 DH, 10 Avenue Abdallah ben Yassine, Tel: 91 27 88). Showers are communal in both these small, clean hotels, and don't expect constant hot water.

The **restaurant** in the **Hotel Riad Larache** is pricey and not particularly memorable, though it is nice to eat in the garden. The very Spanish **Casa de España,** a club for the Spanish population of Larache, will let in non-members and gives a good meal at a very reasonable price (main course from 60 DH, and it has impeccable water closets). To find it from the main square, take the first turn up past the Restaurant Lixus, then the first right opposite the Crédit Agricole. The club has no nameplate, but it's the first door on the left as you go into the street. Decent meals can be had at the **Restaurant Larache** (18 Avenue Mohammed ben Abdallah) (the main course is around 40 DH). The **Restaurant Lixus,** on the main square, is a good place in which to have a coffee or orange juice and watch local life.

Again, once you have visited Lixus (a real must), **sightseeing** in Larache is limited and I prefer just to wander around a bit before sitting down and having a cool drink at a café table in the center of town, in the colonial-style ex-Plaza de España, now Place de la Libération. However, it's worth taking a walk in the **medina** and looking at the outside of the **Stork's Fortress** *(Casbah de la Cigogne)*, built by the Spanish. The **port,** too, is full of life and interest. The **archaeological museum** (indicated on the right as you drive in) is very small and its contents rather limited. The French writer Jean Genet lived for many years in Larache, behind the Christian cemetery in which he is buried. Spanish-speaking Catholic services are held in the **Church of Nostra Señora del Pilar,** Rue Moulay Hassan (Tel: 91 30 99).

For **swimming,** the best beaches are north of the town, on the right bank of the River Loukkos. A small boat takes passengers across the river.

The return journey to Tangier can follow the same route. Alternatively, you can do a circuit via **Ksar el-Kbir** (36 km), and the secondary S603 to Souk el-Kolla (about 50 km), turning left for Khemis des Beni Arouss (another 45 km), before joining the P28 (36 km), and turning left up to Tetouan and back to Tangier. Going straight on at Souk el-Kolla will lead you to **Chefchaouen. Ksar el-Kbir** was said to have been founded in the 11th century, but it was the Almohad Yacub el-Mansour, in the 12th century, who built a protective wall and gave it its name. The Battle of the Three Kings, close to the rivers Makhzen and Loukkos, was fought near here in 1578, a battle that was to change the destinies of both Morocco and Portugal. From the 17th century, the power struggles between the sultans led to the decline of the town, whose greatest claim to fame today is its sugarcane factory. All around here, sugarcane, rice, and, further north, tea, have been planted to help Morocco become less dependent on imports.

Spanish-speaking Catholic **church** services are held in the Church of the Sagrado Corazon de Jesus, Avenue de la Muncipalité (Tel: 91 82 96).

SOUTHEAST OF TANGIER

If at all possible, an excursion should be made to the extremely picturesque town of **Chefchaouen. Chefchaouen,** in the Rif Mountains, is situated on a hillside between the two peaks of the Jbel Ech-Chaouen (the Mountain of the Horns). It is one of the most attractive towns in north Morocco, with a strong Andalusian atmosphere, clearly seen in the architecture and decoration. It is a favorite with visitors for its climate (it's located at 600 m), the charm of its narrow streets and whitewashed houses, and its cascading streams.

By **car** it is easily reached from Tangier by following the P38 southeast towards Tetouan, and turning right before you get into the town (53 km). From here to Chefchaouen is a distance of 60 km (the main road has now become the P28). There is no **train,** but a CTM **bus** leaves Tangier around midday (the journey time is 2½ hours). The CTM has a more frequent service from Tetouan (journey time, two hours), and a daily bus from Kénitra, Rabat, and Casablanca, plus buses from Fès (4-5 hours) via Ouezzane. A much longer bus journey (all day) will take you through the Rif from Chefchaouen to Ketama, Al-Hoceima, and Nador (the total distance from Tangier to Nador is 1,086 km). Other bus companies also cover these towns at different times and at a lower cost. **Big communal taxis** are also a possibility. If you are not planning to return in the day, Chefchaouen makes an attractive stopping point before traveling east or south.

Chefchaouen was founded in 1471 by the Wattasid Mulay Ali ben Rashid to stop the advance of the Portuguese and Spanish installed in

Ceuta and Ksar es-Sghir. Part of the walls of his fortified castle can still be seen. In the late 15th and 16th centuries, and again in the 17th century, it was occupied by Moslems and Jews expelled from Spanish Andalusia. These skilled refugees used their talents and helped the town to prosper, but for centuries it remained shut in on itself, a holy town (with lots of mosques and shrines) into which Christians (but not, of course, Jews) were forbidden to enter. However, three managed to do so—the French explorer Charles de Foucauld spent a night in the town in 1883 (disguised as a Jew), the explorer William Summers was poisoned there in 1892, and the English journalist Walter Harris just managed to get away in 1898. The Spaniards occupied the town in 1920, as part of their Protectorate plans, but were forced to pull out by the rebellion of the Berber tribes of the Rif. Chefchaouen was a central point in this resistance against the Spanish Protectorate, and the Rif Republic was proclaimed in 1922. The rebellion, under the Berber leader Mohammed ben Abdelkrim, lasted five years and the Spanish suffered severe military defeats. From 1924, fierce battles raged around Chefchaouen between the Rifian and the Spanish troops, until the latter were forced to cooperate with the French forces and then managed to gain entry into the town in 1926. Despite being much visited by tourists, Chefchaouen has managed to remain a calm and agreeable place in which to stay a night or two.

The **hotel scene** is good (based on Tetouan tariffs), the most **expensive** being the small but comfortable **** **Hotel Parador** (35 rooms, Place el-Makhzen, Tel: 98 63 24, Fax: 98 70 33), with a restaurant, and the large, rather massive *** **Hotel Asma** (94 rooms, Tel: 98 62 65, Fax: 98 71 58), up on the hill overlooking the town and inconveniently placed if you don't have transport. The views are good from both hotels and both have a bar, restaurant, and a swimming pool (the Hotel Parador might let you use their pool even if you are not a resident).

Medium-priced accommodations can be had at the ** **Hotel Madrid,** 35 rooms, Avenue Hassan II, Tel: 98 74 96, Fax: 09 74 98), but it's not a very good value, or the ** **Hotel Magou** (35 rooms, 23 Rue Mulay Idriss, Tel: 98 62 57). There are plenty of budget-friendly hotels, * or unclassified, including the * **Hotel Panorama** (20 rooms, 33 Rue Mohammed Abderrahmane, Tel: 98 66 15, good views), and the * **Hotel Rif** (Avenue Hassan II, Tel: 98 69 82). The youth hostels are not recommended, and the campsites are a little ways out of town and, again, only to be used if you really have to.

Both the big hotels have **restaurants** (the tourist menu starts at 140 DH in the Hotel Parador, gastronomic at 150 DH; the Hotel Asma's food is rather expensive—130 DH—for the quality). As usual, there is a wide choice of small restaurants, serving meals at 50-100 DH. Try the **Al-Baraka,** (it is difficult to find), Derb M'hatib (Tel: 98 69 88), and **Restaurant Granada** or **Chez Fouad** (close to each other, at the Plaza Uta el-Hammam), and outside the medina you will find the **Restaurant Moulay Ali Berrechid** and the **Restaurant Zouar.**

The places to buy **pastries** are the **Pâtisserie Magou** (10 Avenue Hassan II) and the nearby **Pâtisserie Diafa** (Rue Moulay Ali ben Rachid, which has good breakfasts, too). Both places are a good value. For a **coffee** or **soft drink,** the **Plaza Uta el-Hammam** offers a good view of Chefchaouen life, but all the cafés (which are, by the way, not women-friendly) are inclined to smell strongly of *kif,* as we are now nearing the heartland of its cultivation. For a drink with a view, the terraces of the **Hotel Parador** or the **Hotel Asma** are good choices. **Entertainment,** as known in the Western world, is absent from Chefchaouen, but those who like Andalusian music may be lucky to catch one of the occasional music festivals held in the summer.

For your **sightseeing** tour of Chefchaouen, you could visit the **market** and the **medina,** though you may have had your fill of the former in Tangier and Tetouan. The medina, however, is quite different, and you won't regret your visit. It is only a few minutes from the Hotel Parador and is made up of small winding lanes and sparkling, whitewashed houses, where families can be seen working the looms that still play an important part in the local economy. The different components of medieval Chefchaouen life—Berber, Jewish, and Andalusian—can still be distinguished in the different parts of the medina. Monday and Thursday mornings have particularly active markets, when the countrypeople come in to sell their goods. If you take the road to Ouezzane a short distance from Bab el-Khadem, the south gate of the medina, you will come to a little water mill that is still functional. The 17th century **kasbah,** beside the Plaza Uta el-Hammam, although ruined, is still impressive (it's open 9:00 A.M.- 1:00 P.M. and 3:00 P.M.-6:00 P.M.). It was built in 1672 by Mulay Ismail as part of his plan to consolidate his rule over the country (as usual, this was not always easy), against both the Spanish and the local tribes. Abdelkrim used the castle for a while, but ended up being imprisoned there by the Spaniards in 1926 after his defeat. His cell and iron chains can be seen to the right of the kasbah, while on the left is a small **museum** displaying traditional arts and crafts. Of interest are the wooden "boxes" in which the local brides used to be carried to their wedding. I was actually lucky enough to have seen a wedding procession with one of these swaying contraptions containing the bride, but that was some 20 years ago, and the custom has died out in favor of a hired Mercedes. On the south side of the shady **Plaza Uta el-Hammam** (where a 15th-century Moorish bath still functions, but it's for men only), the **Great Mosque** *(Jamaa el-Kebir)* has an unusual octagonal minaret. It was built in the 15th century by Mulay Ali ben Rashid, the founder of the town. The ruins of the **old Catholic church** can be see from the back rooms of the Hotel Parador.

The Chefchaouen Address List:

Banks—Avenue Hassan II (change, travelers checks, VISA, and MasterCard at BMCE and Banque Populaire).

Bus station *(gare routière)*—Corner Avenue Tariq/Fès, on the west side of the town.

Drugstore—on a small street near the post office.

Police—(Tel: 19).

Post Office—Avenue Hassan II, near the Bab el-Aain entrance to the medina.

Telephone—from the téléboutiques.

Tourist Information—there used to be an office near Place Mohammed V, but it has closed.

FURTHER AFIELD

For those planning to continue south from Tangier, the new expressway, planned to link **Tangier** to **Rabat** (chapter 6), Casablanca, and, eventually, towns further south, starts at Larache (there is a toll fee for a car on the Larache-Casablanca route—55 DH, 255 km). For the moment it is rather empty, except during the summer, but there are pull-offs and filling stations near the Moulay Bousselham and Allal al-Tazi exits. The more interesting, but slower, main P2 from Larache goes through Ksar el-Kbir, Souk el-Arba du Gharb, and Kénitra before arriving in Rabat (190 km). **Souk el-Arba du Gharb** is the most important town on this road before Kénitra.

A continuation **south** from Larache to Ksar el-Kbir (28 km), then east to Ouezzane (44 km), and back up north to Tangier via **Chefchaouen** and **Tetouan** is best done by scheduling a night in Larache and another in Chefchaouen. The old frontier between the French and Spanish Protectorates lay 12 km south of Ksar el-Kbir, at **Arbaoua.** The forbidding concrete hangers making up the customs post have been converted into an ideal place for the local people to sell their goods, often melons, to the crowds of Moroccan workers driving to and from Europe during the holiday period. The new expressway has rather spoiled this flourishing and picturesque business.

The ** **Hostellerie Route de France** (Tel: 07-90 26 08), up a steep road to the right leading to the village of Arbaoua, makes a convenient stopping point and has a reasonably good restaurant. The whole wooded area around here is a **game reserve** (one of the best in Morocco, so they say) where one can shoot wild boar, partridge, pheasants, wild duck, and wood-cock, among other game. It is also possible to make a detour slightly before Arbaoua and visit the birdwatcher's site of **Moulay Bousselham** on the coast, 40 km from Ksar el-Kbir (chapter 6).

Continue south on the P2 before turning left onto the crossgoing road, P23, to **Ouezzane.** Some 15 km after turning off the P2, one can see the ruined walls of **Basra.** Three seasons of archaeological research have been carried out on this early Islamic city, founded by the Idrissids in the ninth century A.D. They have revealed a residential area with house structures, and also the remains of metallurgical and pottery workshops. George Washington University is responsible for the excavations, which are scheduled to continue through 1999, and would probably be ready to supply information to visitors. When not under excavation, the site is closed.

The town of **Ouezzane** (60 km southeast of Chefchaouen) lies on the flanks of the Jbel Bou Hillal, on the southern edge of the Rif Mountains, surrounded by olive and fruit trees. Ouezzane is particularly known as a religious center with no monuments of outstanding interest to the visitor. But it crops up often in the history of Morocco, since its religious leaders played important roles at many times in the past. It was also one of the many places in which Andalusian Moslem and Jewish refugees settled in the 15th century. Its development was due to the foundation in 1727 of a *zaouia* (religious fraternity) by a *cherif,* a distant descendant of Idriss II. The *cherif* founded the Taibya religious fraternity, one of the best-known in Morocco, and built a mosque in which he was later buried. The apogee of Ouezzane's influence as a religious center was reached in the 19th century, when the reigning sultan came and requested the help of the *zaouia.* It is still inhabited by many who consider themselves *chorfa,* descendants of the Prophet, and the tomb of the *zaouia*'s founder is visited by many Moslems. At the end of the 19th century, the *cherif* of Ouezzane married an English woman, Emily Keene, whom he had met in Tangier. He divorced her after 14 years, but they seemed to have remained on good terms, since he later summoned her to his bedside when he was dying. The Cherifa of Ouezzane, as she was called, wrote an interesting book on her life, from which we learn that her husband lived in royal fashion, sometimes supplying food to 600 pilgrims a day. Jews also make a pilgrimage to Ouezzane, to the tomb of a holy man, an Andalusian rabbi named Ba Amrane, who was head of the Jewish community in the 18th century. He died around 1780, and his tomb lies a few kilometers outside the town, on the road to Rabat.

CTM **buses** go to and from Ouezzane to Casablanca once a day, and the Chefchaouen to Fès bus stops at Ouezzane. A more frequent service links the town directly to Chefchaouen. Non-CTM buses also go to much the same places, and the big communal **taxis** are around, too, though it's best to try for one in the morning. Buses and taxis leave from the Place de l'Indépendance.

I wouldn't try to spend the night in Ouezzane, as there's a much better selection of accommodations in Chefchaouen. If you have to, you could head for the **Hotel el-Alam** (rooms under 100 DH, Place de l'Indépendance, Tel: 90 71 82). Much in the same category (though there are no rooms as cheap as the el-Alam) is the **Hotel Restaurant Ouezzane Touristique** (Km 2, on the road to Fès, Tel: 90 71 54).

If you do have time to spare for **sightseeing**, the **Mosque of the Taibya Fraternity** (Place de l'Indépendance) has the octagonal minaret that is a feature of the region. The small green tiles are a 1960s restoration. The nearby *Centre Artisanal* (Craftwork Center) has a good range of the painted furniture and wool rugs that are a specialty of the town.

From Ouezzane the choice is to go southwest, towards **Souk el-Arba du Gharb** and **Rabat** (chapter 6), southeast to Fès (134 km) (chapter 8), or northeast back to Chefchaouen and west along the **Rif** to **Al-Hoceima** via **Ketama** (215 km from Chefchaouen). The first two possibilities are quite straightforward, but the third, the Rif Mountain area, poses a big problem.

It's sad to have to say so, for the scenery is magnificent—but the Rif is dangerous. The U.S. Consulate strongly advises U.S. citizens to avoid the area. Most travel agencies leave it out of their itineraries. All guidebooks to Morocco warn their readers about the dangers. My personal friends wouldn't dream of going there, except in exceptional circumstances. The problem is that this zone, from Chefchaouen to Al-Hoceima, of exceptional scenic beauty, is the center of the marijuana market. The stuff grows everywhere and hard-sell dealers—even tiny kids—are out there along the roadside waiting for you. Well, not just waiting, but chasing you, pouncing on you, bumping into you, pretending to be victims of a breakdown, you name it. *Kif* and *hashish* leave from deserted creeks and coves in little boats and, although the Moroccan authorities are making energetic and successful attempts to stamp out the trade, the task is an uphill one in this wild and rugged area. So, unless you are looking for excitement and adventure and possibly prison (for illegal possession of the stuff), leave the Chefchaouen to Al-Hoceima road to the numerous bandits and police. If you *must* try this route, travel with at least one other person, and preferably go in two cars, making sure you have enough gas, that your tires are in good shape, and that the engine is working well, don't stop, and be very wary. You will be rewarded by stunning views just after going through the small town of Targuist. You can also do the trip by bus from Tetouan or Chefchaouen. I suppose this is safer (I must admit I have not done it). **Ketama** (99 km from Chefchaouen) is the center of the *kif* trade, but if you have to stop overnight, the only possible hotel is the *** **Hotel Tidighine** (64 rooms, Tel: 81 30 16), named after the peak to the southeast, the highest in the Rif (2,448 m).

I am assuming you have reached **Al-Hoceima** by one route or another. It lies around a sandy bay at the foot of the Rif Mountains and is a calm and agreeable holiday town in a beautiful setting—it's just a pity that it is hard to reach.

As well as the Chefchaouen road, a road north from Fès (275 km, also via the unfortunate Ketama), and another from Taza, both go to Al-Hoceima (160 km). Al-Hoceima is connected to Tangier, Tetouan, and Casablanca by scheduled Royal Air Maroc **flights.** The Charif al-Idrissi airport is about 20 kms to the southeast. CTM **buses** come twice a day from Nador, Chefchaouen, Tetouan, Fès, and Meknès, and once a day from Rabat and Casablanca. Other bus companies also have services to and from all-important—and less-important—destinations. **Big taxis** also run to all the main towns, but you need to start your inquiries for an empty place early in the morning and be prepared to wait for the fill-up.

The site was first used in the 9th century. In the 17th century the French tried, without success, to set up a fishing establishment, but it was the Spaniards who finally got the fishing rights from the Moroccan ruler Mulay Rashid, the predecessor of Mulay Ismail, towards the end of the 17th century. The Spanish general Sanjuro built the modern town in 1920, but from 1921 Al-Hoceima was at the center of the Rif war of independence between Abdelkrim and the Spanish. The Berber leader had one of his main bases at Ajdir, only 8 km from the town, and all the surrounding tribes were naturally on his side against the occupying power. In 1921, his forces inflicted a crushing defeat on a Spanish army at Annoual, some 40 km east of Al-Hoceima. An American correspondent, Vincent Sheean, covered the Rif war and was one of the few people to interview the rebel. Americans were also involved in an informal air squadron—the *Escadrille Chérifienne*—set up by the French to counter the activities of an American pilot flying for Abdelkrim. It was composed of volunteer aviators, most of whom were Americans, and it carried out nearly 500 missions in 1925. Of course, the United States was heavily criticized for the squadron's activities, but the American pilots were volunteers and did not necessarily represent the official U.S. position. Abdelkrim's final defeat by the combined Spanish and French forces and surrender in 1926 (20,000 Rifian soldiers against nearly 800,000 troops with air support) put an end to dreams of independence. Spanish occupancy of the north ended in 1956, but Spain still retains the rocky island called Peñon de Velez de la Gomera, some 40 km west of Al-Hoceima and, even more surprisingly, the Peñon de Alhucemas islet, only some 600 m offshore in the bay itself (neither is open to visitors).

Today, Al-Hoceima is a popular holiday resort, not much frequented by Westerners. Its main attractions are the beaches, though the old Spanish part of the now modern town, behind the sea-front hotels, is not unattractive.

Tariffs in the Al-Hoceima region are 174-277 DH or 197-316 DH for the ★★★ and 96-167 DH or 103-207 DH for the ★★. At the top of the hotel list is the ★★★ **Hotel Quemado** (100 rooms, right on the main beach, Tel: 98 33 15, Fax: 98 33 14), a favorite with package tours. Another ★★★ outfit, the **Hotel el-Maghrib el-Jdid** (40 rooms, 56 Avenue Mohammed V, Tel: 92 25 04/05 Fax, 98 25 04) is conveniently situated near the center of the town.

Medium-price accommodations are supplied by the ★★ **Hotel National** (23 Rue de Tetouan, Tel: 98 06 81), very close to the CTM bus station, and the ★★ **Hotel Karim** (51 rooms, 27 Avenue Hassan II, Tel: 92 21 84, Fax: 98 43 40), which is a bit shabby and well in from the beach. There are a number of inexpensive hotels around the Place du Rif, at the south end of the town, not far from the CTM bus station (**Hotel Rif, Hotel Populaire,** and **Hotel Afrique,** for instance), all under 100 DH, but they have communal showers (not always hot) and squat water closets. On the Ajdir road, about a mile out of town, the **Camping Cala Bonita** (45 DH), on the beach of the same name, gets very crowded in summer and the toilet facilities suffer accordingly. Further on, past Ajdir, down a track towards the sea, the French **Club Méditerranée** holiday village still has its traditional straw-roofed huts (Ajdir BP 38, Tel: 80 20 13, Fax: 80 20 14) and is beautifully situated. It's very popular, so advance booking is necessary.

For eating, the **restaurant** in the **Hotel el-Maghrib el-Jdid** is a possibility (the tourist menu is 75 DH, and it has a liquor license). A couple of restaurants in the Avenue Mohammed V, the **Restaurant Paris** (N° 21) and the nearby **Restaurant La Belle Vue,** have slightly lower-priced set menus that are a good value. There are also plenty of fish restaurants, especially around the port. You can have breakfast, or just a coffee, at the **Pâtisserie al-Maghreb al-Fain,** also in the Avenue Mohammed V.

The Al-Hoceima Address List

Airlines—Royal Air Maroc, Aéroport Charif el-Idrissi (Tel: 98 20 63).

Banks—Avenue Mohammed V (cash from VISA and MasterCard at the BMCE and BMCI).

Bus station *(gare routière)*—Place du Rif, south end of town.

Church—Spanish-speaking Catholic, Parroquia de San José, Mision

Catolica, corner Rue Moulay Idriss Alkbar/Rue Embarek el-Bekkay
(Tel: 98 05 12).

Drugstore—Avenue Hassan II.

Post Office—Rue Moulay Idriss Alkbar.

Public Telephone—at post office, but also at téléboutiques.

Taxis—same place as buses.

Tourist Information—Avenue Tariq ibn Ziad (Tel: 98 28 30), but they
generally only have a few pretty brochures.

7. Guided Tours

These are not a feature of Tangier life, unless you have come with an
organized group. Most of the travel agencies listed toward the end of the
chapter can arrange tours to surrounding places of interest.

8. Culture

The patron saint of Tangier is Sidi Bouaraquia. His *moussem* (religious
festival) takes place in the middle of the town, during the Mulud celebrations (July 7 in 1998, 10 days earlier in 1999, and so on).

For visitors, the cultural life of the town is best represented by four museums and a couple of art galleries. The **Kasbah Museum** *(Musée de la
Kasbah)* is situated in the Place de la Kasbah, high up with a good view over
the sea and protected by thick walls. It is housed in the old Royal Palace,
built by Mulay Ismail (Dar el-Makhzen). The entrance is by Bab el-Assa in
the Rue ben Raissouli in the medina (open from 9:00 A.M.-12:00 P.M. and
3:00 P.M.-6:30 P.M. and closed on Tuesdays). Avoid parking inside the kasbah walls if you have come by car. The museum has good examples of
crafts and antiquities, mainly 17th and 18th century. The interior decoration of the building makes a fine setting for the displays of ceramics, carpets, jewelry, *zellij* tiles, musical instruments, leather, and metalwork. There
is a small archaeological section. The gardens lead to the **Café-Restaurant
Detroit** on the second floor, which is usually crowded with tourists, because
of its associations with Brion Gysin, the Rolling Stones, trance musicians of
the 1960s, and the like.

To visit the **Old American Legation,** follow the instructions under section
6, "Sightseeing." The legation no longer has a diplomatic function, but it
houses a fascinating collection of 17th- to 20th-century paintings and engravings of old Tangier, an excellent art gallery, and what is probably the
best research library on Morocco and North Africa. (Altogether not to be

missed.) It still remains U.S. property, but in 1976 was leased to a private foundation. The museum is run by the American Legation Museum Society (3282 N Street NW, Washington DC 20007), a non-profit organization, and is always glad to receive donations (open Monday through Friday from 10:00 A.M.-1:00 P.M. and 3:00 P.M.-6:15 P.M). Groups are advised to arrange a rendezvous with the director, Mr. Kuniholm (Tel: 93 53 17). Entry is free.

A few minutes from the Legation is the new **Foundation Lorin** (44 Rue Touahin), an old synagogue. It has an interesting collection of old photographs and posters of Tangier ("Tangier's Memory"), and makes a useful complement to the Old Legation, as well as a painting workshop for the under-privileged children of the medina (open 11:00 A.M.-1:00 P.M. and 3:30 P.M.-7:30 P.M., with free entry).

The **Forbes Museum** (ex-Palais Mendoub, Rue Shakespeare), about 15 minutes on foot from the Place de la Kasbah, was created by the millionaire publisher Malcolm Forbes to house his extraordinary collection of over 100,000 miniature soldiers. Until recently, it contained many showcases with reconstructions (not always historically correct) of battle scenes such as the Battle of the Three Kings, Waterloo (where Napoleon was defeated in 1815), episodes of World Wars I and II, and the recent Moroccan Green March. I had always thought that the collection had been bequeathed to the town by Forbes before his death, but I've just learned that the Forbes family has sold almost all the collection and that the remaining soldiers are threatened with the same fate (and the house, too). Still, a few displays are there and the museum is well worth a visit. The house and gardens, overlooking the sea, are delightful (with impeccable water closets) (open from 10:00 A.M.-5:00 P.M., closed Thursdays and Sundays).

The **Museum of Contemporary Art** *(Musée d'Art Contemporain)* is lodged in the old, 19th-century British Consulate General (Rue Massella). The building and gardens are a bit shabby, but the museum is worth a visit for anyone interested in contemporary Moroccan painting (open from 9:00 A.M.-12:30 P.M. and 3:00 P.M.-6:30 P.M., closed on Tuesdays).

The private **Galerie Tanjah-Flandria** (6 Boulevard Mohammed V, in the hotel of the same name) is open every day (from 10:00 A.M.-1:00 P.M. and 5:00 P.M.-8:00 P.M.). It displays works by local artists and craftsmen. The **Institut Cervantes** (9 Rue de Belgique) has changing exhibitions by international and local artists.

A new cultural event took place in Tangier in July 1998: the first **music festival,** with music and dance from both sides of the Mediterranean. There were concerts of classical music, Andalusian music, Sufi music, Spanish flamenco, and Portuguese fado. Hopefully, it will become an annual event. An **arts festival** takes place in Asilah in the summer.

9. Sports

Tangier is situated on the shores of the Mediterranean, and a short distance from the Atlantic Ocean. But the polluted Tangier beach is horribly crowded, unless you are there in the depths of winter, and the Atlantic is neither safe nor particularly agreeable. Most big hotels have **swimming pools** and aquatic life is best led here, unless you're a fanatical water-skier and can persuade a motorboat to tow you around the bay (which would be expensive, and water-skiing and all forms of boat hire have, at the moment, been stopped). The Hotel Robinson, at Cap Spartel, will let you use their pool for 50 DH a day. Otherwise, your best bet is to head for the good beaches east of the town, around Malabata, the new tourist complex and Ksar es-Sghir. **Water sports** of all kinds are practiced at the resorts between Tetouan and Ceuta. Good beaches for **swimming** are those around Asilah and Larache. Much further afield, there is good swimming in Al-Hoceima and the bays and creeks around the area. Many big hotels have **tennis courts,** but they are not necessarily accessible to non-guests. The municipal tennis courts are situated in the Avenue de la Paix (Tel: 94 33 24). Guests of the Hotel El Minzah can **ride horses** and **play golf** by arrangement with the hotel. For **golfing enthusiasts,** the Royal Country Club of Tangier has 18 holes, par 72, and a length of 6,050 meters (Tel: 93 89 25). It was redesigned from its original layout by the British golf architect Frank Pennick. The terrain is undulating, with plenty of variety. The club is situated 4 km southwest of Tangier, and close to the Riding Club. There is a 9-hole course at Cabo Negro.

10. Shopping

Tangier is not a particularly good shopping center, and if you are planning visits to Rabat, Casablanca, Fès, or Marrakech, you would do better waiting until then. Having said this, the state-run **Craftwork Center** (*Ensemble Artisanal,* Rue de Belgique) is a good place to go to first. Prices are fixed (no bargaining) and attached to each article. Once you have an idea of the going prices, try your luck in the medina, in the Grand Socco, where haggling will definitely be necessary. Opposite the Hotel El Minzah you'll find the **Bazaar Tindouf** (64 Rue de la Liberté) selling authentic Moroccan and European antiques. It has the reputation of being the best shop of its kind in Tangier, but it is not cheap. Another shop specializing in antiques (as well as kaftans) is **Adolfo de Velasco** (26 Boulevard Mohammed V). The international bookshop, the **Librairie les Colonnes** (54 Boulevard Pasteur, Tel: 93 69 55), has English-language books, as well as a wide selection of books on Morocco, but the books are not always easy to find (closed Saturday afternoons and Sundays). Even if you don't need to buy food, take a look at the **Marché de Fès** (Rue de Fès). It is a charming, hassle-free small market, and stocks a variety of food and flowers, hens, baskets, and spices. (Please don't buy an exotic bird or even a monkey if you see one—this only encourages the capture of more of these unfortunate creatures.) The best hairdresser is **Chez Jean** in the center of town (Tel: 93 77 11), and at the Hotel El Minzah. **Studio Flash** (79 Rue de la Liberté) is a safe place to take your photos and have your camera repaired if necessary. Market day in any of the towns or villages is always worth going to for the pleasure of watching events and also, possibly, to pick up a bargain.

11. Entertainment and Nightlife

Apart from eating, drinking, dancing, or watching the world go by from the terrace of a café, entertainment is short in Tangier. The best cinema is the air-conditioned **Cinema Dawliz** (part of the Dawliz complex), which shows French-dubbed films. There used to be an amateur English-speaking theater group, but this has collapsed with the departure of so many foreigners. Very occasional concerts are given in the French Cultural Center (*Institut Français,* 86 Rue de la Liberté). The Dawliz complex also has **bowling.**

More interesting than the cinema are the bars. A good place for an evening drink is **Caid's Bar** in the Hotel El Minzah. Unfortunately, they have recently jazzed up this very traditional bar and it has lost much of its atmosphere, although it still has a large painting of Caid Maclean. The **Wine Bar,** in the same hotel, is also agreeable. Both are expensive. The **Mirage Piano Bar,** out by Cap Spartel, is a good place from which to watch the sunset across the Atlantic—but you really need a car as night taxis are expensive. **The Pub** (2 Rue Soraya, open from 12:00 P.M.-3:00 P.M. and 6:00 P.M.-2:00 A.M.) serves English beers and *tapas* (drinks from 50 DH). You can also eat there. The **Restaurant Bar Rubis** (3 Rue ibn Rochd) is a popular place for an evening drink. **Dean's Bar** (Rue Amérique du Sud, near the Big Socco) used to be a great haunt for expats, though it's gone down a bit now (it is not advised for women), and there are not many literary memories around. The old **1001 Nights,** frequented by Brion Gysin and his musical friends, is shut. In other towns in north Morocco, there are really only the hotel bars to comfort the thirsty evening drinker—or some pretty rough places.

Most of the big hotels in Tangier have a disco or nightclub. Currently those in the **Hotel Tanjah-Flandria** (open from 9:00 P.M.-3:00 A.M.) and the **Olivia Valere** in the **Ahlan Hotel** (on the Rabat road, see hotels above) are popular. **Regine Club Disco** is at 8 Rue Mansour Ed-Dahbi (open from 9:00 P.M.). Along the seafront, too, there are plenty of more or less dubious nightclubs. It's difficult to recommend any particular one, as they come in and out of fashion with great rapidity. For a rather phony folklore show, with belly dancing and all that—frequented however by Moroccans—try the **Morocco Palace** (11 Rue Prince Mulay Abdallah, Tel: 93 55 64).

12. The Tangier Address List

Airlines—Air France, 7 Rue du Mexique (Tel: 93 64 77); British Airways, Rue de la Liberté (Tel: 93 52 11); GB Airways, 83 Rue de la Liberté (Tel: 93 58 77); Iberia, 35 Boulevard Pasteur (Tel: 93 61 77/8/9); KLM, 7 Rue du Mexique (Tel: 93 89 26); Lufthansa, same address (Tel: 93 13 27); Royal Air Maroc, 1 Place de France (Tel: 93 55 01, Fax: 93 26 81).

Airport—Tangier Ibn Batuta Airport (Tel: 93 51 29).

Ambulances—(Tel: 15).

Banks—American Express (54 Boulevard Pasteur); BMCE, Boulevard Pasteur, open all week. Cash withdrawals with VISA card from BMCE, Credit du Maroc (Boulevard Pasteur) and the SGMB (Boulevard Mohammed V); plus many other banks on Boulevard Pasteur.

Bus Station *(gare routière)*—Place de la Ligue Arab *(Sahat al-Jamia al-Arabia)*; CTM buses: Place de la Marche Verte (Tel: 93 45 70).

Car Rental—Avis, 54 Boulevard Pasteur (Tel: 93 89 60); Budget, 7 Avenue Prince Mulay Abdallah (Tel: 93 79 94); Europcar, 87 Boulevard Mohammed V (Tel: 94 19 38); Goldcar, Hotel Solazur, Avenue des F.A.R. (Tel: 94 01 64); Hertz, 36 Boulevard Mohammed V (Tel: 70 92 27, 70 73 66).

Churches—St. Andrew's (Anglican), Rue d'Angleterre; Parroquia del Espiritu Santo (Cathédral), 55 Sidi Bouabid (Tel: 93 27 62), and Parroquia del Sagrado Corazon, 2 Rue ibn Zohr (Tel: 93 11 47) (both Spanish-speaking); Eglise Notre Dame de l'Assomption, Rue Omar el-Khattab (Tel: 94 04 26) (French-speaking); Chiesa di San Francesco, Mulay Idriss (Tel: 93 22 06) (Italian).

Consulates—France, 2 Place de France (Tel: 93 20 39/40); Great Britain, 4 Boulevard Mohammed V (Tel: 94 15 63) (opposite the Banque du Maroc). There is no U.S. Consulate. Contact the U.S. Embassy in Rabat if necessary (Tel: 07-76 22 65).

Doctors, Emergency—(Tel: 33 33 00).

Drugstore, Night *(Pharmacie de Nuit)*—22 Rue de Fès (Tel: 93 26 19). Each area has a Pharmacie de Garde for Sundays and holidays (address posted up outside any closed drugstore).

Ferry Services—Comanav, Division Passages, 43 Avenue Abou el-Alaa el-Maari (Tel: 94 04 88, 95 05 04, 94 23 50, Fax: 94 35 70, 94 40 22); Limadet Ferry, 13 Avenue Prince Mulay Abdallah (Tel: 93 36 25, Fax: 93 29 13); Transports Maritimes Trasmediterranea, 31 Avenue de la Résistance (Tel: 93 48 83).

Fire—(Tel: 15).

Hospitals and Clinics—Polyclinique de la Sécurité sociale, Route de Malabata (out of town) (Tel: 94 01 99). Day and night emergency service, but if possible call the U.S. Embassy in Rabat for advice (Tel: 07-76 22 65).

Jewish synagogue—an elegant white villa just to the left of the Tourist Office, Boulevard Pasteur.

Police—(Tel: 19).

Post Office—33 Boulevard Mohammed V.

Public Telephone—same address as the post office, open 24 hours a day, 7 days a week. Also téléboutiques, where you can telephone, send or receive a fax (sometimes), and buy stamps.

Railway Station—Gare de Mghogha, by exit road to Tetouan.

Taxis—Big taxi stand next to the bus station, Place de la Ligue Arab *(Sahat al-Jamia al-Arabia)*.

Tourist Information *(Délégation du Ministère du Tourisme)*—29 Boulevard Pasteur (Tel: 93 82 40). Most helpful and well-informed staff; has a list of hotels that can be consulted. Can suggest names of guides. Closed weekends.

Travel Agencies—Carlson Wagonslits, 86 Rue de la Liberté (Tel: 93 16 40); Globus Voyages, 3 Avenue Youssoufia (Tel: 94 29 05); Olive Branch Tours, 11 Rue Omar ibn al-Ahass (Tel: 93 80 83); Voyages Wasteels, Place de la Marche Verte (Tel: 93 81 85, Fax: 93 16 81).

Yacht Club—Port (Tel: 93 85 75).

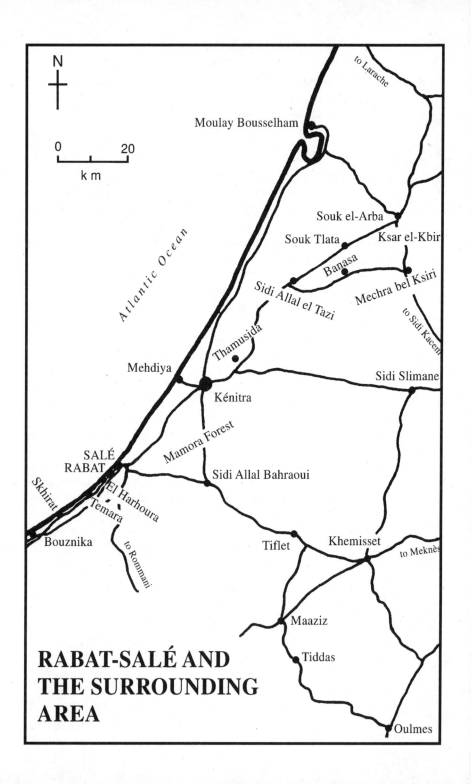

RABAT-SALÉ AND
THE SURROUNDING
AREA

6

Rabat-Salé and the Surrounding Area

1. The General Picture

Rabat and Salé, situated respectively on the left and right banks of the mouth of the Bou Regreg River, on the Atlantic Coast, some 270 km southwest of Tangier, are so intimately linked, both by their past and their present, that they are best taken together. The two agglomerations are often referred to, administratively at least, as Rabat-Salé. But each town jealously guards its individuality and, one has to add, keeps up its rivalry with its neighbor. Rabat is both an old imperial city and a new administrative capital. It was also the residence of the late King Hassan II. It is a well-kept, calm, and peaceful town in which the visitor can relax and enjoy the numerous sights of all periods without fuss or hassle. On the other side of the Bou Regreg River, Salé has an equally rich past and an energetic and fast-growing population. A stay of two to three days is advised in order to take in all the attractions of these two towns.

Early occupation. The earliest record of occupation in Rabat indicates that the Phoenicians, and then the Carthaginians, established a small settlement on what is now called the Chellah, near the mouth of the Bou Regreg

River, in the 3rd century B.C. The Romans continued to occupy the site, called Sala Colonia, in the 1st century A.D., but it was almost certainly inhabited, too, by the local Mauretanian people. Upon the departure of the Romans in the 4th century A.D., the latter, the Berber Berghouatas, set up a small independent state that particularly flourished in the 8th century A.D. They were followers of the Kharijite heresy and for this were attacked and subdued by the Idrissids in the 10th century. Forced to move across the river, they founded the town of Salé.

Almohad and later dynasties. In Rabat, the new powers built a *ribat,* or fortified monastery, on the site of the present Oudaya Kasbah. Later, in 1146, the Almohad sultan, Abd el-Mumen, converted the *ribat* into vast fortified camp, where he assembled his forces prior to the invasion of Spain. At the end of the 12th century, the *ribat,* now called Ribat el-Fath (Victory Fort) became the capital of the Almohad sultan Yacub el-Mansour. After his victory over the Spanish and Portuguese at the battle of Alarcos in 1195, he surrounded the town with over 5 km of fortified ramparts, with five gates. Two of these gates still exist: the gate leading to the Oudaya Kasbah and Bab er-Rouah. Yacub el-Mansour also started, but never finished, the construction of what was to have been one of the biggest mosques in the Islamic world, the Hassan Mosque. With the decline of the Almohad dynasty came the decline of Rabat when the Merinids chose Fès as their capital, though they did build a necropolis on the Roman site of Sala Colonia (Chellah) at the beginning of the 14th century, where they buried their sultans and important officials who had fought in Spain. The Merinids also built the walls of Salé. While Rabat dropped down, Salé climbed up. The town prospered and became an important commercial port, trading skins, wool, and ivory for manufactured goods brought in by English, Flemish, and Italian merchants. In the 16th century the population of Rabat had dwindled to a few hundred families, while Salé continued to enjoy its prosperity.

Corsairs. At the beginning of the 17th century, Rabat started to look up again with the arrival of Moslem Andalusian refugees fleeing from Christian Spain. Salé also benefited from the presence of these skilled craftsmen. In Rabat, they installed themselves in the Oudaya Kasbah and became very successful pirates, even setting up an independent pirate republic with Salé between 1647 and 1638. The raids of the "Sallee Rovers" in the Mediterranean and Atlantic, with their fleet of small, rapid, and well-armed sailing boats—often crewed by adventurers of all nationalities—earned them a terrifying reputation, to such an extent that the foreign powers were forced to negotiate with the Republic to stop the loss of their boats, men, and merchandise. Particularly prized captures were the merchant ships returning from the Americas laden with gold, but the Christian captives also came in useful as slave labor or as a trading commodity to be bought back by their respective countries. The pirates' activities greatly increased the prosperity of both towns. In 1666, Mulay Rashid tried to curtail their activities, but it needed Mulay Ismail's firm hand at the beginning of the 18th century to put an end to all this (albeit only temporarily, for sporadic piracy continued until the beginning of the 19th century).

The modern capital. The establishment of the French Protectorate from 1912 and the choice of Rabat as capital left Salé to itself, while encouraging the growth of Rabat and its transformation into a modern town. The two towns, while still being intimately linked in a love-hate relationship, followed different paths. The French Résident Général made Rabat the country's administrative center, and built a whole new town known as La Ville Nouvelle, leaving the medina untouched. The sultan, Mulay Yusef, was installed in a palace built on the site of the one briefly used by Mohammed III in the second half of the 18th century. Rabat has remained the seat of government and the principal royal residence since Moroccan independence in 1956. It houses all the ministries, foreign embassies, and international organizations, and so is considered the town of civil servants and diplomats. It also has a university. Both Rabat and Salé have grown enormously in the last decades: Rabat's population numbers 634,000, while that of Salé is 635,000. A further 197,000 people live in the neighboring towns of Skhirat and Temara, south of Rabat, which now almost form a single block with Rabat.

2. Getting There

At the moment, Transatlantic **flights** land in Casablanca. In the fall of 1998, Royal Air Maroc (RAM) announced a daily service from Paris to Rabat's airport, situated 10 km to the northeast. Air France also has a daily flight from Paris. From Casablanca, transit is possible once a week to Rabat-Salé by RAM (flight time is ½ hour—but it is much more convenient to take the train).

A very good **rail network** links Rabat with the main towns in Morocco, and this is a much simpler prospect than the plane, since the train lands you in the heart of the city. The train service that runs from Casablanca Mohammed V Airport to Casablanca town goes on to Rabat, Salé, and Kénitra. Departures are roughly every hour or two (first-class single fare to Rabat is 71 DH, second-class fare is 50 DH, and children are half-price). There is no longer a bus from the airport to Rabat, but a big taxi will make the trip (for at least 200 DH).

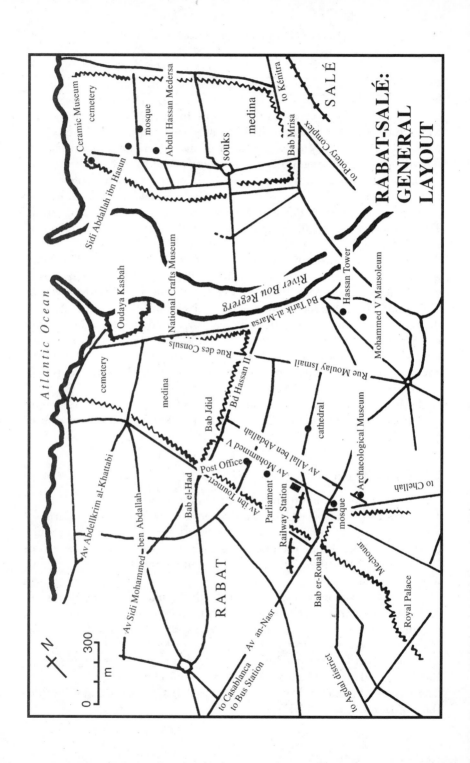

RABAT-SALÉ: GENERAL LAYOUT

SALÉ

to Kénitra

Ceramic Museum

cemetery

mosque

Abdul Hassan Medersa

medina

souks

Bab Mrisa

Sidi Abdallah ibn Hasun

to Pottery Complex

Atlantic Ocean

National Crafts Museum

Oudaya Kasbah

River Bou Regreg

Hassan Tower

Bd Tarik al-Marsa

Mohammed V Mausoleum

Rue des Consuls

Bd Hassan II

Rue Moulay Ismail

cemetery

medina

Bab Jdid

cathedral

Archaeological Museum

to Chellah

Av Allal ben Abdallah

Av Mohammed V

Post Office

Av ibn Toumert

Parliament

Railway Station

mosque

Av Abdellkrim al-Khattabi

Bab el-Had

Bab er-Rouah

Mechouar

Royal Palace

Av Sidi Mohammed — ben Abdallah

RABAT

Av an-Nasr

to Casablanca
to Bus Station

to Aqdal district

N

300

m

0

From Casablanca, fast and frequent trains (travel time about one hour) serve the Rabat suburb of Agdal and Rabat center (station on Avenue Mohammed V). The night train from Tangier to Casablanca (departing Tangier at 10:15 P.M.) and the more recommended day trains stop in Rabat, as do trains from Oujda (two a day, one night service), Fès, and Meknès (eight a day), and Marrakech (six a day). An escalator has recently been installed in the main Rabat station.

Long-distance Greyhound-type **buses** go from Europe to Rabat and other Moroccan towns (see chapter 2). The CTM bus company runs 15 buses a day from Casablanca to Rabat, and all other Moroccan towns are linked to Rabat by bus. Fares are lower than the train. The bus station is a bit out of town and inconvenient, as it means taking a taxi or a bus (N° 30) into the center. The bus station tends to be full of shouting men trying to lure customers into their bus, promising an earlier departure than their rivals, so arrival there can be quite disturbing.

There is no possibility of getting to Rabat by boat, unless you have your own. If you come by car from Europe, you can reach Rabat from Tangier, via the new highway (see chapter 5). The same remarks apply if you have rented a car, say in Tangier.

3. Local Transportation

Depending on what you want to do, how energetic you are, and how much time you intend to spend, you can either take a small taxi, a bus, or walk. I don't advise going places by car, since parking is the eternal problem. Small **taxis** (bright blue) are not expensive. A car will be useful for sightseeing out of town. Taking a **bus** is a bit of a problem in Rabat, since the bus routes are all in Arabic, but someone will certainly direct you to the stop you need.

4. The Hotel Scene

There should be no trouble choosing a hotel in Rabat to suit your tastes. Apart from the new **** **Hotel Le Dawliz,** just across the river, the choice of hotels is very limited in Salé.

The **regional telephone code** is 07 (0 omitted for in-region calls).

EXPENSIVE HOTELS

The three top ***** hotels all charge upwards of 1,450 DH a night, with breakfast around 100 DH. The ***** **Hilton** (220 rooms and suites, BP 450, Tel: 77 12 34, Fax: 77 24 92) is out of town in the Souissi district. It has extensive grounds, conference halls, business center, restaurants, *hammam*, tennis courts, swimming pool—all that one would expect from a ***** hotel but, of course, it is rather large and impersonal. It has recently been taken over by the South Korean Daewoo company. Personal transport or taxi needed.

The ***** **Hotel La Tour Hassan Meridien** (150 rooms, 26 Avenue Abderrahman Annegal, Tel: 72 14 91/70 42 01, Fax: 72 54 08) is more centrally placed and comfortable, and is beautifully decorated in Moroccan Andalusian style. It has conference rooms, a small Andalusian garden, swimming pool, fitness center, and a hairdresser—again all you could want—and has recently been taken over by the KTH hotel chain.

The last ***** hotel, with an excellent view across the Bou Regreg River, is the fairly new **Hotel Safir** (200 rooms, Place Sidi Makhlouf, near the northern exit from Rabat, Tel: 73 47 47, Fax: 72 21 55). As well as the view (if you get the right room), it has a pool and all the normal big-hotel amenities, though it's getting a bit shabby.

Charges fixed for the other hotels in this region are as follows (they vary according to the presence or absence of showers and water closet in the room): **** 367-458 DH or 470-635 DH, breakfast 50 DH for both; *** 183-292 DH or 207-331 DH, breakfast 37 DH for both; ** 100-176 DH or 109-127 DH, breakfast 24 DH for both; * 91-135 DH or 96-154 DH, breakfast 23 DH for both.

The **** **Hotel Bélère** (90 rooms, 33 Avenue Moulay Youssef, Tel: 70 98 01/70 36 89, Fax: 70 98 01) is well placed on the road going down to the station. If you want to spend time in the Archaeological Museum, the **** **Hotel Chellah,** almost alongside it, is the one for you (117 rooms, 2 Rue d'Ifni, Tel: 70 02 09/76 40 52, Fax: 70 63 54). It is also not far from the main street and the station.

A brand-new, very comfortable hotel that opened in August 1998 is the **** **Hotel Majliss** (65 rooms, 6 Rue Zahia, Tel: 73 37 26/27/28/31, Fax: 20 27 46), just to the left of the railway station. It has a bright stuccowork and marble entrance hall, but it's best to ask for a room overlooking the Parliament rather than those facing the railway lines.

In the Agdal suburb you have the **** **Hotel Soundous** (50 rooms, 9 suites, 10 Place Talha, Tel: 67 59 59/19, Fax: 67 58 68), about 10 minutes from the railway station. It has two restaurants, a piano bar, coffee shop, business center, and two conference rooms (as well as an Internet presence: http:www.mtds.ma/soundous).

On the other side of the Bou Regreg River (alongside it, in fact), the new **** **Hotel Le Dawliz** (43 rooms and suites, 750 DH, Avenue du Prince Héritier Sidi Mohammed, Bouregreg, Salé, Tel: 88 32 77/78/81, Fax: 88 32 79) is about five minutes by car from the center of Rabat and the airport, as well as being close to Salé. It has a cool and pleasant reception area with

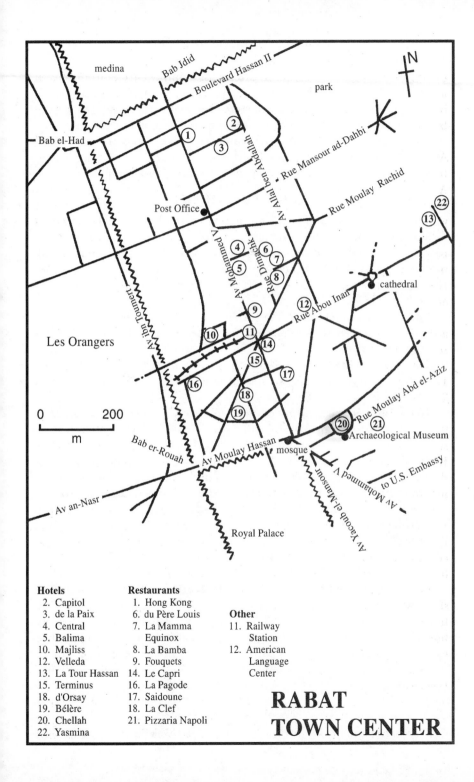

Hotels
2. Capitol
3. de la Paix
4. Central
5. Balima
10. Majliss
12. Velleda
13. La Tour Hassan
15. Terminus
18. d'Orsay
19. Bélère
20. Chellah
22. Yasmina

Restaurants
1. Hong Kong
6. du Père Louis
7. La Mamma
   Equinox
8. La Bamba
9. Fouquets
14. Le Capri
16. La Pagode
17. Saidoune
18. La Clef
21. Pizzaria Napoli

Other
11. Railway
   Station
12. American
   Language
   Center

RABAT
TOWN CENTER

central fountain and large, lurid, orientalist paintings. Its bedrooms, with balconies looking onto the swimming pool, are attractively furnished. It has four restaurants, a piano bar, a coffee shop, and a delightful view from the pool-side terrace across the river to Rabat. This is about the only hotel in Rabat where wheelchair travelers can have a bedroom on the same level as the terrace, pool, dining room, and bar. Within the Dawliz complex are three cinemas, a four-track bowling alley, billiards, and boutiques.

MEDIUM-PRICE HOTELS

There are a number of hotels in the ★★★ and ★★ categories. The ★★★ **Hotel Balima** (71 rooms, Avenue Mohammed V, Tel: 70 77 55, Fax: 70 74 50), is well situated on the main street, opposite the railway station, is functional, with good-sized bedrooms and a restaurant. It's one of Rabat's oldest hotels and its shaded garden café is a much-frequented meeting place because it is so easily recognized.

The ★★★ **Hotel Shéhérazade** (80 rooms, 21 Rue de Tunis, Tel: 72 22 26, Fax: 70 74 50), near the Mohammed V Mausoleum, is a bit out of the way but otherwise alright.

The ★★★ **Hotel Les Oudayas** (4 Rue Tobrouk, Tel: 70 78 20, Fax: 70 82 35), just opposite the Oudaya Kasbah, is also definitely not central, but useful for visiting the kasbah.

To the right as you come out of the train station is the ★★★ **Hotel Terminus** (384 Avenue Mohammed V, Tel: 70 52 67, 70 06 16, Fax: 70 19 26). It's a large, white painted building overlooking the main road (some rooms have balconies), with lots of *zellij* and stuccowork in the rather dark reception area, and is very conveniently placed in the center of town.

Another hotel near the main station is the ★★★ **Hotel d'Orsay** (31 rooms, 11 Avenue Moulay Youssef, Tel: 70 13 19, Fax: 70 19 26). Being at an important intersection, it's rather noisy during the day.

Another ★★★ hotel is the newish **Hotel Yasmina** (55 rooms, corner Rue Mariniyne/Rue Makka, close to the Catholic cathedral, Tel: 72 20 18, Fax: 72 21 00). Its rooms are clean and comfortable, and it is a good value.

In the Agdal suburb, the ★★★ **Hotel Moussafir** is within one minute of the Agdal railway station (95 rooms, 32/34 Rue Abderrahmane el-Ghafiki, Place de la Gare Rabat-Agdal, Tel: 77 49 49, Fax: 77 49 03), but you'll probably need a train, bus, or taxi to get into the center. It has Moroccan-style decoration and a garden with barbecue and music in the summer (there is also a restaurant with international menu at 95 DH, but there are better places to eat).

BUDGET ACCOMMODATIONS

These are ★ and unclassified hotels The ★ **Hotel Velleda** (106 Avenue Allal ben Abdallah, Tel: 76 95 31) and the ⋆ **Hotel Capitol** (same street, N° 34, Tel: 73 12 36) are both pretty simple, but they have elevators. The ⋆ **Hotel de la Paix** (2 Rue Ghazzah, off Avenue Allal ben Abdallah, Tel: 72 29 26) could also be tried.

One of the best cheap hotels (only recently declassified) is the **Hotel Central** (100 DH with shower, 2 Zankat al-Basra, Tel: 70 73 56). It is an unpretentious, rather old hotel, but is a good value, with a little salon where you can have breakfast (10 DH) or a cup of coffee.

There are a number of very cheap unclassified hotels in the medina (around 50 DH), if you continue down Avenue Mohammed V. However, they really are very basic and it's worth spending a bit more and getting something slightly better. One worthy of note in this group is the **Hotel Dorhmi** (313 Avenue Mohammed V, next door to a bank). It is a bit more expensive, at around 100 DH.

The **Youth Hostel** (34 Rue Marassa, Tel: 72 57 69, open from 8:00 A.M.-10:00 A.M., 12:00 P.M.-3:00 P.M., and 6:00 P.M.-10:00 P.M.) is down by the medina and the Bab el-Had gate. It's well placed, but the toilet facilities are not encouraging.

There's a campsite behind the beach at Salé, **Camping de la Plage,** that is not bad, but it gets very crowded (and dirty) in the summer. All the other campsites are along the coast going south towards Casablanca, and thus inconvenient for visiting the town.

5. Dining and Restaurants

Being the capital, Rabat has a relatively large expatriate population, so there is a good choice of restaurants, ranging from the expensive down to the very cheap. A number have their menu and prices posted outside.

HOTEL RESTAURANTS

All the big hotels have one or more restaurants, and it is often handy to eat in one of them. They don't always have the best food, but the following are exceptions. Rabat and Salé cooking is very varied, though following the normal Moroccan gastronomic tradition. The *tajines* here, for instance, have different ingredients from those of Fès.

The **Hilton Hotel** (Souissi, Tel: 77 12 34) has four restaurants, and one of them, El-Andalous, serves Moroccan food. Another, Le Justine, specializes in fish and has a very good selection of French wines. It is expensive (from 350 DH, excluding wine).

Some people feel that the El Mansour restaurant in **Hotel La Tour Hassan** (26 Avenue Abderrahman Annegal, Tel: 72 14 91) serves the best Moroccan food (about the same price).

I've been told that the restaurants in the Agdal district **Hotel Soundous** are excellent. Wood-fire grilled meat is a specialty of the Kanoun Grill in the **Hotel Chellah** (2 Rue Ifni, Tel: 70 02 09).

The **Hotel Balima** does a rather ordinary set meal for 118 DH (meat dishes from 70 DH, snacks in the shape of kebobs for 45 DH, and sandwiches for 40 DH). I think I'd avoid eating in the other hotel restaurants—they're alright, but one can do better elsewhere.

OTHER RESTAURANTS

If you want to eat Moroccan food, a very good restaurant—and an expensive one—is the **Restaurant Dinarjat** (6 Rue Belgnaoui, in the medina, off Boulevard el-Alou—parking here—near Hotel des Oudaias, Tel: 70 42 39, and it is best reserve in advance). This was once a sumptuous private house, and the atmosphere is still that of an Andalusian residence. If you go for the evening meal, you will be met at the medina entrance by a lantern-bearing guide and there will probably be a traditional floor show (main courses around 130 DH, and they are licensed to serve liquor). In fact, the lantern-man is a bit of a joke, as the district now has public lighting.

The **Restaurant La Koutoubia** (10 Rue Pierre Parent, close to the Archaeological Museum, Tel: 76 01 25, closed on Mondays) specializes in *tajines* and used to be very good, but I'm told that the quality is variable and there's quite a bit of dust around (main dish from 60 DH).

Going down the price scale, the **Restaurant La Clef** (next door to the Hotel d'Orsay, on the left-hand side along a small private room between the Rue Hatim and Avenue Moulay Youssef, Tel: 70 19 72) is a handy little restaurant close to the station, serving good Moroccan food. The restaurant is on the first floor and there is a noisy bar below (*harira* 10 DH, salads from 30 DH, *tajines* from 50 DH).

In the Agdal suburb, the attractive **Restaurant Chez el-Ouazzani** (Place ibn Yacine, Tel: 77 92 97, closes at 9:00 P.M.) has good kebobs (a specialty), *tajines,* and *harira* soup (about 50 DH for the kebobs, French fries, and Moroccan salad—no wine). It's often crowded and difficult to find a table.

There are, of course, plenty of other restaurants where you can get the traditional salads, kebobs, and soups—you might come across a real treasure!

International and French dishes can be had at **L'Entrecôte** (74 Avenue al-Amir Fal Ould Oumeir, Agdal suburb, Tel: 77 11 08, closed Sundays), specializing in fresh pasta and grilled meat, as well as fish (the main dish is around 100 DH).

An attractively decorated restaurant serving French food is **L'Eperon** (8 Rue al-Jazair, between the Cathedral and the Place Abraham Lincoln,

Tel: 72 59 01, closed Sundays) in the same price range as the above.

I used to frequently go to the **Restaurant du Père Louis** (Rue Dimashek, behind the Hotel Balima) for a calm, quiet meal (it is fine for single women) in an old-fashioned French decor, but the menu has become very restricted lately, and they've done away with the wine. But it is still not a bad address.

The upstairs restaurant **Le Fouquet's** (Avenue Mohammed V, downhill from the station and on the other side of the road) has a reasonable set meal at 85 DH.

Another fairly standard meal can be had from the **Restaurant Le Capri** (8 Place Mohammed V, on the corner of Avenue Mohammed V, more or less opposite the Hotel Terminus, Tel: 70 90 27) (set meal 65 DH, hamburgers from 30 DH).

A choice of four set menus is offered at the **Equinox** (2 Rue Tanta)— two at 70 DH, one at 75 DH, and one at 80 DH (salad, main dish, and dessert).

Italian food is, of course, popular, and a restaurant I recommend (and so does everyone else!) is **La Mamma** (6 Rue Tanta, Tel: 70 73 29/70 23 00, just behind the Hotel Balima and Avenue Mohammed V). It gets very hot and crowded at midday, but there is a calmer room alongside. They offer specialty pizzas (wide range of fillings, 55 DH), good salads (35 DH), and wine.

The **Pizzaria Napoli** (8 Rue Moulay Abd el-Aziz, Tel: 76 38 02) is a much simpler, quieter place (very suitable for single women) with pizzas and pasta from 50 DH (no wine).

Within the Marjane supermarket complex on the way to Salé, the familiar **Pizza Hut** is just what one would expect. There is another one in Agdal (107 Avenue Fal Ould Oumeir) (both with pizzas from 50 DH).

A modest little Lebanese restaurant, the **Restaurant Saidoune** (467 Avenue Mohammed V, Tel: 70 92 26), tucked away in an arcade, just opposite the Hotel Terminus, serves very reasonable meals (salads 10 DH, *tajines* from 50 DH, Lebanese sandwiches 12 DH). It's also possible to eat vegetarian there (they are closed Fridays).

Good fish restaurants, both near the beach, are the **Restaurant de la Plage** (Plage des Oudayas, Tel: 72 31 48, closed Sundays), below the Oudaya Kasbah, overlooking the sea, and **Borj Eddar** (Plage de Rabat [Sidi el-Yabouri], Tel: 70 15 00/1). Both are fairly pricey, with the main course from 100 DH, but the view is splendid. Both close in winter.

Back in town, **Le Goéland** (9 Rue Moulay Ali Chérif, Tel: 76 88 85, closed Sundays) is expensive (from 150 DH) but the fish and shellfish are excellent and the setting is agreeable.

A much cheaper option is the restaurant **La Bamba** (3 Rue Tanta, just opposite La Mamma restaurant, Tel: 70 98 39). It also has a good reputation and an interesting menu, specializing in fish (Moroccan set meal 110 DH, "classic" set meal 95 DH).

If you are absolutely craving Oriental food, or have had your fill of Moroccan *tajines*, you could try the **Hong Kong** (261 Avenue Mohammed V, Tel: 72 35 94) for Chinese and Oriental cooking (main dish around 60 DH).

La Pagode (13 Rue Baghdad, Tel: 70 93 81), right at the end of this road running parallel to the railway line, offers Vietnamese and Chinese specialties (soup from 45 DH, main dish from 70 DH, open midday and in the evening; closed Mondays). The cooking is good but the service is slow.

The **Fuji** in the Agdal suburb has Japanese specialties (2 Rue Michlifen, Tel: 67 35 83), and in the more distant suburb of Souissi, going out of town, behind the supermarket on the main road, the **Le Dragon D'Or** (Tel: 75 55 77) serves good oriental food, although the service is a bit slow and the price a bit high (from 80 DH, closed Sundays).

OTHER PLACES TO EAT AND DRINK

There is the familiar **McDonald's** in the center of town (Avenue Prince Mulay Abdallah, at the top of the street opposite the train station) where you can eat a chicken or fish burger with french fries from 30 DH in a rather uninspiring decor.

Burgers and kebobs can be had at the nearby **La Bidoche** (about a third of the price) and **Fax Food** (Boulevard Hassan II) (around 20 DH).

If it's roast chicken you're after, the **Taki Fried Chicken** (281 Avenue Mohammed V, down a short alley) might suit you, though it entirely lacks charm or even interest. Still, the chickens look all right, and it's not easy to find a snack joint around here (hamburgers from 15 DH, pizzas 33 DH, chicken 42 DH).

Near the Cathedral, **Le Crépuscule** (10 Rue Laghouat) does pancakes, pizzas, and salads, and is a haunt of Rabat's young.

There are hundreds of places in which to stop and have a coffee, but the terrace of the **Hotel Balima** (71 Avenue Mohammed V), with its well-spaced tables and shady trees, is an obvious choice if you are in the area (the café's public water closet is the squat-bucket-tap kind, with no paper).

Still in Avenue Mohammed V, the **Pâtisserie Quatre Saisons** has a good selection of pastries and pizzas, and upstairs seating.

Rue Tanta (just behind the Hotel Balima) houses **La Dolche Vita,** which has what is considered the best ice cream in Rabat, made by the family that owns the adjoining restaurant, La Mamma.

The **Pâtisserie La Petite Duchesse** (1 Avenue Mulay Abdallah) also has a very good reputation for sweet and savory takeaways and chocolates. The **Pâtisserie Lina** (45 Avenue Allal ben Abdallah) is a nice, quiet coffee shop in which to have tea, coffee, or pastries (women-friendly and no smoking).

And, of course, an absolute must is the **Café Maure** in the Oudaya Kasbah (go through one of the main gates and work your way towards the river, see "Sightseeing" section below). The café has a splendid view over Salé and the mouth of the Bou Regreg River. Mint tea and Moroccan pastries are the specialty. It is a good place in which to linger and relax, but is best in the late afternoon, as it tends to fill up with tourists at other times.

6. Sightseeing

IN RABAT

The order in which you will visit the sights depends, of course, on where you are staying. But for convenience, I will start with the new town (La Ville Nouvelle), although if your time is short (one day), you should head for the oldest historical part of Rabat, the Hassan Tower (and the modern Mausoleum of Mohammed V alongside), the Oudaya Kasbah, and the medina in the morning, and the Archaeological Museum in the afternoon, followed by the Chellah necropolis. A second day will allow a visit to the Abul Hassan Medersa in Salé and whatever of the many other possibilities attracts you.

The **Royal Palace** (near the mosque at the head of Avenue Mohammed V) itself cannot be visited, but you can walk through the parade ground from an entrance near Bab er-Rouah and come out on the other side, towards the Chellah. On the left is a small mosque, dating from the 18th century, where the king kills the ritual ram on the Feast of the Sacrifice. The buildings date from the 19th century, and house not only the king and his family, but the Royal Guard, the royal school, and the royal cooking school (set up by Hassan II to keep up the high standards of Moroccan cooking). The palace itself lies at the end of a vast parade ground, the *Mechouar,* where 500,000 delirious Moroccans assembled to celebrate the return of the sultan Mohammed V in 1955, and on occasion still accommodates a host of personalities coming to pay tribute to the reigning sovereign. In actual fact, the late King Hassan II spent most of his time in the more congenial palace of Dar Es-Salam, a bit out of town. It is not yet known whether his son will follow his example.

While you are up in the palace area, the **Bab er-Rouah** (The Gate of the Winds) (late 12th century) is the finest in the Almohad ramparts, best admired coming up the Avenue de la Victoire (but the ramparts here have been pulled down and redesigned to allow for a smoother flow of traffic into the town). Although somewhat similar to the Oudaya gate, Bab er-Rouah had an evident defensive role. The arched gateway, between two bastions, and its frame are decorated with floral motifs, palmette-scallops, Koranic inscriptions in Kufic letters, and imbricated curves. Moving back down into the centre, the **St. Peter's Cathedral** (*Cathédral Saint Pierre*), Place al-Joulane, was inaugurated in 1921 and the façade restored in 1937. Some of its stained-glass windows are of Arab inspiration. It is the seat of the Bishop of Rabat. Further down, a large building on the left-hand side of Avenue Mohammed V houses the Moroccan Parliament. The **Mausoleum of Mohammed V** (*Mausolée Mohammed V*) lies to the east of the town, beside the **Hassan Tower** (*Tour Hassan*). Both are striking monuments, in totally different ways and of totally different dates. The first is a white, green-tiled pavilion, reached by a flight of steps from the road. Mounted guards, in red and white uniforms, stand watch over the monument, which was built by the late King Hassan II to house the tomb of his father, Mohammed V (his brother, Mulay Abdallah, who died in 1972, also has his tomb there). Visitors walk around a first-floor gallery and can peer down onto the white onyx tomb and admire the rich stuccowork, the black marble, the intricate wood carving of the ceiling, the bronze lamps, and the traditional colored *zellij* mosaics, and listen to the chanting of verses from the Koran (free entry, suitable clothing essential).

The Hassan Tower is the minaret of the mosque started by Yacub el-Mansour in 1194, but never finished. It is considered by some to be the finest Almohad monument. The columns visible today are mostly the result of excavation and reconstruction, from which it is clear that the original plan of the mosque followed the standard Almohad T-shape. The minaret is remarkable for its size—uncompleted it reaches 45 m. Upon completion, the top of the cupola would have measured 80 m. Inside, a ramp winds its way up to the top. The decoration is classically Almohad, sober and simple—interlacing curves, intersecting arcs, net-like designs. It differs on each side of the building. As is customary in Almohad minarets, there are no inscriptions and no floral designs. The reddish-brown stone gives an impression of strength and solidity and hasn't any applied colored tiles as in the Koutoubia mosque of Marrakesh.

The next places of interest are the **medina** and the **Oudaya Kasbah,** both overlooking the Bou Regreg River. The former dates from the 17th century and has no monuments of great interest, though it's worth walking through, and you can work your way to the bustling Rue des Consuls (see "Shopping" section), where the representatives of the various foreign powers were obliged to live until 1912. The Rue des Consuls leads to the Wool Market (*Souk el-Ghezel*), where Christian captives were sold in the 16th and 17th centuries. The old Jewish quarter (*mellah*), laid out by Mulay Sliman at the beginning of the 19th century, is close by, but the synagogues have either tumbled down or are used as storehouses.

From the Rue des Consuls, cross the busy (and dangerous) Boulevard Tarik al-Marsa to visit the Oudaya Kasbah. The name Oudaya comes from the Arab Oudaya tribe who arrived in Morocco in the 13th century and who were finally posted here by Mulay Ismail. The best entrance to the kasbah is the Kasbah Gate *(Bab al-Qasba)* at the top of the hill (no need to take a guide, the kasbah is quite small and bounded by the Bou Regreg River). Unlike Bab er-Rouah, which it resembles, it was not intended to be defensive, despite the towers on either side, since the kasbah lay inside the ramparts built by Abdelmoumen in 1150 (reinforced in the 17th and 18th centuries). It was in fact built around 1195 by Yacub el-Mansour. The gate's style is pure Almohad: outside the pointed, *outrepassé* arch is a blind arch, itself outlined by geometric carvings. The familiar scallop shell can be seen among floral decorations in the corners. Steps lead up to a series of rooms, the first domed, with cusped arches forming the exits. Right from here, the main street, Rue Jamaa, takes you into the kasbah. Have a look at some of the carved wooden doors. At the end of the Rue Jamaa (about 250 m), the **Semaphore Platform** *(Plate-forme du Sémaphore)* provides a good view over the river-mouth to Salé. Halfway up to the left is the Kasbah Mosque, the oldest in Rabat, dating to around 1150, but restored in the 18th century by a Englishman who converted to Islam, Ahmed el-Inglizi. There is a small carpet factory in a corner of the Platform. Going back towards the gate, the second little street on the left will take you into the **Café Maure** (see above).

The **Chellah** lies to the east, outside the city walls. One way to get to it is by walking through the Palace, and turning left out of the gate in the Almohad rampart. From there the walls and monumental gate of the Merinid necropolis are clearly visible (open every day from 9:00 A.M.-6:00 P.M., entry 10 DH including visit to Roman ruins). From a flourishing Roman city, the site became an abandoned mass of ruins in the 10th century, before the Merinids turned it into a huge cemetery at the end of the 13th century, which in turn was destroyed by the Lisbon earthquake in 1755. The entry gate, L-shaped in plan, although richly decorated, is less imposing than the two Almohad gates. It is composed of a pointed, *outrepassé* arch flanked by blind arches, framed by a rectangle filled with floral patterns. The inscription at the top gives the name of the Merinid sultan who ordered the construction of the walls. Once inside, a flat area allows a good view of the Roman town to the left and the Merinid necropolis and minaret to the right. The path downhill is flanked by luxuriant vegetation—fig, olive and orange trees, bougainvillaeas, flowers, and vegetables. On the left the ruins of the Roman Sala Colonia are currently (but slowly) being excavated. Long closed to visitors, it is now open and a guide is there to show you around to look at the temples, public baths and latrines, forum, triumphal arch, shops, and houses that have been brought to light (some items are in the Archaeological Museum). To the right, in the Moslem part of the Chellah, are the minarets of the *zaouia* (religious fraternity) and the mosque of Abu Yusef Yacub, the first sultan to be buried in the Chellah. The mosque is ruined, but the marble and colored tile decoration of the *zaouia* minaret still remains. The minaret has a very photogenic stork's nest perched on the top. The tiny rooms of the students can still be seen, as well as part of the small *medersa* (religious study and boarding center) endowed by Abul Hassan and the *mihrab* (prayer niche indicating the direction of Mecca) at the end of the building, opposite the minaret. In the old days, walking around the *mihrab* seven times was the equivalent of making the pilgrimage to Mecca and gave one the title of *haj*. Around here lie the tombs of Abul Hassan, the best-known of the Merinid monarchs, and his favorite wife, Chems ad-Dawha (Morning Sun, a European converted to Islam), together with the tombs of various local saints (noticeable by their white, domed *kubbas*), scattered in some confusion. Abul Hassan is nick-named "The Black Sultan" because of his black-skinned mother. Further on, usually a bit crowded, is the spring-fed pool, where sterile women come and throw peeled boiled eggs (available on the site) to the sacred eels glid-ing about in the depths. The eels only eat the whites, and the yolks get given to the assembled cats, who obviously know the ropes.

IN SALÉ

Leaving Rabat to cross the river to Salé, there are plenty of saints' tombs to be seen in the medina, as Salé is famous for its saints. They are the scene of numerous pilgrimages, mostly by women looking for solutions to their problems (sterility, ill-health, flighty husband, etc.) (see "Culture" section for the annual pilgrimage to the tomb of Sidi Abdallah ibn Hasun).

The large **Bab Mrisa** (Gate of the Little Harbor) leads into the medina from the main Rabat-Salé road. It is the oldest standing Merinid monument in Salé, built by the sultan Abu Yusef Yacub (see "Chellah" above, also) around 1270. It looks quite Almohad in its decoration, though its propor-tions and curve of the arch are different. The gate was fortified, and its pointed, *outrepassé* arch was high enough (almost 11 m) to allow sailing boats to come up the channel from the river (now silted up) to the dry-docks. They remind one that Salé used to be a famous port. As you walk through the streets, try to imagine Salé as the 17th-century pirate haunt it once was.

From Bab Mrisa the easiest way to reach the **Medersa of Abul Hassan** is probably to try and keep more or less straight down the Rue Ach-Chahid

Ahmed ben Abboud (old *mellah* on the right) past a little square *(Bab el-Khebbaz)*, around the Wool Market *(Souk el-Ghezel)*, turning left after that into the Rue Ras as-Shajara, which will lead you to the *medersa*, and, after some steps, to the *zaouias* of Sidi Ahmed at-Tijani, Sidi Abdallah ibn Hasun, and the Great Mosque. The big cemetery and the Ceramic Museum (see "Culture," section 7) lie ahead. The mosque was originally built by an Almohad sultan at the end of the 12th century, but the minaret and door are recent. The *medersa* was built by Abul Hassan at the beginning of the 14th century. It is thought to be one of the best examples of Merinid decoration. *Medersas* are the only religious buildings open to non-Moslems, so this particularly attractive, small example should not be missed (closed Fridays, entry 10 DH). The entrance is a pointed *outrepassé* arch surrounded by a blind arch, floral decoration, and an Arabic inscription. The interior courtyard is surrounded by a gallery with *zellij*-covered pillars. The painted cedar ceilings and the stuccowork (some of it restored) are admirable. The fourth side of the central court contains the prayer room. On the right as you go in, a rectangular marble panel carved in cursive script bears an inscription about the *medersa's* foundation. A staircase to the right leads up to students' pocket-sized rooms, from which there is a good view over Salé and its houses (reminiscent of Andalusian Spain).

SOUTH OF RABAT

The coastal road **south** from Rabat leads to numerous popular beaches—El Harhoura (12 km), Temara (18 km), Contrabandiers, Sables d'Or, Ech-Chiana (also known as Jawhara), Skhirat (24 km), Bouznika (36 km), Dahomy, David, Mansouria (54 km), and Pont Blondin. Then comes Mohammedia, described in chapter 10. The beaches follow each other so thickly that you scarcely know when you have left one and reached another. When I first came to Morocco, the sands were backed by simple, wooden, one-room beach huts. Development has turned the coast into mini-towns with high-quality villas in some of the classier resorts. The area is also popular for children's vacation camps, run by ministries, banks, and public establishments. The beaches are accessible by car, big taxi, or bus (by a train, too, and the stations are a good way from the beach). If you fancy a swimming session or an afternoon's surfing, remember that the Atlantic waves are big and unpredictable, with a strong undertow.

Archaeologically, this coast has been vital for knowledge of prehistoric man. Caves cut into the fossil cliffs were used when the sea stood much higher than nowadays. Those at Dar es-Soltan, El Harhoura, M'nasra, and Temara have been excavated and have produced Palaeolithic, Neolithic, and Copper Age weapons or pottery, as well as several burials (one has been reconstructed in the Archaeological Museum, see "Culture," section 7). The Contrabandiers cave, fenced in, on the left as you drive down, is theoretically visitable, but I've never found the guardian. You can look in through the iron bars and ponder on the stratigraphy, for there is little else to see.

There are many hotels and campsites along the coast, and plenty of restaurants and cafés. Being highly popular destinations, the quality of these establishments is very uneven. The **Miramar** restaurant at **El Harhoura** serves good fish dishes.

Temara is a very lively destination (now a dormitory town for Rabat) both by day and night. The **Hotel Temara Plage** (Tel: 74 42 30) also has a restaurant.

The new second-class club, **Hotel Club Jasmin** at **Temara** (Route de Temara, Harhoura, Tel: 64 13 52/53, Fax: 64 13 54) has a very good reputation. The town of Temara (inland) boasts a kasbah built by Mulay Ismail. It cannot be visited without permission, as it houses a royal stud farm (but if you do get in, the horses are superb).

The zoo, too, is at **Temara** (see "Entertainment," section 11).

The ** **Hotel La Felouque** (23 rooms, Tel: 74 43 88, Fax: .74 43 88) at Sables d'Or beach has a swimming pool, garden, and a restaurant, but exploits its position as far as food prices are concerned.

The * **Motel Panorama des Sables d'Or** (Tel: 74 42 89), which is quite new, is not bad. The **Sables d'Or** restaurant specializes in fish.

At the **Ech-Chiana** beach the *** **Hotel Le Kasbah** (Tel: 74 91 16/33, Fax: 74 91 53) has a pool, horseback riding, and a disco in summer.

King Hassan II had a summer palace at **Skhirat,** but is said that he rarely used it since the failed coup d'état by army officers during the birthday celebrations in 1971 that ended in the deaths of many guests.

In the spring of 1998, a Saudi-British company (Britannic Hotels Company) came up with plans to build a luxury hotel complex to be called the **Millenium Palace,** pulling down the Hotel Skhirat Beach Hotel (ex-L'Amphitrite).

The **Restaurant La Potinière** at Skhirat (Tel: 74 22 04) overlooks the beach, and gives the impression of an old-fashioned French family hotel, but provides a delicious lunch on Sundays (140 DH, order the day before, closed at all other times).

Mansouria Beach is frequented by line-fisherman hanging their lines into the creek more than by bathers. Inland, the old, ochre-colored **Mansouria Kasbah** (the work of the Alaouite sultan Mulay Ismail) and the minaret of its mosque are clearly visible. Someone thought of turning the kasbah into a hotel a few years ago, but the idea seems to have been dropped.

A short drive east out Rabat, towards Meknès, brings you to the **lake** formed by the dam on the Oued Mellah (about 20 km, reached by turning right 7 km out from Rabat). R'bati and Casablancans go here to surf and swim. It is also good for a picnic.

NORTH OF SALÉ

North from Rabat is not for swimmers—the beaches are notoriously dangerous. But there are other things to do. On the road to Kénitra, the **Bouknadel Exotic Gardens** *(Les Jardins Exotiques de Sidi Bouknadel)* lay 12 km from Salé, on the left, and are badly indicated (bus N° 23 from Salé). This is not a botanical garden in which you can see Moroccan flora, but an attractive collection of non-Moroccan trees (see "Culture," section 7).

To the right lies the **Mamora Forest,** thinly filled with rather spaced-out cork oaks, the bark of which is used to make wine bottle corks, among other things. It makes up half the cork-oak plantations of Morocco, but has suffered a lot of depredation in recent years.

Six kilometers further on, a turn to the left leads to the ****** Hotel Firdaous** (Plage des Nations, Tel: 82 21 31/32, Fax: 82 21 43) and the **Plage des Nations Beach,** which is very dangerous for swimming, but nice to walk along. It is better to use the hotel swimming pool, even though it is open to non-residents. U.S. forces landed here in the November 8-10, 1942 "Operation Torch." Between this beach and Mehdiya, a bit to the north at the mouth of the River Sebou, the cruisers *Texas* and *Savannah,* two aircraft carriers, three destroyers, four escorters, eight transport ships, and 9,000 men were waiting off the mouth of the River Sebou, aiming to land at midnight on November 8. Unfortunately, operations were delayed, which caused the unnecessary loss of lives. Sadly, too, some 300 U.S. soldiers, loaded down with equipment and unable to cope with the heavy swell and undertow, were drowned before even setting foot on the beaches.

About 17 km from Rabat, on the right, a private museum, the **Belghazi Museum** *(Musée Dar Belghazi),* has one of the best and largest collections of traditional Moroccan craftwork I've seen, and should certainly be visited if time permits (see "Culture," section 7).

Further up the coast, 40 km from Rabat, the **beach** of **Mehdiya** proved equally fatal to the landing craft, many of which were overturned by the waves, and soldiers trying to get ashore. At Mehdiya there is a seaside complex, **L'Atlantique** (it is expensive for what you get), and two restaurants, the **Restaurant Belle Vue** (menu 70 DH) and **Le Dauphin** (which is cheaper).

Mehdiya Kasbah is an impressive place, strategically placed overlooking the Atlantic. The site is though to have been occupied by the Carthaginians, then by local Berber people who called it "La Mamora."

The Almohad leader, Abd el-Mumen, fortified it in the 12th century. Then the port of Mehdiya became an active stronghold of English pirates, until the Spanish sent in a fleet in the 17th century and built the fortress more or less as it stands today, except for the massive gateway that was built by Mulay Ismail, who captured the fort in 1681 and called it Mehdiya. Inside the kasbah, an elegant doorway leads to the old palace of the governor. Its outbuildings included a *hammam* (hot baths), a mosque, and stables. In 1795, the reigning sultan ordered the port to be closed, but the fishing port at the mouth of the river is still active. A bit inland from Mehdiya (indicated by a sign), the large **Sidi Bourhaba Lake** is well known to bird-watchers. Luckily it's protected, for the number of migrating species to be seen here (said to total around 200) makes it one of the most important bird sanctuaries in Morocco. Information on the birds for the non-initiated can be had from an office on the east side of the lake, fieldglasses can be rented, and there are circuits laid out that even wheelchair bird enthusiasts can use. The lake is open all day. The best time of year for visiting is winter.

The main P2 road going north heads into **Kénitra** (40 km from Rabat, 10 km from Mehdiya), a town of little tourist interest. It was built in 1913 by the French (and called Port Lyautey at the time) and is today an agricultural and industrial center, with a port still engaged in exporting local products. In 1951, the United States signed an agreement with Morocco for the establishment of seven airforce bases in the country, mostly in the Gharb, and the U.S. still maintains American staff in Kénitra, at what used to be one of the biggest of their bases. It was from here that Moroccan pilots took off in 1972 in an attempt to shoot down King Hassan II's Boeing as he returned from a trip to Spain. Only great presence of mind by the pilot prevented the attempt from being successful.

Kénitra is on the main Casablanca-Tangier and Casablanca-Oujda **railway lines,** as well as being served by a rapid shuttle service to and from Rabat. CTM and other **buses,** as well as **big taxis** go frequently to Kénitra.

The best hotel is the ★★★ **Hotel Safir** (Place de l'Hôtel de Ville, Tel: 37 19 21). It has a swimming pool and it is best to have a room poolside, since the others are noisy. More modest, the ★★ **Hotel Mamora** (also Place de l'Hôtel de Ville, Tel: 37 17 75, Fax: 37 14 46) has a pool and restaurant, and is the next best after the Safir.

The ★ **Hotel La Rotonde** (80 Avenue Mohammed Diouri, Tel: 37 14 01), is, quite honestly, *very* noisy and agitated, but its restaurant is acceptable. French-speaking Catholic *mass* is celebrated in the Eglise du Christ Roi, 17 Rue Mohammed Abdoub (Tel: 37 99 52).

A longer excursion from Rabat-Salé, still possible in a day, is **northwards** to the **Roman** sites of **Thamusida** and **Banasa** and the attractive little **coastal resort** and **birdwatchers' paradise** of **Moulay Bousselham.** All involve taking the P2, though the return could be made along the expressway (entry Moulay Bousselham, 70 km to Rabat-Salé, toll 30 DH). It's not possible to visit these places by train, but the CTM and other buses going north from Kénitra will drop passengers within a few kilometers of Thamusida (which is hard to find).

Thamusida lies about 12 km north of Kénitra. It is really only of interest to those attracted to Roman ruins. About 4 ½ km after the right-hand turn to Sidi Kacem, a track to the left, going more or less northwest (keep to the principal one) leads to the site (5 km). A white *kubba* (saint's shrine) overlooks the site. Current opinion places the foundation of Thamusida around the third century B.C., as no older objects have yet been found. Essentially a military camp, of rectangular shape, it was in the past frequently covered with meters of flood debris from the River Sebou. The site has only been partially excavated, and its interpretation is not easy for the unspecialized visitor. From a small natural hillock, however, the layout of the town becomes apparent: on one side were the houses and shops, on the other the military installations, then further on the baths, and further still a *garum* (fish paste) production area. A broad track and a small archway, some fairly well preserved baths, a three-celled temple, and a couple of towers make up the more recognizable items.

To reach **Banasa,** continue along the P2 as far as the turn on the right to Mechra bel Ksiri (S212), about 30 km from Kénitra (if you arrive in Sidi-Allal el-Tazi you have gone a few kilometers too far). Take this secondary road (keep left at the T-junction) until, after about 25 km, a sign on the left marked "Ruins" (not visible except from the Mechra bel Ksiri direction) indicates a track to the site, also with a white *kubba* as landmark. It's not easy to reach Banasa without some form of transport. Banasa—more strictly Julius Valentia Banasa—was founded at the end of the first century B.C. as a colony for Roman veterans who farmed the surrounding land. It was first identified in 1871, and has been periodically excavated ever since. Material from the site (350 m² of mosaics were unearthed) has been removed to the Archaeological Museum in Rabat. On-going research by a Franco-Moroccan team has concentrated on the baths, the biggest in Morocco, dating from the second century A.D., and improved in the middle of the third century. Visible now are the remains of a paved forum, capitol (the colony's main temple), a possible basilica, smaller temples, houses, shops, and paved roads. A market was perhaps situated behind the shops. Banasa, noted for its baths, has what have been called the Big Western Baths, the Fresco Baths, the Little Western Baths, and the Northern Baths. However, the most inter-esting are undoubtedly the Fresco Baths to the west of the site, where the mosaics and pale red frescos are still in place.

From Banasa, the coastal site of **Moulay Bousselham** (halfway between Rabat and Tangier) is easily reached by turning left on the main road from the ruins, towards Mechra bel Ksiri, then left and northwards to **Souk el-Arba du Gharb**. From here there are regular **buses** and **big taxis** (distance about 45 km). Non-motorized travelers will perhaps give Banasa a miss and go straight from Kénitra to Souk el-Arba du Gharb. Souk el-Arba du Gharb lies in the middle of the Gharb plain, a rich agricultural area often subject to severe flooding. New dams have considerably lessened this risk. This sprawling agricultural town looks as though it contains nothing but cafés, all turning out kebobs. The new expressway, alas, has put many of the butchers, kebob cookers, and cafés out of business, since the Tangier to Casablanca traffic now by-passes the town. From Souk el-Arba du Gharb, the S216 going west winds around a bit before reaching Moulay Bousselham, perched on a hill with a fine view over the sea (bathing there is dangerous) and the lagoon.

The little village is pleasant enough, frequented by Moroccans in the summer, and by birdwatchers (mostly foreign) at any time of the year, but particularly in winter for the migrant species. The appeal of Moulay Bousselham for some people is its large lagoon, Merja Zerga (hired boats are available) and beach, which attract pink flamingos, spoonbills, herons, ducks of all kinds, all sorts of waders, and a number of rare species. Others prefer to make a pilgrimage to a nearby cave, while many prefer to partic-ipate in the important annual *moussem* (religious festival) held in the sum-mer in honor of Moulay Bousselham ("the man with the cloak"), a Sufi saint who is said to have come to Morocco from Egypt in the 10th century. His tomb is one of the white-domed *kubbas*.

The **hotel scene** is very limited. The **Hotel Lagon** (around 200 DH, Tel: 43 26 03) is frankly run-down and cannot be recommended at all. The campsite is noisy and infected with mosquitoes.

My Rabat friends go to a small place calling itself a "Residential Club," **Villa Nora** (bed and breakfast only, 200 DH, Tel: 43 20 71) run by an Englishman (Alan) and his sister. It is reached by a small road off the main street, at the end of the village, on the seafront. It has five old-fashioned but comfortable bedrooms. The owners will provide an evening meal (100 DH) if warned in time. This is a very pleasant little place and the small art gallery on the upper-floor exhibits local talent. Hunting, fishing, bird-watching, surfing, and other water sports can be arranged.

Budget accommodations can be had at the **Hostal Flora** (100 DH, Tel: 91 22 50).

The best of the small **restaurants** are **La Jeunesse** and **l'Océan** (main dish 40 DH). Moulay Bousselham can also be reached direct from Kénitra by the coastal road, S206.

Going **east** after sightseeing in Rabat, a visit to the spa town of **Oulmes** provides a nice change of air (100 km as the crow flies, but by road quite a bit longer). It is possible as a day's outing, but it's better to spend the night there and enjoy the charms of the countryside (it is not on a **bus** route, but possible, of course, by **big taxi**).

Oulmes lies at a height of 1,1257 m, so it is pleasantly cool in summer. Take the road out of Rabat, toward Meknès (the beginning of the motor-way to Tangier and the one under construction to Fès), through the cork-oak **Mamora Forest,** also cut by the north-going road from Salé (roadside baskets of truffles are for sale in the spring). Just after **Tiflet** (50 km), turn right onto the narrow S209, in the direction of Oulmes. You can't miss Tiflet because sellers of straw pom-pomed hats wave their wares at motorists as they drive through. Tiflet is a rather unattractive, straggling town, going in for ribbon-development, but it has a good reputation for kebobs, and you can take your choice from numerous roadside stalls. Some 10 km further on, a small road to the left leads to the **Dayet er Roumi Lake**, set among low hills, where it is possible to fish, swim, wind-surf, picnic, or camp. Back on the S209, continue to **Maaziz** and **Tiddas,** noted for its *moussem* in September, in which gaily decked-out horsemen perform their *fantasia*. The Ziane Berbers are noted for their horseman-ship and *fantasias* here are splendid things to watch (a good date is Throne Day, *Fête du Trône*, always on March 3). After Tiddas, the route be-comes very picturesque and offers good views as it climbs up the green and wooded hilly Zaine country until reaching Oulmes (80 km from Tiflet) The attractions here are the spring (Lalla Haya) from which water bursts out to become a fierce river, the woods, rivers, and ravines, the smell of the aromatic plants, and the invigorating air. It's really an excel-lent place in which to walk around, but it is best not to tease the wild boar who also frequent the woods. The Oulmes water is bottled and sold throughout Morocco.

The ∗∗∗ **Hotel les Thermes** (42 rooms, Tel: 55 23 53/55 22 93) is the only place in which to stay. It has a restaurant offering an international menu (130 DH). To get back to Rabat go either completely by the same route or take a left turn at Maaziz along the S106 to Rommani and the P22 to Rabat (70 km from Rabat).

FURTHER AFIELD

The P1 continues east after Tiflet to reach Khemisset (the expressway was just completed from here) and Meknès (138 km) (chapter 7). Going north, the P2 and the new expressway go to Larache, Asilah, and Tangier (278 km).

7. Guided Tours

Tours of Rabat are not organized—it's fairly easy to get around. But if you want a guide to go with you, your hotel will find you one. Remember to fix the price and the itinerary before setting out, and stick to both. There are also guides at the entry to the kasbah, but you don't really need one.

8. Culture

The **Archaeological Museum** *(Musée Archéologique)* (23 Rue el-Brihi, near the Hotel Chellah and the Moroccan radio and television studios, open 9:00 A.M.-2:00 P.M. and 3:00 P.M.-6:00 P.M., closed Tuesdays, entry 10 DH) is the best of its kind in Morocco. It's just a pity that there are no captions in English. A small photographic display in the entrance hall shows ongoing research. This leads onto the main ground floor room where showcases feature finds from sites dating from the Lower Paleolithic through the Neolithic to the Bronze Age. The skull of Jbel Irhoud Man, once thought to be an African version of the famous European Neanderthal Man, but now proved to be an archaic *Homo sapiens,* almost like us, dated to around 100,000 B.C., shows us that we are not in fact identical. A Neolithic burial from the El Harhoura cave has been reconstructed, and one can also admire the elephant ivory bracelets and bowls found in the Neolithic sand dune necropolis of Rouazi/Skhirat (dated to around 3,000 B.C.) (both sites on the coast just south of Rabat). The first floor contains Islamic and indigenous Mauretanian material, including a very good display explaining the functioning of the 16th-century sugar factories in south Morocco and the excavations in the northern coastal site of Belyounesh. A number of rock engravings from south Morocco are displayed in the little gardens on either side of the ground floor room. The big attraction for most visitors, however, is the large room to the left with Roman objects from the sites of Volubilis, Lixus, Banasa, Thamusida, and Chellah, arranged thematically. This used to be called the *Salle des Bronzes,* because of a collection of superb bronze statues (including the head of a young Berber, thought to be King Juba II), but it contains a lot more than that, with some fine marble heads, gold jewelry, and household items such as oil lamps, grinding stones, and cooking pots.

The **Geological Museum** *(Musée National des Sciences de la Terre)* is hard to find and absolutely not indicated. It is located in the *Ministère d'Energie et des Mines* (Ministry of Power and Mines), one of a series of ministries in an area reached by turning left at the traffic lights when coming from the bus station and Avenue ibn Rochd (red Fire-Brigade building on the corner), down Avenue Ma al-Ainaine, and left at the next traffic lights. The Ministry is a large building about 200 m down on the left. It displays the huge mounted skeleton of a dinosaur found at Tillougguit, near Azilal in the High Atlas, which lived in the area 165 million years ago, along with photographs showing how it was excavated. An original footprint of a dinosaur from Demnate (see chapter 12) is also on view, along with fossils from Taouz and Erfoud (chapter 13). All the items displayed have been found in Morocco. The skulls and bones of early man found during archaeological excavation can also be seen (at the moment the museum is only open from 3:00 P.M.-5:00 P.M. on Wednesdays and Fridays, but groups can visit at other times by appointment, and entry is free).

A museum displaying traditional arts and crafts is the **Museum of Moroccan Arts** *(Musée des Oudayas),* which is reached by going into the kasbah by a smaller gateway down the hill from Bab Oudaya. On your right is a building that used to be Mulay Ismail's palace; one of the rooms is decorated in 17th-century style (open from 9:00 A.M.-12:00 P.M. and 3:00 P.M.-6:00 P.M., entry 10 DH). Going through into the Andalusian garden (a nice place in which to sit and rest among the datura, hibiscus, roses, and seasonal flowers) you'll find, to the right, a series of rooms off an arcade containing an interesting collection of musical instruments and traditional clothing.

Just down the road from the Oudayas is the **National Crafts Museum** *(Musée National de l'Artisanat)* (6 Boulevard Tarik al-Marsa, open 9:00 A.M.-12:00 P.M. and 3:00 P.M.-6:00 P.M.). It is not so much a museum of antique pieces as a display of current Moroccan handicrafts in all their richness—rugs, jewelry, ceramics, embroidery, and leatherwork

If you are a stamp collector, the **Post Office Museum** *(Musée National des PTT),* Rue al-Khalil, off Avenue Mohammed V, going right from the station, has a small collection of stamps, including those issued by the various foreign powers before the Protectorate. Moroccan stamps are often very attractive, featuring birds, animals, rugs, pottery, silverwork, and events of national or international importance (open during post office hours, there is an entry fee, and you'll have to ask someone to let you in).

The **State Bank** *(Banque d'Etat)*, a heavily-guarded building on the corner of Avenue Mohammed V and Rue le Caire, has a mouth-watering collection of Moroccan gold and silver coins from all Islamic periods. Permission is needed to get in, and this may well prove difficult, as the person authorized to give permission to visit is not always there.

Cross the river, by boat if you like (many people do) (departures are on the shore, near the Club Nautique, upstream of the kasbah, and the cost is about 50 centimes). Pay a visit to the **Ceramic Museum** *(Musée Régional de la Céramique Regional)*. Having crossed the road bridge, turn left at Bab Mrisa, go on as straight as you can (Salé's medina is to your right), and left again at the crossroads by the Sidi Abdallah ibn Hasun mosque, towards the tomb of Sidi ben Achir, aiming for the Borj Nord Ouest, which houses the museum (about 2 km). Here there is a splendid collection of antique pottery, including rare Almohad and Merinid pieces.

Some 12 km from Salé, going towards Kénitra, the **Bouknadel Exotic Gardens** *(Les Jardins Exotiques de Sidi Bouknadel)* are worth a visit if you like plants. The gardens are on the left, not clearly indicated (bus Nº 23 from Salé). The gardens were created in 1951 by a French horticulturist who compiled over 1,500 species of plants and trees from outside Morocco with the idea of introducing suitable ones into the country and also to illustrate tropical and semi-tropical habitats. He left his garden to the Moroccan State, but it has unfortunately not been well kept up, and now looks more like a tropical jungle. However, an association for the protection of the gardens has just been formed, so things may improve (open 9:00 A.M.-6:00 P.M., entry 10 DH). The gardens cover four hectares and two circuits (45 or 90 minutes) are indicated by colored signs. It is good for kids, but best avoided by single women.

About 17 km from Rabat the private **Belghazi Museum** *(Musée Dar Belghazi)* has a marvelous collection of traditional Moroccan craftwork. There are literally thousands of pieces exhibited and, they say, as many not on view (entrance is 40 DH—or 100 DH if you want to see the enormous reserve collection). One can lunch there with prior notice (Tel: 82 21 78, Fax: 82 21 79, meal and visit 200 DH). Mohammed Abdelilah Belghazi, who created the museum, filled it with many pieces of traditional furniture and objects that had belonged to his own family in Fès. The museum is a large two-storied building and displays include jewelry, clothing, embroidery, carved doors, *minbars* (pulpits in a mosque that the non-Moslem rarely has the chance to see), shutters, and painted wooden ceilings. Some of the items date from the 17th century. This really should not be missed.

The **National Library** *(Bibliothèque Générale et des Archives)*, about five minutes from Bab er-Rouah (Avenue Ibn Batuta), is open to the public (roughly 10:00 A.M.-12:00 P.M. and 3:00 P.M.-5:30 P.M.), who can consult a vast number of books, newspapers, journals, and old manuscripts (all in French or Arabic). The staff is helpful, but many books listed in the card index are not available.

The United Kingdom has a **Cultural Center,** run by the **British Council** (36 Rue de Tanger, Tel: 76 08 36, off the Avenue Mohammed V, behind the big As-Souna Mosque). It has an information center, library, Internet club, and cafeteria, and organizes language courses, films, musical and theater events, and art exhibitions. The **French Cultural Center** (2 Rue Yanboua, Tel: 76 11 38, near Avenue Mohammed V) does much the same things, only in French.

The **Théatre Mohammed V** (Rue Moulay Rachid, center town) puts on plays, ballets, concerts, and shows, sometimes by visiting companies, but more often by Moroccan groups. The shows are in Arabic, so it's perhaps your chance to try and pick up something of the language. Morocco's classical music is of Andalusian origin and Rabat has its own orchestra, specializing in this type of music, that gives occasional **concerts.**

The celebration of Mulud, the Prophet Mohammed's birthday, is the occasion for a **pilgrimage and procession through the streets of Salé.** As the date changes every year, you'll have to make inquiries as to when it will take place (it was on July 7 in 1998, is 11 days earlier in 1999, and so on). This is an important event in honor of Salé's 16th-century patron saint, Sidi Abdallah ibn Hasun. The Slaoui craftsmen (people of Salé) make large, decorated candles that they place in colorful lanterns and then they march through the streets to the saint's tomb to thank him for past favors. Watch out for pickpockets, since the crowd is dense. There are also a number of *moussems* in the region, but as their dates are never exactly fixed in advance, information is best had from a hotel. On March 3, the Throne Day *(Fête du Trône),* all localities have some sort of celebration, many of them with *fantasias.*

9. Sports

The Hilton Hotel has **tennis courts,** and all the three ***** hotels have swimming pools, but these amenities are not available to non-guests. Non-members cannot play on the courts of the many private tennis clubs, unless invited by a member. **Sea bathing** is practiced by a crowd of youngsters in the mouth of the Bou Regreg, but cannot be recommended because of the proximity to two large towns. The beaches going north are dangerous for other reasons (undertow). The good beaches for sunning and swimming lie south of Rabat, on the coastal road to Casablanca (see above).

The **soft-water lakes** of Dayet er-Roumi Lake (on the road to Tiflet, see above) and the one on the Oued Mellah (see above) are safer for swimming and are also good for **wind-surfing.**

The big sport in Rabat is **golf.** The Royal Dar Es-Salam Golf Club is private, but one can play there as a temporary member on payment of the green fee (around 200 DH) (closed Mondays). Beautifully set among the cork-oaks of the Mamora Forest, it has two 18-hole courses (a red course, 6,702 m, par 73, and a blue course, 6,205 m, par 72) designed by Robert Trent Jones and a 9-hole one (2,150 m, par 32). The late King Hassan II was a keen golfer and the international Hassan II Golf Trophy is played there in November. The club lies a little out of town, on the Meknès road (Tel: 75 58 64/65, Fax: 63 88 21). It also has a good restaurant and a whole health-and-beauty center, including hairdressing.

The Hotel La Tour Hassan has a **fitness center** for its clients, and Thala Forme (Allée des Princesses, Souissi district, Tel: 63 82 94) has a whole range of facilities such as a beauty parlor, massage, sauna, aquabeds, heated indoor swimming pool, and gym. There is a **karting** center on the road to Ben Slimane (just after the exit from the Rabat-Casablanca expressway, direction Ben Slimane).

10. Shopping

Rabat is one of the most important centers for rugs and carpets. Each of the carpet-producing areas of Morocco has its own style, which a connoisseur can easily recognize. The story has it that the R'bati rug had its origin in an Oriental design—a kindly stork one day let a fragment of such a rug drop into the patio of a Rabat house, where the women picked it up and copied it (it's always women and little girls who weave rugs). The Rabat rug has a rectangular frame made up of several designs, enclosing a plain area in the middle of which are one or more medallions. The basic colors are red, green, blue, and pink. It is a "noble" rug, seen in upper- and middle-class houses. Get an idea of what it and other rugs look like and what they sell for (so much the square meter, depending on the number of knots—different grades are indicated on the guarantee label stitched to the back of the rug) by going first to the **State Craftwork Center** (*Ensemble Artisanal*) on the Boulevard Tarik al-Marsa, just down from the Oudaya Kasbah. Also check here on the official prices (fixed) for other items that interest you, before starting bargaining elsewhere. Embroidery is widely practiced in Morocco, and here again towns have their own distinctive stitch—so Rabat embroidery differs from Salé embroidery. The **Rue des Consuls,** opposite the kasbah, is a good place for rugs, as well as a whole range of Moroccan crafts, both ancient and modern (jewelry, pottery, copper and bronze items, and new kaftans). The *fondouks,* old-time overnight lodging for traders and their animals, are also a feature of this busy and attractive road. Market days are Tuesdays and Thursdays. The **Galerie Cheremetieff** (16 Rue Annaba) also sells high quality goods.

The **Pottery Complex** *(Cité des Potiers)* is on the outskirts of Rabat, on the way to Salé. Salé pottery—trademarked "Oulja"—is one of the best known in Morocco, clearly different from the pottery of Fès and Safi (the other urban centers) in colors, design, and fabric. The complex contains about 25 ceramic workshops, where the craftsmen turn, fire, decorate, and sell their goods. Although at first glance all the workshops look as though they are producing identical pieces, in fact new ideas are constantly being incorporated into the traditional shapes and themes. Even if you don't want to buy, these workshops are worth the visit just for *le plaisir des yeux,* the visual pleasure. The complex also has basket-weavers, and a café.

More prosaic, **everyday needs** can be best covered around the Avenue Mohammed V. Women's clothing such as kaftans and *gandouras* are on sale in many shops in this area, and also often in the boutiques of the big hotels. The Marjane Supermarket, on the way to Salé, is also well stocked with local and imported goods.

There are two good **bookshops,** Edition La Porte, ex-Les Belles Images (281 Avenue Mohammed V, Tel: 70 99 58/70 64 76, Fax: 70 64 78) and Librairie Libre Service (46 Avenue Allal ben Abdallah) (mostly French-language). The English Bookshop (7 Rue al-Yamama, close to the station) goes in for second-hand English and American novels, guide books, language courses, dictionaries, and similar English-language material. The American Bookstore (part of the American Language Center, 4 Rue de Tanger) has a small stock of new English-language books including some interesting studies on Morocco. The big hotels and the railway station usually have a few copies of U.S. and British **newspapers.** In theory, detailed **maps** for most of Morocco north of Agadir can be bought at the Division de la Cartographie, 31 Avenue Hassan I (close to the Hotel Chellah, entrance on a corner, then go up the stairs). In practice, the employees make rather a fuss about handing them over and require a request in writing, justifying your request, plus a passport or identity card (open from 9:00 A.M. -11:00 A.M. and 2:30 P.M.-5:30 P.M.). General road maps can be bought from bookshops or the bigger newspaper stalls.

11. Entertainment and Nightlife

For outdoor entertainment there are horse races and an annual Horse Show, in the summer, at Dar Es-Salem (on the way to Meknès). A visit to the zoo (Parc Zoologique National, a few kilometers south of Rabat on the road to Temara; buses N° 17, 41, and 45 will take you there) will please kids, even if it is small compared to some Western zoos. It is Morocco's most important zoo, not only for the number of visitors it gets each year (600,000), but also for the quantity and quality of its animals. It is clean and the animals appear well cared for. It has numerous species of big cats (lions, tigers, and leopards) and birds (entry 7 DH for adults, 4 DH for children, open all week, from 9:00 A.M.-6:00 P.M., from 10:00 A.M. on Sundays).

Various **tennis clubs hold tournaments** in the summer, and they are not always restricted to their own members. They are open to spectators. Ask at the Information Office (address below) for dates. The Dawliz complex, just the other side of the river, has four-lane bowling.

The Cinéma Renaissance (Avenue Mohammed V) is the best of the many Rabat **cinemas** (Arabic or French speaking). There are periodic film weeks organized by the cultural centers, who also put on a number of **music festivals.** The newspapers carry details of dates and showings, or your hotel should be able to advise you.

For an **evening drink,** the big hotels such as the Hilton (transport needed), the La Tour Hassan, the Safir, the Chellah, and the Dawliz are all agreeable locations. The sunset view over Rabat from the Dawliz terrace is splendid. Other **** and *** hotels also have bars, often rather small and noisy (the *** Moussafir in the Agdal district, for instance, is handy if you're waiting for a train, and the Hotel Soundous also has a nice piano bar). The same big hotels have nightclubs (drinks from 60 DH), and the Hotel Balima has a **disco** that is thought to be good, as does the Arc-en-Ciel just behind (Rue Dimachk). At the moment, the Amnesia (Rue Monastir, just off Avenue Allal ben Abdallah) is a favorite, decorated to look like an American bar. You can also play American snooker (entry 100 DH—60 DH during the week). You need to be decently dressed in all these places. As usual, as all over the world, there are always women hopefully waiting to find a kindred spirit (and men on the lookout, too).

Going south along the seaside resorts, you'll find many discos and nightclubs. The in-place for the young set at the moment is the **Bouznika Beach Club,** on the beach at Bouznika (36 km south of Rabat, entry fee of 150 DH includes first drink, beer 60 DH, soft drinks 40 DH, dancing). It is terribly crowded in the summer—but I suppose this is part of its attraction!

12. The Rabat-Salé Address List

Airlines—Royal Air Maroc, Avenue Mohammed V (Tel: 70 97 66) and
    9 Rue Aboufaris al-Marini (Tel: 70 97 00).
Airport—Rabat-Salé (Tel: 76 73 93).

Banks—Many on Avenue Mohammed V. BMCI and Wafabank have VISA cashpoints. In Salé, the Banque Populaire and the BMCE have branches on Rue Fondouk Abd el-Hadi, close to Bab Fès.

Bus Station *(gare routière)*—in Rabat, 5 km out of town on the road to Casablanca; in Salé, near Bab Fès (bus to Rabat just about opposite).

Car Rental—Avis, 7 Rue Aboufaris al-Marini (Tel: 76 79 59); Budget, Rabat railway station (Tel: 76 76 89); Europcar, Hotel Rabat Hilton (Tel: 77 12 34); Hertz, 291 Avenue Mohammed V (Tel: 76 92 27).

Churches—Mass in English twice a month at 5:00 P.M. in the Cathédral Saint Pierre (call Father Barnaby in Marrakech for details, Tel: 04-43 05 85); Mass in French at the Cathédrale Saint Pierre, Place du Golan (Tel: 72 23 01), Eglise Saint Pie X, 40 Rue Jaâfar es Sadik (Tel: 67 02 50), Eglise Saint François d'Assise, Avenue du Président Soekarno (Tel: 72 43 80); Russian Orthodox Church, Bab Tamesna (Tel: 72 74 79); French-speaking Protestant church, 8 Rue el-Mourabitine (for information telephone the church in Casablanca, Tel: 02-30 21 51).

Drugstore, Night *(Pharmacie de Nuit)*—Rue Moulay Slimane (next to Résidence Mulay Ismail). Each district has a *Pharmacie de Garde* for Sunday and holiday openings.

Embassies—Canada, 13 Rue Jaafar as-Sadiq, Agdal (Tel: 67 28 80); United States, 2 Avenue de Marrakech (Tel: 76 22 65, Fax: 76 56 61, open 8:30 A.M.-12:30 P.M. and 2:30 P.M.-6:30 P.M.); Great Britain, 17 Boulevard de la Tour Hassan (Tel: 72 09 05, Fax: 72 09 06, open from 8:30 A.M.-12:30 P.M. and 2:00 P.M.-5:00 P.M., there is always a duty officer on call).

Express Post *(Poste Rapide)*—from the central post office (Tel: 72 21 80).

Fire—(Tel: 15).

Highway emergency service—(Tel: 177).

Hospitals and Clinics, day and night emergency—Hôpital Avicenne (Tel: 67 28 71); Hôpital d'Enfants (children) (Tel: 67 02 27/34/94); Maternité Souissi (maternity) (Tel: 67 02 94/27/34, Souissi suburb); Maternité des Orangers (Tel: 72 27 62); Hôpital Prince Mulay Abdallah (Tel: 78 72 33, Salé).

International and American Organizations—UNICEF, 8 Rue de Marrakech (Tel: 76 00 83); United States Agency for International Development (USAID), Avenue Allal ben Abdallah; Peace Corps, 1 Rue Benzerte (Tel: 70 60 20, Fax: 70 87 01).

Jewish synagogue—Synagogue Talmud Torah, 9 Rue Mulay Ismail (Tel: 72 45 04).

Photocopies—from almost all establishments selling tobacco, stamps, and newspapers.

Police—(Tel: 19).

Post Office—Avenue Mohammed V; in Salé, close to Bab Fès.

Railway Station *(gare ONCF)*—Avenue Mohammed V, Rabat (Tel: 76 73 53); Place de la Gare, Agdal (Tel: 77 23 85); Salé, Place de la Gare.

School—Rabat American School, Rue Ouhad, Agdal. A private, fee-paying establishment, providing an American education from kindergarten to 12th grade.

Taxis—there are always lots of small taxis *(petits taxis)* outside the Rabat and Salé stations. The latter's *petits taxis* (beige) are not allowed into Rabat. Taxi stands in town are indicated. In Rabat, the big taxis *(grands taxis)* wait at the bus station *(gare routière)*, and near the railway station in Salé for north-bound destinations and at Bab Mrisa for Rabat.

Telephone—next to post office and téléboutiques.

Tourist Information—Office National Marocain du Tourisme, corner Avenue Abtal/Rue Fès, Agdal. Only has a few colored brochures.

Travel Agencies—Africa Voyages, 28 Avenue Allal ben Abdallah (Tel: 70 83 04); Carlson Wagonlit Travel, 1 Avenue Prince Mulay Abdallah (Tel: 70 96 25, Fax: 70 96 72).

Yachting and Water-sports *(sports nautiques)*—information from the Yacht Club de Rabat, Quai de la Hassan (Tel: 72 02 54).

7

Meknès and the Middle Atlas Mountains

1. The General Picture

Meknès is the logical continuation after Rabat for the visitor who wants to visit the Imperial cities of Morocco and study and admire some of the finest examples of Islamic architecture. Its medina is one of the six Moroccan sites recognized as world heritage by UNESCO. The advantages of Meknès are threefold: it can boast of urban monuments, Roman ruins—the site of Volubilis is the best preserved in the country—and proximity to beautiful lakes, forests, and mountains. Two days could be spent in the town, a day at Volubilis and Mulay Idriss, and a couple more days set aside to explore the cedar forests and lakes of the Middle Atlas.

Foundation. There seems to have been no occupation of the site until, in the 9th century, the Zeneta Berber Maknassa tribe settled on flat ground overlooking the Bou Fekrane River, attracted no doubt by the vast fertile plain (the Sais). The first to construct buildings more substantial than the little Berber villages were the Almoravids, who, in 1069, built a kasbah in what is now a city district. The town became rich and the Almohads started casting their eyes on it from 1120, although their sultan, Abd el-Mumen,

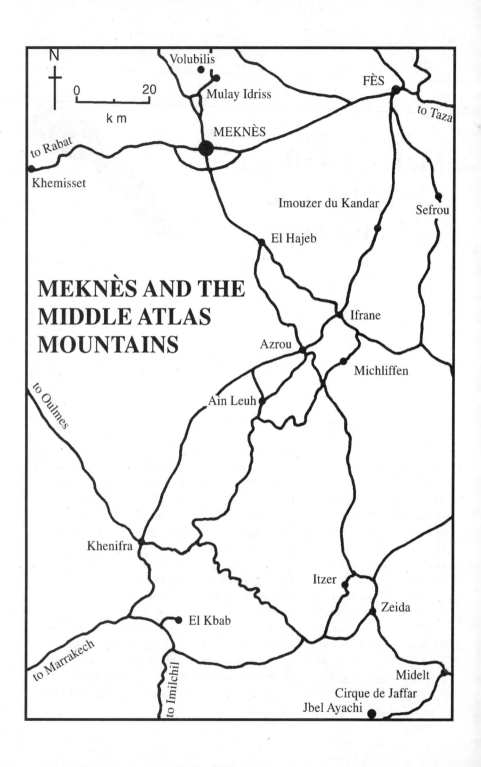

N

0   20

k m

Volubilis

Mulay Idriss

FÈS

to Taza

to Rabat

MEKNÈS

Khemisset

Imouzer du Kandar

Sefrou

El Hajeb

MEKNÈS AND THE MIDDLE ATLAS MOUNTAINS

Ifrane

Azrou

Michliffen

to Oulmes

Ain Leuh

Khenifra

Itzer

Zeida

El Kbab

to Marrakech

to Imilchil

Midelt

Cirque de Jaffar

Jbel Ayachi

succeeded in taking the town only in 1145, after a seven-year siege. The weakening Almohads did not rule long over Meknès, for in the beginning of the 13th century their successors, the Merinids, invaded the region and captured the town. They did not establish their capital here, but built a kasbah, a mosque, a *medersa,* and numerous buildings to house their governor. Meknès declined when the Merinid dynasty crumbled at the end of the 14th century. Although the Wattasids and then the Saadians occupied the town, it only really came into its own when the new Alaouite sultan Mulay Ismail chose it as his capital in 1672.

Sultan Mulay Ismail. Meknès and Mulay Ismail are inextricably bound together, for this powerful, long-reigning figure left an indelible mark on the town. Mulay Ismail was a young man of 26 when he came to the throne. Dark-skinned, of good physique, and extremely strong-willed, he reigned for 55 years. He was a great builder, though not a great architectural innovator. One of his first tasks was to rebuild the city, using (it is said) between 1,000-3,000 Christian slaves and 20,000-30,000 prisoners from the surrounding tribes. The Merinid kasbah and part of the old town were destroyed and a new vast wall of trampled down earth and lime, with huge gates, was constructed. Mulay Ismail built kasbahs for his Black Guard, mosques, hangars in which to store supplies of grain, stables, and gardens. Much of the decorative building materials for the Imperial Town, Dar el-Makhzen, built to house his personal administration and harem (said to contain 500 women), which he built south of the medina, came from the nearby Roman ruins of Volubilis and the El-Badi Palace of his predecessors in Marrakech. Well aware of the need for a strong military force, Mulay Ismail got together an army of 150,000 men, made up of black slaves, immigrant Arabs, Andalusians, and Christians, whom he housed in a military camp beside the palace. He needed a good army to keep his unruly compatriots under control and push the Europeans out of Morocco's coastal towns.

A diplomat too, Mulay Ismail worked to increase commercial exchanges with France and sent missions to France and England. His court in Meknès, in turn, became the destination of western ambassadors coming, often, to buy the release of their countrymen captured by the Moroccan corsairs. Up to 1678, the captured foreigners belonged to their corsair captors, but after that date they became the sultan's personal property. Negotiations with France were particularly difficult, for the French king held far more Moroccan galley slaves than Mulay Ismail did French building slaves. The Alaouite sultan was such an important figure that it is worth recalling a few stories about him, one of which concerned Louis XIV. The French king received one of Mulay Ismail's missions—headed by the ex-pirate Ben Aicha—at Versailles in 1699. Ben Aicha presented such an enthusiastic portrait of the French king's daughter that Mulay Ismail requested her hand in marriage (a request that Louis XIV turned down).

John Windus, who went to Meknès in 1720 with an English mission trying to buy back a number of English slaves, saw the sultan when he was about 74 years and described him as very active for his age. Mulay Ismail's strong personality ensured that a host of legends were attached to his name, some of them certainly true, others not. He had many good qualities, including determination, religious faith, abounding energy, political astuteness, and a certain tolerance towards his Christian slaves, allowing them to live apart in a sort of shantytown and have a Catholic priest to administer to their spiritual needs. He also had many less appealing traits, such as extreme cruelty, ruthlessness, and a fierce spirit of revenge. Stories of the people he put to death on a whim are endless. Many are true, but I won't dwell on them here. With his death in 1727, the civil war that broke out led to the decline of Meknès, a decline hastened by the Lisbon earthquake in 1755.

However, the city maintained its military reputation. Under the Protectorate, a New Town was built in 1920, separated from the Old Town by the Bou Fekrane River (about a 15- to 20-minute walk). It housed an important French military garrison. French farmers settled in the rich surrounding plain and turned Meknès into a thriving agricultural center, also producing Morocco's best wines. When Morocco got back its independence, their farms were confiscated, many of them being taken over by the state (but the well-known wines such as Guerrouane and Ait Soualah continued to be produced).

Today, the town of Meknès gives the impression of being rather overshadowed by the splendors and refinement of Fès, some 60 km away. Yet its vigorous population, around 500,000, is energetic and active and the town has no reason to envy Fès because of its agricultural and horticultural richness and natural beauty of the region. The town itself is a bit noisy and dusty, but I have always found the Meknassi helpful and friendly. It still has a large military garrison and hospital.

2. Getting There

Meknès cannot be reached directly by **air.** Royal Air Maroc flies to Rabat (138 km away) and Fès (only 60 km), but neither of these possibilities are particularly helpful. **Trains** provide the best public transport. Eight arrive every day from Casablanca (80 DH) via Rabat, Salé, Kénitra, and Sidi Kacem; nine times a day from Fès (14 DH); three from Tangier, via Sidi Kacem; three from Oujda via Taza, and five from Marrakech via

Casablanca. Make sure to get off at the station near the center of town (El-Amir Abdelkader, the first halt in Meknès coming from Rabat, the second coming from Oujda). Meknès can also be reached from Belgium, France, and Spain by the **CTM bus** company's international service. Closer at hand, the company runs eight buses a day from Fès (first arrival at 8:00 A.M., the last at 8:00 P.M.), and eight a day from Casablanca (63 DH) and Rabat (first arrival at 11:00 A.M., the last at 11:00 P.M.). A daily bus arrives from Laayoune and Marrakech at 7:00 P.M. and from Dakhla and Agadir at 8:00 P.M. A daily bus also arrives from Azrou and Ifrane, and further afield from Tangier, Oujda, Berkane, Taza, Rissani, and Errachidia. The CTM bus station is conveniently situated in the center of town. Other buses, less reliable than the CTM, also run from these towns.

An expressway links Meknès to Fès (60 km) and Meknès to Khemisset (50 km). When completed it will join Rabat to Fès (198 km), via Meknès. At the moment, the **main P1 road** from Rabat is the direct route (138 km). It is narrow and winding, with a number of blind dips hiding oncoming cars, and traffic is heavy. **Big taxis** (pale grey Mercedes with black roofs) will also take the visitor from Meknès to any other large town.

3. Local Transportation

Within Meknès, local **buses** transport the Meknassi from one end of the town to another. But the visitor is best advised to take a **small taxi** (duck-egg blue) as far as the entrance to the medina and do the rest on foot.

4. The Hotel Scene

Being less of a tourist-catcher than Fès, it is often easier to find a hotel room here than in Fès. There are 14 classified hotels in Meknès and its immediate surroundings. Hotel charges fixed for this region are as follows (they vary according to the presence or absence of showers and water closet in the room): **** 333-457 DH or 426-600 DH, breakfast 44-48 DH or 45-50 DH; *** 166-264 DH or 187-300 DH, breakfast 33 DH for both; ** 91-158 DH or 98-197 DH, breakfast 22 DH for both; * 86-140 DH, breakfast 21 DH.

The **regional telephone code** is 05 (0 omitted for in-region calls).

EXPENSIVE HOTELS

The most expensive hotels are situated in the New Town. The top of the list is the **** **Hotel Transatlantique** (120 air-conditioned rooms, Rue el-Meriniyine, Tel: 52 50 50/51, Fax: 52 00 57), with a very good reputation (the direction is indicated in the center of town). Situated in a residential

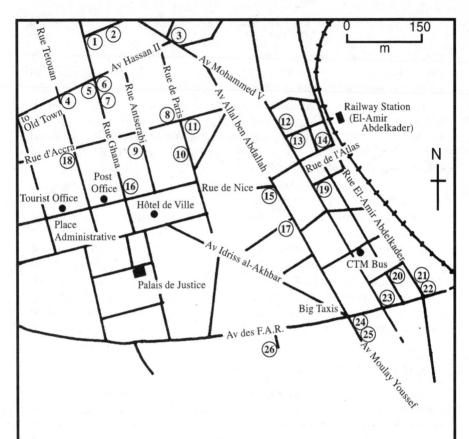

Hotels
8. Nice
13. Majestic
15. Touring
16. Palace
17. Ouislane
18. Rif
20. Bab Mansour
21. Akouas
22. Excelsior
24. Volubilis
26. Panorama

Restaurants and Cafés
1. Gambrinus
2. Metropole Annexe
3. Le Dauphin
   Café Opera
5. Rôtisserie Karam
6. La Coupole
7. Pâtisserie Glacier Florence
9. Mo Di Niro
10. New Mex Snack Grill
11. Pizzaria La Mama
12. Pâtisserie Glacier Miami
14. Pizzaria Le Four
19. Marhaba
23. La Boveda
25. La Case

Useful Addresses
4. Librairie la Ville
   Nouvelle

MEKNÈS
NEW TOWN

area on the edge of the New Town overlooking the medina, it is agreeably decorated and has a very pleasant garden, with two pools, tennis courts, and a restaurant offering a good Moroccan meal. The old part is said to be more attractive than the modern side (the staff is sometimes a bit uninterested in its guests).

For those looking for a slightly cheaper, really centrally-placed hotel with **** amenities, the **** **Hotel Rif** (120 rooms, Rue d'Accra, Tel: 52 25 91/92/93/94, Fax: 52 44 28) is an excellent choice. The hotel, a tall, cream-colored building, is fully air-conditioned, has two restaurants, a bar, swimming pool, and a nightclub with a floorshow.

The **** **Hotel Zaki** (163 rooms, Boulevard al-Masssira, Tel: 52 09 90/ 52 00 63/52 41 73, Fax: 53 48 36) is a most attractive place, interestingly designed, with lots of stuccowork and *zellij,* marble corridors, and tastefully furnished bedrooms (although it has no elevator). It lies in pleasant green surroundings, has a large pool, sauna, two restaurants, piano bar (Arab and Western music), and a nightclub. But it is frankly only suitable for motorized travelers, being about 2 ½ km from the town center on the road to Azrou (a dusty, uninteresting walk). Tourist groups appreciate this quiet, well-appointed hotel.

MEDIUM-PRICE HOTELS

These are *** and ** hotels. The newish *** **Hotel Bab Mansour** (82 rooms, 38 Rue El-Amir Abdelkader, Tel: 52 52 39/40, Fax: 51 07 41) is excellently placed for the railway station (five minutes on foot) and town center. It has a discreet, grey marble outside entrance, rises to five stories (two elevators), has an attractive, spacious reception area, comfortable, well-furnished bedrooms (the back room balconies are very sunny in the afternoon), restaurant, bar, boutique, nightclub with a floorshow, covered garage, conference room (with retro-projector facilities), and a friendly and helpful manager.

The *** **Hotel Akouas** (52 rooms, 27 Rue El-Amir Abdelkader, Tel: 51 59 67/ 68/95, Fax: 51 599 94), only three-years old, is practically opposite the Hotel Bab Mansour (so it is also very convenient for the railway station). It, too, has an attractive, luminous, stucco-decorated reception area, with comfortable, well-furnished bedrooms, a restaurant, bar, and a nightclub, as well as a friendly reception staff. Both these *** hotels receive tourists groups and are very often full (their high season is mid-August to mid-November).

Undoubtedly, the best of the ** group and a good value is the ** **Hotel Majestic** (42 rooms, 19 Avenue Mohammed V, Tel: 52 20 35/52 03 07, Fax: 52 74 27). It is a hotel of long-standing, has recently been completely renovated, and is within three minutes of the railway station (well indicated), with very clean, comfortable bedrooms, two little salons, and a sunny rooftop terrace for breakfast. The manager is very friendly and helpful, and I have also had a warm recommendation from an American couple staying there.

The ** **Hotel Ouislane** (30 air-conditioned rooms, 54 Avenue Allal ben Abdallah, Tel: 52 17 43/52 48 28) is also very central (the entrance is on the corner). Its reception area is rather dark, but its clean and comfortable rooms have balconies. It also has a restaurant and bar.

The ** **Hotel Volubilis** (30 rooms, 45 Avenue des F.A.R., Tel: 52 50 82) is well placed at the top of Avenue Mohammed V, near the CTM bus station. It recently lost its third star and is, in fact, a bit drab and run-down, though the fully-equipped bedrooms are clean and comfortable (those looking onto the small courtyard are very quiet). There are some amusing old tourist posters in the corridors, but the reception hall is very dark during the day until the whole place livens up in the evening thanks to the bar.

The ** **Hotel Nice** (30 rooms, 10 Rue d'Accra, Tel: 52 03 18/52 18 02) is a three-story building with no elevator, but is otherwise pleasant enough and well placed in the center of town.

The ** **Hotel Palace** (40 rooms, 11 Rue Ghana, Tel: 52 04 07), also central near the Hôtel de Ville (the town hall, not another hotel), is another place to head for in this range. It has an agreeable little reception area, clean bedrooms (no elevator), a lock-up garage, and a restaurant.

BUDGET ACCOMMODATIONS

Budget accommodations are represented by * or unclassified hotels. Some of these cheap hotels are not bad at all for the price. The * **Hotel Touring** (35 rooms, 34 Avenue Allal ben Abdallah, Tel: 52 23 51), on the corner with the Rue de Nice, is noisy during the day, but otherwise well situated. It's a bit dark and shabby, but the rooms are clean.

For train travelers, the * **Hotel Excelsior** (41 rooms, 57 Avenue des F.A.R, Tel: 52 19 00, on the corner, practically next door to the Hotel Akouas) is less of a value than the Hotel Touring , but its rooms are clean although pretty basic.

Among the unclassified, the **Hotel Panorama** (25 rooms, 104 DH, Avenue des F.A.R., Rue 8, Tel: 52 27 37) is probably the best, and I would say better than the two * hotels above. It is on a little road off the Avenue des F.A.R., with the Café Chems on the corner and a Shell garage nearby. The large clean rooms come with a complete toilet set-up (shower and water closet) and the back ones have a little balcony looking onto tree-filled garden (expect this hotel to rise in grade shortly).

The **Hotel Continental** (41 rooms, 128 DH with shower, 92 Avenue des F.A.R., Tel: 52 54 71) is just opposite the taxi stand at the head of Avenues Mohammed V and Allal ben Abdallal—you can't miss the word "Hotel" painted high up on its yellow wall. Its rooms are simple but clean, and some have balconies. It's useful for those traveling by the CTM bus.

There are masses of cheapies in the medina, but they only have communal showers (which are generally cold) and shared water closets. The **Youth Hostel** (Tel: 52 46 98) is close to the Hotel Transatlantique (see above), with the usual youth hostel prices and conditions (YHA membership required). It's not bad, and it's cheap.

The Meknès campsite, **Camping Agdal** (17 DH per person, 10 DH per tent) is a pleasant, shady place, but is a 2 km walk from the center of town on the Rabat road. To compensate, it has the attraction of being within the walls of the old town.

5. Dining and Restaurants

To the Meknassi, the town obviously offers gastronomic delights, but this is not really the place for the visitor to taste the top of Moroccan cooking.

HOTEL RESTAURANTS

The two restaurants in the **Hotel Transatlantique,** the **Belle Vue** and the **Ismailia,** are certainly the best in town and have very good reputations. The latter (only open in the evening) offers an excellent Moroccan menu (expensive, main dish 150 DH). The former is open for lunch and dinner (same price).

The **Hotel Rif** does a gastronomic menu at 143 DH that is said to be good.

The **Zaki Hotel** restaurant does a set meal at 157 DH. The restaurant **El-Ambra** in the **Hotel Bab Mansour** specializes in Moroccan dishes and seafood (quality variable).

The restaurant in the **Hotel Akouas** is said not to be bad. The **Hotel Palace** runs the adjoining restaurant (set menu 80 DH).

OTHER RESTAURANTS

Outside of the hotel restaurants, the up-market **Restaurant Le Dauphin** (5 Avenue Mohammed V, entrance behind for non-groups, Tel: 52 34 23) specializes in fish dishes, but also has Moroccan and international cooking (main dish from 90 DH).

The **Palais Terrab** (18 Avenue Zerktouni, Tel: 52 61 00), on the eastern side of town, serves good, traditional Moroccan food.

The **Restaurant Pizzaria Grill La Coupole** (corner Avenue Hassan II/Rue Ghana, Tel: 52 24 83), which is often rather full, serves a wide variety of dishes and is a good value (salads from 30 DH, pizzas from 48 DH, meat from 50 DH). A wooden screen divides the small dining area from the very popular bar, and it has live music most evenings.

La Case (8 Avenue Moulay Youssef, Tel: 52 40 19) serves a good range of French dishes (fish from 110 DH, meat from 75 DH), but I'm told the quality is sometimes uneven (it opens at 7:30 P.M. but at 8:00 P.M. the only person competent to take my order had not arrived, so I left—it is closed Mondays).

A pizzeria most people head for is the **Pizzaria Le Four** (1 Rue de l'Atlas, Tel: 52 08 57), just off Avenue Mohammed V, very near the station, with an amusing kitsch Italian decor and unorthodox square pizzas served on wooden boards. It is licensed to sell liquor (wine and beer—Budweiser and local brands), but it has a poor choice of desserts (pizzas from 34 DH, pasta from 20 DH, open all week except during Ramadan).

Another pizza place is the **Pizzaria La Mama** (Rue de Paris), a lively, friendly place often a bit full (pizzas from 38 DH).

Traditional Moroccan food is served in the **Restaurant Metropole Annexe** (11 Rue Charif Idrissi, close to junction of Avenues Hassan II and Mohammed V). The menu comes at around 90 DH.

The modest little **Restaurant Marhaba** (23 Avenue Mohammed V, Tel: 52 16 32) is recommended for a quick simple meal. It does *harira* soup with delicious bread (3.60 DH), kebobs (18 DH), and good *tajines* (30 DH).

Moroccan food is also served at the **Restaurant Gambrinus** (Avenue Omar ibn el-Hass, near the Restaurant Metropole Annexe), another pretty simple place but a good value (menu 60 DH).

In the medina, it's a pity that tourist groups have spoiled the **Zitouna** (44 Jamaa Zitouna, Tel: 53 02 81), because the Moroccan food used to be good. Its palace-style gives it character, but both the food and the service have deteriorated. It is still worth a try if you're that way.

The two-story **Collier de la Colombe** (67 Rue Driba, in the southern part of medina, very hard to find, Tel: 55 50 41) has the reputation of providing a good Moroccan meal at a reasonable price (menu 80 DH) (international menu also available).

As usual, there are plenty of small, popular restaurants frequented by the local people, which are not expensive but not particularly good.

Some 3 km out of town, on the Fès road, **La Hacienda** (Tel: 52 10 92) is a nice place in which to have lunch on a summer's day, in the shaded courtyard. It provides French, Spanish, and Moroccan cooking, as well as good views over the Zerhoun hills.

OTHER PLACES TO EAT AND DRINK

Hamburgers and French fries can be had from the new **Mo Di Niro** for around 20 DH (14 Rue Antserabi, off Avenue Hassan II). They have a first floor that is calm for women traveling on their own.

The **New Mex Snack Grill** (20 Rue de Paris, also perpendicular to Avenue Hassan II) is maybe not the Tex-Mex you know, but it's not bad (around 40 DH), and they also serve hot dogs and burgers (20 DH).

If you're keen on roast chicken (not likely to cause stomach trouble), they turn on a spit in front of you at **La Boveda,** (35 Rue El-Amir Abdelkader, beside the Hotel Excelsior on the corner of Avenue des F.A.R., from 15 DH) and at the **Rôtisserie Karam** (2 Rue Ghana, just off Avenue Hassan II). A ¼ roast chicken costs around 15 DH.

In the New Town, there are lots of cafés around the Avenue Mohammed V where you can stop and have a coffee or soft drink. Single women will appreciate the first floor of the **Café Opera** (7 Avenue Mohammed V).

The **Pâtisserie Glacier Florence** (Rue Ghana) gets very crowded around 6:00 P.M. Its breakfast of orange juice, croissant, and coffee costs 12 DH.

The **Pâtisserie Glacier Miami** (15 Avenue Mohammed V) also has delicious croissants and ice cream (15 DH and 20 DH, summer only), and has a vast, attractively furnished area with comfortable chairs where you can have breakfast (fried eggs 12 DH, orange juice 5 DH, almond, apple, and banana juice 6 DH).

Pastries, tea, coffee, and fresh fruit juice can be enjoyed at the **Boulangerie-Pâtisserie La Renaissance** (32, Avenue Allal ben Abdallah). It's a bit masculine, but work your way to the back if you prefer. It offers a breakfast of fruit juice, coffee, and croissant for 8.50 DH.

If you are looking for a coffee shop in the medina, try the **Salon de Thé La Comtesse** (underneath the Hotel de Paris, Rue Rouamazin) for Moroccan pastries (also ice cream).

Also in the medina, the cafés in the **Place el-Hedim** (between the big Bab el-Mansour Gate and the Dar Jamai Museum) provide good vantage points from which to watch the crowd.

I must say a word about the *sfenj* (a deep-fried sort of donut with a hole in the middle) which are sold around here from little booths. I personally cannot resist them (they're delicious), but if you have any doubts about eating possibly not 100 percent hygienically-prepared food, then resist the temptation.

6. Sightseeing

IN MEKNÈS

The sights to be seen in Meknès all lie on the other side of the River Bou Fekrane from the New Town. They are almost all the work of Mulay Ismail, and as he had lots of space available, today's visitor often has lengthy walks to reach the principal sites. The main places of interest can be divided into three: **the ramparts,** with their monumental gates Bab Berdane and Bab el-Khemis, the **medina,** and the **Imperial Town.** If you are short of time, visit the **Bou Inania Medersa** (not an Alaouite monument, for once), the **Dar Jamai Museum,** the **Bab el-Mansour,** and the **Heri as-Souani Granary.**

For the motorized traveler, an idea of the fortifications can be had by driving a few kilometers along the crenellated **ramparts** from the New Town, towards Rabat, taking in Bab Berdane and Bab el-Khemis. The old part of the town was enclosed by almost 40 km of ramparts, forming three enclosures, designed to stop successive waves of invaders. Bab Berdane is a good example of Alaouite architecture, based on the Saadian military model. The green ceramic decoration and the *zellij* Kufic inscriptions soften its very massive appearance. Bab el-Khemis has the same solid look and has an inscription (admirably open-minded) that says "I am the gate open to all people, whether they be from the West or the East." Outside the ramparts lies the oldest Moslem cemetery of the town, with the white-domed *kubba* of **Sidi Mohammed Ben Aissa,** founder of the Aissaoua religious fraternity (a close approach is not advised). See the "Culture" section below for details of the annual pilgrimage.

The visit of the medina and Imperial Town is best started at the vast **Place el-Hedim,** lying between the two (there is a car park). In Mulay Ismail's day the square served as a dumping ground for all his building material. On one side is the **Bab el-Mansour** gate, to the other the **Dar Jamai Museum** (see "Culture" section). The monumental gateway, the biggest in Meknès, was started by a Christian architect/slave converted to Islam, just before the death of Mulay Ismail, and completed five years later by his son. It is made up of the usual *outrepassé* arch surrounded by a blind arch, and has black tiles, floral motifs, and an inscription. The towers on either side were not designed to be defensive since the aim of Bab el-Mansour was to impress visitors to the sultan's palace by its size and ornate decoration.

Going into the medina, the road winding around Dar Jamai leads to the Great Mosque and the **Bou Inania Medersa.** The latter was started in the reign of the Merinid Abul Hassan, and finished in the 14th century by his son, Abu Inan. It is smaller than its namesake in Fès, but has the same

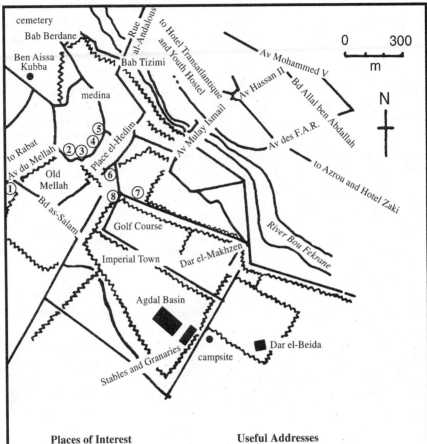

cemetery
Bab Berdane
Ben Aissa Kubba
medina
to Rabat
Av du Mellah
Old Mellah
Bd as-Salam
Rue al-Andalous
to Hotel Transatlantique and Youth Hostel
Bab Tizimi
Place el-Hedim
Av Mulay Ismail
Av Mohammed V
Av Hassan II
Bd Allal ben Abdallah
Av des F.A.R.
to Azrou and Hotel Zaki
Golf Course
Imperial Town
Dar el-Makhzen
River Bou Fekrane
Agdal Basin
Stables and Granaries
campsite
Dar el-Beida

0   300
m
N

Places of Interest
2. Carpenters' Souk
3. Dar Jamai Museum
4. Great Mosque
5. Bou Inania Medersa
6. Bab el-Mansour
7. Mausoleum of Mulay Ismail
8. Koubbat al-Khayatin

Useful Addresses
1. Bab el-Khemis
   Bus Station
   Big Taxis

MEKNÈS: OLD TOWN

lodgings for religious students on the ground and first floors. The bright *zellij* work, the delicate carved plaster, and carved beams of cedar have been restored, but manage to convey a very good idea of the original building. From the roof, there is a good view of the green-tiled roof and minaret of the Great Mosque (founded in the 12th century), the medina, and a number of other minarets of surrounding mosques. The vertical panels of green tiling on the mosques are a feature of Meknès.

As is customary in Moroccan medinas, the **souks** (markets) are grouped according to profession—dyers, tinsmiths, carpenters, carpet makers, spice sellers, and even makers of musical instruments. You can see craftsmen bent over their tools, working away and creating marvels in what, to Western eyes, are very bad conditions (dark and stuffy). In here is Bab el-Jdid, one of the town's oldest gates built in Almohad times, and also an Almohad mosque. The old *mellah* (Jewish quarter) lies to the left of the medina as you face the Dar Jamai Museum, the other side of the road from the Carpenters' Souk.

Going in the other direction from the Place el-Hedim, you'll reach the **Mausoleum of Mulay Ismail,** and the **Imperial Town** with the **Dar el-Makhzen, Agdal Basin, stables,** and **granaries.** The road to the right of Bab el-Mansour leads more or less straight to the **Mausoleum of Mulay Ismail** (on the left), leaving the small, domed Koubbat al-Khayatin (Tailors' *Kubba*) on the right. Mulay Ismail used to receive foreign ambassadors here in the 18th century, and it was later used as a workshop for making military uniforms (from which it gets its name). Close by is the entrance to a vast **underground granary** (once a prison where a few hundred prisoners—Christians, Turks, and local Berbers—were held before Mulay Ismail allowed them to build their own district, equipped even with a church for the Christians). Rather more cheery, the **Mausoleum** is a flamboyant place, reached through a series of courtyards, and can be visited by non-Moslems, decently dressed (shoes left upon arriving at the railings in front of the tombs). The interior dome is supported by 12 columns taken from the Roman site of Volubilis. The funeral chamber is decorated with stuccowork and mosaics and is thickly carpeted. Behind the tombs, two elegant tall French clocks, a gift from Louis XIV, look rather out of place. There are four tombs: those of Mulay Ismail, his favorite wife, and two of his sons. Mulay Ismail's tomb is topped by five bronze balls, usually reserved for the minarets of the mosques (open from 9:00 A.M.-12:00 P.M. and 3:00 P.M.-6:00 P.M., closed Fridays, entry 10 DH). Entry by non-Moslems was decreed by Mohammed V. If you turn left out of the Mausoleum, go back a bit towards Place el-Hedim, left past the Koubbat al-Khayatin, and then left for about 15 minutes (1 km) (the golf course, once an ornamental garden, lies on the left) you arrive at Dar el-Makhzen. Visitors are not allowed in, since it is still a royal palace, but you can swing right until coming to the **granaries, stables,** and **Agdal Basin.** The vaulted **Heri es-Souani** granaries are really impressive and very photogenic. The walls are four-meters thick, the windows small, and the building was kept cool by water circulating under the floor. Some of the 12 wells (14 m deep) connected to the Agdal Basin are still visible. Part of the movie *The Last Temptation of Christ* was shot here. Good views over the palaces can be had from the roof of the granaries (open from 9:00 A.M.-12:00 P.M. and 3:00 P.M.-6:00 P.M., entry 10 DH). The nearby Agdal Basin was used as a reservoir for the palace gardens and a boating lake for the sultan and his family. It has just recently been renovated and is now most attractive. Also not far, Mulay Ismail's stables, which housed 12,000 horses, are vast but rather ruined. Originally, they were made up of some 20 aisles and several thousand columns, and were once thought to have been a granary. Further off can be seen a palace built by Mohammed III at the end of the 18th century, called **Dar el-Beida** (White House) (this sultan was the one who recognized the newly independent United States of America). Mulay Ismail had an ostrich farm here, and it now houses a military academy.

A visit to the **Royal Stud Farm,** a bit out of town on the Azrou road (well indicated), is a marvelous opportunity to see some superb stallions—Arab thoroughbred, Barbs, and Arabo-Barbs. Visitors can look around as they like and admire these animals in their boxes—all with their names and a color to indicate their race and ancestry—or at work. The farm is designed to improve the quality of the Moroccan horse, by providing the best stallions for the mares that are brought in for mating. Entry is free and the pleasant staff seems pleased to be working there.

NORTH OF MEKNÈS

North of Meknès, the holy Islamic town of **Mulay Idriss** (22 km) and the **Roman ruins of Volubilis** (30 km) are easily accessible in the day. Many visitors prefer to make Volubilis their base if their time is limited. Both can be visited in a day if necessary. For the motorized traveler with time to spend, a drive among the olive-groves of the **Zerhoun Massif** (1,118 m), taking a right-turn after Volubilis, up to Nzala-des-Beni Ammer, can be very agreeable, especially in the spring, when the almond trees are in bloom, or in October, when the olives are being harvested. Big sheets are laid out around the trees and whole families vigorously beat the branches to shake down the olives.

Perched on the hillside, **Mulay Idriss** is a holy city, containing the shrine of Idriss I, a fugitive from Arabia, who founded the first Arab-Moslem dynasty in Morocco. It is only in this century that non-Moslems have been allowed in, and they are still not allowed to spend the night there. Upon his arrival in Morocco, Idriss installed himself in Oualili (ex-Volubilis), won the esteem of the neighboring tribes, and was proclaimed sultan in 788 A.D. He died, poisoned, in 791, and was succeeded by his son Idriss II, who chose to make his capital in Fès. But the small town of Mulay Idriss houses the tomb of the holy founder and owes its fame to him, ranking high among the holy towns of Islam. The annual pilgrimage to the shrine, during the *moussem* held at the end of August, attracts thousands of pilgrims from all over the country.

The way to both Mulay Idriss and Volubilis starts with the P6 to Tangier, north of the town, with a right-hand turn onto the P28 after about 15 km. The road winds up through olive trees, vines, and holm oaks. After another 6-7 km, a small road to the right leads to Mulay Idriss (car park in main square). A bus leaves Meknès every hour from the Bab el-Mansour bus station. A big taxi will also make the trip.

There is no **hotel** in Mulay Idriss, but there is a reasonable campsite some 14 km out of Meknès, on the way to Mulay Idriss, **Camping Zerhoun Belle Vue.** It is shady and its little restaurant is not bad.

The **Restaurant el-Baraka** (22 Ain Smen-Khiber) supplies a good Moroccan menu from 100 DH.

Way up the hill, behind Mulay Idriss's shrine, the small restaurant **Dar Diaf** (8 Rue Hofra) is also a possibility, with a splendid view thrown in.

The town is small, but it's not too difficult to find the way up from the big square (bus and taxi stopping place) to the main shop-lined street, through a three-arched gateway on the left, and then on to the **Mausoleum of Mulay Idriss,** built by Mulay Ismail (not really necessary to take one of the numerous guides). Non-Moslems can only go as far as the railings. At the end of a labyrinth of small streets that climb up to the left of the Mausoleum the Sidi Abdallah el-Hajjam terrace provides a splendid view over the sparkling white town, the mausoleum, and the surrounding countryside, including Volubilis on a clear day. Another way up is to go back to the main street, then up a street marked "Municipalité," continue climbing, pass a mosque with a tile-coated, cylindrical minaret, and after another 300 m you'll reach the panoramic terrace.

The visitor who makes his way to **Volubilis** sees the ruins of this old Roman town from afar. While it is true that the most visible monuments date from the first to third centuries A.D., when the Romans occupied Volubilis (then called Oualili, later transformed into Volubilis), a Mauretanian Berber village of roughly-built houses had already existed there for several centuries. It is also almost certain that the site was also

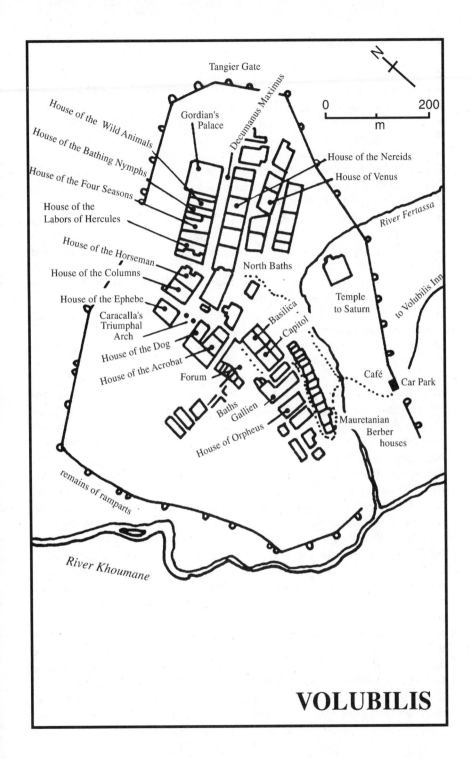

Tangier Gate

House of the Wild Animals

House of the Bathing Nymphs

House of the Four Seasons

House of the Labors of Hercules

House of the Horseman

House of the Columns

House of the Ephebe

Caracalla's Triumphal Arch

House of the Dog

House of the Acrobat

Gordian's Palace

Decumanus Maximus

House of the Nereids

House of Venus

River Fertassa

North Baths

Basilica

Capitol

Temple to Saturn

to Volubilis Inn

Forum

Café

Car Park

Baths Gallien

House of Orpheus

Mauretanian Berber houses

remains of ramparts

River Khoumane

0   200
m

N

VOLUBILIS

occupied in Neolithic times. Before the arrival of the Romans in Morocco, the Berbal tribal leaders had come under the influence of the Phoenicians and Carthaginians who had started frequenting the coast in the seventh century B.C. Towns such as Oualili began to copy the Punic urban and social model. However, in the first century B.C., the Berbers supported the loser in the power-struggle among the Roman generals, were defeated, and a young Berber prince (aged five) was taken captive to Rome. Brought up in the household of the Emperor Augustus, where he was educated in the manner of a young Roman aristocrat, this Berber prince was sent back to Africa by the Romans in 25 B.C. as king of Mauretania. Taking the name of Juba II, he established his capital at Caesarea (Cherchel) in Algeria and his "secondary" capital in Volubilis. His reign lasted almost 50 years, and brought prosperity and cultural prestige to Morocco.

Juba II was responsible for the town's first important monuments. Cultivated and scholarly, he brought in architects who embellished it with public buildings and private houses. But in spite of his efforts, it was only after the annexation of his kingdom by Rome in about 42 A.D. that Volubilis became endowed with buildings whose ruins are admired today.

Roman power in the kingdom was represented by a governor, whose seat was in Volubilis. The Roman town was protected by 3 km of ramparts, with towers at regular intervals and 11 gateways—the northeast one is the most visible today. Its cosmopolitan population is estimated to have reached 20,000. The majority of the townspeople were natives of Morocco, while others were Roman government officials, soldiers of many nationalities, and Greek, Syrian, and Carthaginian merchants. The town prospered from its trade in olive oil (many houses had their own presses), wheat, and trade in wild animals for the Roman games. As in most Roman North African towns, the first monuments were built at the beginning of the third century A.D., especially under the Emperors Septimus Severus and Caracalla. But as their empire shrank, the Roman administration was obliged to leave the southern part of the Moroccan protectorate. Volubilis, the provincial capital, was evacuated around 285 A.D.. However, the departure of the merchants and the Roman army did not mean the end of all activity in the town. The local population continued to live and trade there, altering the urban layout by building their small houses in the middle of the roads and burying their dead in the abandoned villas. Some inscriptions and tombs show that a community of Christianized Berbers continued to occupy the town until the eighth century. When, in 789, Idriss I was proclaimed *imam* (religious leader), Volubilis reverted to its old name of Oualili. The later founding of Fès started its definite decline, and the 1755 Lisbon earthquake finished it off.

Excavations in the town were begun at the end of the 19th century. Many monuments were revealed and restored by French archaeologists, and their work is continued today by teams of Moroccan archaeologists and students. Many of the mosaics are still in place, but the superb bronze and marble statues and numerous small finds have gone to the Archaeological Museum in Rabat. A few mosaics and statues decorate the garden by the ticket office, but precious items are no longer on display, some having been stolen in the past since security is difficult to assure in this out-of-the-way place.

Volubilis is reached by returning to the main road after Mulay Idriss and continuing on a few kilometers. A road to the left marked "Volubilis" leads to a very large parking area in front of the entrance to the ruins (open daily, entry 20 DH). The route to follow in the site is shown and it is perfectly possible to navigate it alone. The site is a very relaxed sort of place and one can wander about as one likes (climbing on the walls is forbidden). Guides are available (about 100 DH for a hour's tour). At least one speaks English, but he may have to be hired in advance.

The nearest **hotel** is the **** **Volubilis Inn** (52 rooms, Tel: 54 44 05, Fax: 63 63 93), situated a kilometer from the Roman site and 3 km from Mulay Idriss. It is often preferred as a base by visitors intending to make only a short visit to Meknès. It is set in calm surroundings, has a small pool, tennis court, two restaurants (one Moroccan under a traditional tent), and a bar. There are very good views from the terrace (telescope provided) and from the bedrooms facing the right direction. The lower floor bedrooms open onto the gardens. People with walking problems should make sure they have a room involving a minimum of steps, since the bedrooms are on several floors. The **restaurants** in the **Volubilis Inn** are the only ones in the area (set meal from 154 DH), but it is possible to eat a reasonable lunch or snack in the shady site restaurant at Volubilis (*tajine* or chicken), or just stop for a soft drink or coffee.

Once on the site, the route goes downhill from the entrance, across the little River Fertassa, then up to the left and through the southern district of the town, where the older **Mauretanian Berber** houses were built. Oil presses can be seen on the left, before one arrives at an exceptional house in this part of the original town, the **House of Orpheus,** so named because of its large mosaic depicting the legendary musician Orpheus taming the wild animals. A mosaic of dolphins decorates the floor of the *triclinium* (dining room), to the left of the entrance (note also the chariot of Amphitrite). Judging from its size, the house was the residence of an important person. A later architect adapted a block of several old Berber buildings to create this single, large, Roman-style villa. Near here is a reconstruction by Meknès high school pupils of an **olive-press** that's worth studying. Two sets of **public baths** *(Thermes)* follow, those of Gallien and the Forum. Some hot rooms and pools can be seen in the former.

On the right lies the **Capitol,** preceded by a stone altar and reached by a flight of steps. It dates to 217 A.D. and some of its Corinthian columns have been restored. The **Forum,** the center of public and administrative life, is reached by a couple of low steps. It is small and oddly shaped by normal Roman standards, and still retains part of its original blue-grey limestone paving. It flanks the vast rectangular **Basilica,** more or less in line with the Capitol. This is probably the most imposing of Volubilis' buildings, covering 1,000m². Its three aisles are separated by a line of seven columns. It was here that people gathered to talk, to hear lawsuits, draw up municipal regulations, and do business. A little further on, to the left, is the **House of the Acrobat** *(Maison au Desultor),* again named because of its mosaic showing a man back to front on a mule or donkey, followed by that of the **House of the Dog** *(Maison du Chien)*—the bronze statue of a dog found here is the spitting image of a modern Moroccan farm dog barking at an intruder. The house—like many others—has two doors: one for people on foot, the other for those being carried in the customary box-like carriage.

Caracalla's Triumphal Arch *(Arc de Triomphe de Caracalla),* next on the itinerary, was built at the end of the main street, with the **Decumanus Maximus,** leading to and from the **Tangier Gate** *(Porte de Tanger),* still visible at its extremity. An inscription on the arch indicates that it was built in 217 A.D. in honor of the Emperor Caracalla and his mother, Julia Domna. Archaeologists have attempted to reconstruct its decoration from the lumps of stone lying around, particularly the statues that once stood in the side niches. The horses and chariot that topped it were probably in bronze.

The orientation of the town changes from here. Flanking the Decumanus Maximus on either side are a series of what were once beautiful villas, with patios and tiled galleries. They still retain a number of well preserved mosaics, showing fish, dolphins, and other marine animals, or mythological scenes. The general layout of these villas is roughly identical: a vestibule leads into an atrium, surrounded on three sides by pillars, containing a basin to collect rainwater. Opposite the entrance a large room, the *triclinium* served as a dining room. In front of these houses were small shops, with up-and-down sliding shutters, much like many Moroccan shops and garages today. The first of these villas is the **House of the Ephebe** (beautiful young man—and indeed he is, but his bronze statue is only visible in Rabat!), then the **House of the Columns** *(Maison des Colonnes)* with differently shaped pillars, the **House of the Horseman** *(Maison du Cavalier)*, with a magnificent mosaic showing Bacchus, helped by a little Cupid, spying on the sleeping Ariadne. The **House of the Labors of Hercules** *(Maison des Travaux d'Hercule)* shows 10 of his tasks, set in little medallions with a rich floral decoration. Continuing along the villas on the right, a well-designed mosaic shows Bacchus (again—but this is only to be expected as he was the God of Wine) and the Four Seasons, and another has bathing nymphs *(Maison des Bains des Nymphes)*. Most of these villas have central basins and mosaic floors other than the main cited attractions (have a look at some of these, too).

Gordian's Palace *(Palais de Gordien)* has a large bath area and is thought to have been that of the governor of the town. Going back down the main paved street (with drainage channels), work your way through the ruins on the left until you reach the **House of the Nereids** and the **House of Venus** *(Maison de Vénus)*, the latter being one of the richest on the site. The numerous marble and bronze busts that were found here (Juba II, Cato) have all gone to Rabat, but the mosaic floors are still there. They show a chariot race with harnessed geese, ducks, and peacocks, Bacchus (this time with the four seasons), Hylas captured by nymphs, and Diana surprised by Actaeon in her bath.

Continuing back towards the Triumphal Arch, you'll see the big **North Baths** *(Thermes du Nord)*, and further on a **stone trough,** with well-worn edges, that collected water from the aquaduct—bits of which can also be seen at ground-level—which the Romans built to bring water from the Zerhoun massif. The visit to the site is not really over, for there is a whole mass of villas around the House of Venus, but the best of the mosaic floors have been seen. For the really keen, ask to see the Christian cemetery that has recently been revealed near the Triumphal Arch, the Temple to Saturn, and the phallic stone tucked away in a villa near here. Volubilis is one of the Moroccan sites scheduled by UNESCO as part of the world heritage.

WEST OF MEKNÈS

West from Meknès, the main P1 to **Rabat** (138 km) goes through attractive, rolling, agricultural country devoted to cereals, olives, and wines for the first 45 km, as far as Khemisset. Work to link Meknès and Rabat by expressway is now finished. After about 30 km, the road twists down to cross the **Oued Beth.** Just after the bridge, the hill on the right was fortified by a wall in Neolithic times and surface finds have included pottery shards and several hundred polished axes. Khemisset is perhaps not worth a special visit, but it merits stopping on the way to somewhere else. Being on the main road, it's easy to get there by bus from Meknès, as well as by big taxi. From Khemisset, the spa town of **Oulmes** (chapter 6) can be reached along a very narrow but picturesque secondary road, the P2572. The **Café-Hotel Royal** on the left in Khemisset is a popular place for a snack.

The Tuesday market is one of the most frequented in the area, where one can see a good selection of rugs woven by the local Zemmour tribes. There is a **Craftwork Center** *(Centre Artisanal)* showing rugs on the right at the beginning of the town. Khemisset also goes in for the highly-decorated, pom-pomed straw hats made in Tiflet (chapter 6), and is noted for its kebobs (all the long-distance buses stop here for a "kebob-and-coffee" pause).

EAST OF MEKNÈS

Going **east,** a motorway now joins Meknès to Fès (60 km) (chapter 8). It runs through rich agricultural land, where many French farmers settled and turned the wild ground into productive farmland. It is possible to visit the most important sights in Fès in a day, but it is strongly advised to spend at least a night in Fès to do justice to this fascinating city.

FURTHER AFIELD

The road going **north** from Meknès, the P6, eventually reaches **Tangier** (chapter 5) via **Sidi Kacem** (46 km) and **Souk el-Arba** (a further 61 km) (chapter 6). The route is not particularly picturesque, apart from a stretch around the **Zeggota Pass** *(Col de Zeggota).* The town of Sidi Kacem is dominated by its oil refining industry. From Sidi Kacem the P3, going west, goes through the Gharb plain before reaching **Kénitra** (84 km) (chapter 6) and Rabat.

It is **south** of Meknès that the best excursions can be made, plunging into the heart of the **Middle Atlas.** This mountainous range can also be reached from Fès. The area is not noted for its historical monuments, but rather for its natural beauty. Several centers are well equipped with hotels and restaurants suitable for all types of traveler. Stretching for 250 km (156 miles), the Middle Atlas has more rainfall than the High Atlas, although its oak and cedar-clad hills are not as high. The highest peak is the Bou Iblane (3,172 m), at the eastern end of the chain. The western end is undulating country, ideal for a rest/cure, trekking, or fishing in the many lakes. Cross-country skiing is also possible from the end of December to the end of February (snow, however, is not guaranteed). The main towns that will be covered here are **Azrou, Ifrane, Khenifra,** and **Midelt.** Only the first two can reasonably be attempted in a day's outing (70 and 65 km respectively from Meknès). Khenifra is only 150 km from Meknès, but the main road is without interest and it would be a pity to miss out on the attractions of the Middle Atlas. The same applies to Midelt, which is 210 km from Meknès.

The first port of call can be **Azrou,** some 70 km from Meknès. The main P21 first goes through **El-Hajeb** (30 km), standing at 1,045 m, which was, and still is, an important military base. There is a good viewpoint here, back towards the plain south of Meknès, but El-Hajeb itself is not particularly interesting, though it has the ruins of a kasbah built by the sultan Mulay Hassan at the end of the 19th century. At El-Hajeb there is a choice of routes—one goes to **Azrou,** the other (to the left) to **Ifrane.** As there is a very attractive road between Ifrane and Azrou, the visitor can do a round trip on the return to Meknès. On past El-Hajeb, you are on top of a plateau with a superb view to the right. *The* stopping place is at a point called **Ito's Viewpoint** *(Belvédère d'Ito),* 15 km before Azrou.

Azrou is an important center for the Middle Atlas Berber tribes, who have lived in the region for many hundreds, if not thousands, of years, and its name comes from the pointed rock at the edge of the town (*azrou* means rock in Berber). Its position, at the intersection of routes from Meknès and Fès to Marrakech or the desert regions in the Tafilalet, accounted for its prosperity. Mulay Ismail built a kasbah here at the end of the 17th century, but it is in ruins and really not worth looking for. The small lively town lies on the edge of a fine cedar forest (which is, unfortunately, declining) with many pleasant walks and picnic places. With luck, you'll see a few Barbary apes. Situated at an altitude of 1,250 m, it is today much appreciated as a summer resort by the inhabitants of Meknès and Fès, or for skiing when there is snow. The French opened a high school in Azrou for Berber pupils, *Le Collège Berbère.* The town also houses a number of holiday camps run by the state or private organizations. Azrou is noted for its rug making (the style is known as Moyen Atlas, off-white with a little pale brown design in the corner) and samples can be seen in the **Craftwork Center** *(Coopérative Artisanale).* It can be reached by **bus, big taxi,** or **car.** The CTM bus company also runs a service to and from Ifrane, Fès, and Casablanca, and even further afield to Agadir, via Beni Mellal and Marrakech, or Midelt and Er-Rachidia (all these last destinations involving many hours of travel).

The **top-of-the range hotel scene** is represented by the **** **Hotel Amros** (83 rooms, Tel: 56 36 81/56 36 63, Fax: 56 36 80), 7 km outside Azrou on the Meknès road. It is agreeable and calm, with a swimming pool, tennis courts, a restaurant, and a nightclub.

This is followed by the *** **Hotel Panorama,** just behind the high school *(lycée)* on the Ifrane/Fès road, 500 m from the town center (40 rooms, Tel: 56 20 10, Fax: 56 18 04). It was completely renovated in 1996 and is comfortable and welcoming, with a wood fire in the vestibule in the winter (the bedrooms also heated, though some are a bit small), a bar, and a restaurant.

Budget accommodations are provided by the * **Hotel des Cedres** (9 rooms, Tel: 56 23 26) and the **Hotel Ziz** (rooms with windows around 70 DH, Tel: 56 23 62), one opposite the other in the center of town (Place Mohammed V), with clean rooms, communal showers, and lots of noises outside.

There is a **Youth Hostel** (Tel: 56 24 96) as you come into the town from Ifrane (youth hostel card not necessary). The cheaper hotels and the Youth Hostel are not recommended for winter lodging, since they don't have heating and you really need a very good sleeping-bag to keep warm.

Dining is limited to the two big hotels mentioned above—food in the **Hotel Amros** is rather ordinary. The three-course set menu in the **Hotel Panorama** is 120 DH (130 DH if you want the local trout). (Friends there in the summer of 1998 found the menu very expensive for what they got— vegetable soup, trout, and caramel cream dessert). The **Hotel des Cedres** also serves the local trout. Other smaller restaurants can usually provide good soup and kebobs. The Azrou trout farm supplies many local hotels.

Lake fishing and **hunting** in season can be arranged by the Hotel Panorama, who will also advise on suitable **walks** and long-distance **trekking** (make sure that the mountain escort they suggest is officially recognized). **Trekking,** with an accredited mountain escort and mules (most convenient for the baggage) can also be arranged through the National Association of Mountain Guides and Escorts, based in Marrakech, but has members resident in Ifrane. The address of the association—ANGAM *(Association Nationale des Guides et Accompagnateurs en Montagne du Maroc),* rather a mouthful)—is given in the Meknès address list. For French-speaking Catholic mass, you need to ring Meknès (Tel: 53 00 36).

Before starting on the various circuits possible from around here, it is worth considering the town of **Ifrane,** which makes an equally good departure point. It lies 17 km from Azrou (the most picturesque route is through a cedar forest, with stunning views) on the Fès road (P24). A turn off this road (which is marked) leads to **Gouraud's Cedar** *(Cèdre de Gouraud),* named after a French general, who was Résident Général for three months. This massive cedar has a 10 m circumference. Ifrane (altitude 1,650 m) was built by the French in 1929 as a summer and winter resort for residents in Fès and Meknès, and is quite different from Azrou. In summer it is deliciously cool, in winter it is a skiing center, and at other times of the year serves, like Azrou, as an agreeable base for excursions. Ifrane is clean, green, and well-watered, with tumbling streams that make one wonder if one is in Morocco (especially if you have come up after a long drive from the dry sands of the desert). Look out for the carved stone Lion of Ifrane, a legacy of the French (it is not far from the Hotel Perce-Neige, but rather hidden by the vegetation).

And you can't miss the storks, which seem particularly fond of the town. The late King Hassan II had a summer palace in Ifrane, and in the early 1990s a private **university** was set up, Al Akhawayn (The Brothers), with a strong American slant and a number of American teachers. It is a pricey establishment, with the majority of Moroccan students from Casablanca, but it does have a sprinkling of nationals from other Arab countries (500 students in all, at the moment). As one drives into Ifrane from Meknès, one sees a mass of little white houses quite unlike the rest of Ifrane's architecture. This district is designed to be the new commercial center of the town, with banks, a supermarket, and all sorts of other shops. The town also boasts a Sports Center, where national and foreign football teams come to train. Ifrane **can be reached** by **car, bus,** or **big taxi.** CTM buses come from Fès, Meknès, Casablanca, Marrakech (via Beni Mellal), and Azrou.

Ifrane is well provided with **hotels,** but in July and August, and during holiday periods, most of them are fully booked. The **most expensive** is the recently-renovated ***** **Hotel Michliffen,** outside the town (106 rooms, 900 DH, Tel: 56 66 07/14/16/18, Fax: 56 66 23). This is an excellent establishment, with a restaurant, game-rooms for kids, and a nightclub.

Medium-price hotels start with the *** **Hotel Perce-Neige** (27 rooms, breakfast 40 DH—too expensive—Rue des Asphodelles, BP 47, Hay Riad, Tel: 56 63 50/51, Fax: 56 71 10). Don't be put off by the long address— Ifrane is so small that all the hotels are very easy to find. The hotel was taken over in 1975 by the Samir Oil Company (but this only means that Samir staff have preferential bookings). The hotel is agreeably furnished, the bedrooms are small, heated, and have balconies, and the reception is very welcoming. It has a restaurant.

The *** **Hotel Tilleuls** (20 rooms and 8 suites, breakfast also at 40 DH; an additional floor is being prepared to increase the number of rooms, Tel: 56 66 29) is a pretty undistinguished place (the only thing I found interesting there was a showcase with the stuffed heads of two wild boar and a Barbary sheep). The staff do their best and it has a bar and restaurant.

The ** **Grand Hotel** (used to cost 300 DH for a double room, Tel: 56 62 03, Fax: 56 64 07, Avenue de la Poste) was closed and said to be in the process of being entirely refurbished.

The * **Hotel Chamonix** (used to cost 200 DH, Avenue de la Marche Verte, Tel: 56 60 28) was also closed, apparently to be enlarged.

Ifrane does not go in for budget accommodations, but the campsite (Tel: 56 61 56, 20 DH per person, per tent, and per car) at the entrance to the town (coming from Meknès) is good (with clean restroom facilities for once).

Hotel restaurants have been mentioned above, with the **Hotel Michliffen** the best, but expensive (the set menu, at 230 DH, is not really worth the price).

The **Hotel Tilleuls** does a tourist menu at 80 DH (more if you want trout), but I couldn't eat there because the chef was off duty (no comment— maybe I was unlucky).

Dinner in the restaurant of the **Hotel Perce-Neige** (menu 120 DH) can be excellent if the chef is there.

Other restaurants include the small, unpretentious **Café Restaurant La Rose,** 7 Hay Riad (in the center of town) that was good and had very rapid and pleasant service. The set meal was 70 DH and—surprisingly—the place was licensed, so we had a bottle of wine (85 DH) with our delicious trout.

The Café-Restaurant La Paix (Avenue de la Marche Verte) is very similar and slightly cheaper, with the advantage of an outdoor terrace. It serves pizzas.

This food section cannot end without a mention of two good places for a snack: the **Cookie Craque** (Avenue des Tilleuls) has a modern decor, pleasant terrace, tasty pastries, savories, pizzas, and ice cream, and, understandably, is often crowded with young men and women (not so often seen together in public cafés), and **Le Croustillant,** a very nice coffee shop, also usually full of people.

Sightseeing close to Ifrane could include a visit to the ski resort of **Michliffen** (17 km south of Ifrane), crossing Tizi n'Tretten pass (1,934 m). Unless you have gone to ski, there is nothing much to do, but in summer it makes a pleasant place in which to walk (you need your own transport). Cross-country skiing is very popular around here as the slopes are not steep enough for high-speed skiing, though the Jbel Hebri is more challenging. Gear can be hired in Ifrane. Excursions on horseback are arranged in the summer by the Hotel Michliffen (the tourist office can also offer advice).

Whether the traveler has his/her base in Ifrane or in Azrou, the **Lake Circuit** *(Circuit Touristique des Lacs)* between Ifrane and Imouzer du Kandar is well worth doing for the beauty of the scenery. As the trip can be done more easily from Fès, details are given in chapter 8.

Seven kilometers out of Azrou, on the P21 road to Midelt, a signpost on the right marked *Circuit Touristique* (Touristic Circuit) points the way to beautiful country lying between Khenifra, on the road to Marrakech, and Itzer, on the way to Midelt (a car is essential, unfortunately, unless a big taxi is hired for the day by a group of friends). This circuit (following the S303) is not advised in winter, when the roads may be under snow or damaged by rain. The traveler can choose what to see from the numerous possibilities—but don't hesitate to be guided by the signposts. The road goes through the cedar forest to the big village of **Ain Leuh** (20 km) (which has a market on Wednesday). There are plenty of tempting little ways into the woods, but watch out not to get stuck in the mud. The older Berber women around here are beautifully tattooed, but you'll see few pretty young tattooed girls, as the custom is dying out. From time to time, through the mist, one can catch glimpses of smoke from charcoal burners' fires, looking rather like Indian wigwams. Small *dayas* (temporary lakes) can be spotted, white-splashed with water lilies. Migrating birds pass down this way in the season. About 30 km further on and to the left (there is a parking place and would-be guides and car-guardians), are the **springs** and **waterfalls** (a 10-minute walk away from the parking area) that are the origin of the big River Oum er-Rbia *(Sources de l'Oum er-Rbia)* which reaches the Atlantic at Azemmour (a distance of 600 km). Further on, try not to miss the marked track to **Aguelmane Azizga,** a blue lake in the middle of cedars and evergreen oaks. After this, **one possible exit** is to turn right, about 20 km after the waterfalls, at the T-junction, and take the S3485 for Khenifra, with a right turn again at **Khenifra** to get back to **Azrou** by the main P24 (to the left at Khenifra the road continues to Kasba Tadla, Beni Mellal, and Marrakech). The **other option** is to turn left and continue along a very winding road (still the S3485) to join the main road at the lead-mining village of Zeida and back up to Azrou by the P21 and the Col du Zad pass. A right turn down the P21 will take you to Midelt.

The **first option** above leads to **Khenifra.** For the traveler in a hurry to reach Khenifra, the quickest route is the main P24 via Mrirt, but the itinerary proposed above is infinitely more rewarding. Khenifra lies on both banks of the River Oum er-Rbia and is a bustling and attractive Berber town. For a long time it used to be only a modest little center for the surrounding Zaine Berber tribes, but then Mulay Ismail recognized its strategic position. He restored the Adekhsan Kasbah and had a bridge built across the river to facilitate the movement of his troops. For once, however, it is not Mulay Ismail who is associated with the town, but the Zaine chief, Moha ou Hammou. At the end of the 19th century, the sultan Hassan I nominated him *caid* and he rapidly gained complete control of the region, in the name of the sultan. Khenifra flourished, became an important trading center, Moha ou Hammou built mosques and lodgings for the traders and, of course, became quite independent of the weakening central rule. Becoming more agressive, his men attacked passing caravans and organized raids for booty as far as Meknès. In these circumstances, it is not surprising that he was a leading figure in the fierce Berber resistance to French penetration at the beginning of the 20th century. Although French forces reached Khenifra in 1914, World War I and the mobilization it required prevented them from winning control until 1921, after epic battles. Today, Khenifra is a busy town with a population of around 15,000 (and still very Berber, although it is now a provincial capital, with offices of the central administration). All of the Middle Atlas is noted for its songs and dances, in particular the Ahidous, and, not only Khenifra, but each village has its own troop of dancers.

Khenifra can be **reached** by **car,** or by **bus** from Meknès or Marrakech. **Hotel accommodation** is very limited. The ⁂ **Hotel Hamou Azzayani** (58 rooms, BP 94, Tel: 58 60 20, Fax: 58 78 74) is disappointing, despite its beautiful situation.

The **Hotel-Restaurant de France** (Tel: 58 61 14, in the west part of town) has a grand name but is a very modest affair and best used only in an emergency.

There is not much **sightseeing** to be done, but the **medina** and **souks** are active and interesting and an excellent place in which to look at the local capes *(selham)* and jewelry. Of the two **kasbahs,** only one, by the bridge, is not completely ruined. Weather permitting, a circuit south of Khenifra by **El Ksiba** and up to **El Kbab** offers splendid views, but since this is rather far from Meknès, and accommodations in Khenifra are poor, it is dealt with in chapter 12. From Khenifra, the main P24 goes right to Azrou and left to Kasbah Tadla and Marrakech (see chapter 12 for these last two towns).

If you decide on the **second itinerary,** joining the main road at Zeida and up left to Azrou, you can see, from time to time, beside the main road the tents of the nomad tribes and their large flocks of sheep and goats. The tents are sometimes made of the traditional black goat and camel wool, and are now often made of multicolored plastic sheeting. In fact, the occupants of these tents are not all-the-year-round nomads; most have a settled village somewhere and move around with their flocks according to the season and the availability of pasturage for their animals. Along this route, some 10 km after the junction, a road to the left leads to the small village of **Itzer,** which is good for the purchase of a rug or two, especially on market day. Back on the main road, just after the **Col du Zad pass** (altitude 2,178 m) a short road (1 km) on the right leads to **Aguelmane de Sidi Ali,** a lake formed in an old volcanic crater that is nice for swimming or a picnic. The Col du Zad marks the dividing point for rivers flowing into the Atlantic (the Oum er-Rbia) and those flowing north into the Mediterranean (the Moulouya). The main road goes through **Timahdite,** another mining town, which is not very attractive, but the storks seem to like the area.

If, from Meknès, you are intent on reaching the **far south** as quickly as possible and skip the enchanting lakes, hills, and valleys of the Middle

Atlas, continue along the P21 from Azrou, through Timhadite down to **Midelt** (140 km from Azrou). On the right after Zeida there's a big sign announcing the **National Barbary Sheep Reserve** *(Parc National des Mouflons).* **Birdwatchers** say they have had some unusual sightings south of Zeida.

If you're not in a hurry and want to do something out of the ordinary, stop for a day or two at the **Timnay Inter-Cultures Tourist Centre,** on the left, a few kilometers before Midelt (BP 81, Midelt 39016, Tel: 58 34 34). This is *not* a ***** tourist complex, but it does offer a number of unusual possibilities despite the pseudo-kasbah central building. They have small, very simple but clean rooms with hot showers (50 DH adult, 30 DH children, with a minimum of 100 DH) in the garden, a shady campsite (18 DH/person, 15 DH/tent, and 15 DH/car, and there is a pool—in the summer only), a small grocery store, and a restaurant. You'll not be coming here for the lodging but for the experience. Created as an "intercultural" center in 1990, its publicized aims are to "initiate visitors in the culture and lifestyle of the nomads and sedentary people of the mountains and upper valleys . . . through reliable means and reasonable prices, adaptable to visitors' financial means." They do this by providing a guide if you have your own 4WD car or motorbike to take you off the beaten track, or they can supply suitable transport themselves (a car, mule, or mountain bike). Their itineraries are adapted to suit all tastes and physical fitness (it's okay for kids and seniors). Prices for the excursions range from 120 DH for a half-day to 300 DH for a full day, per person, with food included. If you don't want to be organized, you can hire a guide and mule. The whole thing is pretty rough and primitive, but the managers are friendly and willing to please. When I first went there, I thought I had discovered something, but I have since found out that the center is pretty well known and that it's best to book in advance to be sure of getting what you want.

Midelt lies at the foot of the Jbel Ayachi and is cold in winter (at an altitude of 1,488 m) and windswept at all times. It has been essentially a mining town (for the mines of Aouli and Mibladen), attracting a mixed population, but the mines are not as active as they used to be. It is also a horticultural center, concentrating on apples. The youth of the town seem to live off selling semi-precious (or fake semi-precious) stones and fossils to the passing tourist, but they are not too insistent and enjoy a bit of a chat. The **bus station** is off Avenue Mohammed V, the main street. You can arrive in Midelt from just about anywhere, if you are prepared for long journeys and several changes, and you can leave in the same way. **Big taxis** also go north and south.

The hotel scene has the new *** **Hotel Restaurant Asmaa** (20 rooms, Tel: 58 04 08, Fax: 58 39 45), on the right, 3 km before the town. It has a large, very ornate hall, a pool (open in the summer only), a restaurant, and a bar. The staff is very welcoming (one speaks English), and I noticed that it was popular with tourist buses.

In the town, the ★★★ **Hotel El-Ayachi** (28 rooms, Rue d'Agadir by Avenue Hassan II, Tel: 58 21 61, Fax: 58 33 07) is an old, established, clean, and comfortable hotel set in a small garden, with a restaurant and a bar (it is also popular with tourists).

Much lower down the scale, the best is probably the unclassified **Hotel-Restaurant Bougafar** (eight rooms on two floors, 120 DH, 7 Boulevard Mohammed V, Tel: 55 30 99). Its rooms are clean, but the water closets are communal.

Dining and Restaurants. The **Hotel Restaurant Asmaa** and the **Hotel Ayachi** both have restaurants, with the set meal at the former slightly cheaper (100 DH compared to 120 DH). Both are licensed.

Cheaper eating can be had at the **Restaurant Fès** (Rue Lalla Aicha), where the standard meal is priced at 70 DH (it is very much in the *harira* soup and *tajine* style, but good).

Nightclubs have not yet reached Midelt, so **entertainment and nightlife** is confined to soft drinks at a café or stronger stuff in the two big hotels.

Sightseeing around here is for nature-lovers. The road southwest (the 3424), to the **Cirque de Jaffar** (26 km), at the foot of the 3,737 m peak of the Jbel Ayachi, is stunningly beautiful. The pass just before the Cirque stands at 2,250 m. This is a mountain road, often muddy, that should be undertaken with prudence, preferably with two cars, or better still a 4WD vehicle. Better still, some would say, it should be done on foot, for a few days (check with the Weather—or "Met"—Office for news before setting out—in the summer freak storms in the mountains can be dangerous). The road, the P3425, continues on past the Cirque and comes out at **Imilchil** (see below), after about 170 km of difficult driving (only for the adventurous). The **climb** up to the summit of Jbel Ayachi is not particularly demanding. The departure point is the village of **Tattiouine** (off the 3424), from where a mule track goes up to the top. Further along the track, a good base for the climb to the western summit of the mountain—particularly suitable for spring skiing—is the village of **Ait Wouchen,** where friends strongly recommend Said Boubker as a guide, who lives near the mosque. Said is a very careful mule driver, he knows the region well, and can provide simple, clean accommodations and good, traditional cooking. Whether going with or without a guide (a village man, for instance), make sure you are properly equipped with climbing boots, water, some food, and warm clothes.

Part sightseeing, part **shopping,** is a visit to the **weaving and embroidery workshop** run by Franciscan nuns in **Kasbah Myriem** ("Mary" in Arabic).

Take a narrow road to the right just before the bridge if coming from the north, or a left before the bridge coming the other way (it is marked). The prices are high compared to local shops, but the quality is much better and, equally important, the women (not little girls) are paid a decent sum for their work (it is closed Fridays and Sundays).

French-speaking **mass** is held in Midelt (Tel: 58 20 67 or the nuns at Tel: 58 24 43 for information). It is not exactly shopping, but if your car is giving you trouble there are some pleasant and competent mechanics on the left as you come in, 50 m before the Total filling station (on the right).

From Midelt the road goes on south to **Er-Rachidia** (chapter 13). All along this road you are likely to see streams of dusty 4WD or motorbikes returning from beating up the Saharan dunes in the south.

This section cannot end without mentioning the possibility of going from Meknès to the famous Berber center of **Imilchil** (altitude 2,000 m). It is not really in the Middle Atlas, but is near enough to be included here. The annual *moussem* and the **Fiancés Festival** attracts visitors from many parts of Morocco and, now, from many parts of the world. It has been called a sort of marriage fair, where members of the Ait Haddidou tribe have assembled since time immemorial to draw up marriage contracts, in which the women (usually divorced) are free to choose their future husbands or reject undesired suitors. The *moussem* does not take place in Imilchil itself, but at a saint's tomb at Ait Haddidou Ameur, about 20 km from the village. Held in September, it has now become pretty official and is losing part of its authenticity, with acts of allegiance to the king and more police and tourists around, but the scene is highly colorful and worth the visit. The whole plateau becomes a tented market, with itinerant merchants (now motorized) displaying their wares, lots of *Ahidous* dancing by the Ait Haddidou, lots of Ait Haddidou women and girls (the former highly made-up) in black woolen capes striped yellow, red or blue with pointed or round hoods (pointed for the divorcees) and colored wool belts, and lots of handsome, young moustached men in white, fingering their silver curved daggers . . . yes, it's still a noteworthy occasion. And to show how international it has become, it has recently opened a site on the Web: http://www.errachidia.org/imilchil/index.html.

Getting to Imilchil is not easy, but one of the simplest routes is certainly this one, through a rather bare landscape—continue on past Midelt as far as the turning on the right for **Rich** (about 60 km), signposted for Imilchil. Past Rich, the track (S3442 becoming the S3443) fords the River Ziz, reaches the pass of Tizi n'Ali, then another ford, and finally turns right at the T-junction for Imilchil (about 150 km from Rich). This is not possible if the River Ziz is high (which it shouldn't be in September).

I've never been to Imilchil with a tourist group, but I'm told the **accommodations** under organized tents is more than primitive, and the toilet arrangements best forgotten. The **food** supplied by the big town hotels for their "camps" is also best forgotten. But it's better than not going at all.

Medium-price accommodations are provided by the small **Auberge du Lac** and the **Hotel Restaurant Izlane** in the village. The manager of the latter, Ali Boudrik, is happy to organize trekking and other mountain activities for visitors. The well-known legend around this *moussem* is that, long ago, a young Ait Haddidou girl and a young Ait Haddidou man decided to get married. But their parents were against the affair. The two young people cried so much that their tears formed the two local lakes high in the hills, called Isli after the boy and Tislit after the girl. Unlike Romeo and Juliet, the story has a happy ending, for the parents finally let their children follow their hearts' desire. (Another version has it that the parents refused and the two young people decided to die together by drowning in the lakes. You can take your pick.) More prosaically, the Peace Corps have participated with the Moroccan state in a reforestation project around Imilchil.

7. Guided Tours

There are guides (false and official) hanging around to show you the sights of Meknès medina, but there are no organized group tours within the town. Your hotel will be able to find you a guide if you need one (fix the price and the itinerary carefully before setting out). Ask at the tourist agencies (see the end of the chapter) for excursions to the surrounding area.

8. Culture

The **Dar Jamai Museum,** Place el-Hedim (medina), is a palatial residence of a powerful 19th-century family, government ministers to the sultan Hassan I, now turned into a splendid **museum** with an attractive Andalusian garden. It belonged to the same family as the Palais Jamai in Fès (now a hotel). The displays cover traditional craftwork (rugs, embroidery, ceramics, jewelry, and woodwork) of Meknès and the surrounding area. One of the rooms is furnished in the traditional style of the period (open from 9:00 A.M.-12:00 P.M. and 3:00 P.M.-6:00 P.M., closed Tuesdays, entry 10 DH). The **French Cultural Center** (*Institut Français,* Rue Ferhat Hached, off Avenue Hassan II) organizes concerts, shows, and video films (closed in August). The annual **pilgrimage** to the tomb of **Sidi Mohammed Ben Aissa,** founder of the Aissaoua fraternity, takes place in the old cemetery just north of the medina at the feast of Mulud, when a very excited crowd of admirers renews their faith in the saint. This is worth watching (from a distance). As for all Islamic feast-days, this one changes its date every year.

9. Sports

Pool **swimming** is possible in many of the hotels. The Hotels Transatlantic and Rif are among the hotels that let non-residents use theirs (100 DH at the Transatlantic, in the summer only, and 30 DH at the Rif). The municipal swimming pools are packed in summer and not recommended for a quiet plunge (or for a clean swim) (one is situated next to the Hotel Zaki, on the road to Azrou). Swimming in the lakes south of Meknès is much more agreeable. **Golfers** will be surprised to learn that there is a little 9-hole course tucked away in the Imperial Town, inside the ramparts, close to Dar el-Makhzen. The Royal Golf of Meknès has a par of 36 and is lit at night. **Line-fishing** is possible in the many lakes surrounding Meknès (a permit should be obtained from the *Délégation Provinciale des Eaux et Fôrets* in Meknès). **Trekking** is also much practiced in the Middle Atlas, and the contact address for a fully-qualified mountain guide/escort is given in the "Address List." Several qualified mountain guides work in the Meknès/Ifrane area. The Timnay Inter-Cultures Tourist Centre, near Midelt, will provide guides and transport (4WD vehicles, mule, or mountain bike) for a variety of excursions (see above). When there is snow, **skiing** is possible at Michliffen, 17 km south of Ifrane (see "Sightseeing" above). **Horseback riding** can be arranged at Ifrane. **Birdwatchers** can look out for rare species around the various lakes.

10. Shopping

It's difficult to suggest where to go to buy locally produced arts and crafts. The **State Craftwork Center** (*Ensemble Artisanal,* Avenue Riad, New Town) allows an idea of going prices but not much else, since the stuff for sale is not attractively displayed or of the highest quality. The **souks** in the medina always have a selection of handicrafts, and American friends have told me that they found the **carpet market** excellent, with a good choice and much lower prices than in the more tourist-visited towns. The best bookshop is the **Librairie la Ville Nouvelle** (Avenue Hassan II), but it stocks only French-language books. American and English **newspapers** are sometimes available in the big hotels, as well as from stands in Avenue Mohammed V.

11. Entertainment and Nightlife

There's not much going except for a **cinema** or two, showing films in French or Arabic. The public tends to be noisy, nut-chewing, and mobile even during the film. The best are around Avenue Hassan II. There are an amazing number of **bars** in Meknès, most of them pretty noisy and male-dominated. **La Coupole** (Avenue Hassan II) is a very animated bar for an evening beer for those not wanting to go to the three **** hotels, and usually has live music (it is noisy with or without music). Thirsty women travelers would be best at the hotel bars, such as the one in the **Hotel Rif**, which is fairly standard but calm. The **Hotel Zaki** has an agreeable piano bar in a nice setting, as well as a nightclub. The **Hotel Bab Mansour** has the calm **Bar el-Andalouse** on the ground floor and organizes an **evening show** in the basement, with Moroccan dancing girls, and a **disco**. The **Diamant Bleu** nightclub, below Hotel Akouas, and the **Bahia** nightclub in the Hotel Rif are also said to be good.

12. The Meknès Address List

Airlines—Royal Air Maroc, 7 Avenue Mohammed V (Tel: 52 09 63).

Banks—Avenue Mohammed V, Avenue Hassan II, Avenue Allal ben Abdallah, Avenue des F.A.R. (the BMCE and the Wafabank have VISA distributors). In the medina, banks are situated in the Rue Sekkakin (near Place el-Hédim).

Bus Station (*gare routière*)—CTM, Avenue Mohammed V; other companies are near Bab el-Khemis in the medina.

Car Rental—Hertz, Avenue Houmane el-Fetouaki; Maroc Voyages, Avenue Allal ben Abdallah; Stopcar, 5 Rue de la Voûte (Tel: 52 50 61); Zeit, 4 Rue Anserabi (Tel/Fax: 52 59 18).

Churches—French-speaking Catholic mass at Notre Dame des Oliviers, Avenue Mohammed V (Tel: 52 78 84).

Consulates—the only one is the French, on the corner of Avenue Mulay Ismail/Rue Ferhat Hached. If necessary, contact the U.S. Consulate in Casablanca (Tel: 02-26 45 50).

Drugstore, Night (*Pharmacie de Nuit*)—Place Administrative, opposite the Hotel de Ville.

Express Post—Call the main post office for information (Tel: 52 25 00).

Golf Club—Royal Golf of Meknès (Tel: 53 07 53, Fax: 55 05 04).

Hospitals and Clinics—Polyclinique Cornette-de-Saint-Cyr, 22 Esplanade du Docteur Guiget (Tel: 52 02 62); also two state hospitals: Mohammed V (Tel: 52 11 34) and Mulay Ismail (central, Tel: 52 28 05).

Photocopies—in many shops selling newspapers, stamps, and tobacco, and some téléboutiques.

Police—(Tel: 19).

Post Office—Place Administrative (New Town), Rue Dar Smen (medina).

Railway Station—main station out east of New Town, on Avenue du Sénégal; more central is the station El-Amir Abdelkader (in road of same name).

Taxis, Big and Little—corner Avenue Mohammed V/Avenue des F.A.R. and outside the El-Amir Abdelkader railway station; Bab el-Khemis (medina). Little taxis also have numerous other stands.

Telephone—in post offices as above, or numerous téléboutiques (also have fax).

Tourist Information—The *Délégation Régionale du Tourisme* (Place Administrative, Tel: 52 44 26) and the *Syndicat d'Initiative* (near Palais de la Foire, Tel: 52 01 91) have the usual colored brochures, but not much else.

Travel Agencies—Carlson Wagonslit Travel, Immeuble Siffiche, 1 Rue Ghana (Tel: 52 19 95, Fax: 52 19 96); Wasteels, 45 Avenue Mohammed V, next to CTM Bus Station (Tel: 52 30 62).

Trekking—for the Middle Atlas contact the office of ANGAM *(Association Nationale des Guides et Accompagnateurs en Montagne du Maroc)*, BP 47, Asni, Marrakech (Tel: 04-44 49 79, Fax: 04-43 36 09). Timnay Inter-Cultures Tourist Centre, outside Midelt (BP 81, Midelt 39016, Tel: 58 34 34), can also arrange interesting trips.

Weather information—(Tel: 02-90 24 24) Particularly for those planning treks in the mountains.

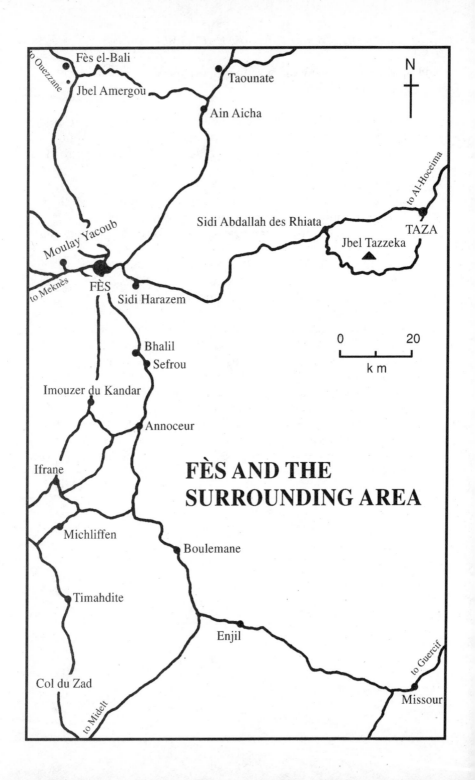

8

Fès, the Spiritual Capital

1. The General Picture

Morocco's Islamic history can be said to start in Fès, and much of the country's later history took place there. Not all Moroccan sultans established their capital in Fès, but its spiritual power has always been such that rulers preferred to have the Fassi (its inhabitants) with them rather than against them. Its medina is the nearest a modern visitor can get to a medieval Arab town, with its labyrinth of little streets and dark cul-de-sacs. The richness of its Islamic monuments is incomparable and the fascination of its age-old markets and craft workshops immediate. It is the oldest of the Imperial Towns and figures on the essential visiting list of most overseas visitors. The most important monuments can be seen in half a day—it's better in a day, and better still at a more leisurely pace over two days.

Beginnings. Fès lies in a hollow in the middle of the fertile Sais Plain, just to the north of the Middle Atlas Mountains. It is on the easy east-west route by which invaders reached Morocco from Algeria and moved on across the plains to the Atlantic. It is also well placed for communication with Tangier and the Mediterranean. Fès was founded by Idriss I, who made it his capital in 789 A.D. His son, Idriss II, increased the size of the first settlement and offered home and welcome to thousands of Arab Moslems from Spain and other North African countries. Refugees fleeing from Andalusia founded the Andalusian district of the town in 818, while those from Kairouan (Qayrawin) in Tunisia, in 825, built another district to which they also gave their name. These new populations, who evicted the local Berbers, were wealthy merchants, craftsmen, and intellectuals with a rich cultural tradition, used to city life. Progressively the town was endowed with a university, the Qarawiyin, mosques, and libraries, and became the religious and cultural center of the country. With all this richness, it was not surprising that it was coveted by foreign Islamic dynasties. It was ruled by Tunisian Fatimid governors until 953, before they were pushed out for a short time by the Idrissids, who were back again shortly thereafter, and then replaced by the Spanish Umayads in 985. In the beginning of the 11th century, they too disappeared, and Fès, independent again, became bigger and richer through its varied crafts and trading contacts, with an important and industrious Jewish community. However, the Almoravid sultan, Yusef ben Tachfin, put an end to this in 1069 when he besieged and captured the city. He knocked down the ramparts that divided Fès in two and surrounded the town with one single rampart and exterior fortress, but preferred to use Marrakech as his capital.

Commerce and culture. In the middle of the 12th century, Fès came under Almohad rule, new silk weaving, leather, and metalworking techniques were introduced by refugees from Andalusia, and trade prospered as never before. Although no longer the political capital, Fès was widely recognized as an unparalleled religious and cultural center. Under the **Merinids,** who made Fès their capital in 1250, it reached its golden age—splendid new palaces were constructed, religious schools established, and business boomed. Merchants traded with China, India, East Africa, and the Middle East, sold wheat, leather, and rugs to Europe, and imported cloth and industrial products from England. The status of Fès as the country's spiritual and cultural capital was maintained. More Moslems and Jews expelled from Spain settled there in 1492. The ups and downs of history after the decline of the Merinids led Fès to be occupied by the Saadian dynasty in 1549. After a brief early period, when the Saadian Abd el-Malik kept Fès as the capital city, for most of the Saadian reign Fès lost its capital status in favor of Marrakech. Episodes of plague, famine, and civil wars at the beginning of the 17th century enormously reduced the population until, in 1666, the new Alaouite sultan, Mulay Rashid, established order in the country and made Fès his capital. Business looked up and the town prospered again, even if his successor, Mulay Ismail, preferred to settle in neighboring Meknès. The calm was broken by a long period of disorder after the death of Mulay Ismail in 1727, before peace and prosperity started to return when Mohammed III took control in 1757. After the death of sultan Hassan I in 1894, the troubled period that marked the reign of his successors, Mulay Abd el-Aziz and Mulay Abd el-Hafid, forced the latter, who had deposed his brother, to call in French forces to quell a violent revolt in Fès. In March 1912, Mulay Hafid signed the Treaty of Fès, initiating a French Protectorate over the country. As was his custom, the French General Lyautey left the old town untouched and had a new, separate modern town built, slightly higher than the original Fès, but practically touching it. The visitor should not be surprised by the names Fès el-Jdid (the New Fès) and Fès el-Bali (the Old Fès)—both are in the old town. During the struggle for independence, Fès and the Qarawiyin were the center of resistance, where the intellectual elite of the country, already active before World War II, drew up their political programs and plans. Many ministers in Morocco's first post-independence governments were Fassi.

Today, most of the businessmen and traders have deserted Fès for Casablanca. Their rich dwellings in the medina have become occupied by poor families from the Rif with their numerous children, many often sharing the house with several other families. The result is a degradation of the urban tissue in the medina, not designed for such an influx of population, which is today estimated at around 200,000. Its medina is on UNESCO's list of world heritage sites and is the object of many restoration projects, for its renovation has become a preoccupying problem. At the end of 1998, the World Bank granted Morocco a new loan of 14 million dollars as a contribution towards this conservation and rehabilitation program. The city's present population, medina and "new town" taken together, probably numbers almost 1½ million. Its many unemployed young people, the poor housing, and general difficulties met with in daily life led to violent rioting in 1990. Even if it is not the administrative or economic capital of the kingdom, Fès represents a spiritual and political force to be reckoned with.

2. Getting There

Royal Air Maroc has a flight from Paris twice a week. The town can be reached by **air** from Casablanca daily by RAM and Regional Air Lines. Flight time is just under one hour. Travelers from Tangier, Marrakech, Agadir, and Ouarzazate have to go through Casablanca. Certain flights from Europe also touch down in Fès. Public transport from Fès-Sais Airport is by the N° 16 local bus to the railway station. Big taxis will do the run (13 km) and they charge around 100 DH.

There is a good, comfortable **train service** from Casablanca (five hours), via Rabat (four hours), and Meknès (one hour). These trains also stop in Salé, Kénitra, and Sidi Kacem. There are nine a day (seven from Casa-Voyageurs, two from Casa-Port), with two arriving in the early hours of the morning (1:30 A.M. and 3:30 A.M.) (100 DH single from Casablanca). Fès can also be reached by train direct from Taza (two hours), Oujda (six hours) (three trains a day in both cases), and once a day from Tangier, changing at Meknès.

The CTM **bus** company runs nine buses a day from Casablanca (80 DH), via Rabat and Meknès, frequently from Meknès (15 DH), once a day from Al-Hoceima (12 hours), three times a day from Tangier (60 DH), and daily from Taza (40 DH), Oujda (65 DH), and Marrakech (100 DH). In the fall of 1998 the CTM introduced a non-stop service from Casablanca to Fès. The CTM has a brand-new, airport-style bus station in the new town that is all marble and stucco—but with no departure and arrival times posted for consultation. The non-Arabic speaker will have trouble using this company from Fès unless this is improved. The many non-CTM buses running services to Fès arrive at Bab Boujeloud in the medina. **Cars** or **big taxis** can use the new fast **expressway** joining Fès and Meknès (60 km) to Khemisset (45 km), designed to continue to Rabat (180 km) and to link up with the highway to Tangier (300 km). A seat in a big, shared taxi should cost around 60 DH from Rabat, 110 DH from Casablanca.

3. Local Transportation

Like all big Moroccan cities, Fès has its network of local **buses.** They are usually crammed with people and not very convenient unless one has a lot of time to spend. Since the bus destinations and stops are all written in Arabic, it may be difficult for a visitor to use this system. Street names, too, are all written in Arabic. If you have come by **car**—your own or rented—I advise you to leave it at the hotel or use it only for eating out in the modern town, where the roads are wide and traffic and parking easier. The medina cannot be visited by car, and it is infinitely easier to take a **little taxi** (red) to one entrance, and pick up another when one comes out the other side. I am happy to say that the unpleasant habit—mentioned by all guide books—of young men on motorbikes or scooters waylaying motorized visitors at the entrance to the town to try to take them to a hotel or guide them to the sights has been almost eradicated. These are the famous "false guides" who are a plague to tourists and, while false guides still exist, the

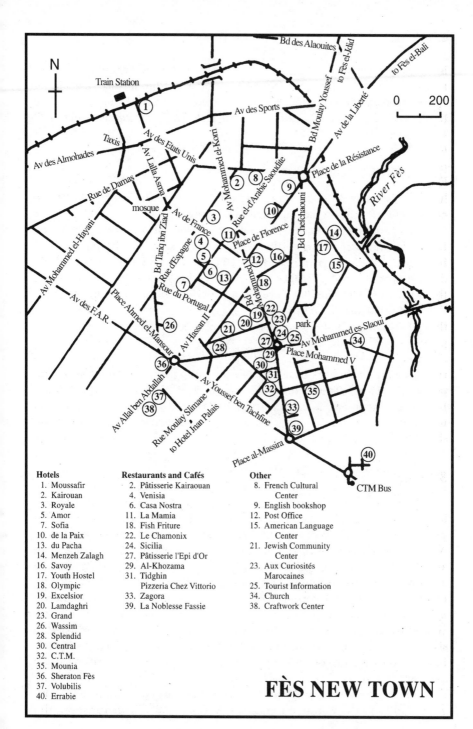

Hotels
1. Moussafir
2. Kairouan
3. Royale
5. Amor
7. Sofia
10. de la Paix
13. du Pacha
14. Menzeh Zalagh
16. Savoy
17. Youth Hostel
18. Olympic
19. Excelsior
20. Lamdaghri
23. Grand
26. Wassim
28. Splendid
30. Central
32. C.T.M.
35. Mounia
36. Sheraton Fès
37. Volubilis
40. Errabie

Restaurants and Cafés
2. Pâtisserie Kairaouan
4. Venisia
6. Casa Nostra
11. La Mamia
18. Fish Friture
22. Le Chamonix
24. Sicilia
27. Pâtisserie l'Epi d'Or
29. Al-Khozama
31. Tidghin
   Pizzeria Chez Vittorio
33. Zagora
39. La Noblesse Fassie

Other
8. French Cultural
   Center
9. English bookshop
12. Post Office
15. American Language
   Center
21. Jewish Community
   Center
23. Aux Curiosités
   Marocaines
25. Tourist Information
34. Church
38. Craftwork Center

FÈS NEW TOWN

authorities have taken energetic and successful steps to curtail their activities. A special branch of the police has been created to ensure that the visitor has a hassle-free time in Fès. If you need a guide, take an official one from your hotel or from the Tourist Office *(Syndicat d'Initiative)* (section 7, "Guided Tours").

4. The Hotel Scene

Fès is not only renowned for its Islamic monuments, but also for its excellent cuisine and high-class hotels. There are 27 classified hotels and any number of unclassified ones. Hotel charges fixed for this region are as follows (they vary according to the presence or absence of showers and watercloset in the room): **** 350-436 DH or 448-693 DH, breakfast 47-50 DH for both; *** 174-277 DH or 197-330 DH, breakfast 34-37 DH for both; ** 96-167 DH or 103-207 DH, breakfast 23 DH for both; * 87-129 DH or 91-146 DH, breakfast 22 DH for both.

The **regional telephone code** is 05 (0 omitted for in-region calls).

EXPENSIVE HOTELS

There are four ***** hotels in Fès, including one classified as a ***** Luxe—the **Hotel Palais Jamai** (125 rooms and 25 suites, a room with a view over the medina can cost 1,850 DH, the others about 500 DH cheaper—but if you are going to splurge, take a room with a view from the balcony—breakfast 130 DH, Bab el-Guissa, Tel: 63 43 31, Fax: 63 50 96). Lying just within the medina walls at Bab el-Guissa, the hotel was an 18th-century palace built by a sultan's *vizir* (minister). The whole building had a face-lift early in 1998, but was closed for a complete renovation at the end of the year. It opened again in the spring of 1999 and has lost none of its oriental charm, while retaining its luxurious and softly-padded atmosphere. Its previous decoration and furniture, in superb Moroccan style, is still there, as are the two restaurants, bars, a swimming pool (heated in winter) set in a charming Andalusian garden, tennis courts, *hammam,* a hairdresser, and a boutique. The new version has an absolutely superb fitness center and a conference room fitted with the latest instantaneous interpretation system, a new panoramic bar—and, of course, all its traditional attractions. Since early 1998, its management has been entrusted to the group Accor and the hotel now has the group's branch label "Sofitel" added to its already prestigious name (let's hope the staff will be more pleasant!).

Some say the ***** **Hotel Jnan Palais** is a better value, but it is in the new town and lacks the unique location of the Hotel Palais Jamai (198 rooms,

34 duplex, 17 suites, 1,700 DH, Avenue Ahmed Chaouki, Tel: 65 22 30, Fax: 65 19 17, e-mail: jp@marocnet.net.ma; web site: www.m-link.com/jnanpalace). Built in 1992, the four-story building lies in the middle of spacious gardens, has smallish but pretty bedrooms, four restaurants, bars, a coffee shop, attractive pool, tennis courts, and a conference center. It is appreciated by tour groups.

The ***** **Hotel Les Mérinides** (90 rooms, 1,100 DH, Avenue Borj du Nord, Tel: 64 52 26, Fax: 64 52 25), a rather unimaginative building from the outside, lies up on the hill and also has a splendid, but more distant, view of the medina. Although damaged by a fire in 1990, the interior has been renovated, and the hotel offers two attractive restaurants (particularly agreeable in summer), two bars, and a swimming pool.

The ***** **Hotel Sheraton Fès** (285 rooms, 1,700 DH, corner Avenue des F.A.R./Avenue Hassan II, Tel: 62 30 06/93 09 09, Fax: 62 04 86) is a large establishment in the new town, tastefully decorated, with restaurants, bars, a swimming pool, tennis courts, and a conference center. It is, of course, up to normal Sheraton standards.

Four hotels are in the **** range. The most attractive (and my favorite) is undoubtedly the **** **Hotel Menzeh Zalagh** (150 rooms—including 18 suites—700 DH, Rue Mohammed Diouri, Tel: 62 28 10/62 55 31, Fax: 65 19 95), lying on the edge of the new town overlooking the medina (good views from the terrace, the dining room, and bedrooms facing that way). The architecture, all in curves, is very pleasing to the eye, the reception area is imaginatively laid out and the bedrooms are tastefully furnished in pale pink. Garden-terraces descend to the level of the swimming pools. The hotel has three restaurants, a grill/snack bar, a piano bar, a wine-tasting bar, nightclub, sauna, *hammam*, and two attractive swimming pools— and lots of charm (with a pleasant staff).

A nice hotel in the new town, but further out, is the **** **Hotel Volubilis** (120 rooms, Avenue Allal ben Abdallah, Tel: 62 11 26, Fax: 62 11 25), almost opposite the Hotel Sheraton (not in any way to be confused with the unclassified Hotel Volubilis on Boulevard Abdallah Chefchaouni). It is pleasantly furnished, has an attractive garden, pool, restaurant, bar, and a nightclub, and is a good value. It is run by the FRAM Tourist Group, so it is often fully booked.

A centrally-situated hotel is the **** **Hotel Sofia** (98 rooms and 4 suites, 3 Rue Royaume d'Arabie Saoudite, Tel: 62 42 65/66/67/68, Fax: 62 64 78). Fully renovated in 1996, it has a pleasant entrance hall, comfortable and well-equipped bedrooms, two restaurants, a bar, a nightclub, and a conference room.

The new **** **Hotel Wassim** is another well-placed hotel in the new town

(102 rooms and 2 suites, Rue du Liban, Avenue Hassan II, Tel: 65 49 39, Fax: 93 02 20). The 10-story building has modern, comfortable bedrooms, two restaurants, two bars, a panoramic terrace, a solarium, a conference room, a nightclub, and a garage. These last two hotels are functional and agreeable, but not particularly interesting.

MEDIUM-PRICE HOTELS

These are *** and ** establishments, with—to my mind—a fairly big difference between the facilities they offer. The *** Hotel Splendid (70 rooms, 9 Rue Abdelkrim el-Khattabi, Tel: 62 21 48/62 67 70/65 02 83, Fax: 65 48 92) is perhaps the best in this category. It is a very pleasant, well-run, functional establishment, with a restaurant, bar, and the (unexpected) attraction of a small swimming pool set in a charming little courtyard. Those interested in modern art will find about 10 paintings by the very well-known Moroccan self-taught woman artist, Chaibia, hanging on the walls of the reception area.

The five-floor *** **Hotel de la Paix** (42 rooms, 44 Avenue Hassan II, Tel: 62 50 72/93 17 97, Fax: 62 68 80) is situated on the finest palm-tree lined avenue in modern Fès. It's a fairly old hotel, but its rooms are fully equipped and comfortable (some overlook the avenue, others the courtyard). It has a restaurant and bar.

An advantage of the *** **Hotel Moussafir** (98 rooms, Avenue des Almohades, Tel: 65 19 02, Fax: 65 19 09) is its proximity to the railway station (on the left of the square as you come out). This chain of modern hotels was originally built by the Moroccan state railway company to cater to rail travelers (now run by the French Accor hotel group—look out for their label "Ibis" in red on the roof). It is white with blue trim, attractively decorated in Moroccan style, and has a small garden, a swimming pool, and a restaurant.

The *** **Grand Hotel** (84 rooms, Boulevard Abdallah Chefchaouni, Tel: 93 20 26, Fax: 65 38 47), although not as grand as its name would suggest, has a pretty entrance and has recently been redecorated. Its bedrooms are comfortable and the hotel has a restaurant, a bar, and a nightclub, and is a good value.

The *** **Hotel Mounia** (86 rooms, 60 Rue Asilah, Tel: 62 48 38/65 07 71/ 65 07 72, Fax: 65 07 73) is tucked away down a small street off Boulevard Mohammed V, opposite the clearly-visible Hotel C.T.M. It's a newish hotel, and the rooms, although small, are comfortable and well-equipped. The hotel has two restaurants and a bar.

In the old town, the *** **Hotel Batha** (61 rooms, 260 DH, Place Batha, Tel: 63 64 41) lies just outside the medina, near Bab Boujeloud. It was closed for a time, but has recently reopened, losing a star in the process. With a restaurant and bar, it is convenient for visiting the old town, but a good walk away from modern Fès.

Some 6 km out of Fès, at **Ain Chkeff,** on the Ifrane road, the *** **Hotel Reda** (Tel: 64 09 78/79), set in a pleasant garden, is said to be good, but not very convenient for visiting Fès.

In the ** category, the choices are fairly varied. The ** **Hotel Olympic,** conveniently situated not far from the post office, has a luminous sign on the roof so it's easy to find (32 rooms, corner Boulevard Mohammed V/ small street, Tel: 93 26 82, Fax: 93 26 65). All the bedrooms are equipped with shower, water closet, and television. The hotel has a restaurant.

Close to the main post office, in the center of town, you have the ** **Hotel Amor** (35 rooms, 31 Rue Arabie Saoudite, Tel: 62 27 24/62 33 04), also within a 15-minute walk from the railway station (clearly signposted). The reception area hall—decorated with green and red tiles outside—has an attractive display of craftwork. Its bedrooms and bathrooms are small but correct, the restaurant is quite pretty, and there is a little bar and patio (and in the evening a technician came at once to repair a faulty bathroom light).

A highly-praised hotel is the ** **Hotel Errabie** (32 rooms, 1 Rue de Tanger, Route de Sefrou, Tel: 64 01 00/64 10 75, Fax: 65 911 63). It's certainly an attractive hotel, spacious, well decorated, with pleasant, fully-equipped bedrooms, a good view from the terrace, and a friendly staff. But it's out of the way unless you are coming by car from Sefrou, getting off the CTM bus, or like walking about 20 minutes through a dusty, commercial zone before reaching the center of town.

BUDGET ACCOMMODATIONS

Two modest but good little hotels in the * category in the **new town** are the small * **Hotel Kairouan** (20 rooms, 84 Rue du Soudan, Tel: 62 35 90) and the * **Hotel Royale** (22 rooms, 36 Rue du Soudan, Tel: 62 46 56). Both are well indicated, clean, central, and only 15 minutes from the railway station. The former has an attractive carved wood doorway and prides itself on having "lots of European water closets" in the corridor. The latter has bedrooms looking onto the street and others onto the courtyard. The * **Hotel Lamdaghri** would do in a pinch (20 rooms, 10 Rue Abbas el-Masaadi, Tel: 62 03 10). It's in a little street off the Boulevard Mohammed V (look out for the Café Zanzibar on the corner), and has recently lost a *. The area is noisy at night.

Some of the unclassified hotels have pretty rustic, squat water closets, are run-down, or have doubtful clients. However, a better value than the

Hotel Lamdaghri is the unclassified **Hotel Central** (34 rooms, 83 DH without shower, 114 DH with shower and water closet, 50 Rue Brahim Roudani, near Place Mohammed V, Tel: 62 23 33).

Not far away is the well-indicated unclassified **Hotel C.T.M.** (25 rooms, 90 DH with shower, 75 DH without, Boulevard Mohammed V), where the water closets are in the corridor, but the rooms are alright and the hot water is said to be on all day. The CTM bus station used to be here in the old days.

The unclassified **Hotel Savoy** (20 rooms, singles 50 DH, doubles 70 DH, 3 people 90 DH, 4 people 120 DH, 16 Boulevard Abdellah Chefchaouni, Tel: 62 06 08) is a very simple place, pretty basic, but friendly, and the clean rooms have washbasins (water closets and showers—5 DH for hot water—in the corridor).

Another unclassified hotel is the **Hotel du Pacha** (24 rooms, 80 DH, 32 Avenue Hassan II, Tel: 65 22 90). Some of the simple, basically furnished rooms have showers, others not. There are communal water closets in the corridor.

As you walk up the Boulevard Mohammed V, you can't miss the unclassified **Hotel Excelsior** (40 rooms, 75 DH, corner Boulevard Mohammed V/ Rue Larbi el-Kaghat, Tel: 62 56 02). The rooms are large, the showers are hot in the evening and morning (so they say), and the water closets are in the corridor. The rooms look onto the road (which is noisy) or the courtyard. It's not a great place in which to stay, but it could be worse.

In the **old town,** in **Fès el-Jdid,** the **Hotel du Commerce** (29 rooms, 80 DH, Place des Alaouites, almost in the new town, Tel: 62 23 31) is a good place to try, with clean but sparsely furnished rooms.

In **Fès el-Bali,** around Bab Boujeloud, there are also lots of of budget accommodations, with the same disadvantages as those in the new town. Two of the best are the **Hotel Cascade** (around 60 DH, Tel: 63 84 42) and the **Hotel Lamrani** (same price, near the Bou Inania Medersa, Tel: 63 44 11), both pretty spartan, but clean.

The **Youth Hostel** (18 Rue Abdesslam Serghini, Tel: 62 40 85) is central (new town). There is only cold water in summer. The **campsite Camping du Diamant Vert** is on the road to Ain Chkef, 6 km south of Fès (bus N° 17 from Fès new town). At the moment it is one of the better Moroccan campsites, with decent water closets, a pool, and a disco (20 DH per person, 30 DH per car, 25 DH per tent, and it is always crammed in July and August).

The newish **Camping International** is also out of town, some 3 km on the Sefrou road (bus N° 38 from Fès new town). It's quite an up-market place, with gardens, two pools (one for kids), restaurants, and shops (50 DH per person, 30 DH per car and per tent).

5. Dining and Restaurants

Fassi cooking is renowned throughout the country and it is only to be expected that some of the best traditional dishes should be served here.

HOTEL RESTAURANTS

Tables should be reserved for the first two of these restaurants. At the top of the list is the **Restaurant Al-Fassia** in the **Hotel Palais Jamai** (evenings only, Tel: 63 43 31). It has a memorable *pastilla* in beautiful traditional Moroccan surroundings, with discreet lute players and an oriental dancer in the evening (around 400 DH for the meal).

The French restaurant in the **Hotel Palais Jamai, La Djenina,** with a French chef, also has an excellent reputation (menu 300 DH) (but it would be a pity to miss out on the splendid Moroccan meal if you are there).

The **Hotel Sheraton Fès** has an good restaurant (Tel: 62 30 06). The setting of the restaurant in the **Hotel Les Mérinides** (Tel: 64 60 40) is attractive, and both it and the **Hotel Jnan Palais** (Tel: 65 22 30) serve classic hotel food of good quality, but they are not really up to the **Hotel Palais Jamai** standard.

The Moroccan restaurant in the **Hotel Menzeh Zalagh** sometimes puts on a show during the meal (tourist menu 180 DH). The more modest **Grand Hotel** (Tel: 62 55 11) also has a very acceptable French restaurant (set menu 113 DH), and friends say that food in the restaurant of the **Hotel Splendid** (Tel: 62 21 48) is not bad at all (four-course meal is 120 DH).

Le Nautilus Restaurant in the **Hotel de la Paix** (Tel: 62 50 72) serves Moroccan and international dishes (set meal 123 DH). The service is often slow and the decor is not particularly appealing, but the food is good.

The two restaurants in the **Hotel Mounia** also serve Moroccan and international food (set meal 102 DH), but I heard that they are not as good as they used to be. The food in the **Hotel Amor** restaurant (spacious, pleasant setting, all stuccowork and *zellij*) is correct (menu 80 DH).

OTHER RESTAURANTS

Tables should be reserved for the **medina** restaurants, as they tend to fill up during the high season. At the top end, there are several good Moroccan restaurants at Bab el-Guissa: the **Restaurant Firdaous** (Tel: 63 43 43) and the newish **Restaurant Les Remparts de Fès** (Tel: 63 74 15). Both are near the Hotel Palais Jamai, but are less expensive (menu 175-400 DH at the latter).

The restaurant **Dar Tajine** (15 Ross Rhi) specializes—as one would imagine—in different kinds of *tajine* (from 150-300 DH).

Dar Saada restaurant in the Souk el-Attarin, Fès el-Bali (Tel: 63 33 43) has been installed in an old Fassi house and is attractively decorated. Well known for its delicious *pastilla* and couscous (around 200 DH), it is at the same time a carpet bazaar. It makes a useful midday halt when visiting the medina. These restaurants, however, are often best in the evening, when there is more "atmosphere" (with music and a show).

The **Palais Mnebhi** restaurant (15 Souiket ben Safi, Talaa Seghira, Tel: 63 38 93—call first to make sure it's open) is also situated in a 19th-century Fassi aristocratic house, and has kept the traditional decor (meals are from 200 DH). The French Résident Général, General Lyautey, lived here in 1912.

A good address in Fès el-Bali used to be the **Palais de Fès** (16 Rue Boutouil, Tel: 63 72 22), in another old Fassi house near the Qarawiyin Mosque. But in August 1998 it burned down—luckily, the owner had another suitable house next door, which is his new restaurant. It is convenient for people visiting the medina as it is open for lunch, but it is inclined to be full of tourist groups.

The **Maison Bleue** (Batha District) is an elegant new Moroccan restaurant in the medina, with a reputation for very good, but expensive, food (350-400 DH/meal).

Finally, cheaper than all the above and still in Fès el-Bali is the **Restaurant Dar Jamai** (14 Funduq Lihoudi—the "Jewish caravansery"— Tel: 63 56 85), which is a bit hard to find but not far from the Hotel Palais Jamai. Makes a very good couscous (80 DH).

In the new town, the top-ranking restaurants specialize in non-Moroccan cooking (though most can propose a traditional Moroccan dish), which is reasonable in view of the quantity of excellent Moroccan places in the medina. At the moment, the best is **Zagora** (5 Boulevard Mohammed V, Fax: 94 06 86), down a little passage (Au Derby shoe store on the corner) with a parking area behind. The manager, Haj Boussellama, who used to run the Mounia restaurant, goes in for high-class, refined, and imaginative cooking at a reasonable price in agreeable surroundings (set menus at 90 DH and 150 DH). He was proud to have been given the *Médaille de Préstige* (highest honor) by the National Tourist and Guide Federation in 1998.

La Cheminée used to be in the Avenue de France, but has recently moved. It is a small, calm restaurant with a good choice of dishes (from 60 DH) served by attentive waiters.

The restaurant previously known as **Le Roi de la Bière** (59 Boulevard

Mohammed V, Tel: 62 53 26) has changed its name to Oued de la Bière on the menus, and **Restaurant Tidghin** outside. It's not particularly noteworthy for the cooking, but the setting is agreeable and it's open during Ramadan (set menu 80 DH).

Out of town, on the road to Immouzzer, the **El Ambra** (47 Route d'Immouzer, Tel: 64 16 87), open only in the evening, is not at all bad—it is best to choose its good grills. The **Restaurant Astor** (18 Avenue Slaoui, Tel: 69 40 12) serves kosher food and has a good reputation.

There are plenty of **pizzerias** around. The best is the **Restaurant Pizzeria Chez Vittorio,** just off the Place Mohammed V (21 Rue Brahim Roudani, Tel: 62 47 30), which, along with the Zagora, is reckoned to be the best place to eat in the new town. Pasta and pizzas cost from 45 DH and beer and wine is available.

Slightly cheaper (but not as good) is the **Restaurant Sicilia** (4 Boulevard Abdallah Chefchaouni, Tel: 62 52 65). The pizzas start at 32 DH for a small one (salads 12 DH, burgers from 30 DH). It doesn't open until lunchtime, but says it stays open until midnight, which can be useful.

The **Restaurant Casa Nostra** (51 Rue Arabie Saoudite, almost opposite the Hotel Amor, Tel: 93 28 41) is an attractive little place, with good pizzas from 30 DH and pasta from 45 DH (they serve soft drinks only).

The **Pizzaria Restaurant Assouan** (4 Avenue Allal ben Abdallah, almost opposite the state craftwork center) also stays open late (until 11:00 P.M.) and has a good choice of pizzas (from 30 DH) and salads (from 25 DH).

The restaurant **Le Chamonix** (50/52 Rue Mokhtar al-Souissi) is down a small street off Boulevard Mohammed V, just opposite the Hotel Excelsior. You can get a reasonable, cheap Moroccan meal for around 50 DH.

The **fast food Al-Khozama** restaurant (23 Avenue Mohammed es-Slaoui) —you can't miss its Pepsi sign—has a standard Moroccan menu for 60 DH, and also does sandwiches (from 15 DH) and pizzas (from 40 DH).

A modest little restaurant with a few tables in a quiet little courtyard, while the others are inside, is the **Restaurant Fish Friture** (138 Boulevard Mohammed V, opposite the Wafa Bank, Tel: 94 06 99, closed Sundays). Soup costs 15 DH, salads 20 DH, an omlette 20 DH, *tajines* 30 DH, and a set meal of salad and fish *tajine* comes at 25 DH.

OTHER PLACES TO EAT

If it's just a snack or sandwich you're after, the Rue de l'Arabie Saoudite is home to lots of sandwich shops: **Le Coin Sandwich** is a good one. Hamburgers, kebobs, and the like can be had at **Venisia Sandwich** (Avenue de France, near the Hotel Amor), but it is not open in the early morning.

Near here, the **Chicken Mac Rôtisserie** offers *harira* soup (4 DH), small *tajine* (9 DH), and a ¼ roast chicken, which you can see turning on a spit (17 DH). **La Mamia** (53 Place Florence, Tel: 62 31 64), in a square just off Avenue Hassan II, opposite the post office, does hamburgers (12 DH), cheeseburgers(14 DH), pizzas (from 26 DH), and more substantial dishes (steak 30 DH), which you can eat at tables on the pavement or in a quiet upstairs dining area.

If you're up Boulevard Mohammed V, **opposite the Hotel C.T.M.,** on the corner, there's a small "restaurant" offering soup for 2.50 DH and *tajine* for 18 DH (you're unlikely to find cheaper!).

Down in Fès el-Bali, near Bab Boujeloud, there are lots of cheap eating places frequented by Moroccans, among which the **Café Restaurant des Jeunes** does a bowl of *harira* and a piece of bread for around 5 DH. Sandwiches can be had from a number of stands.

Many of the rather noisy, masculine **coffee shops** have a quite area upstairs—it's worth looking, since they are convenient for single females. The first floor of the **Boulangerie-Pâtisserie Kairaouan** in the new town (84 Rue du Soudan, on a corner) is an excellent place to sit down and enjoy some delicious pastries.

There's also a little coffee shop in the **Boulangerie-Pâtisserie de Paris** (50 Avenue Hassan II, Tel: 62 64 16) where the pastries are equally good and you can get ice cream. Ice cream is also sold in summer at the **Pâtisserie Glacier Zegzouti** (Avenue Hassan II).

The **Salon de Thé La Noblesse Fassie** (Boulevard Mohammed V, no number, but around N° 36) has delicious bakery smells and is very comfortable. More obviously a coffee shop is the **Salon de thé-pâtisserie l'Epi d'Or** (85 Boulevard Mohammed V)—equally tempting! The cafés where you can sit and drink a coffee and watch Fassi life are numerous along the main streets. In Fès el-Bali, a good shady spot for a coffee (or even more substantial stuff like omlettes and salads) is the **Café Restaurant Noria,** set in the Boujeloud Gardens.

6. Sightseeing

IN FÈS

The new town is a functional and agreeable place in which to sleep and eat, but the monuments that give Fès its fame are mostly in **Fès el-Bali,** with some in **Fès el-Jdid.** Having said this, Avenue Hassan II, which runs more or less from one end of the new town to the other, is one of the nicest places I know in a Moroccan town for a calm stroll after dinner. The broad central pedestrian walk, lined with palm trees, is equipped with stone

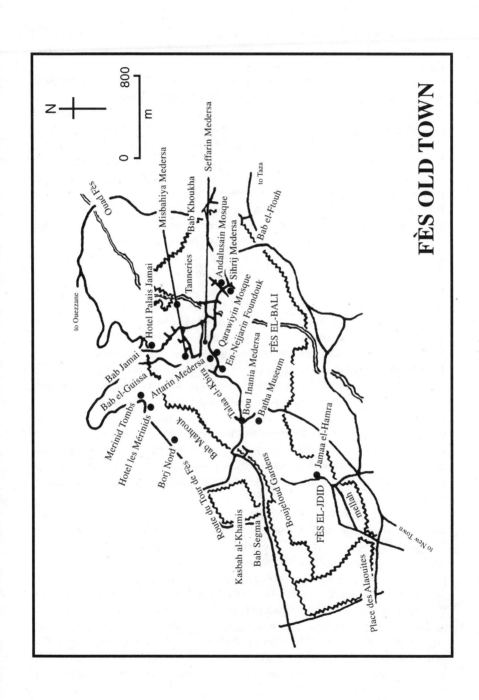

FÈS OLD TOWN

benches. Fountains play at intervals and the traffic is kept away along two one-way avenues, each with a double line of trees. This is a really agreeable, shady place for walking or just sitting.

However, the visitor will certainly first head for the old town. The original 9th-century settlement was in Fès el-Bali (Old Fès), while Fès el-Jdid (New Fès) was a later, 13th-century Merinid addition designed to house their administrators and soldiers. The former presents the greatest interest for the visitor. The **medina** of Fès el-Bali is a confusing place for the visitor, and just a day there will not reveal its secrets. However, the following section suggests some routes that should help to understand the layout. They may not necessarily be those taken by an official (or unofficial) guide, and this is of no importance, provided that you see the things you want to see. If you *do* decide to go on your own, don't panic—you're bound to come out at the other end, where a little taxi will take you back to wherever you want. As in all Moroccan medinas, the shops are arranged by trade or goods— the Spice Sellers' Market, the Carpenters' Market, the Tanners, the Dyers, and so on. Making, buying, selling, and transporting things seems to be the inhabitants' main occupation, and one should not forget that much of the richness of Fès came from the thousands of skilled craftsmen who found refuge in the town throughout the centuries.

It's really impossible to say how long any visit will take—the distances are short (under 1 ½ km from one end of Fès el-Bali to the other)—but the pace employed can vary from a brisk, non-stop walk to a carefree wandering wherever the fancy takes you. The most important monuments have been marked with a *. If you only have half a day, I suggest you look at these while enjoying the markets and the general atmosphere, which contribute enormously to the charm and unique character of Fès. Friday, a holy day, is not a good day for visiting, since many of the workshops and stalls will be closed, as well as some of the buildings normally open to the public.

For **itinerary N° 1** I am partially using that sketched out by Richard Parker in his excellent book on Moroccan Islamic monuments (see chapter 2). It combines part of **Fès el-Jdid** and a good part of **Fès el-Bali** and can be done (rapidly) in a day (leaving out a museum and long dawdling in the markets), at first by taxi (recommended), or by car as far as the Boujeloud Esplanade. Go first to the **Merinid Tombs,** on the north side of the city (the only other Merinid necropolis is at the Chellah, in Rabat). A path to the right just after the hotel leads up to the tombs, and by advancing about 200 m, the whole of **Fès el-Bali** can be taken in, a dense mass of white buildings, green-tiled mosques, and tall minarets. A solid hum of life comes up from the hollow, punctuated five times a day with the muezzin's call to prayer. From here continue along the Route du Tour de Fès, leaving the Hotel des Mérinides on the left, to the **Borj Nord,** now an **Arms Museum** (the entrance is left, just after the fort, see "Culture," section 8 below—it is not advised for a ½ day visit). Its architecture is typical of 16th-century military buildings. Continue past the **Kasbah al-Khamis,** also known as the **Cherarda Kasbah** after a local tribe, built by Mulay Rashid in 1670 for his Fès garrison, go left down the hill, and left again at the walls at the bottom. Behind and to the right is **Fès el-Jdid.** This is estimated to have been the route followed by most early European travelers going to Fès. Go through **Bab Segma** (the Segma Gate), which is flanked by two octagonal towers, built by the Merinid sultan in 1315, and turn right through another little gate to arrive in the **Vieux Mechouar,** the work of Mohammed III (18th century). On the right is the ornate gate to the **Makina,** built for Mulay Hassan by an Italian mission in the late 19th century as an arms factory, and more recently used as a rug factory (the building forms part of the planned Royal City of Arts and Culture).

At the end of the Vieux Mechouar, the **Bab Sbaa** (the Lion Gate) used to guard the entrance to the royal palace. It leads into the **Petit Mechouar,** at the end of which is the huge **Bab Dakaken,** built by the Merinid sultan in 1276 but restored in the 19th century. A visit to the **Mulay Abdallah** district (a "red light" area during the Protectorate), reached by a small gate to the right, will have to be quick. Leave the car in the Petit Mechouar. Once inside, pass an old **water wheel** on the right, a souvenir of the 13th-century model, to arrive at the **Great Mosque of Fès el-Jdid,** founded by the Merinid sultan in 1287, which contains the tomb of the Merinid Abu Inan. You can look into the courtyard before returning to your vehicle. The Mulay Abdallah District is crowded and lively with markets, while the 18th-century **Mulay Abdallah Mosque** has an adjoining sanctuary containing the tombs of several members of the Alaouite family. Cars are not allowed in **Fès el-Bali,** so a visit means **walking.** If this is your choice, after the Petit Mechouar turn left though the arches of **Bab Chems** (the Sun Gate), which leads to **Fès el-Bali.** Leave the **Boujeloud Gardens** (originally royal, but now public) on the right, pass a modern high school, and abandon the taxi (or leave the car at the nearby parking area on Boujeloud Esplanade).

Starting the **walking part** of the itinerary, you will see the **Boujeloud Mosque** and the **Bab Boujeloud** (the Boujeloud Gate) in front of you, with a mass of cheap hotels and cafés. As a help to orientation, to the left from the mosque is the **Place Baghdadi.** Originally built in the 13th century, the **mosque** and crenellated **gate** have been much restored. The latter, although it looks old, in fact only dates from the beginning of the 20th century. A road left from the gate leads to the attractive **Bab ech-Chorfa** (built by Mulay Sliman at the end of the 19th century), which was the gate to an Alaouite kasbah, now a residential area, but still with ramparts. Further on is **Bab Mahrouk,** which takes you the other side of the Fès el-Bali walls (there is a good view up to fine entry gate to the Kasbah al-Khamis, up on the hill). The original Bab Mahrouk was built by the Almohads in 1204 and got its name (Gate of the Burned) because they finished off a rebel under its arch. Turn left just after Bab Boujeloud and swing around into **Talaa el-Kbira** (the Big Ascent—though it actually goes down from where you are), the main route through Fès el-Bali. Although the road can still get very muddy when it rains, the recent paving is a great improvement. It leads into the heart of the medina and is very crowded. Squeeze to one side when a laden donkey comes along, its driver shouting *"Balek!"* ("Watch out!"), but don't miss looking at the multitude of little shops (some are really miniature in size). Many of the alleys are covered over with rushes and are cool and shady. A hundred meters or so down the Talaa, and clearly visible by its minaret, is the *Bou Inania Medersa, the most impressive of Fès' *medersas* (residential religious schools), built by the Merinid Abu Inan around 1350 (it was recently restored). It can be visited (open from 8:00 A.M.-5:00 P.M., closed Friday mornings, entry 10 DH), and the visitor is at once confronted with a wealth of decoration in the shape of *zellijs,* cursive script inscriptions, and carved stucco panels. The square courtyard, with a small ablutions fountain in the middle, is also decorated from top to bottom, and beautiful *musharabiya* (carved, openwork wooden screens) hide the surrounding galleries and students' rooms. Unlike many *medersas,* this one had its own mosque, complete with *minbar* (pulpit) and minaret. Up the stairs from the hall, the decorated gallery running around the courtyard has a beautiful carved ceiling. Another flight of stairs leads to the roof. Just across the street an ingenious **water clock,** fixed into the wall and dating to 1317, was a technological wonder of its day. It seems that a water-activated weight dropped into one of the 13 brass bowls and a window opened to mark the hour. When I first saw it, some years ago, it was in a pretty bad state, and only some carved cedar consoles and a row of arched windows could be seen. Since then it has been under renovation and invisible to the visitor.

Some 300 meters further on, you might notice a *fondouk* (caravansery) on the left and on the right a venerated spot where Mulay Idriss is said to have rested and decided to found the town of Fès. Further on, the road divides and becomes the ech-Cherabliyin road. Keep right, and after the fountain and *hammam* (baths), you'll find the **Cherabliyin Mosque** (Slippermakers's Mosque), founded by the Merinid sultan Abul Hassan in 1342. The mosque has been restored many times, but its minaret is a fine example of Merinid art, both for its elegant proportions and its polychrome *zellij* decoration, divided into registers by lines of bricks.

Further on, one of a number of lanes on the right leads to the *En-Nejjarin **Square, Fountain,** and **Fondouk.** The Nejjarin ("Carpenters") caravansery dates from the mid-18th century and has a most beautiful doorway. Its attractive fountain is much photographed. The *fondouk* has recently been renovated and turned into a museum (see "Culture," section 8 below). In the little workshops around the square, carpenters turn out wonderful tables with the simplest of tools. Working your way out of the Nejjarin Square, you'll quickly reach the **Suq el-Attarin** (Spice Sellers' Market). This souk is the center of a large number of shops selling a variety of articles and all are reached by a labyrinth of little alleys. The Attarin Souk itself specializes in **spices** and **herbs** and attracts hordes of customers. The everyday ingredients are heaped in front of the booth, the more precious ones stocked at the back. Note the piles of henna and all sorts of other local cosmetics in the **Suq el-Henna,** to the right just before the Spice Sellers' Souk, with its square and 15th-century fountain. Once in the Spice Souk, you will see an ornamental gate on the right, leading into a colorful lane full of shops selling silk braid, tassels, and belts. The minaret of the **Mulay Idriss Zaouia** and **Mosque** can be seen at the end of the lane. Today's visitor may not visit the *zaouia,* but can go through the **horm** (sacred precinct) of the *zaouia,* which was a traditional place of asylum, though up to the 20th century it could not be entered by non-Moslems. Remains thought to belong to Mulay Idriss II were found here in 1308 and reburied in the same place, a shrine being erected in his memory. Circling around the shrine, the visitor reaches a door through which his tomb can be glimpsed. Other doors are sometimes open and one can admire the carved wooden ceilings. Many people, especially women, come here to seek the saint's *baraka* (divine power)—the cult of the saints and holy men is strong in Morocco.

At this stage, some visitors will be feeling like **lunch,** or at any rate a pause (most of the medina's inhabitants will also be stopping to eat). See section 5 of this chapter for restaurants, but as a reminder, Dar Saada is right here (you need to have booked in advance). Back a bit, the restaurant Palais des Mérinides is near the Ech-Cherabiyin Mosque. The Palais de Fès restaurant is further on, near the Qarawiyin Mosque. For pastries, the Pâtisserie Kortouba is after the Atterin Medersa and before the Qarawiyin. Somewhat further away, about 500 m up a street to the left by Dar Saada, is Bab el-Guissa, where you have the Restaurant Ferdaous and the restaurant in the Hotel des Remparts, as well as the Hotel Palais Jamai (200 m right of Bab el-Guissa) (advance booking is advisable). For more "budget" eating, the Restaurant Dar Jamai isn't far from the Hotel Palais Jamai. The itinerary can obviously be stopped here and taken up the following morning or afternoon.

After the Dar Saada restaurant, on the right, a quiet covered market, the **kissaria,** sells things such as ready-made clothes, shoes, perfume, and jewelry. The entrance to the ***Attarin Medersa** is at the end of the Attarin souk. The *medersa* was built by the Merinid sultan Abu Said in 1323. At the time, it was considered the finest of its kind in Morocco, and still is today. Of course, it has been restored, but the original motifs have been preserved. As you go in, note the fine engraved patterns on the big bronze-covered doors and the beauty of the *zellij,* and the carved stucco and cedar in the courtyard, which is overhung by the galleries characteristic of *medersas.* The whole effect is breathtaking, and despite the richness of the decor, the overall impression is very harmonious. The prayer hall, which can be visited, has an elegant *mihrab* (a niche indicating the direction of Mecca), flanked by black marble columns, but it is otherwise very simple. From the first floor there is a good view down onto the souks. Another climb leads to the roof (not always allowed), from where you can see the Merinid Tombs up on the hill, the tall Mulay Idriss minaret in front, and, particularly, the minaret, courtyard, and roofs of the Qarawiyin Mosque just opposite (open 9:00 A.M.-12:00 P.M. and 2:00 P.M.-6:00 P.M., closed Friday mornings, entry 10 DH).

It is unfortunate that non-Moslems cannot enter the ***Qarawiyin Mosque,** for it is the most important example of Almoravid art in Morocco, and the oldest religious foundation in the country (it was begun in 857). It is one of the biggest Islamic **universities,** along with Al Azhar in Egypt and the Zitouna in Tunisia, though not necessarily the oldest, since its educational function only started in the 13th century under the Merinids. In 933 it became the principal mosque of the district founded by the Tunisian emigrants from Qayrawan, but it was the Almoravids who expanded it between 1135 and 1144 and gave it the magnificent decoration for which it is noted today. They were responsible for the stalactite domes under the central roof, for a superb wooden *minbar* (pulpit), only slightly younger than their *minbar* in the Koutoubia of Marrakech, and many other embellishments. According to the well-known local legend, the people of Fès hid the elaborate Almoravid decorations under a coat of plaster to protect them from destruction by the stern, puritanical Almohad conquerors (in fact, in the 1950s, the legend was found to be true). However, the Almohads did add an enormous latrine, one of the earliest in Morocco, and provided the mosque with a brass chandelier considered the finest to have survived since the Middle Ages, apart from the one in Taza. Succeeding dynasties all added their part, among them the Merinids, who built another latrine and a library, and three *medersas* around the mosque. It really is a pity that the visitor has to rely on published photographs to visualize all the beauty of this mosque, but some consolation can come from looking at the minaret, which is the oldest part of the building visible from outside and, in fact, Morocco's oldest monumental Islamic structure that can be seen by ordinary visitors (exactly dated to 956). By walking around the building, one may be lucky to find a door open through which to peer. There are plans to create a "City of Art and Culture" (including a library, museum, and a theater) adjoining the mosque. The mosque itself is in the process of being restored and renovated.

Just down the principal road from the Attarin Medersa there are a couple of gates, through the first of which you can look into the courtyard of the Qarawiyin Mosque. The second **(Bab al-Medersa)** is opposite the rather derelict Merinid **Misbahiya Medersa** (1346). The *medersa* has a floor of Italian marble and an Andalusian ablutions basin given by the Saadians. It is being restored by the Foundation Hassan II, and may not be open yet. The road then swings to the right, passing the **Funduq at-Titawan** (14th century), an old caravansery used by Tetouan merchants to store their goods and stable their mules while they lodged on the first floor. It is now used as a carpet shop. (The Palais de Fès restaurant used to be near here). Keep going alongside the Qarawiyin (on the right), to arrive at the **Seffarin Square** (Brassworkers' Square), a pretty noisy place and a monumental gate to the **Qarawiyin Library** (1349, restored in 1948). It contains many thousands of books, including some unique early Korans and manuscripts (it is not open to the public). From the square, the road forks, the left branch leading down and left to the **Seffarin Medersa,** indicated by a large door with carved stucco and a cedar overhang. There are actually three *medersas* here, two relatively modern, but the third (in ruins) was built by a Merinid sultan some time before 1285 and was the first of the Fès *medersas*. Keen visitors can distinguish a little of the original decoration and a small brick minaret. From the Seffarin Medersa, the colorful **Dyers's Street** *(As-Sabbaghin),* along the river, used to be lined with little workshops containing the cauldrons used for dying wool and thread, but now seems to be occupied by metalworkers. Going back to the **Seffarin Square,** a very twisting lane to the right (Rue Mechatine—Combmakers' Road) leads (250 m), not to an Islamic monument, but to the unforgettable **Tanners' District** *(Derb Debbaghin)* (don't take an earlier road right—it goes down to the river). This is on all the tourist itineraries—understandably—and so tends to be crowded with visitors. The tanneries are best visited in the morning, so try and fit it into your morning schedule. The *tanning basins are memorable to the eyes and to the nose. The visitor could find his way there by smell alone. Here skins of sheep, goat, cow, and dromedary are treated and then dyed. Preparing the skins is a laborious business, involving scraping, soaking, and pegging out for drying. The locals have got things pretty organized, and for around 10 DH people are taken up to the top of a house to look down on the basins, full of colored dye, skins, and bare-legged men tramping them up and down in the stinking liquid. As all the guidebooks say, this is real medieval technology (which does pose problems to the municipality due to the water pollution it causes).

Retrace your steps and go left and left again to the **Qantrat Bayn al-Mdoun** (Bridge Between the Towns) over the River Fès, leaving behind the Qarawiyin sector of the town for the **Andalusian** sector. Go uphill as straight as you can (not easy), and through a gateway (fountain behind on the left), to arrive at the monumental gate of the *Andalusian Mosque** at the top of the slope. It was founded by the sister of the pious woman who paid for the building of the Qarawiyin Mosque in the second half of the 9th century, and its minaret, at least, is contemporary with that of its bigger counterpart. It was rebuilt by the Almohads and its monumental gateway dates from the beginning of the 13th century (it has been much renovated since them). The Merinids added a fountain and library. It's difficult to take in more of this large building other than the gate, with its beautiful horseshoe arch, surrounding stuccowork, Koranic inscription, and carved wooden overhang. The mosque is, at the moment, being restored and renovated, but with a scrupulous respect for its original form. The *Sihrij Medersa,** considered to be the prettiest after the Attarin and Bou Inania, is reached by going right and then left from the entrance to the Andalusian Mosque (only a small lane divides it from the latter). It was built by the Merinid Abul Hassan (he was crown prince at the time) in 1323 to house the students studying in the Andalusian Mosque. Again, it is much restored (in particular the carved cedar and *musharabiya* or "wooden screens"), its original decoration has been faithfully copied, and the simple *zellij* work is old (open 9:00 A.M.-12:00 P.M. and 3:00 P.M.-6:00 P.M., closed Fridays, entry 10 DH). The neighboring **Sebbaiyin Medersa** is not open to the public.

If you want to get out of the medina altogether from here, its quite easy to reach **Bab el-Ftouh** (buses and taxis) by turning left from outside the entrance to the Andalusian Mosque, then right (mosque walls on your right), and taking a good-sized road running pretty straight to Bab el-Ftouh (500 m). If you want to continue the visit, it's quite complicated getting back across the river from here, over the Sidi el-Aouad bridge, so I suggest you retrace your route to the **Seffarin Square.** From here, take the right branch at the fork previously mentioned, and turn up right after about 50 m to the **Cherratin Medersa** (Ropemakers' *Medersa*). This is a comparatively recent building, having been founded by the Alaouite Sultan Mulay Rashid in 1670, and also one of the largest (it could house 160 students). The students' cells are arranged on three stories around small courtyards, but otherwise the *medersa* follows the usual lines and is not particularly noteworthy.

From the Cherratin Medersa it is about 1 km to **exit** by the south gate of **Bab el-Jdid** (buses and taxis), along the Boulevard Mohammed el-Alaoui. Transport is also possible from the **Er-Rsif Square,** only some 250 m along the same boulevard. The **Er-Rsif Mosque,** dating from the reign of Mohammed III (second half of 18th century), has quite an impressive minaret decorated with green ceramic tiles. **Alternatively,** if you are a souk and medina glutton, you can turn right out of the **Cherratin Medersa,** go to the top of the lane, then right to the Qarawiyin Mosque, and then left to the Attarin Medersa. From here you can get up to the **Bab el-Guissa Mosque, Medersa,** and **Gate** (buses and taxis), and leave the medina, or turn right for the Hotel Palais Jamai. The mosque and *medersa* were built by Mohammed III in 1760 and restored some 100 years later (it is not open to the public). The first gate to be built here dates from the 11th century, and was built by a local Berber chief. Depending on where you want to exit, you could **also go back** the way you came to **Bab Boujeloud.** This way, you could follow a Moroccan saying: "Going down, look; going up, buy," and pick up something you'd spotted on the way down.

A **different itinerary (N° 2),** if you **don't want to walk** (and thus miss out on Fès el-Bali), continues by car or taxi (parking not allowed) after the Petit Mechouar though a double arch down the principal road in Fès el-Jdid —passing various markets and, on the left, a couple of mosques, one of which, **Jamaa el-Hamra,** has a 14th-century minaret—to arrive at **Bab Semmarin** (the Farriers' Gate) (about 600 m). This gate constitutes, in fact, the principal entry into Fès el-Jdid. It was built in 1924, on the site of an earlier Merinid gate. From here, a right turn leads to the Grande Rue des Mérinides, which runs through the *mellah* (Jewish quarter), and out into the **Place des Alaouites.** The Jews were noteworthy jewelers and the district still specializes in this craft. The *mellah* (now inhabited by Moslems) was established here by the Merinids in 1438 in a district that had been occupied by some of their troops. Previously, the Jewish population had lived around the Qarawiyin Mosque, and they were moved here, both to be closer to the Merinid administration (for their own protection) and probably also to allow the construction of the many new *medersas*. They were obliged to pay an additional tax to the sultans and there were many restrictions on what they could do outside the *mellah* (such as wearing shoes or riding on the back of an animal). Although its Jewish population has left for the New Town or further afield, the *mellah's* characteristic balconies, doorways, and windows opening onto the street continue to confer a particular flavor to the district. There are still some synagogues (not in use). In spring 1998, the Foundation for the Judeo-Moroccan Cultural Heritage (based in Morocco) invited a group of Spanish architects to study the possibility of restoring a number of these old synagogues, so they may come to life again. With the help of UNESCO, a Jewish family of Moroccan origin, now settled in France, is also busy restoring its family synagogue. On the left is the old Jewish cemetery, extremely well kept and full of flowers. A small collection of Jewish objects are exhibited in a little building in the grounds. Another very busy shopping road right from Bab Semmarin, also coming out at the Place des Alaouites, skirts the *mellah* to the north. To its right is the **Royal Palace** *(Dar el-Makhzen)*, which is not open to the public. However, one can walk to the open space in front of the palace and admire the **monumental gates** that were built as part of Hassan II's renovation and enlargment plans (1969-71).

A **variant on this itinerary (N° 3)** starts at the Place des Alaouites and does N° 2 in reverse, but includes, at the end, a visit to the **Museum of Moroccan Arts and Crafts** *(Dar Batha)*. The exhibits are housed in a palace built by the sultans Mulay Hassan and Abd el-Aziz between 1886 and 1907. The museum gives an excellent idea of Moroccan crafts (see "Culture," section 8). It can be reached from Bab Boujeloud by taking any of the roads going right (not the one straight ahead into Fès el-Bali), to the Place de l'Istiqlal (about 200 m).

A **final suggestion** for motorized travelers is an early morning or evening drive around Fès (12 km), taking in most of its famous gateways and allowing good views over different parts of the city. From the new town, take the Boulevard Moulay Hassan, turn left along the Boulevard des Alaouites (beginning of ramparts), right along the Boulevard des Saadiens, right again at the next big intersection (Meknès road to the left), and left up the hill by Bab Segma. The road turns around the Kasba des Cherarda, passes the Borj Nord, the Hotel des Mérinides, and the Merinid Tombs (view point—see itinerary N° 1 above). Continue the Route du Tour de Fès down to Bab el-Guissa and Bab Jamai (Hotel Jamai is on the right) and swing south to the Bab Sidi Boujida and Bab Khoukha (both a bit in, on the right). Keep on following the walls, turning westward after the junction with the Taza road on the left, to Bab el-Ftouh (note the cemetery up on the hill to the left), the Borj Sud (has a good view), and the final climb up to the new town.

AROUND FÈS

The **thermal springs** of **Moulay Yacoub** are situated some 18 km north-west of Fès (end of the road). About 10 km along the main P1 from Fès to Meknès, a small road on the right (marked) leads to the springs, well known for their beneficial effects on skin diseases and rheumatism (bathing, *not* drinking). The center has recently been improved and there are swimming pools and massage parlors. Moulay Yacoub can be reached by **big taxi.**

The ****** Hotel Thermes** (120 rooms, 600 DH, Tel: 69 40 70/71, Fax: 69 40 65) is set among trees, is very comfortable and well kept, and the food is good. The hotel runs a shuttle service to the thermal springs.

Another thermal center lies 15 km east of Fès, at **Sidi Harazem,** 1 km off the main P1 to Taza. The village is watered by a hot spring, whose mineral-rich water is recommended for liver and kidney ailments. Sidi Harazem water is bottled and sold throughout Morocco, and is drunk regularly by those worrying about kidney stones. A swimming pool is available for bathers (a few DH for use of the changing room). The site is not particu-larly attractive, but worth a visit if you're going that way. In May an impor-tant *moussem* takes place around the tomb of Sidi Ali ben Harazem, a 12th-century saint and learned man from the east. Sidi Harazem can be reached by **bus Nº 28.**

The one hotel, the ***** Hotel Sidi Harazem** (64 rooms, 320 DH, Tel: 69 00 57), has a restaurant and is fine for an overnight stay.

WEST OF FÈS

A new expressway now links Fès **westwards** to Meknès (60 km) and Khemisset (a further 45 km). It also allows for a quick and easy journey to Rabat (198 km). It is possible to visit the Roman ruins of Volubilis, 30 km northwest of Meknès, in a day, but it is strongly advised to allow longer to cover both Volubilis and the important monuments in Meknès itself (chapter 7).

SOUTH OF FÈS

The attractive little mountain town of **Imouzer du Kandar** (40 km) is sit-uated at an altitude of 1,650 m in the Middle Atlas, and is much appreci-ated by the Fassi, who go there to picnic in the spring and summer. It is reached by **car, bus,** or **big taxi** along the main P24 to Ifrane and Azrou.

There is a good hotel, the *** Hotel des Truites** (146 DH, Avenue Mohammed V, Tel: 56 30 02), where you can enjoy a lunch of trout, and perhaps wild boar, while admiring the view. The region is dotted with lakes, and flowers fill the prairies in the spring.

Of the two other hotels, the ** **Hotel Royal** (207 DH, Tel/Fax: 66 30 80) and the *** **Hotel Chahrazed** (277 DH, Place du Marché, Tel: 66 30 12), the latter is the more agreeable. An Apple and Pear Festival is held in Imouzer du Kandar in September.

A delightful **Lake Circuit** (*Circuit Touristique des Lacs*) starts about 10 km south of Imouzer du Kandar, where a left turn takes in the **Dayet Aoua** (a "daya" is a lake, usually shallow) and **Dayet Ifrah.** The area actually contains five lakes, thick with all sorts of birds and ideal for walking and picnicking.

At Dayet Aoua, the ** **Hotel-Restaurant Chalet du Lac** (20 rooms, 207 DH, Tel: 66 32 70/66 31 97) also makes a good overnight stay, with a high-quality meal: the lunch or dinner "gastronomic menu," prepared by two Frenchwomen, costs around 180 DH (it is best to make a reservation). It is possible to swim, fish, and hire a rowboat here. The road comes out just south of **Ifrane** (total about 40 km from Imouzer du Kandar), from where the return to Fès is by the main P24 (see chapter 7 for Ifrane and possible continuation on to Azrou and further southwest).

East of the Imouzer road, but still **south** from Fès, the visitor can take the P20 for a day's outing to the little walled town of **Sefrou** (28 km). The inhabitants of **Bhalil,** a small town just before Sefrou, were said to have had Christian origins, and it may be that it was occupied in the 1st century A.D. by the Romans. Not yet up in the mountains, **Sefrou** (altitude 850 m) lies in the middle of a well-watered plain, and was already known as a commercial center in the 12th century, where merchants from the north met those coming up from the south. The early inhabitants were Berbers converted to Judaism, who adopted Islam in the 8th century, at the time of Mulay Idriss. An important Jewish colony from south Morocco and southern Algeria settled in Sefrou in the 13th century, and its *mellah* remained important until the 1950s, implanted in the middle of the medina. A stroll in the medina is pretty calm and hassle-free, and one can watch the local craftsmen turning out jewelry, pottery, and metalwork. Today's population numbers about 40,000. A pleasant walk (1½ km) is up the gorge of the River Aggai (marked *Cascades*), with its **waterfalls** and **caves.** One of these caves, called **Kef el-Moumen** or **Kef el-Youdi** (Jew's Cave) is a place of **pilgrimage** for both Jews and Moslems. Legend has it that it contains the tomb of the biblical prophet Daniel. Regular **buses** leave from Fès. Sefrou is famous for its cherry orchards and a Cherry Festival is held here in mid-May (*Fête des Cerises*). The religious festival and pilgrimage to the tomb of Sidi Lahcen Lyoussi takes place in August.

The **hotel scene** is not good, with only one decent hotel, the ** **Hotel Sidi Lahcen Lyoussi** (22 rooms, 207 DH, Route de Sidi Ali Boussaghine).

It has a pool and licensed bar, and it's also the best place to eat, apart from the **Restaurant Café Oumnia** (near Boulevard Mohammed V), which does a standard, but decent, tourist menu for 60 DH, and a number of cheap snack bars near the market.

FURTHER AFIELD

Fès is a real center of a spider's web of roads, offering communication in all directions. Some 20 km **south** of Sefrou, on the main road to **Boulemane** (106 km from Fès), across the Kandar Massif of the Middle Atlas (splendid views), and further on to Midelt (chapter 7) and the far south, a road on the right at Annoceur joins the **Lake Circuit** *(Circuit Touristique des Lacs)* mentioned above. This is a charming itinerary, and Fès can be regained in a circular movement. If planning to take the route in winter, make sure from the Gendarmerie that it is open, for the Tizi Abekhnane pass is up at 1,769 m and may be blocked by snow at times between November and April. After the pass, the stretches of wood and pasturage give way to a bleaker landscape, announcing the desert region of the Tafilalt.

Three roads **north** allow the visitor to reach **Ouezzane** (chapter 7)—one is the P28 (branching off the main road to Meknès), 134 km of rather uninteresting scenery; another, slightly shorter (the 4050, 130 km), direct from Fès, is more or less a short-cut, since it joins the P28 just before crossing the River Sebou; and the rather longer (157 km) and marginally more interesting P26 to **Fès el-Bali** (87 km) (not to be confused with the district in Fès of the same name). In the first half of the 12th century the Almoravids built a stronghold just before Fès el-Bali—the **Jbel Amergou Fortress**—to control the surrounding country. Perched on the Jbel Amergou (683 m), it has a sheer drop on one side of 300 m and is still a spectacular place to visit (1 km northwest of the village of Moulay Bouchta, 79 km from Fès). Apart from some good views over the plain from time to time, none of these routes are particularly scenic, and are only of interest in that they allow access from Fès to the attractive town of Chefchaouen, and eventually Tetouan and Tangier (all chapter 5). The Mediterranean coastal town of **Al-Hoceima** (chapter 5) can be reached from Fès by a road going northeast, the S302 (275 km) via Ain Aicha, which is rather boring until **Taounate** (81 km), after which it starts climbing up into the Rif Mountains to reach **Ketama** (a further 79 km) and right to Al-Hoceima. The stretch between Taounate and Ketama is really beautiful, as is the next bit on from Ketama, at least as far as **Targuist** (see chapter 5 for warnings about the dangers of driving in the Rif). Targuist was the last refuge of **Abdelkrim,** who led a revolt of the Rif tribes against the Spanish (and later the French) between 1921 and 1926.

The east-bound P1 (after the deviation for Sidi Harazem above) continues on to **Taza** (120 km). There are some fine scenic stops along the way, the big Mulay Idriss I dam lies to the left, and, after the low Touahar pass (556m), the road arrives in Taza. Before reaching Taza, however, the **Jbel Tazzeka Circuit,** including waterfalls, lakes, and deep caves—it's speleological country—should not be missed, even if you don't intend to spend days underground. It is perfectly possible to have a quick look at this splendid region—known as the **Jbel Tazzeka National Park**—on your way to Taza by **big taxi,** but your own transport is, of course, preferable. Although the road distance is only about 80 km, to do it nicely, the Jbel Tazzeka Circuit requires a day (right turn at **Sidi Abdallah des Rhiata,** 90 km from Fès), so you need to make a really early start from Fès, or spend the night in Taza and set off early from there. From **Sidi Abdallah des Rhiata,** the narrow, winding, climbing road (S311) runs along the gorges of the River Zireg before turning east to swing around the southern side of the **Jbel Tazzeka** (1,980 m). Leaving the cork oaks behind, the plateau landscape seems very bare, though the Jbel Tazzeka slopes are covered with conifers. After the Bab Taka pass (1,459 m) the now run-down village of **Bab Bou-Idir** used to be a highly appreciated summer resort for the families of the French garrison stationed in Taza during the Protectorate.

Dayet Chiker, to the right, is usually dry, but it is linked to an underground water system and can suddenly become quite deep. Just after the pass, a bad track climbs steeply to the top of Jbel Tazzeka, where there is a television relay station—and a splendid view covering the Rif Mountains in the north and the Atlas to the south. Further on, the **Friouata Caves** are marked on the left *(Gouffres)* and are one of the prime attractions of the region (reached by car or a stiff half-hour walk from the roadside). The huge mouth of the cave system is 30 m wide, and drops sheer down, almost 100 m, before reaching the sloping floor. A narrow series of steps carved out of the cave wall leads down (there is a shaky handrail) to the first level, with further steps descending to a vast, tall chamber with a rich stalactitic decoration, off which leads more galleries and chambers. The slippery surface slows down progress, which is otherwise horizontal and easy, before the visit stops (or it did for me!) at a deep shaft (approximately two hours and 7 km in a straight line from the mouth). There is a guide (entrance fee is 3 DH), but you should have your own flashlight, shoes with a good grip, and old clothes. If you want a guide all the way (not essential), it'll cost you around 100 DH. There are superb stalactite formations in some of the distant rooms, but you'll need over two hours to get to them. The Friouata system, probably the deepest in Morocco, has been explored by speleologists, including the famous Frenchman Norbert Casteret, and is thought to have wide ramifications. The **Chiker Caves** *(Grottes du Chiker)*, a few kilometers further on, on the right, are connected to the Dayet Chiker and form an underground river explored over 2 km. Casual visitors cannot enter, and cavers should get in touch with the Tourist Office *(Syndicat d'Initiative)* in Taza for information. Actually, the whole of this area is riddled with caves like a Gruyère cheese, and is a paradise for speleologists. Next, a road to the left (marked Ras el-Ma) leads to the **Ras el-Oued Waterfalls** (they "fall" after winter rains only) and then into Taza. Stouthearted travelers in a 4WD vehicle could take a right turn after the Chiker Caves and follow the 4822 road down to **Merhaoua, Tamtrouchte,** and **Ait Makhlouf** to join the main P20 road just south of **Boulemane.** Superb scenery is guaranteed, but you really need to be well equipped and have a good map. The road could be blocked by snow from November to April.

Being off the main circuit, **Taza** does not attract many tourists. It is, however, one of Morocco's oldest towns, and its key position in the narrow corridor between the Rif Mountains and the Middle Atlas has meant that all invaders (or simple travelers) came along here on their way west, or established a base from which to penetrate further inland. Traces of prehistoric occupation are numerous, but the first historical mention is of a Berber fortification dating from the 10th century. In 1074 it was captured by the Almoravid Yusef ben Tachfin, and then in 1132 by the Almohad sultan, Abd el-Mumen, who made it his temporary capital. Faced by constant attacks by the Beni Merin tribe from the Sahara—who were later to found the Merinid dynasty—the sultan surrounded the town with ramparts. These were reinforced in the 14th century, when the Merinids got control of the country, and again in the 15th century by the Saadians, for Taza had lost none of its strategic importance through the ages. In the 17th century, the first Alaouite sultan, Mulay Rashid, used Taza as a base for attacking Fès. Under Mulay Ismail, the fortress served to prevent the Turks of Algeria from using the Taza Corridor to invade the country.

A pretty grim episode followed at the beginning of the 20th century, when an exiled court official returned to Morocco and claimed in Taza, in 1902, that he was the eldest son of the late sultan Hassan I and rightful heir to the throne occupied by the young sultan Abd el-Aziz . Calling himself **El Rogui** (the Pretender), he persuaded the Berber tribes, always ready for a fight, to rebel against the sultan and he remained master of Taza until 1909. By then his underhanded dealings with the Spanish over mining rights in the Rif and his rough treatment of the local people had lost him the support of the tribes and Mulay Abd el-Hafid, the new sultan, managed to capture him. The Rogui used to ride around on a donkey and rapidly became known as **Bou Hamara** (owner of the she-donkey) and was not a particularly tender-hearted man. However, he came to a very sticky end at the hands of Mulay Hafid (he was squeezed into a cage attached on the back of a camel, displayed to gaping crowds, thrown to the sultan's private lions—who didn't finish him off—then shot and burned). After the establishment of the French Protectorate in 1912, Taza became an important military base.

It is made up of two towns, the old and the modern, which are still quite separate. The New Town lies off the main Fès-Oujda road, while the Old Town is up the hill to the south, called Low and High Town respectively by the inhabitants, who number around 120,000. The Old Town is remarkably rich in ancient Islamic monuments for such a small town, and it is a pity that non-Moslems cannot get in to see them.

There is no **plane** service to Taza, but RAM has flights to Fès and Oujda, from where Taza can be reached by **train, bus,** or **big taxi.** However, Taza is easily and comfortably reached by train from Fès (three a day, about 40 DH) and Oujda (three a day, about 50 DH), and there is a day train or a night one with sleepers from Casablanca. There are frequent **bus** services from Fès and Oujda, and less frequent ones from Casablanca (two a day) via Rabat, Meknès, and Fès, and from Al-Hoceima. **Big taxis** also do the Fès-Taza, Oujda-Taza, and Al-Hoceima-Taza run (around 50 DH per person).

There is not a great choice of **hotels** in Taza. The most expensive in the **medium-price** range is the ★★★ **Hotel Friouato Salam** (58 rooms, 277 DH, Bab Bou Idir, Tel: 67 25 93/98, Fax: 67 35 67), but it is most inconveniently placed, being outside both parts of Taza (although slightly closer to the old town). Its grounds are well looked after and it is alright for motorized travelers looking for an overnight stop or a base from which to explore the region. It has a restaurant, bar, and a tennis court.

The ★★ **Hotel Dauphiné** (26 rooms, 167 DH, Avenue Prince Héritier Sidi Mohammed, Tel: 67 35 67) is situated at the southern edge of the New Town, just by the Place de l'Indépendance. The decor is in old Art Deco style, and the hotel has a certain charm. The rooms overlooking the square have balconies and the hotel has a bar and restaurant.

Budget accommodations can be provided by the fairly new **Hotel de la Poste** (20 rooms, around 80 DH, Place de l'Indépendance), and the **Hotel Guillaume Tell** (about the same price, also Place de l'Indépendance, Tel: 67 23 47), both with reasonably clean rooms. There is no decent hotel near the station (Taza lacks the Moussafir chain of station hotels), and while the **Hotel de la Gare** is useful for trains, buses, and taxis, since it is only about 200 m from these amenities, it cannot be recommended on any other count (the better rooms, with shower, cost around 120 DH).

In the Old Town, I'm told by Taza friends that the **Hotel de l'Etoile** (39 Rue Moulay Hassan, to the left as you come in, Tel: 27 01 79) has very basic but clean rooms for around 40 DH—and there, at least, you are in the thick of the medina, inside the ramparts.

The **dining and restaurant** situation is equally limited. The **Hotel Friouato** has a restaurant (set meal 123 DH), and I've eaten an acceptable but not memorable meal there. A meal of equal quality can be had at the **Hotel Dauphiné** (tourist menu 80 DH).

Cheap "eats" can be had around the bus and taxi terminals, while standard *harira* soup, *tajines,* and kebobs are served in slightly more attractive surroundings in the **Restaurant Majestic** (Avenue Mohammed V) (main dish around 35 DH).

The **Hamburger Youm Youm** (close to the Place de l'Indépendance) does (naturally) hamburgers and French fries (15 DH). Breakfast, as well as pastries, can be had at the nearby **Café Boulangerie Pâtisserie Amsterdam.** Coffee and (sometimes) snacks are available in a number of cafés in the medina.

For **sightseeing,** head for the medina, 1½ km from the Place de l'Indépendance (bus from the Place, or little taxi). The oldest parts of the **ramparts,** mostly in ruins, date from the 12th-century Almohads. The **bastion** set into the ramparts at their eastern extremity is the work of the Saadian Ahmed el-Mansur in the 16th century; its construction was clearly influenced by the European military architecture of the time. If you want to take a walk around the ramparts (3 km), excellent views can be had from the northern gate, the **Bab er-Rih** (the Gate of the Wind). Close by, inside the walls, is the **Great Mosque,** built by Abd el-Mumen in the 12th century, and added to by later sultans, but it's difficult to see much of it (it is, of course, not open to non-Moslems). Continuing down the road from here, away from Bab er-Rih, the visitor passes a couple of other **mosques** (note the curious minaret of the second, the **Mosqué du Marché**) before coming to the **Abul Hassan Medersa** (Merinid, 1323) with a carved cedar lintel and an interior *zellij*-decorated courtyard (it can be visited if anyone can be found to open it). Close by is the **Andalusian Mosque** (12th century) and the *mechouar* (assembly ground). The **souks** are close to the Mosqué du Marché. Rugs woven by the Berber women of the local Beni Ouarain tribe are sold here. They are considered by some experts to be the most authentic of all Berber rugs, but rarely figure in books on Moroccan rugs. A typical Beni Ouarain rug has an overall losange design on an off-white base. A final place of interest might be the house of **Bou Hamra,** just beside the Andalusian Mosque, with some remaining carved plaster decoration—but no brass commemorative nameplate to say he lived here!

The Jbel Tazeka circuit can easily be done using Taza as a base.

The **evening drink** will have to be taken at the **Hotel Friouato** or the more animated, popular bar in the **Hotel Dauphiné.**

The main P1 road continues east to Oujda (223 km), via Guercif (65 km) (chapter 9).

The Taza Address List:

Banks—BMCE, Avenue Mohammed V; Banque Populaire, Avenue Moulay Youssef; Wafabank, Boulevard Hassan II.

Bus station *(gare routière)*—north of New Town, near main Fès-Oujda road.

Church—French-speaking mass at the Eglise de la Sainte-Famille, 91 Rue Sultan Abou el-Hassan (Tel: 67 37 93).

Express Post—*Poste Rapide* from the central post office.

Gendarmerie Royale—(Tel: 17).

Photocopies—téléboutiques and most tobacco shops.

Police—(Tel: 19).

Post Office—just off Place de l'Indépendance.

Railway Station—just north of main Fès-Oujda road, New Town.

Taxis, Big—by bus station, north of New Town, near main Fès-Oujda road.

Telephone—in post office and also téléboutiques.

Tourist Information (ONMT)—Avenue Tetouan, behind Place de l'Indépendance.

7. Guided Tours

Tours of the Fès medina are not formally organized (unless you can sneak in among an organized tourist-group visit). There are, however, lots of **official guides** for individual travelers. There are also **false guides** who crowd around the visitor on all occasions, offering their services, despite attempts (increasingly successful) by the authorities to curb their activities. The guide problem is two-fold. On the one hand, the official guides are more expensive (120 DH/morning) but competent (on the whole), as opposed to the false guides who are cheaper, and know the medina well (but not necessarily its history). Most guides are generally bent on leading visitors to "their" shops, where they get a commission on purchases, a practice that is often to the detriment of a proper visit to the monuments. Official guides can be hired through your hotel, or from the *Syndicat d'Initiative*, where the tariffs are posted. Some speak English (Competent women guides are also available). Fix clearly beforehand the things you want to see, and those that don't interest you. For a first visit, or when time is short, it is preferable to have a guide, official or unofficial. If you do decide to take the latter, he is very likely to get into trouble with the police who patrol the medina.

8. Culture

The **Museum of Moroccan Arts** *(Musée des Arts Marocains)* is one of the country's most interesting folk museums. It is situated in the Palais Dar Batha, and is consequently often called the "Batha Museum," about a 5-minute walk from Bab Boujeloud, in the Place de l'Istiqlal, to the right as you face the gate from the outside, past the Sidi Lezzar Mosque. The building is a late 19th-century Hispano-Mauresque palace, with rooms opening onto the usual central courtyard with plants and a fountain. Its carved wooden doors and painted ceilings are masterpieces. The museum contains a rich collection of antique ceramics, Fès-stitch embroidery, rugs, ancient navigating instruments, wooden carving, stuccowork, and *zellij* (open 8:30 A.M.-12:00 P.M. and 2:30 P.M.-6:00 P.M. , closed Tuesdays, entry 10 DH).

The Borj Nord contains a **Weapons Museum** *(Musée d'Armes)* exhibiting a very fine collection of swords, daggers, antique rifles, and pistols (which used to be in the Batha Museum). Some of the cannons are presents from European sovereigns to the Moroccan sultans. If you can get up onto the roof, there are some good views (open 9:00 A.M.-12:00 P.M. and 3:00 P.M.-6:00 P.M., closed Tuesdays—but it is unfortunately more often closed than open). Spring 1998 saw the inauguration of a new museum, the **Nejjarin Woodworking Museum** *(Musée Nejjarin des Arts et Métiers du bois)*, situated in the *Fondouk Nejjarin* (Carpenters' *Fondouk*), Place Nejjarin (Tel: 74 05 80), Fès el-Bali. It is the first private museum (created by the Foundation Mohammed Karim Lamrani) specializing in woodworking arts and crafts. This newly renovated caravansery, classified as a historical monument in 1916, displays ancient woodworking tools and a fine collection of old sculptured wood. This is a marvelous opportunity to visit both an old *fondouk* and a fascinating museum, and the top floor coffee shop has a beautiful view over the medina (open 9:00 A.M.-12:00 P.M. and 2:30 P.M.-6:00 P.M., closed Tuesdays, entry 10 DH). Plans are in the air for the creation in Fès el-Jdid of a **Royal City of Arts and Culture** *(Cité Royale des Arts et de la Culture)*, made up of two squares, the big and little Mechouar, the old arms factory, Dar el-Makina, and a garden.

Fès is not only noted for its cooking, but also for its **Andalusian** music, called Ala. It is a classical, courtly music, played by a string and percussion orchestra, accompanied by a solo singer and choir. The Fès Ala orchestra is one of the best and gives occasional public recitals. The *Association Fès*

Sais and the *Association Art & Musique en Méditerranée* organized, for the second time, a week of Western and Eastern classical music early in September, called the *Académie International de Musique de Fès* (Tel: 63 39 89 for details). Other concerts are given from time to time.

The **French Cultural Center** *(Institut Français)*, Rue Loukili, New Town (Tel: 62 39 21), has a program of events including concerts, talks, video films (all in French), and art exhibits. The **Spanish Cultural Center** *(Instituto Cervantes)*, at 7 Rue Abdelkrim el-Khattabi (Tel: 62 22 51), organizes occasional exhibitions, concerts, talks, and plays (in Spanish). There is a **Jewish Community Center** at 24, Rue el-Hsin al-Khasar (a discreet, unnamed building just opposite the Hotel Splendid), which welcomes Jewish visitors.

9. Sports

There is an attractive 9-hole **golf** club, the Royal Golf of Fès (3,168 m, par 37). It lies a few kilometers outside Fès on the Imouzer road and was designed by Cabell B. Robinson. It has the advantage of not being crowded (and has a good restaurant). As you play your way around, you can enjoy good views of the Middle Atlas. Most big hotels have **swimming pools** and the Hotel Menzeh Zalagh lets outsiders use its pool (50 DH a day) (this is a good bargain, for the hotel is a most attractive place). The Municipal Swimming pool is crowded and not particularly clean. Guests at the Hotel Errabie can use the facilities of the U.S.F. sporting club just beside the hotel (heated swimming pool, volleyball, and basketball). **Lake swimming, fishing,** and **rowing** is possible at Dayet Aoua (see Imouzer du Kandar above). The big hotels have **tennis courts,** for use by guests only.

10. Shopping

There is an abundance of things to buy in the **medina,** and the only problem will be having to make a choice. Have a good look around, and don't be fooled by endless glasses of mint tea into buying a rug you don't want at a price you don't want either. Try the **State Craftwork Center** *(Ensemble Artisanal)* on Avenue Allal ben Abdallah (next to the Hotel Volubilis and a bit up from the Sheraton) if you want to look calmly around with no pressure to buy. It is usually well stocked, the prices are indicated, and there is no bargaining, but a reduction is offered for the purchase of several items (open daily 9:30 A.M.-12:30 P.M. and 2:30 P.M.-6:30 P.M.). Kitty Morse, the well-known Californian cookery expert who was born and brought up in Morocco, recommends the follow large **rug**

bazaars: Palais Vizir (35 Derb Touil Blida), Aux Merveilles de Fez (opposite Attarin Medersa), and Palais Andalous (15 Derb Selma).

All the **big hotels** have **boutiques** where books, clothes, jewelry, and other items are, often, at quite reasonable prices. The Boutique of the Hotel Palais Jamai has a good collection of jewelry and elegant clothing. For the whole range of Moroccan handicrafts at very reasonable prices, one of the best shops (highly recommended) is the **Curiosités Marocaines** (12 Boulevard Chefchaouni, Tel: 62 23 94), next to the Grand Hotel. All the prices are shown on the goods and you are free to look around and handle them without any hassle. The owner, Jacques Mamane, is firm about not letting in tourist guides, so often responsible for high prices. Fès is famous for its blue and white **pottery,** and there is a Potters' District on the hill above the road to Taza (near Bab el-Ftouh). It is easy to pick out due to the smoke from the ovens. While it's interesting to see the stages in the production of the ceramics, the articles themselves and the prices are not particularly appealing.

English-language books, mostly language-learning and novels, are stocked at the English bookshop, 68 Avenue Hassan II. Newsagent stands along Boulevard Mohammed V have **foreign newspapers** and **magazines,** which can also be found in all the big hotels.

11. Entertainment and Nightlife

The best **cinemas** are L'Empire (60 Avenue Hassan II) and the Rex (recently renovated), both of which show French- or Arabic-speaking films. A few years back, Fès started a **Sound and Light Show** *(Son et Lumière),* modeled on the successful French event. So far, the Fès version is the only one in Morocco. In 45 minutes it tells the story of Fès's glorious past with the help of modern technology such as laser beams, sound effects, and pictures projected onto the Borj Sud walls, near Bab el-Ftouh. It takes place every night except Sundays; opening times vary according to the season (information is available from Immeuble La Mamela, Apt. #65, Place de Florence, Tel: 93 18 93, Fax: 93 18 93, the *Syndicat d'Initiative,* and the bigger hotels). Don't let the hotels charge a commission on the sale of tickets. The official price has been dropped to 50 DH.

At the end of May, the **Fès Festival of Worldwide Sacred Music** *(Festival de Fès des Musiques Sacrées du Monde)* is attended by spectators from throughout Morocco and even further afield. It is a cultural event not to be missed, as it brings together singers and choirs from all over the world from a variety of cultural and spiritual backgrounds—Gregorian chant, Negro Spirituals, and Sufi songs, to name just a few. Information and tickets are available from the Palais Batha (Bab Boujeloud) or the Tourist Office.

If you are not spending the evening in one of the big hotels, enjoying a Moroccan **dinner with music and dancer(s),** you'll be hard pushed to find an interesting place in which to have just an **evening drink** other than in a hotel. There are a few bars around in the new town, but these are definitely all-male affairs and can get a bit rough as the evening draws on. All the **big hotels have bars,** some more appealing than others. Possible choices are those in the Hotel Palais Jamai (marvelous pianist), Hotel Jnan Palais (attractive), the Hotel Mérinides (splendid view over the medina), the Hotel Wassim (English bar and snack bar), the Grand Hotel, the Hotel Sofia (bar and English pub), Hotel Splendid (comfortable bar, but it's nice to have a drink by the pool in summer), Hotel Menzeh Zalagh (piano bar, pub bar, "Happy Hour" from 7:00 P.M.-8:00 P.M.—two drinks for the price of one—marvelous view), the Hotel Sheraton Fès (spacious), and the Hotel Volubilis (full of tourist groups). The ** Hotel Amor has a nice little bar and outside patio (good in summer). **Nightclubs** and **discos** function in most of the big hotels, often with a floor show: Hotel Wassim, Hotel Sofia, Grand Hotel, and Hotel Menzeh Zalaga. Plan to pay from 50-150 DH for entry and the first drink.

12. The Fès Address List

Airlines—Royal Air Maroc, 52 Avenue Hassan II (Tel: 62 04 56).

Airport—Fès-Sais, Route d'Imouzer (Tel: 62 47 12).

Banks—many on Boulevard Mohammed V; VISA distributors: BMCE, Place Mohammed V, Place de Florence; Société Générale Marocaine de Banques, Boulevard Mohammed V.

Bus station *(gare routière)*—CTM, new station up near the Place Atlas; non-CTM from Place Baghdadi, near Bab Boujeloud.

Car Rental—Avis, 50, Boulevard Chefchaouni (Tel: 62 67 46); Budget, bureau Grand Hotel, Boulevard Chefchaouni (Tel: 62 09 19); Europcar, 41 Avenue Hassan II (Tel: 62 65 45); Hertz, bureau Hotel Sheraton Fès, Avenue des F.A.R. (Tel: 62 28 12); Maroc-Car, 53 Rue Compardon (Tel: 62 53 76); Zeit, 35 Avenue Mohammed es-Slaoui (Tel: 62 55 10).

Church—French-speaking mass at the Eglise Saint-François, Avenue Mohammed es-Slaoui (Tel: 62 24 81).

Drugstore, Night—at the Municipalité, Boulevard Moulay Youssef (from 8:00 P.M.-8:00 A.M.).

Express Post—from the central post office (Tel: 62 24 00).

Fire—(Tel: 15).

Gendarmerie Royale—(Tel: 17).

Golf Club—see under section 9, "Sports."

Hospitals and Clinics—best contact U.S. Embassy in Rabat (Tel: 07-76 22 65, Fax: 07- 76 56 61).

Jewish Cultural Center—24 Rue el-Hsin al-Khasar (opposite Hotel Splendid).

Jewish Synagogue—Synagogue Saadoun, Boulevard Mohammed V.

Photocopies—most tobacco stores and téléboutiques.

Police—(Tel: 19).

Post Offices—corner Boulevard Mohammed V/Avenue Hassan II; near Batha Museum, Fès el-Bali.

Railway Station *(gare)*—Place de la Gare, north side of New Town (Tel: 62 50 01), about a 20-minute walk from Avenue Hassan II and main post office.

Taxis, Big and Little—big taxis from railway station, Avenue des Almohades; also from Place Baghdadi bus station, Bab Mahrouk, and Bab el-Ftouh; small ones will stop on demand, or have specially indicated stands.

Telephone—in the post office and téléboutiques.

Tourist Information—the *Syndicat d'Initiative,* Place Mohammed V, has the usual colored brochures, a list of hotels, tariffs for guides, and can advise on hiring guides. Helpful staff.

Travel Agencies—Carlson Wagonlit Travel, Immeuble Grand Hotel, Boulevard Mohammed V (Tel: 62 29 58, Fax: 62 44 36).

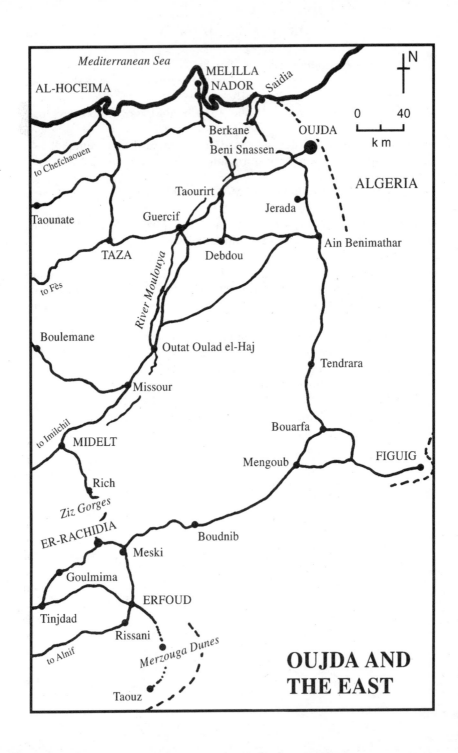

9

Oujda and the East

1. The General Picture

Oujda is not a town—visited by many Western travelers. This is a pity, since, although it's not particularly rich in ancient monuments, its surrounding country and Mediterranean beaches to the north are attractive. It is a frontier town, only 10 km from the Algerian border (about double to the frontier post), and has a character all to itself.

Situation and distant past. The town lies in the middle of a fertile plain, hemmed in to the north by the Beni Snassen hills and to the south by the Monts d'Oujda. Neither of these massifs reach a great height: 1,532 m for the Beni Snassen, 1,167 m for the Monts d'Oujda. The River Moulouya, one of Morocco's most important rivers, reaches the Mediterranean Sea at the western limits of the province of Oujda, of which the town is the capital. Apart from the Oujda and Triffa Plains and the Beni Snassen Hills, the region going south is one of arid steppes and a scrubby sort of vegetation.

The distance between the two hill formations varies from 30-50 km, so it is understandable that Oujda has been the favorite way into Morocco throughout the ages. Archaeological excavations have shown that the region was inhabited at least since Middle Palaeolithic times, around 50,000 years ago. One of North Africa's most important Upper Palaeolithic sites, Pigeons' Cave in Taforalt in the Beni Snassen massif, is only 40 km from Oujda. Later Neolithic people of the area are also known from their excavated sites.

Strategic importance. The town itself was founded in 994 A.D. by a member of the nomadic Berber Zenata tribe, Ziri ibn Attia. He made it the capital of his zone of influence, which extended as far south as Sijilmassa and lasted for nearly 80 years. Oujda's strategic position, as gateway to Algeria and further east, led to its capture by the Almoravids in 1070, and then by the Almohads in 1206. Both dynasties strengthened the fortifications, only for it to become the scene of struggles between the Merinid dynasty and the Algerian rulers of Tlemcen. After the Merinids, the Saadians won control of the town, then the Alaouites became its masters, until the return of the Turks installed in Algiers. The Turks were finally ousted by the Alaouite sultan Mulay Sliman at the beginning of the 19th century, but Moroccan ownership of Oujda was short-lived, since the French occupied it in 1844 in retaliation for Moroccan support of the Algerian leader Abd el-Kader, fighting to rid his country of the French occupying forces. Abd el-Kader's defeat at the Battle of Isly in 1844 meant that the French became firmly settled in Algeria, but it was not until 1857, and again in 1907, that they repeated their occupation of Oujda. From that date the town became effectively part of Algeria, until the Treaty of Fès in 1912 established a French Protectorate over Morocco and Oujda returned to the Moroccan crown, albeit under French rule. Unlike later French planning, the new European town was built right up against the medina.

Since then, Oujda has grown steadily, living off trade, agriculture, sheep-raising, wine-production, and mining. With a population of nearly 400,000, it is by far the largest town in eastern Morocco. Short-lived fighting with Algeria in the early 1960s closed the frontier, and flooded the town with Moroccan refugees from Algeria. When the two countries resumed normal relations, Oujda again became a lively meeting place for merchants and travelers from both countries, as well as a transit point for Algerian workers in Western Europe whose easiest way home for the holidays was via the Moroccan Mediterranean ports. Goods, too, would arrive in Oujda from the Spanish enclave of Melilla, on the Mediterranean coast to the northwest, to be bought in bulk by Algerians for resale in Tlemcen, Oran, or Algiers. Moroccan livestock, principally sheep, were easily sold in Algeria. This flourishing commercial activity was halted in the summer of 1994, when the frontier was again closed, and the town's economy has felt the pinch. At the time of writing, however, there were hopes of its reopening. Some 25,000 students attend the three university facilities.

2. Getting There

Oujda can be reached easily by **plane** from Casablanca. Royal Air Maroc does four flights a week (1 hour, 40 minutes flying time) and Regional Air Lines does six. Air France sometimes has a flight from Paris, depending on the season. RAM flies from Paris twice a week and from Marseilles once a week. Oujda can be reached from Marrakech and Agadir by connecting flights in Casablanca. The Oujda-Angads Airport is 15 km north of the town and a taxi shouldn't cost more than 50 DH (there is no public transport from the airport).

From Casablanca, sleepers and couchettes are available on the night **train** leaving Casa Voyageurs station at 8:28 P.M., calling in at Rabat, Meknès, Fès, and Taza on the way, and arriving in Oujda at 7:05 A.M. the following morning. This is an agreeable, if not particularly fast, way to get to Oujda. The other night train, leaving at 10:30 P.M., arriving at 9:00 A.M., only has couchettes. It can also be boarded at Rabat, Meknès, Fès, and Taza in the middle of the night or early in the morning (not advisable). A direct day train leaves Casa Voyageurs at 10:00 A.M. and arrives in Oujda at 8:30 P.M., stopping at Rabat, Meknès, Fès, and other intermediate towns. Oujda can be reached by train from Tangier, after a change and long wait at Meknès. It used to be possible to continue into Algeria by train, but this is not possible as long as the frontier is closed. The railway station is just under a kilometer from the town center. Supratours, which works in collaboration with the national railway company, sells combined bus/train tickets to Oujda from Agadir.

For short distances, the CTM **bus** is about as convenient as the train, though you can do the whole long journey by bus from Casablanca (one a day, 140 DH). Rabat, Meknès, Fès, and Taza are on the same route and the CTM buses can be picked up in these towns. There isn't any alternative to the bus to get to Oujda from Nador (140 km) and Al-Hoceima (293 km), on the Mediterranean coast, and Bouarfa (268 km) and Figuig (376 km) in the south. Figuig is the other frontier post with Algeria, but it is closed at the moment. Non-CTM buses do much the same thing, with many daily several departures from Meknès and Fès, more from Nador (because of its proximity to Melilla, source of Spanish goods), a few from Al-Hoceima, Saidia, Bouarfa, and Figuig. **Big taxis** go frequently to Taza, less frequently to Nador, and really only in the summer to the seaside resort of Saidia (unless you book one specially).

3. Local Transportation

There are **buses,** but, as always, you'll avoid complications by taking a **small taxi.**

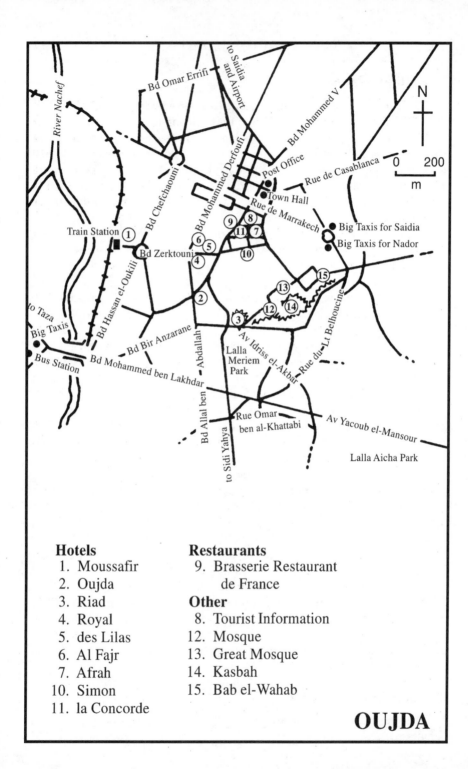

Hotels
1. Moussafir
2. Oujda
3. Riad
4. Royal
5. des Lilas
6. Al Fajr
7. Afrah
10. Simon
11. la Concorde

Restaurants
9. Brasserie Restaurant
   de France

Other
8. Tourist Information
12. Mosque
13. Great Mosque
14. Kasbah
15. Bab el-Wahab

OUJDA

4. The Hotel Scene

Oujda's hotels did a flourishing trade when the frontier was open with Algeria. There are 23 classified hotels in and around Oujda (including 5 in the *** category). At the moment, the hotels are in no way filled (which has advantages for the visitor, but it's depressing for the hotels). Some are practically closed. Hotel charges are fixed for this region and are as follows (they vary according to the presence or absence of showers and water closet in the room): **** 318-396 DH or 407-487 DH, breakfast 43 DH for both; *** 158-252 DH or 179-287 DH, breakfast 31-34 DH for both; ** 87-152 DH or 94-188 DH, breakfast 21 DH for both; * 79-117 DH or 83-133 DH, breakfast 20 DH for both.

The **regional telephone code** is 06 (0 omitted for in-region calls).

EXPENSIVE HOTELS

There's nothing in the top-class, **** or *****, category in Oujda, but a good hotel is the *** **Hotel Moussafir** (Place de la Gare, Tel: 68 82 02, Fax: 68 82 08). Like all hotels in this chain (now run by Ibis), it is situated beside the railway station, almost 1 km from the town center. It is attractively furnished and well kept, with a garden and a restaurant.

The *** **Hotel Oujda** (105 rooms, Boulevard Mohammed V, Tel: 68 50 63, Fax: 68 50 64) is more centrally placed, with comfortable, well-equipped rooms, a restaurant, bar, and a small swimming pool. Unfortunately, at the moment, it is more or less closed for lack of trade.

MEDIUM-PRICE HOTELS

Several hotels are classified in this category. The ** **Hotel al-Fajr** (48 rooms, on a small street off Boulevard Mohammed Derfoufi, Tel: 70 22 93) is modern and bright and the rooms are well-fitted, clean, and comfortable.

The ** **Hotel des Lilas** (38 rooms and 10 suites, Rue Jamal ed-Din el-Afghani, Tel/Fax: 68 08 40) has been spruced up recently and its rooms, too, are well equipped.

Right in the middle of the town, the ** **Hotel la Concorde** (36 rooms, 57 Boulevard Mohammed V, Tel: 68 23 28) is a comfortable, friendly place, with a restaurant and a bar.

The ** **Hotel Riad** (Avenue Idriss el-Akbar, Tel: 68 83 53) is another reasonable choice. As all these hotels were virtually closed at the time of writing, so intending travelers should check first.

BUDGET ACCOMMODATIONS

There are several * and unclassified hotels. Two of the best are the * **Hotel Afrah** (15 Rue de Tafna, Tel: 68 65 33), all done up with traditional *zellij,* horseshoe arches, and carved plasterwork, and the ⋆ **Hotel Royal** (13 Boulevard Zerktouni, Tel: 68 22 84).

Down the scale, the small ⋆ **Hotel Simon** (1 Rue Tarik ibn Ziad, Tel: 68 63 04) is one of the best of the cheaper hotels. In the medina, several unclassified hotels offer rooms, with communal showers, for around 60 DH.

There are three campsites, including one adapted to physically disabled people.

5. Dining and Restaurants

There's not a great choice of restaurants in Oujda, which is better known for its excellent Beni Snassen wines.

HOTEL RESTAURANTS

The **Hotel Moussafir** has a restaurant that is well kept without being memorable. It is licensed, so even if the meal is not extraordinary it can be washed down with some good local wine.

OTHER RESTAURANTS

Moroccan food is served at the **Restaurant Wassila** (Rue de Tafna, next to the Hotel al-Fajr). You can get a meal of *harira* soup, salad, and a *tajine* for around 50 DH.

The **Brasserie Restaurant de France** (Boulevard Mohammed V) is not as grand as it sounds, but it has a license and its international cuisine is not too bad.

OTHER PLACES TO EAT

Cheap snacks can be had near **Bab el-Wahab,** but they are not particularly appetizing.

The **Pâtisserie Colombo** (80 Boulevard Mohammed V) does breakfast (10 DH), as well as selling delicious pastries. Do try the Oujdi specialty, *makrout* and *qaik,* the latter a delicious, hard, dunking-type cookie.

The **Café Le Trésor** (Boulevard Mohammed V, near the Town Hall) serves an early morning breakfast (12 DH).

6. Sightseeing

Although dating from the 10th century, Oujda fell into the hands of so many of the rival powers that were struggling to become masters of northwest Africa that little remains of its past. The most animated part of the **medina** is around the **Bab el-Wahab** gate (more correctly called Bab Sidi

Abd el-Wahab). Only the eastern side of the **ramparts** remains today, and Bab el-Wahab is the best preserved of its three gates (the others are Bab Oulad Amrane and Bab Sidi Aissa). On the left from this gate, there is not much to see of the **Great Mosque** (founded by Abu Yacub at the end of the 13th century), or the **kasbah** (further left), but the *kissaria* (covered market), more or less straight on from the gate, is lively and leads to the **Water Market** square (Souk el-Ma), where water for irrigating the gardens used to be allocated, sometimes at a very high price. From here the exit into the Rue de Marrakech by the **Bab Oulad Amrane** is quite easy.

AROUND OUJDA

About 6 km southeast of Oujda, the little oasis of **Sidi Yahya** (exit along the Boulevard Sidi Yahya) is the last resting place of many local saints (indicated by the whitewashed *kubbas*), and very popular with local people. **Buses** and **big taxis** go here. Sidi Yahya ben Younes is the patron saint of the town and the annual pilgrimage to his tomb takes place in September. He is held in great esteem by Moslems, Jews, and Christians, and is believed to be none other than Saint John the Baptist. One of the other saints buried here is reputed to cure rheumatism, so it is not surprising that the place is thronged with people, who hang bits of colored cloth in the trees and kill a cock or hen to obtain a blessing. The **Cave of the Houris** *(Ghar al Houriyat)*, said to be frequented by these handmaidens of Paradise (the reward of all good Moslems), adds to the religious attraction of this little oasis.

Northeast of Oujda the P1 road leads to the frontier posts between Morocco and Algeria. The frontier being closed at the moment, there is no reason for taking this route, particularly since security is extremely severe.

NORTH OF OUJDA

For a **plunge in the waters of the Mediterranean,** take the main road **north** (P27) to the seaside resort of **Saidia** (60 km), next to the Algerian frontier. Saidia has the usual collection of restaurants and cafés, is full of Oujdis in summer (July and August), and has an excellent beach (18 km long), where you're unlikely to see many bronzing foreigners. **Buses** (18 DH) and **big taxis** (25 DH) go from Oujda. Many hotels are only open in the summer (in winter, prices are lower in the establishments that stay open).

The top of the **hotel scene** is the *** **Hotel Rimal** (Boulevard Mohammed V). It is well placed near the beach, overlooking the sea, and has a restaurant.

Medium-price hotels are the ** **Hotel Atlal** (44 Boulevard Hassan II, Tel: 62 50 21) and the ** **Hotel Hannour** (opposite Place du 20 Août, Tel: 62 51 15).

Budget accommodations are best at the * **Hotel Paco** (Boulevard Hassan II, Tel: 62 52 10, Fax: 62 22 22).

Of the three campsites, the **Camping al-Mansour** (Tel: 62 51 65) is thought to be the best, but it is several kilometers out of town, and non-motorized travelers may prefer to try their luck at the **Camping Essi,** only a couple of hundred meters from the beach (but much less well kept).

Restaurants are not a specialty of Saidia. The center of town is the best place to look around, and it should be possible to have a soup (5 DH), salad (10 DH), and *tajine* or chicken (35-60 DH).

Apart from **swimming** and **walking** along the beach, **birdwatchers** can look out for rare species to the west of the town, especially towards the mouth of the River Moulouya (10 km).

Nightlife is pretty low key in Saidia, apart from a festival in August.

Really only for motorized travelers (if you have your own car, or a motorbike or big taxi), a **circuit of the Beni Snassen massif** is worth the effort (approximately 180 km). It is apparently rich in wild animals, and you may just be lucky enough to see a fox or a lynx. There are several possible approaches, but the easiest route is the main P27 (as for Saidia above) to **Berkane** (60 km). The latter, a relatively recent town (founded at the beginning of the 20th century), is the commercial center for the rich agricultural Triffa plain and for the wine-producing Beni Snassen hills.

The best **hotel** here is the *** **Zaki.** The narrow S403, 10 km after Berkane, climbs up to the little village of **Taforalt,** best known by prehistory buffs for its **Grotte des Pigeons,** where Upper Palaeolithic populations, physically close to the European Cro-Magnons, lived between 23,000 and 10,000 years ago (this site is not open to the public). They buried their dead in the cave and about 100 skeletons were recovered from excavations. That these people cared for the members of their society is shown by the bones of an almost totally handicapped woman who managed to live to a good old age, thanks to care and attention from her fellow humans. Going east from here, the mountain road winds along to the **Grotte du Chameau** ("Camel Cave," open to the public), where a stalactite vaguely like a camel had the reputation of curing sterility, and then north for the splendid 9-km long **Zegzel Gorge,** and back to Berkane. For those not wanting to go back to Berkane and not minding missing out on the gorge, the S403 continues southwards to Sidi Bouhria and Oujda. For the adventurous in a 4WD vehicle, a road to the right after the cave, then right at the final T-junction to join the 5319, then left, will bring you out on the P27, some 25 km north of Oujda. This route runs through the heart of the massif, is dangerous, and should not be undertaken lightheartedly.

NORTHWEST OF OUJDA

Going northwest, the main P27, after passing through Berkane, crosses the River Moulouya, to arrive in **Nador** (140 km from Oujda), situated on the Mediterranean coast about 13 km south of the Spanish enclave of Melilla. I'm sorry to displease the natives of Nador, but there is really nothing to take the visitor there, unless it's to buy kitchen gadgets and audio-visual material smuggled in from Melilla. The new airport, which had been planned for several years, opened in the summer of 1999. The old one will be turned into a vast industrial center. Nador is the capital of a province whose economic resources are agriculture, citrus fruits, wine-producing grapes, and, to a certain extent, industry and the savings brought in by many of its overseas workers. The Comanav **shipping company** runs a **ferry** there from Sète (France) in the summer. Supratours provides a combined **bus** and **train** service once a day from Casablanca and intermediate towns—departure by the 8:45 P.M. train to Taourirt, where passengers board a bus for Nador, arriving at 7:30 A.M. Nador can be reached by CTM **bus** daily from Oujda. Buses also link Nador with Al-Hoceima, Tetouan, Tangier, Taza, Fès, Meknès, Rabat, and Casablanca. The **bus station** lies to the south of the town. Big taxis also have their terminus here. A **local bus** goes to the frontier post with Melilla, and **big taxis** will also do the run.

The **regional telephone code** for Nador is 09 (0 omitted for in-region calls).

The Hotel Scene. Nador has 13 classified hotels and 43 unclassified. Hotel charges fixed for this region are slightly higher than in Oujda. They vary according to the presence or absence of showers and water closet in the room: **** 350-436 DH or 488-532 DH, breakfast 47 DH for both; *** 174-277 DH or 197-316, breakfast 34 DH for both; ** 96-167 DH or 103-207 DH, breakfast 23 DH for both; * 87-129 DH or 91-146 DH, breakfast 22 DH for both.

Two **** hotels are the **** **Hotel Ryad** (Avenue Mohammed V, Tel: 60 77 15/16/17/18, Fax: 60 77 19) and the **** **Rif** (Avenue Youssef ben Tachfine, Tel: 60 65 35), both of which are well kept.

Down the scale, the ** **Hotel Méditerranée** (Avenue Youssef ben Tachfine, Tel: 60 66 11) offers clean and simple accommodations.

Dining and Restaurants. You could try the **Restaurant Majid** (3-5 Boulevard Kaid Ahmed Riffi), which is said to be good, or play it safe with a pizza in the **Pizzaria/Heladeria Villanapoli** (124 Boulevard ibn Khaldoun).

Sightseeing will, I think, be limited to **birdwatching.** Nador's lagoon, the **Sebkha Bou Areg,** is considered to be a unique ecosystem along the Mediterranean. In the winter it regularly welcomes thousands of birds, including pink flamingos and grebes, and the avocet is said to nest here.

Catholic mass is celebrated in Spanish in the **church** of Santiago el-Mayor, 5, Rue Moulay Hassan ibn el-Mehdi (Tel: 09-60 46 49).

If you have your passport and all your papers in order, 13 km of road north of Nador will bring you into a little bit of Spain-in-Africa—**Melilla,** jutting out into the sea. Originally a Phoenician trading post (Russadir) in the 5th century B.C., it later came under Carthaginian, then Roman rule. After the Vandal invasion in the 5th century A.D. and an occupation by the Byzantine rulers, it entered into the Moslem sphere of influence in the 10th century. From then on, Melilla was fought over by the succeeding Umayad, Fatimid, Idrissid, and Almoravid dynasties. The latter took the town in 1080, were dislodged by the Almohads (1272), who were in turn ousted by the Merinids. Its advantageous position led the town to become an important outlet for the trans-Saharan caravans coming up from Sijilmassa, in the Tafilalet. Under the Merinids, Melilla became one of the ports for Fès and Taza, trading with Italy and Spain. The troubled period at the end of the Merinids led to it falling into disgrace under the Wattasids and its easy capture in 1497 by a Spanish nobleman in the service of the Duke of Medina-Sidonia, who handed it over to the Spanish crown in 1506. After this, life for the Spanish inhabitants was a succession of sieges and blockades. But they held on behind their fortifications, and the Protectorate period from 1912 saw its port improved (already a free-zone since 1887) and relative prosperity thanks to mining and agricultural activity in the hinterland. It was from Melilla in July 1936 that General Franco launched his rebellion against the Spanish republican government (many Moroccans from the Rif—not necessarily Nador—joined his army). However, Morocco's independence in 1956 cut Melilla off from its inland contacts and an even worse blow was struck when the French farmers from the nearby district of Oran in Algeria, who were frequent shoppers, left Algeria for good in 1962.

This loss, I think, is amply balanced by the tax-free goods coming in from Spain which find their way, by one means or another, into Nador and further south. Today, the town has a population of around 70,000. Its occupation by the Spanish is a constant source of irritation to Morocco, and its return is periodically demanded. These days, the important military garrison is particularly on the alert because of the very unsettled situation in Algeria. Illegal Algerian refugees stream into the town, and a very primitive camp has been built for them while their requests for political asylum are examined. Unrest by the large Moslem population also bursts out from time to time in response to new Spanish legislation, and the town has a strange feeling to it. It is divided into the Old Town *(Melilla la Vieja)* behind the ramparts, and the New Town, the center of which is the **Plaza de España** (look out for examples of Art Deco).

Melilla can be reached by **air** from Madrid or Malaga with the Spanish company Air Iberia. The Trasmediterranea shipping company runs **ferries** from Malaga and Almeria. **Cars** travelling into Melilla from Morocco will be examined at the frontier post of Beni Enzar, which is where **buses** and **big taxis** drop their passengers coming from Nador. A few hundred meters separate the Moroccan and Spanish customs and police, and a local bus leaves Beni Enzar regularly for the center of Melilla (20 minutes).

Dirhams and Spanish pesetas can be changed in Melilla. The **exchange rate** in the summer of 1998 was around 5.3 DH/100 pesetas. It is best go to a bank for this operation, rather than through a street dealer. Prices in this section are quoted in pesetas (ptas).

There are plenty of **hotels** in Melilla, and they are more expensive than in Morocco. At the top of the list are the **Parador de Melilla** (count on 15,000 ptas for a good double room, Avenida de Candido Lobera, Tel: 68 49 40, Fax: 68 34 86) and the **Hotel Rusadir** (14,200 ptas, Calle Pablo Vallescá, Tel: 68 12 40, Fax: 67 05 27).

Medium-price hotels that can be recommended are the **Hotel Avenida** (8,000 ptas, 24 Avenida de Juan Carlos I Rey, going away from the Plaza de España, Tel: 68 49 49, Fax: 68 32 26) and the **Hotel Anfora** (10,500 ptas, Calle Pablo Vallescá, Tel: 68 33 40).

Not really **budget accommodations,** but lower down the scale, is the **Hotel Nacional** (5,500 ptas, 10 Calle Primo de Riviera, Tel: 68 45 40, Fax: 68 44 81). If none of these suit you, or are full (they are in summer, particularly, and at Spanish holiday periods), or you want one of the cheapest hotels or guest houses, I suggest you ask at the Tourist Office (address below).

The best **hotel restaurant** (and one of the most expensive) is in the **Parador** (from 3,500 ptas/meal). For other restaurants, a very good three-course meal can be had at the **Barbacoa de Muralla** (Calle Fiorentina, in the Old Town), which will set you back at least 4,000 ptas.

Fish is on the menu at a number of restaurants, including the **Restaurant Los Salazones** (15 Calle de Alcaudete) and the **Restaurant Granada** (36 Marqués Montemar). Neither of the establishments are near the center of town, the first being down near the Paseo Marítimo, the second in the industrial district, south of the New Town.

You may find it more convenient to hunt around for one of the restaurants or snack bars around the Avenida de Juan Carlos I Rey, including pizzerias and the **Cafetería Nuevo California** (no, not really Californian), which is a café/bar downstairs and a restaurant on the first floor.

Of course, in the best Spanish tradition, there are plenty of cafés and *bodegas* (bars) serving *tapas* (snacks) and drinks. They say that one of the best places is the **Onubense Bar** (5 Calle General Pareja). Or try the **Cervecería** (23 Calle General O'Donnell). Another late-night place, but this time for ice cream, is the **Heladería La Ibense** (also on Calle General O'Donnell). There's said to be a good **disco** on the Carretera de Alfonso XIII.

Apart from a walk through the **New Town** and a glance at the duty-free articles in the bazaar-like shops, **sightseeing** is more interesting in the original **Old Town** (also known as Medina-Sidonia). Entrances are by the **Puerta de Santiago** (with the coat of arms of the Emperor Charles V), after the Plaza de Armas (to the west), or the **Puerta de la Marina** (to the south). A lot of reconstruction work has gone on here (and is still going on in some areas), but it is just about possible to appreciate the **fortress** built by the Spaniards, the **ramparts,** and the **St. James Chapel** (Santiago). The **Iglesia de la Concepción** has an interesting interior (if it's open) and the **Municipal Museum** *(Museo Municipal)* has a fine collection of ancient pottery and coins (*Bastión de la Concepción,* part of the ramparts) (open weekdays from 9:00 A.M.-1:00 P.M. and 5:00 P.M.-7:00 P.M.).

Swimming is a no-go activity in Melilla, although the Parador Hotel's pool is open to non-residents. **Shopping,** too, is of no particular interest, unless you want some duty-free articles. Gas, too, is cheaper here, so it's worth stocking up if traveling by car (can be had from a supermarket on road to the Beni Enzar frontier post).

The Melilla address list:

Airlines—Air Iberia, Avenida de Juan Carlos I Rey.

Banks—most of them are along the Avenida de Juan Carlos I Rey.

Boats—Trasmediterranea, Plaza de España (closed Saturday afternoons and Sundays).

Bus station—buses to and from the frontier leave from the Plaza de España.

Post Office *(Correos y Telégrafos)*—Calle Pablo Vallescá.

Telephones—Calle Sotomayor, other side of Parque Hernández from Plaza de España, and public phone boxes.

Tourist Information—Paseo del General Macias, near Plaza de Toros (the inevitable bullring), southwest of the Plaza de España (Tel: 68 40 13). It can provide quite a lot of helpful information.

To **return to Oujda** avoiding Berkane, take the south-bound S412, turning left at its junction with the P1 towards El-Aouin and Oujda (about 150 km). That untiring builder, the sultan Mulay Ismail, erected a kasbah at **El-Aouin** in 1679, which was later restored by Hassan I, to protect camel caravans from marauding tribesmen.

FURTHER AFIELD

Travelers wanting to **continue their journey west** after Melilla should return to Nador and take the main P39 to **Al-Hoceima** (154 km) (chapter 5). The main P1 **west** from Oujda (or from the above junction) goes through the Taza Corridor, which, from prehistoric times, has always been an easy passage from Algeria and eastern Morocco through to the Atlantic. The road goes through **Taourirt** (a much disputed strategic point in the 13th and 14th centuries) and **Guercif** (158 km from Oujda), before arriving at Taza (a further 65 km) and **Fès** (120 km) (see chapter 8 for Taza and Fès). The total distance from Oujda to Fès is 343 km.

South from Taourirt, the S410 leads to Debdou (60 km), a town surrounded by orchards and pleasant wooded country. In the 14th and 15th centuries, an important **Jewish community** settled here, fleeing persecution in Spain. They were expert jewelry makers, weavers, tailors, shoemakers, and farmers. Many were scribes, capable of teaching Hebrew law. The French explorer Charles de Foucauld, traveling through Morocco at the end of the 19th century disguised as a Jew, noted that the Jewish merchants in Debdou traded constantly with Tlemcen in Algeria. However, they never had an easy time, and the *mellah* was frequently the target of attacks by the local Moslem population. At the beginning of the 20th century, Bou Hamara (a Taza chief claiming to be the rightful heir to the throne) imprisoned ten important Jews and confiscated their goods. Not much of this vigorous Jewish past remains now, after the departure from Morocco of the last members of the community in the 1960s.

From Debdou it is possible to reach Guercif by the secondary 4991 road, turning right at the junction with the road from Guercif to **Outat Oulad el-Haj.**

Guercif, a quiet town that has recently been much developed thanks to irrigation, has had a stormy past. In the 11th century it was described by an Arab geographer as a "flourishing town." Up to the beginning of the 13th century, it formed the northern limit of the territory grazed over by the nomadic Beni Marin, who then began to make warlike incursions further north before inflicting a severe defeat on the Almohad army in 1248. This gave them the chance to spread their wings, capture Taza and Fès, and found the Merinid dynasty. Its 18th-century kasbah, built on the site of the Merinid walls, has pretty much disappeared. Some 37 km past Guercif, at the big village of **Msoun,** one can see, on the right, the remains of another Mulay Ismail kasbah and of the giant storage silos used by the local Berber tribes. The **Col de Zhazha** pass, after Msoun, marks the watershed between the basin of the River Moulouya, flowing into the Mediterranean, and the River Sebou, flowing into the Atlantic.

From **Guercif,** for those who want to reach **Midelt** or **Er-Rachidia** by the quickest route from Oujda and who enjoy long drives through flat country, the S329 south via Outat Oulad el-Haj and Missour is just the thing (264 km to Midelt). To the right, after leaving Guercif, the summits of the **Jbel Bou Iblane** (3,172 m) are generally snow-covered from December to May and attract cross-country skiers, while the more southerly Bounasseur peak reaches 3,326 m. The small town of **Outat Oulad el-Haj,** perched on an eminence overlooking the River Moulouya (130 km), has numerous adobe *ksour* (fortified villages) half-hidden by plantations of olive, pomegranate, and fig trees. **Missour** (179 km) is another important oasis on the River Moulouya. The Peace Corps had a rabbit husbandry project involving some 50 women here in 1997 After a further 70 km, the road reaches the main north-south road between Midelt and Er-Rachidia, 15 km south of Midelt.

Back in Oujda, it's a long haul **south** down to **Bouarfa** and **Figuig** (376 km). Few people go there who don't have to. The P19 starts off all right, through the Monts d'Oujda (lead and zinc mines to the left, Jerada coal mines to the right). The first town on the way is **Ain Benimathar** (83 km), formerly known as Bergent, followed after a further 115 km by the small town of **Tendrara.** The province of Figuig begins some 50 km north of Tendrara. It is one of the least populated provinces of Morocco, and its inhabitants are mostly nomads or live in the oasis of Figuig. Its landscape is characterized by *hamadas* (plateaus), broken by occasional depressions or low hills. The region is classed as semi-arid, with steppe vegetation. The local esparto grass is collected and sent away to be processed elsewhere. It can be very hot in summer and swept by icy winds in winter.

Bouarfa (70 km from Tendrara) is, at the moment, the provincial capital and home to an important contingent of Moroccan troops, especially vigilant because of the troubles in Algeria. Manganese, copper, and lead are mined in the neighborhood. There is nothing to retain the tourist here, but (rather surprisingly) it can be reached once a week by **train** from Oujda or by **daily buses** (the journey takes all day). A daily bus from Er-Rachidia also runs to Bouarfa (290 km). There is a small **hotel** and a few cafés in the town. Another small hotel is being built, just beside the *Province* (provincial headquarters). When one knows how many people in south Morocco suffer from severe eye diseases, it was good to hear, in the fall of 1998, that Bouarfa's Hassan II hospital will shortly be endowed with an ophthalmological section, in part thanks to the Lions Club of Oujda. The Chinese government has also recently provided the hospital with surgical equipment.

Figuig is 108 km from Bouarfa and is altogether a more interesting proposition than Bouarfa and considerably bigger. Once a convenient way into Algeria, its frontier post is, of course, closed at the moment, so it is the end of the line for all travelers. Figuig does not seem to have had much of a recorded history, though the area has certainly been occupied for many thousands of years. A few kilometers from the center of the town, a rock shelter in the Col de Zenaga pass into Algeria contains numerous engravings of Neolithic age, as do several other caves in the neighborhood. The oasis is said to date from the ninth century (its inhabitants claim it is older than Fès), and contains 100,000 palm trees. The water to support the immense oasis and its small cultivated plots under the trees comes from springs that flow along man-made, underground canals called *foggara,* or *rhettara,* one of southern Morocco's most ingenious constructions. Short but fierce fighting took place here between Morocco and Algeria in 1963 over a frontier problem. There are plans to create a national park some 40 km south of Bouarfa, which would protect the Houbara bustard and the rare gazelles that have escaped being shot by unauthorized hunters. Figuig is famous for its dates and for its woolen *burnous* (capes). The women weave a local style of carpet that keeps the natural colors of the wool (white, brown, grey, and black).

Figuig can be reached by **bus** direct from Oujda or Bouarfa. There are plans to run a **tourist excursion** on the railway from Oujda to Bouarfa, and from there a bus will run to Figuig (but this is still only in the planning stage). By **car,** it is essential to have a full gas tank before leaving Bouarfa; Figuig has a petrol station, but a local mechanic recommended that some friends not fill up there. The road goes through stony and sandy desert. It is tarred all the way, and sometimes a bit sand-covered, of course, but is mostly a single "track" with quite steep edges, so passing other vehicles can be difficult (the last 35 km are better). I am advised that, while it is not necessary to have a 4WD vehicle, it is preferable to have two cars and to keep your eye on the road, especially if you encounter a sandstorm (always possible).

The **hotel scene** is—as one might have guessed—limited. The town has suffered from a bad reputation for its former hotels, and two have been closed by the Municipality (the Hotel Sahara and the Hotel Melliase). At the time of writing, the ✶✶ **Figuig Hotel** (5 rooms, Tel: 89 93 09) is the only recommended place to stay, and, as it is used for official visitors, it will probably keep up decent standards. The hotel was the former campsite, the Diamant Vert. The rooms are small but very clean (each has its own bathroom) and there are superb views across the oasis from the balcony. It has a large terrace (being improved), also with splendid views, a restaurant, and a swimming pool. Camping is possible at the hotel, which has tents in the garden for guests wanting to sleep under the desert skies. The

Figuig Hotel is also the only place to have a simple but good **meal.** There is no menu as such, you just discuss what you would like—the salads and kebobs are said to be excellent. And in season (fall) there will certainly be dates, for which Figuig is famous. There are a number of small cafés for a coffee or mint tea while you watch local life.

The town is built on two levels and is divided into seven *ksour* (fortified villages), each still a small medieval town on its own, unspoiled and intact. From the upper level there is a wonderful view across the oasis and into Algeria (3 km). A stroll around the palm groves, which abound with birds and a rich variety of trees, plants, and crops, is the best **sightseeing** that can be done, and my friends said they could have spent whole days just wandering through the trees and around the water-collecting pools, enjoying the cool shade and the sunny open spaces. Each *ksar* has its own character and interesting sights, and the hotel will arrange for someone to show you around the *ksour,* the old Jewish district, and the irrigation system. Almost no tourists go to Figuig and the atmosphere is friendly, hassle-free, and relaxed. **Birdwatchers** have a marvelous time. On the drive from Bouarfa, my friends (experts in this field) spotted various large raptors, ravens, crowned sand grouse, desert wheatears, and warblers. From the hotel terrace in Figuig they saw swallows, martins, and bee eaters, and even a short-toed eagle which hovered over them as they sipped their mint tea (was it close enough for them to measure its toes?)

All in all, Figuig is a charming place with friendly people and a wonderful spot in which to relax and unwind, and to enter into age-old Saharan oasis life, well off the beaten track (but admittedly the road to get there is a long one). Turning your back on Figuig along the road to Bouarfa (fill your tank with gas here), you have the choice of going back north to Oujda or west to Er-Rachidia (chapter 13). The P32 road to Er-Rachidia (290 km), passing through Boudnib, brings you out 23 km south of Er-Rachida, at Meski, and back into another world, where you will possibly feel a touch of regret at having reached "civilization" again.

7. Guided Tours

There's not much demand for guided tours in Oujda, but your hotel can probably find you someone to show you around.

8. Culture

There are, unfortunately, few cultural activities in Oujda likely to interest the passing traveler, though there is a **Museum of Traditional Arms** in the Lalla Meriem Park, one of Oujda's two parks; the other is the municipal park, baptized Lalla Aicha. The **French Cultural Center** *(Institut Français),* on Boulevard Mohammed Derfoufi, organizes temporary art exhibitions, concerts, and talks (French-speaking). The warlike traditions of the eastern Moroccan tribes have greatly influenced Oujda's **local dance.** The groups are made up of white-robed, turbaned men, gunpowder boxes slung across their shoulders. They wield long, old-fashioned rifles and advance and retreat with a shoulder-shaking movement, supposedly representing an infantry charge. If you have the chance to see them perform, don't miss it.

9. Sports

The nearest **swimming** is at the seaside resort of Saidia, on the Mediterranean (60 km).

10. Shopping

All the usual necessities of life can be bought in Oujda's New Town, but, although Oujda is well known for its engraved daggers, there are few opportunities to buy attractive handmade articles.

11. Entertainment and Nightlife

The **Cinema Royal** (street joining Boulevards Mohammed V and Mohammed Derfoufi) shows French and Arabic films only. For a late night drink, the **bars** are all pretty rough. You may find it more agreeable to go to the Hotel Moussafir, where women in particular will feel more at ease. **Birdwatchers** will enjoy the marshy areas around the mouth of the River Moulouya (west of Saidia), east of Nador, and in the oasis of Figuig in the far south.

12. The Oujda Address List

Airlines—Royal Air Maroc, Boulevard Mohammed V (ground floor Hotel Oujda) (Tel: 68 39 09).
Airport—Oujda-Angads (Tel: 68 32 61).
Banks—many on Boulevard Mohammed V. The BMCE and BMCI have ATMs.
Bus station *(gare routière)*—CTM buses leave from behind the Town Hall; other companies leave from the bus station at the western end of Boulevard Mohammed ben Lakhdar, on the other side of the River Nachef.

Car rental—Avis (Maroc Voyages), 110 Boulevard Allal ben Abdallah (Tel: 68 39 93): Budget, Immeuble Kada, Boulevard Mohammed V; Europcar (Carlson Wagonlit Travel), Place Mohammed V (Tel: 68 25 20); Hertz, Immeuble El Baraka N° 2, Boulevard Mohammed V (Tel: 66 38 02).

Churches—French-speaking mass at Eglise Saint Louis, 11 Rue d'Acila (Tel: 68 24 81).

Consulates—the U.S. does not have a consulate in Oujda. Telephone the Embassy in Rabat if in difficulty (Tel: 07-76 22 65). Canada does not have a consulate either, so telephone the Canadian Embassy in Rabat (Tel: 07-67 28 80).

Drugstore, Night (*pharmacie de nuit*)—behind the town hall, opposite the CTM bus station.

Express Post—telephone the main post office (Tel: 68 23 00) for details.

Fire—(Tel: 15).

Gendarmerie Royale—(Tel: 17).

Hospital—telephone the U.S. Embassy in Rabat if needing serious medical care (Tel: 07-76 22 65).

Photocopies—at many shops selling tobacco, stamps, and newspapers, and at some téléboutiques.

Police—(Tel: 19).

Post Office—Boulevard Mohammed V.

Railway station—end of Boulevard Zerktouni (Tel: 68 27 01).

Taxis, big and little—big ones leave from the bus station (*gare routière*) or the Place du Maroc. Small ones have stands in several places.

Telephone—at main post office, but also more easily from the téléboutiques.

Tourist Information—Place du 16 Août. Has the usual colored brochures, but not much else.

Travel Agencies—Carlson Wagonlit Travel, Place Mohammed V (Tel: 68 25 20, Fax: 68 19 68); Europa Voyages, corner Boulevard Zerktouni/Rue Moulay Ahmed Laghrani (Tel: 68 26 27); Maroc Voyage Tourisme, 110 Boulevard Allal ben Abdallah (Tel: 68 39 93).

10

Casablanca and the Atlantic Coast

1. The General Picture

Casablanca is situated on the Atlantic Coast, more or less halfway between the Mediterranean Sea to the north and the barrier of the High Atlas Mountains to the south. It is the country's economic capital, and is the first Moroccan town seen by travelers on a direct transatlantic flight. At first glance, the scene is more or less familiar—modern airport, big buildings, public transport, traffic police, businessmen with portable phones clamped to their ears . . . on a smaller scale than in the U.S., but familiar sights all the same. This is an illusion. Casablanca is not a miniature and rather poor copy of an American city but a successful blend of Moroccan and Western civilizations, as the visitor will soon find out.

The distant past. Leaving aside the prehistoric people who lived on the outskirts of the present city around one million years ago, Berber fishermen were the first to inhabit Casablanca, installing themselves in the 10th century B.C. on a hill situated in the southern part of the town (the present Anfa district). The natural harbor here offered a convenient port of call for Phoenician traders going down the coast three centuries later. A

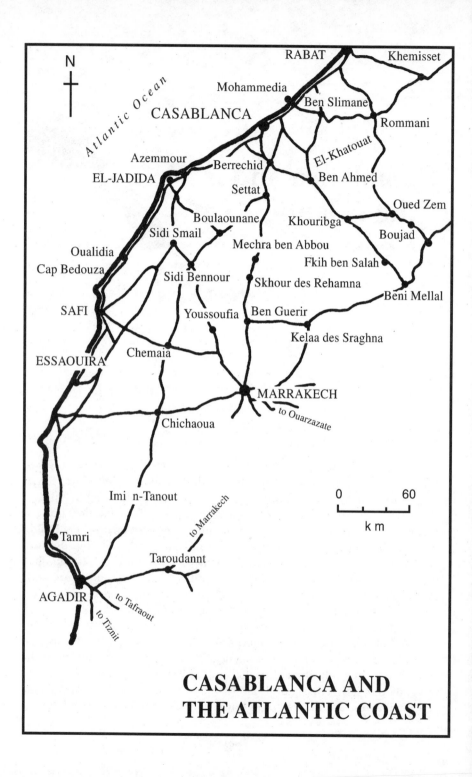

CASABLANCA AND
THE ATLANTIC COAST

Roman wreck from which were salvaged 169 silver coins shows that the Romans, too, appreciated this useful creek. The next news of Casablanca comes from the 7th century A.D., when history shows that a large Berber tribe, the Berghouata, settled in the area between the rivers Bou Regreg to the north and Oum er-Rbia to the south. For four centuries their independent kingdom flourished, until it was defeated and destroyed by the Almoravids in 1068.

An important trading center. It was not until the 14th century, under the Merinids, that Anfa came to life again and began to look like a real Islamic town, complete with wall, mosque, *medersa,* and governor. Trade flourished, particulaly with the Spanish, and local wheat, leather, and wool were exported from its excellent port. Leon the African, whose *Description de l'Afrique* was published in 1550, described the town as full of mosques, palaces, and shops, and its inhabitants as well-dressed and cultured. However, pirate ships, also taking advantage of the harbor, installed themselves there in the 15th century. Their raids around Lisbon resulted in the infuriated Portuguese sending a large fleet and attacking Anfa, whose occupants had all fled in terror, in 1468, and destroying it. Contrary to what is often written, there is nothing to indicate that the Portuguese returned and built fortifications in 1515 or in 1575, though they did carry out raids on the surrounding countryside. Nor was the town empty for 300 years, for little by little the inhabitants returned and resumed their commercial activity. In 1630, for instance, the Portuguese came and bought large quantities of wheat in Anfa, since there was a shortage in Portugal. Flemish and Portuguese ships are known to have regularly put in to Anfa to take on fresh water and supplies. Pirates returned to work, too, at the end of the 16th century. The 1755 Lisbon earthquake, with its wide-ranging repercussions, destroyed the town again, and its Jewish population, merchants and their families, were among the first to leave. Reconstruction of the town started again in 1770, under the sultan Mohammed III. The sultan, to please a Spanish trading company, authorized its name of Dar el-Beida (see legend under "Sightseeing") to be translated into the Spanish "Casa Blanca" (white house). By the middle of the 19th century, Casablanca had regained its place as an important business center, exporting local produce and importing, among other things, a newly-discovered delight—tea. European steamships were frequent visitors, and by the end of the 19th century trade had became thoroughly international, and Europeans flooded into the town. The population grew rapidly from 600 in 1830 to nearly 8,000 in 1868.

French occupation. In conformity with the Act of Algeciras in 1906 (in which the United States participated), the French started important port-improvement work. The first narrow-gauge railway line was built in 1907, provoking a prompt and angry response from the local population, who murdered a number of European workers, claiming that the line impinged on a Moslem cemetery (in fact, it only ran along the beach). The French Ambassador in Tangier, in favor of stronger action in Morocco, no less promptly sent a ship down to Casablanca. A small landing-party met with great resistance from the united local tribes, which had also seized the occasion to invade and loot the town, causing a great loss of life. The French, accompanied by a Spanish contingent, briefly bombarded the town and order was restored. When the French protectorate was established in 1912, the first Résident-Général (General Lyautey) decided to make Casablanca the country's economic capital. New commercial and residential districts were built, leaving—as was Lyautey's habit—the old medina untouched. By 1920, Casablanca had become Morocco's principal port, and so far it has not been overtaken. New jetties in recent years have increased its capacity.

During World War II, Casablanca was home to spies and intrigue of all kinds. Even if the film *Casablanca,* starring Humphrey Bogart and Ingrid Bergman, was filmed in a Hollywood studio, it well reflected the feeling of the city. On November 8, 1942, 35,000 U.S. troops landed in Morocco, half of them on beaches near Casablanca. After some sad but short (three days) fighting between the U.S. and French forces faithful to Vichy, General Patton established his military headquarters in Casablanca and the Allies started their successful march across North Africa, joined by Moroccan and French troops. General Eisenhower was the overall commander-in-chief. The Allied dead were buried in the Ben M'Sik cemetery. The coffins of the U.S. soldiers and sailors were later transferred to America, but there is still a U.S. War Memorial in the cemetery. The popular Moroccan singer, Houcine Slaoui, recorded well the local atmosphere after the arrival of the American troops with his song "Bye, bye! Chewing gum," [refrain: "All you hear is . . ." (in Arabic) "Okay, Okay, Come on! Bye, bye!" (in English)] in which he sang that the Americans distributed chewing gum, sweets, cigars, and dollars, and that even the old Moroccan women put on make-up and drank rum with the Americans. In January 1943, the Anfa Conference saw President Roosevelt, British Prime Minister Winston Churchill and French Generals Giraud and de Gaulle meet in a hotel situated in the elegant Anfa district of Casablanca to plan the Sicily and Normandy landings. The President twice received the sultan of Morocco, Mohammed V, in his Anfa residence, and promised to help Morocco win back independence. Despite Morocco's hopes, independence failed to materialize after the war.

When, in 1953, the sultan was deposed and exiled to Madagascar, his people refused to recognize the French-appointed successor, Mohammed ben Arafa. Boycotting of French products, such as cigarettes, gave way to violence—the explosion of a bomb in the central Casablanca market on Christmas Eve 1953 and another in the Mers Sultan area in July 1954 (killing a total of 24 French civilians) were but some of the many actions undertaken by Moroccan nationalists throughout the country. Finally, negotiations resulted in the return of Mohammed V in November 1955 and four months later the Protectorate came to an end.

The modern town. Today, Casablanca is Morocco's biggest town, with a population not far from 3 million. Despite decentralization efforts, it still remains the country's industrial pole. As such, it attracts increasing numbers of rural people in search of work and its population is ever-growing. Nationals of many countries live and work in Morocco's most cosmopolitan of cities. Numerous congresses, seminars, and international meetings are held here, and the permanent grounds of the *Foire* (fairground) have year-round exhibitions and commercial fairs attracting exhibitors from many foreign countries.

2. Getting There

Visitors from the United States or Canada coming by **air** will land at Mohammed V airport (formerly known as Nouasseur), about 30 km south of the town. Royal Air Maroc (RAM) runs a flight direct from JFK Airport in New York 6 times a week in the summer, 4 times a week at other times. RAM has 3 flights a day from Paris, 1 a day from Lyon, 12 a week from Marseilles, 4 a week from Bordeaux and Toulouse, 3 a week from Nice, and 2 a week from Strasbourg. Royal Air Maroc and British Airways both do daily flights from London, and other European companies also serve Casablanca. A total of 30 RAM flights come in from African and Middle Eastern countries each week.

Trains run regularly from the airport into Casablanca (first-class single fare for adults is currently 34 DH, 17 DH for children between 4 and 12, second class is 22 DH for adults, 11 DH for children) and Rabat (first-class single fare for adults is 71 DH, children 36 DH, second class for adults is 50 DH, children 25 DH). By **train,** Casablanca can be reached from Europe, through Spain with a connecting boat across the Strait of Gibraltar and a connecting train down to Casablanca. By road, **long-distance buses** from many European cities do much the same thing, reaching Casablanca by the new expressway. Travelers coming from Europe by **car** also follow the same route (there are frequent boat crossings). There is no

boat service to Casablanca, unless you can get yourself a berth on a cargo ship aiming to discharge in its port.

Once in Morocco, it is easy to reach Casablanca by **air**. Both RAM and the private Regional Air Lines run services from the following towns, though flights are not always direct: Tangier, Tetouan, and Al-Hoceima in the north; Oujda in the northeast; Rabat and Fès in the center; Marrakech, Agadir, and Ouarzazate in the south; and Laayoune and Dakhla in the far south. There used to be a flight to and from Tantan, but this has been stopped. All **trains** home into Casablanca, which serves as a distribution point between north and south. There's scarcely a train you can catch that won't take you to Casablanca. If catching a train to or from Casablanca, make sure you're going to the right station since there are two and this can lead to confusion. Casa-Port is situated near the port, as its name implies, and Casa-Voyageurs further inland. Check carefully the station from which your train is scheduled to arrive or depart.

Single travelers do best by avoiding the night trains to and from Casablanca and the port town of Tangier. Coming into Casablanca from Tangier and intermediate stations, day trains leave Tangier at 8:40 A.M. and 4:40 P.M., arriving in Casa-Port respectively at 2:30 P.M. and 10:35 P.M. Leaving Casablanca for Tangier, the best bet is the 6:45 A.M. departure from Casa-Port, reaching Tangier at 12:35 P.M. This is considered to be the "boat train." Sleepers and couchettes are available on the night train from Oujda leaving at 9:30 P.M., arriving in Casa-Port at 7:34 A.M. the following morning. The only day train from Oujda leaves at 10:00 A.M. and arrives at Casa-Voyageurs at 8:10 P.M.

A more frequent service runs from Fès (to Casa-Port or Casa-Voyageurs), stopping at Meknès, with six trains a day. The journey can take from just under 4 ½ hours in a "rapid" to nearly 6 hours in an "ordinary." Unless you are a train fan, try and choose one of the quicker trains. The Marrakech to Casablanca train, once humorously called the "Marrakech Express" on account of the inordinate length of time it took to cover the 240 kilometers between these two towns, has now been spruced up, has air-conditioning, and makes the trip in 3 ½ hours. Eight trains run from Marrakech to Casablanca (either Casa-Port or Casa-Voyageurs), and it is a comfortable and agreeable way of traveling. Good ones are the 9:00 A.M. departure from Marrakech, arriving at Casa-Voyageurs at 12:13 P.M., and the 4:00 P.M. departure, arriving at Casa-Port at 7:28 P.M.

A fast and frequent service between Casablanca and Rabat was introduced a few years ago, to serve the numerous commuters between these two cities. Known officially as the *Navette* (Shuttle), it was at once nicknamed "Aouita" after the Moroccan athlete Said Aouita, then holder of

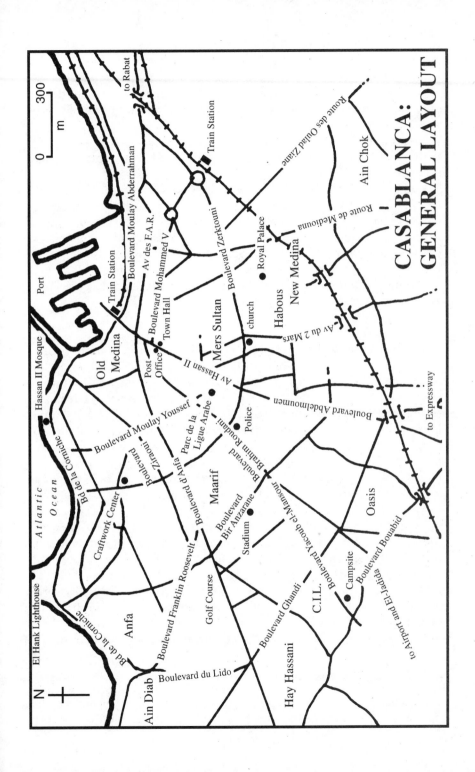

CASABLANCA:
GENERAL LAYOUT

N

Atlantic
Ocean

El Hank Lighthouse
Hassan II Mosque
Port
Bd de la Corniche
Craftwork Center
Boulevard Zraouini
Boulevard Moulay Youssef
Old Medina
Train Station
Post Office
Town Hall
Boulevard Mohammed V
Av des F.A.R.
Boulevard Moulay Abderrahman
to Rabat
Train Station
300
0
m

Boulevard Zerktouni
Royal Palace
New Medina
Habous
church
Mers Sultan
Av Hassan II
Police
Parc de la Ligue Arabe
Boulevard d'Anfa
Maarif
Boulevard Bir Anzarane
Stadium
Boulevard Brahim Roudani
Boulevard Abdelmoumen
Av du 2 Mars
Route de Mediouna
Route des Oulad Ziane
Ain Chok
to Expressway
Oasis
Boulevard Bouabid
Boulevard Yacoub el-Mansour
C.I.L.
Campsite
Boulevard Ghandi
Hay Hassani
Golf Course
Boulevard Franklin Roosevelt
Anfa
Ain Diab
Boulevard du Lido
Bd de la Corniche
to Airport and El Jadida

many middle-distance running records. Unfortunately, its reputation has become a bit tarnished, with passengers complaining of frequent delays. Still, I am very glad to take it if I have to go to Rabat for the day and don't want to drive.

A last word on train services within Morocco generally: check on departure times before turning up at the station and, in Casablanca, make sure you've got the right one.

Casablanca is also reached by the **internal bus** companies, of which the recommended line is the CTM. CTM buses arrive from Tangier six times a day, from Fès and Meknès seven times a day, from Marrakech six times a day, Agadir seven times a day (some are night buses), and Dakhla once a day (18-hour journey via Agadir). Several other towns are also served by the CTM. A good network of **roads** links Casablanca to towns all around the country, with an expressway from Rabat and, in the north, Larache.

3. Local transportation

Within Casablanca, it is possible to travel by **train** from suburbs such as Ain Sebaa to the main stations, and out to suburbs such as Oasis on the other side. But these trains, designed to help the chronic transport problem, are of very little use to the visitor. There is no **subway,** but in the spring of 1998, yet another feasibility study was commissioned by the Minister of the Interior, so perhaps, one day, it will materialize. At the moment, the mass of the Casablanca population travels by **bus**—though you might think that it traveled by car, in view of the dense circulation. The buses, both municipal and private, are generally very crowded, except at really off-peak times. There is a set fare (2 DH in the municipal, 3.30 DH in the private). I do not advise you drive around Casablanca by **car,** rented or other, unless you know the town well or really have to for business reasons. Parking is a hassle and driving a nightmare, except for the steely-nerved. Parking meters are installed in many central streets and have to be constantly fed (2 DH/hour) if you don't want to have your car "booted." Best leave the car and take a little red **taxi.** There are plenty of clearly-marked taxi stands, and the vehicles have meters. A journey in from the nearer suburbs to the center shouldn't cost more than 10 DH, but taxi-hiring for late-night dining out of town will be much more expensive.

4. The Hotel Scene

Casablanca is very well equipped with hotels, from the ***** down to the unclassified. Low season hotel charges fixed for this region are as follows

Fantasia—*rider and horse ready for a display of warlike horsemanship.*

Oudaya Kasbah, Rabat.

Oudaya Kasbah, Rabat.

Cedars, Middle Atlas.

Permanent salt water river in arid desert, Saharan Morocco.

Mosaics in a Roman villa in Volubilis.

Kairouan Mosque, Fès.

Hassan II Mosque, Casablanca.

Cannon and defensive bastion, Essaouira.

Fishing boats at Essaouira, Atlantic Coast.

High Atlas village.

Boys at work in the Coppersmiths' market, Marrakech.

Pottery sellers in Marrakech market.

Camel and Saharan tribesman, Mhamid, south Morocco.

Prehistoric rock engravings of shields, Jbel Rat Mountain, High Atlas.

Rock engraving of bull in south Morocco.

Kasbah Dar Glaoui, Ouarzazate.

Tinerhir Oasis.

Ahouach dance, Tata, south Morocco.

Palm grove at Erfoud.

Miles of sand dunes at Merzouga, near the Algerian frontier.

(they vary according to the presence or absence of showers and water closet in the room): ★★★★ 493 DH or 799 DH, breakfast 53 DH or 67 DH; ★★★ 186-306 DH or 213-347 DH, breakfast 37 DH for both; ★★ 108-180 DH or 113-227, breakfast 26 DH for both; ★ 94-133 DH or 100-160 DH, breakfast 24 DH for both.

The Casablanca **regional telephone code** is 02 (0 omitted for in-region calls).

EXPENSIVE HOTELS

These are hotels in the ★★★★★ category. The best at the moment is the ★★★★★ **Hotel Royal Mansour Meridien** (182 rooms and suites, 1,700-3,300 DH, breakfast 170 DH, 27 Avenue des F.A.R., Tel: 31 30 11/31 21 12, Fax: 31 25 83/31 48 18). Very central, it has large, comfortable, and attractively furnished bedrooms and bathrooms, a restful reception area with an interior, glass-domed garden, three restaurants, a health center, conference rooms, and quiet and efficient service. It is a meeting place for all the elegants.

Down the road a little is the huge ★★★★★ **Hotel Sheraton,** part of the well-known hotel chain (304 rooms, from 2,400-2,800 DH, breakfast 130-155 DH, 100 Avenue des F.A.R., Tel: 31 78 78, Fax: 31 51 36). An unattractive exterior hides an imaginative interior, with an entrance hall full of discreet lounges at different levels, although the bedrooms are rather small. It is less classy than the Hotel Royal Mansour, but well equipped with three restaurants, a nightclub, a karaoké bar, roof-top pool, squash court, fitness center, sauna, *hammam,* a business center, and conference rooms.

The ★★★★★ **Hyatt Regency** (229 rooms, 2,300-2,600 DH, Place des Nations Unies, Tel: 26 12 34, Fax: 22 01 80) overlooks the Place des Nations Unies (ex-Place Mohammed V). From the outside, it is a rather dull, cube-like building. Inside, however, it is more exotic. The hotel has three restaurants, a bar, a nightclub, pool, squash, a fitness center, and conference rooms.

Downtown (transport is useful), near the sea, the ★★★★★ **Melia Riad Salam** (150 rooms, slightly cheaper at 1,500 DH, breakfast 110 DH, Boulevard de la Corniche, Tel: 39 13 13, Fax: 39 13 45) also offers all the facilities one would expect in a charming setting. It has five restaurants, a garden, attractive pool, disco, and conference rooms. The attached **Institute of Sea Water Therapy,** *Le Lido,* has an international reputation.

The ★★★★★ **Holiday Inn, Crown Plaza** (158 rooms, 22 suites, 2,100 DH, Rond-Point Hassan II, Tel: 29 49 49, Reservations Tel: 29 50 10, Fax: 29 30 29, Reservations Fax: 29 30 35), rises pillar-like at a very busy intersection, and is central for the banks but a bit away from the shops. It has three

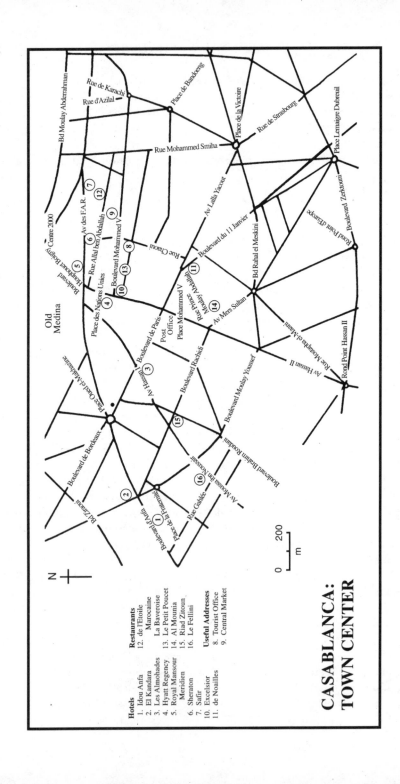

CASABLANCA:
TOWN CENTER

Hotels
1. Idou Anfa
2. El Kandara
3. Les Almohades
4. Hyatt Regency
5. Royal Mansour
   Meridien
6. Sheraton
7. Safir
10. Excelsior
11. de Noailles

Restaurants
12. de l'Etoile
   Marocaine
   La Baveroise
13. Le Petit Poucet
14. Al Mounia
15. Riad Zitoun
16. Le Fellini

Useful Addresses
8. Tourist Office
9. Central Market

0   200
m

N

restaurants (one alongside the roof-top pool), a sauna, *hammam*, massage, a nightclub, and conference rooms (they say their beds have been imported from the United States). It seems to be the only Casablanca hotel with facilities for people in wheelchairs.

In the ***** range, the **Hotel Safir** (311 rooms, 1,300-1,600 DH, breakfast 75-100 DH, 160 Avenue des F.A.R., Tel: 31 12 12, Fax: 31 65 14) is another large, well-placed hotel used for meetings and conferences. It has two restaurants, a nightclub, and a sauna.

The **** **Hotel Toubkal** (9 Rue Sidi Belyout, Tel: 31 14 14, Fax: 31 11 46) is conveniently central, and also has a good reputation.

The quiet, well-kept **** **Hotel Idou Anfa** (220 rooms, 85 Boulevard d'Anfa, Tel: 20 02 35, Fax: 20 00 29) is owned by a Berber who ensures that it is one of the "cleanest" (morally-speaking) in town. It is recommended for single women clients. An unpretentious establishment, it has functional bedrooms and it is not very attractively decorated, and has three restaurants, a pool, sauna, and conference/exhibition rooms.

Another good, well-kept hotel on the Boulevard d'Anfa is the **** **Hotel el-Kandar** (213 rooms, Tel: 26 29 37/26 27 91, Fax: 22 06 17). It has four restaurants, a sauna, a piano bar, a nightclub, a conference room, and a business center.

The **** **Les Almohades** (138 rooms, Avenue Hassan I, Tel: 22 05 05, Fax: 22 05 05), part of the French Accor chain, has comfortable and well-equipped rooms, restaurants, and a bar.

The **** **Kenzi al-Mounia Hotel** (24 Boulevard de Paris, Tel: 20 32 11) has recently changed hands and is a lively establishment, and well placed in the center of town. It has a restaurant, piano bar, and a nightclub.

Downtown, beside the sea, the newish **** **Hotel de la Corniche** (Boulevard de la Corniche, Tel: 36 27 82, Fax: 39 11 10) has rooms overlooking the sea (most with balconies), and a small pool.

MEDIUM-PRICE HOTELS

These are the *** category. A quiet, clean, friendly hotel with large bedrooms, in a busy, noisy road, handy for the Casa-Port station, is the *** **Hotel Plaza** (27 rooms, 18 Boulevard Houphouet Boigny, Tel/Fax: 29 76 98). (A friend's father stayed here for a whole month and said it wasn't all that noisy.) Here you are right in the middle of a series of stores selling carpets, leather wallets and slippers, and pottery—the whole range of Moroccan handicrafts.

The *** **Hotel de Noailles** (22 Boulevard du 11 Janvier, Tel: 26 05 83, Fax: 22 05 89) is another friendly hotel, of long-standing, located in a busy shopping zone. It has a calm bar and coffee shop on the first floor.

If you are arriving late by train, or planning an early morning departure, the *** **Hotel Moussafir** (Place de la Gare Casa-Voyageurs/Boulevard ba Ahmed, Tel: 40 19 84, Fax: 40 07 99) is useful, as it is just beside the station. This hotel chain was, in fact, designed for rail travelers (*moussafir* means traveler) and has recently been taken over by the French Accor/Ibis chain. The Casablanca version is not up to its Rabat and Oujda counterparts, despite its modern Moroccan decoration and small interior garden.

The *** **Hotel Bellerive** (32 rooms, 38 Boulevard de la Corniche, Tel: 39 13 57, Fax: 39 54 93), nicely placed beside the sea, is also a good value.

The *** **Hotel le Dawliz** (20 rooms, 6 suites, Boulevard de la Corniche, Tel: 39 69 43/39 12 25, Fax: 39 14 29) has bedrooms pleasantly furnished in modern style, two restaurants (with Asiatic, Moroccan, and international menus), a piano bar, and a terrace overlooking the sea. It is just next door to the four Dawliz cinemas, which include an art gallery and a coffee shop.

BUDGET ACCOMMODATIONS

I would say that there are not many budget accommodations in Casablanca that one could really recommend. There are plenty of small, cheap hotels for under 100 DH a night, but most of them are pretty "sleazy." If you can manage a higher price, try and do so.

In the ** range, good ones are the ** **Hotel de Lausanne** (31 rooms, 24 Rue Tata, Tel: 26 86 90) and the ** **Hotel Astrid** (12 Rue Ledru-Rollin, Tel: 27 78 03, Fax: 29 22 72), both of which are clean and well equipped.

The ** **Hotel Excelsior** (2 Brahim el-Amraoui, off the Place des Nations Unies, Tel: 20 02 63) used to be one of the top hotels in Casablanca at the beginning of the century, but it's seen better days. There should be no surprises here, but it's not a particularly good value.

At the bottom of the list there is the **Youth Hostel** (Auberge de Jeunesse, 40 beds, 6 Place Ahmed Bidaoui, ex-Place Amiral Philibert, Tel: 22 05 51), in the old medina, looking onto a small square near the ramparts (YH card not essential). It is about as clean as these places usually are, with unappealing water closets.

The campsite, **Camping Oasis,** is in the residential Beausejour district, a 10 DH taxi ride from the center of town (buses possible) (Avenue Mermoz, Tel: 25 33 67). The shops are close and the trees are shady, but the water closets and the rest are up to—or rather down to—usual Moroccan campsite standards. The place is constantly threatened with demolition, being a very desirable development area.

There are many camping and caravaning sites along the coast just south of the town, including the **Camping Tamaris** (Tamaris beach), which is very crowded in summer, as many local people camp there for their August holiday (10 DH per person, the same for a tent and a car).

5. Dining and Restaurants

Casablanca is home to many national and international companies and, as such, has a population attached to high-class eating, both for their own upper management staff and for visiting VIPs. One wouldn't come to Morocco just to eat in Casablanca, but once you are there you can certainly count on eating well.

HOTEL RESTAURANTS

The hotel restaurants indicated here are not given in any order of preference—it all depends on what you are looking for. For Moroccan food, the **Restaurant La Douira** in the Hotel Royal Mansour is very high-class. It is small, attractive, and has excellent food, and there are often a couple of well-known musicians playing Andalusian music. As it's small, booking several hours in advance is advised (it is expensive). Their French restaurant, the **Volubilis,** is also good, but the service is a bit slow. They do a good-value barbecue in the summer on the roof-top terrace.

The Moroccan restaurant in the Hyatt Regency, the **Dar Beida,** is getting better and is now very good. They put on an evening show (friends were particularly impressed with the dancer energetically twisting around with a tray of tea-glasses on her head). The service is good. The midday buffet in their **Golden Gates** restaurant is also substantial and varied, and their Mediterranean restaurant, **L'Olivier,** does a very good dinner.

For Oriental thrills, you could try an evening meal (not memorable) in the **El-Bahia** restaurant in the Holiday Inn Hotel. Entertainment in the dining area around the pool in summer is provided by the Sheraton, but I wouldn't go there just to eat.

For anything but thrills, the **Restaurant Les Elysées,** in the Hotel Idou Anfa, does good French cooking (small helpings), and the service is a bit slow, but it's calm and agreeable if you want to talk rather than go for a gourmet meal. There is piano music (sometimes) in the evening.

The **Hispania Restaurant** in the Riad Salam Hotel is surprisingly inexpensive for this ***** hotel (fish dishes from 110 DH), and in its Italian Pizzeria restaurant, **Le Jardin,** you can eat your pizza on the terrace just beside the sea (pizzas from 50 DH, pasta from 55 DH).

OTHER RESTAURANTS

For Moroccan food one of the best is the **Restaurant al-Mounia** (95 Rue du Prince Mulay Abdallah, Tel: 22 26 69, closed Sundays), set in a small garden, which makes summer meals particularly pleasant (it is always full in the evening). The staff is agreeable and efficient. Count on around 80 DH for an excellent main dish.

Excellent Moroccan food is served at the attractive **Riad Zitoun** (31 Boulevard Rachidi, Tel: 22 39 37), near the Belgian and Greek Consulates. It has a quiet upstairs eating area and was opened recently by the son of Al-Mounia's late proprietor (main dish from 80 DH).

The **Imilchil** (27 Rue Vizir Tazi, Tel: 22 09 99) is around the same price, and does a good Moroccan meal in an attractive but rather cramped setting. A cheaper Moroccan option is the **Restaurant de l'Etoile Marocaine** (107 Rue Allal ben Abdallah, Tel: 31 41 00), where your main dish shouldn't cost more than 50 DH (no alcohol).

For high-class French cooking the choics are numerous. The furthest out of town, on the coast near the sanctuary of Sidi Abd er-Rahman, is **Ma Bretagne** (Boulevard de la Corniche, Sidi Abd er-Rahman, Tel: 39 79 79, closed Sundays), which has recently been completely redecorated. The cooking is refined (the chef is French), and although fish is a specialty, all their dishes are excellent. The service at one time had a bad reputation, but it is now very good. If you are not "motorized," this can be an expensive outing (120 DH for the main dish, plus a taxi there and back).

On the Boulevard de la Corniche, out from the center, but not so far, near El-Hank lighthouse, the two restaurants **La Mer** (Tel: 36 33 15, closed Sundays) and **Le Cabestan** (Tel: 39 11 90) have good views over the sea (if you can get a window table—regular clients tend to have first choice). My personal preference is for the latter, but both have an excellent menu, specializing in fish (around 100 DH for the main dish in either place). They are very popular for business lunches and dinners, so they are crowded—it is best to make a reservation.

Still along the Boulevard de la Corniche, **La Réserve** (Tel: 36 71 10) is also a favorite with many of my friends. It is quieter than Le Cabestan, and slightly less expensive. It limits itself to fish (usually big fish caught the same day), and the service and sea views are good (reservation advisable).

Le Retro 1900, in the Centre 2000 near the port (Boulevard Moulay Abderrahman, Tel: 27 60 73, closed Sundays), with its Art Deco decor, is an amusing place, pretty smart, with a friendly staff and a rather special atmosphere. Its menu is very good, but expensive (count on around 200 DH).

Perhaps the best value for refined French cooking is **La Gondole** (also in Centre 2000, Tel: 27 74 88/29 47 40), which is cheaper than Le Retro 1900. Under direct French management, this restaurant has a varied and interesting menu (from 80 DH for the main dish), and is an excellent place for an evening meal. It's a big favorite with my French friends.

As good as La Gondole, but more pricey (count on 250 DH for the menu) is the rather chic **L'Atelier** (2 Rue Pierre Curie, Tel: 22 21 65, closed Sundays), which does very good French cooking. It has a contemporary art gallery on the ground floor, which you can look at without having to eat in the restaurant.

For good meat, there is nothing in my mind that beats **L'Entrecôte** (78 Avenue Mers Sultan, Tel: 27 26 74, closed Sundays). It only serves an entrecôte steak, kept warm on a hot-plate on the table in front of you, preceded by a salad, and followed by a very wide selection of desserts. It's a very good value (steak 90 DH), and enjoyed by meat-eating kids.

Other French cooking is supplied by the restaurant **Chez Milhet** (1 Rue Ahmed Sitou, Tel: 31 11 88), which hasn't changed much since the 1930s. It's not a very classy affair, and is frequented by old French *pieds-noirs* (French people long-resident in Morocco) who come to enjoy good family cooking (main dish from 70 DH). There is a noisy bar at ground level, but a quiet restaurant on the first floor.

The **Brasserie La Bavaroise** (129 Rue Allal ben Abdallah, opposite Chez Milhet, Tel: 31 17 60), though it used to be kept by Germans (who imported German beers), does nice French food and has a big selection of French wines (special guests are given a wine key and can inspect the cellar). It has attentive service, but it's inclined to be crowded with local people at lunchtime. It is a good value (main dish from 70 DH). Choose the *plat du jour.*

Le Petit Poucet (86 Boulevard Mohammed V, Tel: 27 54 20) has rather a faded glory atmosphere, not looking as though it had changed since the French aviator and writer, St. Exupéry, ate here when stopping in Casablanca on his trans-Sahara Toulouse-Dakar flights in the 1920s. His photograph and some of his letters hang over the bar. The food, too, is a bit "faded" ("diluted French" says one of my friends), but it's good enough and not expensive (100-120 DH/meal).

For a cheap meal, the department store **Alpha 55** (Avenue Mers Sultan, near the French Consulate) has a restaurant on its sixth floor, with good views over the city, where you can have a three-course meal for 60 DH.

Turning now to restaurants dealing almost exclusively in fish, you have **Le Restaurant du Port de Pêche** (inside the fishing port, Tel: 31 85 61), where the fish is good and fresh, but the noise is considerable. It's not for a quiet romantic evening (main dish from 50 DH). Downstairs there's a "working man's" restaurant, cheap and cheerful (25 DH/main course).

For something quieter, **L'Ostrea** is just opposite (Port de Pêche, Tel: 44 13 90). It's good for a late lunch (between 1:30 P.M. and 2:00 P.M.). Get a window table with a view over the port (it *is* a fishing port, so there are naturally fishy smells around) and choose the day's freshly-caught fish, whatever it is, following the waiter's advice. L'Ostrea has its own oyster park down the coast at Oualidia.

In the busy shopping street leading to the port, **Le Taverne du Dauphin** (115, Avenue Houphouet Boigny, closed Sundays) is also popular, serving delicious fresh fish and other seafoods.

In the Centre 2000, the **Restaurant Le Chalutier** is a possibility (Tel: 20 34 55, main dish). Along the Boulevard de la Corniche, opposite La Réserve, the **Restaurant La Criée** (on the first floor) offers good views and decent fish (Tel: 36 71 05) (main dish from 80 DH), while downstairs next door, **La Pierrade** goes in for meat (main dish from 70 DH).

For ethnic food, the Italian restaurant **Le Fellini** (36 Avenue Moussa ibn Noussair, Tel: 22 82 56) is popular and has live music in the evening. But it is expensive for what it gives—I think one pays more for the music than for the food (starters from 40 DH, pasta from 70 DH, meat from 100 DH).

The **Sorrento** (5 Rue de Cluny, Maarif) does a variety of pizzas and pasta (which can be washed down with a jug of sangria). A favorite of mine, it's a friendly sort of place where one can exchange a word or two with diners at the next door table (the tables are *very* close together), but it's crowded unless one goes early (closed during Ramadan) (pizzas and pasta from 60 DH).

The **Don Giovanni** (89 Rue Ibnou Mounir, also in the Maarif, Tel: 25 19 19/25 19 65) is also an attractive restaurant, rather larger than the Sorrento, and definitely less convivial (pizzas from 50 DH, pasta from 60 DH).

Italian food can also be had at the **Restaurant Casablanca** (32 Rue Abou Ishak el-Marouni—ex-Rue Mont d'Or—Tel: 99 11 39) in the Maarif, but, despite the candles on the tables in the evening, there's not much atmosphere and the "Casablanca" decor is limited to a few small, old photographs of the town. However, it has the advantage of being open during Ramadan (appetizers 45-80 DH, meat or fish 80-125 DH).

For a Spanish splurge, try **La Dorade** (Avenue de la Côte d'Emeraudes, Ain Diab, Tel: 94 43 77/94 43 78) (very expensive—main dish from 150 DH).

Down the scale, but still Spanish, **La Corrida** (35 Rue el-Araar, ex-Gay Lussac, Tel: 27 81 55, closed Sundays and in September) is tucked away off the Boulevard du 11 Janvier. Surprisingly, it has a shaded front garden, and is very pleasant for a calm, summer's evening meal. The whole place is decorated in the Spanish style and is still run by Madame Solange Marmaneu, whose husband was killed in the attempted coup d'état at Skhirat in 1971. It does a nice cold *gaspacho* soup for 25 DH and a fish or meat dish for 75 DH, with a big pitcher of sangria (95 DH).

In the Spanish line and much cheaper, the **Restaurant de la Presse** (32 Boulevard Brahim Roudani/corner Rue Oussama Ibnou Zaid, Tel: 25 05 43), opposite the CTM bus depot, is very handy for a quick brasserie type meal in the Maarif. You can sit on a stool at the counter and have a meal with beer or wine pretty quickly; the table service is slower (fried fish 35 DH, main dish from 40 DH, and *paella* 40 DH).

The **Restaurant Beyrouth** (7 Rue Karatchi, Tel: 30 87 98) has seen a lot of changes in the past few years, but its Lebanese meal is now considered good by my Lebanese friends, who also eat at the **Restaurant Baalbeck,** on the Corniche (3 Boulevard Océan Atlantique, Tel: 39 11 93). Call in advance, so that the chef can prepare something nice.

For Oriental cooking, one of the best is the **Restaurant Vinh-Along** in the Mers Sultan district (22 Rue Attaouss, ex-Rue Belfort, Tel: 44 64 57, closed Mondays). It cooks Vietnamese specialities and also has "takeaway."

The **Restaurant La Tonkinoise,** in the Ain Diab district (Avenue de la Côte d'Emeraude, Tel: 39 11 87), also has a reputation for good Vietnamese food and a friendly staff, and I have enjoyed eating at **Le Tonkin** in the center of town (first floor, 34 Rue Mulay Abdallah—pedestrian zone— Tel: 22 19 13).

The **Golden China Restaurant** in the Maarif is closed, but has opened attractively decorated new premises in the center of town (12 Rue el-Ouraibi Filali, Tel: 27 35 26). It's recommended by friends for its Chinese gourmet cooking (set menus 150 DH and 180 DH, not licensed for liquor, closed Sundays). **La Pagode** (95 Rue Ferhat Hachad, Tel: 27 71 85) is another good place for Chinese food.

The **Restaurant Au Nid d'Hirondelle** (384 Boulevard Zerktouni, Tel: 20 64 42) serves a very nice Chinese meal (main dish from 50 DH, closed during Ramadan). (The **Restaurant Mekong** is closed altogether.)

For those wanting beef, the Brazilian **Restaurant Papagayo** (23 Rue Zaid Ibnou Rifaa, Maarif, near the Twin Towers) might suit you. It does more than kebobs, and gets pretty crowded.

OTHER PLACES TO EAT

The very modern **Subway** (4 Boulevard Bir Anzarane, Maarif, Tel: 23 46 19) is a good place for large sandwiches of all types, including turkey, chicken fajita, and vegetarian (from 18 DH), and salads and soft drinks. It does a Kid's Pack for 33 DH, and has a large panoramic view of New York on the wall for the homesick.

The **Boga-Boga,** just off the Corniche (Rue Tempêtes, Tel: 94 91 36) does good salads and pancakes, but you can also get a slightly more substantial meal.

Then, of course, there's a **McDonald's**—three in fact. The most popular is on the Corniche overlooking the sea (6 Boulevard de la Corniche,

Tel: 39 79 38), with the usual hamburger range (Big Mac 23 DH, child's meal 28 DH, breakfast of coffee and croissant 7.50 DH), and the additional attraction of a games' park for kids. The others are in the center of town, 8 Boulevard Mohammed V (Tel: 48 25 34) and 53 Rond-Point Mers Sultan (Tel: 22 64 27).

There are four **Pizza Huts** (142 Boulevard Ghandi, Tel: 94 13 94; 67 Boulevard Moulay Youssef, Tel: 47 36 36; in the Marjane supermarket complex a few kilometers out of town on the way to the airport, Tel: 21 32 03; and 207 Boulevard de la Résistance, Tel: 20 24 64). Their menus come at 50 DH, 78 DH (pizza, dessert, and soft drink), and a junior menu at 39 DH. They do takeaway and home delivery.

A life-size cowboy and a Red Indian mark the entrance to the newly-opened **Schlotzsky's Deli** (10 Rue Madame Rolland, between the Boulevards d'Anfa and Massira al-Khadra, Tel: 36 96 96, open from 10:30 A.M.-11:00 P.M.). Pizzas cost from 50 DH, and a very wide variety of sandwiches (with soft drink and packet of French fries) starts at 32 DH. It also does home (or office) delivery.

The **U.S. Seaman's Center** (118 Boulevard Moulay Abderrahman, Tel: 30 99 50) provides hamburgers in a casual, friendly atmosphere.

You can buy delicious ices from **Dairy Queen** (225 Boulevard d'Anfa— look out for the big plaster ice cream outside). The attraction of the American, soft-serve Dairy Queen ice cream is that it's prepared in front of you (from 15 DH). Hot dogs, chicken, and french fries are also on sale from 25 DH. There's no particular charm to this very modern place, but you can take your ice cream and eat it elsewhere (it claims it is the 5,750th sales point of this American group).

For a really up-market ice cream establishment, there is nothing to beat **Oliveri** (132 Avenue Hassan II), where you can order mouth-watering combinations of ice cream and cake, topped with little meringues, or eat ices (around 20 DH) and drink fruit juice in the coffee room.

American donuts are offered by the first fast-food establishment specializing in them, **Dunkin Donuts** (corner Boulevard d'Anfa/Boulevard Moulay Youssef)—there are 52 varieties, sold from 7 DH for one, 38 DH for six.

Casablanca is a large city, with three main commercial districts: downtown, Mers Sultan, and Maarif. Tired shoppers wanting to ease their feet over a fruit juice or cup of tea will probably want something near. If downtown, **Le Trianon** (32 Boulevard Mohammed V) is a recommended coffee shop with good, sugary eats.

Women travelers can retreat to the coffee shop on the first floor of the **Hotel de Noailles** (22 Boulevard du 11 Janvier) or have a quiet tea or coffee at the **Pâtisserie de l'Opéra** (50 Boulevard du 11 Janvier).

In the Maarif, **La Colombe d'Or** (corner Rue Ibnou Nafis/Rue de l'Atlas) is a good stopping place. Near the sea, in the Ain Diab area (while waiting for a movie, for instance), you could try the **Salon de Thé Dawliz,** in the Dawliz complex on the Corniche.

In the residential Riviera/Oasis area, the newly-opened coffee shop **Le Napoléon** (corner Rue Baudelaire/Boulevard Ghandi) has delicious pastries. Down along the Corniche, the **Restaurant Revolver** sells pastries which you can enjoy over a coffee or fruit juice on its terrace. Freshly-pressed orange juice can be had from many cafés around town and is delicious.

6. Sightseeing

There are no Islamic monuments of any great age in Casablanca, but the visitor should not miss the unique opportunity of visiting the new **Hassan II Mosque.** The **Old** and **New Medinas** are interesting in different ways, and many of the **buildings in the center of the modern town** are fascinating examples of different architectural and decorative styles.

IN CASABLANCA

The center of the modern town makes a convenient starting point for a visit. This is easily recognisable by the huge and unsightly Hyatt Regency and the large, traffic-congested area in front of it now called **Place des Nations Unies,** formerly Place Mohammed V. From here a network of roads branch out east, west, south, and north, including Avenue Houphouet Boigny, which leads to the port and Avenue des F.A.R. and Boulevard Mohammed V, going towards Mohammedia and Rabat. To the right of the Hyatt lies the **Old Medina** and the **Clock Tower** (*Tour de l'Horloge*), a 1990s version of an early 20th-century tower.

If you are bent on shopping, head down the **Avenue Houphouet Boigny.** Just before the station, on the right, is the white dome (*kubba*) of the **sanctuary of Sidi Belyout,** the town's patron saint. Otherwise a tour of the surroundings offers a marvelous selection of **architectural styles.** Opposite the Hyatt Hotel is the Hotel Excelsior, still looking much as it did in 1920. The facade of the big building at the corner of Avenue Houphouet Boigny is a good example of the "boat style" of the 1950s. Along Boulevard Mohammed V—alas, very degraded commercially—N° 3 and N° 40 are splendid examples from the 1930s; the decorative motifs of N° 58 are reminiscent of the Italian Renaissance; a head of the god Pan, surrounded by bunches of grapes, decorates the pediment of N° 95. Balconies, arcades, pillars, and porticos break up the facades, while a glance up at the tops of many of the older buildings in this central area (don't miss the Rue du

Prince Mulay Abdallah) reveals an extraordinary wealth of decoration, from sculpture and stucco to colored tiles. Along Boulevard Mohammed V, the **Central Market** *(Marché Central)* is a real feast for the eyes—pyramids of fruit, vegetables, and spices vie with each other for the most colorful display.

Architecturally interesting, too, is the newly-named **Place Mohammed V** with its luminous fountain (built at the end of the 1970s) and administrative buildings: the Town Hall *(Préfecture)* (1930), Law Courts *(Palais de Justice)* (1925), and post office (1918, but recently renovated), all of Hispano-Moorish inspiration. The State Bank *(Banque du Maroc)*, with its mixture of stone and marble, is another imposing building in this sector. Continuing along Avenue Hassan II, the French Consulate lies to the left, and further on is the **Parc de la Ligue Arabe,** once a leafy park in which to walk, but now rapidly being planted with coffee shops. On the far side of the park, the **Eglise du Sacré Coeur,** built in 1930, is still an impressive structure, but is no longer used as a church. A functioning Catholic church, with magnificent modern stained-glass windows designed by a master craftsman from the French cathedral town of Chartres, is **Notre Dame de Lourdes,** built in 1953, along Boulevard Zerktouni.

Back at the Place des Nations Unies, a walk through the **Old Medina** *(Ancienne Medina)* (advisable in the daytime only) can be preceded by a short visit to **St. John's Church** (road to left of Hyatt Regency), the oldest standing foreign church in Casablanca (building began in 1905 and was finished in 1906) and a classified monument. Between 1942-1945 there was a strong American military presence in Morocco and the church was often filled to overflowing. General George Patton attended the church regularly and donated an oak pulpit in memory of those who had fallen in the battle for Casablanca.

The few craftsmen working in the medina don't make traditional objects, but go in for cheap suitcases, and the shops sell manufactured goods for local people. But the medina is rich in history and is well worth a visit. Some of its buildings are more than 100 years old. It was here that foreign consuls lived in the 19th century and a few old buildings survive. The Maison Tazi (now housing a school) was built before 1902 for the German consulate, and the Maisons Acherki date from 1893 and were used by an English administration. The town's first patron saint, **Sidi Allal el-Kairouani,** and his daughter, Lalla Beida, have their sanctuary in here. Sidi Allal was said to have left Kairouan in Tunisia in the 14th century, hoping to reach Senegal by boat. But he was shipwrecked off Casablanca and saved by local fishermen. Upon the death of his wife, he asked his daughter to join him and she, too, was shipwrecked off Casablanca. But she was unlucky and drowned. She was buried facing the sea, later to be joined by Sidi Allal. The sanctuary (and from there the town) took the name of *Dar el-Beida* (white house) from the whiteness of Lalla Beida's skin. There's a different legend about the origin of Casablanca's name, involving a woman accused of immorality, but that's another story.

Working your way through the medina, you can come out, via the Place Ahmed Bidaoui (ex-Place Amiral Philibert) onto the big Boulevard des Almohades that circles the medina alongside the ramparts. To the left, after about 300 m, opposite the fishing port, lies **La Skala** and the 18th-century fortified bastion of the **Bordj Sidi Allal al-Kairouani,** its cannons pointing seawards, which has been restored. It can be studied from the outside, but is closed to the public. Another charming little *kubba*, in the middle of a quiet square, is that of **Sidi Bou Smara,** who struck the ground with his stick during a drought and caused water to spring out. The people wouldn't let him go after that, so he used to sit under a tree he had planted, and today people stick a nail *(mesmar)* in the tree's trunk to implore his favor. The shrine lies just inside the medina, up a small street as you return towards the station and the **Centre 2000.**

The **New Medina** was planned by French architects in the 1930s, as an improved version of an old Moroccan medina designed to house an ever-increasing local population. Its most impresssive building is the **Mahakma du Pacha** (1948) in the **Habous** district, in Neo-Hispano-Moorish style, as are the buildings in the Place Mohammed V. It was originally planned to house a tribunal and reception room for the Pacha of Casablanca. The Habous is also a thriving shopping area, much frequented by Moroccans (see "Shopping" below).

The opposite of all this is the chic **Anfa** district, at the other side of town. The rich and elegant villas are built on the hill of the original Casablanca settlement, Anfa. Many of the Consular representatives have their private residences here, alongside rich Casablanca businessmen. In 1943, after the U.S. landings on the Moroccan coast, the Allies decided to hold an international conference to decide on the course World War II was to take in Europe. Casablanca was chosen as the site, and the Anfa hill was transformed into an entrenched camp, protected by General Patton's troops, ready to receive President Roosevelt, British Prime Minister Winston Churchill, and the two French generals Giraud and de Gaulle. The Hotel Panoramique (alas, destroyed and replaced by a modern appartment block) and 18 villas were requisitioned to receive the illustrious visitors. President Roosevelt, his son Elliott, and his two secretaries, Averell Harriman and Harry Hopkins, plus his North African representative, Robert Murphy, were installed at the Villa Es Saada, at the top of the hill.

Churchill lived in the nearby Villa Mirador, now the home of the U.S. Consul-General. Other generals and admirals (including General Marshall, Chief of Staff; Admiral King, Commander-in-Chief of the U.S. Fleet; and Generals Eisenhower, Clark, and Patton) were scattered around in different villas, with their British colleagues. President Roosevelt twice met the sultan Mohammed V in his Villa Es Saada, once at an official dinner where the Crown Prince, the late king Hassan II, was also present. Photos of the Anfa Conference hang in the hall of the Casablanca Consulate and can be studied on request.

Down from Anfa, and left along the coast a few kilometers from Ain Diab, the **sanctuary of Sidi Abd er-Rahman** is beautifully sited on a rock promontory cut off from the mainland at high tide, and can't be missed. It is visited all year-round by people hoping for the saint's blessing *(baraka)* to cure them of their ills (often mental troubles). Non-Moslems cannot visit the shrine, but can walk around and admire the breakers crashing on the rocks (N° 90 bus from Place de la Concorde).

Two or three kilometers inland, important archaeological excavations on Lower Palaeolithic sites are periodically undertaken. Visits are allowed when the Franco-Moroccan teams are at work. Try contacting the Institute of Archaeology in Rabat for information (*Institut National de l'Archéologie et du Patrimoine,* Tel: 07-75 68 84/75 09 61).

Back along the Corniche, past the **El Hank Lighthouse,** the high minaret of the **Hassan II Mosque** is visible for miles around (N° 11 bus from Sidi Belyout). Although it comes last in this list, it is an absolutely essential visit, one of the rare chances to see the inside of a Moroccan mosque and a marvelous display of Moroccan craftsmanship. The visitor can walk right around the mosque, built out into the sea, and admire the huge doors and exterior decoration, but the interior can only be visited with an official guide (see "Guided Tours" below for conditions of entry). The building was started in 1980, financed by public subscription (in theory, it was voluntary, but in some cases over-enthusiastic administrators forced things a bit), and opened on August 29, 1993, after additional meters had to be added to the minaret (200 m high) and adjustments made to the laser beam that flashes out from the very top over a distance of 35 km. Whole books have been written on the mosque, and justice to its splendor cannot be done in few lines here—particularly as the obligatory guide explains things very well. A few figures, however, will give an idea of the size of the building, which is the biggest Moslem monument in the world outside of Mecca: 25,000 believers can assemble in the prayer room, which has a sliding roof, and 80,000 on the esplanade outside. It is said to have cost US$800 million. The interior is breathtaking—a profusion of *zellij,* stucco, carved wood, marble, and granite, all of the highest quality. The basement holds two ablution rooms (one for men, one for women) with fountains, basins, and *zellij* decoration, and a *hammam* designed after the model current in ancient times. The minaret, purely traditional in style, has two interior elevators. The mosque is completed by a *medersa*, library, and museum. In the evening, the road just inland allows a beautiful view of the mosque, its secondary buildings, fountains, and illuminations set against the setting sun.

NORTHEAST OF CASABLANCA

The expressway northeast to Rabat allows an easy day visit to the small coastal resort town of **Mohammedia** (30 km) for a game of **golf,** a **swim** in the sea, or a **meal** in one of its fish restaurants—or all three! The Samir oil refinery is situated here, and although the port is busy with oil tankers, it also houses the best yacht club in the area. By car, the best exit is the first, marked Mohammedia Ouest, then left towards the sea, to the port, and then left to the golf club (all marked). The town can be reached by frequent trains or buses from Casablanca.

The **regional telephone code** is 03 (0 omitted for in-region calls).

The **top hotel,** the ***** **Hotel Miramar** (188 rooms, 740 DH, breakfast 65 DH, Rue de Fès, Tel: 31 24 40/43, Fax: 32 46 13), just behind the beach, with a tennis court, swimming pool, restaurant, bar, nightclub, and conference rooms, has been closed due to an industrial dispute for over a year.

The *** **Hotel Samir** (46 rooms, 34 Boulevard Moulay Youssef, Tel: 31 07 70/31 07 74, Fax: 32 33 30), also quite close to the beach, with a tennis court, restaurant, bar, and nightclub, is a shade better than the *** **Hotel Sabah** (42 Avenue des F.A.R., Tel: 32 14 51/55, Fax: 32 14 56).

There's not much choice lower down the scale, but the **Hotel de la Falaise** (Rond-Point Pasteur) could be looked at. The **Camping International Loran,** on the coast, 7 km south of the town, cannot be recommended. The other campsite, **Camping International Oubaha,** 5 km north at Mansouria, gets very crowded in summer and is not much better than the first one.

Dining in the **Hotel Samir** or the **Hotel Sabah** is always a possibility for a meal without surprises (113 DH). However, most of my friends prefer to go elsewhere. But wherever you go, choose the fish, making sure it's the day's catch.

The **Restaurant du Port** (1 Rue du Port, Tel: 32 24 66) serves wonderful fish dishes, including big, salt-baked fish (main dish from 70 DH, set meal 150 DH, not licensed).

The **Restaurant La Frégate** (Rue Oued Zem, Tel: 32 44 47) is a favorite, with good fish and *paella.* The **Restaurant de la Place** has recently changed hands and has improved. Cheap "eats" can be had from the very popular

Pizzaria Eurosnack (Rue Mansour ed-Dahbi) serving hamburgers (around 15 DH) and pizzas (from 40 DH).

As well as **golf** and **swimming,** it is possible to practice **watersports** and **horseback** riding. The Hotel Samir is a good place for information on water-skiing and riding. There is a Catholic French-speaking **church,** the Eglise St. Jacques (Tel: 32 21 03).

The expressway continues from Mohammedia on to Rabat and Kénitra (chapter 6).

Another day excursion **northeast** from Casablanca involves continuing on the expressway past Mohammedia until reaching the Ben Slimane exit (25 km), and turning right for the little town of **Ben Slimane** (15 km), renowned for its excellent climate.

There is a good hotel here, the ***** Hotel Ziaida** (Avenue Lalla Aicha). Apart from its 9-hole golf course, there is nothing special to do, but another 15 km leads to a left turn down the narrow S1058 into the middle of the **El-Khatouat massif.** This is a fine, rugged place for walking, with splendid views and is a favorite with hunters—there are plenty of partridge, hare, and even wild boar. The vegetation is made up of evergreen oaks and sweet-smelling scrub. The first of several Foresters' Houses (*Maison Forestière,* M.F. on the maps) is reached after about 15 km.

If weather permits, you can work your way through southwards and come out on the main P22 from Rommani to **Oued Zem** or the P13 from Oued Zem to **Khouribga** (33 km) and Casablanca (a further 109 km). **Oued Zem,** on the road from Casablanca to Kasba Tadla, Beni Mellal, and the High Atlas, is an administrative and commercial center, but is unlikely to attract the traveler's attention.

Nor is **Khouribga,** except for the fact that it is the focal point for Morocco's biggest export—phosphates. The white pyramid-shaped rejected material from the open-cast mines can be seen from a distance. Khouribga is the capital of the province of the same name. It has a big hotel, the ****** Hotel Safir** (Boulevard Moulay Youssef, Tel: 03-56 35 50/ 56 23 50, Fax: 03-56 10 40), and a large, lively market on Sunday. The French-speaking Catholic **church,** Eglise Sainte Barbe, is situated at 2 Avenue Allal ben Abdallah (Tel: 49 45 52).

SOUTH OF CASABLANCA

South from Casablanca, a visit to the **Boulaounane Kasbah** (130 km) is easily done in the day by **car** or **big taxi.** The main P7 (in the direction of Mohammed V Airport) goes through the up-and-coming industrial town of **Berrechid** (30 km) before arriving at **Settat** (a further 30 km). The University and the Royal Golf Universitaire de Settat (see "Sports" below) lie to the left just before Settat (if traveling by car, note that there is a long stretch before the town where the speed is limited to 40 km/hour). Settat was used as a stopping place by sultans traveling from Fès to Marrakech, and in the town, on the right, the **kasbah** can be seen, which was built by Mulay Ismail in the 17th century. Settat strikes the visitor by the quantity of large, imposing, modern buildings, many of them administrative. This is understandable, since its parlimentary representative is Mr. Driss Basri, the current Minister of the Interior. Settat can be reached by frequent **train** or **bus** from Casablanca. Its annual cultural and tourist festival takes place in September. At the entrance to the town, a road to the right, the S105, goes to Boulaounane Kasbah (70 km).

The **** **Hotel du Parc M'Zamza** (Tel: 40 39 41, Fax: 40 20 08) is on the right before entering Settat, and the ** **Al Massira** is in the town itself (3 Place Mohammed V, Tel: 40 20 72, Fax: 40 10 92).

Boulaounane Kasbah, a veritable fortress, dominates a meander in the River Oum er-Rbia. It was built by Mulay Ismail in 1710, and his name and date of construction are written above the impressive gateway. The big walls, with their seven towers, are still standing, but unfortunately, the interior is very much in ruins. A square tower and a very small mosque complete with minaret are still visible, but the visitor will have to use his imagination to visualize the palace, which is said to have housed the most beautiful of Mulay Ismail's women. The view from the kasbah, however, is stunning, and the river below makes a good picnic and bathing site. Around the kasbah lie the vineyards producing the famous Boulaounane Gris wine. From here, the S105 continues towards the coast and the town of **El-Jadida** (see later).

From Settat, the P7 continues south, without any great interest, crossing the River Oum er-Rbia at **Mechra ben Abbou**—lots of young men beside the road try to sell bunches of wild flowers, necklaces, and fish from the river—going through **Skhour des Rehamna** (there is a nice little café with clean water closets and strange decoration, on the right at the very end of the town), the big airforce base at **Ben Guerir** (a satellite landing place, too), and **Sidi Bou Othmane** before reaching Marrakech (chapter 12). For those interested in history, it was in Sidi Bou Othmane that El Hiba, the son of the charasmatic Saharan leader Ma el-Ainin, hearing that the sultan Mulay Abd el-Hafid had signed the Protectorate treaty with the French, declared himself sultan in 1912 and faced French forces with 10,000 Saharan tribesmen. The latter had been told that the enemy's bullets would not harm them because they had the *baraka* (blessing) of their leader . . . but French cannons and rifles proved the contrary.

Long before El Hiba, an old dam a short distance (1½ km) off the main road was probably built by the Almohads in the 12th century. Some 105 m long, it was designed to supply water to nine cisterns for the irrigation of

the surrounding plain. The cisterns, long parallel half-underground chambers with vaulted ceilings, are quite well preserved. The turn off to reach
the dam is on the left, almost opposite the Gendarmerie, but it is really
only of limited interest.

SOUTHWEST OF CASABLANCA

Southwest of Casablanca, along the coast, the towns of **Azemmour** (76
km) and **El-Jadida** (16 km further on) are rich in history and should not
be missed if time allows (a day will do to cover them both). By **car,** both
towns can be reached by the P8, leaving Casablanca at the entrance to
the divided two-lane highway to the airport, and by frequent **bus** services
by the CTM and other companies. There are **buses** from Azemmour to
El-Jadida (about 5 DH), but a **big taxi** is probably simpler. The main road
is a very busy one, congested with trucks bringing up fruit and vegetables
from the very fertile zone (often grown in hideous plastic-covered green-
houses). I wouldn't try to stay in Azemmour—there is a better choice in
El-Jadida—but there are **cafés** in the main Place du Souk where one can
have a decent coffee or soft drink.

Lying about a kilometer from the mouth of the River Oum er-Rbia,
Azemmour was probably frequented by the Phoenicians and the
Carthaginians in the second half of the 1st century B.C. Around 1376 it was
briefly occupied by a member of the Merinid dynasty, but it is not until the
end of the 15th century that it became known as a town where Portuguese
ships called in to peacefully buy wheat, cloth, and horses. In 1513, the
Portuguese captured the town and built a fort with ramparts and towers,
before being forced by the Saadians to pull out in 1541. A splendid **view**
can be had from a point just before crossing the river. Tall, whitewashed
houses drop down directly into the river—it is here that well-known
Californian-based cookbook writer Kitty Morse has an old house, beautifully restored by her late father. The **medina,** to the right, through one of
the big gates in the ramparts, is a maze of little streets (with a horde of pestering children and a large quantity of rubbish). Many of the doors of now
rather dilapidated houses have a distinctly Portuguese look to them.
Among the buildings to look out for are the **old Portuguese church,** now
a mosque, and, within the ramparts themselves, the ruined **Dar el-Baroud
fortress.**

To walk along the **ramparts** (restored in 1998), it is best to go in at the
main entrance, protected by a tower, at the Place du Souk, where you will
hopefully find the guardian. A short staircase leads to a platform that allows views of both the River Oum er-Rbia and the rest of the ramparts
(looking down into the houses in the medina is not as attractive as it used

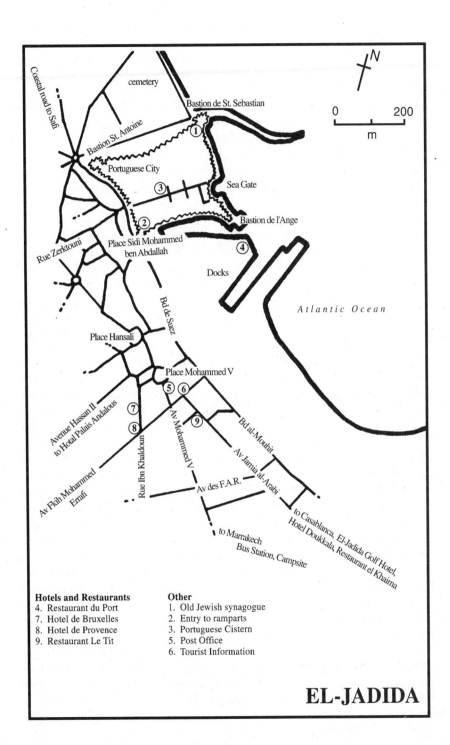

Hotels and Restaurants
4. Restaurant du Port
7. Hotel de Bruxelles
8. Hotel de Provence
9. Restaurant Le Tit

Other
1. Old Jewish synagogue
2. Entry to ramparts
3. Portuguese Cistern
5. Post Office
6. Tourist Information

EL-JADIDA

to be, since the houses have now increased in height with the addition of ugly concrete blocks). There used to be a very important Jewish community in Azemmour, and although they are no longer there, the **synagogue** is still open and can be visited. The old Jewish **cemetery** is a little way out of town towards the river mouth. The *moussem* (religious festival) of the patron saint, Mulay Bouchaib, takes place in September.

The town of **El-Jadida** is an altogether more important place, with a population around 200,000. One of the best natural harbors on the Atlantic, it is probable that the Phoenicians and Carthaginians took advantage of the site. The Portuguese landed on the beach in 1513 and, after building a fortress, started the construction of the town, known as Mazagan. After the loss of Azemmour and Agadir, they started fortifing their town in 1542. Part of their string of strongholds along the Moroccan coast, it soon became one of the most important Portuguese commercial centers on the Atlantic. Briefly Spanish from 1580 until its return to the Portuguese crown in 1640, it was won back in 1769 by the sultan Mohammed III. In 1815 it was reconstructed and given its original name of El-Jadida. In the second half of the 19th century, the town housed an important Jewish community, most of whom left in the 1950s for the United States or Canada. It almost became Morocco's main port under the Protectorate, until frantic speculation caused Résident Général Lyautey to prefer to develop Casablanca. The recent creation of the port of **Jorf Lasfar** to the south, specializing in the exportation of phosphates coming from the rich deposits around Khouribga, has given a fresh boost to the area and a vast new industrial zone is planned. In the summer, El-Jadida is a favorite resort and its August *moussem* in Mulay Abdallah (see below) attracts thousands of visitors.

At one time El-Jadida could be reached by **train,** but the service has recently been stopped. Local demand may lead to its return. El-Jadida can be reached by **car** or **bus** (as for Azemmour above). For **local transportation,** the **little taxis** (white) are the most convenient.

The **regional telephone code** is 03 (0 omitted for in-region calls).

At the top of the **hotel scene** (transport needed) is the **** **El-Jadida Royal Golf Hotel,** 7 km north of the town, marked "Royal Golf d'El-Jadida, Club Med" (107 rooms, 900 DH, BP 116 El-Jadida Principal, Tel: 35 41 41/48, Fax: 35 34 73). It is run in conjunction with the French Club Med, so there are a certain number of organized activities (open to all). Set between a eucalyptus forest and the beach, it has a big pool, tennis court, restaurants, a piano bar, *hammam,* sauna, and a pretty garden, and is alongside the challenging 18-hole golf course (see "Sports" section). It is very welcoming and has a pleasant atmosphere. The management can arrange horse-drawn buggy trips in the area (600 DH per half-day for two people), and the beach is nearby for seaside walking.

Medium-price accommodations are available in El-Jadida itself. I have mixed feelings about the ✱✱✱ **Hotel Doukkala** (81 rooms, Rue Jamia al-Arabia, on the sea side of the main road into town, Tel: 34 37 37). At the moment an El-Jadida friend affirms that it is still the best hotel in town, even if it is not as good as it was some years ago. Official delegations, ministers, and high civil servants stay there. Tour groups go there, too, and seem to find it all right, but foreign friends say it is rundown. Maybe it depends on when you're there. It is right on the sea, has a swimming pool, tennis court, restaurant, and bar, and I suspect that its size and amenities account for its success.

The smaller ✱✱✱ **Hotel Palais Andalous** (36 rooms, Boulevard Docteur Delanoe, ex Rue Curie, Tel: 34 37 45, Fax: 35 16 19) (it is not easy to find—take the Avenue Hassan II away from the town center) is to my mind a much better value. As its name implies, this hotel was once a pasha's palace and is of pure traditional style, with lots of colored *zellij* and stucco. It has an attractive interior courtyard surrounded by little Hispano-Moorish salons, and a restaurant and bar.

Lower down the scale, the small ✱✱ **Hotel de Provence** (18 rooms, 42 Avenue Fkih Mohammed Errafi, off the Place Mohammed V, Tel: 34 23 47, Fax: 35 21 15), with a bar and restaurant, is still a good address (it was once owned by an Englishman and is still a member of the British Chamber of Commerce).

For those interested in **budget accommodations,** there are plenty around, but they are very crowded in the summer, as El-Jadida is a favorite seaside resort. In this category, the ✱ **Hotel de Bruxelles** (40 Rue Ibn Khaldoun, Tel: 34 20 72) has very simple but clean rooms, with shower and water closet. Avoid the campsite.

Dining and Restaurants. The **El-Jadida Royal Golf Hotel** food is good (buffet lunch, set meal only in the evening), but not worth making a journey to get there (186 DH).

The restaurant in the **Hotel de Provence** has good Moroccan and French food (100 DH for a three-course meal). The **Restaurant el-Khaima,** facing the beach, almost opposite the Hotel Doukkala, offers reasonable Moroccan food (meal around 100 DH).

For a change from Moroccan or fish dishes, the **Restaurant Le Tit** (off Avenue Jamia al-Arabi, near the post office) serves "international" dishes (120 DH set menu). The **Restaurant du Port,** inside the port, at the very end, is well situated and its fish dishes are generally excellent (set menu 100 DH).

Kebobs are served at reasonable prices in many **small restaurants** with tables and chairs on the pavement (with salad, around 50 DH/meal, depending how many kebobs you eat).

It is possible to have a sandwich with your coffee at the small, new **Café La Marquise** (Place Mohammed V). The **Hotel Doukkala,** the **Palais Andalous,** and the **Hotel de Provence** have bars suitable for an evening drink, and any coffee shop will provide soft drinks. The **Royal Golf Hotel,** of course, also has a bar and it is most agreeable to sip your drink around the pool and watch the sun set over the Atlantic.

Sightseeing will concentrate on the **Portuguese City** *(Cité Portugaise),* more obviously a citadel typical of the military architecture of the 15th century. The structure cannot be missed as you come into the town from Casablanca and continue straight on, past the Place Mohammed V, and to the right of the Place Sidi Mohammed ben Abdallah (well indicated). The Portuguese **ramparts** had five **protruding towers** *(bastions),* four of which were rebuilt when the town was captured by Sidi Mohammed in 1769. This type of tower, invented by the Italians, was a military novelty at the time, with 360° views of the enemy. The **walkway** can be reached from the **Bastion du Saint-Esprit,** the first entrance to the fortress. A splendid view over the **city** and the **Sea Gate** *(Porte de la Mer)* (the Portuguese forces left from here for waiting ships when they abandoned the town) can be had from the **Bastion de l'Ange.** Two other towers protected the south of the city. Within the ramparts lay the elegant houses of the Portuguese officials and merchants, the **Church of the Assumption** (not in use) and, beside it, a **mosque** with a minaret built on the ruins of a five-sided watchtower (probably the only five-sided minaret in Morocco).

Beside the **Bastion de St. Sebastian,** facing the sea in the northern corner, is the Jewish **synagogue,** now abandoned. The most photographed building in El-Jadida is certainly the spectacular underground **Portuguese Cistern** *(La Citerne Portugaise)* (open every day from 8:30 A.M.-12:00 P.M. and 2:00 P.M.-6:00 P.M., entry 10 DH). It can be reached from the main entrance to the city, along the main street, Rue Mohammed Ahchemi Bahbai (which also leads to the Sea Gate). The building, constructed in 1514, was initially used for storage, until, in 1542, it was transformed into a freshwater cistern, necessary in the event of a siege. The vaulted ceiling is supported by 25 pillars, a shaft of light comes in from a round hole in the roof, and the few inches of water covering the floor produce unbelievably strange reflections. (Orson Welles filmed part of his *Othello* here). Oddly enough, the cistern, which was buried under a mass of rubble, was only discovered by chance in 1916.

There is a French-speaking Catholic **church** in El-Jadida, the Eglise Saint-Bernard (Rue Assoudane, Tel: 35 26 16), attended by a fairly large

Christian community working mainly in the Jorf Lasfar phosphate complex, but also in Casablanca.

By taking the main P8 road (in the direction of Safi) and then left along the S105, you can return to Casablanca via Boulaounane Kasbah (66 km) and Settat (see above). The coastal road out of El-Jadida (in the direction of Oualidia) leads to **Sidi Bouzid** (7 km), which used to be a very simple place, but is now a thriving seaside resort, with lines upon lines of small villas, and lots of cafés and restaurants—and lots of people in August. Its beach looks nice, but the water is reported to be rather polluted. The **
Hotel Hacienda (Tel: 34 83 11) calls itself a private club, but is, in fact, open to the public. It has a pool, a tennis court, and a restaurant.

Going out of Sidi Bouzid, turning right towards the sea, one comes across the **Auberge Beauséjour,** but it didn't impress me much (it's okay for the sunset). Five kilometers further on, the village of **Mulay Abdallah** is situated beside the remains of the 12th-century *ribat* (fortified monastery) of **Tit** (the Almohad fortress said to have existed in El-Jadida is, in fact, this *ribat* south of the town). The ruins (which are not easy to find) are not particularly appealing for the casual visitor, but they do have historical interest.

Tit seems to have been built by a local Berber family to ward off attacks from the sea, and in 1513 it was captured by the Portuguese, only to be recaptured by the Wattasids a couple of years later, when its population is said to have been deported to somewhere near Fès. Mulay Abdallah was abandoned when the Portuguese arrived in the 15th century and much later became a small fishing village. The minaret of its *zaouia* dates from the end of the 12th century/early 13th century and is decorated in a style close to that of the Koutoubia minaret in Marrakech and the Tour Hassan in Rabat. Mulay Abdallah is well-known throughout Morocco for the huge *moussem* that is held there in August. Up to 200,000 people attend the festivities, which includes displays and *fantasias* by almost 15,000 richly harnessed horses and their riders from among the best in the country. If you like crowds and horses, this is an event not to be missed.

FURTHER AFIELD

Continuing further afield still, **south** from El-Jadida to **Oualidia** (167 km from Casablanca) down the coast along the pretty coastal S130, hungry or tired travelers can stop at the small * **Villa La Brise** at **Sidi Moussa** (37 km from El-Jadida on the coastal road, Tel: 34 69 17). Set above the road, with a lot of greenery, it looks out over the lagoon (boat-hire is possible) and has 24 simple double rooms, with water closet and shower, for 160 DH (half-board—breakfast and one additional meal—340 DH). It has a swimming pool, a restaurant (set meal 80 DH or 90 DH, said to be all right), and a bar. The nearby beach of Sidi Abad is one of the few that is reasonably safe. There are a couple of animated Friday markets on the way down to Oualidia, and numerous beaches, cafés, and restaurants. The road is a busy one, with trucks loading the vegetables and fruit that are grown in this fertile strip of land alongside the road.

The attractive little seaside resort of **Oualidia** makes a good destination for a meal or a night (76 km from El-Jadida). A day-excursion from Casablanca is also possible, but won't leave much time for swimming or surfing. Oualidia's name comes from the Saadian sultan El Oualid, who built a kasbah here in 1634 (now ruined). It is a favorite weekend destination for people from Casablanca and Marrakech, who appreciate its beach and wide lagoon protected by a rocky reef, which makes it a safe bathing place (but dangerous when the ebb tide races between the rocks). It is also known for its windsurfing and oyster beds. It can be reached by **car** or **bus** from El-Jadida or direct from Casablanca.

The **regional telephone code** is still 03 (0 omitted for in-region calls).

One of the most agreeable **hotels** is the *** **Hotel-Restaurant L'Hippocampe,** by the beach (signposted) (23 bungalows, singles 460 DH half-board, doubles 695 DH half-board, 2 suites at 1,500-2,000 DH, Tel: 36 61 08/36 64 99, Fax: 36 64 61). It has comfortable rooms (with impeccable water closets) opening onto a flower-filled little garden and a swimming pool. Nautical sports, boating, and kayaking can be arranged.

At the ** **Motel-Restaurant à L'Araignée Gourmande,** near the campsite and beach (15 rooms, half-board 200 DH per person, Tel: 36 64 47, Fax: 36 61 44), ask for a room overlooking the sea. **Reservations** are strongly advised for all hotels during the summer season.

The rooms in the * **Auberge de la Lagune,** on the main road with a good view over the bay, are rudimentary, but the staff is helpful and friendly (10 rooms, Tel: 36 64 78).

At the bottom of the range, the **Camping Oualidia Les Sables d'Or** is not bad for its kind (around 10 DH per person, per tent, per car). The **Hotel Chems** has been closed for some time.

For a **meal, L'Hippocampe** is popular at all times in the season and at other times for Sunday lunch, with fresh seafood, oysters, and lobsters a specialty. I usually eat there, but friends have found the food very average, with **L'Araignée Gourmande's** restaurant much better, serving oysters, seafood, and lobsters (menu at 75 DH).

La Langouste is also another reasonable eating-place. Fish is a specialty everywhere. **Surf** or **fun-board** enthusiasts can go to Surfland, near the beach, for equipment and/or instruction.

Some 40 km after Oualidia, it's worth stopping near the fort-like lighthouse at **Cap Beddouza** to admire the view across the Atlantic. Just before the lighthouse, a very fine, long beach makes a tempting place to swim (the **Auberge Bedouza** offers simple meals). Cap Beddouza is thought to have been the Cap Seloeis, where the Carthaginian admiral Hanno built a shrine in honor of Neptune.

Next comes another **Sidi Bouzid** and **Safi** (30 km). During World War II, part of General Patton's invasion forces landed with great ease near **Sidi Bouzid,** on November 8, 1942. A giant, **** hotel was in construction here, and almost completed, in the summer of 1999. The **Restaurant Refuge Sidi Bouzid** (see below) is indicated. The high cliffs just before Safi don't leave much chance of getting down for a swim.

The **general picture** of **Safi** is of a surprising mixture of **phosphates, sardines, pottery,** and **Portuguese.** A day should be enough to visit the main sights. The beginnings of the town are vague—it was first mentioned in the 11th century, under the name of Asfi, and other historians recorded that it was an active port in the 12th century and had a *ribat* (fortified monastery) by the 14th century. But it is only in the 15th century, with the arrival of the Portuguese, that Safi's history becomes better known. In 1481, the Portuguese established a trading post there, and in 1508 they seized the town, building a surrounding wall and a separate fortress overlooking the sea. They were masters of Safi until 1541, when the Saadian Mohammed ech-Cheikh forced them to retire. Safi remained Morocco's most important commercial port during the 17th century, trading with Europe. By the 19th century it had declined, but fortunately sardine fishing and canning, together with phosphate exportation, have revived it.

The huge silver-colored phosphate complex, however, has added nothing to the charm of Safi. Luckily, it is situated outside the city center, and the town is pleasant enough and little visited by tourists. The fishing port has several hundred registered boats, particularly active in summer, when they get their sardines off the Western Saharan coast and around Safi. A large part of Safi's canning industry deals with sardines, of which 90 percent find their way onto the European market. The 30-odd canning factories employ a largely female staff. More romantically, it was from Safi, in 1969, that Thor Heyerdahl launched his papyrus-built boat, *Ra I,* in an attempt to prove that the Egyptians could have reached and colonized the Americas. After the shipwreck of his first boat, Heyerdahl's second attempt with *Ra II* in May 1970 was successful in reaching Barbados.

A Jewish *moussem* is held in the synagogue every year in August and receives visitors from Europe, America, and Canada. The Jewish Sanctuary of Oulad ben Zmirour Bessaba is near the Hotel Safir.

Safi can be reached by **car** from El-Jadida by the main P8 (a good, fast road) or by the coastal 121. The CTM and all the usual **bus** companies run services to Safi from Casablanca and El-Jadida (four runs a day from

Casablanca by CTM). In the fall of 1998, the CTM launched a new non-stop service from Casablanca. **Local transport** is assured by **bus** and **little taxi** (white).

The **regional telephone code** for Safi is 04 (0 omitted for in-region calls).

Hotel charges fixed for this region (the same as Casablanca) are as follows (they vary according to the presence or absence of showers and water closet in the room): **** 793 DH or 799 DH, breakfast 53 DH or 67 DH; *** 186-306 DH or 213-347, breakfast 37 DH for both; ** 107-180 DH or 113-227, breakfast 26 DH for both; * 94-113 DH or 100-160, breakfast 24 DH for both.

The **hotel scene** has one hotel in the **most expensive** category, the **** **Hotel Safir** (90 rooms, Avenue Zerktouni, Tel: 46 42 99). The hotel has a spacious hall, a restaurant, bar, swimming pool, tennis court, conference rooms, and a nightclub. It is excellently situated, behind a large gate in the middle of a superb garden, with breathtaking views over Safi and the Atlantic.

The *** **Hotel Atlantide** (48 rooms, Rue Chawki, quite close to the Hotel Safir, Tel: 46 21 60) is vast and imposing and also has a very pretty garden and splendid views over the town. It is an old-established hotel and used to be the only good one in Safi. It is now run by the OCP Phosphate group and is consequently equipped with many conference rooms (which accounts for its deceptively large appearance). It has a restaurant and bar, and a swimming pool was under construction in the summer of 1998. Avoid the ground floor bedrooms, as they are not used much and tend to be a little musty.

The *** **Hotel Assif** (72 rooms, Avenue de la Liberté, near Place Mohammed V, just opposite the central market, Tel: 62 23 11, Fax: 62 18 62) used to be a ** establishment, but part of it is only 12 years old, with a new part added in 1996. It is a very flashy place, all pink and purple with shining white corridors, the rooms are large, comfortable, and well-equipped, with a little balcony, the reception staff very welcoming, and it can be warmly recommended. It has a restaurant.

Much less central is the ** **Hotel Anis** (Rue de R'bat, Tel: 46 30 78) (the ** **Hotel Les Mimosas** is not recommended).

As always, **budget accommodations** (around 100 DH) are difficult to propose. There are plenty of small hotels around the port and the medina, but the rooms are mostly small and the establishments noisy. Try the **Hotel L'Océan** (around 60 DH, Rue de R'bat, not far from the Hotel Anis, Tel: 46 42 07), which has washbasins and communal showers.

The campsite **Camping International Sidi Bouzid** is 3 km out of town on the Sidi Bouzid road (marked), and not very practical for travelers without transport (it is possible with a little taxi). It has some trees, a good view (not near the sea), hot showers (10 DH), and a pool (20 DH if in use) (12 DH per person, 10 DH per tent, 10 DH per car).

The **Hotels Safir** and **Atlantide** both have restaurants. The restaurant of the **Hotel Assif** provides an excellent meal, specializing in fish (vegetable soup 18 DH, a huge plate of grilled shrimp 47 DH, meat from 70 DH).

I have friends who strongly recommend the **Restaurant La Trattoria** for lunch (2 Route d'Aouinate, out of town, Tel: 62 09 59). The Italian dishes are supervised by the owner (fish, pasta, and main dish around 80 DH).

Le Refuge Sidi Bouzid, also out of town to Sidi Bouzid (3 km), by the sea, with a good view (Tel: 46 43 54) is also thought to be one of the best.

Back in town, I didn't enjoy my meal at the **Restaurant de la Poste** (40 Place de l'Indépendance, Tel: 46 31 75) and found the **Restaurant Gegene** (11 Rue de la Maraine, near Place de l'Indépendance, Tel: 46 33 69), serving fish, and the **Restaurant de Safi** (N° 3 same street), serving kebobs (slightly cheaper), a better value. For excellent grilled sardines and the like, try the **medina,** near the Big Mosque (around 30 DH with French fries, salad, and soft drink).

The **Castle of the Sea** *(Dar el-Bahr)* is a small, remarkably well preserved monument (restored in the 1960s) overlooking the sea, just outside the medina. Entry is by a staircase in a little lane. It was built by the Portuguese in the 16th century to protect the northern approaches to the port and to house the governor of the town. In the 17th and 18th centuries, the Moroccan sultans lodged here when visiting Safi. Many of the 17th-century cannons up on the platform were made in Spain, Portugal, Holland, and France. On the right of the entrance, the tower that held the prisoners can be visited (open 9:00 A.M.-12:00 P.M. and 2:30 P.M.-6:00 P.M., entry 10 DH). The **medina** is filled with craftsmen's workshops, small eating places, and merchants of all kinds. Behind the **Big Mosque** are the ruins of the **Portuguese Chapel.** The **Kechla** *(Borj el-Dar),* east of the medina, is housed within the 16th-century Portuguese ramparts. Access is through a massive gate in the walls, with crenellated towers. Inside is an open space (a parade ground or *mechouar*), and a little oratory. A mosque, a garden, and a palace *(Dar el-Makhzen)* were added in the 18th century. The building now houses the **National Ceramic Museum** *(Musée National de Céramique)* (open every day except Tuesday, from 9:00 A.M.-12:00 P.M. and 2:00 P.M.-6:00 P.M.—but I've often found it closed). The **Potters' Area** *(Quartier des Potiers)* lies to the north of the medina, outside the walls, and is well worth a visit, if only to watch the different stages in the production of the well-known Safi pottery: wheel-turning, firing, and decoration. Safi pottery does not reach the high technical level of Fès, but its designs are colorful and ingenious.

The Safi address list:

Banks—Place de l'Indépendance.

Church—mass in French at Eglise Saint-Vincent-de-Paul (16 Rue de Chefchaouen, Tel: 46 23 38).

Post Offices—Place de l'Indépendance; Sidi Mohammed Abdullah (off Place Mohammed V).

Telephones—same as the post office, but easier in the téléboutiques.

Tourist Information—*Syndicat d'Initiative*, Avenue Moulay Youssef (off Place Mohammed V).

The main P8 leads to the town of **Essaouira,** some 140 km further south (350 km from Casablanca). If you're really keen on ruins (but otherwise not worth the detour), the coastal 6537 road, 33 km south of Safi, brings you to **Souira Kedima** and the ruins of a small Portuguese fort built in 1521 and evacuated in 1525. Some 10 km further, after the ford, can be seen the ruins of **Kasbah Hamidouch,** built in the18th century by Mulay Ismail to keep an eye on movements north and south. Back on the main road, a sign soon announces that the "Argan Route has begun," but, in fact, it's hard to see these trees hidden among the olive trees.

Essaouira is an absolutely delightful little town on the coast, as yet unspoiled (and frankly a haven of calm compared to the hassles of Marrakech). Its small fishing port is lively and the medina is one of the cleanest in Morocco, with narrow streets, whitewashed houses, and blue-painted doors. Essaouira's inhabitants are polite and non-pestering. It never gets hotter than around 25°C, even when inland temperatures are around 40°C. On the other hand, it's windy . . . and an ideal place for surfers (the World Cup Flysurf Pro was held here in June 1999, attracting the world's best surfers for four days of competition). Half a day will get you through the sights, but it would be a pity not to profit from the exceptional charm of the town and stay overnight. But watch out—in August it is absolutely packed!

Essaouira can be reached by **air** twice a week from Casablanca (45 minute flight), now that the Essaouira-Mogador Airport has been opened, and by **car** or **bus.** The CTM does two daily runs from Casablanca, and other buses run from Safi and Agadir. Once there, it's small enough to be inspected on **foot,** though **bicycles** can be hired from a man near the Place Prince Moulay Hassan.

Long before any humans set foot in Essaouira, the region was inhabited by giant reptiles. In 1998, the fossilized bones of one of these large beasts were discovered east of the town, on the right back of the River Qsob. They date to the Jurassic period (195 million years ago).

The Phoenicians came here in the 7th century B.C., followed by the Carthaginians. Excavations on one of the offshore islands unearthed a

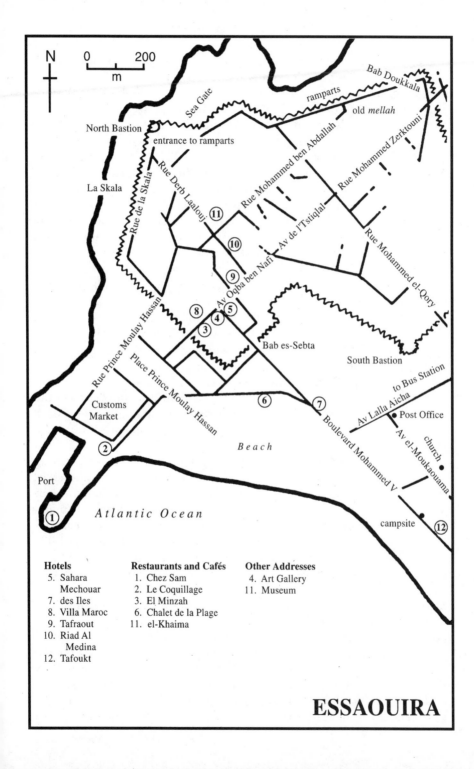

Hotels
5. Sahara Mechouar
7. des Iles
8. Villa Maroc
9. Tafraout
10. Riad Al Medina
12. Tafoukt

Restaurants and Cafés
1. Chez Sam
2. Le Coquillage
3. El Minzah
6. Chalet de la Plage
11. el-Khaima

Other Addresses
4. Art Gallery
11. Museum

ESSAOUIRA

pottery sherd inscribed with the name of the Carthaginian admiral Hanno. A Greek voyager in the 4th century B.C. noted that the people who inhabited the coast around Essarouira were very fond of elephant ivory, since they drank out of ivory goblets, the women had ivory necklaces, and "even" the horses had ivory ornaments. At the end of the 1st century B.C., Juba II, king of Mauretania, established a center for the production of the famous purple dye obtained from the local *murex* shellfish. In the 10th century A.D., the town became known as Amogdur, after its Berber patron saint, Sidi Mogdul, and exported from its port produce from all over southern Morocco. The Portuguese, always on the move, installed a trading post there in the 15th century, and in 1506 built a small fort (now ruined) to protect the entrance to the port. They encouraged trade and the exploitation of the sugar cane plantations of the interior, but didn't stay long in the town. Essouira had no truly safe port, and the Portuguese doubtless preferred to concentrate their energies on El-Jadida, Safi, and Agadir.

The Saadian sultan Abd el-Malik rebuilt the place a bit in 1628, but it was not 1764 that the town really took off, thanks to the Alaouite sultan, Mohammed III, who decided to turn it into a naval base. It seems that Sidi Mohammed's choice of Essaouira came from his desire to punish Agadir, a town which openly defied him and took the lion's share of European trade. Determined to do a good job, the sultan entrusted the design of the new town to a French prisoner. So its roads were straight, cutting each other at right angles, and the whole place was surrounded with French-style ramparts. Mogador became re-baptized Essaouira ("the picture," said to refer to the Frenchman's plan), and Sidi Mohammed set about making a commercial success of his new town. The foreign consuls established in Rabat and Agadir were ordered to take up residence in Essaouira, rich Moroccan families were invited to settle there, and an important community of Jewish merchants, with their intimate knowledge of European languages and business methods, help trade to expand. By 1780, almost 1,000 Europeans were involved in a dozen commercial enterprises and 40 percent of maritime trade passed through Essaouira. It was here that U.S. Consul General, Thomas Barclay, landed in June 1786 on his way to Marrakech to negotiate a treaty of friendship with the Moroccan sultan. Under the Protectorate, the improvement of the ports of Agadir, and especially Casablanca, halted much of this trade, though it was then that the modern town grew up outside the ramparts. Plans are afoot for the "development" of the town, including an ambitious series of museums, galleries, and art schools, perhaps financed by the European Union. For the sake of visitors, let's hope that Essaouira retains its simple charm and doesn't get spoiled by all this expansion.

The **regional telephone code** is 04 (omit the 0 for in-region calls).

There are 27 hotels in Essaouira: 7 classified, ranging from **** down to the 20 non-classified. Low season hotel charges fixed for this region (the same as Marrakech) are as follows (they vary according to the presence or absence of showers and water closet in the room): **** 403-503 DH or 516-1,155, breakfast 53-88 DH for both; *** 201-319 DH or 227-460 DH, breakfast 40 DH for both; ** 110-191 DH or 119-290 DH, breakfast 26 DH for both; * 100-147 DH or 105-169 DH, breakfast 25 DH for both. High season charges are slightly more.

At the moment, the **most expensive hotel** is the **** **Hotel des Iles** (well indicated) (75 rooms, the only hotel suitable for wheelchair travelers, since most of the rooms are ground-floor, level with the swimming pool, Boulevard Mohammed V, Tel: 78 46 20, Fax: 47 24 72). It struck me as being a little bit shabby when I visited it, but it has now been repainted. As well as the nice pool, it has a restaurant, a bar, and (apparently) a night-club. The staff is very helpful and pleasant.

Slightly cheaper, but I would rate it higher on aesthetic grounds, is the *** English-run **Hotel Villa Maroc** (15 rooms, 10 Rue Abdallah ben Yacine, just within the ramparts, from 600 DH, Tel: 47 31 47, Fax: 47 28 06). It is made up of two Moroccan houses put together, and many of my friends will only stay there. It has, indeed, a very special atmosphere (very intimate) and is beautifully furnished. The plumbing is not top-notch, but the water is hot and breakfast can be taken on the roof-top. It's a good place to go in September (otherwise book well in advance).

The *** **Hotel Riad al-Medina** (27 rooms, 9 Rue Derb Laalouj, in the medina, Tel: 47 27 27, Fax: 47 29 07) used to be the private house of a pacha, then was turned into the Hotel du Pacha in the 1960s and recently renovated, so it looks just like a superior Moroccan house, built around a central courtyard. In the hippie days it was frequented by celebrities such as Jimmy Hendrix, Cat Stevens, and others. It has a restaurant and sauna.

A *** hotel, on the right as you come into town, is the blue and white painted **Hotel Tafoukt** (40 rooms, Boulevard Mohammed V, Tel: 47 25 04, Fax: 78 44 16). It's a friendly place and has a restaurant and bar, though the rooms are small (some with balconies overlooking the sea) and it's over a kilometer out of town.

Moving down to the **medium-price hotels,** there is the ** **Hotel Sahara** (70 rooms, Avenue Oqba ben Nafi, Tel: 47 22 92) (not a very attractive building) that looks across at the ramparts and is conveniently located.

For **budget accommodations,** there is the * **Hotel Mechouar** (27 rooms, Avenue Oqba ben Nafi, next door to the Hotel Sahara, Tel: 47 28 28) and the **Hotel Tafraout** (around 100 DH, 7 Rue de Marrakech, in the medina, Tel: 47 21 20), which is pretty simple (not all the bedrooms have showers).

A British woman, **Jane Loveless** (16 Rue el Yamen, Tel/Fax: 47 63 47) has one or two pleasant rooms for rent with kitchen facilities (140 DH double). All the other small hotels, under 100 DH—and there are about a dozen which could reasonably be tried if you don't mind roughing it—are pretty rudimentary with cleanish rooms, but shared toilet facilities. Among these, I've had good reports on the **Hotel Majestic** (50 DH), which has been freshly painted and is relatively clean (basin in room, but communal water closets and showers). The town campsite, **Camping International** (along Boulevard Mohammed V, on the right, past the Hotel des Iles), is not good. The French Accor group has plans to open a hotel and thalassotherapy (a form of water therapy) institute in Essaouira in the near future, to be called the Sofitel Thalassa (the hotel will have120 rooms, with the thalasso institute able to welcome 80 guests). Keen followers of this specialty should look out for its arrival.

Alternative hotel accommodations are provided at the **Auberge Tangaro,** 5 km out of town on the Agadir road (indicated on the right) (little blue taxis will go there) (17 rooms, half-board only at 450 DH per person), in a calm and beautiful setting, quite romantic (there is no electricity). There is a **campsite** next door to the Auberge. Shortly after the turn off for the Auberge Tangaro, the **Hotel Jasmin** (with adjoining campsite) could be tried if all is booked up in Essaouira.

The **Hotel Villa Maroc** provides just about the best place for **dining** (evening only, order in advance), in a refined setting with a delicious and unusual menu. If you want a more animated, crowded atmosphere, **Chez Sam** is where you'll find it (at the very end of the fishing port, Tel: 47 35 13). It serves excellent fish dishes and is highly recommended by anyone who has eaten there, but I personally found it slightly overrated (set menu from 100 DH, licensed for beer and wine).

On the way to Chez Sam, **Le Coquillage** has much the same fish menu at much the same price. The restaurant **El Minzah** (3 Avenue Oqba ben Nafi, Tel: 47 23 08) has a good set menu at around 80 DH.

Just about opposite the Hotel des Iles, the restaurant **Chalet de la Plage** (Boulevard Mohammed V, Tel: 47 29 72) is an excellent choice for a lunch looking out over the sea. They serve fish, of course (menu around 100 DH, licensed). For those fed up with fish, Moroccan cooking can be sampled at **Restaurant el-Khaima** (Rue Derb Laalouj, on the square, Tel: 47 30 52) for around 80 DH/set menu (licensed). It is inclined to be crowded with tour groups at lunchtime. The list of small restaurants would be long. Most of them provide very good fried or grilled fish.

Nightlife in Essaouira is limited to a soft drink at one of the many cafés or a nip of something stronger at the **Hotel des Iles** (which says it has a nightclub) or the **Chalet de la Plage.**

The **port** is a good place to start visiting **Essaouira.** It lies at the foot of the ramparts and is extremely lively, especially when the boats come in and discharge their catch. There are generally one or two wooden fishing boats under construction on the quayside. From there, plunge into the **medina** and get to the entrance to the **ramparts** and the **North Bastion** *(Bastion du Nord)* protecting the **La Skala battery,** with its 18th- and 19th-century cannons (at the end of Rue de la Skala, off Rue Prince Moulay Hassan). (Orson Welles shot scenes for his *Othello* here as well). The 200-meter long Skala was one of several gun batteries that Mohammed III placed around the bay—at the entrance to the port, on one of the islands, and to the south of the town. Along the ramparts to the right is the **Sea Gate** (Bab el-Bahr), its date carved on the pediment (1184 in the Moslem calendar).

After the Skala and the ramparts, a stroll back along the Rue de la Skala enables the visitor to look at the tiny **workshops** under the ramparts where Essaouira's master craftsmen turn out the wooden objects for which the town is famous. This is an absolute must, for the visit is both fascinating and provides an occasion for a bit of **shopping** (not much bargaining)—anything from large tables to small boxes, made from the local thuya wood, inlaid with the wood of lemon and walnut trees and mother-of-pearl. The **medina** is also a charming place in which to wander around. It has **markets** specializing in jewelry, spices and herbs, carpets, and clothing. The Rue Mohammed Zerktouni runs through the old *mellah* (Jewish district), in the very northeast corner of the medina, as far as Bab Doukkala. There may well have been at least 4,000 Jews in Essaouira at the end of the 19th century (the old Jewish cemetery lies on the sea-edge and is frequently washed over by the waves; however, some of the Hebrew inscriptions are still legible). At present, this run-down district is estimated to house 7,000 people—far too many for the age of its buildings—and a pilot project is in the air to improve living conditions there. Outside the Bab Doukkala gate can be seen the **European cemetery,** recalling Essaouira's cosmopolitan population in the 19th century. There is, in fact, still a functioning **Catholic church** in the town, the Eglise Notre Dame de l'Assomption, serving the few Europeans working in the area and summer tourists.

It is possible to **hire a boat** and go out to the **islands** *(Les îles Purpuraires),* now a **bird sanctuary.** In Sultan Hassan I's day there was a prison, and before that the islands were well known for its *murex,* a purple-producing shell. This can usually only be done out of the nesting season (the protected bird is Eleanora's Falcon and it is in residence from the spring through the fall). Ask for information at the *Syndicat d'Initiative* (Rue du Caire, just inside the ramparts, Tel: 47 36 30). **Birdwatchers** with binoculars can watch the falcons, gulls, and waders around the port and along the seashore.

The **Sidi Mohammed ben Abdallah Museum** (Rue Derb Laalouj, opposite the Restaurant el-Khaima) is located in an old palace and displays local craftwork, including musical instruments and Jewish and Arab jewelry and textiles (open 9:00 A.M.-12:00 P.M. and 2:30 P.M.-6:30 P.M., closed Tuesdays, entry 5 DH). It is well worth the visit for an idea of the rich, age-old traditions that are still cherished. Much more recently, Essaouira has achieved a big reputation as an **artistic center,** a reputation it already had to a certain extent from the middle of the 18th century, when poets, writers, and craftsmen settled there.

The **Frédéric Damgard Art Gallery** (Avenue Oqba ben Nafi, Tel: 78 44 46, Fax: 47 28 57) was certainly not responsible for the flowering of so much young local talent, but its creation by an inspired Dane gave these self-taught painters and sculptors the chance to make their work known. Many have become well-known outside Morocco, for their works—"primitive," "naïve," "pop"—have a great appeal (open 9:00 A.M.-1:00 P.M. and 3:00 P.M.-7:00 P.M. Other galleries are also open for a visit.

In June 1998, Essaouira hosted the first **International Festival of Gnaoua Culture,** bringing together concerts, exhibitions, and speakers from many countries to listen to and look at the multiple aspects of Ghaoua music and culture (see "Music" section, chapter 3). The second "edition" of this festival was held in 1999.

Sportswise, Essaouira caters almost exclusively to wind-surfers, and is Morocco's best-known location for this sport. In any event, it's a chilly place for a swim, although there are marvelous long stretches of sand. The best beaches for surfing lie south of the town, as far as **Diabet** and **Cap Sim** (Marrakech and Agadir road). Diabet used to be well known in hippie circles, but has now dropped out of the international scene. The Ocean Vagabond Windsurf Center, on the beach on the left as you come in, promises all sorts of surfing possibilities, as well as equipment. Horseback riding on the beach in the summer can be arranged from here. About 15 km out of Essaouira, on the P8 road to Agadir, a road to the right leads to a white-domed sanctuary (the *kubba* of Sidi Kaouki) (27 km from Essaouira). The road doesn't quite reach **Sidi Kaouki beach,** a great surfing destination. About 500 m from the shrine, near the beach, the **Résidence Kaouki Beach,** run by the Hotel Villa Maroc of Essaouira (10 rooms, Tel: 47 31 47, Fax: 47 28 06) is much appreciated by surfers. It is clean and comfortable, has communal showers, no electricity, and good food. It's a fun place to go to with kids or a group of friends. But the bathing is very dangerous, and only suitable for experienced surfers. Along here, too, is the **Auberge de la Plage,** at the end of the paved road on the left (information from Cobra Tours at Mirleft—Agadir—Tel/Fax: 08-71 90 56). It's run by an Italian and a German girl, who are both most welcoming. The latter has a horse-back riding club and arranges rides in the neighborhood.

The Essaouira address list:

Banks—Place Prince Moulay Hassan.

Bicycle rental—Restaurant Chez Toufik (in small road just off Avenue Moulay Hassan).

Car park—there's a big parking area, by the Customs port area.

Church—mass in French at Eglise Notre Dame de l'Assomption (behind the post office, Tel: 47 58 95).

Post Office—Avenue Al-Mouqawama.

Telephones—next to the post office, but best use the numerous téléboutiques.

Tourist information—Rue du Caire. Quite helpful, and has small French-language books on the town.

Back on the P8 road, going south, 163 km further on will see you in **Agadir** (chapter 11). The road, not designed for fast driving, winds and climbs around the tail end of the High Atlas, with some stunning views as it nears Agadir. There are many more argan trees here than before Essaouira, and the amber-colored liquid sold in bottles from plastic-covered stalls is not honey but argan oil. The road passes beside immense stretches of golden sands and through numerous small seaside resorts, with cafés, beach umbrellas, and beach huts.

7. Guided Tours

There are no guided tours of Casablanca. Daily tours of the **Hassan II Mosque** are accompanied by the mosque's own guide (English, French, and Spanish speaking tours, but arrive early to get the language/tour you want), included in the price of the entry ticket (the only way for a non-Moslem to see the inside) (visits daily except Friday, 9:00 A.M., 10:00 A.M., 11:00 A.M., and 2:00 P.M., entry 100 DH. They last about an hour). There are, of course, plenty of town guides around, but their services are not necessary in Casablanca. The town's streets and directions are well indicated, and it's not difficult to get around, with the help of the small taxis.

8. Culture

As yet there are no **museums** in Casablanca, though plans are always in the air. On the other hand there are plenty of private **art galleries,** exhibiting and selling the works of contemporary Moroccan artists and, from time to time, paintings by foreigners. **Venise Cadre** (65 Rue Allal ben Abdallah,

Tel: 31 05 76) only takes well-established artists, while the **Galerie Nadar** (5 Rue Al Manaziz, Maarif, Tel: 23 00 18) is prepared to take risks with rising talent. The **Al Manar** gallery (Dawliz Complex, Boulevard de la Corniche) has interesting exhibitions of well-known and less well-known artists.

The **Galerie Bassamat** (2 Rue Pierre Curie, Tel: 20 26 45, same management as the restaurant L'Atelier above) is also well worth a visit. In the "air" for a long time, a "museum" of modern and contemporary art, baptized *La Villa des Arts*, opened its doors in June 1999. Created by a private foundation, and using a beautiful villa that had been empty for many years, the museum-gallery will put on long-term exhibitions of Moroccan artists (Boulevard Brahim Roudani, opposite the police station). **Carrefour des Arts** (Corner Rue Daguerre/Chereuil, just off Boulevard du Phare) not only has exhibitions, but workshops for children and talks on cultural subjects. Various **hotels** (such as the Safir and Idou Anfa), **banks** (Espace Wafabank, 163 Avenue Hassan II), and **bookshops** (Librairie Omar el-Khayam, 283, Boulevard Ziraoui, Tel: 21 31 98) have occasional exhibitions. The **Frédéric Damgard gallery** in Essaouira (see "Sightseeing") puts on regular exhibitions of modern artists.

There are several national **cultural centers.** The **American Cultural Center, Dar America** (10 Place Bel Air, Tel: 22 14 60), has a library that can be consulted and occasional talks and video films (mostly about American life and politics). The **French Cultural Center** (*Institut Français de Casablanca,* 121 Boulevard Zerktouni, Tel: 25 21 21), the **German Institut Goethe** (Place du 16 Novembre), and the **Spanish Instituto Cervantes** (31 Rue d'Alger) all exhibit young and unknown artists from time to time and put on concerts and exhibitions.

9. Sports

Sports in Casablanca are mainly **aquatic,** though **golf** enthusiasts are at the center of a network of good courses. The Hotel Royal Mansour can organize golf weekends throughout Morocco (ask for their "Golf Package"), but three 18-hole and two 9-hole courses are within easy distance of Casablanca and there is a 9-hole course in the town itself. Green fees vary from between 250-300 DH, and caddies cost around 70 DH. In Casablanca itself, the 9-hole **Anfa Golf Club,** 2,710 m, par 35 (Rampe d'Anfa, Tel: 36 10 26/ 36 53 57, closed Monday) is a nice little course, but inclined to be crowded. It's also not playable when there is horseracing, as the routes cross.

The **Royal Golf de Mohammedia** is the nearest 18-hole course (28 km north of Casablanca, closed Tuesdays). It was opened in 1924 and its challenging 18 holes cover a distance of 5,917 m, partly beside the sea, for a par of 72. It's full of charm, but the pollution from the oil refinery is a bit disagreeable. The **Royal Golf de Benslimane** is a nice little 9-hole course, par 36 (25 km along the expressway, exit Mohammedia Est, toll 8 DH, then a further 15 km). Further out (70 km south of Casablanca), the **Royal Golf of El-Jadida,** (18-holes, 6,270 m, par 72), is one of the most recent courses to be constructed. Designed by Cabell B. Robinson, it is a beautiful course set in superb surroundings (300 DH at the weekend, 250 DH during the week, 75 DH to rent a ½ series of six clubs, caddie obligatory, 70 DH). It has the advantage of an excellent hotel attached (see El-Jadida above). The three courses in Rabat, at the **Royal Dar es-Salam** golf club, are described in chapter 6. The 9-hole **Royal Golf Universitaire de Settat** (70 km south of Casablanca), 3,215 m for a par of 37, is a new course, using part of the race-course, is not particularly interesting, but unencumbered and a caddie is not obligatory. It's good for a game on the way to Marrakech, perhaps.

The beaches around Casablanca are dangerous for **swimmers.** The majority of young Casablancans go to the closest, **Ain Diab,** so it's very crowded, or around **Sidi Abd er-Rahman.** Football is popular on all the Casablanca beaches. Otherwise, the best beaches are northeast in **Mohammedia** (see entry below) or southeast to **Dar Bouazza, Tamaris, Jack Beach,** and others. In addition to the hotels and clubs (such as Sun Beach and Tropicana), public pools are limited to the **Tahiti** (12 pools, 5 of them for adults), which has direct access to the beach, the **Miami** (9 pools, 5 for adults, more sheltered from the waves than the others), and the **Kon-Tiki** (12 pools, mainly for children). The last one also has a heated indoor pool and four restaurants. The price for these three establishments is roughly the same: 45-50 DH during the week, a bit more at weekends and holidays.

The **Miami Fitness Club** (Boulevard de la Corniche, Ain Diab, Tel: 94 97 83, Fax: 94 97 86) also has a heated pool (see prices below). **Windsurfing** is practiced at Mohammedia, Oualidia, and Essaouira (see earlier), a long way from Casablanca, and the Oued Mellah lake, nearer at hand (see chapter 6, Rabat). For further information, ring Surfland, or Jeff Blakeman Surf School (21 Rue Ilya Abou Madi, Gauthier, Tel: 27 75 70, Fax: 36 61 10).

Squash can be played at the **Hotel Sheraton,** the **Hyatt Hotel,** and the **Miami Fitness Club.** This last place has a whole set-up of gyms (men and women separated), muscle-building equipment, badminton and volleyball room, jacuzzi, sauna, *hammam,* beauty parlor (water therapy, massage, hairdressing, etc.), and a restaurant (25 DH entry plus 120 DH the meal), as well as a heated pool and a squash court (entry to the club is 200 DH/day).

Horses can be ridden along the sands and in a number of riding schools on the outskirts of Casablanca. Contact the stables listed in the address list below. Outside of Casablanca, horseback riding can be arranged at several places much further down the coast, including Sidi Kaouki, south of Essaouira.

If you are into **yoga,** the *Association Marocaine de Yoga* (A.M.Y.), 21 Rue des Asphodels, will give information on all the yoga professors and classes in Casablanca and even elsewhere. For **tai-shi** (tai-chi) enthusiasts, try Tel: 52 23 12 for information. Communication may be difficult, as this is a fairly low-level activity and there's not always someone at the end of the line (and even if there is he may only speak Arabic).

10. Shopping

Two areas in Casablanca provide a concentration of shops selling Moroccan articles: **Boulevard Houphouet Boigny** and the **Habous** (New Medina). They sell all kinds of things, from carpets to kaftans and *gandouras* for women, leather slippers, wallets, brass trays, and teapots—whatever you fancy. The shops in the Habous particularly are frequented by Moroccan women and I regularly pick up a cheap cotton *gandoura* there. There is only one way of going shopping in these areas—go and have a look into all the shops before deciding. Then start the bargaining technique (see chapter 3). The articles in **Aux Curiosités Marocaines** (8 Boulevard Houphouet Boigny) and **Le Petit Bateau** (just opposite), both run by an Indian family, are not particularly cheap, but the prices are fixed and there isn't any bargaining. As always, it's good to have a look around and check prices at the **Craftwork Center** (*Délégation de l'Artisanat*, 195 Boulevard de Bordeaux, off Boulevard Zerktouni, almost at the sea). **Aux Arts Islamiques** (15 Passage Tazi, off Avenue Hassan II, near Place des Nations Unies, Tel: 26 16 12), has authentic Berber amber necklaces, silver bracelets, rings, and fibules—you name it (not exactly cheap). For amusing little gifts, Moroccan and other, the **Citron Vert** (81 Rue Abou Salt Andalussi, Maarif, Tel: 25 69 20) is a good address.

If going down the coast to **Safi,** don't miss looking around the potteries. Safi is one of the big Moroccan pottery centers. Further south, the town of **Essaouira** is renowned for its woodworking, and you can buy anything from a tiny box to a large table (see "Sightseeing" section for details on Safi and Essaouira).

If you want to give a terribly expensive gift of imported china, silver, or glass to a special Moroccan friend, there is **Rhapsodie** (2 Boulevard du Phare, off Boulevard Abdellatif ben Kaddour).

For easy shopping for everyday stuff, the **Romandie II Hyperpermarket** (305 Boulevard Bir Anzarane) is well stocked with imported goods. I cannot recommend the **Marjane Supermarket** (on the fringes of Casablanca, on the Route de Bouskoura, the road to Mohammed V Airport) which has a lot of goods on display, but most of the registers are closed when I go there, so it's a real pain trying to pay and get out. **Alpha 55** (Avenue Mers Sultan, near the French Consulate) is a fairly low-class department store, but if you want to buy some socks or hankies, it'll do.

The **American Bookstore** (beside the American Language Center, 1 Place de la Fraternité, Boulevard Moulay Youssef) is the only place for English-language books. It stocks a range of subjects: business, economics, literature, social sciences, Islam and the Arabic World, modern fiction—including translations of Moroccan authors—and non-fiction. There are also a few titles for kids. Good bookshops for French-language books, including some very fine illustrated works, are **Carrefour des Livres** (71 Rue des Landes, Maarif) and **Librairie Omar Khayam** (283 Boulevard Ziraoui, Tel: 20 31 98). Two recommended photographic studios are **Studio Jauson** (Place du Puy de Dôme, Maarif, Tel: 25 08 20), which has a nice selection of large unframed photographs of Morocco, and **Central Color** (50 Rue d'Alger, Tel: 27 69 68). Both are very reliable for developing and printing. Many other smaller studios will produce passport photographs while you wait.

The shop with the best reputation for Moroccan pastries in Casablanca is **Bennis,** in the Habous area of the New Medina (2 Rue Fkih el-Gabbas—but anyone will tell you where they are). They've also opened up a branch downtown (112 Avenue du 2 Mars). Their New Medina shop is always crowded with Moroccans buying a wide variety of sticky, honey-coated, or almond pastries to take away (especially during Ramadan, when these sweet items are a must). The **Pâtisserie La Normande** (213 Boulevard Mohammed V) goes in for French-style pastries.

Also on Boulevard Mohammed V (N° 32), the **Pâtisserie-Confiserie Trianon** does very temping French pastries and chocolates, and so does **La Petite Friande** (338 Rue Mostapha el-Maani). If you're hankering for delicious chocolates, there are a number of specialized shops: **La Dragée d'Or** (221 Boulevard d'Anfa), **Chereau** (25 Rue el-Kadi Iass), and **Jeff de Bruges** (opposite Carrefour des Livres, 37 Rue du Marché, Maarif).

11. Entertainment and Nightlife

Casablanca offers a wide range of entertainment and nightlife, but in the small towns such as El-Jadida, Safi, and Essaouira the only places to enjoy a drink (other than a fruit juice or coffee) are the big hotels.

The best **movie theaters** in Casablanca are the **Rialto Cinema** (35 Rue Mohammed el-Quorri, Tel: 26 26 32), which has recently been reopened after extensive renovation, providing seating for 1,100 people (its 13 x 8 meter screen is one of its improvements), the **Dawliz Complex** (Boulevard de la Corniche/Rue de Nantes, opposite McDonald's, Tel: 36 48 81), with two projection rooms (it's clean and with comfortable seating), its downtown counterpart, the **Dawliz Habous** (Tour des Habous, Avenue des F.A.R., behind the Hotel Sheraton, Tel: 31 48 22), and the **Lynx Cinema** (150 Avenue Mers Sultan, Tel: 22 02 29).

The **Sindibad Amusement Park** (down the coast at Sidi Abd er-Rahman) is a good place to take small kids (but don't wander off into the surrounding woods) (take bus N° 90 from Place de la Concorde, near the Hyatt Hotel). They have indoor and outdoor karting areas.

Many Moroccan families picnic on the weekends or exercise their dogs in the **Bouskoura** forest (on the left, just outside Casablanca on the road to the airport—14 km from the center of town). The **Zoo** at **Temara** is also a possibility for bored youngsters (see chapter 6), and it's better than the small **Casablanca Zoo** at Ain Sebaa, which is, however, much closer. **Horseracing** takes place at the Anfa Golf Club every Friday afternoon (except during Ramadan). There is an outdoor **karting** center on the way to Benslimane (about 5 km after the exit from the expressway).

For an **evening drink,** depending on your tastes, you have the bars in **all the big hotels.** These are the best places for women travelers. The glass-domed garden area in the **Hotel Royal Mansour** is particularly agreeable. In the **Hyatt Regency** you can find The Casablanca Bar, to the left, that aims to recall the film *Casablanca.* The piano is there, but not much else except a few photos of the stars. Don't expect exciting spies and the1940s atmosphere (soft drinks from 25 DH, beer 40 DH, spirits from 80 DH; during the "happy hour" the second drink is free) (Interesting tidbit: Ronald Reagan was scheduled to play the role of "Rick," but it went to Humphry Bogart instead).

Another piano bar can be found in the **Kenzi al-Mounia Hotel** (and a "happy hour"). The Panoramique Bar at the top of the **Hotel Idou Anfa** (16th floor) has the advantage of a splendid view over the town ("happy hour" is 6:00 P.M.-8:00 P.M.). The "happy hour" at the **Hotel el-Kandar** is from 7:00 P.M.-8:00 P.M. The **Hotel Sheraton** has a karaoké bar.

For a **drink** and a look at local life, especially in the summer, there is nothing better than a stroll along the **Corniche** that starts, approximately, at the far side of the Hassan II Mosque (bus N° 9 goes to Ain Diab, N° 15 to the El Hank Lighthouse, both from Place Oued el-Makhazine, near the Hyatt Hotel, N° 90 to Sindibad Amusement Park, N° 11 to the Mosque, both from Place de la Concorde). There are lots of cafés, restaurants, nightclubs, and drinking places. Local animation is guaranteed.

The Churchill Club (1 Rue de la Méditerranée, Ain Diab) is an English-speaking club reserved for members, but temporary membership is possible for a month's stay and more casual visitors can telephone **Miloud** (Tel: 36 72 80) and arrange to be signed in by a member. It's a good place for a drink or a meal in a British atmosphere (but not quite like a UK club, for all that). The **U.S. Seaman's Center** (near the port, 118 Boulevard Moulay Abderrahman, Tel: 30 99 50) is a casual, friendly place with a bar, pinball machines, and a restaurant.

English-speaking women (of whatever nationality) with time to spare can come as paying guests to meetings and functions of the **American International Women's Club,** held in The Churchill Club. It's an ideal place in which to meet women from many countries, including Morocco. Meetings take place on the first Thursday of every month (from 9:00 A.M.), and there are lunches or teas on most of the other Thursdays (Tel: 36 72 80 or call in at The Churchill Club for information).

Evening drinking and **music** is also well provided for along the Corniche. **Armstrong's** (behind the Villa Fandango) plays jazz, blues, and soul music, is noisy and crowded, but the clients are okay (no entry fee, drinks around 100 DH). The **Caf'Conce,** off the Corniche, has all kinds of music, plus salads and soups (drinks from 90 DH). The **Lido,** next to the Riad Salam Hotel (see above), is a good place for a drink (beer 25 DH), and you can play American snooker there.

Jimmy's Discotheque and Piano Bar is another popular rendezvous in the Lido. The **Tex-Mex** is currently popular with young people (bar, music, American snooker, no dancing; no entry fee, drinks from 80 DH). Alas, nothing seems to have replaced the **Banana Café,** which went up in smoke a few years back. They had a marvelous singer (American, French, and English songs) and you could eat there. All the **big hotels** have **bars** where one can have a quiet drink, often with piano or other music.

Late-night entertainment can be had in the Moroccan restaurant in the Hyatt Hotel and the **El-Bahia** restaurant in Holiday Inn Hotel, both of which have an **evening show** with dinner. The **Kenzi al-Mounia Hotel** puts on an evening show (dancers or musicians).

Discos and nightclubs can be found in all the big hotels, in shady areas around the port, and around the up-market Ain Diab and Corniche area. The hotels are the best bet, but many—especially the young—find them dull and expensive. In any event, all nightclubs are frequented by "working girls." Single women travelers will get "tempting" offers, and unaccompanied men will also be solicited for a drink or two.

Caesar's, in the Sheraton, appeals to a slightly older crowd and is comparatively "clean" (entry about 200 DH, drinks from 200 DH, bottle of whisky 900 DH). The **Black House** in the Hyatt Regency has been improved recently. It attracts younger people, with lots of Saudis and Moroccans (drinks from 100-150 DH).

Most of the other discos and nightclubs are concentrated along the Corniche in the Ain Diab district. Practically none of them have a street number. Roughly in order, coming from the center of town, you have **Le Village** (11 Boulevard de la Corniche, just after the Lido, on the left, opposite Tahiti pool) catering to a very young crowd (under 20), mostly Moroccan. The **Villa Fandango** (Rue Mer Egee, just behind restaurant Croc Magnon, Boulevard de la Corniche) is a good place, very crowded, mostly frequented by people in their 30s. Further along from Le Village, **La Notte,** a low building marked "Restaurant, Bar, Nightclub" (25 Boulevard de la Corniche, Tel: 36 73 61) (noisy) is also very popular with well-heeled youngsters (under 25) from the Casablanca American School and the French Lycée Lyautey (entry 100 DH, including first drink, next drinks from 100 DH). It has a reputation for being well kept and won't let in unaccompanied males.

The **Balcon 33** (33 Boulevard de la Corniche), another low, whitepainted building, opposite the Miami swimming pools, is a restaurant until 11:00 P.M. (food average and fairly expensive at around 200 DH/meal, and service is not very good) and then graduates into a nice nightclub with dancing (mixed ages). Further along on the right after the Hotel Bellerive and before the Hotel Suisse, a very Moroccan nightclub with *chkhiats* (professional women dancers/"working girls") is the rather quaint **Tio Pepe** (Boulevard de la Corniche, near Hotel Atlantis, Tel: 36 01 89), where you can also eat and dance.

Outside Casablanca, a big attraction with the young crowd at the moment is the **Bouznika Beach Club,** on the beach at Bouznika (about 45 km north east of Casablanca, off the expressway). Entry is 150 DH, including the first drink (then beer 60 DH, soft drinks 40 DH, and dancing).

12. The Casablanca Address List

Airlines—Air France, 15 Avenue des F.A.R. (Tel: 29 40 40); British Airways, Place Zellaqa (Tel: 22 94 64 for reservations, Tel: 33 95 24 for information); Iberia, 17 Avenue des F.A.R. (Tel: 27 96 00); KLM, 6 Boulevard Houphouet Boigny (Tel: 20 32 22); Lufthansa, Tour des Habous, Avenue des F.A.R. (Tel: 31 23 71); Royal Air Maroc, 44 Avenue des F.A.R. (Tel: 31 11 22); Sabena, 41 Avenue des F.A.R. (Tel: 31 39 91); Swissair, Tour des Habous, Avenue des F.A.R. (Tel: 31 32 80).

Airport—information Airport Mohammed V (Tel: 33 90 40).

Ambulance—the *Sapeurs-Pompiers* (Fire Brigade) have an emergency ambulance service (Tel: 15).

Banks—Citibank Maghreb, 52 Avenue Hassan 11 (Tel: 22 41 68); other banks: BMCE, 140 Avenue Hassan II (Tel: 20 04 77), Wafabank, 163 Avenue Hassan II (Tel: 27 41 31); all the banks have one or more agencies in each district. VISA card distributors: Crédit du Maroc, Avenue Hassan II, by the post office and 48, Boulevard Mohammed V. ATM machines in the big banks (a good safe place is the BMCE, Boulevard d'Anfa, near the U.S. Consulate).

Bus stations *(gare routière)* —CTM, 3 Rue Léon l'Africain, near Avenue des F.A.R. (Tel: 44 81 30); pending the opening of the new station right out of town, other bus companies go from the Benjdia station, corner Boulevard Lahcen-Ou-Ider/Rue Liborne. A new station on Route des Oulad Ziane became operational in the spring of 1999.

Car Rental—Avis, 19 Avenue des F.A.R. (Tel: 31 11 35); Budget, Tour des Habous, Avenue des F.A.R. (Tel: 31 37 37); Europcar, 44 Avenue des F.A.R. (Tel: 31 37 37, Fax: 31 03 60); Hertz, 25 Ruede Foucauld (Tel: 31 22 23); and many at Mohammed V Airport.

Churches—St. John's Anglican Church, 24 Rue Guedj, near the Hyatt Hotel (pulpit donated by General Patton) (Tel: 25 71 20 for information); English-speaking Catholic mass twice a month at Notre Dame de Guadalupe (CIL district) (Sundays at 10:30 A.M.) and twice a month at Christ-Roi (call the American priest, Father Barnaby, in Marrakech for information—Tel: 04-43 05 85); French-speaking Catholic mass at Notre Dame de Lourdes (Rond-Point d'Europe, Tel: 26 57 98), Christ-Roi (44 Boulevard Abdelmoumen, Tel: 25 49 63), Carmel St. Joseph (56 Boulevard Abderahim Bouabid, ex-Jerrada, Oasis district, Tel: 25 44 27), Chapelle Anfa-Maarif (13 Avenue Ain Harrouda, ex Jeanne d'Arc, Tel: 36 19 13), Saint François, Rue d'Azilal, Tel: 30 09 30). French-speaking Protestant service, Temple, 33 Rue d'Azilal (30 21 51); Greek Orthodox, 2 Rue Hatim al-Assam (ex Rue de Namur) (Tel: 27 68 92); Russian Orthodox, 13 Rue Blinda (Tel: 27 98 55) (not always functioning).

Consulates—U.S. Consulate General, 8 Boulevard Moulay Youssef (Tel: 26 45 50); French Consulate, Rue du Prince Mulay Abdallah (Tel: 48 93 00).

Doctors, Emergency—SOS Médecins (Tel: 44 44 44).

Drugstore, Night *(pharmacie de nuit)* —corner Boulevard d'Anfa/Place Oued el-Makhazine.

Express Post—DHL World Wide Express, 52 Boulevard Abdelmoumen (Tel: 25 58 28) or the *Poste Rapide* from the central post office.

Fire *(Sapeurs-Pompiers)* —(Tel: 15) (the Fire Brigade also runs an emergency ambulance service).

Gendarmerie Royale—(Tel: 177).

Golf Clubs—see under "Sport," section 9 above.

Horseback Riding—Club de l'Etrier, Rue Omar el-Khaayam, Quartier des Stades (Tel: 25 37 71); Ferme Equestre, Route d'Azemmour, Sidi Abd er-Raham (south of Casablanca, near restaurant Ma Bretagne).

Hospitals and Clinics—Best get in touch with the U.S. Consulate for advice.

Jewish Community Center—Communauté Israelite de Casablanca, 22 Rue Jaber ben Hayane Hanus (Tel: 29 52 46); Communauté Israelite, corner Rue Djazzet/Adrienne Lecouvreur (Tel: 22 28 61/27 69 52).

Jewish Synagogue—Synagogue Benaroch, 24 Rue Ibnou Rochd; Synagogue Beth-el, 61 Rue Jaber ben Hayane Hanus (Tel: 28 71 92); Synagogue Em-Habanim, 14 Rue Ibnou Rochd.

Photocopies—at many shops selling tobacco, stamps, and newspapers, and at a number of téléboutiques all over the town (for phone and fax, too).

Police—(Tel: 19).

Post Offices—main office corner Avenue Hassan II/Boulevard de Paris, but local offices in every district.

Railway Stations—Casa-Port (Tel: 27 18 37); Casa-Voyageurs (Tel: 24 38 18).

Schools—Casablanca American School, Route de la Mecque, Californie (Tel: 21 14 16/21 14 17, Fax: 21 48 88). Founded in 1973 to provide an American education in Casablanca, fee-paying, day pupils only, kindergarten to 12th grade; George Washington Academy, 14 Rue Mohammed ben Brahim, Oasis (information from Global I.E., 82 Rue Soumaya, Palmiers, Tel: 99 09 61, Fax: 99 09 62, e-mail: info.globalie.org). An initiative of Global I.E, registered in the U.S.A. as a not-for-profit corporation (cheaper than the Casablanca American School). At the moment preschool, kindergarten, and primary only, but extension planned.

Shipping Companies—Comanav, 7 Boulevard de la Résistance (Tel: 30 30 12, Fax: 30 84 55).

Taxis, Big and Little—Big taxis wait at the Airport and at Boulevard Hassan Seghir and Boulevard Yacoub el-Mansour. Small taxi stands are all over the place or you can hail a passing vehicle.

Telephone—Boulevard de Paris, just around the corner from the post office, or all the téléboutiques.

Tourist Information—98 Boulevard Mohammed V (Tel: 22 14 31). Only has colored brochures and a list of Casablanca hotels that can be consulted but not taken away.

Tour Operators, special trips—Globe Trotters, 67 Rue Lagramta, Oasis (Tel: 25 13 65, Fax: 25 15 22), specializing in adventure, sports, and theme travel; Team Travel Services (English-speaking), Résidence Eugénie, 209 Boulevard d'Anfa (Tel: 94 12 42/45, Fax: 94 12 50), a dynamic young team specializing in sports, adventure, motivation seminars, and training sessions; Menara Tours, branch office: 57 Place Zellaga (Tel: 31 18 62, Fax: 30 60 21).

Travel Agencies—Carlson Wagonlit Travel, 60/62 Rue el-Oraibi Jilali, (ex-Rue de Foucauld) (Tel: 20 30 51, Fax: 27 40 54/48 28 42); Olive Branch Tours (one of the oldest-established), 35 Rue el-Oraibi Jilali (Tel: 22 03 54/22 39 19, Fax: 26 09 76/20 36 79, e-mail: olivetour:open.net.ma).

Vaccination center—Institut Pasteur du Maroc, Place Charles-Nicole, off Boulevard Abdelmoumen (for rabies, amongst others) (Tel: 22 16 36).

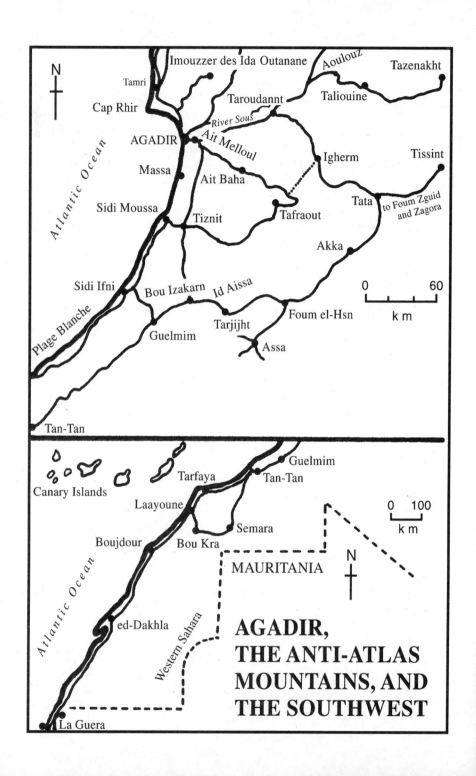

N

Imouzzer des Ida Outanane
Aoulouz
Tazenakht

Tamri

Cap Rhir

Taroudannt
Taliouine

River Sous

AGADIR
Ait Melloul

Atlantic Ocean

Massa
Igherm
Tissint

Ait Baha

Sidi Moussa
Tata
to Foum Zguid
and Zagora

Tiznit
Tafraout

Akka

Sidi Ifni
0   60

Bou Izakarn   Id Aissa
k m

Plage Blanche
Foum el-Hsn

Guelmim
Tarjijht

Assa

Tan-Tan

Canary Islands
Tarfaya
Guelmim
Tan-Tan

Laayoune
0   100

k m

Semara

Boujdour
Bou Kra

MAURITANIA

N

Atlantic Ocean

ed-Dakhla

Western Sahara

**AGADIR,
THE ANTI-ATLAS
MOUNTAINS, AND
THE SOUTHWEST**

La Guera

11

Agadir, the Anti-Atlas Mountains, and the Southwest

1. The General Picture

Agadir lies at the western end of the wide Sous plain, backed by the mountains of the High Atlas and Anti-Atlas. It is a seaside resort, claiming to enjoy 300 days of sunshine a year. It is not too hot in summer, mild in winter, and attracts visitors all the year round. Most are happy to relax on its beaches during the day and wander around the town or watch a show in their hotel in the evening. Some make Agadir their base for visiting the Anti-Atlas Mountains or the sub-Saharan regions to the south. Others combine the two. Certainly, if you've come up from a hot dusty trip in the desert, the swimming pools and comfort of Agadir's hotels are most welcoming.

Foundation. The history of the town starts with its name. Agadir in Berber or Arabic means a "fortified granary." These solid buildings, often perched on a rocky eminence, can still be seen today overlooking many villages in the Anti-Atlas and Atlas Mountains. It is believed that some time before the 12th century A.D., a group of Berber fishermen installed themselves near a spring on the edge of a large, sheltered bay. They used a cave as their granary, their "agadir." Between 1325 and 1470 the port was shown on European maps under the name of the Berber tribe that lived there.

Battles and trade. At the end of the 15th century, the Portuguese were becoming more and more active in south Morocco and in 1500 and 1504 the Spanish governor of the Canary Islands tried, unsuccessfully, to get hold of Agadir. However, it was the Portuguese king in 1513 who acquired the small fort that had been built there privately in 1505 by one of his countrymen to protect the bay. He enlarged the fort, calling it Santa Cruz do Cabo de Aguer. In this way, the new Portuguese possession controlled the sea and land routes to sub-Saharan Africa, the source of gold and slaves. Less than 30 years later, in 1541, the Portuguese governor of Agadir was forced to surrender and leave the fort after a six-month siege by the Saadian sultan, Mohammed ech-Cheikh. In 1540, the sultan built a kasbah on the hill overlooking the bay to support his troops in their attacks against the Portuguese. The confusion following the end of the Saadians' reign at the end of the 17th century helped the powerful Berber Tazeroualt leaders, opposed to the new Alaouite dynasty, to become masters of this whole region. They turned Agadir into an important port where cloth and wheat from Europe were exchanged for African gold and sugar-cane from the plantations in the Sous plain around the town. The Alaouite sultans managed to restore central authority in the 18th century. They took their revenge on Agadir by shutting the port and concentrating trade on the expanding town of Essaouira, to the north.

Modern Agadir. Just before World War I, in 1911, the German Kaiser William II sent the cruiser *Panther* into Agadir Bay, with the idea of installing a naval base there and extending his country's influence along the West African coast. The French reacted quickly and reached an agreement with the Germans ("you take part of the Congo, and we'll keep an eye on Morocco"). In the 1930s, after the installation of the French Protectorate in 1912, Agadir became an important stopover for the French *Aéropostale* pilots such as Saint-Exupéry and Mermoz, who landed on improvised landing strips (lit at night with burning branches) on their transatlantic postal flights from Toulouse. Progressively the port was enlarged, and fishing (particularly sardines), agriculture, and canning industries brought prosperity back to the town. This tranquility was brutally broken on the night of February 29, 1960, when an earthquake struck Agadir, killing more than 15,000 inhabitants and destroying most of the houses. With courage and determination, the town was rebuilt, the new residential buildings following strict anti-seismic regulations. International NGOs also came in to help—the British *Save the Children Fund* and the German-based Protestant association *Eirene*, for instance. By 1962, a new port and industrial zones were created at the northern end of the bay, and hotels and houses along the 10 km of beach. Hotel construction continues, and today Agadir and its province offer 22,000 beds in classified hotels while its airport is the second most important, after Casablanca, for tourist arrivals. It was in Agadir in 1975 that Hassan II launched his call to the Moroccan people to undertake a peaceful march into the Spanish Sahara—the Green March, *Massira el-Khadra*.

The temperature never drops below 16° C in winter and never exceeds 27° C in summer. The quality of Agadir's beaches—six miles of them—the range of sporting activities, the wide choice of accommodations, and the variety of its surroundings make it an ideal destination for visitors looking for a rest, for those with young children, for "water-babies" of all ages, and for the adventurous looking for a base from which to explore the hinterland. They won't find Agadir a very "Moroccan" city (for a taste of popular Moroccan life one has to go down to Inezgane or Ait Melloul) but it is clean and hassle-free. The urban population of Agadir, Inezgane, and Ait Melloul combined is slightly over 400,000.

2. Getting There

By **air,** Agadir is linked to Paris by 4 flights a week. RAM runs 3 flights a day throughout the week from Casablanca, with a flight time from Mohammed V airport to El Massira airport of just over an hour (special weekend rates). Regional Air Lines does 17 flights a week. RAM passengers coming into Casablanca from the United States or Canada have a connecting flight to Agadir. Agadir can be reached from all major cities in Europe via Casablanca. There is no bus link between the airport and Agadir. For travelers on a shoe-string and not in a hurry, a bus leaves from the airport car park to Inezgane about once an hour, and from Inezgane another bus (or taxi) goes to Agadir. The state railway company (ONCF) does a **combined train-bus** service with Supratours from Casablanca: passengers travel by a morning train from Casablanca to Marrakech, where they transfer to a coach arriving in Agadir five hours later.

Seven CTM **buses** leave Casablanca for Agadir every day (nine-hour journey, 140 DH). Agadir can be reached by bus from Taroudannt (85 km), Marrakech (273 km), Essaouira (173 km), Laayoune (649 km), and several other towns, including Dakhla in the far south (a nine-hour journey by the CTM). **Big taxis** do the same runs, also covering intermediate destinations. By **car, motorbike,** or even **bicycle,** the visitor will find the main roads into Agadir well maintained and usable throughout the year. The sailing port provides good shelter for **yachts** and other small boats.

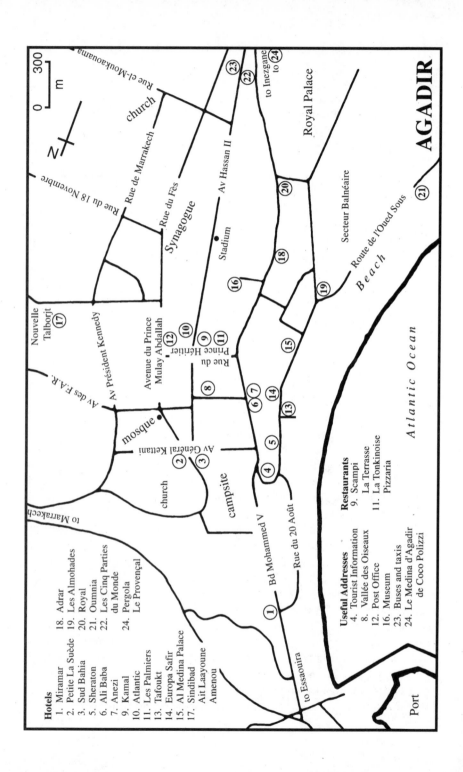

3. Local Transportation

Within Agadir, only **big taxis** (blue) are allowed to do runs to and from the airport (22 km). They have a fixed price: 150 DH during the day, 200 DH at night. A big taxi will also take you almost anywhere you want out of town—to nearby Taroudannt, for instance—for a negotiable fee, but officially it is 3 DH/km if you rent it specially. **Small bright orange taxis** can only do in-town travel (check the meter or fix the price before setting off). They are limited to three passengers.

The **local bus service** covers the principal town destinations (including Inezgane and Taghazout). Motorbikes (about 200 DH a day), **scooters,** and **bicycles** (20 DH/hour) can be hired, but you're probably just as well off walking and taking taxis—Moroccan streets are dangerous! There are plenty of car rental firms if you want to travel further afield for a few days (see "Address List" below).

4. The Hotel Scene

There are 83 classified hotels in the province of Agadir, most of them in the town itself, so it should be possible to find a room (the bed capacity is just over 21,000). But remember that Agadir is a seaside resort and at Easter, in the peak of the summer season (August), and during Moroccan school and religious holidays, the more popular establishments will be full. Some have special summer rates, even for individual travelers. Book in advance if you can. High season hotel charges fixed for this region are as follows (they vary according to the presence or absence of showers and water closet in the room): **** 421-523 DH or 439-847 DH, breakfast 53-72 DH for both; *** 209-333 DH or 238-380 DH, breakfast 40 DH for both; ** 116-200 DH or 122-249 DH, breakfast 26 DH for both; * 105-155 DH or 109-178 DH, breakfast 25 DH for both. Low season charges are 30-100 DH less.

The **regional telephone code** is 08 (0 omitted for in-region calls).

EXPENSIVE HOTELS

There are many **** or ***** hotels in Agadir. Most of them are huge and cater to package tours, which get a lower price than those offered to independent travelers. All have air-conditioning, but not all rooms have balconies overlooking the sea.

The ***** **Hotel Europa Safir** (254 rooms, 1,050 DH, Boulevard du 20 Août, Tel: 82 12 12/84 11 66, Fax: 82 34 35) is part of the Safir chain of hotels and has all the usual amenities of this type of hotel: pool, restaurants, bar, a nightclub, *hammam,* and conference rooms.

The ***** **Melia al-Madina Salam** (206 rooms, 825-1,138 DH, Boulevard du 20 Août, Tel: 84 53 53, Fax: 84 53 08), part of the Salam chain of hotels, is considered by some to be the best in Agadir. It is attractively designed in Moroccan style, has an unusually-shaped pool in a setting of plants and flowers, three restaurants (international, Italian, and Moroccan—the buffet is highly praised), bars, billiards, tennis courts, *hammam,* sauna, and a fitness center.

The ***** **Hotel Sahara** (273 rooms, 1,200 DH, Boulevard Mohammed V, Tel: 84 06 60, Fax: 84 07 38), a huge establishment, also has all the usual amenities: pool, tennis court, restaurants, a bar, and a nightclub.

The ***** **Hotel Sheraton Agadir** (195 rooms, 1,250-1,450 DH, Boulevard Mohammed V, Tel: 84 32 32, Fax: 84 33 39) offers the same services.

Also along Boulevard Mohammed V, the main road parallel to the sea, are the **** **Hotel Anezi** (257 rooms, Tel: 84 09 40/84 07 14, Fax: 84 07 13), and the **** **Hotel Adrar** (170 rooms, Tel: 84 04 37/84 07 17, Fax: 84 05 45). Still on Boulevard Mohammed V, the **** **Hotel Oasis** (132 rooms, Tel: 84 33 13/14/15/16, Fax: 84 22 60) adds a heated pool, tennis, disco, and a fitness club to the normal run of amenities.

The **** **Hotel Tafoukt** (135 rooms, Boulevard du 20 Août, Tel: 84 07 27, Fax: 84 09 71) is another hotel with "its feet in the sea," as they say—that is, with direct access to the beach—part of which they have appropriated for their straw beach huts. It also has its own pool, a restaurant, and attractive gardens.

The **** **Hotel Les Almohades** (320 rooms, Boulevard du 20 Août, Tel: 84 02 33, Fax: 84 01 30), run by the French Accor hotel group, is a massive place, functional enough, but without a great deal of character.

Integrated in the **** **Iberotel Tikida Beach** (Chemin des Dunes, Tel: 84 54 00/84 15 10, Fax: 84 58 62) is the **Institut Marin d'Agadir,** offering the full range of thalassotherapy services. The **** **Hotel Amadil** (Route de l'Oued Sous, Tel: 84 06 20, Fax: 82 36 63) is popular with package tours, but it's a bit far from the center for non-motorized travelers.

Full-board **"clubs"** are a good choice for visitors enjoying a heap of organized activities on the spot. The first-class club **Agadir Beach Club** (350 rooms, BP 310 Secteur Balnéaire, Tel: 84 43 44, Fax: 84 08 63) is highly praised by my friends. Situated on the water's edge, it has a variety of rooms from studios to suites (some of the rooms are a bit so-so), four restaurants, and a large pool surrounded with greenery and protected from the wind (as well as a *hammam,* conference rooms, and so on) and is good for families with children.

Another rather similar affair is the third-class club **PLM Dunes d'Or** (450 rooms, Tel: 84 01 50, Fax: 84 05 74), a huge sports and seaside complex, somewhat out of town in the Secteur Balnéaire, which again has all the amenities one would expect, but which is in the process of changing hands.

The first-class club **Club la Casbah** (Boulevard du 20 Août, Tel: 84 09 50), practically on the beach as well, has a good reputation and all sorts of things to occupy the visitor: beach, tennis court, cinema, shop, restaurant, bar, and nightclub.

The **Valtur VVT** (350 rooms, Parcelle 34 [STB], Tel: 84 44 85/95, Fax: 84 33 75) is another first-class club, a few minutes from the seafront. This vast establishment is run like a fully-contained village, with multiple activities: restaurant, bar, large swimming pool, tennis courts, a theater, a disco, organized activities for adults and children, and a casino nearby. It is popular with Italians and Germans, though a few Americans come there on a package from the United States.

The third-class club **Club Sangho** (Boulevard Mohammed V, Tel: 84 03 42), now run by the Accor Group, is normally good, but the service is sometimes sloppy. All the usual club amenities and activities are at your doorstep.

MEDIUM-PRICE HOTELS

These are the *** and ** hotels. The *** **Hotel Kamal** (128 rooms, Avenue Hassan II, Tel: 84 28 17, Fax: 84 39 40) is central, has a big, bright hall, a small garden, and comfortable, well-equipped bedrooms.

The *** **Hotel Moussafir** is out of town (1 km) on the Marrakech road (112 rooms, 12 suites, Rue Oued Ziz, Tel: 23 28 42/43/44, Fax: 23 28 49). The Moussafir chain (now Ibis/Accor) is normally near a railway station, but there isn't one in Agadir. It's a beautiful little hotel, with a small pool, restaurant, and a bar, and much less invaded by big groups.

Along Boulevard Mohammed V, you have the *** **Hotel Ali Baba** (105 rooms, Tel: 84 33 26, Fax: 84 12 47), which has a restaurant, a nightclub, and a tennis court.

The *** **Hotel Sud Bahia** (246 rooms, Rue des Administrations Publiques, off Avenue du Général Kettani, Tel: 84 07 41, Fax: 84 08 63) is an old hotel, rather dark, and not well placed for sea views, but it is only 10 minutes from the beach. The bedrooms are comfortable and the atmosphere is agreeable. It has an international restaurant, snack restaurant, pool, bar, and a nightclub.

The *** **Hotel Oumnia** (180 rooms, Route de l'Oued Sous, Tel: 84 03 52) is better situated, beside the beach, and has a restaurant, tennis court, and a nightclub.

The ** **Hotel La Pergola** (Km 8, Route d'Agadir-Inezgane, Tel: 83 08 41/ 83 31 00), 8 km along the road to Inezgane, just before the turn off to Inezgane, is still run by a Frenchwoman and is a good value (excellent restaurant).

Just after the turn off to Inezgane is the ** **Hotel Le Provençal** (Km 9, Route d'Agadir-Inezgane, Tel: 83 12 087 12), which used to be run by the sister of the owner of the Hotel La Pergola. It's still quite family-style and much appreciated, even if not as much as it was in the old days.

The ** **Hotel Miramar** (Boulevard Mohammed V, Tel: 84 07 70) is away from the center, on the left as you come in from Essaouira. It's an old place, but good for the price and is particularly noted for its excellent restaurant.

The ** **Hotel Royal** (98 rooms, Boulevard Mohammed V, Tel: 84 06 75) and the ** **Atlantic Hotel** (54 rooms, Avenue Hassan II, Tel: 84 36 61, Fax: 84 36 60) are both well situated, more or less in the center of town. The latter is just off the main street, in a cul-de-sac and consequently quiet. The rather bleak three-story building (no balconies or elevator) is very functional, the rooms are comfortable, the sanitary equipment excellent, there is a pleasant little garden behind, and the staff is helpful (a recommended address).

Just around the corner from the Hotel Kamal and the Atlantic Hotel the modest ** **Hotel Les Palmiers** (29 rooms, Rue du Prince Héritier Sidi Mohammed, Tel: 84 37 19) is a good value, with a restaurant and a bar (also open for breakfast—24 DH—for non-guests from 6:00 A.M..

The ** **Hotel Petite Suède** (18 rooms, Avenue Hassan II, just off Avenue du Général Kettani, Tel: 84 07 79, Fax: 84 00 57) has nothing Swedish about it, but it's well-kept, and although of long standing, has recently been renovated.

The ** **Hotel Sindibad** in the busy shopping area known as the Nouvelle Talborjt, around the Place Lahcen ou Brahim Tamri (Tel: 82 34 77, Fax: 84 24 74), is a 15-minute walk from the Boulevard Mohammed V and is the best of a series of small hotels in this area.

BUDGET ACCOMMODATIONS

There are a **number of budget-price hotels** around the Place Lahcen Tamri, including the * **Hotel Ait Laayoune** (9 rooms, Rue Yacub el-Mansour, Tel: 82 43 75) which is quite well kept, but small and often full. Just opposite, the * **Hotel Amenou** (Tel: 84 56 15) is not bad, but both hotels have communal showers.

At the southern end of the Avenue Hassan II, in a far from pretty district, the * **Hotel Les Cinq Parties du Monde** (Tel: 84 54 81/84 25 04) has the advantage of being near the bus station, so it's noisy, but it's clean and has a restaurant.

The **campsite** is not exactly luxurious, but is one of the best of its kind, with trees but rather hard ground. It is often pretty full with Dutch or German caravaners who spend a few winter months there, which may explain the comparative cleanliness of the toilet facilities. It lies just off the northern end of the Boulevard Mohammed V (15 DH per person, per tent, per car). There's another campsite 18 km out of town, at the **Camping International Taghazout** on the road to Essaouira (it is pretty dirty and often short of water).

There is also accommodation in **"Résidences"**—furnished studios and apartments with kitchen facilities. They can be a good value if you don't want to eat out all the time. There are lots of them around, and prices vary enormously according to size and season. The Résidence Tislit in the Rue du Prince Héritier Sidi Mohammed would give you an idea of their potential, and the Tourist Office can advise on others (but all are heavily booked throughout August).

5. Dining and Restaurants

Agadir is not the place for gastronomic delights, though the Agadir people themselves—the Gadiri—may think otherwise. Many package-tour visitors have meals included in the price, which doesn't stimulate very high-class restaurants. But it is possible to eat well in Agadir, both expensively and cheaply.

HOTEL RESTAURANTS

All the big hotels have two or three restaurants, serving international and Moroccan meals. Most are not particularly inspiring, but Agadir is the sort of place where the tourist can generally find all he needs on the spot—lodging, food, swimming, and shopping—and it is often convenient to eat in the hotel restaurant. In fact, it is probably impossible to eat a first-class Moroccan meal other than in one of the big hotels (but they are always very expensive).

Among those with a particularly good reputation is the **Marrakech Restaurant** in the **Agadir Beach Club Hotel,** the restaurant **Le Président** in the **Hotel Europa Safir** (Boulevard du 20 Août, Tel: 82 12 12), and the restaurant in the **Hotel Miramar** (Boulevard Mohammed V). The latter does pretty expensive French cooking, Italian pasta, and excellent fish, is open for lunch and dinner, and is frequented by businessmen. Its little shaded terrace is agreeable in summer.

It's also enjoyable to eat in the pool-side restaurant of the **Hotel Tafoukt** (Boulevard du 20 Août, by the beach). The buffet restaurants, Moroccan and international, in the **Al Medina Palace Hotel,** also on the Boulevard du 20 Août (Tel: 84 53 53), have been highly praised.

The restaurant belonging to the **Hotel Les Palmiers** (Rue du Prince Héritier Sidi Mohammed) is a good value with a set menu (Moroccan or international) at 70 DH. It also provides snacks. A couple of kilometers further on, the restaurant in the **Hotel La Pergola** has a reputation for good French cooking, with many dishes quite out of the ordinary prepared by the French owner.

Going the other way, the restaurant in the **Hotel Moussafir** is appreciated by my Agadir friends (but it is a bit far to go just for a meal).

The Pizzeria in the **PLM Dunes d'Or Hotel** is said to be good (and useful if you want to continue the evening in the nightclub). The **Hotel Anezi** also has a pizzeria, but it's probably more interesting to go to one of the similar, very lively places along Boulevard Mohammed V.

OTHER RESTAURANTS

At the top end, the **Restaurant La Tour de Paris** (Avenue Hassan II/ Avenue du Général Kettani) goes in for fine French cooking and is a nice place for a meal, but it's perhaps not worth the price (180 DH).

Le Bistro Romain (19 Avenue Hassan II), not a bistro or Roman, does the usual range of Moroccan food, including *tajines,* couscous, and fish dishes. For a Moroccan meal in a traditional setting, with music and traditionally-dressed waiters, the best place is the **Restaurant Darkoum** (Arabic for "your house"), situated on Avenue du Général Kettani (set menus from 180 DH).

Mister Picolo (Boulevard du 20 Août) also serves a French cuisine. The **Restaurant Scampi** (Avenue Hassan II, across the road from the Atlantic Hotel and almost next door to the Hotel Kamal) is an attractive little restaurant sheltered from the street by a hedge (set menu 100 DH, good selection of Moroccan wines, and the service is slow but pleasant).

A more refined setting is provided by the restaurant **La Terrasse,** belonging to the Hotel Kamal (Rue du Prince Héritier Sidi Mohammed, Tel: 84 28 17), raised up from street level (set menu 120 DH).

The restaurant **La Tonkinoise Chez Redy** (Rue du Prince Héritier Sidi Mohammed, Tel: 84 25 27), is sister to the one in Casablanca, and serves Vietnamese specialties.

There are pizzerias galore in Agadir, and you could try the Boulevard du 20 Août for the **Restaurant La Mamma** and **Restaurant Pizza Pino,** or the Avenue Hassan II for the **Pizzaria La Siciliana, La Dolche Vita,** and **Via**

Venetto (all from 45 DH). All the Hassan II pizzarias are crowded in the summer.

Another "snack" place is the **Restaurant Igloo** (Rue du Prince Héritier Sidi Mohammed), which does a simple meal of salad, main dish, and dessert for 55 DH.

For a good fish meal—and after all, Agadir is an important fishing port—the **Restaurant du Port** is one of the best. It's inside the fishing port, on the right, and not easy to find.

There are also a whole lot of **cheap little eating places** around here, just outside the port, about 500 m from the campsite, where you can eat fresh grilled sardines (not advised for squeamish stomachs, as cleanliness is not guaranteed). They are very popular with Moroccan families—fix the price before starting and check the bill (unlicensed).

A cheap Moroccan meal (*tajine*, 40 DH) can be had from the **Restaurant Tafoukt** in the Place Hassan II (not to be confused with the hotel of the same name).

Another collection of **cheap restaurants** (30-40 DH for salad and main dish) much frequented by Moroccans—and increasingly by visitors who want to get out of the tourist circuit—is the Nouvelle Talborjt shopping area around the Place Lahcen Tamri (off Rue el-Mahdi ibn Toumert, about a 15-minute walk from the Boulevard Mohammed V—see Hotel Sindibad above).

OTHER PLACES TO EAT

The **Boulangerie-Pâtisserie Tafarnout** (corner Avenue Hassan II/Rue de la Foire) offers a very large selection of delicious pastries, both Moroccan and French, to take away or eat in the coffee shop. It is also possible to have breakfast there, sitting at an outside table.

Le Traditionnel (Avenue du Prince Mulay Abdallah) can also be recommended for its Moroccan pastries. Another coffee shop, selling pastries and ice cream, is **La Maison du Pain** (19 Avenue Hassan II, close to the Hotel La Petite Suède.

The up-market restaurant **La Tour de Paris** (corner Avenue Hassan II/ Avenue du Général Kettani) has a mouth-watering choice of breakfast pastries and excellent coffee, to be enjoyed at a table in the open-air.

The **Salon de Thé Navarro** (Avenue Hassan II) also sells ice cream. **Le Dome** (Avenue Hassan II) does an ordinary breakfast for 16 DH, and a cooked one for 30 DH (from 8:00 A.M.-12:00 P.M.).

The **Restaurant Pizzaria** (corner Rue du Prince Héritier Sidi Mohammed/Boulevard Mohammed V) is shaded and has noisy music, and serves hamburgers and frankfurters, as well as pizzas.

6. Sightseeing

IN AGADIR

The town is worth a stroll around, if only to compare it with other Moroccan towns you have seen or will see. The Boulevard Mohammed V more or less divides it into the seaside resort on the one side, the modern town on the other. An evening drink in the center or a cheap meal in the Nouvelle Talborjt, just about covers the attractions. The fishing port is another place to visit, if you don't mind the fishy smells. Otherwise the tourist attraction is the partially restored Saadian **kasbah** on the hill (236 m high) overlooking Agadir's bay. It was built in 1540 as a strongpoint from which to lay siege to the town, then held by the Portuguese, and reinforced in the 18th century. After the 1960 earthquake only parts of the ramparts and the gate remained standing. The latter has an inscription in Dutch ("Fear God and respect the King") recalling that a Dutch trading post was established here in 1746. Unfortunately, the site is crowded with tourist buses and the inevitable sellers of "souvenirs," with the saddled camel waiting for the "souvenir" photograph. But the view is superb, especially at sunset. On the outskirts of Agadir (about 5 km from the center), on the road to Inezgane, **La Medina d'Agadir de Coco Polizzi,** an artifically-created medina, is nevertheless interesting for a chance to see traditional craftsmen at work (a sight otherwise lacking in Agadir).

NORTH OF AGADIR

The exit north from Agadir goes through the unattractive industrial zone, smelling strongly of fish in the summer. After 12 km up the P8 coastal road towards Essaouira, a narrow, winding road on the right climbs up to **Imouzzer des Ida Outanane** (50 km). The landscape is a mixture of bare hills, deep valleys, bright green oases, and picturesque little villages, and is certainly the best short excursion from Agadir. In the spring the almond trees are in bloom and in the fall the olives are harvested. It can also be reached by a daily **bus** (departure behind Hotel Sindibad), which returns the next day. About 30 km after the turn, a particularly attractive valley has been nicknamed "Paradise Valley." Imouzer itself, the principal town of the Berber Ida Outanane tribe, lies at an altitude of 1,250 m and dominates the surrounding country. It is famous for its honey (Honey Festival in mid-August) and its spectacular waterfalls (the big one needs rain to make it work), reached by a paved road (4 km) or a path from the hotel. Twenty years ago one could expect to meet a troop of wild pigs wandering around, but times they are a-changing. Good walks and longer treks can be made around this area.

The only hotel is the *** **Hotel des Cascades** (27 rooms, Tel: 82 60 16), which has a swimming pool and a tennis court. It's beautifully situated, very well kept, and has a lovely garden. There's a cheaper, small hotel at Tifrit, some 18 km before Imouzer: the **Hotel Tifrit** (half-board around 320 DH). **Dining** is restricted to the restaurant in the **Hotel des Cascades** (set menu 143 DH) or the **restaurant/café** near the waterfalls for a snack. A picnic is recommended.

Returning to the main north-bound road, the visitor will arrive at a whole series of beautiful golden beaches, less crowded in August than those of Agadir. Access to some is direct from the road, others lie at the foot of cliffs. **Taghazout** (18 km) has become a real little seaside resort, with villas, restaurants, cafés, shops (surfboards for sale), a mosque, and a school. Buses go here, but no further. It's not a particularly good place in which to pass the night—the campsite is mentioned above and you are strongly advised not to camp just anywhere or to accept offers of accommodation in private houses. The beaches continue after Taghazout, and a particularly popular one, 25 km from Agadir, is equipped with beach umbrellas, tents, up-market villas, cafés, and so on. A landmark is the lighthouse of **Cap Rhir,** jutting out into the sea, followed by **Tamri,** thick with banana plantations, with an easily accessible beach. **Imessouane** is a beautiful little fishing port off the main road, with good surfing and camping possibilities—but plans are underway to establish some sort of industrial fishing complex there. And so we move up to **Cap Tafelney** (also off the main road) and **Essaouira** (chapter 10).

EAST OF AGADIR

East of Agadir, the town of **Taroudannt** can be visited in the day (85 km), but a longer stay is recommended. The town, protected by its red adobe walls, looks as though it hasn't changed for centuries. It has, of course, but the visitor is plunged into the atmosphere of a busy little Berber commercial town and it is, for this reason, a most agreeable place. Although it may have been nicknamed "the little Marrakech," it has only the ramparts in common with the large metropolis of Marrakech.

The town has had quite an agitated past, being the capital of an independent little kingdom in the 11th century A.D., taken over by the Almoravids in 1056, then independent again under the Almohads, destroyed in 1306 by the Merinids, and blooming again when the Saadian sultan, Mohammed ech-Cheikh, built a kasbah and made it his base for attacking the Portuguese in Agadir. Trade in sugar, cotton, rice, and other products from the rich Sous agricultural lands made the town an important center for the caravan routes. In the 17th century, Taroudannt became part of the independent Berber Tazeroualt kingdom, in open rebellion against the

Alaouite dynasty. This was unfortunate for the town, since it was continu-
ally attacked by the Alaouite military forces and finally captured by Mulay
Ismail, who killed most of the inhabitants. When, in the 18th century, the
port of Agadir was closed by order of the sultan, Taroudannt and all the
region declined in importance. It sprang back into life when El Hiba, the
son of the Saharan leader Cheikh Ma el-Ainin, declared himself sultan in
1912 after the signature of the Treaty of Fès by the legitimate sultan,
Mulay Abd el-Hafid, and made Taroudannt the base of his resistance to
French penetration until 1913. But El Hiba's dreams had already come to
an end in August 1912, when his forces were defeated by the French just
north of Marrakech. Today, Taroudannt, against a backcloth of the snow-
capped summits of the High Atlas in winter, is calm and welcoming, traditional in the best sense of the term, and a good destination for the
individual traveler.

There is no **plane** or **rail** service to Taroudannt. **To get there,** take the
main P32 which passes by the Agadir airport. The very busy road, crowded
with trucks, tractors, mule-drawn carts, motorbikes, and bicycles, goes
alongside an almost continuous line of plastic hangers for bananas and
tomatoes, orange groves, and accompanying constructions. Taroudannt
can also be reached from Agadir by branching off from the P40, which
goes **northeast** to Imi-n-Tanoute and Marrakech (310 km). The road to
Marrakech (chapter 12) is attractive enough as far as Imi-n-Tanoute, a busy
market town, but then goes through flat, cultivated country of lesser interest. There's no particular reason to go to Taroudannt by this route,
which is, however, convenient if coming from Marrakech and wanting to
go there direct. Some 60 km along this P40 (5 km after the village of
Imouzer) a small road to the left (indicated) leads to the very long underground river/cave of **Wit Tamdoun** *(Grotte de Wit Tamdoun),* claimed to be
the second most important underground system in Africa (for experienced, well-equipped speleologists only). Some 20 km further along the
main road, the Tamzaourt dam on the right helps to irrigate the Sous valley.

The visitor to Taroudannt can also take a CTM or Satas **bus,** which leave
several times a day from Agadir, three times a day from Marrakech, twice a
day from Ouarzazate, and once a day from Casablanca. **Big taxis** also make
the trip. For **local transportation** one only really needs a pair of feet, since
the town is small, but you can hire a horse-drawn buggy *(calèche)* (40 DH
for a 1 ½-hour tour) or use a **small taxi** to do a tour of the crenellated ramparts, pierced by five huge gates.

The **hotel scene** includes one of the best hotels in Morocco, the *****
Hotel Gazelle d'Or (23 rooms), 2 km southwest of Taroudannt (they'll
pick you up at Agadir or Marrakech). This is a most select place, once the
hunting lodge of a French baron, used by royalty and the jet set, and is up

to its high reputation. The spacious bungalows (with marble bathrooms, telephone, heating, and fireplace) are hidden in glorious gardens, and have recently been renovated with impeccable taste. The grounds contain a swimming pool (heated in winter), tennis courts, a croquet lawn, and riding stables (advance booking is compulsory, casual visitors are not welcome, a single room in a bungalow costs 1,470 DH for one, double room in a suite is 3,510 DH; breakfast 114 DH, the other meals of corresponding price; Tel: 85 20 39, Fax: 85 25 37).

The **** **Hotel Melia Palais Salam** (143 rooms, Tel: 85 23 12, Fax: 85 26 54), set in the ramparts, is a beautiful 19th-century Pasha's residence decorated with the finest of Moroccan craftsmanship. There are 95 rooms in the original part of the building (including 2 suites and 34 duplex rooms built around small courtyards filled with banana trees and fountains) and 43 in the new wing (23 suites and 4 apartments). The whole hotel is compact, rustling with controlled jungle vegetation, yet there is space for two charming pools and two restaurants (sauna, tennis, and horseback riding are available). The staff is attentive and helpful.

Medium-price accommodations are offered by the ** **Hotel Saadiens** (56 rooms, Tel: 85 25 89, Fax: 85 21 18). It is situated in the medina and is well indicated. The bedrooms looking onto the patio and pool are preferable to the front ones, which are a bit noisy. I've always found the staff cold and unhelpful, but I may have been out of luck. It has a restaurant and a bar.

Among the **budget accommodations,** I've found the best to be the **Hotel Taroudannt** in the medina (31 rooms, around 100 DH, Place al-Alaouyine, near the bus station, Tel: 85 24 16). It is a bit dilapidated and the plumbing's not always too good, but it has a charming courtyard filled with trees and a pleasant staff. Other little hotels concentrated around this square and the nearby Place el-Nasr are all pretty basic (around 50 DH), but worth looking at if that's your price range.

Dining and Restaurants. At the top end, the food at the **Hotel Gazelle d'Or** is phenomenally good. The next best is undoubtedly the **Hotel Melia Palais Salam,** which has a good Moroccan and French restaurant (186 DH).

One can eat well in the **Hotel Saadiens'** panoramic restaurant on the top floor (unlicensed) (106 DH), but again I find the more simple **Hotel Taroudannt** a better bet. It does Moroccan food, but also provides good French cooking (around 50 DH for the main dish, or set menus at 70 DH and 90 DH), accompanied by Moroccan wines or beer.

Among the **"cheapies,"** those around the **Place al-Alaouyine** all do standard salads, *tajines,* and the eternal caramel cream (*crème caramel*) (one of the legacies of the French Protectorate) (about 40 DH/meal—and really, the *tajines* are no worse than in a higher-class restaurant).

The **Hotel/Restaurant Roudani** is as good a place as any, and is a recommended place in which to have breakfast and watch the Roudani (people of Taroudannt) passing by. Don't stare at the women or attempt to take photographs, but note that many of the women drape themselves with elegant (but hardly practical) indigo blue wraps.

There are not many **sights to see** in Taroudannt itself, but it's well worth having a stroll around the **souks.** Look particularly at the **Berber jewelry** (not always real silver, though it may look like it) and the stone carvings. Before their departure, the Jewish craftsmen were responsible for much of southern Morocco's silver jewelry. The **Moroccan Jewish community** still holds a *moussem* (religious festival) in December near Bartzou Nbahmou, some 25 km from Taroudannt, attended by Jews from Casablanca, Rabat, and Fès, as well as many members of the Jewish community resident in France, Belgium, England, and Canada. Some of the small shops have real treasures, though the prices may not be particularly low. **The markets** on Thursday and Sunday, held just outside Bab el-Khemis, are entertaining events just to watch (get there early). There is a **mass** in French at the Eglise Notre Dame des Sept Douleurs, 72 Rue du 20 Août (for information call Tel: 85 25 14 or the nuns at Tel: 85 04 09).

About 7 km northwest out of Taroudannt on the Ameskroud road (which, if you turn left at the junction with the main P40, will bring you back to Agadir), after a small village, take a large track to the right just after the Salama gas station for 1½ km to reach the well-preserved remains of a huge **aquaduct straddling the River Ouar,** which is visible from quite a distance. Three archways are still standing, topped by their water-bearing channel, while the remains of the others and the channels that led up to the aquaduct can be followed. The construction formed part of the network of canalisations bringing water to the sugarcane factories for which the Sous area was famous under the Saadians. The remains of several of these factories, including traces of the giant water-turned wheel working the machinery, can be seen south of Taroudannt and also west of Marrakech, near Chichaoua (chapter 12).

South of Taroudannt, turning right after 8 km along the Marrakech road, **Tioute Kasbah** used to be a real pleasure to visit (35 km). Alas, its painted wooden ceilings, *zellij*, and other decoration were ripped out a few years ago and, with the help of a lot of cement, the kasbah has been turned into an expensive restaurant. The oasis is still an attractive place in which to take a walk. But Tioute has a romantic history: when Agadir was captured by the Saadians in 1541, the Portuguese governor and his daughter were imprisoned in the kasbah by one of the victorious Saadian chiefs. The chief found the young Portuguese girl sufficiently appealing to marry her. They must have led an idyllic life, even eating their meals together (quite unheard of in the traditional Moroccan system). Inevitably, perhaps, the other wives were furiously jealous and successfully eliminated the intruder with a strong dose of poison (her father was freed).

Trekking in the western end of the High Atlas is possible from Taroudannt, either totally on foot or preferably with a mule, since food and water will have to be taken along with a tent, sleeping bag, and personal equipment. It is suggested that anyone wanting a few days' of not too heavy walking should get in touch with Tigouba Adventures (Bab Targhount, Immeuble 1, 1st floor, BP132 Taroudannt, Tel: 85 35 01), a specialized trekking agency (best contact well in advance). The hotels Palais Salam or Saadiens in Taroudannt might also be able to advise on suitable routes and guides. If trekking independently, complete equipment and detailed maps are essential, as the area is lightly populated.

SOUTH OF AGADIR

The main P30 road south of Agadir, passing through Inezgane and Ait Melloul, eventually goes to the far south (if really stuck in Inezgane, the ** **Hotel Hagounia,** on the main road through the town, by the traffic lights, is the best). About 60 km from Agadir, a small road to the right marked "Massa" leads to the **Parc National Souss-Massa,** near the mouth of the **Oued Massa,** an important **bird sanctuary.** Massa was used by sailors from Genoa in the 11th century, then the Portuguese established a trading post there before it became the center of an important religious community. The reserve was created in 1991 and is supported by the World Wildlife Fund. The WWF representative is based in Agadir and can be contacted for information (Tel: 33 38 80). Depending on the season, the birds to see include flamingos, herons, and cranes, and smaller fry such as warblers, shrikes, sand martins, and some ducks. Forty oryx antelopes, a number of hartebeeste, and 39 ostriches from the Chad were recently introduced into the park, but I've never been able to see them. To reach the park, take the turn to the village of Massa (5 km) then right to Sidi R'bat until the way is barred by a tree trunk. The rest has to be done on foot. The small campsite at Sidi R'bat, on the water's edge just outside the reserve, was shut down recently and I wouldn't advise camping alone around there. Whale bones on the beach in the 16th century led to the improbable story that Jonah landed at Sidi R'bat after being thrown up by this creature. Rather less improbable is the legend that it was from this beach that Oqba ibn Nafi, the 7th-century Arab conqueror, plunged his horse into the Atlantic after crossing North Africa.

Another easy day out from Agadir can be had by taking the same main road through Inezgane and Ait Melloul to **Tiznit** (90 km) and **Sidi Ifni**

(70 km). **Tiznit** was built in 1881 by the Alaouite sultan Hassan I as a fortified base from which to put the southern Moroccan tribes under his control. Although it developed into an important trading center, it really only struck the headlines of the time when **El Hiba,** son of the Saharan chief Cheikh Ma el-Ainin, proclaimed himself sultan in Tiznit's mosque and vowed to chase out the French and the legitimate sultan, Moulay Abd el-Hafid, who had signed the Treaty of Fès in 1912, establishing a French Protectorate over Morocco. El Hiba, known as the "Blue Sultan" from the blue robes he wore like all the Saharan tribesmen, rapidly won over the tribes in the Sous, and other supporters arrived from around the River Draa, and the Sahara as far as Mauritania. Two of his brothers occupied Taroudannt and Agadir, and he established his capital in the former town. By the end of August, almost all south Morocco was in his hands, but El Hiba and his 5,000 tribesmen were defeated by the French at Sidi Othmane, north of Marrakech. El Hiba retired south and died in 1919. The military base of Hassan I later housed another garrison, when the French used it as one of their southern fortifications.

The traveler can get to Tiznit by **bus, car,** or **big taxi.** CTM buses go from Casablanca four times a day and frequently from Agadir, Marrakech, Tafraout, and Guelmim. It is also possible to reach Tiznit direct from London or Paris with Eurolines (see chapter 2). **Little red taxis** run around the town.

Top-class accommodations are limited in Tiznit to the *** **Tiznit Hotel** (40 rooms, Rue Bir Inzaren, left around the big traffic circle at the entrance to the town, Tel: 86 24 11, Fax: 86 21 19). It is not very attractive from the outside, but the spacious hall opens onto an interior courtyard, which is delightfully calm, with a plant-surrounded swimming pool. The bedrooms are large and comfortable (the best overlook the pool). It has a large restaurant, three bars, and a nightclub (if there are enough tourists around). At the moment, this is the best hotel with a pool between Agadir and Laayoune (649 km), and is very appreciated by motorists coming up from the south.

Medium-price accommodations are provided by the fairly new * **Hotel de Paris** (20 rooms, Avenue Hassan II, right-hand road from the traffic circle, Tel: 86 28 65, Fax: 60 13 95), which has a restaurant and a good reputation.

The best **budget accommodations** are in the **Hotel Mauritania** (16 rooms, 100 DH, Tel: 86 36 32), but it is a bit out of town, on the road to Bou Izakarn. It has a bar and restaurant.

Unclassified cheap hotels worth going to are the **Hotel Belle-Vue** or the **Hotel des Touristes** (both off the Place al-Mechouar and both under 100 DH).

The **best hotel restaurant** is the one in the **Hotel de Paris,** which does a better meal (main dish from 45 DH) than the **Hotel de Tiznit** (set meal

143 DH). The **Hotel Mauritania** also does a reasonable evening meal for about 45 DH.

A cheaper Moroccan meal (around 40 DH) can be had at the **Restaurant Essaraha** (Boulevard Mohammed V) and sandwiches and French fries from the **Restaurant el-Bahia** for slightly less (same road).

Tiznit has always had a reputation for its jewelry making. The **jewelry market** is the best place to see people at work and their finished products. The Berber fibula and bracelets are unlikely now to be of silver, but rather of an alloy called "German silver" by the experts. It's difficult for "ordinary" people to tell the difference (see chapter 2). There's also a market selling **older jewelry** and you might pick up a bargain.

The **minaret of the Great Mosque** is also a curiosity, with its poles sticking out at the top. I wouldn't bother to be lured by would-be guides into seeing the **Blue Spring** *(Source Bleue)*, also called *la Source de Lalla Tiznit* or *Source de Lalla Zninia,* unless you want to muse over the legend of a "woman of easy virtue" who repented and lived there as a holy woman, so holy that God forgave her and caused a spring to burst out from under her feet. She eventually became a saint and gave her name to the original village of Tiznit. Cheikh Ma el-Ainin, the charismatic 19th-century Saharan leader, is buried in Tiznit and a *moussem* is held at his tomb in August.

For **Aglou beach** (17 km), follow the sign *Centre Ville* then the blue one marked *Aglou Plage*. The beach is good for surfers and relatively clean. **Sidi Ifni** (70 km from Tiznit) is reached by a road going southwest out of Tiznit, which is clearly marked. It doesn't become attractive until it reaches the coast at Gourizim and turns south along the cliff edge The first village of importance is **Mirleft** (45 km), a small holiday center for mainly local people. It is appreciated for its many beaches, to both the north and south, and for its cliffs dropping down into the sea where sea bass and other prize fish are just waiting to be hooked by an experienced fisherman. The beaches, however, are dangerous, especially when the tide is going out.

The few **hotels** and **cafés** here are pretty basic. The **Hotel Tafoukt** is about the best. Mirleft is the headquarters of **Cobratours,** a travel organization run by an Italian couple who propose unusual itineraries for small groups or individuals (tailor-made if you want). Their program is called "Unknown Morocco," and they offer sports activities (including hiking, mountain biking, and horseback riding) combined with contact with the local inhabitants and their culture (address: BP 85350 Mirleft, Tiznit, Tel/Fax: 71 90 56/71 91 05).

After a further 30 km, the road reaches **Sidi Ifni,** built on a rocky plateau high above the Atlantic. It has had a rather curious history and the thick mist that hangs over it much of the time adds to its unusual atmosphere. The Spanish were already installed there in the 15th century to watch over the route to the newly (re)discovered Canary Islands. At that time they called their post Santa Cruz del Mar Pequeña. The Saadian rulers ousted the Spanish in 1524, but the latter were back again in 1934 when they built a complicated system for hoisting their ships up out of the water, since there was not much of a port at the time. For some 30 years the town was mainly occupied by Spaniards, whose occupation was fishing. It was not until 1969, 13 years after Moroccan independence, that Spain agreed to give the enclave back to Morocco. That side of old Sidi Ifni is a bit shabby, but the town is changing rapidly and the fishing port is active.

Sidi Ifni can be reached by **bus** from Agadir, Tiznit, Guelmim, and Marrakech. But plenty of **big taxis** make the run from Agadir more frequently (50 DH), via Tiznit. The **best hotels** are the modest * **Hotel Belle Vue** (16 rooms, 9 Place Hassan II, Tel: 87 50 72) and the **Hotel Suerte Loca** (from 100-150 DH depending on whether you are in the new part or not, Avenue Moulay Youssef, Tel: 87 53 50). The latter is a very friendly, almost homey sort of place (and likely to be full at holiday times).

Down on the beach is the rather scruffy **Hotel Ait Baamrane** (20 rooms, around 130 DH, Tel: 87 52 67). There are a number of **cheap hotels** near Avenue Mohammed V (around 50 DH) with amenities (or lack of them) corresponding to their low price. The **restaurant** in the **Hotel Suerte Loca** is a very good value—ask for fish caught that day (main dish around 40 DH).

A short walk around the town will probably cover the **sightseeing.** The architecture is a mixture of traditional Moroccan and the Spanish version of 1930s Art Deco. The ex-Plaza Mayor, now Place Hassan II, has a Spanish air to it, and the Spanish church is still standing, but the old consular building is closed, the very Spanish balustraded esplanade is a bit shaky, the old hoisting equipment is still there but broken and rusty, and the airstrip is abandoned. But the rising Moroccan population and the activity in the port disperse any nostalgic feelings. There are said to be plans to turn the town into the top seaside resort of the south, but as yet this project has not got under way.

Agadir is best regained by the same route or, if time permits, by the 7129 to Guelmim (44 km) and back north to Bou Izakarn (40 km) and Agadir (158 km).

FURTHER AFIELD

From Taroudannt, the traveler not wanting to return to Agadir can continue eastwards along the P32. After about 60 km, a road to the left leads to **Marrakech** (210 km) via the **Tizi n'Test pass.** This used to be the only road from Marrakech to Agadir until the much easier route by Imi n'Tanoute was built. The road is narrow, winding, climbs steeply, and is beautiful (81 km to the pass). If you are thinking of taking it to reach Marrakech, check with the Gendarmerie that it is open, since heavy rain or snow can cause it to be blocked. On the right, just before the pass, there's a spring and a little café, good for a snack. Going down the other, northern side of the Atlas, the road passes the historic mosque of **Tinmal** (chapter 12).

After the junction of the Tizi n'Test road, the P32 continues east via **Aoulouz, Taliouine,** and **Tazenakht** to arrive at **Ouarzazate** (294 km, chapter 13). From **Aoulouz,** a very rough road runs through the old volcanic region of the Jbel Siroua, coming out the other side at Anezal (148 km) This is a favorite area for trekkers and the scenery is spectacular. Some of the villages still use their fortified granaries *(igherm)* to store their foodstuffs, and even their precious documents. Both vehicles and trekkers should be properly equipped (4WD and full camping gear). Information on qualified mountain guides and escorts for the Jbel Siroua area can be obtained from the *Délégation Provinciale du Tourisme,* Ouarzazate (Tel: 04-88 52 91).

Taliouine offers two **accommodation** possibilities: the ****** Hotel ibn Toumert** (100 rooms, Tel: 04-88 22 25, Fax: 04-88 23 19), next to the ruins of one of the kasbahs which belonged to the Glaoui, Pasha of Marrakech, and the modest, unclassified four-room **Auberge Souktana,** 4 km before the village (120 DH) (sleeping on the roof terrace is possible). Both do **meals** (set meal in the hotel 143 DH, Auberge from 50 DH). **Tazenakht** is known throughout Morocco for its handwoven rugs (see Ouarzazate, chapter 13).

Only 8 km out of Taroudannt on the same P32, the road to the right passing the turning to **Tioute** (see above) continues **south through the heart of the Anti-Atlas** and is the one of the gateways to sub-Saharan Morocco. The road, bordered on each side by bare plateaus or orchards of almond trees, climbs in steep curves up to the small town of **Igherm** (82 km). Just before pulling into Igherm, a pretty rough unpaved road (just over 100 km), the 7038, goes off on the right to Ait Abdallah, Ait Ourhaine, and **Tafraoute.** Many of the villages along this route have well-preserved **granaries,** which can be visited. Igherm stands at 1,900 m and is usually pretty cold and windy. The whole region is home to the Berber Soussi, many of whom have emigrated to the big towns of Morocco, where they run most of the small grocery stores, or even further afield to Europe. There's a gas station, but not much else apart from a small market with rather tired vegetables, a bakery, and a few cafés. There are several copper mines in the area, and by the 11th century Igherm's copper products were being exported to sub-Saharan Africa. Some of the black-swathed women still carry the copper water pitchers for which Igherm was renowned, but most prefer the cheaper version made out of old airplane or tractor tires.

The next 100 km stretch of road south is relatively recent. The ochre-colored hillsides are bare of trees, and the exposed rock strata heave up and down like gigantic prehistoric serpents, today's witness of past geological upheavals. A left-hand turn at the T-junction brings the visitor into the large oasis of **Tata** (200 km from Taroudannt), a good place for a night's stopover.

Tata is the seat of provincial government, the center of some 30 *ksours* (plural of *ksar,* a group of houses protected by high adobe walls), and the junction of three rivers having their origin in the Anti-Atlas. Its dark-skinned inhabitants may be the descendants of the prehistoric cattle-herders who lived in the Sahara at a time when the climate was wetter—around 6,000 years ago—and who were pushed north by increasing aridity and desertification. Or they may be the remains of the black troops brought up into Morocco by the Almoravid invaders in the 11th century A.D. Their occupation today is date production, though the big problem in recent years has been a lethal sickness that killed off many palm trees. Locusts are another plague much feared in the southern provinces, though here, luckily, energetic measures are taken by the state to plane-spray the infected zones. Tata can be **reached by bus** from Taroudannt, Tiznit, or Agadir.

The top **hotel** is *** **Le Relais des Sables** (55 rooms, 18 with air-conditioning, which is precious in summer when temperatures can reach 40° C, Tel: 80 23 01, Fax: 80 23 01), a fairly new establishment at the entrance to the town, equipped with a restaurant and small swimming pool (not always open, call first).

My favorite for many years is the simple, friendly ** **Hotel La Renaissance,** further into town (44 rooms, not air-conditioned, Tel: 08-80 20 42). The hotel was started by a Tata man who worked many years in France before returning to open a small hotel (on the left-hand side). Apart from its lower price, its only real attraction is the shady little garden. Inside, 17 rooms are arranged around a courtyard (the plumbing is deficient). The success of his hotel prompted the owner to open his annex, an unattractive but more functional building on the right (27 rooms).

There is a **campsite** further along off the main road. Both **Le Relais des Sables** and **La Renaissance** serve a standard Moroccan meal (143 DH and 92 DH respectively).

An opportunity to see a **fortified granary** *(igherm)* in an excellent state of conservation can be had by taking a good track on the left just after the village of El-Khemis, marked El-Ayoun, turning right to **Jbair** (opposite the El-Ayoun turning). The Jbair granary is a square, stone-built construction of four stories. It owes its good condition to a private person who had the good idea to persuade an old village man to live there and be its guardian (small tip required for being shown around).

An easy excursion eastwards to **Tissint** by the now-tarred road should not be missed (about 80 km). Some 2 km short of Tissint, there is a superb, plunging **view** down into the blue riverbed—not the Grand Canyon, but not bad for a desert. The village of Tissint is noted for its waterfall and salty pools in which one can bathe, a remarkable sensation in the middle of a hot, dusty trip. About 10 km after Tissint, it's well worth stopping to cross the river and climb the low **Jbel Fergoussat** on the other side, where there are a number of **rock engravings** (mostly ostriches) near the top. The view is also splendid from here and worth the climb, even for those not into rock art. The road continues on to **Foum Zguid** and up north to **Ouarzazate,** or by unpaved road to **Zagora** (chapter 13).

From Tata (buy gas and have tires repaired before leaving), in a generally western direction, the well-kept 7084 eventually becomes the P30 and joins the main north-south road at Bou Izakarn (245 km). Before doing so, however, it goes through country rich in **prehistoric art engraving (petroglyph) sites.** Two accessible sites are those of **Tiggane** (25 km from Tata and 5 km from the village of Tiggane) and **Madaoui** (a few kilometers further on), both indicated by noticeboards on the left of the road. The engravings were done perhaps 5,000 years ago (perhaps a bit more recently), but at any rate, at a time when animals such as rhinoceros, elephants, and antelopes frequented the area since they are favorite subjects of the prehistoric hunter-herdsmen who engraved their images on the sandstone outcrops. Remember that these sites are protected and there are heavy penalties for damaging the engravings.

The scenery all along this stretch is bare and stark, broken occasionally by scattered acacia trees and herds of camels or goats. To the right lies the 500-km long Jbel Bani, stretching from the Atlantic to Zagora in the east. It's a formidable barrier, broken only from time to time by a *foum* (mouth), where a river has cut its way through the sandstone. These *foum* are all occupied by oases, profiting from the underground water and rich soil left by the downpouring rivers. A sudden rise in water level can turn the normally dry riverbeds into raging torrents, destroying the adobe houses and causing the death of animals and humans.

There's not much going on at the oasis of **Akka** (62 km from Tata) apart from the souk on Thursday, but if you're into rock engravings, ask for Mouloud Tarabit in Akka (try the Café Tamdoult). He knows most of the rock art and other interesting sites around (remunerated at about 100 DH/day). Again, make sure not to run afoul of the law concerning the "Moroccan national heritage." Just before the oasis of **Icht** (81 km from

Akka), the road (now the P30) goes straight on to Bou Izakarn and left to **Foum el-Hsn,** at the moment housing an important military garrison (police control on the road, passport essential). This little town used to be an important stop for camel caravans coming up from Black Africa laden with gold and slaves. A road from Foum el-Hsn goes down to the oasis of **Assa** (80 km), once an important center with a 13th-century *zaouia* (religious fraternity), but it is sometimes blocked by the military.

About 60 km further on, a track on the right, marked "Souk Tnine Waday" and "Amtoundi," leads to the **fortified granary of Id Aissa** and the village of Amtoundi (don't worry if you've missed the turn off, there is another, rather easier, but longer road [30 km], which leaves from Taghjicht, about 12 km further on). This is a magnificent example of the fortified granaries of south Morocco and deservedly popular, which means that there are streams of 4WD tourist agency vehicles pouring in from Agadir, especially around 11:00 A.M. By 3:00 P.M. all is calm again, and it is a good time for a quiet appreciation of this magnificent building (tip to the guardian) and for a walk in the surrounding oasis.

There's one small **hotel** in the village, **Hotel Taregua,** but it's often closed. They'll do a **meal** if it's not too late. More sure accommodations are available back on the main road, at Taghjicht. I don't give the **Auberge Tarjijht,** up the hill on the left before reaching the village, many stars, but it is always open and convenient at the end of a long day (25 rooms, 120 DH double room, without water closet). They will do a standard **dinner** if necessary (licensed bar), but we've always cooked food in the bedroom without any problem.

About 20 km on from Tarjijht, a turning on the right (marked) leads to **Ifrane de l'Anti-Atlas,** once inhabited by the oldest Jewish community in Morocco (8 km). The *mellah* is claimed to have been settled in the 6th century B.C. by Jews fleeing from Babylonian persecution—but archaeological research has proved that the tombs date from the 1st century A.D. The population of the region was one of the last to be converted to Islam and Christian communities were still living there in the 12th century A.D. The synagogue, already in a bad state when I first visited it in 1974, has been ransacked, the houses in the *mellah* destroyed, and the tombs in the Jewish cemetery are scarcely recognizable. However, in 1998, the Foundation for the Judeo-Moroccan cultural heritage announced plans to restore the synagogue and the cemetery.

After **Bou Izakarn** (20 km), the road clings to the side of the mountain as it climbs up out of the plain to reach **Tiznit** (67 km) and **Agadir** (a further 91 km). South from Bou Izakarn, the P41 goes to Guelmim and Tan-Tan. Bou Izakarn has a 30-room, ** hotel, the **Hotel Anti-Atlas.**

South of Agadir, an agreeable shorter circuit taking in **Ait Baha,**

Tafraout, and **Tiznit,** for a total distance of some 350 km, is most comfortably done in two days. The main road from Agadir passes through Inezgane and Ait Melloul, both hustling, bustling places with trucks puffing out diesel fumes. At Ait Melloul, leave the P30 road going to Tiznit and take instead the S509 to **Ait Baha** (50 km), a large agricultural center. A *** hotel was opened here in March 1998, the **Al Adarissa** (32 rooms). It has a large restaurant and a coffee-room, all in Moroccan style, and being new, it will probably stay clean and functional for a while. From here to **Tafraout** (86 km) the road is mountainous, winding, and narrow, but the views are magnificent. In early February, the countryside is a mass of blossoms and a delightful sight. It's the scenery visitors go for, so good weather is needed. Look out for the *igherms (agadirs),* the fortified granaries, often perched on a rocky point slightly apart from the villages. Their walls follow the shape of the rock to such an extent that it often hard to know where nature gives way to man. The one at **Tioulit,** on the right, can be visited. Tafraout lies in the middle of a valley—the Ameln Valley—surrounded by pink granite rocks, suspended at a height of 1,200 m. Erosion has turned the rocks into great rounded bundles heaped up on each other. In 1984, a Belgian artist had the idea of painting some of them bright blue . . . is it art?

Work in the fields and orchards is almost entirely done by women— Tafraout men were among the first to be employed in Europe after the war. The "new rich" immigrant workers are responsible for the concrete houses, built with their overseas earnings. The women around here are dressed in black, with a bit of colored embroidery here and there. They are very independent.

Tafraout can be reached by **bus** direct from Agadir or Tiznit, or from further afield via Agadir. The most expensive **hotel** is the **** **Hotel Les Amandiers** (Tel: 80 00 88, Fax: 80 03 43) up on the hill overlooking the town. Tour groups come here and it has a restaurant and bar.

In the lower range, the **Hotel Salama,** in the town (150 DH, Tel: 80 00 26, Fax: 80 04 48), has recently been done up, and the rooms are large and comfortable.

Budget accommodations are best provided by the **Hotel Tafraout,** looking onto the Place al-Massira at the northern end of the Avenue des F.A.R. (100 DH, Tel: 80 00 60).

There are two more hotels in the town, very basic, the **Hotel Tanger** and the **Hotel Reddouane** (both with rooms around 50 DH). The campsite, **Camping Les Trois Palmiers,** is small and stony, but not bad, with reasonable toilet facilities (10 DH/person, 10 DH/tent, 8 DH/car).

The **restaurant** in the **Hotel Les Amandiers** is okay, but not worth going to specially (set meal 143 DH). The restaurant **L'Etoile du Sud** (opposite the post office on Avenue Hassan II) is definitely out to catch the tourist, but the Moroccan meal is not bad (set menu 70 DH) and the waiters are friendly (too friendly, perhaps).

Sightseeing around Tafraout includes a visit to **two rock engravings (petroglyphs) at Tazka,** depicting domestic cattle but called gazelle *(gzal)* by the local people. They are easily reached on foot along the road to the little village of Tazka (1½ km from town center) and lie in a narrow valley full of gardens and trees. The most visible engraving, on a vertical rock face, is 1.20 m long, the other, slightly bigger, is on the upper surface of a large block just below. There's so much vegetation around that they are not easy to find, so it's probably best to be guided by one of the numerous children who will have been watching you. The engravings date to some unknown prehistoric period, probably the 1st millennium B.C. Two other readily reached rock-art sites are shown on a map displayed in the Hotel Les Amandiers, and someone here will help you to find them, though only one **(Tirmtmart)** is really worth the visit.

The Tafraout area is ideal for **excursions** on foot for the day or for longer treks, or gentle drives around to admire the countryside and the numerous abandoned villages, perched defensively on hilltops. A particularly interesting one is the **Agadir n'Tark** (also called **Agadir n'Tarhaout**), reached by the road going south to Agard-Oudad, Taloust, and Tarhaout. A couple of kilometers after Tarhaout, on the left, the fortified village of Agadir n'Tark is clearly visible, abandoned but still giving a very good idea of its layout (just over 20 km from Tafraout). A steep mule trail on the west side leads up to an impressive gate, which is still standing. Inside the ramparts is the granary, a mosque, ruined houses, and little lanes.

Independent trekking is easily done from Tafraout by equipped walkers (there are villages up in the hills, but no official rest houses) with a good map. If a guide or information is wanted, the Hotel Les Amandiers, or the shop Maison Touareg, in the center of town, can probably help. As an idea for negotiating a price, the tariff for an accredited mountain escort is currently 160 DH a day in the High Atlas, and should be a good bit lower for a casual guide in this area. By the way, I must repeat that there are absolutely *no* Touareg in Morocco. The Touareg are desert dwellers living in South Algeria, Mali, and Niger.

A good road goes northeast from Tafraout to **Ait Abdallah,** but then becomes so rough that it is only suitable for stout nerves or 4WD vehicles. It arrives, after 100 km, at Igherm (see above, route from Taroudannt to Tata) via a series of typical Berber villages with their **fortified granaries** set slightly apart on an easily defended hill. Some of these granaries can be visited—**Agadir Tasguent** and **Ait Ourhaine,** for instance.

The **return to Agadir** is along the 7057, towards Tiznit. The scenery is absolutely stunning as far as Tiznit (107 km): deep valleys, Berber stone and adobe villages perched on the hillsides, terraces of cultivated crops rising up one above the other, and almond and argan trees in profusion. The **Kerdous Pass** *(Col du Kerdous),* some 50 km from Tafraout, stands at 1,100 m and for the tired or thirsty traveler there is an excellent hotel here, the ★★★★ **Hotel Kerdous** (39 rooms, Tel: 86 20 63, Fax: 86 28 35), with a restaurant and bar. About 20 km short of Tiznit, the land flattens out, and the 95 km to Agadir are quickly covered.

This whole circuit can, of course, be taken in the other direction, starting on the Tiznit road and ending with the beautiful, but slow, mountainous route by Ait Baha.

A really **long trip south** from Agadir will take you past Tiznit (93 km), down to Guelmim, Tan-Tan (331 km), and eventually Laayoune (649 km). **Guelmim** (formerly called Goulimime), a long, straggling, pink-colored town, is one of those desert towns that grew in importance at the time of the Green March into Spanish Sahara in 1975, but it is not particularly noteworthy now. It had a glorious past from the 10th to the 14th centuries, when it lay on the camel caravan route from the Niger, Mali, and Senegal and traded with Timbuktu, but it declined when the trade in gold, spices, indigo, and slaves ceased. Until the 1930s, too, it had an immense annual camel fair which, in a good year, saw 40,000 roaring and foaming beasts bought and sold. The "blue men" from the desert would come in and watch, fascinated, the kneeling women "dance" the famous Saharan dance, the *guedra,* involving erotic movements of the upper body, that would doubtless compensate them for their hard nomadic life. Slightly outside the modern town, the little streets of old Guelmim have probably little changed since those heroic days (they are worth a stroll). But my impression of today's weekly camel market (Saturdays) is that there are as many tourists as camels, though this may change with current plans to bring the camel back into favor because of its ideal adaptation to desert conditions (at the moment, the town of Settat, near Casablanca, is the place to buy or sell a camel). The best time of year to see camels around Guelmim is at the beginning of June, after the crops have been harvested, when the neighboring tribes bring their animals in to graze off the stubble. And there are camel races in April.

The CTM **buses** run from Agadir and there is one a day from Laayoune and Casablanca. SATAS buses also come to Guelmim. **Big taxis** may often be more convenient, and are hardly more expensive. The long-distance buses and big taxis have their base 1 km out of the town, on the Agadir road.

The **hotel scene** starts with the ★ **Hotel Salam** (19 rooms, at the big intersection in the town, going towards Tan-Tan, Tel: 87 20 57), painted brick-red, so it can't be missed. It has a restaurant and bar.

For **budget accommodations** there are a number of hotels offering rooms at around 50 DH, but it's difficult to recommend one over another, since they all have more or less clean rooms and cold showers (avoid the **Hotel de la Jeunesse** if you can).

The town campsite, just outside the town, would do in a pinch. The best **restaurant** is in the Hotel Salam (set meal 92 DH) and **cheap standard Moroccan meals** (around 50 DH) can be had at the **Café de la Poste** and the **Café Le Diamand Bleu** (both Route de Tan-Tan).

Accommodations **outside** Guelmim may be more appealing if you are motorized. At **Abino,** about 15 km north of the town, on the road to Sidi Ifni, there is a simple but comfortable hotel, the **Hotel Abeino** (100 DH, Tel: 87 04 23, Fax: 87 04 22), after the village, with a restaurant and bar. The little oasis has hot springs, organized for bathing.

About 40 km west of Guelmim, in the direction of Plage Blanche (13 km tarred to Tiseguenane, then 18 km of good track), the **Fort Bou Jerif** campsite is an ideal place to head for if you have a car, and an absolute must for those hardy travelers intending to drive down to Mauritania (BP 504, Guelmim, Fax: 87 30 39). The general direction is indicated on the right of the main road into Guelmim. This big campsite, set in a little oasis at the foot of a ruined French Foreign Legion fort, is run by a French couple and offers simple rooms and beds under a nomad tent and an excellent restaurant (130 DH for the set meal, including wine). But it is far more than a campsite—the latest information and tips for traveling down into Mauritania are exchanged here in a stimulating atmosphere of adventure (well, maybe some periods are calmer than others). Hikes or Land Rover trips in the neighborhood can also be arranged. The **Plage Blanche** is made up of 50 km of white beach and is a marvelous place for walks.

For a really quiet retreat in a very modest establishment, instead of going straight on to Tan-Tan, bear left at the first traffic circle and keep left at the second for the **Auberge Tighmert** (indicated at the intersection, on the right, as 12 km, but it is, in fact, 15 km). This is the road to **Fask/Asrir** (note camel-crossing road sign). Turn right for Asrir (famous palm grove) and continue along the paved road as far as a school and a red, kasbah-style building on the right (marked), and you can't miss it. This is the **Auberge Tighmert** (17 rooms, 150 DH, telephone should have been installed by the end of 1998), with clean, very simple rooms with water closet and shower, a restaurant, bar, and *guedra* dancers (so they say . . . I doubt it). The Fask road leads to the oasis of **Assa** (100 km), from where a roughish road goes northeast to **Foum el-Hsn** (70 km) (both described above).

The 125 km of road from Guelmim to **Tan-Tan** may not be inspiring, but it is well maintained, with traffic mostly limited to trucks bringing fish up from Tan-Tan or Dakhla. The landscape is typically sub-Saharan—stone-covered plateaus *(hamada)* (which means it's a *reg* and not an *erg*, which is a **hamada** covered with sand dunes), broken by dry river beds and a few hills. Occasional sand-devils twist and turn, sucking up grains of sand. There are not many signs of life, as most of the villages lie some way off the main road, but there is the occasional café (best fill up with gas before leaving Guelmim).

Tan-Tan is a sprawling, white-colored town, for many years part of the Spanish zone of southern Morocco and only handed back in 1958. The ex-Spanish fort can be seen up on the hill. Before the Spaniards came, nomads used to gather here to draw water from the well, and the town owes its name to the noise, "tin, tin," made when the bucket was let down. The presence of water encouraged the Spaniards to establish themselves here, and it became a strategic point in the 1940s. Tan-Tan used to be the principal town of a poor province living off herding and the end of the line for public transport. Most of the bus passengers got off here, and in the late 1960s the hippies and others wanting to go down to what was then the Spanish Sahara and from there across to the Canary Islands and then to Dakar all scrambled into Land Rovers or hired places on trucks to do the last sandy stretch to the frontier at **Tah** via **Tarfaya.** This was an epic journey which could last 24 hours, depending on how many times the vehicle got stuck in the sand. When the Moroccans moved into the Spanish Sahara in 1975 and made Tan-Tan their departure point, all this changed. The road has been paved as far as Laayoune and even further, to Dakhla (ex Villa-Cisneros). After the Green March, the town became full of trucks and soldiers going backwards and forwards, but although still containing an important military garrison, the town has now quieted down. The improved port is active with small fishing boats. The camel races and the *moussem* of Sidi Mohammed Laghdaf, one of Cheikh Ma el-Ainin's numerous sons, have not been held for several years.

Royal Air Maroc used to have a **flight** to Tan-Tan from Casablanca/Agadir, but this was stopped in 1998. The town can be reached daily by CTM **bus** from Casablanca, and from nearer towns such as Agadir, Laayoune, Dakhla, and Marrakech, as well as by **big taxi** from Agadir. The CTM bus station is in the main road. The **little town taxis** are blue and cream.

The **hotel scene** is not brilliant. I think the best hotel is the **Hotel al-Aoubour** (51 Avenue Hassan II, Tel: 87 75 94) on a corner on the left as you drive straight through the town. It has four rooms with shower and water closet, and six others (communal shower and water closet) opening onto a small open courtyard. The rooms are pretty basic, but clean, and all cost 100 DH. It has a restaurant.

After that, there is the **Hotel Bir Anzarane** (30 rooms, 100 DH, Avenue Hassan II—keep on down the main road and you'll see a big building at the fork, after the river—Tel: 87 78 34). The post office is clearly visible at the end of this road. Again, the rooms are pretty basic, with shared showers and water closets. It also has a restaurant.

The newish **Tan-Tan Club,** just outside the town on the Laayoune road, has been taken over by the United Nations at the time of writing and is closed. It is said to have three rooms and three to four dormitories with communal showers and water closets.

After these two, there are a few **cheapies** (50 DH), such as the **Hotel Tiznit,** hidden in a small street to the right as you get into Tan-Tan, just before the first fork, which are best avoided if possible.

The **campsite** at the entrance to the town is not inspiring, and it is just as cheap to go for a small hotel.

Dining and Restaurants. The **Hotel al-Aoubour** serves the best simple meal (main dish 30 DH). The next best is the restaurant in the **Hotel Bir Anzarane** (same price). There are plenty of cafés around, and one at the entrance, on the right, opposite the filling station, does good coffee and warm croissants.

Just before Tan-Tan, the P41 changes direction and goes west for 25 km to **Tan-Tan Plage,** where the fishing port is situated. Like any small port, this is worth a visit and a walk out along the breakwater. There are a number of holiday villas, small restaurants (not at all bad), and cafés around the beach. A large "seaside resort" has been under construction for some time, but it has not taken off yet, and the hotel has not been officially named.

From Tan-Tan it is possible to drive direct to **Semara** (220 km), which is now the capital of the Moroccan province of the same name, pending the results of the referendum to decide the fate of this ex-Spanish territory. The route is pretty monotonous but avoids Laayoune. Deviations to either side of the road are not advised, since this area was the scene of heavy fighting after the Green March in 1975 and mines are still hidden under the sands.

The road from Tan-Tan to **Tarfaya** (236 km) runs along the coast, which is sometimes low and flat, and sometimes backed by cliffs. It is paved all the way, though sometimes lightly covered by blown sand. Lone figures can be seen fishing from the cliffs and there is an occasional shack. Camping is possible anywhere around here.

The area at the mouth of the **River Chebeika** (30 km from Tan-Tan Plage) is particularly appreciated by fishermen, and keen Casablancans go there for a fortnight's camping and fishing. It's a good place for bird-watchers, too. But the low moving sands, strong winds, and powerful currents make this whole coast very dangerous for shipping, and just north of Tarfaya several wrecks can be seen only a few hundred yards from the shore. One of the crew of the Brazil-bound English vessel *Montezuma*, Alexander Scott, was shipwrecked here in 1811. Captured by fierce nomadic tribes, the account of his wanderings, escape, and final ransom by the British representative at Essaouira makes poignant reading. Another sailor, the American James Riley, captain of the 220-ton brig *Commerce*, out from Gibraltar laden with wine, was also shipwrecked and captured in the same area in 1815 and eventually wrote a book about his adventures.

A small village of fishermen is installed at **Sidi Akhfennir,** about 60 km further on. Among the cafés there's a very good little fish restaurant, the **Café de France,** where you can get delicious, freshly-caught fish (the **Café des Pêcheurs** is also a good one), and gas becomes tax-free. Ask the Caid for permission to fish in the lagoon or in the sea around here. The road makes a curve inland at **Foum Agoutir** (70 km from Tarfaya) to avoid the Sebkhat Tazra. *Sebkha*—below sea level depressions covered with a thin film of salty water—are familiar sights around here and, when it rains (which it rarely does), the local people use them for cereal cultivation. This now-desolate region was occupied, perhaps occasionally, by prehistoric people who left behind their stone tools and burial mounds, but no trace of settlement.

Tarfaya became one of the far-flung outposts of the British empire (in a way) when, in 1875, the Scotsman Donald MacKenzie built an offshore trading post just opposite the village. The building was known as **The Sea House** *(Casa del Mar)* and one can walk out and see its ruined walls. Mackenzie left eight years later, and, in 1920, the Spanish established a small garrison as part of their occupation of southern Morocco under the Protectorate treaty. Tarfaya was an important stopover for the *Aéropostale* service from Toulouse to Dakar and South America in the 1920s. The statue of a small copper airplane recalls this period. In recent years there have been attempts to make a port in Tarfaya, but the strong underwater currents bring down so much sand as the wind and sea erode away the cliffs that the port became rapidly blocked. Research has been undertaken on oil shale deposits here, but for the moment their exploitation is too expensive.

For non-motorized travelers, the **only way to get to Tarfaya** is by one of the infrequent **buses** or **big taxis.** There is no hope of finding a **hotel,** but it is possible to get a simple **meal** from one of the cafés.

Some 110 km of road separate Tarfaya from Laayoune. The whole Western Saharan zone consists of a line of coastal dunes, followed inland by a vast *hamada*. The landscape is flat, passing close to a number of *sebkha* before arriving at **Tah,** the old frontier post, the small village of **Dawra,** and **Laayoune.** A monument in Tah celebrates the visit that sultan Hassan I made here in 1885 as part of his campaign to force obedience from the dissident tribesmen, and also that of the late king, Hassan II, after the success of the Green March.

Laayoune lies on the left bank of the area's longest river, the **Saguiet al-Hamra,** starting 400 km away in the Zemmour hills to the east. As one crosses the bridge into the town, its blue waters can sometimes be seen before it gets lost in the sand on its way to the sea. To judge from prehistoric tools and rock engravings, Laayoune—like the whole region—was occupied in prehistoric times, but the town itself was built by the Spaniards in the 1930s as the capital of their Saharan possession. They never turned it into anything very grand, but since the Green March in 1975 it has become the center of Moroccan administration in the territory, pending the results of the referendum to decide its final fate. Much money has been poured into the town since 1978, and it is now better equipped with hospitals, schools, and training colleges than many towns elsewhere in Morocco. The airport has been modernized, and electricity and drinking water facilities extended. Laayoune port lies 24 km from the town and is mainly used by fishing boats. International fishing fleets make big hauls further out into the Atlantic, and their activities cause a certain amount of friction. A short distance down the coast, a big shipping terminal, its quay sticking way out into the sea because of the shallow water, exports the phosphates mined in Bou Kra, where the deposits are among the richest in the world. The phosphates travel on a conveyor belt direct from the mine, a distance of 100 km. The belt was set up by the Spanish, with machinery made by the big German firm Krupps, but it and the terminal have been improved by the Moroccan government.

Laayoune is the headquarters of the United Nations mission (MINURSO) responsible for the organization of the referendum. Population density for Laayoune province is low—4.1 inhabitants per km^2—with 95 percent living in Laayoune town. Laayoune has quite a number of foreign residents, mostly Spaniards working for the phosphates, or Spanish and Mauritanian shopkeepers.

Royal Air Maroc runs a **regular air service** to Laayoune from Casablanca and Agadir, three times a week. Three CTM **buses** arrive from Agadir and Tiznit every day, with one from Casablanca (315 DH). SATAS buses also serve Laayoune. **Big taxis** are also available.

The Hotel Scene. The ***** **Hotel Parador** (33 rooms, from 900 DH, Rue Oqba ben Nafi, Tel: 89 45 00, Fax: 89 36 24) is the most **expensive.** Until very recently it was difficult to get rooms here, as they were reserved for the United Nations team, but this has changed, and it is now possible for ordinary visitors to be lodged. It is as elegant as all the old Spanish Parador chain, and has a pool and restaurant.

After that, the ***** **Hotel Al Massira** (75 rooms, from 900 DH, 12 Rue de la Mecque, Tel: 89 42 25) is big, new, and up to the Parador standard, with a pool, a restaurant, and a bar. But it is often fully booked by tourist groups. Both these hotels are run by the French Club Med.

Dropping down a bit, you have the **** **Hotel Nagjir** (Place Dchira, Tel: 89 41 68, Fax: 89 41 69), which has a restaurant, a bar, and—sometimes—a disco.

In the **medium-price** range, there is the *** **Hotel Lakouara** (40 rooms, Avenue Hassan II, Tel: 89 33 78), which is a good value, and the ** **Hotel el-Alia** (34 rooms, 1 Rue Kadi el-Ghalaoui, Tel: 89 41 44).

Among the **budget accommodations,** you have the * **Hotel Marhaba** (36 rooms, also on Avenue Hassan II, Tel: 89 32 49), which gets pretty full since it's one of the best of the cheap hotels.

The **cheaper** hotels (around 50 DH) are popular with soldiers and the water is always cold.

The **campsite** at the beach (Laayoune Plage) is pretty rock-bottom. A big tourist complex is planned for Laayoune Plage, but is unlikely to take off until the political problem has been solved.

Good **restaurants** are not a specialty of Laayoune, and it's best to go for the **Hotel Parador** or **Hotel Al Massira.** Cheap *tajines,* roast chicken, salads, kebobs, and the like can be had in cafés and restaurants along Avenue Hassan II or Rue de la Mecque. The **Restaurant Le Marelka** (78 Avenue Hassan II) is one of the best.

A **stroll around the modern town** to admire its new buildings (Place du Mechouar, for instance), and note the domed architecture designed to keep out the heat, a visit to the very small **aviary** (the *Colline aux Oiseaux,* near Avenue Price Mulay Abdallah), and the **Craftwork Center** (*Centre Artisanal,* Rue de la Mecque), and you've probably done about all the **sightseeing.** The old **Spanish church** (not far from Avenue Hassan II) can only be looked at from the outside. The Saturday **market** is a lively event, mainly concerned with the buying and selling of goats and camels.

The Laayoune Address List:

Airlines—Royal Air Maroc, Place Dcheira, Immeuble Nagjir.

Banks—BMCE, Place Hassan II; Banque Populaire, Avenue Hassan II/ Boulevard Mohammed V and Place Dchira.

Bus station *(gare routière)*—CTM bus, Rue de la Mecque; SATAS and others, north out of town.

Express Post *(Poste rapide)*—Check with the main post office (Tel: 89 48 01) for details.

Post Office—end of Avenue Hassan II.

Taxis—north-bound big taxis leave from northwest end of Avenue Hassan II; south-bound from south of the town.

Telephone—at the post office and in téléboutiques.

Tourist information *(Délégation Régionale du Tourisme)* —practically opposite the Parador (Tel: 89 16 94), with the usual colored brochures, but not much else, though the staff is helpful (closed weekends).

The main road follows the coast down to **Boujdour** (200 km) and **Dakhla** (340 km further). The Portuguese landed in **Boujdour** in the 15th century. Today, it is frequented by people wanting to fish from the cliffs. There is only one small, new, clean **hotel,** with much *zellij* decoration (shared water closet and shower), and some of the little **restaurants** are not bad. The road down to **Dakhla** is long and uninteresting. It lies at the end of a 40-km peninsula jutting out into the sea like a curved beak, and was founded by the Spanish in 1884. Known as Villa Cisneros, it was a busy little town when I first visited it in the early 1970s, its port trading with Mauritania and the Canary Islands, but now it is very military.

Dakhla can most easily be **reached by air.** Royal Air Maroc has three flights a week from Casablanca, via Agadir and Laayoune (RAM office, Avenue des P.T.T., Tel: 89 70 49). By **bus,** there is a daily CTM and SATAS service from Laayoune and Agadir (often full, book early). An air-conditioned CTM bus does the nearly 1,700 km trip daily from Casablanca (via Agadir) in 18 hours (460 DH). **Big taxis** are an alternative. **Motorized travelers** heading for Mauritania (visa needed) and destinations further south have to assemble their vehicles here to join the twice-weekly convoy (Tuesdays and Fridays at 12:00 P.M.). Permission must be had beforehand from the police, the gendarmerie, and customs. All vehicle papers must be absolutely in order. Any deviation from the authorized route is highly dangerous because of the minefields on either side, which will remain even when the future of the area has been settled. Some 350 km have to be covered before the Moroccan frontier post is reached. The road is good until within about 10 km of the Mauritanian frontier, when it becomes definitely bad. Getting permission from the Mauritanian administration for the return journey is time-consuming and expensive. Experienced friends who have done the trip there and back have said that the whole thing was a nightmare and they wouldn't try again.

The **most expensive hotel** is the ★★★ **Hotel Doums** (43 rooms, Avenue al-Walla, Tel: 89 80 46, Fax: 89 80 45). The **Hotel la Sargha** is closed.

Again, the **cheaper accommodations** tend to be full of soldiers and are very rudimentary. The best possibilities for clean, simple rooms (communal water closets) are the very basic **Hotel al-Wahda, Hotel Sahara** (single room 60 DH, Avenue Sidi Ahmed Laaroussi, Tel: 89 77 73), and **Hotel Miramar** (no telephone).

The **campsite, Camping Moussafir,** is situated 6 km outside the town on the main road and, for once, is well kept (10 DH per person, same for tent and car). The **Hotel Doums** is the best place in which to **eat** (licensed), though there are some cheap restaurants around.

There is nothing much to see in Dakhla and no great incentive to go there, unless it is to fish, both by line and from a boat. The waters off Dakhla are excellent fishing grounds for professional fleets and sea-fishing by individuals is reputed to be equally rewarding. The Tourist Office in the town can help to arrange trips (Tel: 89 82 28) and the Casablanca-based company Sochetour organizes exclusive fishing trips (72 Boulevard Zerktouni, Casablanca, Tel: 02-27 75 13).

The immense underground water reserves that were discovered inland from Dakhla some years ago promise to bring a new source of wealth to the area. Banana farms are starting up and the Royal Farm at Dakhla exports tomatos and garlic to the United States. Two nature reserves are scheduled, one near the coast to protect the last small colony of monk seals, the other with gazelles and ostriches—the natural inhabitants of the region before they were exterminated by hunters—and possibly members of the cat family. The French owner of the Casablanca-based tourist agency Globe Trotters (67 Rue Lamgranta, Casablanca, Tel: 02-25 13 65, Fax: 02-25 15 22) has a farm just north of Dakhla, and plans to organize short excursions to the various national parks, flying from Marrakech or Agadir with Royal Air Maroc, from a comfortable hotel base in one of these towns.

The only other town in these Saharan provinces that can be visited is **Semara,** 240 km east of Laayoune. It was founded as a *ribat* (fortified religious center) around 1887 by Cheikh Ma el-Ainin, a learned, holy man who had lived in Mauritania before settling in Semara with his religious fraternity. Cheikh Ma el-Ainin chose Semara, so it is said, because a patch of rushes showed him there was water—the site is, in fact, close to the Saguiet el-Hamra river. The building, a partially fortified settlement, was built by Moroccan workers with material brought into Tarfaya by Moroccan and Spanish steamers, and then transported to the site by camels. The architects were from Morocco and Mauritania, and the construction was done as much as possible in dry-stone, with some adobe. It included a mosque, library, Koranic schools, public baths, and grain storage pits. About 50 wells were dug and palm trees planted. From here the Cheikh directed his opposition against the Spanish and French. His hostility to foreign penetration had already started 1883, and the Moroccan sultan Hassan I helped him with arms and ammunition, but resistance reached a head in 1913 when the *ribat* was attacked and partially damaged by French troops moving up from the south. Ma el-Ainin and his followers had already fled. It was briefly occupied by the Spanish, then left to crumble into ruins.

Semara can be **reached** from Laayoune and Tan-Tan by **bus** or **big taxi.** The few **hotels** are unclassified and pretty horrible. The **campsite** about 10 km north of Semara on the Tan-Tan road is okay if you are motorized. One or two small café-restaurants can provide a **cheap meal.**

Not a great deal remains of Ma el-Ainin's *ribat,* but it is worth a visit. One can easily imagine the impression of strength and power this large stone building gave to the nomadic Saharan tribes, more used to a camel-hair tent. Its walls are constructed with single flat or double courses and chevron patterning, and the numerous arcades and pillars of the mosque are fine examples of classic Moorish architecture. Some of the interior rooms are also still in quite a good state, though disintegrating every day through neglect. A Moroccan association based in Tan-Tan has been created to restore this important souvenir of the past.

7. Guided Tours

Guided tours of Agadir are not necessary (and even would-be guides are not too insistent). But there are plenty of tour operators providing excursions to the surrounding country—either in 4WD vehicles or minibuses. Most of the destinations they propose can easily be done by ordinary bus: Marrakech, Taroudannt, and Tafraout. The longer tours are more promising. As an example, **Karam Voyages** (Avenue Hassan II) proposes an excursion to Tata and Akka by 4WD on Thursdays for 1,395 DH, which includes two lunches, dinner, and a night's lodging. Their day trip to Massa on Tuesdays and Fridays by 4WD (departure 8:00 A.M., return 5:30 P.M.) costs 395 DH (lunch included). A half-day in Taroudannt (departures 8:00 A.M. and 2:00 P.M., return 12:30 P.M. and 6:30 P.M.) costs 175 DH (without lunch). Other agencies offer different possibilities, and it is worth shopping around (and negotiating if out of season).

8. Culture

Agadir's only **museum** owes its creation in 1992 to the talent and devotion of a Dutchman, Bert Flint. Resident in Marrakech, he acquired over his many years in Morocco an incomparable collection of traditional Berber arts and crafts from south Morocco, from the end of the 19th century to the present. A few years ago, he handed it over to the Municipality of Agadir, so that it could be appreciated by the general public. Photographs of the architectural traditions, elements of interior decoration and furniture, from wooden shutters and doors to rugs and simple cooking utensils, costumes, jewelry, pottery, and basketwork are among the displays. Housed under the municipal theater, in a square just off Boulevard Mohammed V, opposite the Hotel Salam, it is open every day except Sunday (from 9:30 A.M.-1:00 P.M. and from 2:30 P.M.-6:00 P.M., entry 10 DH). It is definitely not to be missed. My only complaint is that there are not enough captions and explanations.

The **American Cultural Center** (6 Impasse de Baghdad) gives a series of concerts in the summer, and organizes other periodical cultural activities.

9. Sports

This being a coastal area, **water sports** are the most obvious. But **horseback riding** and **golf** are also practiced in Agadir itself. The Atlantic Ocean is cold, but in Agadir Bay the sea is calm and the beaches clean. In front of the beach hotels you may be asked to pay for a place in which to spread your things. Pedalos, various types of water-skis, and surfboards can be rented at the southern end of the Agadir beach, but they are not cheap (from 100 DH/hour depending on what you want). Also along the beach, you'll find **horses** and **camels** ready for a trot or gallop along the sands. The Hotel Adrar (Boulevard Mohammed V, Tel: 84 04 37) and Hotel Les Almohades (Boulevard du 20 Août, Tel: 84 02 33) will both organize **horseback riding.** Try the Royal Club Equestre (on the right, just before Golf Les Dunes, 2 km along the road to Inezgane) for further information. Going north out of Agadir, towards Taghazout, the Ranch Hotel Pyramid (Route de l'Oued Sous-Bensergaro, Tel: 83 47 05) runs donkey-back excursions for children between 10 A.M. and 12:00 P.M. (100 DH) and horseback riding excursions for beginners or experienced riders from 8:00 A.M.-10:00 A.M. (200 DH).

Sports Evasion Maroc, in the center of town near the Hotel Sud Bahia (Rue des Administrations, off Avenue du Général Kettani, Tel: 84 01 22) can arrange not only horseback riding but **sea-fishing trips.** Shark-fishing every day is proposed by Atlantic Loisirs (25 Boulevard du 20 Août, complexe Tagadirt, Tel: 84 00 74). Departures are at 9:30 A.M. with a return at 5:00 P.M. Karam Voyages (Avenue Hassan II) runs shark-fishing trips every day from 9:30 A.M., returning at 4:30 P.M. (325 DH). Sea-fishing can also be arranged from Dakhla, in the very south. Information on deep-sea fishing can be had from Sochetur, 72 Boulevard Kerktouni, Casablanca (Tel: 27 75 13).

Line-fishing is much practiced from the cliffs much further south, around Mirleft for instance, and south of Oued Chebeika (see "Sightseeing" above). **Sea excursions** on the *Jana II* for the day (departure 10:30 A.M., return at 5:30 P.M.) or half-day (departures 9:30 A.M. and 1:00 P.M., return at 12:30 P.M. and 4:00 P.M.) are run by Wonder Cruise s.a.r.l. (BP 908, New Town, Tel: 84 82 51). The day cruise costs 600 DH per person and includes an aperitif and lunch and the half-day cruise costs 300 DH (aperitif only). Karam Voyages also does a shorter sea cruise every day (departure 9:00 A.M., return 3:00 P.M.), rather more cheaply (485 DH including lunch on board).

Golfers are lucky in Agadir. There are two golf clubs—the Dunes Golf Club *(Golf les Dunes)* (on the right, 2 km along the Inezgane road, Tel: 83 46 90) and the Agadir Royal Golf Club (10 km further on, on the left, Tel: 24 12 78). The former is made up of three 9-hole courses that can be combined, all with a par of 36. The Yellow course covers 3,050 m, the Blue is slightly longer at 3,174 m, and the Red 3,204 m. The Dunes Golf Club belongs to the Club Med holiday association, but is open to the public for payment of a green fee (around 200 DH) (handicap card compulsory). Clubs can be rented. The latter is a 9-hole course, par 36, 3,600 m. Both clubs are set in attractive surroundings, combining eucalyptus and palm trees with lakes and fountains. Several international competitions are held on the Agadir courses. There is a restaurant, Restaurant Lakersaba, conveniently placed next door to the Royal Golf Club.

Non-members can play **tennis** at the Royal Tennis Club, Avenue Hassan II, where they can also rent equipment and the services of a coach.

10. Shopping

Agadir itself is not the place to pick up a bargain carpet or piece of pottery. There is no local handicraft, so what is sold has been made elsewhere. Prices are relatively high, since the shops cater to the tourists, many of whom have not had the chance to see good and cheaper stuff elsewhere. Bearing this in mind, have a look at the traditional craftwork in the *Complexe Artisanal* (Rue du 29 Février), which applies fixed prices. The **big hotels** have boutiques, where the quality is often not bad at all. Cool and cheap Moroccan clothing can be found in the **Nouvelle Talborjt** district. For everyday necessities and food for a picnic, the **Uniprix Supermarché** (corner Avenue Hassan II/Rue du Prince Héritier Sidi Mohammed) stocks a wide range of goods, including beer and wine. The **Central Market** *(Marché Central)* (just off Avenue du Prince Mulay Abdallah) is the place for all fresh food, including fish, meat, and vegetables. A good range of books in English, including second-hand novels, is sold at the **Crown English Bookshop** on Place Hassan II (up on the first floor), and newspapers are available in the **big hotels** and at many kiosks in the center of town and around the seafront. Color films can be bought or printed and developed quickly at a number of **photographic shops** around town. All have automatic machines and the quality is the same everywhere. Many do while-you-wait passport photographs.

11. Entertainment and Nightlife

There is a small sort of **zoo-aviary-children's playground,** called **Bird Valley** *(Vallée des Oiseaux)* between the Boulevards du 20 Août and Hassan II. It mainly has cages of birds, including peacocks, but there are some monkeys, an antelope or two, llamas, and some unusually well-fed goats. It has quite a bit of greenery and a small waterfall, and is a pleasant place to visit (open every day except Mondays from 9:30 A.M.-12:30 P.M. and 2:30 P.M.-6:30 P.M., entry 5 DH, children 3 DH). **Birdwatchers** can watch free-flying birds at a number of waterside sites such as the mouth of the River Sous and further south in the Oued Massa park (see "Sightseeing" above).

There are not many **cinemas** in Agadir. Try the **Rialto** (off Avenue Mulay Abdallah) or see if the **Alliance Franco Marocaine** (5 Rue Yahchech) has a film or play programmed. Everything will be in Arabic or French.

Outside of the hotels, nightlife does not go on very late in Agadir. The animated **Boulevard du 20 Août** is full of restaurants-bars where you can stop and have a **drink. Beer** can be had from many cafés and restaurants along the **seafront.** For a quieter drink in comfortable surroundings, the big hotels are the best bet. Most of them have bars with some sort of music in the evening. The **Alhambra Cabaret** (Boulevard du 20 Août) puts on a show appreciated by tourists. If the dancers sometimes look a bit tired, it's understandable—the season is long. The **Cabaret Les Lords** in the **Agadir Beach Club** is said to be good. In the big hotels and beach club "villages" you have discos and nightclubs. Be wary of "working girls" looking for unaccompanied males. The best **nightclub** at the moment is the one in the **Hotel Sahara** on the Boulevard Mohammed V, followed by the one in the **Hotel Agadir Beach Club.** The **Byblos** nightclub in the **Hotel PLM Dunes d'Or** (Secteur Balnéaire) used to have a very good reputation, but may have declined a bit lately. The **Casino Le Mirage** offers Black Jack, English roulette, poker, and pinball machines (open every evening from 9:00 P.M.-4:00 A.M., pin machines from 5:00 P.M.). It's out in the Club Valtur Village (Parcelle 31, Secteur Balnéaire, Tel: 84 87 77, Fax: 84 87 74).

12. The Agadir Address List

Airlines—Royal Air Maroc, corner Avenue du Général Kettani/Avenue Hassan II (Tel: 84 07 93).

Airport—Al Massira (Tel: 83 90 01).

Banks—Crédit du Maroc, Avenue des F.A.R. (Tel: 84 01 88) represents American Express; all major banks have branches in Agadir (Avenue du Général Kettani, Avenue Hassan II for instance); the BMCE (Avenue du Général Kettani) has a credit card distributor and ATMs.

Bus Station *(gare routière)* —Nouvelle Talborjt.

Car Rental—Avis, Avenue Hassan II (Tel: 84 17 55, at airport Tel: 83 92 44); Budget, Bungalow Marhaba, Boulevard Mohammed V (Tel: 84 46 00, Fax: 84 53 09, at airport Tel: 83 91 01); Europcar, Bungalow Marhaba, Boulevard Mohammed V (Tel: 84 09 39, at airport Tel: 83 90 71); Hertz, Boulevard Mohammed V.

Churches—Eglise Sainte-Anne, 115 Rue de Marrakech (Tel: 82 22 51, Fax: 84 81 33), Mass in French: Saturday and weekdays at 6:30 P.M.; mass (polyglot) Sunday 10:00 A.M. and 7:00 P.M.

Consulates—the U.S. does not have a consulate in Agadir, and the UK has closed theirs. Contact the U.S. Consulate in Casablanca if necessary (Tel: 02-26 45 50).

Drugstore, Night *(pharmacie de nuit)*—Immeuble Baladia, next to the post office.

Express Post *(Poste rapide)* —Contact the main post office (Tel: 84 26 90) for details.

Fire *(Sapeurs-Pompiers)*—(Tel: 15).

Fishing—see "Sports," section 9 above.

Gendarmerie Royale—(Tel: 17).

Golf Clubs—see "Sports," section 9 above.

Horseback riding—see "Sports," section 9 above.

Hospitals and Clinics—call the U.S. Consulate in Casablanca for advice (Tel: 02-26 45 50) or try the Clinique Al Massira, Avenue du Prince Mulay Abdallah (Tel: 84 32 38). Avoid the public hospital.

Photocopies—at many shops selling tobacco, stamps, and newspapers, and at some téléboutiques.

Police—(Tel: 19).

Post Office—Avenue du Prince Mulay Abdallah.

Sailing and Sea Excursions—see "Sports," section 9 above.

Taxis, Big and Little—big taxis to Inezgane and Tiznit leave from Place Salam, at the south end of the town, for Taghazout from the Nouvelle Talborjt; little ones can be had all over town at stands marked "Taxis."

Telephone—in main post office, but easier to use the numerous téléboutiques (fax, too).

Tourist Information—*Délégation du Tourisme,* Rue du Prince Héritier Sidi Mohammed (Tel: 84 63 77), or better, *Syndicat d'Initiative* (junction Boulevard Mohammed V and Avenue du Général Kettani, Tel: 84 03 07).

Tour Operators—lots around junction Avenue Hassan II and Avenue des F.A.R., and Rue du Prince Héritier Sidi Mohammed. Shop around for the best offer (see "Guided Tours").

Travel Agencies—Carlson Wagonlit Travel, 26 Avenue des F.A.R. (Tel: 84 15 28, Fax: 84 60 96); Globus, 119 Avenue Hassan II (Tel: 82 13 59); Menara Tours, 341 Avenue Hassan II (Tel: 82 11 08); Olive Branch Tours, 125 Avenue Hassan II (Tel: 82 52 97).

Yacht Club—Agadir Yacht Club, Port d'Agadir.

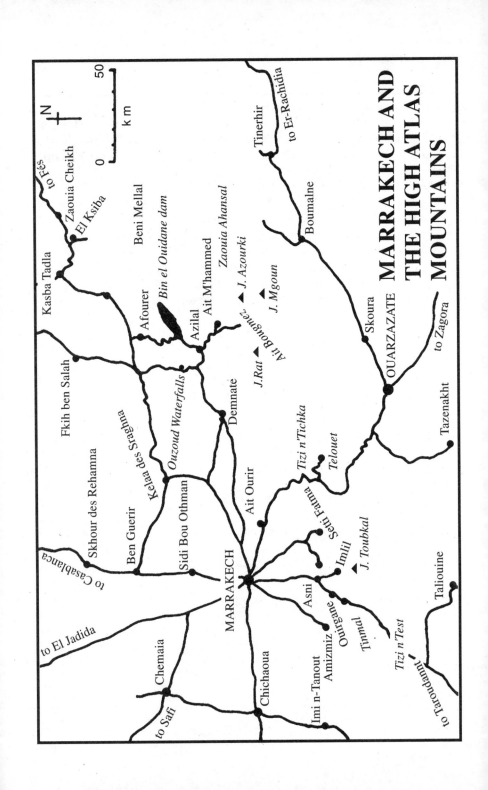

MARRAKECH AND THE HIGH ATLAS MOUNTAINS

12

Marrakech and the High Atlas Mountains

1. The General Picture

Marrakech lies in the Haouz plain, on the northern edge of the High Atlas Mountains, on the left bank of the River Tensift. It is a crossroads town, with routes going north, south, east, and west. Although separated from southern, Saharan Morocco by the imposing heights of the High Atlas, Marrakech already has a warm, desert feeling to it. It was once the capital of the kingdom, giving its name to the whole country. Its buildings and ramparts are a pinkish red, palm trees are very much at home in temperatures that can reach well over 35° C in summer, and the pace of life is slower. It is difficult to imagine visiting Morocco without experiencing Marrakech. And it is an experience—not always enjoyable on a first contact, but always enriching. It's worth staying around for a few days just to get into the spirit of the town, its animated souks, and storytellers in the Place Jemaa el-Fna. It has a wide choice of hotels and restaurants, a lot of nightlife, three golf courses, and the High Atlas Mountains close by for rugged sport. Outside of high summer, the temperature is always agreeable and the climate especially advised for asthma sufferers.

The founding of Marrakech. The Haouz plain around Marrakech had been inhabited from Neolithic times at least by simple Berber farmers, whose stone implements have been found in several places. The arrival of Arab conquerors and Islam in northern Morocco in the 7th and 8th centuries A.D. probably affected life little in the Haouz—at that time Sijilmassa, further to the east, was the main southern town. It was not until 1070 that the advancing Saharan Almoravid army, under Abu Bakr, having conquered Sijilmassa and Fès, camped some 200 m north of the actual Koutoubia Mosque, where Abu Bakr decided to found a new city. A plain, a river, a well, and suitable stone for building rendered the choice propitious. A stone fortress and the first adobe mosque were built and the new town was called Marrakech. This name was mentioned for the first time in an 11th century manuscript in the Qarawiyin library in Fès and meant "the country of the sons of Kush" (black people), since many of the troops accompanying Abu Bakr were black Africans from Mauritania. Abu Bakr had to leave precipitiously and his cousin, Yusef ben Tachfin, took control, finished the mosque, had houses built, minted gold coins, and arranged for the gold and ivory laden trans-Saharan caravans to arrive in his new creation. Marrakech was to be the Almoravid capital for 100 years, the center of power that extended from the Atlantic Ocean to Algiers, and from the Tafilalet to the River Ebro in Spain. His son, Ali ben Yusef, introduced Andalusian craftsmen to Marrakech, built the ramparts and many of its gates, a new palace, a mosque, and a garden. Ali is credited with the introduction of the underground water canal system *(rhettara)* used to irrigate the gardens.

Rise and Fall. In 1125, the fiery and pious preacher Ibn Tumert settled in Tinmal, in the mountains south of Marrakech, preaching his moral reform, and continuing his revolt against the Almoravids installed in Marrakech. Ibn Tumert died around 1128, but his followers, the Almohads, captured the nearby town of Aghmat and laid an unsuccessful siege to Marrakech in 1130. They succeeded, under Abd el-Mumen, in capturing the city in 1147, after a long siege. By that time the population was famine-stricken and the Almoravids' Christian mercenaries tired and discouraged. Abd el-Mumen had the good idea of promising to spare the lives of the mercenaries, but the Almohads nevertheless killed off at least 7,000 inhabitants and sacked the town, destroying many public and religious buildings. In exchange, they built the first Koutoubia mosque (on the site of the Almoravid fortress) and created the Menara Gardens. Abd el-Mumen's son, Yusef, enlarged the town and made it into a center of Arab philosophy, attracting countless poets and scholars. Yusef's son, Yacub el-Mansour (known as "the Victorious"), followed the same policy, building a kasbah, an imperial city, palaces, mosques, a hospital and gardens, while continuing his conquests in Spain. Commercial links with Andalusia were encouraged, with Marrakech exporting leather, sugar, and ceramics.

After this period of prosperity at the end of the 12th century, Marrakech declined with the death of Yacub el-Mansour in 1199. For half a century, dynastic troubles adversely affected the town. The situation became worse when a new family, the Merinids, who had made their capital in Fès, captured the town in 1269. The trans-Saharan gold route abandoned Marrakech for Fès, and when the Merinids seized Sijilmassa in 1274, the gold market was lost, trade declined, houses and palaces fell into ruins, two-thirds of the town became uninhabited, and the remaining population fell victim to a rapid Portuguese attack as far as the town gates in 1522. It may have been with relief that the famine-struck inhabitants of Marrakech welcomed the arrival of a new dynasty, the Saadians, in 1525.

Renaissance. With the Saadians, firmly established as the new rulers of Morocco, Marrakech came to life again. At first only their southern capital, the town became the capital of all Morocco once they had consolidated their empire. Two Saadian sultans were mainly responsible the renaissance of Marrakech in the second half of the 16th century: Mulay Abdallah and his younger brother, Ahmed el-Mansur. After the victory over the Portuguese at the Battle of the Three Kings in 1578, the latter started ambitious building projects in Marrakech, helped by the capture of Timbuktu and three tons of gold in 1591, the sugar exported to Europe from the sugarcane plantations, and the production of Moroccan leather goods, known as *maroquin* (morocco). In Europe, Morocco—the shortened form of Marrakech—was used to designate the whole empire. Between 25,000 and 70,000 people lived in Marrakech at that time. The Jewish population, living in its *mellah*, was the most important in the country, and the Europeans were diplomats, businessmen, or, sometimes, prisoners. In the first half of the 17th century, this affluence was compromised by insecurity, palace revolutions, and wars.

Then a new dynasty came to the fore, in the shape of the Alaouite family from the Tafilalet. The new sultan, Mulay Rashid, captured Marrakech in 1669, but preferred to make Fès his capital. His successor, Mulay Ismail, established his capital in Meknès, removing from Marrakech all traces of his Saadian predecessors. It was not until the middle of the 18th century that Mohammed III restored many of the buildings that had been destroyed and built a new palace. He improved existing gardens and created new ones, including that of the Mamounia (now part of the Mamounia Hotel grounds). His successors, Hassan I and Mulay Abd el-Aziz, continued to build new and imposing palaces in Marrakech. Recognizing the help given to him by the head of the Glaoui family, chiefs of the Berber Glaoua tribe, Hassan I made the Glaoui Pasha of Marrakech. Glaoui kasbahs already occupied strategic points, both in the High Atlas and in the south, but now the family wielded almost unlimited power.

The French Protectorate. In 1907, Mulay Abd el-Hafid, Abd el-Aziz's half brother and rival, set himself up as a champion against European penetration into Morocco and declared himself sultan in Marrakech. Indeed, hostility to the establishment of the French Protectorate in 1912 was strong in south Morocco. The Saharan leader, El Hiba, attempted to resist the French advance but his troops were defeated at Sidi Bou Othmane, just north of Marrakech. The town's position as capital of Morocco was now lost in favor of Rabat. The French relied heavily on Thami el-Glaoui to keep order in southern Morocco and during his heyday many foreign statesmen, including Winston Churchill, were entertained by the Glaoui in Marrakech or his High Atlas palace of Telouet. The French called him the "Black Panther." In 1953, with his help, the French Résident-Général organized a so-called popular uprising against the legitimate sovereign, Mohammed V, who was deported to Madagascar. On Mohammed V's triumphal return in 1955, the Glaoui crept back on his knees before his king and asked to be forgiven. He fell into disgrace, his goods were confiscated, and his kasbahs crumbled into ruin. Few tears were shed for him among the people he ruled over in Marrakech and the south, and he died a year later. Much of his wealth came from the hashish trade, prostitutes, and mining rights, and his harem is said to have contained 200 women or more.

Marrakech today. Following customary French practice, the new town (*ville nouvelle*), with its central districts of Guéliz and Hivernage, is distinct from the old city (medina). About 1½ km separates the old from the new. Pinkish-red ramparts surround the medina, which contains the souks and the Place Jemaa el-Fna. Hivernage contains mostly hotels and apartments, while Guéliz is the active commercial center. Official 1997 figures gave a population of around 800,000 for the town of Marrakech, but this is probably an underestimate. At rush hours, one gets the impression that they are all on the roads, either in cars or on bicycles (Marrakech is flat and ideally suited for this form of transport). The town has become an essential destination for holidaymakers and tourism is its main source of income. Even if it lies in second place behind Agadir, its easy access allows many tourists to make a day excursion there from Casablanca or Agadir, while perhaps fewer plan to spend their whole holiday there. Marrakech is also a favorite venue for seminars, company meetings, and national and international congresses. The town was host to delegates signing the international GATT trade agreements in 1994 and to a General Motors worldwide congress in February 1998. Over now are the days when young Westerners "went Morocco" in Marrakech, wearing Moroccan clothes and eating *tajines* in the Place Jemaa el-Fna when they weren't smoking *kif.* Marrakech has been cleaned up since then.

2. Getting There

Marrakech is easily reached by **air.** A daily Royal Air Maroc flight direct from Paris was inaugurated in the fall of 1998. British Airways has 2 flights a week from London. Air France also does a direct flight from Paris once a week. RAM runs 3 flights a day from Casablanca, connecting with trans-Atlantic and European services. Regional Air Lines also has 10 flights a week from Casablanca. Flights from other towns are possible, via Casablanca. The airport, Marrakech-Ménara, is 5 km southwest of the town and a taxi shouldn't charge more than 50-80 DH (negotiate before climbing in).

By **rail** there is a good service from Casablanca, with eight trains running throughout the day. Some are "ordinary," stopping everywhere, so it's better to choose one of the "rapids," six of which leave Casablanca (Port or Voyageurs station) every day, covering the 240 km in 3½ hours in comfortable, air-conditioned cars. Travelers coming from Tangier during the day will have to change trains in Casablanca, but there is a night train with couchettes which is direct. Coming to Marrakech from Oujda sometimes entails changing in Casablanca. Supratours and the Moroccan state railways run a combined bus-rail connecting service daily from Agadir and all towns further south as far as Dakhla (this is, in fact, an all-night affair).

CTM **buses** run six times a day from Casablanca (65 DH), twice a day from Fès (via Beni Mellal), three times a day from Agadir, and four times a day from Ouarzazate. The CTM started a new non-stop line from Casablanca in the fall of 1998. It also runs buses from Safi, Er-Rachidia, M'Hamid (via Zagora), Laayoune, and Tan-Tan (both via Agadir). Other bus companies have services from all the big towns, as well as from places such as Demnate, Asni, and the Ourika Valley.

By **car,** Marrakech is an easy 240 km from Casablanca, 176 km from Essaouira, 273 km from Agadir, across the High Atlas via Imi n'Tanout, 483 km from Fès, and 204 km from Ouarzazate, across the High Atlas by the Tizi n'Tichka pass. The only route likely to be affected by rain or snow is the last one, but it rarely remains closed for more than a few hours.

3. Local Transportation

As usual, the **little taxis** (sandy-colored) are the simplest method of getting around, although the distances are not so great as to rule out walking. It shouldn't cost more than 10 DH for a normal in-town trip. They
only take three passengers. Local **buses** are a perfectly reasonable way of
getting around, but they are pretty full. The N° 8 is a useful one, going
from the train station to the Place Jemaa el-Fna, via the post office and
Bab Doukkala. N° 1 and N° 20 go from the Place Jemaa el-Fna down
Avenue Mohammed V to the Guéliz area. An attractive way of getting back
if tired after a session in the medina to the hotel (or vice-versa) is to take
a **horse-drawn buggy** *(calèche)* (not just reserved for tourists). These
calèches are much used in Marrakech, both for in-town journeys and for
an outing in the palm grove, and are a most agreeable way of going
around. Like taxis, they should have the tarif on view: 60 DH an hour. It
shouldn't cost more than 10-15 DH to get back to the new town from the
medina, a few dirhams more if you want to go further. They take four passengers, and the fee should be clearly arranged beforehand. For those
with strong nerves, **bicycles** and **scooters** can be rented, but there is always
the parking problem Voyages FRAM (see "Guided Tours," section 7) will
rent you a bicycle for 70 DH a half-day, 120 DH for the whole day. They
can be had much more cheaply from places near the Place Jemaa el-Fna
(see "Address List," section 12).

4. The Hotel Scene

One gets the impression sometimes that there are nothing but hotels in
the new town. Official figures give 77 classified hotels for the whole
Marrakech area, not to mention all the small unclassified ones. Even so,
there are times (school holiday periods, Moroccan feast days, and springtime) when the upper categories are booked up, so reserve beforehand if
you can. Understandably, not all these hotels can be mentioned here. If
you are planning a trip in high summer, it is advisable to take a hotel with
air-conditioning. Hotel charges fixed for this region are as follows (they
vary according to the presence or absence of showers and water closet in
the room): **** 403-503 DH or 516-1,155 DH, breakfast 53-88 DH for both;
*** 201-319 DH or 227-460 DH, breakfast 40 DH for both; ** 110-191 DH
or 119-290 DH, breakfast 26 DH for both; * 100-147 DH or 105-169 DH,
breakfast 25 DH for both.

The **regional telephone code** is 04 (0 omitted for in-region calls).

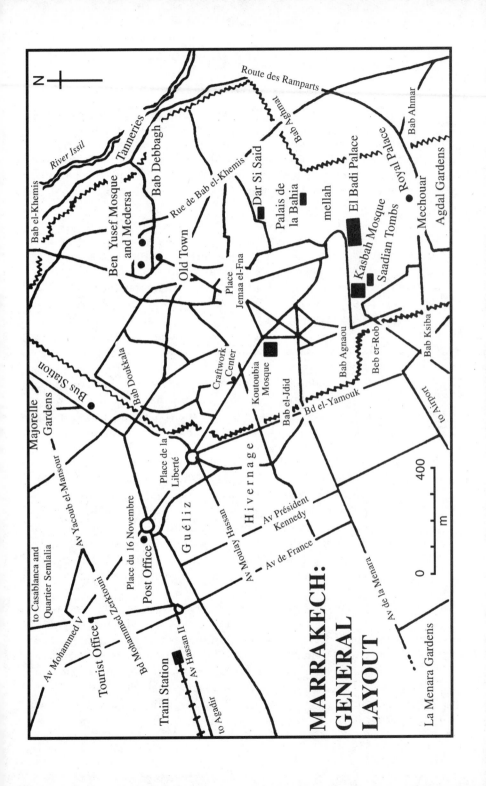

EXPENSIVE HOTELS

There are 25 hotels in the ***** and **** categories. Undoubtedly, the ***** luxury **La Mamounia,** frequented by the jet set, royalty, and international VIPs, comes out top of the list (170 rooms, 56 suites, 3 villas, from 1,700 DH single in the low season to 30,000 for a suite; prices are lower for package tours; Avenue Bab el-Jdid, Tel: 44 89 81, Fax: 44 46 60/44 49 40). The hotel has been patronized by the famous since it opened at the end of the 1920s, and guests have included Paul Valéry, Ravel, Arletty, Rita Hayworth, Eric von Stroheim, Orson Wells, Richard Nixon, Jimmy Carter, Henry Kissinger, the Rothschilds, and the Rockfellers. British Prime Minister Winston Churchill used to come and paint from its terrace, looking towards the snowy summits of the Atlas Mountains. The latest V.I.P. in the Mamounia was Hillary Clinton, who had a short stay there in March 1999. In short, the Mamounia's past history is unique, its vast gardens are superb, its newly-renovated Art Deco style is eye-catching, and its bedrooms contain an exact copy of the famous 1929 Leleu armchair. It has five restaurants, five bars, a casino, nightclub, boutiques, swimming pool, tennis courts, squash, billiards, jacuzzi, body building, beauty center, sauna, *hammam,* massage, conference rooms, and a ballroom. It has everything you could want from a luxury hotel (but I'm not the only one to find the bar staff arrogant—unless, of course, you are the U.S. President!). If you're really set on staying in the Mamounia, you'll have to book months ahead, since it is much sought after.

Another in the ***** category is the **Palmeraie Golf Palace** (314 rooms and suites, 1,200-1,990 DH, Circuit de la Palmeraie, Tel: 30 10 10/31 34 60, Fax: 30 50 50/30 20 20). It lies in the palm grove, has luxurious bedrooms, eight restaurants, four bars, a nightclub, boutiques, five swimming pools set among palm trees, tennis courts, squash, horseback riding, a fitness center (jacuzzi, sauna, *hammam,* massage), and, of course, the 18-hole Palmeraie Golf Club course within its extensive grounds. Here again, everything you could need is here without setting a foot in the turbulence of the town.

One of the best in this category is the ***** **Hotel es-Saadi** (160 rooms and suites, 1,400-1,600 DH, breakfast 90 DH, Avenue Quadissia, Tel: 44 88 11/44 70 10, Fax: 44 766 44), well situated in the Hivernage district, close to the markets. This is a much-frequented hotel, with attractively furnished bedrooms, a good restaurant, bars, boutiques, a swimming pool (heated in winter), tennis courts, *hammam,* sauna, massage, a nightclub, and gorgeous gardens. In addition, the staff is friendly and helpful (not always the case in Marrakech, alas).

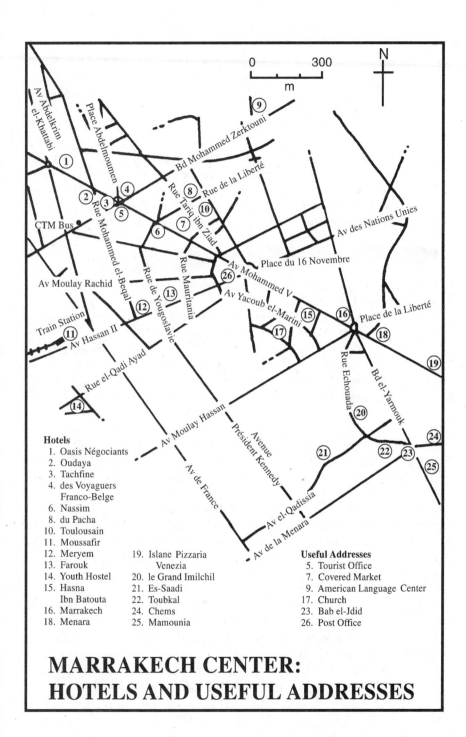

Hotels
1. Oasis Négociants
2. Oudaya
3. Tachfine
4. des Voyaguers
   Franco-Belge
6. Nassim
8. du Pacha
10. Toulousain
11. Moussafir
12. Meryem
13. Farouk
14. Youth Hostel
15. Hasna
   Ibn Batouta
16. Marrakech
18. Menara

19. Islane Pizzaria
    Venezia
20. le Grand Imilchil
21. Es-Saadi
22. Toubkal
24. Chems
25. Mamounia

Useful Addresses
5. Tourist Office
7. Covered Market
9. American Language Center
17. Church
23. Bab el-Jdid
26. Post Office

MARRAKECH CENTER:
HOTELS AND USEFUL ADDRESSES

Another one I like is the recently-renovated ***** **Hotel Kenzi Semiramis** (180 rooms, 1,250 DH, buffet breakfast 85 DH, Route de Casablanca, Quartier Semlalia, Tel: 43 13 77, Fax: 44 71 27/44 72 00). The interior decoration is superb, with lots of inside plants, and the spacious bedrooms are attractively furnished. The hotel has three restaurants and a pool-side buffet, a delightful swimming pool, tennis courts, archery, table-tennis, and boutiques. If warned in advance, they can arrange to look after your kids while you hop on the hotel shuttle bus service for a game of golf or horseback riding at the Amelkis Golf Club. Excursions, treks, and *calèche* trips can be organized. The only inconvenience is that it is situated at the far end of the Guéliz district, away from the shopping center and even further from the medina.

The ***** **Imperial Borj** (217 rooms, 1,100 DH, breakfast 70 DH, Avenue Ech-Chouhada, Tel: 44 73 22, Fax: 44 62 06), an elegant hotel opened in 1990, has an original interior decoration, restaurants, bars, a swimming pool, boutiques, a nightclub, and conference rooms.

Friends much enjoy the ***** **Sheraton** (1,700 DH, Avenue de la Ménara, Tel: 44 89 98/44 62 62, Fax: 43 78 43/44 89 72), which they say is not a typical Sheraton. The bedrooms are attractive, the swimming pool very nice, and the restaurant excellent.

Early in 1998, the good quality ***** **Mansour Eddahbi** (441 rooms, same price range, Avenue de France, Tel: 44 80 43/44 82 22, Fax: 44 90 81) came under the management of the U.S. Westin Hotels & Resorts company, who were intending to rename it the Westin Mansour Marrakech. The hotel has six restaurants, swimming pools, tennis courts, a health club, bars, a nightclub, and a jazz club. Situated near the town's conference center, the new management intends to cater to the meetings market, as well as the tourist trade.

Another ***** outfit is the **Hotel Kenzi Farah** (ex-Safir Farah) (290 rooms, 1,200 DH, breakfast 60 DH, Avenue Président Kennedy, Tel: 44 74 00/44 81 26, Fax: 44 87 30). Its swimming pool is heated in winter, and the hotel has restaurants, bars, a sauna, *hammam*, a conference room, and a host of recreational facilities including tennis courts and golf practice.

Another very luxurious, select establishment, this time in the old town, is the newly-opened **Maison Arabe** (5 rooms and 6 suites, around 1,000 DH, Rue Fatima Zohra, almost opposite the Bab Doukkala Mosque, Tel: 39 12 33). It is said to combine Hispano-Moorish architecture, Berber craftsmanship, and European comfort. Its individualized rooms are exquisitely furnished, with cedar ceilings, thick rugs, and tasteful furniture, so you get the impression you are really a guest in an authentic Moroccan palace.

The **Palais Rhoul,** another swanky place in the Palmeraie next to the Palmariva Palace, has its suites charmingly arranged around a swimming pool and offers every comfort to its guests.

A good **** hotel is the **Melia Tichka Salam** (130 rooms, 8 suites, Route de Marrakech, Quartier Semlalia, Tel: 44 87 10, Fax: 44 86 91). A French architect and an American decorator got together to produce an absolutely delightful hotel of great charm in the style of an old Moroccan mansion. The bedrooms are attractively furnished, there are two restaurants and a pool-side buffet, two bars, a small but imaginatively-designed pool (heated in winter), boutiques, *hammam,* and massage. Golf can be arranged. The garden is small and the hotel lacks the space of its neighbor, the Semiramis Hotel, but is otherwise highly recommended.

Still in this district, the **** **Hotel Tafilalet** (84 rooms, Avenue Abdelkrim el-Khattabi, Route de Casablanca, Tel: 44 98 18, 43 80 69/76, Fax: 44 75 32) has always been noted for its pleasant staff, as well as for its attractive bedrooms, reception areas, heated pool, boutiques, restaurant, and pool-side grill. It has facilities for people in wheelchairs, and is often full.

The **** **Nassim Hotel** (52 rooms and suites, 115 Avenue Mohammed V, Tel: 44 64 01, Fax: 43 67 10) is a rather austere building apart from its very glossy entrance, with agreeably-furnished bedrooms looking onto a small patio swimming pool. It is extremely well placed in the heart of the new town. It has a restaurant, two bars, a coffee shop, a fitness center, and and boutiques. The receptionist said they were full nearly all year round.

The **** **Safir Siaha** (293 rooms, Avenue Président Kennedy, Tel: 44 89 52, Fax: 44 69 27) is a favorite with U.S. packaged tours. The bedrooms are rather small, but the reception areas and garden are beautiful, and the swimming pool is delightful.

The huge **** **Atlas Hotel** (304 rooms, Avenue de France, Tel: 44 70 51, Fax: 43 33 08) is also popular with U.S. groups.

The French tour company FRAM runs the **** **Hotel Les Idrissides** (341 rooms, 44 Avenue de France, Tel: 44 87 77) and the **** **Hotel Chems** (1 Rue Houmane Fetouki, Tel: 44 48 13/17, Fax: 44 05 47), so they are often full.

Another **** hotel, but well outside the town, is the **Iberotel Tikida Garden** (206 rooms and 8 suites, Circuit de la Palmeraie, Tel: 30 90 99, Fax: 30 93 43). It is quiet and attractively designed, with two restaurants, a pool-side buffet, bars, a disco, a heated swimming pool, tennis courts, archery, large garden, fitness center, boutiques, and free shuttle service to the two nearby golf courses. It is well provided with conference rooms.

The **** **Hotel Les Almoravides** (105 rooms, Arset Jnane Lakhdar, off Avenue Mohammed V, Tel: 44 51 42, Fax: 44 31 33), another good hotel in this category, is just behind the **Craftwork Center** (*Ensemble Artisanal*), halfway between the old and new towns. It has comfortable rooms, a restaurant, a boutique, a small garden arranged around the swimming pool, a tennis court, mini-golf, a large shaded parking area, and a helpful staff (and always looks full).

Out along the Casablanca road, in the Quartier Semlalia, the **** **Hotel Amine** (112 rooms, Avenue Abdelkrim el-Khattabi, Tel: 43 63 76, Fax: 43 81 44) is a calm hotel, frequented by tourist groups, with a big pool surrounded by plenty of greenery. It has a restaurant and bar.

The **** **Hotel Le Marrakech** (350 rooms, Place de la Liberté, Tel: 43 43 51, Fax: 43 49 80) is well placed on the way to the old town, but it's another of those enormous establishments catering a lot (but not exclusively) to tourist groups. It has two restaurants and a snack service, bars, boutiques, and a swimming pool (heated in the winter).

The first-class club **Palmariva Palace** (316 rooms, 685 DH per person/day half-board, Km 6 Route de Fès, Tel: 44 91 49, Fax: 44 91 50) is also out of the way, but warmly recommended by friends who go there regularly. Lots of sports are included in the price: tennis, swimming, and mini-golf (horseback riding is extra). It is very good for small kids from 4 through 12. It has a restaurant, *hammam*, and a sauna, as well as club-style entertainment for adults and kids all day.

MEDIUM-PRICE HOTELS

This category comprises *** and ** establishments, of which there are respectively 20 and 15 in Marrakech, mostly in **Guéliz**. The *** **Hotel Toubkal** (124 rooms, Rue Haroun Errachid, Tel: 44 88 72, Fax: 44 89 87) has comfortable rooms, a restaurant, a pretty garden, and a pool.

The *** **Hotel Oudaya** (77 rooms and 15 suites, 147 Avenue Mohammed el-Beqal, Tel: 44 85 12, 44 71 09, Fax: 43 54 00) has been warmly recommended. Its comfortable bedrooms are well equipped, there are two restaurants—one with a splendid view over the town—a bar, and a swimming pool.

Two hotels close to each other in the Guéliz district are the *** **Hotel Amalay** (40 rooms, 87 Avenue Mohammed V, Tel: 44 86 85/44 90 23/ 43 13 67, Fax: 43 15 54) and, just around the corner, the *** **Hotel Tachfine** (Rue Mohammed el-Beqal, Tel: 44 71 88, Fax: 43 78 62). Both have a restaurant and a bar.

The *** **Hotel Ibn Batuta** (52 air-conditioned rooms, Avenue Yacoub el-Marini, Tel: 43 81 60/63, Fax: 43 40 62) is well placed between Guéliz and the medina, its rooms are pleasant, it has a restaurant (but no pool), and the reception staff is helpful.

Practically back to back with the Ibn Batuta, the ***** Hotel Hasna** (247 Avenue Mohammed V, Tel: 44 99 72, Fax: 44 99 94) has well-equipped rooms, a restaurant, and a small pool.

The ***** Hotel Le Grand Imilchil** (94 rooms, Avenue Ech-Chouhada, not far from the medina, Tel: 44 76 53, Fax: 43 01 71), with pleasant but small-ish rooms, has a good reputation. It has a restaurant (so-so), a small pool, and a garden, and attracts a lot of clients.

Another near the medina, but still pretty calm, is the ***** Hotel de la Ménara** (Place de la Liberté, Tel: 43 64 78, Fax: 44 73 86), also with a garden and a swimming pool.

The ***** Hotel Islane** (44 rooms, 279 Avenue Mohammed V, Tel: 44 00 81/83, Fax: 44 00 85) is situated between the new and old towns. Its rooms are comfortable and some have good views but are noisy, and the others have no view and no noise. Its rooftop restaurant also offers splendid views of the Koutoubia Mosque.

The ***** Hotel Meryem** (97 rooms, 154 Rue Mohammed el-Beqal, Tel: 43 70 62/65, Fax: 43 70 66), situated just off Avenue Hassan II, near the railway station, is another good-value hotel. The bedrooms looking onto the patio pool are the nicest. The hotel has two restaurants, a small pool, sauna/massage, a boutique, and a helpful reception staff.

The ***** Hotel Moussafir** (now part of the Accor/Ibis chain, 103 rooms, Avenue Hassan II, Tel: 43 59 29/30, Fax: 43 59 36), just beside the train station, is another hotel handy for train passengers. It's attractively decorated but without much character. It has a restaurant, a bar, and a swimming pool (personally I found the woman at the reception desk pretty unhelpful—perhaps she was having a bad day).

In the lower range, the **** Hotel du Pacha** (39 rooms, 33 Rue de la Liberté, Tel: 43 13 27, Fax: 43 13 26), situated behind the central market, is an old hotel that has recently been done up. The rooms are pleasant, and those looking onto the courtyard are quieter (not all have air-conditioning). It seems that half-board is required from March to the end of May.

The **** Hotel Oasis Négociants** (33 rooms, 50 Avenue Mohammed V, Tel: 44 71 79) is not a bad choice, but it's nearly always full. Its rooms are comfortable and there is a restaurant.

In the **medina,** the **** Hotel Restaurant de Foucauld** (33 rooms—most air-conditioned—Avenue el-Mouahidine, Tel: 44 54 99, Fax: 44 13 44) is a very good address. It's only a few meters from the famous Place Jemaa el-Fna, so the front rooms are a bit noisy, but it's clean and friendly. American friends were very enthusiastic. The restaurant is in the basement.

The ** **Grand Hotel Restaurant Tazi** (61 rooms—air-conditioning, TV, phone—corner Avenue el-Mouahidine/Rue de Bab Agnaou, Tel: 44 27 87, Tel/Fax: 44 21 52), in the same area, has a small, top-floor swimming pool, a restaurant, a bar, and a lock-up garage. Some rooms look onto the pool, others onto the road.

BUDGET ACCOMMODATIONS

The top here are obviously the * hotels but there are not many of them in the new town. One of the best in **Guéliz** is probably the * **Hotel Toulousain** (44 Rue Tariq ibn Ziad, close to Avenue Mohammed V, Tel: 43 00 33), which has a quiet, interior courtyard and a friendly atmosphere.

Two other possible Guéliz addresses for cheap hotels are the * **Hotel des Voyageurs** (26 rooms, 40 Boulevard Mohammed Zerktouni, off Avenue Mohammed V to the right coming down from the medina, Tel: 44 72 18) and the * **Hotel Franco-Belge** (21 rooms, 62 Boulevard Mohammed Zerktouni, Tel: 44 84 72). Both are a bit shabby but clean enough.

Another that I go to from time to time when money is low is the **Hotel Farouk** (42 rooms, 100 DH, 66 Avenue Hassan II, Guéliz, Tel: 43 19 89, Fax: 43 36 09), where the rooms are pretty basic, but they have sparkling little bathrooms with hot showers and water closets. The top floor rooms open onto a terrace roof, where one can sit and read if one likes. Its ground floor restaurant is good for breakfast, but the meal is pretty ordinary (50 DH). It is under the same management as the Hotel Ali in the medina.

In the **medina,** the backpackers' hotel and rendezvous is undoubtedly the friendly **Hotel Ali** (42 rooms, 70 DH single, 120 DH double, with water closet and shower, breakfast 15 DH, Rue Mulay Ismail, Tel: 44 49 79, Fax: 44 05 22). It, too, is only 50 m from the Place Jemaa el-Fna, and is a bustling, friendly place, full of trekkers, mountain guides, and backpackers. I have friends who have been going there for years. Reservations are essential from spring through the fall (same management as Hotel Farouk).

About the same price, the * **Résidence CTM** (60 rooms, 132 DH with breakfast, Place Jemaa el-Fna, Tel: 44 23 25) has a terrace café with fine views, and its bedrooms, although very simple, are clean and adequate.

There are a couple of small, cheaper places in the same area—the **Hotel Ichbilia** (27 rooms, 100 DH double, 60 DH single, communal shower and water closet, 1 Rue Bani Marine, a little pedestrian road just behind Hotel Ali, Tel: 39 04 86), with pretty little rooms on the first floor around an interior courtyard, and a restaurant, and the **Hotel La Gazelle** (28 rooms, 100 DH double, 60 DH single, communal shower and water closet, 12 Rue Bani Marine, Tel: 44 11 12), where the rooms are also arranged around a courtyard.

There is a **Youth Hostel** on the Rue el-Jahid (Tel: 43 28 31). It's not easy to find, a few minutes from the station (YHA card necessary).

The municipal **campsite** in the town has been closed and the ground used for more lucrative purposes. It has been replaced by the **Camping Firdawz,** 9 km out of Marrakech on the Casablanca road (on the left just, after the Agip gas station) (37 DH for camping car and two people). This is a new campsite and when I was there everything was clean and in working order. Let's hope that it stays this way (popular with caravaners).

5. Dining and Restaurants

Marrakech has a good reputation for restaurants, which come in all forms and at all prices. The top category restaurants require guests to be correctly dressed (jacket and tie for men, strictly no shorts).

HOTEL RESTAURANTS

Practically all the hotels mentioned above have their own restaurant, with prices in relation to their category. All serve perfectly adequate meals, and it is often convenient to eat in the hotel if you are staying there, but a few are particularly noted for their gastronomic delights. And a few are worth going to especially. Having said that, the restaurant **Le Marocain** in **La Mamounia** is probably one of the best for Moroccan food, and certainly one of the most expensive (set meal 700 DH). Its Italian restaurant (**L'Italien**) and the pool-side luncheon buffet are said to be good (250 DH for the latter).

The Moroccan and Italian restaurants in the **Palmeraie Golf Palace** are held to be good by golfing friends who eat there a lot.

Other friends enjoy the pizzas around the pool at the **Hotel Sheraton.** The **El Menzeh** restaurant in the **Kenzi Semiramis** does high-quality Moroccan cooking, and I enjoyed the Italian specialities in its **La Strada** restaurant. The **Hotel Es-Saadi** has a good restaurant.

People tell me that **Hotel Hasna's** restaurant serves reasonable Moroccan and international meals (set menu 130 DH).

The ** and lower hotel restaurants serve standard Moroccan set meals from 80 DH, which are all right but certainly not memorable. The **Grand Hotel Restaurant Tazi** has a rooftop restaurant (set meal 96 DH) offering good views over the Place Jemaa el-Fna if you don't want close contact with the crowd while you eat.

An exception to the set menu type, the **Hotel Ali** (not to be confused with Chez Ali!) has an evening buffet service for its backpacker guests (50 DH for them, 60 DH for outsiders). It is also okay for vegetarians. The **Hotel Foucauld** also has an evening buffet.

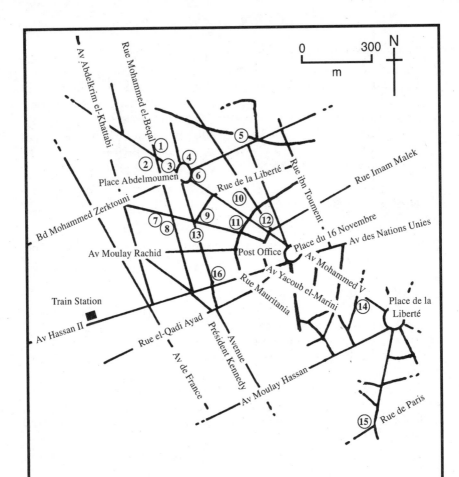

Cafés and Restaurants

1. Brasserie Le Petite Poucet
2. Restaurant La Petite Auberge
3. Café Renaissance
4. Café Les Négociants
   Restaurant Le Jacaranda
   Boule de Neige
5. Restaurant Le Dragon d'Or
6. Restaurant L'Entrecôte
7. Glacier Oliveri
8. Restaurant La Trattoria

9. Pâtisserie Al Jawda
10. Le Café Cantanzaro
11. Pâtisserie Mirgon
12. Snack Sindibad
13. Bagatelle
    Restaurant Rôtisserie la Paix
14. Pizza Hut
15. Chez Gérard
16. Vila Rosa

MARRAKECH CENTER: CAFÉS AND RESTAURANTS

OTHER RESTAURANTS

Most require prior reservations. This is best done by yourself, in person, or by telephone, or by the hotel reception. Avoid all other offers of help, from taxis or guides for instance, who are often more interested in taking you somewhere else.

For a top-class Moroccan meal in a superb setting, the **Yacout,** hidden away in the medina is among the best (79 Sidi Ahmed Souissi, Tel: 38 29 29, Fax: 38 25 38). This is an old palace complete with fountain, converted into a restaurant, and decorated by American designer Bill Willis. Drinks accompanied by Andalusian music are taken upstairs, where there is a splendid view over Marrakech (expect to pay around 600 DH for the meal). Reservations are essential.

Another highly recommended restaurant—some say the best—of a similar type serving a gastronomic meal of traditional Moroccan food in sumptuous surroundings is the **Stylia** (34 Rue el-Ksour, more or less off Rue Sidi Yamini, Tel: 44 35 87/44 58 37), hidden away in a maze of streets (a doorman will direct you there). It is possible to order a kosher dinner. Here again, reservations are essential (bookings can be made through Voyages FRAM, 450 DH including hotel transfer—see "Guided Tours," section 7) (open every day, from 8:00 P.M.).

In the same class is the **Restaurant Le Tobsil** (25 Zaouia el-Hadar, Riad Laarous, Tel: 44 40 52). Another refined restaurant in the medina, a beautiful converted palace, is the **Dar Marjana** (15 Derb Sidi Ali Tair, Tel: 44 11 10/ 44 57 73, Fax: 42 91 52), where gourmet Moroccan meals (some say the best in Marrakech) are accompanied by a floor show (not always as good as the food). Plan on paying around 600 DH for the meal, and reservations are essential.

The **Dar Fez,** still in the medina (8 Rue Boussouni el-Gza, Riad Laarous, Tel: 38 23 40/38 22 13) is said to be good. Rather different, but a very popular tourist rendezvous, is **Chez Ali,** out of town (Circuit Jaffaria, La Palmeraie, Tel: 30 77 30, 30 44 28/29/31), where diners eat under tents in the middle of the palm grove and watch traditional dancing followed by a *fantasia,* a display of warlike horsemanship. Yes, it's touristy, but enjoyable all the same. Reservations are essential (meal with show around 500 DH).

Still in Moroccan food, but slightly cheaper, the **Restaurant Ed Douira** (14, Derb Jdid Hay es-Salam, Tel: 44 28 02), next door to the Palais de la Bahia, offers a couple of menus in a traditional setting (it is also open for lunch). It's often difficult to find a table since its location attracts tourist groups (around 400 DH).

The **Al Fassia** restaurant, in Guéliz (232 Avenue Mohammed V, Tel: 43 40 60) has an attractive garden and serves a good set lunch (around 140 DH) and an equally good meal in the evening (main dish from 80 DH).

The food in the **Restaurant Dar el-Baroud** (275 Avenue Mohammed V, entrance down the side street, Tel: 42 60 09), close to the medina, is said to be good, and it has a show in the evening (main course from 85 DH).

There are several other restaurants serving high-class Moroccan food, generally with a floor show or music in the evening, such as **Ksar Es Saoussan, Dar Mounia, Dar Es Salam, Le Ryad, Le Marrakchi, Le Palais Gharnatta,** or the **Kasbah Restaurant.** All have been recommended to me in one way or another. Their prices vary from "expensive" (600 DH) to "modest" (300 DH).

Coming down from these high-class restaurants, there are any number of **small places** around the **Place Jemaa el-Fna** serving adequate Moroccan food, either as a three-course set menu from 60-80 DH, or as individual dishes. The **Argana** (on the far side of the square, well indicated by colored lights) is frequented by friends.

I've eaten perfectly reasonable meals at the **Café Restaurant Iceberg,** just around the corner, left out of the Hotel Ali (set menu 60 DH).

For the brave with good stomachs, **booths** set up on the square itself serve *harira* soup, French fries, snails, kebobs, and so on (the kebobs are a safe choice).

Leaving Moroccan food aside, the restaurant **Le Pavillon** (Rue Fatima-Zohra, next to the Hotel La Maison Arabe), by Bab Doukkala in the old town, proposes a very refined French gourmet menu for around 600 DH.

There are also a number of excellent restaurants in the Guéliz and Hivernage districts. The **Bagatelle** (101 Rue de Yougoslavie, Tel: 43 02 74) is an attractive French-run restaurant serving unusual dishes, as well as the more standard French cuisine. In summer one can eat out under vine-covered latticework (main dish from 50 DH, closed Wednesdays).

For grilled meat, try the **Restaurant Rôtisserie la Paix** in the same road (N° 68, Tel: 43 31 18), where you can also sit at tables outside under the trees. Apart from the grills, the other food is not up to the Bagatelle standard (it's open for lunch and dinner).

At the **Restaurant Le Jacaranda,** also French-run (32 Boulevard Mohammed Zerktouni, Tel: 44 72 15) you can choose the good set menu (90 DH lunch time, 150 DH in the evening) or pick from a wide choice of dishes. The place looks a bit old-style, with whitewashed walls and a big fireplace, combined with a friendly atmosphere (closed Tuesdays).

Also on Boulevard Mohammed Zerktouni (N° 55, Tel: 44 94 28), the **Restaurant L'Entrecôte** offers several interesting meat menus (including one for children) in a pleasant setting (meat dishes from 80 DH). But you can also choose fish or Italian specialities (open from 12:00 P.M. and again at 9:30 P.M., closed Sundays).

The **Vila Rosa** restaurant (64 Avenue Hassan II, Tel/Fax: 43 08 32) has recently come under French management and serves superb and imaginative French meals in a delightful setting, with a wide selection of Moroccan and French wines (starters 50-80 DH, meat 105-120 DH, open evenings only, with a jazz bar from 6:00 P.M.).

In the Hivernage district, near the Mamounia Hotel, **Chez Gérard** (corner Avenue Ech-Chouhada/Rue de Paris, Tel: 43 77 55) is a restaurant recommended by several friends for its good French cooking (main course from 80 DH).

Further down the scale, **Le Petit Poucet** (56 Avenue Mohammed V) is straight out of French Protectorate days, with a standard three-course menu which is not memorable, but well kept.

If you've had enough of Moroccan or French cooking, the nearby Vietnamese restaurant **Le Dragon d'Or** (10 Boulevard Mohammed Zerktouni, Tel: 43 06 17) is excellent (main dish from 80 DH).

Everyone looking for a good Italian meal heads for the restaurant **Le Catanzaro** (Rue Tariq ibn Ziad, Tel: 43 37 31), behind the Central Market. It's maybe gotten a bit too popular, because it is often crammed with people, especially at weekends and holiday periods, but the grilled meat and pizzas are particularly good (pizzas from 40 DH, main dish from 70 DH, closed Sundays).

Another Italian restaurant is **La Trattoria** (179 Avenue Mohammed el-Beqal, Tel: 43 26 41). This restaurant, hidden behind a huge gate, owes its interior decoration to American designer Bill Willis (also responsible for the Hotel Melia Tichka and the Yacout restaurant) and its cuisine to its Italian manager/cook. It has a gourmet meal (pasta from 60 DH, meat and fish dishes from 100 DH, closed Mondays, reservations necessary) (some friends haven't found it a good value for money, but others disagree).

Cheaper pizzas (from 40 DH) can be eaten at the **Pizzaria Venezia,** at the top of the Hotel Islane (279 Avenue Mohammed V), pleasantly shaded and with a good view of the Koutoubia Mosque, and even cheaper (20 DH) in **La Petite Auberge** next to the Hotel Oudaya (Avenue Mohammed el-Beqal). And there is always **Pizza Hut** (6 Avenue Mohammed V).

OTHER PLACES TO EAT

The snack bar **Café Snack Sindibad** (Avenue Mohammed V) is nice for breakfast (15 DH) and for salads and simple meals. The **Glacier Oliveri** (Boulevard Mansour Eddahbi) is the best place for ice cream (it's a branch of the well-known Casablanca ice-creamery). They also make milk shakes, fruit juices, and serve breakfasts.

Boule de Neige (corner Avenue Mohammed V/Rue de Yougoslavie) is a popular place for ice cream. **Chez Mirgon** (Avenue Mohammed V) is good for pastries, as is **Al Jawda, Chez Mme Alami** (11 Rue de la Liberté) which has delicious but expensive Moroccan pastries.

In **Guéliz,** two essential places in which to stop and have coffee or breakfast while watching the Marrakchis go by are the **Café Renaissance** and the **Café Les Négociants** (opposite each other on Place Abdelmoumen). In the former, an elevator goes up to the top terrace where one has a good rooftop view while avoiding beggers and annoyances.

The **Panarea Club** and the **Jet d'Eau,** mentioned in some guide books, were both closed and up for sale in summer of 1998. In the **old town,** around the Place Jemaa el-Fna, there are a number of cafés with rooftop terraces giving good views over the square (the prices are generally higher than at the sidewalk tables).

The **Pâtisserie des Princes** (32 Rue de Bab Agnaou), near the Hotel Ali, is a pleasant, quiet place to go to for a good breakfast, pastries, or ice cream. If you're thirsty and waiting to catch a train, a little stall outside the **railway station** sells delicious fresh orange juice for 3 DH a big glass.

6. Sightseeing

The location of Marrakech meant that there was plenty of space in which to build, so the visitor has to move around quite a bit to get in all the sights. The new town, with the Guéliz and Hivernage districts in the center, contains modern shops, car rental firms, travel agencies, the big hotels, and many of the restaurants serving French or international meals. The main post office is here, as well as the vast *Palais des Congrès,* host to numerous international conferences. But the great majority of places of interest to the visitor are in the medina. In no order of preference, the things to see are the *minaret of the **Koutoubia Mosque,** the * **Place Jemaa el-Fna,** the *souks, the *Almoravid Cupole *(kubba),* the **Ben Yusef Mosque,** and *medersa, the **El Mansour Mosque** (also known as the **Kasbah Mosque**), the *Saadian Tombs, the **El-Badi Palace,** the **Palais de la Bahia, Dar Si Said** (museum), and the *mellah.* If your visit has to be short, don't miss * sites. In the new town, try to see the **Majorelle Garden** (and its little museum). A tour of the **ramparts,** a classic tour of the **palm grove,** and a stroll in the **Menara** and **Agdal Gardens,** with perhaps a saunter through the **gardens of the Mamounia Hotel** (meal or drink obligatory) just about finishes the list. When the king is in residence (generally in winter), certain monuments may be closed to the public.

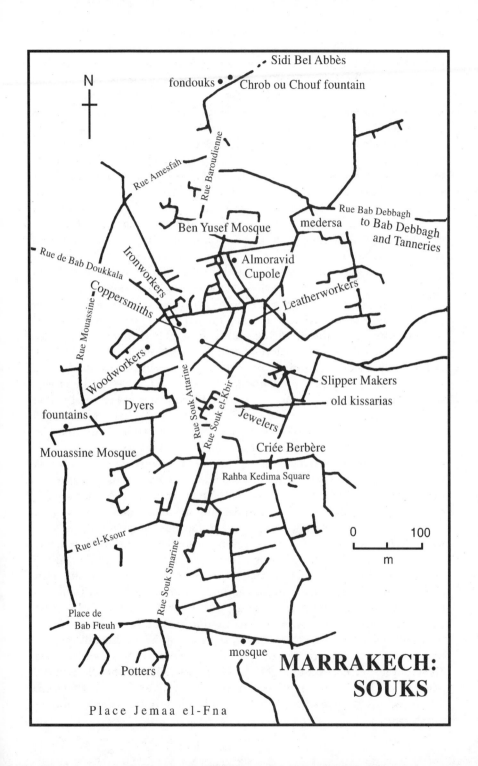

Tackling the medina first, the easiest place to start with is the **Koutoubia Mosque** (the Booksellers Mosque), its minaret visible from afar. The Almohad's first mosque was built here in 1147, on the site of an earlier Almoravid stone fortress (at the end of the 11th century), and excavations have revealed some of these early foundations. The construction of the mosque we see today was started, only a few years after the first one, by the sultan Abd el-Mumen and finished by his grandson Yacub el-Mansour. Its minaret is the oldest of the three famous Almohad minarets—the Tour Hassan in Rabat and the Giralda in Seville (Spain)—and introduced a new architectural style in North Africa. It is almost 70 m high, but its perfect proportions (1 to 5) disguise its size and account for its harmony. It is built of roughly-cut stone and contains six rooms, one above the other, with a ramp curling around them (it is not open to non-Moslems). The decor of the minaret is particularly striking, and the curvilinear motifs introduced by the Almohads differ on each side. Below the four golden balls is a ribbed dome, surrounded by a saw-toothed parapet. Only remnants of the bands of rich enamel tiles that made up the decoration of the minaret now remain—the best photographs are taken from the southeast and southwest, particularly in the afternoon. Scaffolding during six years of restoration work has, for long, spoiled the aesthetics of this magnificent building, but at the end of July 1998 the renovated minaret was revealed to the public.

Close to the Koutoubia Mosque lies the **Place Jemaa el-Fna,** best visited in the early evening, when the animation is at its highest and the food booths have been set up to serve soup, salads, fruit, kebobs, and other delights. Place Jemaa el-Fna is a public theater, where jugglers, acrobats, storytellers, musicians, snake charmers, dentists, water-carriers, and sellers of miracle medicines, love potions, or sticky stuff to make your hair grow or win back an unfaithful husband all compete to attract a circle of attentive, credulous, fascinated spectactors and doubtful or potential buyers. Most performers won't start their act until the public has coughed up a few centimes! Even if you don't understand Arabic, just watching any of these actors is a show in itself, with the punch line often left in the air until more money is forthcoming. It's a fascinating place and always slightly different each time one goes there. Just wander around in the crowd (with money, papers, and camera well tucked away) and enjoy the scene. By the way, photograph-taking will cost you money and may often be refused.

Across the other side of the square, the **souk** of the medina also throbs with life and color. As in Fès, you can't really get lost, though you may not come out just where you thought you would. In 1956, Hitchcock used the alleys of the medina to shoot sequences of his thriller *The Man Who Knew Too Much.* A pottery market lies to the left just before entering the souk. I won't dwell on the attractions of a walk through the Marrakech markets—their names are evocative enough. Smells, sounds, and colors invade the narrow alleys, people, bicycles, motorbikes, and the occasional car or donkey jostle for space, and keen merchants vie with each other to lure you into their little shop or to buy an article from the heap of goods piled up in front of them. A good entrance to the souk, starting from the Place Jemaa el-Fna, is along the Rue Souk Smarine (cloth and kaftan sellers) which divides into Rue Souk Attarine (spices) and Rue Souk el-Kbir. To the right, just before the fork is Rahba Kedima Square (sheepskins) and, nearby, the old slave market and the **Criée Berbère** (carpets). You can circle around from here and continue down Rue Souk el-Kbir, past the jewelers' souk, the old *kissarias* (covered markets), and the leatherworkers. If you take the left-hand road, down Souk Attarine, off to the left before reaching the slipper, coppersmiths', and ironworkers' souk, you'll come to the dyers and woodworkers. Personally, unless you want to buy something in particular, I'd advise just wandering through and enjoying the sights. Once you've been through a couple of times, you'll be quite at home in the maze of alleyways.

After the leatherworkers' souk, the Rue Souk el-Kbir leads down to the **Almoravid Cupole** *(kubba)* and the **Ben Yusef Mosque** and *Medersa*. The *kubba* (indicated in the square in front of the mosque, entry 10 DH) is the only complete building in Morocco surviving intact from the Almoravid period. It's not very impressive, being a small rectangular stone, brick, and cement construction with a dome on intersecting ribs and a small basin. But according to Richard Parker, it contains "a remarkable repository of Almoravid-Andalusian decorative motifs" and is the only place in Morocco where they can be seen in their original position by non-Moslems. If you look closely you'll notice that the arches over the doors are all different and that the brick dome is decorated with a zigzag pattern unusual in Morocco. It's particularly worth going down inside (most of it is now below ground level). The dedicatory inscription indicates that it dates from the reign of Ali ben Yusef (first half of the12th century) and was probably part of the ablutions area of his big mosque. Looking up at the dome, you'll notice a scallop or palmette in the center of the floral motifs (all different) filling the branches of the eight-pointed star. This is said to be the earliest use of the scallop design in Morocco.

Quite close to the *kubba* and easily recognizable by its minaret, the **Ben Yusef Mosque** is one of the oldest in Marrakech, but successive restorations have left nothing of the early architecture. The original mosque was built in the 12th century, in honor of Sidi Yusef ben Ali, one of the town's seven patron saints, who, despite being a leper, had an unfailing faith in

God. It presents no great interest to the visitor (closed to non-Moslems). But to the right is the **Ben Yusef** *Medersa,* one of the largest and finest in Morocco, which should not be missed even if time is short (its restoration in the 1960s carefully followed the original designs) (entry 10 DH, closed from 12:00 P.M.-2:30 P.M.). Descriptions by Arab historians indicate that the *medersa* was founded by the Merinid sultan in the mid-14th century, but it was completely rebuilt by the third Saadian sultan, Mulay Abdallah (elder brother of Ahmed el-Mansur) around 1564. It became the most important residential religious college in North Africa, attended (supposedly) by 800 or 900 students. The long, dark entrance corridor leads into a square hall which opens onto a large courtyard with carved wooden arcades on two sides, a prayer room opposite the entrance, and a white marble basin in the middle. The *medersa* is notable for its characteristic Andalusian architecture and decoration, where plasterwork, *zellij*, marble, and cedar combine in perfect harmony. Practically no space is left undecorated. On the first floor, a few of the 132 tiny rooms look out onto the street, and the others onto small interior patios, both unusual features for a *medersa.*

The Rue Bab Debbagh, going eastwards, leads quickly to **Bab Debbagh** (the Tanners' Gate) and the **Tanneries.** As in Fès, the tanners set up their vats near running water (the River Issil), outside the ramparts, and a little way from the center of the medina so that their evil-smelling vats would not disturb the population. They have been installed there since the 12th century.

The visitor keen to visit every corner of the medina can return to the Ben Yusef Mosque (leaving it on the right and the *kubba* on the left) and turn right along Rue Baroudienne, keeping more or less straight until arriving at the Sidi Bel Abbès district of the town and **Bab Taghzout,** the gateway to the old Almoravid sector, marking the entrance to the Sidi Bel Abbès district. Sidi Bel Abbès, also one of Marrakech's patron saints, was born in Ceuta in the 12th century and was particularly active in favor of the blind. Nearby, the large **Chrob ou Chouf fountain** (Drink and Look) of carved wood carries inscriptions in Koufic script. A couple of **cavaranseries** *(fondouks)* can be seen around here, and many more are hidden away in this rambling old district.

Other visitors would do better working their way back to the Place Jemaa el-Fna. A slightly different route from the way out, passing near the *Copper Market* and the **Dyers' Market,** leads to the **Mouassine Mosque** and **fountain.** The mosque is a large, 16th-century (Saadian) building with three large carved doorways. The fountain is divided into three parts: two for thirsty donkeys and one for humans. From the mosque, a straightforward road (Rue Mouassine) leads to **Bab Fteuh** and **Place Jemaa el-Fna.**

Starting off again at the **Place Jemaa el-Fna,** but going in quite the opposite direction, a circuit can take in **Bab Agnaou,** the **Kasbah Mosque** (also known as **El Mansour's Mosque**), the **Saadian Tombs,** the **El Badi Palace, Bab Berrima,** the **Palais de la Bahia,** and the **Dar Si Said** museum. To my mind, this is far too much to do without a good stop in the middle of the day, or two separate outings. Roughly speaking, this is the "court" area of the old town, where many splendid palaces were built and where, in fact, the late king, Hassan II, had his palace (not open to the public).

Bab Agnaou (probably meaning "the Gate of the Hornless Ram") is reached from the Place Jemaa el-Fna, down the Rue de Bab Agnaou. It is one of the most imposing of the gates leading into the kasbah constructed by Yacub el-Mansour at the end of the 12th century. Built of blue Guéliz stone, its broken, *outrepassé* arch is framed in a rectangle of floral motifs (note the palmette in each corner). The gate is a fine example of an Almohad military gate, with a decor similar to Bab er-Rouah in Rabat, and was the main entrance the sultan passed through on his way to the kasbah. Old texts indicate that the bodies and heads of condemned prisoners were displayed here.

Close to Bab Agnaou is **Bab er-Rob,** originally built in the Almohad period. Built of brick and adobe, it's not a particularly impressive gate. One of the Merinid sultans is also said to have exposed the heads of 600 rebels here early in the 14th century. The **Kasbah Mosque** (El Mansour's Mosque) is easily identified by its baked brick minaret, decorated with one of the favorite Almohad designs cut into the turquoise tile background. It was built by Yacub el-Mansour, probably between 1185 and 1195, when the rest of the kasbah was being built. It was restored under the Saadians and again by the Alaouite sultan Sidi Mohammed ben Abdallah. In the 16th century it was nicknamed "the Mosque of the Golden Apples," legend having it that the three golden spheres at the top of the minaret were made from the gold jewelry of Yacub el-Mansour's wife (the same story also circulates about the three golden balls on the Koutoubia minaret).

The **Saadian Tombs** are entered by a little passage off Rue de la Kasbah, beside the mosque. The monument is made up of two mausoleums constructed in the 16th century to contain the tombs of the Saadian sultans. It is decorated in the Alhambra style—lots of carved stucco, cedar, and marble—although it is about 200 years younger than the Alhambra and became a royal necropolis when the second Saadian sultan Mohammed ech Cheikh was buried here in 1557. His eldest son built a *kubba* for him and was, in turn, buried here in 1574. The first mausoleum is made up of three rooms. The first room, an oratory, was apparently not designed for burials. It contains a magnificent *mihrab* (a niche showing the direction of Mecca) and the tomb of a later Alaouite sultan, Mulay Yazid. Another son, the sultan Ahmed el-Mansur, greatly embellished the monument, and he and his sons have their tombs in a second room—"The Room of the Twelve Pillars"—whose gilded cedar dome is supported by 12 grey marble pillars from Carrara in Italy. From the dome hang carved pendant or sta-lactite ornamentation *(muqarnas)*, and the walls are covered with delicate *zellij*. The sultan's tomb is the middle one. Inscriptions and interwoven arabesques on the floor indicate the burial places of the sultan and his family. The tombs of the children, wives, and concubines of the Saadian princes lie in a richly decorated third room. The much venerated mother of Ahmed el-Mansur, Lalla Messaouda, has her tomb in the second build-ing, called the "Kubba of Lalla Messaouda," less splendid than the other chambers, but nevertheless with fine painted stucco stalactites and delicate inscriptions carved on cedar. Outside the chamber, in a little tree-filled garden, are the tombstones of the dynasty's servants and loyal soldiers. Sixteen Saadian sultans have their last resting place here. When Mulay Ismail managed to capture Marrakech in 1677, he seems to have been im-pressed by the beauty of this monument (or perhaps he was superstitious), for he sealed off the tombs behind a solid wall rather than destroy the building as he destroyed the nearby Badi Palace. The mausoleum was only revealed in 1917 (open every day from 9:00 A.M.-12:00 P.M. and 2:30 P.M.-6:00 P.M., closed Friday mornings, entry 10 DH). If you want, someone is there to show you around (tip expected). There's so much detail to look at in the Saadian Tombs that it's worth trying to get to them before the tourist crowds or after they have gone.

It's quite easy to reach the **El-Badi Palace** (no need for a guide) by returning to Bab Agnaou and turning right along a broad road to the Place des Ferblantiers (Tinsmiths' square). Here you can't miss **Bab Berrima** gate with its solid towers, where a narrow, high-walled street leads to the ruins of the El-Badi Palace. The palace can also be reached directly from the Place Jemaa el-Fna, by taking the Rue de Bab Agnaou for some 300 m and then turning left along Avenue Houman el-Ftouaki to the Place des Ferblantiers. The huge **Dar el-Badi** (Palace of the Incomparable) was the work of the Saadian Ahmed el-Mansur (Mansur ad-Dahabi), after his vic-tory at the Battle of the Three Kings in 1578, and its construction lasted a good 25 years. The money for this sumptuous palace came from compen-sation by the defeated Portuguese, gold from Black Africa, and exporta-tions of sugarcane—"a kilo of sugar for a kilo of marble." No pains were spared to make this palace a showpiece of Saadian splendor: craftsmen from Morocco and Europe worked on the construction and decoration and building materials were imported from Italy (Carrara marble), France, Spain, and even India. The building was not the sultan's residence, but was used for enormous and impressive receptions. The 360 rooms were laid out around a large interior courtyard (135 m by 110 m) containing ornamental ponds and flowerbeds. Faced with such richness, it is not surprising that in the 17th century the Alaouite sultan Mulay Ismail stripped the palace of its furniture, *zellij*, exotic building materials, and decorations and carted them off to embellish his new capital in Meknès. He left El-Badi in ruins, and today's visitor sees only a number of adobe walls in good condition (their marble and plaster covering was among the items removed), a large courtyard, and the remains of four pavilions, probably summer houses. A new gallery in the small, refurbished museum of El-Badi houses (since May 1998) the intricately carved and beautifully delicate *minbar* (pulpit) from the Koutoubia Mosque. This masterpiece of Islamic art has had a varied history, beginning its life at the hands of craftsmen in Cordova in 1137. It had been ordered for the Marrakech mosque of the Almoravid sultan, Ali ben Yusef, and was transported there, assembled, and installed by 1147. Although the Almohads, upon their arrival in Marrakech, destroyed the Almoravid mosque (it had a faulty orientation), they transfered the magnificent, inlaid wood *minbar* to their own new mosque. The Almohad mosque was also found to be incorrectly oriented, a new version was built (known as the Koutoubia), and the *minbar* transfered yet again. In 1992, it traveled back to Spain to be on display at the Al-Andalus exhibition in Grenada. But over the centuries it became increasingly fragile, and in 1996 a U.S./Moroccan team (the U.S. side represented by the Metropolitan Museum of Art) began its restoration. It is impossible to do justice to what the director of the American museum estimated as "one of the marvels of its age and one of the finest works of art ever produced by the craftsmen and artists of the Moslem world." I can only suggest you have a look yourself or read up on it in an excellent book on the subject (see chapter 3). It will undoubtedly be the masterpiece of the planned museum of Islamic art. For many years now, the Marrakech Folklore Festival has been held in the spring in the marvelous setting of the Badi Palace, but after being stopped for several years it was scheduled to reappear in June 1999. The palace is open from 8:30 A.M.-12:00 P.M. and from 4:30 P.M.-6:30 P.M. (entry 10 DH). The present-day **Royal Palace** *(Dar el-Makhzen)* lies just behind El-Badi. It was built by the Almohads in the 12th century, altered by the Saadians in the 16th century, and again in the 17th century by the Alaouites. Recently restored, it is not open to the public.

After the El-Badi Palace, the visitor can return (slowly) to the Place Jemaa el-Fna via the **Palais de la Bahia** and **Dar Si-Said.** Those interested in traces of the past Jewish populations can go and have a look at the *mellah*, just a little east of the El-Badi Palace and entered from the Place des Ferblantiers. It's rather run down now and the Jews have left, but its architecture is different from other parts of the town. There are one or two synagogues, one of which is still functioning. To reach the **Palais de la Bahia,** cross the Place des Ferblantiers away from the *mellah,* keeping to the right, and turn right soon after into the Rue Bab Rhemat, where you should see a long tree-lined avenue and the entrance to the Palace (not clearly indicated, but next to the Restaurant Ed Douira). The **Palais de la Bahia** (the "Beautiful") is a 19th-century house, built for Ba Ahmed, an all-powerful *vizir* (minister) during the reigns of the sultans Hassan I and Mulay Abd el-Aziz. Many hundreds of craftsmen from Fès worked on the building for seven years, using traditional wood, carved stucco, and *zellij.* Ba Ahmed was small and rather fat, so he had everything built on ground level. When he died in 1890, his many enemies were quick to plunder his sumptuous residence, but it has been extensively restored and was lived in by General Lyautey, the French Résident Général under the Protectorate. The palace lies in a large garden with fountains, and contains a series of rather secretive rooms opening onto sheltered courtyards, with no apparent architectural unity, but not without charm. It's a pleasant place in which to dawdle, but the guide is always in a hurry. The only rooms open to the public are the council room (note the *zellij* and the cedar ceiling), the main marble-paved courtyard complete with fountains, and the apartments of the favorite wife or concubine (Ba Ahmed had 4 of the former and 24 of the latter) (open from 9:00 A.M.-12:00 P.M. and from 2:30 P.M.-6:00 P.M., with longer hours in summer, entry free, but paid guide obligatory).

Continuing from the exit, take the road Rue Riad Zitoun el-Jdid for some 200 m to reach **Dar Si Said** on the right (clearly marked). This old palace belonged to Si Said, Ba Ahmed's brother, and is now the **Museum of Moroccan Arts** (see "Culture," section 8). It's well worth a visit for its interior decoration, even if you are not all that hooked on Moroccan arts and crafts (splendid as they are!) (open from 9:00 A.M.-12:00 P.M. and 2:30 P.M.-6:00 P.M., with shorter hours on Fridays, entry 10 DH, closed Tuesdays). While you are in the neighborhood, don't miss a quick visit to **Dar Tiskiwin,** where there is a small display of traditional handicrafts (see "Culture," section 8).

A **tour of the ramparts** (about 10 km, though the circuit can be shortened), preferably in a horse-drawn buggy (1-1½ hours for a cost of 100 DH) or, more actively, on a bicycle, is best done in the evening, when the sun is setting over the High Atlas Mountains, which are often topped with snow. The red ramparts, the green palm-trees, the white, snow-clad Atlas Mountains—you'll see them often on postcards and tourist posters, but they are still beautiful. The adobe-cement ramparts, 8-10 m high, date from the beginning of the 12th century, with later changes by succeeding dynasties. They are broken by 10 monumental gates in the Hispano-Mauresque style, used later for the gates in other Moroccan towns. Start at the **Place de la Liberté** (new town, about halfway between the Koutoubia and the main post office, going clockwise, the itinerary passes first the ruins of **Bab el-Raha,** then **Bab Doukkala,** in a very crowded, busy district of the town (the bus station is here). The name comes from the rural area lying north of Marrakech. This large, Almoravid gate has a broken, *out-repassé* arch with a square tower on each side. Behind the arch, a crooked passage leads from a small courtyard into a vaulted chamber, followed by another archway leading into the town. The next gate, **Bab el-Khemis,** the most northerly point in the ramparts, is flanked by two protective bastions and leads to the Souk el-Khemis (the "5th Day" or "Thursday" market). It has a small tomb of a saint just outside. **Bab ed-Debbagh** (the Tanners' Gate), leading to the tanners' area, was originally Almoravid, but has been rebuilt several times. It was designed to defend the eastern entrance to the medina, so that once past the entrance (parallel to the ramparts), one goes through a vaulted area, then right, then right again into another chamber, then twice left and finally right to enter the medina. The next gate, **Bab Aylen,** is another right-angled construction designed for defensive purposes. It is really of historical interest only, since it was here that the Almohads were defeated in 1130 when they first tried to capture Marrakech. Moving around, you will arrive at **Bab Aghmat** (or "Rhmate"), opening onto the road to Aghmat, the most important town in the area before the Almoravids founded Marrakech (going the other way, the road leads to the Palais de la Bahia). It was originally built by the Almoravids but has since undergone many changes. The Almohads' successful entry into Marrakech in 1147 after a long siege was through this gate. The *zaouia* of **Sidi Yusef Ben Ali,** the leper, one of Marrakech's patron saints, lies just opposite Bab Aghmat. His tomb attracts many humble visitors and an annual pilgrimage to the tombs of the seven patron saints was set up by Mulay Ismail to counteract the influence of the pilgrimage of the seven Regraga saints around Essaouira, but 18th-century Moslem theologians protested against this practice and it was stopped. **Bab Ahmar** (the Red Gate) is much more recent. It is an 18th-century Alaouite construction designed to allow the sultan direct access to the palace. When royalty is not in residence, the gate leads to the exterior *mechouar* (parade ground) adjoining the **Royal Palace** (*Dar el Makhzen*). The inner *mechouar* leads to the **Agdal Gardens** (see further on) and *big mechouar,* where *fantasias* are held on feast days. From Bab Ahmar, the road back to the Place de la Liberté continues around past **Bab Ksiba** and straight down the Boulevard el-Yarmouk, passing **Bab el-Jdid** (the New Gate), to your departure point, Place de la Liberté (missing Bab er-Rob and Bab Agnaou, beside the Saadian Tombs, on the road to the Place Jemaa el-Fna).

Another excursion in Marrakech better done by horse-drawn carriage or bicycle is a **circuit of the palm grove** (*Circuit de la Palmeraie*). This, again, is a pleasant thing to do after a tough day's walking, and the *calèche* will cost you from 150-200 DH for a circuit of 1½-2 hours (the driver usually tries to make the shorter trip for the higher price). The circuit starts at the bridge over the River Tensift, to the north of the town, where there are usually a number of *calèches* waiting for customers. Originally the circuit covered about 20 kms, but so many palm trees have been ripped up and so many buildings have taken their place that a much shorter outing is enough (14 km) to get an idea how attractive this area used to be. There are said to be 150,000 palm trees, whose origin sprang (according to the legend) from the very first Almoravid camp before the town was built. The desert warriors camping there had brought with them their usual food of dates, and some of the pits they carelessly threw around fell into the holes made by the lances they had stuck in the ground.

A different and perhaps more agreeable outing is to **La Menara Gardens.** A word of warning: this is not an organized garden with flowers and bushes. It is really an olive grove, with the addition of a large ornamental pool and pavilion. It's a 2½ km walk from behind the Koutoubia Mosque, along the Avenue de la Menara, but it makes a pleasant place to stroll in, especially in summer. The pool dates from the 12th century and is filled by a complicated system of water channels. The little pavilion on the water's edge is Saadian in origin, but was completely renovated in the late 19th century (entry 5 DH). It used to be the romantic (and secret) meeting-place of the sultans, one of whom (so it is said) had the charming habit of throwing his night's companion into the water at sunrise.

The **Agdal Basin Garden** lies south of the Royal Palace and a double-wall allowed access from the palace in complete privacy. Nowadays, it is best reached from the inner *mechouar.* It is also an agreeable place for a walk but, although it has a greater variety of vegetation, including fig, apricot, and orange trees, as well as olive trees, it again is not a laid-out, ornamental garden, but rather a vast orchard. The Almoravids created this haven of calm and peace in the 12th century, supplying it with the irrigation channels that are still used today. The garden was enlarged by successive Saadian sultans, and rearranged by the Alaouites at the end of the 19th century. It is about 3 km long and there are lots of paths among the trees.

The biggest of the two ornamental pools dates from the Almohad period, while the ruins of the **Dar el-Hana** (House of Happiness) date from the Saadians. A little colonnaded building, with a richly decorated ceiling and turquoise-colored tiles, stands in the middle of the garden.

Finally, to finish activities in Marrakech, a drink or coffee in the **Mamounia Hotel** gives you the chance to wander thorough its *real* **gardens,** which are splendid (trees, plants and flowers of all kinds), and the **Hivernage district** of the new town, full of hotels and high-class apartments, is also good for an evening walk.

WEST OF MARRAKECH

Due **west,** the P10 goes to the busy little town of **Chichaoua** (73 km). Although it doesn't look like much, the town has had quite a past. The region is inhabited by the Arab Ouled Bou Sbaa tribe, who originally came to northwest Africa in the 13th century. Installed south of the High Atlas Mountains, in the Tafilalet, and the valley of the River Draa, they were pushed westwards to their present area in the 14th century. They are noted for their woven rugs, and in the 1930s the French authorities set up a workshop to improve the quality. Ouled Bou Sbaa rugs are characterized by lozenge designs on a dark red base, and also by the stylized representation of animals (unusual in Moroccan rugs). In the past, the red color came from the madder plant, but now chemical dyes are used. Both dyers and weavers can be seen if you ask someone to show you the way. Chichaoua used to be an important sugar-producing region in the 16th century, under the Saadians. About 5 km along the S511 road to Chemaia, at the end of an unpaved road on the right (1 km), one can see a number of imposing walls which are the remains of the sugar factory. It is also possible to see bits of an aquaduct that brought water to the sugarcane plantations and the factory. Morocco's sugar was exported to many European countries and was an important source of revenue at the time.

SOUTH OF MARRAKECH

There are two pleasant day excursions in the High Atlas Mountains south of Marrakech: to the **Ourika Valley** and the area around **Ouirgane,** though it is nicer to overnight there. A visit to the winter sports center of **Oukaimedan** can be combined with the Ourika Valley. The restored **Almohad mosque of Tinmal** can be visited as part of the trip to Ouirgane, on the way south to Taroudannt, or as another day's outing from Marrakech. Many mountain sports can be practiced in this part of the High Atlas, such as skiing, trekking, hiking, mountain biking, rafting, and rock climbing, and a specialized center has been set up in **Amizmiz**. **Imlil** is the starting point for good climbs into the heart of the mountains and up the **Jbel Toubkal,** North Africa's highest peak.

For the **Ourika Valley,** take the S513, which goes through the rather uninteresting Haouz plain, before starting to climb and swing left alongside the river Ourika (in the direction of Arhbalou). Just before leaving the plain, the road passes close to **Aghmat,** founded by a Berber tribe before the arrival of Islam. Trade brought prosperity to the town, which became the capital of the region at the end of the 10th century before being captured by the Almoravids and losing its status in favor of Marrakech. As the road climbs, the scenery becomes more and more attractive, with ochre-colored villages visible high above the other side of the river, with fields and orchards at water level. Violent storms in 1995 and again a short time later caused the River Ourika to overflow its banks, with enormous damage to property and loss of life. Since then the road has been repaved and it is now forbidden to camp beside the river. Despite some rather hideous constructions, the valley is very attractive, particularly in the spring. Lots of Marrakchi come here in the summer, to get away from the heat of Marrakech (the villages stand at around 1,200 m). It is possible to reach the various villages in the valley by **bus** (about 1½ hours from Bab er-Rob) or by **big taxi,** and, of course, by **car.**

The **hotel scene** is not bad. There is the **** **Ourika Hotel** (339 DH, breakfast 35 DH, full-board for 2 people 957 DH, special reduced rates for groups, Vallée de l'Ourika, B.P. 870, Tel: 02-12 09 99), about 9 km after the turn off to the Ourika Valley, right beside the road to Oukaimedan. It has a small sloping garden, splendid views, a nice log fire in winter, a restaurant, and a pleasant staff. The swimming pool is only filled in summer.

There are lots of hotels and restaurants along the valley itself but the one I recommend is the ** **Hotel Restaurant Ramuntcho** (14 rooms, 250 DH, breakfast 30 DH, Vallée de l'Ourika, Aghbalou, Km 50, Tel: 48 45 21, Fax: 48 25 22), which lies up on the right. It has an attractively decorated whitewashed restaurant and bar, and a terrace overlooking the valley. The bedrooms are small but comfortable.

A very homey stay is proposed by a French couple in their house, **Dar Piano,** at Arbalou, just after Ramuntcho, on the other side of the road (three rooms with washbasin and shower, 250 DH with breakfast, Tel: 02-12 10 73). The owners are busy enlarging the terrace so that breakfast can be eaten there, overlooking the river.

Meals can be had in the Ourika Hotel, which offers lunch or dinner for 140 DH, and at the Hotel Restaurant Ramuntcho (set menu 170 DH). Dar Piano also proposes a Moroccan menu everyday, and a French one if it is

ordered in advance (main dish 80 DH). This is a nice friendly place, with a good view over the river.

About 6 km after Ramuntcho's, a bridge across the river is the starting point of treks to the **Yagour Plateau,** well known for its rock engravings. These petroglyphs were carved in the sandstone rocks during the Bronze Age period and later. They represent daggers, arrow or lance heads, shields, humans, and animals. The highest point of the plateau is the Jbel Meltsen (3,595 m) and the plateau itself stands at around 2,500 m. It's a pretty stiff 45-minute climb up to the village of Anammer, where a mule and its driver can be hired. If you are not in a hurry, hang around the bridge and ask a passing villager to send along a mule or two (the tarif for a mule and driver is 75 DH a day and one mule will carry the gear of two people). There are no accommodations or shops on the plateau, so trekkers should be fully-equipped. The mule drivers often know where to find the rock engraving sites, but experienced mountain guides (160 DH a day) know a lot more about the country and can be hired from **Setti Fatma,** a village perched high up at the end of the road (65 km from Marrakech). A nice hike (count on camping one or two nights on the plateau) starts in the Ourika Valley and comes out in the **River Zat Valley** (about 20 km), upstream of the village of Arba Tighedouine. If going from west to east, it should be possible to pick up a truck going back to Marrakech after the Wednesday market at Arba Tighedouine. The names and addresses of authorized mountain guides and current tariffs can be found in the free booklet issued by the Moroccan Tourist Office, *The Great Trek through the Moroccan Atlas.* Experienced guides can also be contacted in Marrakech through the Hotel Ali (Rue Mulay Ismail, near Place Jemaa el-Fna, Tel: 44 49 79).

The big attraction of **Setti Fatma** is its series of waterfalls on the other side of the river, which can be reached by an easy climb. In August, Setti Fatma has its one-day *moussem* in honor of Lady Fatma, who—many years ago—distributed her riches to the poor of the valley. There's lots of dancing and festivities to be seen (find out date from the Marrakech Tourist Office). Accommodations are very limited, and about the best places are the **Hotel Asgaour** in Setti Fatma itself, or the **Auberge Tafoukt,** 3 km before Setti Fatma. Both are pretty basic. There are also a few restaurants serving the standard *tajines* or kebobs.

Back at the point where the S513 turned off to Arhbalou, the road continues in a series of sharp bends up to the mountain-resort of **Oukaimedan** (74 km from Marrakech, altitude 2,650 m). There is **no public transport** for non-motorized travelers, but a certain number of vans and trucks go up and down and it is sometimes possible to hitch a ride. **Big taxis** will also make the journey. Olive, poplar, walnut, ash, and oak trees progressively give way to a more austere landscape as the trees thin out. The views plunging deep down into the valley are absolutely splendid and are, in fact, the best part of the trip, since the village of Oukaimedan doesn't present any great interest unless you are going to ski, walk, look for butterflies or birds, or study the rock engravings. The engravings are easy to find if you use the book *Gravures rupestres du Haut Atlas,* on sale at the Anghor Hotel and the French Alpine Club (it also covers sites on the Yagour Plateau and the nearby Jbel Rat). For skiers, there are 25 km of ski runs and three ski-lifts (one going up to 3,300 m), as well as wide open spaces for cross-country skiing. Skis and boots can be rented. There are a variety of attractive treks around Oukaimedan, some of them involving spending a night in a local's house (or camping). In mid-August the local tribesmen bring their herds and flocks up from the valleys to graze on the rich pastures until the first snow falls. They spend the summer months in small stone buildings called *azibs.* At the end of 1997, the Canadian government provided 13.5 million DH to increase the attractions of this modest resort by improving the road and the communications network. However, as yet, Oukaimedan remains fairly basic, although there are good, if limited, accommodations.

The **most expensive hotel** is the *** **Hotel Kenzi Louka** (100 rooms and suites, Tel: 31 90 80, Fax: 31 90 43 for bookings). This hotel is part of the Kenzi hotel group (as is the Hotel Semiramis in Marrakech) and was opened at the end of 1997. Its big attraction is an indoor heated swimming pool, but it also has a restaurant, a bar with panoramic view, sauna, *hammam,* jacuzzi, a fitness center, and a disco. Its sports staff offers activities such as archery, trekking, ski lessons, mountain biking, mountaineering, and visits to the rock engravings.

A smaller, simpler, but very agreeable hotel is the French-run ** **Hotel de l'Angour** (17 rooms, 310 DH per person, full-board, Tel: 31 90 05, Fax: 31 90 06), which has warm, comfortable bedrooms, good cooking, and a bar. Here, too, the visitor can get information on the rock engravings.

Finally, the **French Alpine Club** (*Club Alpin Français*) has a warm comfortable chalet (80 beds, dormitory 40 DH in winter, room 46 DH, cheaper in summer, Tel: 31 90 36, Fax: 31 90 20) where simple accommodations are available to members and affiliated clubs. As yet, no U.S. club is affiliated, but people who are not members of the club can be "invited" by the manager (space permitting). Good, filling food is provided in a friendly atmosphere (set meal 80 DH).

Ouirgane is reached by the S501 road from Marrakech, uninteresting as far as Tahanaoute. The road then becomes distinctly more attractive as it enters the Moulay Brahim gorges, passing below the village and *zaouia* of **Moulay Brahim,** the scene of an important *moussem* at the Islamic feast of

Mouloud. **Asni** (47 km from Marrakech, altitude 1,150 m) makes a good stop for the traveler not in a hurry and its Saturday morning market is worth watching.

The best **hotel** is the *** **Grand Hotel du Toubkal** (26 rooms, Tel/Fax: 31 92 03), but a strike by the staff has had it closed for many months now. When open, it is comfortable and friendly, and its restaurant serves a good enough meal. It also has a swimming pool.

Several fully-qualified guides live in Asni and can be contacted through the guides' office (postal address B.P. 22 or 47) (check carefully that they really are authorized guides—there are said to be false ones around). **Ouirgane** is about 15 km south of Asni and is a favorite haunt of Marrakchis and Casablancans in search of peace and calm. It's worth spending a night there to enjoy all the area has to offer. **Buses** run regularly from Marrakech to Ouirgane via Asni.

There are two hotels: the **** **Résidence de la Roseraie** and the ** **Le Sanglier Qui Fume.** They are totally dissimilar and cater to different types of guests. Both are very highly recommended.

The **** **Roseraie** (30 rooms, 770 DH per head, half-board only, Tel: 43 20 94, Fax: 43 20 95; for reservations Tel: 43 91 28, Fax: 43 91 30 in Marrakech) is about 500 m before Ouirgane, before the river, and its little rough road on the left is marked. It has beautiful gardens, is discreet, calm, and relaxing (it's *not* the place for noisy kids), and the rooms are comfortable and tastefully furnished. It has an indoor heated swimming pool and *hammam* and can organize excursions on horseback. It's an excellent place to recover from city stress. Reservations are advisable. The hotel will collect guests in Marrakech.

The ** **Sanglier Qui Fume,** run by a French couple, is a very lively place (16 rooms, 226 DH half-board, Tel: 48 57 07—but both it and the Roseraie have trouble with their telephones). It is on the road and clearly visible. The bedrooms are comfortable and attractive (with bathrooms, but the water is not always piping hot), with good log fires. Its restaurant is very popular with tourist groups (French and Moroccan cooking) (couscous on Fridays) (large set meal 110 DH). It, too, has a swimming pool (50 DH for non-residents) set in an attractive garden and can arrange all sorts of activities, such as rafting, trekking, and short walks. It's an excellent value. Market day in Ouirgane is Thursday.

Just before Ouirgane, in the **Marera Valley,** Françoise and Christian, a French couple who ran the Sanglier Qui Fume for a year, are building a small place (eight rooms), the **Auberge du Dahu.** Some rooms should be ready now (up a rough road on the right) (Tel: 48 56 20 for information).

A rather different kind of excursion can be had by taking a rough road on the left 1 km after Asni. This will lead you to **Imlil** (17 km, altitude

1,740 m), along what was a highly cultivated valley until freak summer storms in 1995 poured down a mass of erratic boulders which crushed trees and crops in their mad course. There is **no bus** to Imlil but **big taxis** will make the journey. Imlil is the departure point for a whole range of **excursions,** including the climb to the summit of **Jbel Toubkal** (4,167 m), the highest peak in North Africa. The area around the Toubkal is a Moroccan National Park. Imlil was also used as one of the settings for Martin Scorcese's movie on the Dalai Lama, *Kundun.*

Accommodations are simple but adequate, and there are food shops around for stocking up before setting out on a trek. The French Alpine Club has a mountain hut with caretaker in the middle of the village (38 beds, sleeping bag needed) and, at the entrance, the **Hotel El-Aine** (12 rooms, 30 DH per person, communal showers and water closets) is fairly rudimentary, but clean and calm.

The **Kasbah du Toubkal,** run by a Berber guide, is a recently restored stone-built kasbah about 10 minutes from the center with a commanding view of the valley. It was put into shape by a small British company, Discovery, Ltd., which won a Green Globe Award for Sustainable Tourism, and particularly focuses on mountain activities. It has a few very pleasant rooms with bathrooms (100 DH per person, Imlil BP 31, Asni, par Marrakech). Information about it is best obtained from the **Hotel de Foucauld** in Marrakech (Avenue el-Mouahidine, near the Place Jemaa el-Fna in Marrakech, Tel: 44 54 99, Fax: 44 13 44), or from the UK direct from the British geologist responsible for the scheme (Tel: 44 (0) 1883 744392, Fax: 44 (0) 18833 744913, e-mail: info at discover.ltd.uk, html//www.discover.ltd.uk/net/.

Further on towards the nearby village of **Aremdt,** the **Atlas Gîte** (three double rooms with bathroom, 60 DH per person with breakfast) is an excellent place to stay. It is run by a Frenchman long installed in the Atlas Mountains, who will help with hiring guides and mules. The meals are said to be delicious. There are four classified *gîtes* (lodging houses) in Aremdt, which provide very simple accommodations (communal showers and water closet) and meals (about 30 DH per person per night, breakfast 15 DH, meal 35 DH). Whatever you are doing in this area—long treks with tents and mules or short daily walks—you should be warmly dressed, suitably shod, and preferably have a detailed map. Authorized guides and mule drivers can be hired in Imlil, though if you are just going to climb up the Toubkal a guide is not necessary. The climb is not too difficult in summer, but winter ascents need special equipment.

Count on spending a night at the halfway **Toubkal** mountain hut (3,207 m altitude) and the round trip in the day. At the moment the hut sleeps 35, but it is in the process of being enlarged, as the number of visitors is ever increasing. There are other French Alpine Club mountain huts in the region, at **Tazarhart** (3,000 m, 22 beds) and **Tachdirt** (2,314 m, 23 beds). Trekking on the **Tazarhart** plateau requires appropriate equipment and is best done with a guide. The 2½-hour walk from Imlil to the **Tachdirt** valley is an easier proposition and is highly recommended for its beautiful landscape and villages. All in all, trekking and hiking around here is a great experience, bringing the visitor into contact with sturdy and independent Berber populations, proud of their traditions and way of life. Taking on a guide will ensure you get the maximum out of your trip and will enable easier contact with the local people.

Some 36 km separates Ouirgane from **Ijoukak,** just north of **Tinmal mosque. Buses** from Marrakech to Taroudannt stop in Ijoukak. Before reaching the turn off to Tinmal, you can see on the right the large ruined kasbah of **Talat n'Yacoub,** the seat of the powerful High Atlas Goundafi family, who at one time were the masters of the region until pushed aside by the Glaoui family. Although one would not think so now, Tinmal is one of Morocco's most important historical sites. It was founded by the reforming preacher Ibn Tumert, the father of the 12th-century Almohad dynasty, who sought refuge in the Atlas Mountains after having incurred the anger of the reigning Almoravid sultan by his fiery preaching against the central power. Once installed, Ibn Tumert made Tinmal a spiritual center of great influence. He rallied many tribes to his cause and although he died before dislodging the Almoravids, his lieutenant Abd el-Mumen fulfilled his ambition by capturing Marrakech in 1147. The fortified mosque of Tinmal was built by Abd el-Mumen near the tomb of Ibn Tumert, and Abd el-Mumen was buried there. But once the Almohads had settled into Marrakech, Tinmal and its mosque declined in importance, although the tombs and mosque became a place of pilgrimage. Tinmal was captured and sacked by the Merinids toward the end of 1275, and the beginning of 1276, but enough remained of the ruined mosque for its size and beauty to be appreciated by visitors. It had five aisles and a gallery on each side of the courtyard. The central aisle leading to the *mihrab* is wider than the others. The *mihrab* is a little niche rather unusually built into the minaret. The mosque has recently been partially restored (in 1997), thanks to private funding, but still has no roof. While the visitor can now wander in security through the building, enjoying the chance to see the inside of a mosque and admiring the austerity of its massive pillars and solid walls, restoration has made it difficult to discern the new from the old (5 DH entry fee to the guardian and a small sum to the man or boy who says he's been "guarding" your car).

A very short excursion south of Marrakech for those interested in country markets, with a bit of history thrown in, can be to **Tameslohte** (18 km) and **Amizmiz** (54 km). The two *zaouias* (religious fraternities) of Tameslohte, distinguished by their green-glazed roofing tiles, were founded by a learned holy man in the 16th century. They had an important political and religious role in the past, particularly in the 19th century, but the saint's descendants live in what is now a rather dilapidated kasbah modeled on those of the High Atlas. An "eco-development" project financed by the European Union and the P.N.U.D. aims to restore the building before it falls down completely. The Tuesday market in Amizmiz is one of the most important Berber markets in the region, noted for its pottery. A highly-recommended **multi-activity center** has been set up by an Englishman near **Amizmiz**—"Life in Outdoor Pursuits" (Caet, Draa Souk, Amizmiz, Tel: 45 44 08, Fax: 45 41 42). The English director, Matthew Low, is an experienced, qualified mountaineer and his center organizes trekking, kayaking, rock-climbing, and other activities, as well as providing full board and lodging.

SOUTHEAST OF MARRAKECH

Going in this direction, the main P31 road from Marrakech goes to **Ouarzazate** (204 km), but a turn off 12 km after **Ait Ourir** (29 km) will take you alongside the **River Zat** to the village of **Arba Tighedouine** (16 km). From here mule trails lead up to the **Yagour Plateau** and its rock-engravings (described earlier). It's a nice walk, even if you are not into rock art. No mules are available at Arba Tighedouine, but the climb is much less stiff than the route starting at the Ourika Valley and there are several villages at the beginning of the journey. Two days should be enough to reach the paved road and "civilization" in the Ourika Valley.

NORTHEAST OF MARRAKECH

In this direction, the **sightseeing** consists of the **Imi n'Ifri "natural bridge"** *(Pont Naturel)* and **dinosaur tracks,** both near Demnate, and the **Ouzoud Waterfalls** *(Cascades d'Ouzoud)* further on towards **Azilal.** The **Ouzoud Waterfalls** are undoubtedly the most spectacular of these attractions and a fairly long day's drive, or a 2-day outing if traveling by bus, will get you there. By **car,** the **shortest route** is the secondary 6206 and 6207 to **Demnate** (about 100 km), which continues to **Azilal** (72 km) (the turn off to the waterfalls is 22 km before Azilal). Two daily **buses** from Marrakech to Azilal stop in Demnate. **Big taxis** make the run from Marrakech to Demnate and Azilal (65 DH). I'm told the hotel in Demnate is horrible.

The walls surrounding the small town of **Demnate** are pierced by two imposing gates. Its kasbah belonged to the Pacha of Marrakech, Thami el-Glaoui. From the town, take the east-bound CT6715 as far as the huge natural archway or **"bridge"** of **Imi n'Ifri,** carved out by the river Mahseur. The bridge can be used by pedestrians and a path leads down to the pools at the bottom, where one can go under the archway, which is full of stalactites and little caves. From Imi n'Ifri an unpaved road (CT6712) leads to the **dinosaur tracks** (7 km). The tracks (unfortunately highlighted in white paint when I last saw them) are on sloping reddish slabs on the left-hand side of the road (one is exhibited in the Geological Museum in Rabat). Unless you want to continue as far as the **Jbel Rat** and climb to its summit (3,797 m), hike around its base, or look at the **rock engravings** (13 sites), it's best to turn back here. If you have a 4WD vehicle and are really keen on walking, continue to the ford and go right or left to the last villages (36 km and 45 km respectively, a three-hour drive from Demnate along a very bad, rough road). Get someone from the village to show you the way to the **Tizi n'Tirghyist** rock art (or buy *Gravures Rupestres du Haut Atlas,* on sale in Marrakech or Casablanca, which will show you the way). This route is not the easiest way to the Jbel Rat—a much simpler way is the one going towards the **Ait Bougmez Valley** (see "Further Afield").

Back in Demnate, to reach the **Ouzoud Waterfalls,** one should continue eastwards along the S508 towards **Azilal,** turning left 22 km before reaching this town. From Azilal it is pretty easy for the non-motorized traveler to find a place in a **big taxi** going to Ouzoud (38 km). Some 16 km after the turn off, you will find yourself in a large parking area (payment required) beside these impressive falls that hurtle down about 100 m into a limestone basin in the river. The whole zone overflows with luxuriant vegetation and forms one of the most attractive sites in the Middle Atlas. Unfortunately, it attracts a large number of false guides, hustlers, and other nuisances of all kinds. A small path goes down to the pools and another path, overlooking the waterfalls, leads to a dozen little watermills, which are still in use. In the evening the noise of the local monkey inhabitants (Barbary apes) fills the air. They live in the many little caves around the falls. There are several campsites, all pretty filthy (about 20 DH for a tent and one person), and there is also a cheap hotel (also dirty). A short and agreeable walk up from the waterfalls leads to **Tanaghmelt,** a small village with a labyrinth of lanes and alleys. Its popularity will be its undoing, however, since it's becoming very tourist-oriented. Going the other way, a very rough, difficult, unpaved road (the 1811), best suited to hikers, mountain bikers, or thrill-loving drivers of 4WD vehicles, leads, after 8 km, down through the superb canyon of the **Oued el-Abid.** However, if you want to come out on the main P24 (about 25 km west of Afourer), you'll need to cover 25 km.

An alternative route for those just wanting to visit the **Ouzoud Waterfalls**—on the way to Fès for instance—is to go by **car** or **bus** along the main P24 road towards **Beni Mellal** (194 km). There's no need to go as far as Beni Mellal (unless you want to spend the night there), since the turn off for the waterfalls, marked **Afourer,** is 19 km before Beni Mellal. At Afourer (5 km), a magnificent mountain road clings to the hillside before reaching the **Bin el-Ouidane Dam,** one of Morocco's biggest, and **Azilal** (see "Further Afield" for information on Beni Mellal, Afourer, the dam, Azilal, and trekking in the mountains). From there the west-bound road to **Demnate** brings you, after 22 km, to the turn off for the waterfalls.

FURTHER AFIELD

The **north-bound** P7 goes to **Casablanca** (240 km). It is a road noted for its accidents, and not particularly interesting from a sightseeing point of view. The epic battle by Saharan warriors against the French in 1912 at **Sidi Bou Othmane** was mentioned in chapter 10.

Northwest from Marrakech, a straightforward and uninteresting road (the P9) goes to **El-Jadida** (197 km), branching off for **Safi** (157 km) after about 50 km, becoming the P12. Both roads go through phosphate country.

The P10 **west** to Chichaoua continues to **Essaouira** (176 km from Marrakech). It is also the road that most vehicles start on to go to **Agadir** (273 km), the south-bound P40 branching off at Chichaoua.

South of Marrakech, an alternative route to **Taroudannt** (222 km), and from there to **Agadir** (82 km), is by the S501 via **Asni** (see earlier) and the **Tizi n'Test** pass (2,092 m). This trip will take at least five hours. The road is not as well maintained as the more frequented route via Imi n'Tanout, and can be blocked by snow or falling rock in winter. After the Haouz plain, the road winds up to the pass (magnificent views) through picturesque stone-built villages, then down the southern side of the High Atlas Mountains. Walnut trees, almond trees, and a wide variety of vegetables are grown in the carefully-cultivated little plots, and the visitor will not see the crowds of idle youths so conspicious in the towns. The road is full of bends and very narrow. If you spot a truck or bus coming towards you, dive into the first especially prepared passing place (usually tucked into the mountainside) and let the oncoming vehicle negotiate the difficult, precipitious, side. A few kilometers after the pass, on the southern flank of the High Atlas, a small café can provide hot coffee or an omlette while you admire the view.

Southeast of Marrakech, the P31 is the main route, across the High Atlas, to **Ouarzazate** (204 km) and the Saharan south. Fill up with gas before setting out if you are **motorized.** Travelers by CTM **bus** will find four departures a day from Marrakech, and a shared place in a big taxi shouldn't be difficult to find. The road has been carefully planned and is well maintained. Snowploughs go quickly into action if the road is blocked, and the situation rarely lasts more than a few hours. At first the direction is Fès, along the P24, then the road turns off to the right and goes through a flat, rural countryside as far as **Ait Ourir** (36 km), a large agricultural and administrative center. Shortly after, a road to the right marked **Arba Tighedouine** runs alongside the **River Zat** before becoming very rough as it climbs up towards the **Yagour Plateau** (see earlier for **treks** and **rock-engraving sites** on the plateau). The main road continues southeast, with some splendid views as it climbs progressively out of the plain and goes through thick natural forests of evergreen oak, little villages, planted walnut trees, and densely cultivated terraces. It is possible to see the Yagour Plateau on the right at the first mini-pass, **Tizi n'Ait Imguer** (1,470 m), about 67 km from Marrakech. After **Taddert** (the last place for a meal or coffee north of the Tizi n'Tichka pass), the road climbs stiffly for 14 km in a series of tight bends before arriving at the **Tizi n'Tichka pass** (altitude 2,260 m). All along the way, sellers of fossils and semi-precious minerals, both false and authentic, try with unceasing hopefulness to get the passing traveler to stop and buy their wares. The journey down the other side to Ouarzazate is described in chapter 13.

   Northeast of Marrakech, a long drive along the P24 takes the traveler to **Fès** (483 km). The road as far as the first important town, **Beni Mellal** (194 km), runs more or less parallel to the High and Middle Atlas chains on the right, passing through rich agricultural land irrigated by an extensive scheme originating in the **Bin el-Ouidane Dam** in the mountains. Beni Mellal is a provincial headquarters and a very busy administrative and commercial town. The province has a population of 906,000, half of whom are urban, and the town is said to be one of the fastest-growing in Morocco. The fact that it is little visited by tourists makes it a very authentic (if not architecturally pleasing) town. Its kasbah was built around 1688 by Mulay Ismail, but has been renovated several times. The town can serve as a jumping off point for trips into the High Central Atlas. All the main banks have branches in Beni Mellal, there are lots of gas stations, shops, a few drugstores, a tourist office (on Avenue Hassan II), and a clinic *(Clinique des Oliviers)*. The post office and the bus station *(gare routière)* are situated in the Boulevard Mohammed V, which lies off the main P24 road. Regular **bus** services run to Beni Mellal from Marrakech, Fès, Casablanca, and Azilal, as do the **big taxis.**

   The **regional telephone code** for Beni Mellal is 03 (0 omitted for in-region calls).

The Beni Mellal region has its own set of tariffs for hotels. The ★★★★ **Hotel Ouzoud** (60 rooms, 457 DH, breakfast 48 DH, Route de Marrakech, Tel: 48 37 52, Fax: 48 85 30) is about 3 km outside the town on the Marrakech side. This is an oldish place, set in an agreeable garden, with a restaurant, a bar, and tennis courts, but both it and its restaurant are expensive for what is offered.

The ★★★★ **Hotel Chems** (77 rooms, 457 DH, breakfast 48 DH, Km 2, Route de Marrakech, Tel: 48 34 60/48 30 08, Fax: 48 11 00) is also out of town, but has always been popular with travelers.

Good value comes from the ★★★ **Hotel-restaurant el-Bassatine** (63 rooms, 330 DH, breakfast 36 DH, Tel: 48 22 47, Fax: 48 68 06), just outside Beni Mellal on the road to Fkih ben Salah. Its bedrooms are air-conditioned, and the hotel is pleasant and well maintained. It has a restaurant and a swimming pool.

In the town, there is the ★ **Hotel Ain Asserdoun** (154 DH, breakfast 23 DH, Boulevard des F.A.R., Tel: 48 34 93), a new hotel with clean rooms equipped with hot shower and water closet. It also has a restaurant.

The ★ **Auberge du Vieux Moulin** is also outside the town center, on the Kasba Tadla road (10 rooms, 154 DH, breakfast 23 DH, Tel: 48 27 88). It's another hotel of long-standing, but is well maintained. Its bedrooms have bathrooms and hotel water, and it has a restaurant and a bar.

A cheap hotel is the **Hotel el-Amiria** (80 DH, Avenue des F.A.R., Tel: 48 35 31), which has simple, clean rooms, but the showers are communal.

One of the best **restaurants** is the one in the **Auberge du Vieux Moulin,** which serves an excellent French meal in an old inn atmosphere and has a well-stocked wine list (set meal 84 DH). The **Hotel Ain Asserdoun** has a tourist menu that is not bad (84 DH). A restaurant that is said to serve a good and copious meal is unnamed, but squeezed in between a couple of other restaurants at 155 Boulevard el-Hansali (Tel: 48 14 48)—try to find a table upstairs (main dish around 50 DH). The best **coffee shop** is the **Salon de Thé Azouhour,** 241 Boulevard Mohammed V.

Local **sightseeing** in the immediate neighborhood of Beni Mellal could be to the **kasbah,** but it is not particularly interesting, and to the **Ain Asserdoun spring** *(Source d'Ain Asserdoun).* The spring lies about 3½ km out of town (you can take a bus or small taxi and walk the last bit). Its water supplies the town, and the spot must have been very attractive in its natural state. Now the pools are all cemented and surrounded by a public garden, so the whole thing has become very formal (and crowded on weekends), but it is still quite agreeable. A narrow road from there climbs up to the ruined fort of **Ras el-Ain** (1 km), where there is a splendid view over the Tadla plain. It's worth making a short excursion **south** of Beni Mellal (but take the main road west, back towards Marrakech, and turn left after 11 km, at the village of Oulad M'barek) to the small mountain town of **Ouaouizarht** (32 km) and the **Bin el-Ouidane Dam.** The lake makes a good place for walking and picnics. There is a **bus** service from Beni Mellal to Ouaouizarht. Motorized travelers can continue south, leaving the lake on their right, along a charming mountain route flanked by evergreen oaks (liable to be under snow from December to February) to the village Tilougguite (42 km) and the principal attraction of the outing (another 10 km)—the **Cathedral** *(La Cathédrale)*. (The dinosaur exhibited in the Geological Museum in Rabat came from near Tilougguite.) Not a religious building, the Cathedral is a line of 800-meter high cliffs, both impressive and awe-inspiring. A day's outing will probably end here, but people having two to three days to spare and a suitable vehicle (4WD), can continue through a **fossil forest** of long-dead trees, to arrive at **Zaouia Ahansal** (51 km, count on four to six hours from Tilougguite). Zaouia Ahansal is a small administrative center, with a post office and a public health dispensary (don't count on it being supplied with medical supplies), and a contact point for qualified mountain guides.

Simple **accommodations** (3 GTAM classified second-class *gîtes*) are available in the villages of Agoudim and Tahgia. All this area is superb trekking country, but adventuring through it requires careful preparation and a good guide. The only people likely to be seen are shepherds with their flocks of sheep and multi-colored goats.

Excursions of two or more days into the **High Atlas** starting from **Beni Mellal** involve taking the main P24 road in the direction of Marrakech, and turning left after 19 km for **Afourer.** There is nothing much here except a good hotel, the ****** Le Tazerkount** (600 DH, breakfast 50 DH, Tel: 44 01 01/44 02 01, Fax: 44 00 94). This is a very attractive, ochre-colored hotel, with bedrooms overlooking a beautiful swimming pool, a bar and a restaurant, tennis courts, *hammam,* a fitness center, and (apparently) a disco. It is recommended as a stop to or from the rigors of the mountain, and is certainly the best in the area. From Afourer, the road climbs before descending to the **Bin el-Ouidane Dam** (30 km). The road crosses the dam, which is guarded by soldiers. Stopping or photographing is forbidden. It is Morocco's third largest dam, with a capacity of 1,060 million cubic meters and has been operational since 1955, supplying a good part of central Morocco's electricity requirements The lake is popular with fishermen, hikers, and holiday makers. About the only place to stay is the *** Auberge du Lac** (154 DH), which is well placed beside the river, but pretty basic. It has a restaurant (set meal 84 DH, licensed to sell liquor).

Fishing in the lake is allowed from the beginning of April to the end of September, but a fishing permit (for this area) must be obtained from the *Délégation Provinciale des Eaux et Forêts* in Beni Mellal, Azilal, or Marrakech. The garrison town of **Azilal,** 27 km from the dam, has grown enormously since becoming the provincial capital, but it is far from beautiful, and there is nothing to retain a visitor. If you *do* have to spend the night here, the best hotel is the ** **Hotel Tanout** (184 DH with bathroom, 147 DH shower only, Tel: 48 82 81), at the entrance to the town (coming from Beni Mellal). It is clean and the staff is helpful.

A reasonable **meal** can be found at the **Restaurant Le Passage** (Avenue Hassan II, near the mosque). There are daily **buses** to Azilal from Marrakech and Beni Mellal. The agency **Azourki Randonnées** (81 Avenue Mohammed V, Tel: 03-45 83 32) specializes in trekking, ski-trekking, canyoning, rafting, and kayaking, and it's a good idea to get in touch with them if you need advice.

The **Ait Bougmez Valley** and the **Jbel Rat** are both reached by taking the tarred road from Azilal to **Ait M'hammed** (20 km). The **Ait Bougmez Valley** in particular is a fabulous area for **resting, walking,** or **trekking** (78 km from Azilal). The valley lies at 1,800 m, and is dominated by the **Jbel Azourki** (3,682 m), a favorite with skiers using mules to carry their equipment up to the snow-line. But south of the Azourki summit, the **Jbel Mgoun** rises even higher (4,068 m) and a climb to its summit is also popular. A wide range of treks have their starting point in this "hanging valley," which has been the object of a very successful Franco-Moroccan project integrating mountain tourism (construction of simple lodging and training of professional, fully-qualified mountain escorts), craftwork (wood-carving and rug-making), and agriculture. As a result, the number of visitors has increased and the inhabitants themselves have seen their standard of living improve. It is a quiet and gentle place, well-watered, and criss-crossed with low mud-walled irrigation channels *(seguia),* blocked or opened according to the time of day. Fields of potatoes, carrots, and turnips are carefully tended by men and women, constantly at work. Walnut and fruit trees thrive. Life is apparently idyllic, but winter snowfalls can be very heavy, covering everything with a thick white carpet. I haven't met anyone who has spent a few days in the valley who has not been enchanted by the beauty of the stone and adobe houses, the charm of the little paths running through the vegetable plots, and the calm of the local people (pestering children are generally quickly reprimanded by an older villager). There are plenty of good, gentle walks if stiff treks out of the valley do not appeal.

To reach this delightful spot, take the tarred road to the right about 4 km before **Ait M'hammed,** cross the Tizi n'Oughbar pass, and follow the valley of the river Lakhdar. Go left at the fork (50 km from the Ait M'hammed turn off) to arrive in the first villages of the **Ait Bougmez Valley.** The main village is **Tabannt,** more or less in the middle. It is hideous, a terrible contrast with the adobe villages in the rest of the valley. It is the seat of local government *(caidat),* has a post office, a public health dispensary (not well-equipped), and a mountain guide contact point.

For accommodations, far and away the best place to stay is the **Auberge Imelghas** (about 5 rooms, 150 DH, reservations through Bernard Fabri, Atlas Sahara Trek, 72 Rue de la Liberté, Marrakech, Tel: 44 93 50, Fax: 44 96 99). It is clean, comfortable, tastefully decorated, has good sanitary equipment, and provides a nice meal (80 DH). There are at least 7 second-class *gîtes* (simple lodging houses), and 11 unclassified ones (look out for the GTAM triangular label), in different villages throughout the valley. Tariffs for *gîtes* depend on their classification, and a night's lodging currently costs from 15 DH in an unclassified one to 30 DH for second class; with breakfast from 12-15 DH and a simple meal (starter, main dish, dessert, and mint tea) 30-35 DH. A recommended second-class *gîte* is **El Ouakhoumi,** also at Imelghas, which is comfortable and clean, with hot showers. Meals are cooked by the owner, Abdallah, who intends to keep up high standards. A small workshop, **Atlas Sculpture,** near the village of Agouti, sells wooden bowls, spoons, and carved statues made by three young men from the valley trained under the development project mentioned above.

Anyone interested in superb **treks** of 4-15 days should contact a mountain guide or be really independent and get hold of the little book *Randonnées pédestres dans le Massif du Mgouna,* which proposes eight itineraries starting from **Tabannt** or **Zaouia Ahansal.** They include a marvelous trek through the mountains, involving walking in the Mgoun river, coming out on the southern side of the Atlas, at **Kelaa des Mgouna** (7 days) (chapter 13). All routes take the visitor along narrow mountain paths, across rich pasture land, through picturesque Berber villages, or up the bare slopes of a rocky mountain. An absolute must if you want to see a particularly Moroccan speciality.

Back at the **fork in the road coming from Ait M'Hammed,** the road not leading to the Ait Bougmez Valley ends up in the tribal lands of the **Ait Bouwili,** around the foot of the **Jbel Rat.** The river can be crossed if the water is low and taken as far as **Souk Sebt Bouwili** (13 km). There are a few shops here and a *gîte* run by Hassan and his wife, Hadda. Hadda will be pleased to show you and (hopefully) sell some of her woven blankets and rugs (one of the aspects of the development scheme mentioned earlier). Hikes or simple walks start from here. A six-hour walk is needed to make the round trip to the first rock-art site at the **Tizi n'Tirghiyst pass.** The engravings have been carved into the sloping sandstone strata and show round, decorated shields, scenes of combat between two groups of armed warriors, daggers, and a number of curious "idols," looking a bit like something from outer space . There are about a dozen other rock-art sites in the area, but the trek around the foot of the Jbel Rat, or even a climb up to its summit (the scene of a yearly pilgrimage by the local people) and around and down into the Ait Bougmez Valley are favorite itineraries.

If you've decided to leave trekking into the mountains for another visit, or it's simply not your thing, continue along the main road to **Kasba Tadla,** 30 km after Beni Mellal. It has a fortress built in 1687 by the Alaouite sultan, Mulay Ismail, since the site was particularly strategic, allowing the central government to control the activities of the turbulent Berber tribes of the Middle Atlas and prevent their incursions into the fertile plains. **Buses** from Marrakech and Fès stop in Kasba Tadla. The best **accommodations** are in the *** **Hotel Bellevue** (330 DH, Rte Ple 24 Marrakech-Fès, Tel: 41 87 31/32/33), on the main road just outside Kasba Tadla, after the junction with the Casablanca road. This hotel has been well designed, with large bedrooms overlooking the gardens and a swimming pool, and has a restaurant.

On the right, 22 km after Kasba Tadla, a narrow road leads to **El-Ksiba** (9 km), a pleasant little mountain town overlooking a valley richly planted with walnut, orange, apricot, and olive trees. There is no **bus service** but a **big taxi** will make the run from Kasba Tadla. About the only **accommodations** worth mentioning here are in the **Hostelerie Henri IV** (Tel: 41 50 02), in a lovely woodland setting. It has comfortable rooms and a reasonable restaurant. Friends say they have seen monkeys in the trees around here. This is quite possible, as the area is noted for its wildlife.

Motorized travelers can continue southeast along this route (liable to be blocked by snow between November and March), to **Tizi n'Isly** and around in a circle to join the P33 17 km before its junction with the main Kasba Tadla-Khenifra road. Southwards from Tizi n'Isly, the road goes to **Imilchil** (61 km) (chapter 7), but for this you really should have a 4WD vehicle. If you are so equipped, this makes a superb drive, where you are not likely to meet with hordes of tourists (or local people, either). For travelers who are not motorized, the only hope is to catch a truck going to Imilchil on market days (Fridays and Sundays). During the Imilchil *moussem* (see chapter 7) there is, of course, much more of this casual transport.

The stretch of the Fès road after the turn off to El-Ksiba runs through more attractive country as the Tadla plain is abandoned for the Middle Atlas. About 25 km after **Zaouia Cheikh,** at Zaouia Ait Ishaq, the new ** **Hotel Le Transatlas** (217 DH, breakfast 24 DH, 24 Route Principale) catches the eye with its harmonous architecture and makes a good coffee and pit stop. A little further on, the campsite that was under construction should now be finished. Zaouia Cheikh is a departure point for line-fishing in the Middle Atlas rivers (information and permit from the *Délégation Provinciale des Eaux et Forêts* in Marrakech, Beni Mellal, or Azilal). The main P24 road continues to **Khenifra** (99 km) and **Azrou** (82 km) (chapter 7) before reaching Fès (chapter 8).

7. Guided Tours

Many travel agencies in Marrakech organize tours around the town and further afield. For instance, **KTI Voyages** (173 Avenue Mohammed V, Tel: 44 61 84, Fax: 43 10 97), **Ménara Tours** (41 Rue de Yougoslavie, Tel: 44 66 54), and **Pampa Voyage Maroc** (213 Avenue Mohammed V, Tel: 43 10 52) organize tours of the town. The last named will also help with made-to-measure itineraries and transport further afield. FRAM (245 Avenue Mohammed V, Tel: 43 95 99, and their offices in the FRAM Hotels Chems and Les Idrissides) do "Marrakech by Night" on Sundays and Wednesdays (2 hours, 50 DH); a guided tour of the main monuments on Mondays (4 hours, 60 DH); a horse-drawn carriage excursion in the palm grove on Monday, Wednesday, and Thursday afternoons (2½ hours, 60 DH); and a visit to the souks on Wednesday afternoons (2 hours, 60 DH). They also propose day excursions to Moulay Brahim, Essaouira, Ourika Valley, the High Atlas, and Ouarzazate (minimum of 6 people for the Atlas outing and one day's notice), and mini-circuits to the Dades Valley, Todra Gorge, and Zagora. KTI Voyages also run day trips to Ourika or Ouirgane (200 DH), Essaouira (300 DH), Ouarzazate (400 DH), and other places. Shop around and see what are the best offers going. Many of these out-of-town destinations are easily and more cheaply reached by bus, but arranged excursions are useful for those short on time.

Official guides can be hired from the main hotels or the tourist office (around 150 DH a day, 120 DH ½ day). Settle on the price beforehand and avoid the unofficial ones.

8. Culture

The Museum of Moroccan Arts, on Riad Zitoun el-Jdid, just north of the Palais de la Bahia, is housed in the former residence **(Dar Si Said)** of the brother of vizir Ba Ahmed. The building is of interest from a decorative point of view (see "Sightseeing," section 6) and its collections of Moroccan antique and traditional craftwork from Marrakech and south Morocco make it one of the best museums of its kind in the country. Among its treasures are carved wooden doors from the High Atlas, inlaid shutters, Berber jewelry, muskets, gunpowder boxes, silver daggers, leatherwork, carpets from many regions, pottery from the religious center of Tamgroute in the Tafilalet, and a carved marble ablution basin dating from the late 10th century, which has a floral decor similar to that used in Cordova, showing that it was probably imported from southern Spain (open from 9:00 A.M.-12:00 P.M. and 4:00 P.M.-7:00 P.M. , with shorter hours in winter and on Fridays, entry 10 DH, closed Tuesdays).

When visiting the Dar Si Said Museum, it is worth droppping into the **Maison Tiskiwin** (8 Rue de la Bahia, Tel: 44 33 35, almost next door to the Dar Si Said Museum), where there is a good collection of traditional handicrafts displayed in the house of Bert Flint, a Dutch authority of Moroccan handicrafts and author of many books on the subject. Bert Flint has spent much of his life in Morocco and his carefully-presented collection is a useful complement to its bigger neighbor. Some articles combining tradition and modernity are also on sale (knock on the door to get in, closed in the afternoons, entry around 10 DH).

A new cultural center, the **Marrakech Museum** *(Musée de Marrakech)*, in the Place Ben Yusef, in the heart of the medina, organizes talks and concerts, as well as exhibits of paintings and traditional crafts.

The **Jardin Majorelle** (entrance in a small street off Avenue Yacoub el-Mansour, Guéliz, not clearly indicated but about a 10-minute walk northwest of Bab Doukkala) houses a small but interesting **museum** of local arts and crafts, as well as a collection of paintings by the French painter Jacques Majorelle (others can be seen in the Mamounia Hotel). Many of his pictures were used as tourist publicity for Morocco (reproductions are not available, but there is a beautiful illustrated book of his work on sale in Casablanca bookshops). Majorelle lived here from 1922 to 1962, and designed the only real **garden** open to the public in Marrakech. A stroll along the paths among the rich vegetation is a delight (open from 9:00 A.M.-12:00 P.M. and 3:00 P.M.-7:00 P.M., shorter hours in winter, entry 15 DH, no children or dogs). The property is now owned by the couturier Yves Saint-Laurent, whose house is not open to the public.

The **American Language Center** (3 Impasse du Moulin, near the Majorelle Garden, new town) has a small library and organizes films, talks, and musical events from time to time (open from 9:00 A.M.-12:00 P.M. and 3:00 P.M.-7:00 P.M.). The **French Cultural Center** *(Institut Français*, off Route de la Targa) not has only language classes, but puts on occasional films, plays, talks (in French), and exhibitions (open from 8:30 A.M.-12:00 P.M. and 2:30 P.M.-6:30 P.M.). For many years now, Marrakech has housed a

Folklore Festival in the spring, with groups from all over Morocco performing their traditional dances. This has been held in the evening in the El-Badi Palace and is an enchanting spectacle. Unfortunately, it has not taken place for several years, but in June 1999 it was again an attraction. It should not be missed (information from the Tourist Office, hotels, or travel agencies).

9. Sports

The sport most easily and evidently practiced in Marrakech is **golf.** Golfers have the choice of three courses. The Marrakech Royal Golf Club, 18 holes, 6,200 m, has a par of 72. It is the oldest of the Marrakech courses (created in 1960) and lies in the middle of an immense 100-hectare park (Tel: 45 58 64). The Amelkis Golf Club, 18 holes, 6,657 m, par 72, is one of the newest golf courses in Morocco. It is situated in beautiful surroundings just opposite the Royal Golf Club. It's a very technical course where one can combine the pleasure of playing with the contemplation of the High Atlas Mountains (Tel: 44 92 84/88). The Palmeraie Golf Club, 18 holes, 6,214 m, par 72, was designed by Robert Trent Jones, and is also very technical. It lies in the beautiful setting of the Marrakech Palm Grove, and has its own ***** hotel to boot (Tel: 30 10 10 for the hotel and information). Non-members can play on all these courses for a green fee of around 200 DH, with caddie obligatory (100 DH). The Semiramis Hotel provides a **golf practice net** for its guests, and the hotels Palmariva, Tikida Garden, and Les Almoravides have mini-golf.

In Marrakech, **horseback riding** at the Amelkis Golf Club can also be arranged through the Semiramis and Mamounia hotels, and is also offered by the Palmariva hotel. Information can be had from the Riding Club (*Equitation,* Km 4 on the road to Asni, Tel: 44 85 29). Many of the big hotels have **tennis courts.** The Royal Tennis Club (Rue Oued el-Makhazine, Tel: 43 19 02) is able to supply information on local tennis tournaments. The Mamounia Hotel has a **squash court** and one or two hotels offer **archery** and **table-tennis.** The municipal **swimming pool** gets terribly crowded, but the Hotel Moussafir lets non-guests use its pool for 50 DH a day, and so does the Palmerie Golf Palace (80 DH a day). The Tikida Garden hotel rents out **mountain bikes** to its guests. **Trekking, kayaking,** and **mountaineering** in the High Atlas can be arranged through specialized agencies in Morocco and elsewhere (see chapter 2), through hotels in Marrakech, and on the spot in the Ourika Valley, Oukaimedan, Amizmis, Imlil, and the Ait Bougmez Valley.

The **ski resort** of Oukaimedan, equipped with three ski-lifts, is only 70 km from Marrakech. Skiing could be possible from mid-December thru to March, since the lifts start at 2,600 m and rise to 3,300 m, but Moroccan weather is fickle and sufficient snow can never be guaranteed. An attractive proposition is the combination of ski plus mule, which permits skiers to reach high, untouched snow slopes aided by mule porterage. Equipment can be rented in Oukaimedan. Information on this can be had from the Club Alpin Français in Casablanca, 1 Rue Aknoul, BP 6178, 20000 Casablanca (Tel: 02-27 00 90, Fax: 02-31 90 20). **Freshwater line-fishing** is possible in many rivers and dams in the High and Middle Atlas (permits and information are available from the water and forest ministry— *Délégation Provinciale des Eaux et Forêts*—in Marrakech, Beni Mellal, or Azilal). A popular international **marathon** takes place in Marrakech in January.

10. Shopping

The **state craftwork center** *(Ensemble Artisanal)* on Avenue Mohammed V, near the Koutoubia Mosque, is laid out with imagination and has good displays of craftwork for sale, painting exhibitions, calligraphy, and lots of people at work making slippers, wooden bowls, rugs, and so on. Prices are fixed, so it's a good place to shop without hassle or to get an idea of going prices before launching into the bargaining process. The **markets** in the medina need little introduction. Everything's there: carpets galore, leather slippers, belts, jewelry, carved wood, kaftans, *jellabas,* pottery, baskets, spices, herbal remedies, and a mass of other things needed by a Marrakchi household. For very expensive, but genuine, antiques, look in at **La Lampe d'Aladin** (99 Rue Semmarine) in the medina. An excellent, but also expensive, place for arts and crafts is **Al Badii,** *Art, Antiquités et Créations* (54 Avenue Moulay Rachid, Guéliz, Tel: 43 16 93). Good quality modern leather goods (jackets, handbags, suitcases, attaché cases, and such) can be bought at the **Galeries Birkenmeyer,** on Rue Muhamed al-Baga in Guéliz. **Le Vendôme,** Avenue Mohammed V, is also a good address for leather goods. **Hotel boutiques** often have clothing or jewelry for sale at prices that are not too outrageous, and the top-class hotels have U.S. and British newspapers and books on Morocco in English. The **bookshop** of the **American Language Center,** 3 Impasse du Moulin, Guéliz, also stocks books in English. U.S. and British newspapers are available at some kiosks along Avenue Mohammed V (especially the one in front of the Avis car rental office). **Photography** stores are best looked for here, too.

11. Entertainment and Nightlife

For an evening beer or other pre-dinner drink, the top place to go to at least once is the piano bar in the **Mamounia Hotel,** particularly if you are not actually staying there—if the door porters will let you in! (correct dress is essential). The pianist is usually American. The **Hotel Melia Tichka Salam** has a pleasant little piano bar, with an electric piano playing all on its own. Live jazz is offered in the **Kenzi Semiramis** hotel bar. The **Tikida Garden** hotel has a piano bar with an orchestra functioning until midnight. A drink without music at the **Palmeraie Golf Palace** is very agreeable, especially in the spring and summer when the freshness of the evening and the surrounding vegetation can be appreciated. Almost all the **big hotels** have a bar beside their swimming pools, which are also pleasant in the summer (Hotel Es-Saadi, Hotel Meryem, Hotel Oudaya, and so on). **Les Almoravides** has a "Happy Hour" around 6:30 P.M. when the second drink is free. Many of the lower-level places sell beer (the **Brasserie Le Petit Poucet,** Avenue Mohammed V, for instance).

More exotic late night entertainment is not lacking in Marrakech, apart from the restaurants mentioned above, which provide a floor-show with their meal (**Yacout, Stylia, Le Tobsil, Dar Marjana, Chez Ali, Restaurant Dar el-Baroud, Ksar es-Saoussan, Dar Mounia, Dar es-Salam, Le Ryad,** and **Le Palais Gharnatta**). The **Villa Rosa Restaurant** has a jazz bar, **Le Millésime,** going from 6:00 P.M.. There is also **The Casino** (next door to the Hotel es-Saadi), which has a floor show, the **Grand Casino** in the Mamounia Hotel (fruit machines, blackjack tables, and roulette), the disco **Diamant Noir** next to the Hotel le Marrakech (it can't be missed with its yellow and black Chevrolet truck outside), the karaoké disco in the **Hotel Kenzi Semiramis,** the disco **Le Joy** in the Tikida Garden hotel, and the nightclub in the **Palmeraie Golf Palace.** Entry to all these places is between 50 DH and 100 DH and includes the first drink. The casinos require jacket and tie for men, smart clothing for women.

12. The Marrakech Address List

Accidents, road—(Tel: 43 07 99).

Airlines—Air France: reservations (Tel: 02-29 40 40); British Airways: reservations (Tel: 02-22 94 64), Flight information (Tel: 02-33 95 24, local representative: Ménara Tours, 41 Rue de Yougoslavie (Tel: 44 66 54, Fax: 44 61 07); Royal Air Maroc, 197 Avenue Mohammed V, Guéliz (Tel: 43 62 05).

Airport—Marrakech-Ménara (Tel: 44 78 65)

Ambulance—(Tel: 44 37 24).

Banks—the BMCE, Avenue Mohammed V, opposite the tourist office, has an ATM and you can get a cash advance on VISA or MasterCard; the BMCE branch in Rue Mulay Ismail, near Place Jemaa el-Fna has a similar service; American Express is represented by Voyages Schwarz, Immeuble Moutaouakil, 1 Rue de Mauritanie, Guéliz (Tel: 43 66 00); the BMCI, near Hotel de Foucauld, Place Jemaa el-Fna, has an exterior cash point.

Bus station *(gare routière)*—Bab Doukkala (Tel: 43 39 33)—but best go personally for information or tickets (don't wait until the last minute before buying a ticket).

Car Rental—Avis, 137 Avenue Mohammed V (Tel: 43 37 27, Fax: 44 94 85); Budget, 68 Boulevard Mohammed Zerktouni (Tel: 43 11 87); Concorde Car, 154 Avenue Mohammed V (Tel: 43 11 16); Europcar, 63 Boulevard Mohammed Zerktouni (Tel: 43 12 28, Fax: 43 27 69) (also has 4WD); Goldcar, Hotel Semiramis, Route de Casablanca (Tel: 43 13 77); Hertz, 154 Avenue Mohammed V (Tel/Fax: 43 46 80); Lune Car, 111 Rue de Yougoslavie (Tel: 43 43 69/44 77 43, Fax: 44 73 54) (best reputation for 4WD vehicles); Pampa Voyage Maroc, 2nd floor, 213 Avenue Mohammed V (Tel: 43 10 52). The Hotel Ali and the Grand Hotel Tazi, in the old town, can arrange reliable car rental for their guests.

Churches—Eglise des Saints-Martyrs, Rue el-Imam Ali (Tel: 43 05 85) (just opposite a mosque), French language Mass weekdays and Saturdays 6:30 P.M., Sundays 10:30 A.M. and 7:00 P.M.; French-speaking Protestant Temple: 89 Avenue Moulay Rachid (Tel: 43 14 79); for information on English-speaking Anglican services, call the English clergyman in Casablanca (Tel: 02-25 71 20); English-speaking Catholic mass is held in the Parish Hall of the Catholic Eglise des Saints-Martyrs, Guéliz, every Sunday at 10:30 A.M. (call American Father Barnaby for information, Tel: 04-43 05 85).

Consulates—there is no U.S. Consulate in Marrakech. If in trouble, call the Consulate in Casablanca, 8 Boulevard Moulay Youssef (Tel: 02-26 45 50).

Doctors, Emergency—at the night drugstore below.

Drugstore, night *(pharmacie de nuit)*—Rue Khalid ibn Oualid, off Place de la Liberté, new town.

Express Post *(Poste rapide)*—(Tel: 43 18 71 for information).

Fire *(Sapeurs-Pompiers)*—(Tel: 15).

Gendarmerie Royale—(Tel: 17).

Golf Clubs—see under section 9, "Sport."

Guides—hotels and the Tourist Office can advise on official guides and their tarifs.

Horse-drawn buggies *(calèches)*—many waiting at the Place Jemaa el-Fna and outside big hotels.

Hospitals and Clinics—Ministry of Health public hospital Ibn Touffail, Rue Abdelouahad Derraq, Guéliz (emergency—*urgences*); the Polyclinique du Sud, 2 Rue de Yougoslavie (Tel: 44 79 99) is good but expensive.

Jewish Synagogue—Beth, Impasse des Moulins, Guéliz (Tel: 44 87 54) and Synagogue Bitoun, Rue Arset el-Maach, medina (Tel: 44 82 66).

Photocopies—from most tobacco stores and some téléboutiques.

Police—(Tel: 19).

Post Offices—Place du 16 Novembre, Guéliz; Place Jemaa el-Fna.

Railway Station—Avenue Hassan II (Tel: 44 65 69).

Taxis, Big and Little—big ones wait at Bab er-Rob, Place Jemaa el-Fna, and near Bab Doukkala; little ones have stands all over town or can be hailed in the street.

Telephone—next to the main Guéliz post office but also at the téléboutiques.

Tourist Information—the **Office du Tourisme,** Place Abdelmoumen, Guéliz (Tel: 44 88 89) has the usual glossy brochures, a list of the classified hotels and, perhaps, the free booklet *Welcome to Marrakech* (closed Sundays); an office called *Informations Touristiques GRIT Marrakech,* on Avenue Mohammed V, does not, in fact, supply tourist information, so they are not very welcoming. But they have the glossy brochures and a plan of the town with the hotels on sale for 20 DH. They will help out in an emergency.

Tour Operators and Travel Agencies—Atlas Sahara Trek (72 Rue de la Liberté, (Tel: 44 93 50, Fax: 44 96 99) (recommended—run by a French expert in treks and adventure trips); Carlson Wagonlit Travel, 122 Avenue Mohammed V (Tel: 43 16 87, Fax: 43 23 41) (specializes in tickets); Ménara Tours, 41 Rue de Yougoslavie (Tel: 44 66 54, Fax: 44 61 07); Nouvelles Frontières, 34 Rue de la Liberté (Tel: 43 36 05, Fax: 43 39 34); Pampa Voyage Maroc, 213 Avenue Mohammed V (Tel: 43 10 52/43 87 30, Fax: 44 64 55) (recommended); Voyages FRAM, 245 Avenue Mohammed V (Tel: 44 95 99/ 44 98 66), and their branches in the FRAM Hotel, Les Idrissides, 6 Avenue de France (Tel: 43 67 87/44 87 77) and the FRAM Hotel Chems, Avenue Houman el-Ftouaki (Tel: 44 48 13/44 48 14) (specializes in group travel).

13

Ouarzazate, the Kasbahs, and the Sahara

1. The General Picture

Situated at an altitude of 1,160 m in the middle of a bare plateau, Ouarzazate lies south of the High Atlas Mountains, well placed at the center of routes going north, south, east, and west. It is the capital of a large province, the northern limits of which run along the southern side of the High Atlas, its southern boundaries disappearing into the desert. It is essentially populated by Berbers, responsible for the construction of the numerous fortified dwellings, kasbahs, for which the region is famous. It is one of Morocco's major holiday destinations, not so much for the attractions of the town, but as a base from which to visit the kasbahs of the Dades and Draa Valleys, and from which to set off on excursions into the desert. Ouarzazate offers the best selection of good quality hotels south of the Atlas, fewer than Agadir to be sure, but architecturally more in harmony with the landscape. Hot and dry in summer, Ouarzazate can be very cold in winter, with icy winds sweeping down from the High Atlas Mountains.

Although surface finds of Palaeolithic tools have been made all around Ouarzazate, the town is a modern creation. Certainly the Glaoui family,

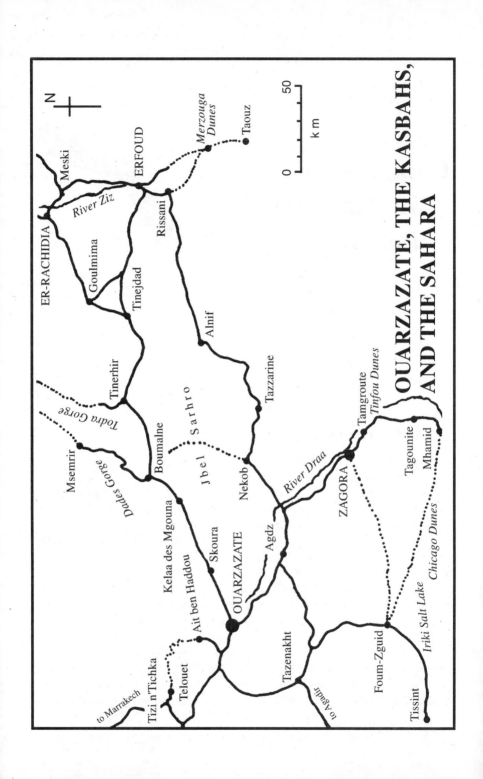

OUARZAZATE, THE KASBAHS, AND THE SAHARA

Pashas of Marrakech in the late 19th and 20th centuries, had a kasbah here, but Ouarzazate was really only created by the French at the end of the 1920s, when they turned it into a garrison town as part of their pacification of the Berber tribes of south Morocco after the establishment of the French Protectorate in 1912. It took off as a major holiday resort in the mid-1980s and has been booming ever since, with an increasing number of new top-class hotels. It has also acquired a vocation as a film-making location, with Morocco's biggest studios welcoming many international film companies. *Lawrence of Arabia* was filmed here in the 1960s, and in 1996 Martin Scorsese used Ouarzazate as the setting for his latest film, *Kundun,* the story of the Dalai Lama's childhood and adolescence. It seems that the beauty and uniqueness of the Tibetan landscapes could best be recreated here! And the Atlas Studios were able to provide the base for the construction of the Dalai Lama's residences (parts of the film were also shot in Marrakech and Casablanca).

2. Getting There

Ouarzazate can be reached direct by **air** from Paris twice a week with RAM. The airport lies a couple of kilometers north of the town (little taxis available, shouldn't cost more than 30 DH). RAM has four flights a week from Casablanca. There is no train to Ouarzazate, but CTM **buses** run from Marrakech (four a day), Casablanca, and Rabat (once a day), and SATAS makes a run from Agadir, via Taroudant, and from Casablanca and Fès via Marrakech. Other companies run from Er-Rachidia and Zagora and many intermediate towns and villages. By **car,** there are very good roads from Marrakech (204 km), across the Tizi n'Tichka pass, from Agadir (375 km), and from Fès (687 km) via Midelt and Er-Rachidia. **Big taxis** make the trip from Marrakech or Er-Rachidia.

3. Local Transportation

A **car** is pretty mcuh essential if you are to get the most out of your stay in and around Ouarzazate. They can be rented from several firms in the town (see "Address List"). You *can,* of course, use the **bus** or **shared taxi,** but this way you'll miss out on most of the attractions of the area, just whizzing past kasbahs and oases without having time to enjoy them. If you are hardy, bicycles allow more scope for individual choice—but you'll find going south to Zagora, for instance, entails a pretty stiff climb.

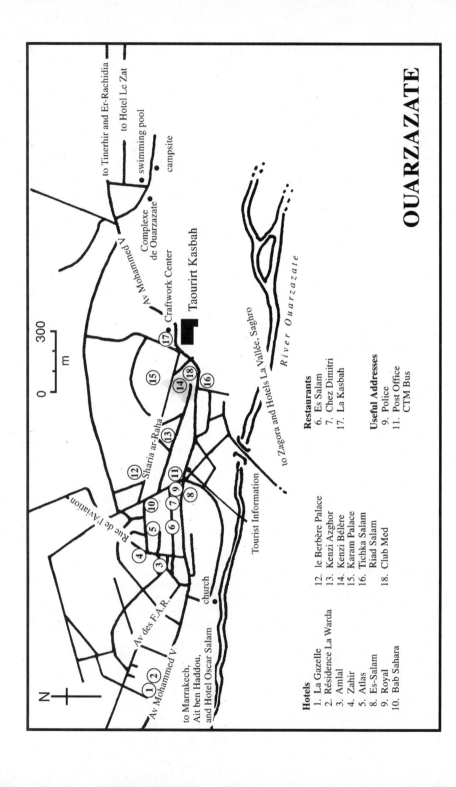

OUARZAZATE

N

0   300
m

to Tinerhir and Er-Rachidia
to Hotel Le Zat
swimming pool
campsite

Av Mohammed V
Complexe de Ouarzazate

Craftwork Center

Taourirt Kasbah

River Ouarzazate

to Zagora and Hotels La Vallée, Saghro

Tourist Information

Sharia ar-Raha

Rue de l'Aviation

Av des F.A.R.

Av Mohammed V

church

to Marrakech,
Ait ben Haddou,
and Hotel Oscar Salam

Hotels
1. La Gazelle
2. Résidence La Warda
3. Amlal
4. Zahir
5. Atlas
6. Es-Salam
7. Royal
8. Club Med
9. Royal
10. Bab Sahara
12. le Berbère Palace
13. Kenzi Azghor
14. Kenzi Bélère
15. Karam Palace
16. Tichka Salam
     Riad Salam
18. Club Med

Restaurants
6. Es Salam
7. Chez Dimitri
17. La Kasbah

Useful Addresses
9. Police
11. Post Office
    CTM Bus

4. The Hotel Scene

There are 32 classified hotels in the province of Ouarzazate, with a capacity of 5,500 beds. This is way behind the provinces of Agadir and Marrakech, but does mean the traveler should be able to find a room. As the town has only recently sprung into the tourist limelight, most of the hotels are big, new, and pretty up-market. For a large choice of good hotels, Ouarzazate is by far the best place south of the High Atlas Mountains (excluding Agadir) and an excellent base for excursions. Hotel charges fixed for this region are as follows (they vary according to the presence or absence of showers and water closet in the room): **** 318-440 DH or 407-770 DH, breakfast 43-70 DH for both; *** 158-275 DH or 179-378 DH, breakfast 32-41 DH for both; ** 87-152 DH or 94-194 DH, breakfast 21 DH for both; * 79-117 DH or 83-133, breakfast 20 DH for both.

The **regional telephone code** is 04 (0 omitted for in-region calls).

EXPENSIVE HOTELS

The two ***** hotels are **Le Berbère Palace** (225 rooms, from 850 DH, Quartier Mansour Eddahbi, Tel: 88 31 05, 88 21 39, Fax: 88 30 71, 88 20 20) and the **Hotel Riad Salam** (70 rooms, from 800 DH, Rue Mohammed Diouri, off Avenue Mohammed V, Tel: 88 33 35, Fax: 88 27 66). The former (part of the Meridien chain) is a rather amusing place, rigged out as a *ksar*, with tastefully-decorated rooms entered from little streets (lined with bushes and flowers, which is unusual for a real *ksar*) within the walls. It has a restaurant, bar, *hammam*, boutiques, fitness center, Jacuzzi, swimming pool, mini-golf, tennis courts, and six conference halls, and is an attractive place in which to pass a few nights. The latter, looking like a kasbah from the outside, just before the Taourirt Kasbah (this one is real), has two restaurants, bars, sauna, tennis courts, and a pleasant amount of greenery around the pool.

The Kenzi chain runs three **** hotels: the **Hotel Kenzi Bélère,** the **Hotel Kenzi Azghor,** and the **Hotel Kenzi Ourida.** The **Bélère** (264 rooms, 22 Avenue Prince Moulay Rachid, near Sharia ar-Raha, Tel: 88 28 03, Fax: 88 31 45) is huge and modern, but nice enough, built around a swimming pool, with two restaurants, boutiques, tennis courts, and a nightclub. The **Azghor** (106 rooms, Avenue Prince Moulay Rachid, Tel: 88 60 00/88 63 53, Fax: 88 24 13/88 63 53), is a charming hotel, recently renovated in southern Moroccan style, with a restaurant, a bar, boutiques, a disco, a good swimming pool, tennis courts, and an attractive garden.

The **** **Hotel Oscar Salam** (65 rooms, Tamassint, Tel: 88 22 12, Fax: 88 27 66), 5 km from the town center coming from Marrakech, with pleasant rooms, a restaurant, and a swimming pool, is a good value.

Friends have enjoyed the **** **Hotel Tichka Salam** (Avenue Mohammed V, Tel: 88 22 06, Fax: 88 56 80). It has a restaurant, a bar, a garden, and tennis courts.

The second-class club category **Club Méditerranée,** part of the French group of holiday villages (Avenue Prince Moulay Rachid, close to Taourirt Kasbah, Tel: 88 26 50, Fax: 88 24 14) is up to the club's usual high standard, with multiple tourist and sports activities, and evening entertainment.

The **** **Karam Palace** (147 rooms, Avenue Prince Moulay Rachid, Tel: 88 25 22) has a restaurant, a nightclub, and tennis courts, and also offers apartments from 500 DH.

MEDIUM-PRICE HOTELS

The choice is not enormous in this range. The *** **Hotel Le Zat** (Ain Kdif, Tel: 88 25 21, Fax: 88 53 94) is out of town on the Tinerhir road. It has a restaurant, a bar, tennis courts, and a disco. Coming into Ouarzazate from Marrakech, the long-established ** **Hotel La Gazelle** used to be the only decent place in which to stay (30 rooms, Avenue Mohammed V, Tel: 88 21 51, Fax: 88 47 27). But it is not as friendly as it used to be, is often full, and unwilling to take guests who don't want to eat dinner there. Apart from that, it is a good value and has a large courtyard in front for parking.

If you are with a group of friends and dead set on doing your own cooking (but come provided with equipment), you could try a place grandly called **La Résidence La Warda,** Avenue Mohammed V, on the left as you come into Ouarzazate from Marrakech (prices vary according to the customer, but shouldn't be more than 150 DH for a double room with bathroom and refrigerator).

BUDGET ACCOMMODATIONS

There's not a great deal of choice here either. The * **Hotel Zahir** (Avenue al-Mouahidine, Tel: 88 57 40), with a restaurant, is up a road to the left just before the mosque.

The * **Hotel Bab Sahara** (39 rooms, Avenue al-Mouahidine, near the old bus station, Tel: 88 47 22) is a good one to try. There is also the * **Hotel Amlal** (28 rooms, Lot du Centre, Tel: 88 40 30, Fax: 88 46 00), just off the road leading to the **Hotel Zahir** (see above). It's pretty simple, with the bedrooms looking onto a central patio, but the breakfast is substantial.

A good choice in this category is the unclassified **Hotel Es-Salam** (50 rooms, 80 DH with shower, cheaper without, Avenue Mohammed V, Tel: 88 25 12) which is pretty basic, but clean.

The **Hotel Royal** and the **Hotel Atlas** are not recommended except in a pinch.

Out of town, 2 km down the road to Zagora, the **Hotel-Restaurant La Vallée** (120 DH for the new rooms with toilet facilities, less for the older ones with communal showers, Tel: 88 26 68, Fax: 88 28 20) is pleasant and friendly, and has a pool and a restaurant.

Just after the above (after the bridge), the **Hotel Saghro** (25 rooms, around 100 DH, Tel: 88 43 05) is basic but clean (although a bit noisy). The municipal **campsite** is one of the better Moroccan versions, without being exactly luxurious. It's a bit out of town, past the Taourirt Kasbah, going east (Quartier Sidi Daoud, Tel: 88 26 50), and is indicated. It's fairly shaded, but the ground is very hard (10 DH/person, 7 DH/tent, 6 DH/car). A few simple rooms are also available.

5. Dining and Restaurants

HOTEL RESTAURANTS

Most people advise eating in the big hotels, as the choice otherwise is not very wide. The **Berbère Palace** restaurant is a good one, as is the **Kenzi Bélère,** both in the upper price range (set menu from 165 DH). The restaurant in the **Riad Salam** is said to have gone down recently. The restaurant of the **Kenzi Azghor** has a reputation for delicious *tajines,* or you can go for grills and salads (set menu 165 DH). The **Club Med** also provides excellent (and copious) meals, with some sort of show or music every evening. The **Hotel La Gazelle** provides French or Moroccan meals in a rather family-style setting, but is often very full (set meal 83 DH). Out of town, about 2 km, the **Hotel-Restaurant La Vallée** serves a good meal under big Moroccan tents, but it tends to be full of tourist cars at lunch time. The **Hotel Saghro,** ½ km further on, also has a good restaurant, serving couscous, kebobs, or *tajines* (unlicensed) (main dish from 50 DH).

OTHER RESTAURANTS

Outside of the hotels, one of the most attractive places to eat is the **Tifoultoute Kasbah** (7 km out, along the P31 Marrakech road, then left, Tel: 88 28 13). This was one of the Glaoui's strongholds when he was Pasha of Marrakech, and it has been beautifully restored. It serves Moroccan meals (set menus at 80 DH or 130 DH). In town, an up-market place is the **Complexe de Ouarzazate,** near the campsite, on the road to Tinerghir (Tel: 88 31 10), where the restaurants serving Moroccan meals under big tents are placed around the swimming pool (set menus from 100 DH). Tastefully decorated, it is open at midday, with a floorshow in the evening in the spring and summer.

Chez Dimitri, on Avenue Mohammed V, used to be the center of all life in Ouarzazate in the late 1920s, when the town was little more than a military post. It was living a bit too much on its reputation, but is now very good, friendly, and has a good selection of dishes and a wide range of wines and alcohol (Dimitri followed the French troops in their advance and ran the gas station, food store, dance hall, telegraph post, and Foreign Legion bar) (closed Fridays, meal with wine around 180 DH). Friends have recommended **La Kasba** restaurant (Tel: 88 20 33), opposite the Taourirt Kasbah, though the decor is perhaps slightly better than the meal (set menu 120 DH). Cheap roasted chicken (cooked outside) can be had in a **little unnamed restaurant** opposite Chez Dimitri (20 DH/portion). Another cheapie is the **Restaurant es-Salam** (Avenue du Prince Héritier Sidi Mohammed/corner Hotel Atlas) which offers a choice of menus (salad, main dish, and fruit), all around 60 DH (unlicensed).

6. Sightseeing

IN OUARZAZATE

A visit to the **Taourirt Kasbah** (eastern end of Avenue Mohammed V) gives an idea of just one of the many kasbahs owned by the Glaoui family, Pasha of Marrakech from the 19th century. Thami Glaoui strongly supported the French in the 1930s, and his cooperation was a big plus for the French because his rule ensured calm and security in the region (at a high price, some would say). An opponent of the sultan Mohammed V, he and his family fell into disgrace with the sultan's return from exile and the end of the French Protectorate in 1956. The Glaoui family has been called "The Lords of the Atlas," and anyone traveling south from Marrakech will constantly see the ruins of one of his kasbahs. Taourirt Kasbah, adobe-built on a stone foundation, was one of the largest, housing several hundred members of the family and servants. It has been partially restored and includes courtyards, reception rooms, living quarters, and gloomy little kitchens (open from 9:00 A.M.-12:00 P.M. and 3:00 P.M.-6:30 P.M. through the week, at least in summer). Entry is 10 DH, and a guide can be hired for a negotiable fee if you want the inside details (check his English first if you are not sure of your French).

AROUND OUARZAZATE

Another Glaoui kasbah is that of **Tifoultoute,** about 7 km **northwest** of Ouarzazate, along the P31 Marrakech road and then left (marked). Taxis will make the run for non-motorized travelers. It is said to be over 250 years old, and has also been restored. It houses a restaurant serving typical

Moroccan meals (see "Dining and Restaurants" above) with traditional Berber dancing and music (in the summer). A few rooms are sometimes available (150 DH).

Further along the P31 Marrakech road, the **Ait Benhaddou Kasbah** must be one of the most visited sites in south Morocco (34 km from Ouarzazate, turn off on the right after 22 km, marked). It is magnificently perched on a hill overlooking the river and has been heavily (but carefully) restored. It should be remembered that *all* adobe buildings have to be regularly restored, so we are never looking at anything terribly old, even if they are ruins. Ait Benhaddou is a UNESCO supported site, and was largely rebuilt for films such as *Lawrence of Arabia* and *Jesus of Nazareth*. Efforts are being made to encourage the local people to return and live there. Vehicles have to be left at the group of craft shops and hotel/restaurants, and the river crossed on foot (there are stepping stones). It's worth the visit, but there's no need to hire a guide—just keep climbing up once you are in among the buildings. It's possible to spend the night comfortably at the **Hotel Restaurant La Kasbah** (double room, half-board 300 DH/person, Tel: 89 03 02, Fax: 88 37 87). Cheaper accommodations close by are provided by the **Auberge el-Ouidane** (around 100 DH, Tel: 89 03 12). Both these places have beautiful views of the kasbah. More basic still (communal showers), but clean, is the **Auberge al-Baraka,** the first you come to (around 70 DH, Tel: 89 03 05). The best place to eat is the **Hotel Restaurant La Kasbah,** much frequented by tourist groups, but with two dining rooms and a large terrace overlooking the kasbah (set meal 80 DH). But you can also get a meal in the two auberges.

Continuing another 5 km along the road past Ait Benhaddou brings you to another Glaoui kasbah, that of **Tamdaght.** The road goes through the river to reach the kasbah about 1½ km further on, but it is not advisable to cross the river unless you have a 4WD. It is better to leave the car at the café beside the river and walk the rest.

For those pressed for time, a short excursion **east** along the P32 can be made to **Skoura** (about 42 km), the first part of a much longer trip recommended along the Dadès Valley (see "Further Afield" below). The Skoura oasis is said to have been founded in the 12th century. On the right, just outside Ouarzazate, the **El-Mansour Eddahbi dam** has allowed the irrigation of much agricultural land, as well as a reforestation program. The oases, in fact, start about 30 km east of Ouarzazate, but the Skoura kasbahs are the best preserved. One of the most accessible (and most visited!) is the one just off the main road on the left, 2 km before Skoura (Kasbah Ben Moro), whose owner will take you around. The outside of the beautiful Amerhidil Kasbah can be admired, but not visited. Other kasbahs lie further into the oasis (some of which can be visited; recommended is the Dar Ait Sidi el-Mati, not so tourist oriented as the first one), and it is delightful just to walk through the oasis and admire the date palms, fruit trees, irrigation channels, and little plots of vegetables. If you like being accompanied by a crowd of small children, go ahead. Otherwise, try to find an adult who will act as a bodyguard and guide (remunerated). There are a few cafés around, but not much in the way of eating places. A short motorized excursion along a north-bound paved road to **Toundoute** (21 km), thick with almond tree blossoms in early spring, gives a good idea of the local environment. Salt mines are exploited at Toundoute.

NORTH OF OUARZAZATE

A longer trip, but still possible in a day, is to the spectacular crenelated stronghold of the Glaoui family at **Telouet** (220 km round trip). The visit is highly recommended, although the building itself is sadly neglected. In its heyday it must have been a splendid place, more a palace than a kasbah, and it was the Glaoui family's most prestigious building, strategically placed to guard the caravan route from the Sahara across the Atlas Mountains to Marrakech. It is reached by **car** along the P31 road to Marrakech, with a turn to the right (indicated) after 94 km (just before the Tizi n'Tichka pass). If you are not motorized, it is easy to get the **bus** to drop you off at the turn, but the next 21 km to the village and kasbah of Telouet will be hard going. The building is fairly new, dating from the late 19th and early 20th centuries, when El Haj Thami el-Glaoui enlarged and embellished it. It contains room after room of what must have been sumptuous reception halls when fully furnished, two of which still retain their Andalusian-inspired decoration. Some *zellij* and plaster work and a few painted ceilings also remain, but it really is a pity that nothing is done to recreate its earlier splendor. A caretaker will open it up for you (5-10 DH remuneration per person suggested).

Telouet can also be reached by one of Morocco's most attractive routes, a rough track requiring a 4WD and often undertaken by mountain bike enthusiasts. If you are tempted by this, I would suggest that it is best to take the main route as far as Telouet (as above) and return to Ouarzazate by the track via Achahoud and Ait Benhaddou (47 km to the main road) rather than the other way around. In either case, this route can only be used if the rivers to be crossed are not overflowing (information from the Gendarmerie in Ouarzazate).

SOUTHWEST OF OUARZAZATE

For people interested in rugs, the journey to **Tazenakht** and back (170 km round trip) is easily done in a day by **car** or **big taxi.** Take the

Marrakech-bound P31, turning off to the left after some 30 km (in the direction of Agadir). The SATAS **bus** to Agadir will drop passengers at Tazenakht, but it will be difficult to get back. There is really nowhere to stay or eat, and the visit is purely for the rugs. If you do want to spend the night there, the **Hotel-Restaurant Etoile de Tazenakht** is probably the best. It is cheap, simple, and clean. Tazenakht has an important craft cooperative, where the Berber women from the surrounding areas bring in their flatwoven rugs, the dominant colors of which are black and orange, though other colors can be incorporated. In the old part of the town one can see women at work in their homes.

FURTHER AFIELD

Northwest of Ouarzazate, the P31 goes to **Marrakech** (204 km), after the turnings to Ait Benhaddou and Telouet, crossing the High Atlas Mountains by the **Tizi n'Tichka pass** (altitude 2,260 m). It is the highest road pass in Morocco and links north Morocco to the Saharan regions of the south. The landscape up to the pass is bare and bleak, except for the villages and patches of green in the cultivated plains and valleys. A small community of Franciscan priests and nuns is established at **Agouim** (about 70 km from Ouarzazate, up a track on the left) where they have a woodworking training school for boys and a weaving cooperative for girls and women, which you are welcome to visit and buy some of their work. After Agouim, if you are into rock art and have the time, take a track to the left to **Tainant** (3½ km), leave the car at the village, and continue on foot a few kilometers (keeping to the left, following the stream) to reach, on the left, a wide prairie. The engraved rocks are mostly on the edge of the red sandstone plateau, to your left. Engraved circles and crescents are the dominant themes and could be around 3,000 years old. Plan on four hours for the round trip, plus the time you need to look for the engravings (camping is possible). Back on the main road, 3½ km further on, the village of **Igherm n'Ougdal** still has its fortified granary *(igherm)*, which can be visited.

A few kilometers before the pass, a café on the right is judged by tour guides to provide a "suitable" pit-stop, while the one at the top is considered less suitable. All along the way, boys and young men will attempt to sell you amethysts and other stones (including intriguing shiny red and orange crystals that will prove to have been dipped in ink if washed). The descent down the other side, made up of hairpin turns, is pretty steep to begin with, but it is well kept and drivers are unusually cautious. If the pass is blocked by snow, this is indicated by the snow barrier well before. Down on the northern slope, 14 km from the pass, the village of **Taddert** seems to be made up entirely of little restaurants selling kebobs and *tajines*, and is a favorite stop for truck-drivers. The road flattens out about 50 km from

Marrakech, where it crosses the **River Zat.** Before the River Zat, a road on the left to **Arba Tighdouine** leads (eventually) to the **Yagour Plateau** and its rock engravings (chapter 12). Although the distance from Ouarzazate to Marrakech is not very long, count on 3½ hours for the non-stop run.

Southwest of Ouarzazate, after **Tazenakht** (see above), it is possible to continue by car or bus to **Taliouine** and **Agadir** (chapter 11) (Ouarzazate to Agadir is 375 km). It is also possible to link up with the P31 Ouarzazate-Zagora road at **Agdz** (about 110 km). This road starts off from Tazenakht as the 6810 to Foum-Zguid, turning east after 22 km to the mining center of **Bou Azzer** and Agdz. Once at Agdz, turn left for **Ouarzazate** or right for **Zagora.** It is a slow and unfrequented road, mostly used by vehicles from the numerous mines in the region. Part of it is dirt road only, which is not dangerous but stony (watch out for tire punctures).

From Tazenakht, instead of turning off towards Agdz, the motorized traveler can continue down the fairly-recently paved road south to the oasis of **Foum-Zguid.** This road (the 6810) goes through some pretty oases, but is probably only worth taking if a long round trip is envisaged westwards from Foum-Zguid to Tissint and Tata (tarred road, 150 km, see chapter 11) or if traveling in a 4WD vehicle. Foum-Zguid has been out of bounds for most people for some time, due to the unsettled situation around the southern frontier, but now it is perfectly open for visitors.

The **hotel situation** is limited, but the **Hotel Berbère** on the main road looked all right, and at least had clean water closets when I was there. It is possible to camp among the palm trees on the western edge of the village, across the river. With a 4WD vehicle, **Zagora** can be reached by a flat unpaved road, which presents no particular difficulties, except for patches of sand from time to time (about 120 km). There is no public transport. The route, along the 6953, starts about 10 km north of Foum-Zguid, just before the river, and goes through a typical desert landscape of flat, stony *hammada,* with sand dunes to right and left. It is more and more frequented by tourist Land Rovers from Zagora (mostly yellow ones from the Hotel La Fibule du Dra in Zagora), but it is not exactly crowded. Road maps show another, longer dirt road (150 km) (the 6961) from Foum-Zguid to **Tagounite,** south of Zagora, via **Zaouia Sidi Abd-en-Nabi,** but for this you really do need to be well equipped with gas, water, and other essentials, and be prepared to lose sight of the road from time to time under sand. This route takes you past the extensive, dry, **Iriki Salt Lake** and the superb **dunes of Chigaga.** Water is available at the little locality of Zaouia Sidi Abden-Nabi, and again at the spring of **Sidi Abd er-Rahmane** (there are leeches in the water, but it's not a real problem). Camping, of course, is possible anywhere (the Hotel La Fibule has a bivouac/café at the spring). A good paved road goes from Tagounite to Zagora (90 km).

Southeast from Ouarzazate, the **Draa Valley** as far as **Zagora** should not be missed. It is just possible to do the round trip in the day (330 km) and return in the evening to a shower and the comforts of a good hotel in Ouarzazate, but I do not recommend it. The CTM, SATAS, and smaller **bus** companies have frequent services to Zagora, stopping at Agdz. **Big taxis** also make the run. The road (P31) as far as Agdz (73 km) climbs and snakes up the bare sides of the Anti-Atlas Mountains. There are some spectacular views across to the east, towards the jagged peaks of the Jbel Sarhro, and the plain where the River Draa, now joined by the River Dades, can be seen working its way southeast. The *Cascades du Draa* (Draa Waterfalls) (62 km), indicated on the left, are not, to my mind, worth the detour unless you tackle the 10 km of easy but stony dirt road in the spring, when water will perhaps be falling (they say you can swim in the seven little pools).

The stark mountains suddenly give way to a green, open valley as the road drops down into **Agdz.** Agdz is a pleasant little town, with some shops stocking interesting bits of Berber jewelry and others selling rugs. The best hotel is by far the ★★★ **Hotel Kissane** (30 rooms, Tel: 84 30 44, Fax: 84 32 58, on the right as you come in from Ouarzazate). It has a swimming pool and a restaurant. There are a couple of cheap hotels (under 100 DH) in the main square: The **Hotel Restaurant Draa** and the **Hotel des Palmiers.** The **Camping Kasbah de la Palmeraie** (shown on the left) is one of the better Moroccan campsites, and has the attraction of being beside a real kasbah.

The next 92 km lead the traveler through a succession of palm groves, orchards, cultivated vegetable plots, and kasbahs. It is here that the charm of the Draa Valley makes itself felt. The River Draa, one of the longest in Morocco, rises in the High Atlas, is joined by the River Dades just south of Ouarzazate, and winds southeast down to Mhamed (south of Zagora). There it suddenly turns west and gets lost in the sands some way before a final burst of energy allows it to reach the Atlantic Ocean north of Tan-Tan Plage. On its long journey to the sea, it brings life to countless oases.

The large, not very attractive village of **Tinzouline** is about 60 km south of Agdz, and is well known to prehistorians for the **rock engraving sites** found in a dry river valley, some 10 km across a (very) stony plain to the right. Coming from Zagora, a sign indicates their presence: *Gravures Libyco-Berbères* (pictures of small, pecked horsemen and foot soldiers, possibly dating to around the end of the first century B.C.). Unfortunately, storms in recent years have shifted massive quantities of rock down the valley, rendering access by car difficult and considerably damaging the engravings. So now, unless you are very keen, I do not think the detour is worth it. If you do want to try your luck, take a dirt road beside the school and ask any small child to guide you. The Peace Corps has been running women's literacy classes here for a few years.

Hotels
1. Riad Salam
3. Tinsouline
4. des Amis
   Vallée du Draa
5. Camping Sindibad
6. Camping de la
   Montagne
7. de la Palmeraie
9. Reda
10. Kasbah Asmaa
11. La Fibule du Dra
12. Camping d'Amezrou

Useful Addresses
2. Banks
8. Gendarmerie

to Ouarzazate

Bus Station

Bd Mohammed V

Avenue Hassan II

River Draa

Post Office

CTM Bus

Palm Grove

to Mhamid

0   200
m

N

ZAGORA

It seems unkind to say so, but the next stop, **Zagora,** is a place in which you arrive in order to leave for somewhere else. It is the jumping-off point for excursions by Land Rover, camel, or foot. It is the gateway to the desert, and a much-photographed sign at the end of the town proudly proclaims: "52 Days to Timbuktu (by camel caravan)."

Historically-speaking, important Jewish communities lived in this area in the past. In the 11th century, the Draa Valley was occupied by the Almoravids, and their leader Abu Bakr built a fortress in Zagora in 1056. Its remains can still be seen on the flanks of the Jbel Zagora. If you have the time and the energy, it's worth climbing up here for the view and the sunrise, taking the road to Tamgroute after the Hotel La Fibule (count on a hour) (a 4WD can get half the way up). In the 16th century, the Saadians started their conquest of Morocco from the Draa Valley. Market day is Wednesday, with dates the specialty in the fall.

Zagora has boomed in recent years and a number of decent hotels are now available. Unfortunately, the number of would-be guides and hustlers has increased to keep pace with the tourist expansion. A wide range of ploys are used to lure the unwary into buying something quite unwanted ("please write me a letter in English" is a standard one). Arrange guide fee or other prices beforehand.

The most **expensive accommodations** are provided by three hotels. The ****** Hotel Reda** (155 rooms, in the palm grove by the river on the road to Mhamed, Tel: 84 72 49/84 70 79, Fax: 84 70 12) is tastefully designed, and the rooms are simple but functional. It caters a lot to tourist groups and has a restaurant, bar, unusual swimming pool, and tennis courts.

The ****** Hotel Riad Salam** is part of the widespread Salam chain (109 rooms and 7 suites, Tel: 84 74 00, Fax: 84 75 51). Situated at the entrance to the town, on the left, its architecture is attractive and many of the rooms overlook the swimming pool. It has two restaurants and a bar.

The ***** Hotel Tinsouline** (88 rooms, Avenue Hassan II, Tel: 84 73 18) is also a harmonious building, with a restaurant and bar.

Two hotels that offer more modest accommodations are the ***** Hotel La Fibule** (31 rooms, Tel: 84 73 18, Fax: 84 72 71) and the ***** Hotel Kasba Asmaa** (20 rooms, 50 DH for tented accommodations, Tel: 84 75 99, Fax: 84 75 27). I often stay in La Fibule, which is on the road to Mhamed, on the right just after crossing the river. It has a pool, attractive garden, a very large dining room, and rooms ranging from very simple to more sophisticated. Unfortunately, it is very popular and often full, with the perhaps inevitable result that some of the staff have become definitely unhelpful.

The **Hotel Kasbah Asmaa,** also after the river, on the left, is an architecturally pleasant place, traditionally decorated, with a swimming pool, a splendid garden, and a restaurant.

The best of the **budget accommodations** is the * **Hotel de la Palmeraie** (60 rooms, 20 DH on the roof if you have your own sleeping bag or blanket, Tel: 84 70 08, Fax: 84 78 78), at the end of the town on the right. It's clean, functional, and friendly, but not particularly inspiring.

A couple of unclassified hotels, also on the same main road, are the **Hotel Vallée du Draa** and the **Hotel des Amis,** the first better than the second. A double room in either is under 100 DH, half of that with communal showers.

There are three **campsites,** one in the town, off Avenue Hassan II near the Hotel Tinsouline **(Camping Sindibad),** the other two on the road out, past the Hotel La Fibule **(Camping de la Montagne,** up a rough road to the left, and **Camping d'Amezrou,** nearer the Fibule, on the right). They are okay if not too crowded, but the sanitary equipment of the Sindibad and d'Amezrou is usually not up to standard.

The best places to eat are in the restaurants of the **Hotel Kasbah Asmaa** or the **Hotel de la Palmeraie** (three-course meal with wine from 100 DH at both). The **Hotel Riad Salam** does a good meal, but is a good deal more expensive (set meal 165 DH). The **Hotel des Amis** does a standard Moroccan meal for around 30 DH. Otherwise, I don't think there is much to choose from between the many little restaurants lining the Boulevard Mohammed V.

Excursions in 4WD vehicles or with camels are a specialty of the **Hotel La Fibule.** You can ring them in Ouarzazate (Tel: 88 57 00), and they'll even come and meet you in Marrakech or Ouarzazate. Check out the price, which is pretty high and depends on the number of people involved. All the big hotels, plus the Hotel de la Palmeraie, have a wide range of possible organized excursions. Shop around for good offers, especially if it's not the high season. Favorite destinations are the **dunes of Tinfou** (terribly touristy, but beautiful all the same) (24 km), the **superb, more distant dunes of Chigaga,** and the **Iriki Sale Lake.**

A 120 km unpaved road west from Zagora (the 6953) leads to **Foum-Zguid,** where the tarred road begins (see earlier).

The principal road continues down to **Mhamid** (96 km). The first place of interest after Zagora is the village of **Amazraou** (3 km), containing an old kasbah called the "Jews' kasbah." The *mellah,* where Jewish silversmiths used to produce local jewelry, is now occupied by Moslems. It's a touristy sort of place, too, with lots of kids wanting to show you the way, but a walk around is nevertheless very agreeable.

Tamgroute (22 km from Zagora) is a long-established religious center, well known for its library (marked *Librairie Coranique*) and *zaouia* of the Naciryin fraternity. The village has several mosques and houses the mausoleum of the 17th-century scholar, Sidi Mohammed ben Nacer, who founded the Koranic school of Tamgroute, which still trains religious teachers. I was told that about 200 students come to study here from all over Morocco. The *zaouia* is regularly visited by people suffering from mental disorders, who hope that the saint's blessing will cure them. Although many of the most precious books, some of them on gazelle skin, have been removed from the library, the visitor can still admire illuminated Korans, as well as historical, medical, and astrological works and dictionaries, some of which date from the 13th century. It is difficult to appreciate these outstanding books because of poor lighting and display, so the ordinary visitor may not find them very impressive. More down to earth, Tamgroute is also a pottery center, where craftsmen turn out characteristic green (manganese and copper) and brown (antimony and copper) glazed tiles, dishes, and candlesticks. Multitudes of small children will offer to show you around the village—an offer worth accepting! **Jnan Dar** (Tel: 84 86 22), opposite the *zaouia*, run by Abdessadek Naciri and his Swiss wife, Doris, has been recommended by many friends. This restaurant and inn, built in kasbah-style, is just opposite the Koranic library. At the moment there are seven simple but clean double rooms, with outside hot showers and water closet. Visitors can also sleep or take a siesta under two large nomad tents in the middle of a garden. Sadek's specialities are very good grilled meat and *mechoui* (grilled lamb), but visitors can also just drink mint tea or have a soft drink (set meal 70 DH). Sadek will also organize camel excursions in the desert.

A further 7 kilometers brings the visitor to **Tinfou** and its dunes (no need for a guide, you're not going to get lost in the Sahara here). A couple of hotels house guests a few hundred meters from the dunes: the **Hotel Repos du Sable** (120 DH, Tel/Fax: 84 85 66), beside the road, and the new ✸✸✸ **Porte du Sahara** (360 DH, BP 28 Zagora, Km 25, Tel: 84 85 62, Fax: 84 70 02) 1 km from the road, at the foot of the dunes. The second is run by a German woman and has been highly recommended to me for its comfort, excellent cooking, and delightful atmosphere. The first is said to be an easy-going sort of place with good food; 4WD and camel excursions can be arranged. It is perfectly feasible to take a 4WD vehicle off into the sand and camp behind a more distant dune or hill.

The next village of any size is **Tagounite** (70 km from Zagora), from where a rough road (4WD only) goes to Foum-Zguid (150 km, see earlier). After the Beni Selmane pass, cutting across the Jbel Bani, the road goes through the small village of Ouled Driss and finally reaches **Mhamid**, which is the end of the line for tourist vehicles. On the left after the pass lies the huge pre-Islamic necropolis of **Foum er-Rjam**, containing many thousands of tumuli (a conical heap of stones under which someone was buried), a few of which have been excavated, one producing a date of around 500 B.C. (not visible from the road). The River Draa divides the village of Mhamid in two, and the Algerian frontier is only 40 km away. A CTM bus leaves for Mhamid every day from Zagora, returning the next morning. The Monday market is a lively affair. Don't count on anything much in the way of hotels here. Both the **Hotel-Restaurant Iriqui** and the **Hotel Sahara** are very basic, but you can always sleep on the roof. **Camping** in the dunes is possible, and there are several **campsites** along the way. Water is a problem, whatever your form of lodging. Both "hotels" provide reasonable Moroccan meals and can arrange camel excursions into the desert.

The **same P31 southeast from Ouarzazate** is joined some 30 km south of Agdz by a now-paved road (starting off as the 6956) leading to **Rissani** and **Erfoud** (240 km). There are not many advantages of this itinerary over the Dades Valley one outlined below, but it is useful for those wanting to do the circuit Ouarzazate-Rissani-Ouarzazate, or for trekkers wanting to tackle the Jbel Sarhro.

The road goes alongside the oases of **Nekob** and **Tazzarine** (about 100 km from Agdz). A trek through the stark but magnificent **Jbel Sarhro,** the eastern end of the Anti-Atlas, which separates the oases of the Dades Valley from those of Nekob and Tazzarine, could start at Nekob (or from the Dades Valley). The Jbel Sarhro was the scene of fierce fighting in 1933 between the nomadic Ait Berber Atta tribe and the advancing French forces. The tribe had already unsuccessfully resisted the arrival of the French in the Tafilalet region to the east, and the Jbel Bou Gafer, in the Sarhro massif, was their last refuge. The trail goes through superb rough volcanic country, with high passes (2,200 m) and deep cultivated valleys. Count on at least five days to come out in the Dades Valley. Really independent backpackers, carrying all their stuff, should be well equipped with a map, tents, sleeping bags, food, and water. It is doubtful if mules and guides can always be hired in Nekob, but the National Association of Mountain Guides and Escorts has an office at Nekob which is supposed to be open on Mondays (*Bureau des Guides et Accompagnateurs en Montagne de Nekob,* Nekob, Tel: 5 at Nekob) and another in Agdz (Tel: 84 30 80), open on Fridays. Those wanting to be sure of logistic assistance are better off arranging things in Ouarzazate, where the provincial tourist delegation (*Délégation Provincial du Tourisme*) can provide a list of qualified guides. The crossing can also be made by 4WD vehicles (preferably from north to south). Practical information on all aspects of trekking in the Atlas, with the names of guides, addresses of mountain huts, mule hire charges, and so on, is contained in the free booklet *The*

Great Trek through the Moroccan Atlas, published by the National Tourist Office in Rabat and, theoretically, widely available.

If you want to see the numerous rock engravings around Tazzarine (10 sites dating from a time when the climate was less harsh than today), your best bet is to go to the **Hotel-Restaurant Bougafer** in Tazzarine, where they are ready to show you around the oasis and the rock-art sites. The hotel (45 very basic rooms) provides the best overnight stop in the area and quite a good meal (50 DH). Buses go through Tazzarine from both Zagora and Erfoud. A very rough and rocky road from **Tazzarine** down to **Zagora,** via the Tizi n'Tafilalet pass, is only possible for 4WD vehicles or hardy back-packers. On past Tazzarine, the 6956 road becomes the 3458 and goes through the pleasant little oasis of **Alnif,** where there are two gas stations and two very simple hotels, **La Gazelle** and the **Restaurant-Hotel Bougafer.** After Alnif, keep east along the 3454 road to join the main north-south P21 road at **Rissani,** 22 km south of the more important center of **Erfoud** (see later).

Back in Ouarzazate, **going northeast,** the P32, following the valley of the River Dades between the High Atlas Mountains and the Jbel Sarhro, has been called the **Kasbah Route** *(La Route des Kasbahs).* Kasbahs, splendid adobe buildings embellished with characteristic decorative patterns, one of southern Morocco's particular attractions, are particularly numerous along this valley. A CTM bus travels daily along this road from Ouarzazate to Er-Rachidia, stopping along the way (but it may be difficult to get a place to continue the journey). The first part of the route, as far as the oasis and kasbahs of **Skoura,** was described above (in "Around Ouarzazate"). Some 45 km after Skoura (83 km from Ouarzazate), a new and charming little hotel, **L'Auberge Pont d'Almou** (10 rooms, Tel: 83 69 13) makes a delightful stop, either to have a mint tea, eat a meal in the flower-filled garden under a caidal tent, or spend the night in complete calm. After Skoura (50 km) the oasis of **Kelaa des Mgouna** is well-known for its production of rose water. The factory can usually be visited, and in the spring the hedgerows are a mass of pink flowers. At the moment, there is a glut of rose water, and production has slowed down. The **Rose Festival** *(Fête des Roses)* is a colorful event held in May, in which rose petals and rose water are liberally scattered in the streets and there is lots of dancing. Many in the important complex of kasbahs are in ruins, but enough remains for their original decoration to be appreciated. There is a *** hotel, the **Hotel Les Roses du Dades** (102 rooms, 275 DH, Tel/Fax: 88 38 07), near the kasbah, with a pool and a restaurant, and the unclassified **Hotel du Grand Atlas** (on the main street, Avenue Mohammed V). Kelaa des Mgouna is the center for treks north up into the **Mgouna massif** (summit

4,068 m) and south into the **Jbel Sarhro**. Information about guides and mules can be had from the office of the mountain guides and escorts *(Bureau des Guides et Accompagnateurs en Montagne du Mgouna)*, Hotel du Grand Atlas (Tel: 84 30 80).

After a few more kasbahs, another 24 km brings you to **Boumalne du Dades**, where there is a bank, a good choice of hotels, and some shops. The town is an administrative center, situated at the opening of the spectacular **Dades Gorge**. Boumalne, with various lodging possibilities, makes a good center for a number of excursions if you are not in a hurry.

The **most expensive accommodation** is at the **** **Hotel el-Madayek** (360 DH, Tel: 83 00 31, Fax: 88 22 23), up the hill to the left going out of town. It has a restaurant and a bar, but caters a lot to groups, is noisy, and not particularly welcoming, and is, in my opinion, over-rated.

The new *** **Hotel Kasbah Tizrouine** (half-board 250 DH per person, possibility for tented lodging, Tel: 83 06 90, Fax: 83 02 56) is a much better proposition. It is 2 km out of town, towards Er-Rachidia, is built in traditional style architecture, has beautiful views, and is a very good value. It can also organize treks and excursions.

A comfortable, friendly, **budget-priced** hotel is the * **Hotel Restaurant Chems** (15 rooms, 110 DH, Avenue Mohammed V, Tel: 83 00 89) on the right at the eastern end of the town. Try and get a room with a balcony and a good view. Another one in the same price range is the * **Hotel Vallée des Oiseaux** (12 rooms, about 500 m after the Hotel Chems, Tel: 83 01 72).

Budget accommodations can be had from the only fractionally cheaper **Hotel al-Manadire** (100 DH with shower, 50 DH without, Avenue Mohammed V), practically next door to the Hotel Chems. The **Hotel Camping Le Soleil Bleu** (8 rooms, 100 DH, 20 DH for sleeping on the roof, Tel: 83 01 63) is up a turning to the left just before the Hotels Salam and Madayek. The owners organize excursions that are particularly appreciated by birdwatchers. Also in this category, you have the **Hotel Adrar** (27 rooms, 60 DH, Tel: 83 03 55) at the entrance to the town, on the left coming in from Ouarzazate, and the very out-of-the-way **Hotel Salam** (15 rooms, 60 DH, communal hot showers, Tel: 83 07 62), up the hill on the left at the very other end of the town, near the Hotel Madayek. Both have restaurants and the Hotel Adrar can arrange treks.

For **dining and restaurants** in Boumalne it is probably best to head for one of the hotels, according to your budget. The **Hotel Kasbah Tizrouine** restaurant has an excellent reputation and is probably the best value (full meal 80 DH). The **Hotel Madayek** restaurant is expensive, but licensed (set meal 138 DH). Lower down the scale, the **Hotel-Restaurant Chems** and the **Hotel Adrar** both do good meals (about 80 DH). Cheaper food (salads, kebobs, or *tajines*) can be had in a number of little restaurants along Avenue Mohammed V.

Around Boumalne, the most obvious trip is up the **Dades Gorge.** However, you really do need some sort of transport. Trucks come up this way on market days (Wednesdays for Boumalne, Saturdays for Msemrir), and it is generally possible to negotiate a place in a big taxi. The road is good but twisting, with sheer drops, canyons, and splendid views, dotted with villages and kasbahs. The tarred road ends after about 27 km, but ordinary cars can probably get as far as **Msemrir** (40 km). After this, a 4WD is definitely required to continue. From Msemrir a loop can be made to link up east with the **Todra Gorge** and **Tinerhir** via Ait Hani (42 km), or the High Atlas range can be crossed (snow permitting—check weather conditions first with the Gendarmerie) with an exit on the north side via **Imilchil** (see chapter 7). This is an extremely difficult drive, and should only be undertaken by very experienced, well-equipped drivers with at least two vehicles. These are bleak, deserted landscapes, with rugged climbs and difficult river passages. There are a surprising number of simple little **hotels** in the gorge, nearly all with **restaurants.** A simple double room, some with splendid views, often costs under 100 DH. More expensive hotels are in the **Auberge des Gorges du Dadès** (Tel: 83 17 10) in the village of **Ait Oudinar** (140 DH with shower, Tel: 83 17 10), which is recommended by friends, and the **Hotel La Kasbah de la Vallée** (120 DH with shower, Tel: 83 17 17), 2 km further on. For those wanting to spend a few days in the area, there are plenty of interesting day treks from different points in the gorge (a map or a guide is essential). The village of Ait Oudinar makes a good departure point.

Boumalne is also a good point from which to tackle the crossing of the **Jbel Sarhro,** either by car (small Renault 4 or 4WD), mountain bike, or on foot. The rough road comes out at Nekob (see above), after about 70 km of pretty rough riding. What has been called the **Bird Valley** (*La Vallée des Oiseaux*), because of its interest to birdwatchers (between December and March), is reached by turning right just after Boumalne, indicated for Ikniouin, and bearing right for Tagdilt after 8 km (a rough track). Shown as "picturesque" on the map, it takes you a little way into the Jbel Sarhro without too much difficulty. The **Todra Gorge** (see later under Tinerhir) can also be visited from Boumalne, where there is a bigger choice of accommodations.

A not very exciting 53 km gets the traveler to the huge oasis of **Tinerhir,** where there are hotels, gas stations, banks, and a few restaurants. CTM buses come here from Ouarzazate and Er-Rachidia, though it is often difficult to get one of the few available places when one wants to leave. Watch out for false guides here, who'll tell you certain hotels are closed in order to lure the unwary traveler into fifth-rate establishments. The **hotel scene** is not bad. The *** **Hotel Sargho,** perched up on the hill with splendid views (62 rooms, Tel: 83 41 81, Fax: 83 43 52) was in the process of changing hands when I stayed there and was in a rather run-down state. It has a restaurant, a bar, and a decent-size pool. At the moment, the new *** **Hotel Kenzi Bougafer** (70 rooms, Tel: 83 32 80, Fax: 83 32 82), a kasbah-style building at the entrance to the town as you come in from Ouarzazate, is a better proposition if you don't mind doing without the view. It has two restaurants, a bar, and a pool. A **medium-price hotel** is the new *** **Hotel Tomboctou** (14 rooms, Boulevard Bir Anzarane, just off Boulevard Mohammed V—indicated—Tel: 83 46 04, Fax: 83 35 05), with pleasant rooms and a knowledgeable manager who rents out mountain bikes and can advise on excursions in the area (there's a good circuit in the oasis).

Dropping down in category, the ** **Hotel Todra** (37 Avenue Hassan II, Tel: 83 42 49), with a bar a and restaurant, is also a possibility.

The best of the **budget accommodations** is undoubtedly the **Hotel de l'Avenir** (12 rooms, 100 DH, Rue Zaid Ouhamed, behind the central square, above a butcher's shop, Tel/Fax: 83 45 99).

The **campsite Camping Ourti** (8 DH/person, 7 DH/car, 6 DH/tent) is on the right as you come in from Ouarzazate, and the **Camping Almou,** indicated at the entrance to the town, is further out. As usual, the sanitary installations in both places leave much to be desired.

The best **hotel restaurants** are those in the **Hotel Saghro** and the **Hotel Kenzi Bougafer,** both serving international and Moroccan menus (set meal 110 DH), and the **Hotel-Restaurant Tomboctou,** which offers Spanish as well as Moroccan dishes (the manager is a Spanish Catalan).

Another hotel producing good Spanish and Moroccan food is the more modest **Hotel de l'Avenir,** where the owner is a Spanish women married to a Moroccan (serves a *paella*). Outside of the hotel restaurants, the best is the **Restaurant La Kasbah** (Avenue Mohammed V, Tel: 83 44 71), with an excellent set meal and a wide choice of dishes. The cheapest places for salads and kebobs are along the Avenues Mohammed V and Hassan II.

The best way to **visit Tinerhir** is to get someone recommended by your hotel to accompany you so that you can enjoy its main attractions, which are a stroll through the oasis (40 km of palm trees towering above small, bright green cultivated plots), a walk through the medina with its spice merchants, carpenters, and weavers, and a visit to the old village of Ait el-Haj Ali, usually called the "Jewish district." The Glaoui, Pasha of Marrakech, had one of his many kasbahs up on the hill in Tinerhir, beside the Hotel Saghro, but it is very ruined and not visitable.

The spectacular **Todra Gorge** starts 15 km north of Tinerhir. Parts of the film *Lawrence of Arabia* were filmed here. There's no public transport, but **big taxis** are available at Tinerhir. The road passes first through a series of palm groves and villages before crossing a river and becoming hemmed in by tall cliffs. It's not the Grand Canyon, but it is quite impressive all the same. A small stream runs along the foot of the cliff, at one point fed by a **spring** held to be sacred by local women *(Source des Poissons Sacrés)*. It is forbidden to catch the fish in the stream, since they are considered to be the work of the saint responsible for the spring. The gorge progressively narrows to about 20 m and a whole cluster of restaurants and small hotels have sprung up in recent years at the point where the tarred road stops. The cliffs at this point reach some 300 m, casting an almost perpetual shadow over the gorge, unless you arrive in the early morning. Trekkers or 4WD vehicles can continue up the gorge (bad road surface), past the restaurants, and link up with the Dades Gorge by a west-bound track at **Ait Hani,** or go north to **Imilchil** (see Boumalne section for the difficulties). There are a couple of very basic places to sleep in some 17 km up from the end of the tarred road. The gorge is crowded with local people on the weekend and at midday with tourists and their buses. However, calm returns in the evening, when the beauty of the spot can be appreciated.

There are a number of small **hotels** on the way up to the gorge and at the end of the road. Nothing **** here, but basic, clean rooms or tented accommodations are available for under 100 DH. For instance, the **Hotel Restaurant Les Roches** (25 rooms, Tel: 83 48 14) charges 20 DH for a night under a tent, 60 DH for a double room without shower, and 150 DH for one with a shower (including breakfast).

There are also three **campsites,** all with a few simple rooms and rather deficient sanitary installations. The **Hotel-Restaurant Yasmina** (Tel: 83 42 07) is a good place for a meal (rooms, too), as is the **Hotel-Restaurant Les Roches.** Both are crowded with tourists at lunchtime. There is a téléboutique, so travelers can phone friends to warn them that they have decided to stay the night.

The road continues another 47 km to **Tinejdad,** where the secondary 3451 goes off right directly to **Erfoud** (115 km) while the main P32 goes up to **Er-Rachidia** (90 km). Tinejdad is a large oasis with a café or two, and one unclassified hotel, the **Hotel Gheris,** opposite the market. But it is well worth stopping a couple of kilometers short of the town and visiting the **museum-shop-art gallery Chez Zaid** (Tel: 05-78 67 98). I found it badly indicated when I was there with American friends, but I'm told that it is now clearly marked. The front garden contains a Berber tent and agricultural implements and articles of everyday use (not for sale), while inside there is a good collection of jewelry, pottery, and wooden bowls for sale—or just "for visual pleasure," as the Moroccans say. The prices are fixed and not particularly low, but the articles are genuinely old and of good quality.

If you are in a hurry to reach **Erfoud** and the **sand dunes** of south Morocco, take the 3451 from Tinejdad. A bus leaves Tinejdad for Erfoud and Rissani once a day. The road is narrow, but goes through a series of *ksour* (fortified villages) and oases. Parts may sometimes be covered with blown sand. This route lets the traveler see an ingenious underground irrigation system characteristic of the region, the *rhettara* or *foggara*. Attention is drawn to these underground channels by conical heaps of earth thrown up at regular intervals. The earth comes from the excavation of vertical shafts that link up with slightly-sloping galleries, along which water which has been captured from springs or groundwater higher up flows, sometimes over many tens of kilometers. The advantage of this system is the absence of evaporation, otherwise very high in this hot, Saharan region. Families, too, have been known to shelter their children in these galleries in periods of extreme heat. With the extension of piped water, most of this extensive network has fallen into disuse.

The town of **Erfoud** is described later.

The P32 from **Tinejdad** to **Er-Rachidia** passes through **Goulmima** and its oasis, containing numerous *ksour*. The old *ksar,* at the end of a 2-km track on the right, is still inhabited and worth a visit. Many of the adobe walls are crumbling, but the main entrance, the narrow lanes, and the wooden doors of many of the houses hint at its ancient splendor. There's a small simple hotel-restaurant, the **Hotel Ghéris,** opposite the market, and a very small place in the palm grove where one can eat and spend the night—**Les Palmiers** (Tel/Fax: 78 40 04).

Er-Rachidia lies at the crossroads of north-south and east-west communication lines, on the right bank of the River Ziz, which has its source in the High Atlas. The town (known then as Ksar es-Souk) was created by the French as an administrative and military post for the Foreign Legion, and is still home to a very important Moroccan army contingent, as well as being a provincial capital. It is, frankly, an unattractive town, long and straggly, but it has a number of large-town amenities and has recently been endowed with a **** hotel (it's always had a host of small places), which makes it a reasonable proposition for a stopover. Previously a regular victim of severe flooding, Er-Rachidia now has an important dam, which has enabled large areas to be irrigated (the dam has also produced a micro-climate, said by friends who live there to be unfavorable for their date palm trees upstream of the dam). The Mulay Ismail University has some departments here.

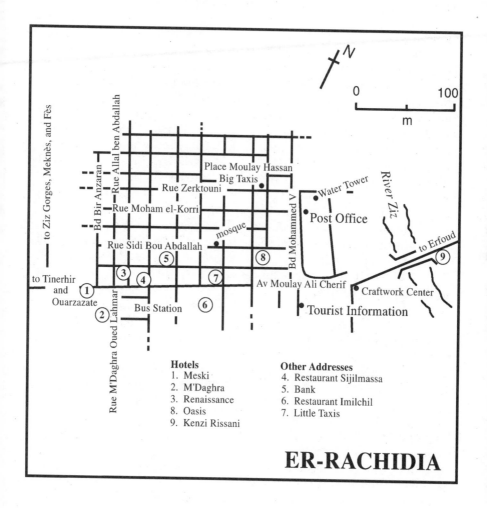

Hotels
1. Meski
2. M'Daghra
3. Renaissance
8. Oasis
9. Kenzi Rissani

Other Addresses
4. Restaurant Sijilmassa
5. Bank
6. Restaurant Imilchil
7. Little Taxis

ER-RACHIDIA

Er-Rachidia can be reached by CTM **bus** daily from Casablanca/ Marrakech/Ouarzazate and all intermediate towns. The CTM also runs a service from Meknès and Azrou in the north and from Rissani/Erfoud in the south. Other companies make do the five-hour trip from Bouarfa, near the Algerian frontier to the east (see chapter 9). **Big taxis** run from Erfoud and Meknès/Fès. **Little blue taxis** run about in the town.

Hotel charges fixed for the Er-Rachidia and Erfoud region are as follows (they vary according to the presence or absence of showers and water closet in the room): **** 333-415 DH or 426-847 DH, breakfast 44-72 DH for both; *** 166-264 DH or 187-300 DH, breakfast 33 DH for both; ** 91-158 DH or 98-197 DH, breakfast 22 DH for both; * 83-122 DH or 86-140 DH, breakfast 21 DH for both.

The **regional telephone code** is 05 (0 omitted for in-region calls).

Way at the **top** of the **hotel scene** is the **** **Hotel Kenzi Rissani** (60 air-conditioned rooms, BP 3, Route d'Erfoud Tel: 57 21 86/57 25 84, Fax: 57 25 85). It's just outside the town, on the right hand side of the road to Erfoud, after the river. Recently in the hands of the Kenzi chain of hotels, it is now an excellent place in which to stay, the reception is friendly, and it has two restaurants, a bar, a boutique, and a central patio swimming pool surrounded by trees and plants.

Some hotel stars have been lost recently and ** hotels demoted to *. This may change shortly. At the moment, there are three **medium-price hotels:** the * **Hotel M'Daghra,** (29 rooms, 92 Rue M'Daghra Oued Lahmer, Tel: 57 40 47/48/49, Fax: 79 08 64), down a street on the right just at the beginning of the town, with pleasant rooms with telephone, and a restaurant and little Moroccan-style room for mint tea; the * **Hotel Oasis** (46 rooms, 4 Rue Sidi Bou Abdallah, parallel to the main road, on the left, near the mosque, Tel: 57 25 19, Fax: 57 01 26), with a bar and a restaurant; and the * **Hotel Meski** (25 rooms, Avenue Moulay Ali Cherif just before entrance to town coming from the north, Tel: 57 20 65, Fax: 57 12 37), which has big rooms (ask for one on the garden side) but no air-conditioning, an imposing entrance, a restaurant, a noisy bar, and a swimming pool (not always functional).

The best **budget accommodations** are provided by the unclassfied **Hotel Restaurant Renaissance** (20 rooms, 70 DH, 19 Rue Moulay Youssef, perpendicular to the main road, at the beginning of town, Tel: 57 26 33), with collective showers and the possibility of sleeping on the roof.

A **campsite** is indicated on the left as you go out along the Erfoud road, after the bridge. Otherwise, the nearest campsite is the **Camping Source Bleue de Meski,** 23 km along the Erfoud road (see later).

Dining and Restaurants. The **top** is the restaurant in the **Hotel Kenzi Rissani** (tourist menu 160 DH, gastronomic menu 200 DH). The **Hotel Oasis** is said to do a good meal (licensed) (80 DH). The **Hotels M'Daghra** and **Meski** both do a set meal for 75 DH and 76 DH respectively.

The **Restaurant Imilchil** (main road, on the right, Tel: 57 21 23), with a licence, has a pleasant dining room and a little garden, and serves a set meal for 80 DH. A cheap place serving the usual Moroccan salads and *tajines* is the **Restaurant Sijilmassa** (on the main road, on the left before the above), where a simple meal will set you back about 40 DH.

French-speaking Catholic **mass** is held in the Fraternité Saint Jean Baptiste (Tel: 57 34 77 or call the nuns at Tel: 57 33 51 for information).

There is no **sightseeing** to be done in Er-Rachidia, but the first part of the road north to Midelt (P21) goes through some spectacular scenery. After 12 km, the **Hassan Addakhil dam** can be seen on the right, the road following the River Ziz as it winds its way through the **Ziz Gorges** and passes through a tunnel, built by the French Legion (officially the Foum Zabel Tunnel and unofficially the **Tunnel du Légionnaire**), which is guarded by the military. The road continues northwards, leaving **Hammate Moulay Ali Cherif** on the left. There are hot springs (50° C) here, rich in sulfates and magnesium, and when I first came down this road you could see people burying themselves in the sand/mud to enjoy its therapeutic qualities (good for arthritis and rhumatism). Now the whole thing has been commercially organized (the word *hammam* means hot bath), and a café/hotel has been installed. In August 1998, an unusual mortality among the fish population in the River Ziz was noted between this spot and Kerrando, a bit further north, due to the exceptionally high air temperatures and the low water level. However, to reassure ecologists, the Ministry responsible for rivers and forests said that this would have little effect on the survival of the fish in question, characterized by great powers of reproduction.

Travelers can continue up the P21 to **Midelt,** via the Tizi n'Talrhemt pass, where the desert is left behind as the landscape changes, and **Meknès** (chapter 7). From the town of **Rich** several tracks lead up to the High Atlas, including a fairly easy route to Imilchil (chapter 7). Even in these remote areas, many satellite dishes can be seen stuck up on the roofs of small, concrete-block houses. I am told by a Moroccan friend in the business that the sale of solar panels has greatly increased, to power this satellite television in the absence of wired electricity.

For **handicraft shopping** in Er-Rachidia, have a look in at the craftwork complex *(Complexe Artisanal)* on the right hand side as you leave Er-Rachidia for Erfoud (closed Saturday afternoons and Sundays). The **banks** are rather scattered, but there is a branch of the BMCI on Boulevard Mohammed V (up to the left near the Erfoud exit) and a BMCE branch further on, in the Place Moulay Hassan (the water tower acts as a guiding point). The **post office** is around here, too, on the same road as the **police station.**

The south-bound P21 out of Er-Rachidia to **Erfoud** (98 km) and the **Tafilalt** now passes through a *desert landscape*—not golden, romantic sand dunes but flat, windswept expanses of hard soil scattered with stones and supporting a rare weather-beaten bush or shrub. The occasional women on the road are often draped in white or in what looks like a pale, printed sheet, imported from the Canary Islands via the Western Sahara. The turn to the **Meski Spring** *(Source Bleue de Meski)* is marked to the right (23 km). This little oasis is very popular with tourists and locals alike, and one can swim in the cemented pool. It's crowded and dirty in the spring and summer.

The **campsite** is here, too (7 DH/person, 10 DH/tent, 10 DH/car). I personally find this camping ground horrible—it's filthy and noisy. But it's maybe all right if you like local music all night, and I know others that highly recommend it.

Just before Meski, the P32 goes off to the left to **Boudnib, Bouarfa,** and, eventually, **Figuig** (247 km, chapter 9).

There are some fleeting views of the River Ziz in the distance, with its string of bright green oases, some *ksours* (including the **Maadid Ksar,** in very good condition), and flimsy sand barriers—and then you are in **Erfoud** and in that part of Morocco known as the **Tafilalet,** home of the present Alaouite dynasty. Two rivers, the **Ziz** and the **Rheris,** run side by side for 25 kilometers, providing water for immense palm groves, the region's main source of income. More than 1.2 million date palm trees have been recorded, producing between 20,000 and 35,000 tons of dates a year.

Erfoud, although in the heart of a long series of oases, only became an organized town during the Protectorate. Resistance to the French in the Tafilalet by the Ait Berber Atta tribe had started in 1916 and lingered on sporadically until the 1930s. The establishment by the French of an important military and administrative center in Erfoud was necessary to control Morocco's Saharan fringes and the dissident tribes. Historically speaking, the nearby town of **Rissani** and the now ruined city of **Sijilmassa** were much more important. The greatly-reduced River Ziz runs south of the town, continuing its way down to get lost in the sands far in the desert.

Erfoud is only reached by **road.** The CTM **bus** company runs three services a day from Fès and two from Meknès. There are six bus arrivals daily from Er-Rachidia, one from Tazzarine, and a frequent service from Rissani. **Big taxis** run regularly from Er-Rachidia and Rissani.

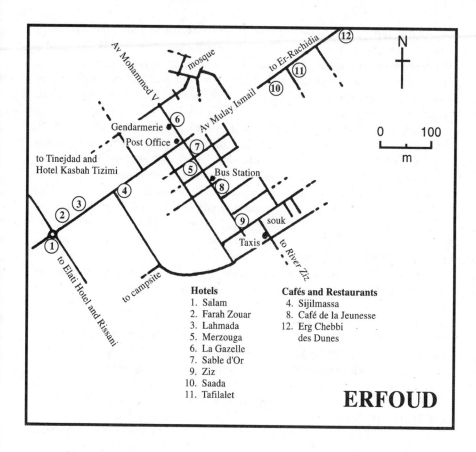

Hotels
1. Salam
2. Farah Zouar
3. Lahmada
5. Merzouga
6. La Gazelle
7. Sable d'Or
9. Ziz
10. Saada
11. Tafilalet

Cafés and Restaurants
4. Sijilmassa
8. Café de la Jeunesse
12. Erg Chebbi
    des Dunes

ERFOUD

At the **top of the hotel scene** is the **** **Hotel Salam** (100 rooms, 15 suites with TV, 40 luxury rooms, Route de Rissani, Tel: 57 66 65), at the Rissani end of the town, on the left. The hotel is agreeable—cool and calm inside after the heat outside, kasbah-style architecture and decoration, and rooms looking onto the central patio swimming pool. It has a restaurant, a bar, and a boutique.

Another **** hotel is the **Elati Hotel** (Route de Rissani, BP 14, Tel: 57 73 72, Fax: 57 70 86), 2½ km out on the Rissani road. It is an enormous place, always full of people, with large comfortable rooms, a restaurant, and a bar. The rooms looking west over the desert have the best views.

The **** **Hotel Tafilalet** (70 rooms, Avenue Mulay Ismail, Tel: 57 65 35/ 57 68 81, Fax: 57 60 36) on the main road, on the left coming in from Er-Rachidia, is a very lively place, much frequented by tourists, highly decorated with *zellij*, stucco, *mushrabiya* (carved, open-work wooden screens), painted ceilings, and an interior fountain. All this is very impressive—more urban Fès than Berber Sahara. The hotel has two restaurants, an Andalusian bar, snack bar, and a pool. The bedrooms overlooking the garden are particularly attractive.

The new *** **Hotel Kasbah Tizimi,** under dynamic management, is highly praised. It is another pleasant kasbah-style building (about 500 m out along the Tinejdad/Tinerhir road, Tel: 57 61 79, Fax: 57 73 75), with comfortable rooms looking onto a central patio, an attractive restaurant, and a pool.

There are several **medium-price hotels.** One is the ** **Hotel Restaurant Ziz** (40 rooms, 260 DH half-board, 3 Avenue Mohammed V, Tel: 57 61 54/ 57 68 11) in the center of town, near the market. It has a restaurant and a friendly, helpful staff.

The well-indicated ** **Hotel-Restaurant Farah Zouar** (21 rooms, with 17 more being added, 6 air-conditioned, with telephone and TV, corner Avenue Mulay Ismail/Tinerhir road, opposite the Hotel Salam, Tel: 57 62 30, Fax: 57 62 30) has a high, light interior courtyard onto which look the clean, comfortable bedrooms (not much of a view). It is under the same ownership as the Hotel Tafilalet.

Still in this category, the ** **Hotel-Restaurant Lahmada** (23 rooms, Avenue Mulay Ismail, at the Rissani end, on the right, Tel: 57 69 80, Fax: 57 60 97) has rather small, badly-lit rooms and tired carpets, but the staff is pleasant and helpful (it's a pity that the view is over a dry water channel full of rubbish).

Finally, the * **Sable d'Or** (10 rooms, Avenue Mohammed V, Tel: 57 63 48), above a noisy bar-café, has clean, simple rooms with hot showers and water closet.

The best of the **budget accommodations** could well be the rather unattractively situated **Hotel Saada,** above a gas station beside the BMCE bank, on the left coming from Er-Rachidia (10 rooms, 70 DH without shower, 80 DH with shower, 48 Avenue Mulay Ismail, Tel: 57 66 89). It is possible to sleep on the roof for 20 DH (shower included), where a nomad tent has been rigged up and the view is "panoramic." It is not to be confused with the Café-Restaurant Essada opposite, which has a bad reputation.

The **Hotel Merzouga** (14 rooms, 80 DH with shower, 114 Avenue Mohammed V, Tel: 57 65 32) has clean, basic rooms, but is noisy, particularly in summer.

Finally, the **Hotel-Restaurant La Gazelle** (six rooms with shower and water closet, 100 DH, three with wash-basin only, 80 DH, Avenue Mohammed V, opposite the Gendarmerie, Tel: 57 60 28) has pretty basic rooms, a basement restaurant, and is very noisy in summer.

Practically all the hotels have **restaurants.** At the top end, the restaurants in the **Hotel Kasbah Tizimi** and the **Hotel Salam** (buffet 182 DH) are good, and the meals are served in attractive surroundings. The **Hotel Tafilalet** has a large, ground-floor restaurant, sumptuously decorated, offering a good international menu (143 DH), and a first-floor Moroccan restaurant. The **Elati Hotel** is also said to serve a good meal (154 DH).

Down the line, I think there is nothing much to choose for quality between the **Hotel-Restaurant Ziz** (set meal 85 DH), the **Hotel-Restaurant Farah Zouar** (rather uninspiring dining room, good set meal 80 DH), the **Sable d'Or** (set meal 69 DH), the **Hotel-Restaurant La Gazelle** (basement dining room, large set meal 60 DH), and the **Hotel-Restaurant Lahmada** (set meal 60 DH). A really cheap place is the **Hotel Saada,** advertising a meal for 35 DH.

The **Café-Restaurant des Dunes** (Avenue Mulay Ismail, entrance to Erfoud, near the gas station Ziz, on the left, Tel: 57 67 93) has been recommended to me by French Alpine Club friends for its copious and succulent meals at very reasonable prices. Practically next door, stuck between the Ziz filling station and the Hotel Tafilalet, the **Restaurant Erg Chebbi** (on the first floor) proposes good international and Moroccan dishes at a variety of prices. The **Café-Restaurant Sijilmassa** (Avenue Mulay Ismail), with tables shaded by tamarisk trees, does a cheap, simple menu concentrating on salads and kebobs, and is usually full of local people (good for a coffee or fruit juice). The **Café de la Jeunesse** (Avenue Mohammed V) is really very rudimentary and correspondingly cheap.

Erfoud itself is worth a short walk around, and the Hotel Salam exhibits and sells attractive little **paintings** of local landscapes by a Swiss artist semiresident in Erfoud. If you wander down toward the river, you will come across a series of shacks where dozens of men are hammering away non-stop to extract from their matrix the fossils for which the region is famous, surrounded by heaps of broken stone. The fossils are not for sale yet, but you will see them all over Morocco, glistening white bullet-shaped ortho-ceres and snail-like goniatites on a highly polished black background, often made into tabletops. These creatures date from around 200 or 300 million years ago.

Towards the end of October, Erfoud celebrates its Date Festival.

Excursions to various places around Erfoud, by camel or 4WD vehicles, are organized by the Hotel Tafilalet, whose enterprising director is re-sponsible for the annual motorized *Raid de l'Amitié* (Friendship Rally), which takes place in the region in the springtime. Excursions can also be arranged by the Hotel Salam.

But the **sightseeing** attraction is undoubtedly the **Merzouga Dunes,** more correctly known as Erg Chebbi (50 km). The village of Merzouga is about 50 km south of Erfoud, and the dunes a further kilometer (also pos-sible from **Rissani,** the departure point for **collective taxis,** see later). The great thing is to be there for sunrise over an unending sea of undulating sand, or for sunset when the colors change from warm yellow to rich pink (or the other way around, if you spend the night on the spot). The dunes are the highest in Morocco and one of the most unforgettable sights in the country, frequently used by film companies. In wet years, water fills a small depression about 2 km west of the village and birdwatchers may be lucky to see pink flamingos. Many other desert-loving birds can be seen here, if you get away from the main crush of visitors. **Normal tourist cars** can get to the dunes if care is taken in the sandy patches. A guide is not necessary. A lot of "sharks" hang around to trap visitors along this itinerary, pretend-ing that such and such a place is closed or that they are the only ones to know the route, or that there are terrible dangers all around . . . don't believe them. Leave Erfoud by Avenue Moulay Hassan, cross the river, and continue along the tarred road for 17 km. Take the left track at Km 17 and follow the green and white markers for the **Kasbah Derkaoua,** and then the line of telegraph poles to the village (count on two hours). If you do take a guide, negotiate the fee beforehand. If you are not motorized, refuse all street offers of transport to the dunes, and arrange the excursion with one of the hotels, such as the Hotel Salam or the Hotel Tafilalet (the lat-ter has an annex at the foot of the Merzouga Dunes). The smaller ho-tels will also offer to rustle up an old Land Rover and take you, but your visit will inevitably be short. For a sunrise visit, the departure is usually around 4:00 A.M. and you'll be back around 9:00 or 10:00 A.M.

It is a pity there are so many of these hustlers around the dunes as well. Remain firm, and once at your destination take the time to wander off the main path and enjoy the beauty of this spectacular site.

There is an extraordinary choice of **accommodations** on the way to Erg Chebbi, and also once you are there. The most expensive is the **Auberge-Kasbah Derkaoua,** well indicated, about 6 km after the end of the paved road to Merzouga (10 rooms, 2 bungalows, half-board single 250 DH, half-board double 400 DH, add 70-100 DH for full-board, Tel/Fax: 57 71 40). You are still about 25 km from the dunes, but this is an absolutely charming, comfortable place run by a Frenchman with corresponding high culinary standards. It is so popular that reservations are essential (closed in January, June, July, and part of August).

At the **foot of the dunes** there are nine café-restaurant-auberge establishments, often of rather doubtful quality, especially concerning the food (shortage of water, absence of refrigerators, and high temperatures—which can reach 40° in Erfoud in July). The visitor is advised to bring his/her own food (don't forget that food prices here will be far higher than in Erfoud).

I warmly recommend the kasbah-like **Ksar Sania** (11 rooms, 100 DH, 25 DH under nomad tent, 1½ km after the village, the last of the café-hotels, in a little oasis on the way to Taouz, at the foot of the dunes, Tel/Fax: 57 72 30), run by a French couple, where you spend the night in great comfort and eat in total security (excellent French meal for 80 DH) in attractive surroundings (watch out for rivals saying it is closed). A reservation is recommended.

After that, there is the **Auberge Merzouga,** an annex of the Hotel Tafilalet in Erfoud (14 rooms), where the rooms are not up to the Erfoud standard, but the nomad tents a good alternative. Most of the places around the dunes offer the possibility of tented accommodations and this is probably the best bet to enjoy the desert atmosphere. Look around to see what accommodations look the most pleasing—double rooms are around 60 DH, tents 20 DH.

From Merzouga, 4WD vehicles can take a trail (one of many) pretty well due south to **Taouz** (25 km). There is a military post here, as the Algerian frontier is very close, and the gendarmes will want to see your identity papers. The interest of Taouz lies in three **rock engraving sites** and a series of well-conserved **pre-Islamic tombs,** 3½-4 km from the post, dating perhaps to the first millennium B.C. Without a detailed map it is difficult to find them, so get someone from the post to show you the way. The engravings are mainly of pecked domestic cattle, but around the summit of the first site

(Jbel Ouafilal) there is a series of "chariots," depicted more or less in plan. The tombs, a little further on, are of dry-stone construction, often with a short passage containing a couple of side niches. They are in excellent condition, but I have heard that more and more tourists are going to see them, with all the risks that this entails.

In the Kem Kem Mountains south of Taouz, practically in Algeria, a paleontological team from the University of Chicago made a dramatic discovery in 1995 when they excavated the skull and teeth of several members of the **dinosaur family.** The remains included the teeth of a huge man-eating theropod, an animal that was probably bigger than the 40-foot long *Tyrannosaurus rex* known in North America. The local people knew the Americans were looking for "animal bones" in these hills and *National Geographic* reported the event in 1996.

It is possible from Erfoud to go to **Ouarzazate** by taking the secondary 3451 road, linking up with the west-bound P32 at **Tinejdad** (see above).

From Erfoud the P21 continues to **Rissani** (22 km), part of the vast network of Tafilalet oases. The *rhettara* (underground water canals) noted on the way into Er-Rachidia (see earlier) are present here, too. The town, now embellished with a grandiose triumphal archway, has an old history. It was an active center for trans-Saharan trade as early as the 8th century. At the beginning of the 13th century, a descendant of the Prophet Mohammed, the *cherif* Hassan Ad-Dakhil, a native of Arabia, arrived in the Tafilalet. Legend has it that the tribal chiefs of the region called for his help, while he was still in Arabia, to end a terrible drought. The *cherif* was successful, he settled in Rissani, and his descendants became the independent rulers of this Saharan province, at the head of the caravan routes to and from the sources of gold and slaves. After the decline of the Saadian dynasty, the Filali (Alaouite) family—aided by the powerful religious fraternities established in the Tafilalet—started open revolt against the central power in 1633, under Mulay Ali Cherif and his sons. By 1670, the first Alaouite—a son of Mulay Ali Cherif—had established the new dynasty. Mulay Ali Cherif has a magnificent mausoleum here, partially destroyed in 1955 by floods from the River Ziz, but restored immediately. Today, Rissani is a quiet little oasis town though, unfortunately, a lot of persistent children and hustlers tend to spoil the visitor's pleasure. It has a **Center for Alaouite Studies** *(Centre d'Etudes et de Recherches Alaouites)* and a small museum with a few objects and some interesting aerial photographs.

Rissani can be reached by CTM **bus** from Erfoud and Er-Rachidia, and other destinations further north. **Big taxis** run frequently from Erfoud. **Local transport** to Merzouga is available every afternoon in the form of a red and white van, and 4WD taxis also make the run on the Tuesday, Thursday, and Sunday market days.

The **hotel scene** is best represented at the top level by the ∗∗∗ **Hotel Kasbah Asmaa** (30 rooms, some with air-conditioning, Tel/Fax: 57 54 94), a large, attractive building beside the road about 4 km outside Rissani coming from Erfoud. The rooms are well equipped and comfortable, looking onto a central patio. It has two restaurants, a bar, and a good swimming pool. The management can arrange excursions to the dunes.

Budget accommodations are best from the ∗ **Hotel Sijilmassa** (Place al-Massira al-Khadra, Tel: 57 50 42, Fax: 57 50 42), where the rooms are big and simple, but clean. There's not much choice apart from these two, the **Hotel el-Filalia** (50 DH), near the bus stop, being pretty run-down (unless it has changed), but with the best views over the palm grove as far as the Merzouga Dunes. The best **restaurant** is undoubtedly that in the **Hotel Kasbah Asmaa** (set meal 87 DH), followed by one in the **Hotel Sijilmassa**. There are a number of cheap places around the town center.

Coming into Rissani one can see the ruins of the 17th-century *ksar* built by that powerful Alaouite sultan Mulay Ismail to keep his sons away from his capital in Meknès. More ruins can be seen by taking the **Touristic Circuit** *(Circuit Touristique)* (21 km of sometimes rough going) through the palm groves south of Rissani. After the gateway into the town and the first traffic circle, bear left then right by the Hotel Sijilmassa to get onto the circuit. The first building of importance is the **mausoleum of Mulay Ali Cherif** (non-Moslems can possibly peer in through the open door and admire the glazed tiles, courtyard, and mosque). Behind it lie the ruins of the 19th-century **Abbar Ksar** *(Ksar Abbar)*. According to historical sources, the *ksar* was a royal residence where the sultan Mulay Abderrahman kept some of his riches, protected by a series of walls and a cannon or two, and guarded by 500 slaves. The building also housed an enormous harem in which the wives of the deceased sultans were kept.

A few kilometers southeast of the above is the **Oulad Abd el-Halim Ksar,** thought to be one of the finest to be seen in the Tafilalet. Built at the end of the 19th century, it was the palace of Mulay Rashid, the sultan Mulay Hassan's elder brother, governor of the region. The guards' quarters were on the ground floor, kitchens, storerooms, and reception rooms were on the first floor, and the private apartments of the governor on the second floor. Its imposing entrance, solid ramparts, and decorative elements can still be seen.

The last important site before getting back into Rissani requires much imagination, for very little remains of the prestigious caravan city of

Sijilmassa, known in the Middle Ages throughout the whole North African world. Founded around 757 A.D., Sijilmassa was the first Islamic city in Morocco, the second in North Africa after Kairouan in Tunisia, and the capital of the Tafilalet. A vital focal point for trans-Saharan caravans, the city lived off trade in gold, ivory, ostrich feathers, salt, and slaves. In 1053-1054, it was captured by the Berber Almoravids in their north-moving campaign to extend their power and control this lucrative trade themselves. The town flourished under their rule. The 11th-century Arab geographer El Bekri described Sijilmassa as protected by a wall with 12 gates; inside were beautiful houses, many with gardens, magnificent public buildings, a mosque, public baths, and rich irrigated fields. It was still important under the succeeding Almohads. A strategic garrison town, it protected the desert to the south as far as Timbuktu and was still one of the biggest towns in the Arab west under the Merinid dynasty, who captured it in 1274, thereby assuring themselves of the caravan trail from Gao to Fès. Then civil wars destroyed its supremacy and it slowly sunk into decay, to be replaced by Rissani. It finally disappeared in 1818, when it was reduced to ruins by the Berber Ait Atta tribe. The Middle Tennessee State University, in collaboration with Moroccan archaeological institutions, has been conducting research on the site since 1988.

The **dunes of Merzouga** can be reached from Rissani (40 km) but the route is much more difficult to find than from Erfoud and you should take a guide (see earlier for local transport).

After a dozen kilometers out of Rissani along the secondary 3454 road, a curious flat-topped hill, **Gara Medouar,** looms up from the flat and stony plain, about 1½ km off the road to the right. As the visitor approaches, by car or on foot, a 100 m-long stone wall, about 7-8 m meters high and 2 m thick, can be seen to bar the entrance to what is in fact a hollow hill. In the spring of 1998, a film company took over the place and used it to film **The Mummy** (supposedly set in the Valley of the Kings in Egypt). A small breech in the wall which enabled one to get inside has now been enlarged and made to look like an important gateway, with a *paved road* leading up to it where before there was just sand. Once inside, it becomes apparent that the whole thing is a vast, natural forteress, protected by this massive wall of carefully-quarried stone. However, not only has the wall been much damaged, but the interior is strewn with plastic bottles and the remains of plaster (it seems that the film company built some constructions here). The function and date of the monument are uncertain, but it was possibly a refuge for families fleeing from Sijilmassa in times of trouble. From Rissani, this secondary road leads to the main north-south **Ouarzazate-Zagora** road (240 km, see earlier).

7. Guided Tours

For non-motorized travelers, it is strongly a[c]
sions at least to the kasbahs of the **Dades Valle[y]**
impressive sand dunes of **Merzouga** are also o[n]
sions organized from Ouarzazate, but this wil[l]
three, days. The big hotels all offer various p[o]
longer stays. These are all pretty expensive com[p]... to public transport,
but have the advantage of allowing stops when desired. The car rental
alternative is more advantageous in many ways. The big hotels in Zagora—
particularly La Fibule—arrange a host of day or longer excursions into the
desert from here, either in 4WD vehicles or on camelback. Excursions to the
Merzouga sand dunes are best done from nearer at hand. They are organized
by the Hotel Kenzi Rissani in **Er-Rachidia** and by the big hotels in **Erfoud.**
Abdeslam Sadoq, owner of the Hotel Tafilalet in Erfoud, is particularly
dynamic in this field. He runs the Tafilalet Adventure and Discovery Travel
Agency (*Tafilalet Aventure & Découverte,* Boulevard Mulay Ismail, Erfoud,
Tel: 05-57 75 18/19, Fax: 05-57 60 36, e-mail: Tafilalet at dial.elan.net.ma),
and proposes a whole range of itineraries in the desert from **Erfoud.**

8. Culture

The cultural intake will probably be confined to a study of the superb
architecture and decorative designs of the **kasbahs** for which the region is
noted. Many have been restored, but others are, alas, no more than ruins.
The average life of a kasbah is around 100 years, but they need constant
upkeep and the hideous concrete building blocks offer a much easier
solution to the housing problem. Don't miss the chance to watch the **traditional dance,** the *ahouach,* where the Berber women form an undulating
circle around the musicians squatting in the center. It is, of course, best to
stumble into a village where this dance is taking place for the benefit of the
local people, but a second best will probably have to be an organized event
put on by a hotel. A **Rose Festival** takes place in Kelaa des Mgouna in May,
and the *moussem* for the patron saint of Ouarzazate, Sidi Daoud, is held in
the town at the end of August. A **Date Festival** takes place in Erfoud at the
beginning of October.

It's hardly culture, but if you have time, visit the **Association Horizon** in
Ouarzazate (Avenue de la Victoire, off Avenue Mohammed V, just opposite the Taourirt Kasbah). This private, non-profit association aims to get
handicapped children integrated into society. The center is well equipped
and its dedicated staff always appreciates a visit.

Ouarzazate, there is a public **swimming pool** near the campsite, in Complexe de Ouarzazate, on the way out of town towards Tineghir. All the big hotels have pools and most let non-residents use them, for a fee of around 40 DH. The big hotels have **tennis courts.** For **golf** enthusiasts, the Royal Golf of Ouarzazate is a 9-hole course, par 36, 3,150 m, showing up as a patch of bright green in the ochre-colored desert surroundings. The green fee for visitors is between 250 DH and 300 DH, and the obligatory caddie costs around 100 DH. The Hotel Riad Salam can organize **horseback riding. Mountain bikes** can be rented and circuits proposed at the Hotel Tomboctou in Tinerhir. **Mountain trekking** departure points (with or without a guide and a mule) are Kelaa des Mgouna, Boumalne du Dades, and the Dades Gorge for the High Atlas, and Nekob, Kelaa des Mgouna, and Boumalne for the Jbel Sarhro. **Birdwatching** around Boumalne and Merzouga is generally rewarding.

10. Shopping

The state-run **craft cooperative,** Coopartim (*Ensemble Artisanal,* opposite the Taourirt Kasbah in Ouarzazate) offers a good choice of handicrafts, at fixed prices (closed on Sundays). The region is particularly noted for its rugs, woven by the Berber Ouzguita women, and displayed at **Tazenakht.** The Ouarzazate and **Tamgroute** potters also produce characteristic ware. There are a number of craft shops in the **Tourist Complex,** out towards the campsite. The **big hotels** all have their boutiques selling kaftans, jewelry, postcards, and newspapers, and many **small tourist shops** in all the big towns will try to sell you *cheiches* (long, narrow, light-weight "scarves" that the locals wind around their heads as a protection against the wind and the sand)—but their prices are exorbitant (shop around before buying). Don't be fooled by the "Touareg" line—again, there are no Touareg in Morocco. Shops also sell rugs and pottery, for which you must bargain (having seen local prices and deciding how much you want to pay—but prices are high in Ouarzazate).

For everyday necessities, and a very good selection of canned food, cheese, wines, beer, and so on, the **Dimitri Supermarket** (Avenue Mohammed V, Ouarzazate) is undoubtedly the place to head for. The **municipal market** (for fresh food) is behind the Place du 3 Mars. Outside of Ouarzazate, the shops in **Agdz** have a good selection of rugs and jewelry, and I recommend **Chez Ziad** at Tinejdad (if you are going to go along the Dades Valley) for old pottery, wooden objects, and jewelry. The **Craftwork Center** in Er-Rachidia has samples of local handicrafts for sale. Fossils are on sale all over the place, but there are some reasonably-priced specimens on the road leading down to the **Ait Ben Haddou Kasbah.** Otherwise, the fossil home is the Erfoud/Rissani area.

11. Entertainment and Nightlife

For that evening or late night drink in Ouarzazate, the traveler will have to head for one of the big hotels. Most have some sort of floorshow or music in the evening. Try the **Club Med,** the **Complexe de Ouarzazate,** the **Hotel Tichka Salam,** the **Hotel Le Zat,** the **Kenzi Bélère,** the **Kenzi Azghor,** the **Riad Salam,** or the **Berbère Palace.** In all the other towns in the region, evening drinking is limited to the big hotels.

12. The Ouarzazate Address List

Airlines—Royal Air Maroc, 1 Avenue Mohammed V (Tel: 88 50 80/ 88 51 02).

Airport—2 km out of town (Tel: 88 23 48).

Banks—along Avenue Mohammed V. The Crédit du Maroc does credit-card cash withdrawals.

Bus station *(gare routière)*—for the CTM, Avenue Mohammed V; for Satas and other small companies, the new station, about 1 km northwest of the town.

Car rental—Avis, Avenue Mohammed V (Tel: 88 43 10); Budget, Résidence Al-Warda, Avenue Mohammed V (Tel: 88 28 92); Hertz, 33 Avenue Mohammed V (Tel: 88 20 84/88 34 85); Inter Rent, Europcar, Place du 3 Mars (Tel: 88 20 35); Yousri Car, 51 Avenue Mohammed V (Tel: 88 55 90).

Church—French speaking mass at Eglise Sainte-Thérèse, 7 Rue Da ou Gadim, Avenue Mohammmed V (near the mosque) (Tel: 88 25 42).

Consulate—there is no U.S. or Canadian consulate in the region. Call Casablanca (Tel: 02-26 45 50) or the Embassy in Rabat (Tel: 07-76 22 65) if in need.

Drugstore, Night *(Pharmacie de Nuit)*—in the town hall *(municipalité)* opposite the post office.

Fire *(Sapeurs Pompiers)*—(Tel: 15).

Gendarmerie Royale—(Tel: 17).

Golf Club—see "Sports," section 9 above

Hospital—Avenue Mohammed V, a bit before the Taourirt Kasbah (Tel: 88 24 44).

Photocopies—most tobacco stores and téléboutiques.

Police—(Tel: 19).

Post Office—Avenue Mohammed V.

Taxis, Big and Little—Place Al Mouhadine.

Telephone—from the post office and also the téléboutiques.

Tourist Information—Avenue Mohammed V, next to the post office.

Tour Operators—Holiday Services, Avenue Mohammed V (Tel: 88 29 97);
    Ksour Voyages, Place du 3 Mars (Tel: 88 28 40).

Travel Agencies—see "Guided Tours," section 7 above.

Index

471